American Government

Origins, Institutions and Public Policy

Seventh Edition

James W. Ceaser

University of Virginia

KENDALL/HUNT PUBLISHING COMPANY
4050 Westmark Drive   Dubuque, Iowa 52002

Cover Image © 2002 PhotoDisc, Inc.

Contents

Preface

This textbook combines the traditional and the modern approaches to the study of American politics. The traditional approach emphasizes constitutional law, the formal characteristics of political institutions, and American political thought; the modern approach focuses on political culture, the policymaking process, and political behavior. Few teachers of American politics hold that the distinction between these two approaches is absolute, and almost all would say that students should receive extensive exposure to both. Yet all too often materials available for classroom use reflect the research interests of scholars who concentrate their work in one of these areas. Our aim in this textbook has been to integrate these two approaches so that students can understand the interconnections between political thought and the formal structures of politics on the one hand, and the policymaking process and political behavior on the other.

We employ a mode of analysis that begins by looking at politics from the perspective of the constitution maker or legislator—that is, one who consciously and rationally considers how to found and maintain the basic structure of a political system. We use the term "constitution" in its original and general sense to refer to the constituent elements that define a political order. In the United States, the Constitution (that is, the written document) is obviously one of these elements, but others include fundamental political beliefs, major laws, and the evolutionary development of institutions. The focus of this book is therefore as much cultural and behavioral as it is

legal. The reader is placed in the position of a constitution maker or founder who is called on to analyze past changes from a constitutional perspective and who is asked to apply this same mode of thinking to major contemporary issues. By this method we seek to avoid a passive presentation of the mere facts of American politics and challenge the reader to consider the significance of these facts for efforts to adapt and maintain the constitutional system.

Political development in the United States has never, of course, been solely the product of conscious and rational efforts by constitution makers. Accordingly, we present other factors that have shaped the system's development, including influences deriving from sociological, economic, and technological causes. Where possible, however, we view these factors from the standpoint of the legislator having responsibility for constitutional maintenance. For example, in treating the increasing influence of the mass media on the electoral process, we not only describe the developments that have taken place but also ask the reader to consider what changes (if any) legislators can and should adopt in response. This approach, we believe, encourages readers to think in terms of political alternatives and to assess the consequences of contemplated reforms.

Learning about politics involves expanding one's capacity to distinguish momentary influences from those that shape the character of a constitution over the long term. Throughout the text, we make use of political theory, comparative politics, and historical development in an effort to escape viewing yesterday's political crisis as the sole basis for political analysis. Our goal is to train readers to perform the mental act of checking day-to-day events against larger forces influencing constitutional change. Thus, although we have made every effort to include the most up-to-date materials, we have deliberately avoided faddish attempts to "peg" the book to the latest political crisis or problem.

Books with a traditional emphasis often glorify the founding generation and engage in the stale exercise of measuring the present system against the standards of the original authors of the Constitution. We have naturally assigned an important place to the nation's founders, both because the founding itself presents the clearest instance of a conscious and full-blown experiment in constitution making and because the founders have included many of America's best political thinkers. Nonetheless, our theme of constitution making implies that a constitution must be adapted to fit the requirements of each generation. No system can be maintained without being reformed to meet new needs and challenges. We have viewed the development of the American system as a process and a dialogue, bounded in large measure by the original principles but constantly facing new questions that the founders either could not have resolved or did not resolve. It is precisely because the task of maintaining the political order falls in some measure to every generation, including our own, that we believe it is essential to think about politics from a constitutional perspective.

While the theme we have adopted may seem distinctive, it lends itself readily to a standard arrangement of the material. Part One presents the overall approach of the book, analyzes the origins of the republic, traces the broad outlines of constitutional development from 1789 to the present, and treats the division of power between the central government and states. Part Two deals with public opinion and with the various links between the public and the formal institutions of government. Much of the material in this section falls into the area of political behavior, but readers will quickly see how political behavior is shaped by constitutional influences. Part Three treats the institutions of the federal government. It includes a chapter on the separation of powers between the president and Congress, an addition made to help students understand the interaction between these two branches. Part Four looks at the policymaking process and analyzes the major substantive areas of public policy. Basic choices in the realm of policy are dealt with in terms of their constitutional significance, and each chapter in this section considers not only what policy choices have been made but also how and by whom they are made. This section enables the reader to consider the effects of the allocation of power on governmental decisions.

A good companion for this text is *Readings in American Government,* edited by Mary P. Nichols and David K. Nichols, published by Kendall/Hunt in 1996. Their selection of readings follows closely the ideas discussed in this book and provides excellent primary source materials for a constitutional perspective on American politics.

The current edition of this text, prepared by James Ceaser, is the sixth revision of the original book that was published in 1984. In the original edition, James Ceaser wrote what are currently chapters 1, 2, 5, 6, 7, and 8 and directed the preparation of chapters 9, 13, and 17, which were drafted, respectively, by William Connelly, Alan Tarr, and David Clinton. Joseph Bessette wrote chapters 10, 11, and 12; Laurence O'Toole wrote chapters 4, 14, and 15; and Glenn Thurow wrote chapters 3 and 16. Several persons helped in researching materials for the second and third editions: Randall Strahan, Andrew Busch, John Young, John Dinan, Andrew Hall, Brian Menard, Jason Robinson, Scott Fischer, Glenn Ellmers, Brad Watson, Cary Federman, Bruce Larson, and James Yoho. In preparing the fifth edition, Professor John Young of Andrews University assisted in revising chapters 6 and 10 for the sixth and seventh editions. Research assistance was provided by Patrick McGuinn, Richard Skinner, Michael Cairo, Joshua Johnson, Joshua Dunn, Ben Bogardus, Richard Drew, Robert Hume, Kathleen Grammatico, Patrick Roberts, Greg J. Lindskog, Robert Saldin, Zachary Courser, Daniel Disalvo, and Gavin J. Reddick.

Part One

The Fundamental Principles

1

The Study of American Politics

CHAPTER CONTENTS

America's political tradition is a blend of continuity and change. Since the founding of the republic over two centuries ago, Americans have looked for guidance in their fundamental political beliefs to the great founding documents of the Declaration of Independence (1776), the Constitution (1789), and the Bill of Rights (1791). On the occasion of almost every inauguration, presidents draw from the principles of the founding. The great struggles for equality in American history—the antislavery movement, the civil rights movement, and the women's rights movement—have all invoked the "self-evident truths" of the Declaration. In the conflicts over the rightful powers and the proper arrangement of the government, from the great battles over states' rights in the nineteenth century to recent struggles between the president and Congress over authority in budget-making foreign policy, Americans continually return to the words of the Constitution and the ideas of the founders.

Yet in looking to their origins, Americans do not always find the same answers. Contending parties claim fidelity to the same documents and principles, but they may understand and interpret them differently. The documents that provide the foundation for continuity sometimes serve as grounds for controversy. New circumstances may also require that the original principles be expressed in new ways. Abraham Lincoln, who began the Gettysburg Address in 1863 by looking back "four score and seven years ago" to the Declaration of Independence, ended by calling for a "new birth of freedom." Franklin Roosevelt, who opened his state of the union address in 1944 by speaking of the Declaration and the Bill of Rights, concluded by calling for a "second Bill of Rights" and a "new basis of security."

A recurrence to original principles is an enduring feature of American politics. As one political scientist observed: "Other nations often see constitutions come and go every generation . . . [but] the United States has still had only one Constitution and one system of government based on one set of political ideas."[1] Change has taken place in large part through reinterpreting the original elements. The founding generation, amid profound disputes of its own, struck a balance among the nation's fundamental principles. Within the basic framework established by the founders, each succeeding generation has faced the responsibility of maintaining those principles and adjusting that balance anew. It is a responsibility that cannot be escaped. Today is no exception. Beneath the daily contests for influence among our politicians and the struggle for advantage by interest groups, choices must often be made about the meaning of liberty and equality, the role of government in society, the relations among the institutions of the government, and the place and purpose of the United States in the world. These choices in turn alter the character of the nation's political system and profoundly shape the future course of American politics.

The significance of the original principles in America's political development suggests the need to study American politics by beginning with the founding and by observing how the founding principles have been interpreted and perhaps modified by successive generations. The main purpose of such an inquiry is not to retrace American history, but to introduce a way of thinking about politics that can help citizens meet the ongoing challenges of preserving the political system.

Thinking as a Constitution Maker

Imagine, then, that you were asked to create a new form of government for the United States. Where would you begin? What questions would you ask, and what standards would you apply? Founding a government is clearly a daunting assignment. But it was one Americans had to confront in the critical period from the days before the Revolution through the ratification of the Constitution.

Fortunately, the major elements of the founding are not lost in the mists of time, like King Arthur's legends, but remain surprisingly accessible to us. America originated with certain deliberate acts of constitution making. When the leaders of the American Revolution declared independence from Great Britain in 1776, they presented an official document, The Declaration of Independence, which sets out the reasons for the break and states the principles of legitimate government. Eleven years later, faced with the failure of the nation's first government under the Articles of Confederation, the founders assembled in Philadelphia to devise a new government. We have today an extensive record of their deliberations at the Constitutional Convention published in James Madison's Notes, as well as a famous commentary on the Constitution, *The Federalist*, which was written during the debate over the ratification to explain the purposes of the proposed government.*

The frame of mind of many of the founders is also known to us. The leading proponents of the new government, among whom were George Washington, James Madison, and Alexander Hamilton, were keenly aware of the importance of the moment and of the unique opportunity it presented. They saw themselves as constitution makers engaged in an undertaking that was potentially no less momentous than the founding of the great ancient governments of Athens, Sparta, or Rome. The stakes were high. To fail might spell the doom for the cause of self-government not just in the United States, but everywhere. As Alexander Hamilton noted at the Convention, "we were now to decide forever the fate of Republican Government."[2]

The way the founders went about the task of proposing the government provides us further instruction. Most governments in the world until then had been established by leaders who took power by force and justified their rule by appeals to myths or supernatural accounts. The American founding relied to a remarkable extent on reason, in which the various arguments for and against the proposed form of government were debated and discussed. The founding provided a kind of test of whether a group of political leaders, taking into account both political theory and practical interests, could devise and agree on a form of government and then win consent for it from the public in an open contest. *The Federalist* begins by observing that it was for Americans "to decide the important question whether societies of men are really capable or not of estab-

lishing good government from reflection and choice, or whether they are forever destined to depend for their political constitutions on accident and force." (*Federalist* 1)

Finally, we know much about the reasoning that the founders relied on in crafting the new government. Some founders studied in depth previous political systems, beginning with those of ancient Greece and ending with the recent state constitutions. The question of how to form and maintain governments was a central concern of a body of knowledge they called "political science" or the "science of politics." ("Science" in this case, incidentally, did not refer to knowledge in which every proposition could be tested and confirmed with mathematical certainty, but a systematic body of thought that sought to establish important relationships.) Yet existing political science could provide them no more than general guidance. Each case had its unique features that derive from the special qualities of its people and history. Creating a government is always a matter of judgment that must fit a government to the particular character or "genius" of a people. In addition, the founders were innovating. The form of government they proposed—a republican government in a large nation—was something that had never been attempted before. Like doctors performing a pioneering operation, they were developing new ideas in political science, even as they relied on its basic categories to guide them. To critics who dismissed their plan as visionary, the founders replied: "why is the experiment of an extended republic to be rejected merely because it may comprise what is new?" (*Federalist* 14)

The document the nation adopted in 1789, known as the "Constitution of the United States of America," serves as the basis of our government today and is the world's oldest written constitution still in use. Yet our form of government today differs in many respects from the one created in 1789. Through amendment, interpretation, and the accretion of practice and precedent, the original system has been modified. If

---

* The delegates at the Constitutional Convention decided that their deliberations would be kept secret. James Madison, who took notes of the speeches, waited until his death to have them published. *The Federalist* was written in 1787 and 1788 by Alexander Hamilton, James Madison, and John Jay. It consists of eighty-five separate essays, and the references in this text will give the number of the essay from which the quotation is taken (for example, *Federalist* 10).

the founders were miraculously to return today, they would certainly recognize the outline of their handiwork, but they would no doubt also be surprised at some of its features.

The government of the United States has changed and will continue to change. The question therefore is not whether we become constitution makers—we must—but whether we base our own decisions on "reflection or choice" or allow change to occur by "accident," without the benefit of the kind of systematic thought that went into creating the government. Although we in this generation do not face the same responsibility of establishing a framework of government, the task of preserving and maintaining a political order, though perhaps a less glorious task than founding a new one, requires no less attention and understanding. The need to think like constitution makers therefore is nearly as important today as it was at the founding. As Daniel Webster once said, preserving the government demands that we not only value the "importance of the achievements of our ancestors," but also learn how "to keep alive similar sentiments and to foster a constant regard for the principles of the Revolution."[3]

To think like a constitution maker means to ask four basic questions that America's founders confronted:

1. What are the ends or purposes of society as a whole?

2. What role should government play in society?

3. Who governs, and how are the institutions of government to be organized and power distributed?

4. How can the nation provide for its security and promote its interests in the world?

These four questions help us not only to understand the task of constitution making, but also to analyze the character of any political system or constitution. By a constitution (with a small c), we mean the basic form of government, also referred to as a "political order" or "political system." But we prefer "constitution" because it recalls at least the possibility of making or constituting something. As defined by the *Oxford English Dictionary,* a "constitution" in its

political sense is the "mode in which a state is constituted or organized . . . the arrangement of its parts or elements, as determining its nature and character." Analysis of the four questions stated above provides a key for describing any given constitution. Once we have set forth the ends of society, the role of government, who governs and the way power is distributed, and the nation's basic posture toward security and foreign affairs, we have characterized the essentials of that constitution.

Using the term constitution as the basic unit of analysis risks creating confusion, because Americans identify the word with our written legal document. The issues raised by the four questions posed above, however, go beyond matters that are addressed or fully answered by our Constitution. There is, therefore, a crucial distinction to be made between our constitution (with a small c) and our Constitution (with a capital C). Our constitution is made up of a set of dominant beliefs, key laws, and established practices that are more than our Constitution and that may on occasion even deviate from it. Our constitution includes the driving force of certain ideas, the interpretation of these ideas in the context of changing circumstances, and the development of major institutions that are not directly provided for by the Constitution. The Constitution, for example, says nothing about political parties, even though parties have become integral parts of the current framework of government.

Calling attention to the significance of extra-Constitutional developments, far from minimizing the influence of the Constitution, allows us to understand its importance in shaping American politics. Those who wrote and amended the Constitution sought to influence decisively the character of the political order. And they succeeded. (By contrast, the written constitutions of some nations are merely public relations documents that have no bearing on how these nations are actually governed.) Because the Constitution establishes the basic outline of our governmental structure, and because Americans believe that it should, the Constitution must be taken very seriously. But no written document can fully contain or define a constitution. The founders themselves were well aware of this fact, and all the more so because the Constitution left much of the job of governing to the states (which had their own written constitutions). Thinking constitutionally, therefore, requires going beyond a legal analysis to consider the fundamental factors that structure a political order.

In this chapter, we shall look at the four basic questions a constitution maker must ask and explore how they have been approached in the United States. The concepts discussed will all be examined in more detail later in the book. The object for the moment is less to master a body of facts than to get a sense of what these questions mean in the context of American politics.

The Ends of Society

A constitution maker must first consider the broad purposes to which society as a whole is devoted and the kinds of human beings it develops. Politics is so important as a human activity because constitutions help shape what people value and how they lead their lives.

This formative dimension of politics can best be seen by looking at a few examples from outside of American politics. Consider, for example, the constitutional changes in Eastern Europe that occurred in the late 1980s. Before then the communist governments in these states allowed only one official view to be heard on the state-owned television; only one political party was permitted; ownership of almost all property was by the government; the teaching of history and social science was based exclusively on Marxist-Leninist principles; and the practice of religion was either discouraged or forbidden. The whole structure of these societies was transformed by the revolutions that toppled these governments. Suddenly, the airwaves opened up to different views; opposition parties organized and openly expressed their ideas; elements of private enterprise began to develop; religious services were held publicly for the first time; and old textbooks in history and social studies were abandoned. When these constitutions changed, there were changes in how people led their daily lives and developed as human beings.

Iran, over the past generation, offers another instructive example. Until its revolution in 1979, Iran was governed by an authoritarian ruler (the shah), who, while placing strict limits on the range of permissible political activity, sought to modernize the nation's economy and to introduce many western customs. The daily life of an Iranian urban middle-class person thus began to resemble that of someone similarly situated in London or New York: people could purchase what they wanted, dress as they pleased, and entertain themselves by going to a nightclub, the movies, or the theater. All this changed abruptly in 1979 after a revolution brought to power a group of Islamic fundamentalists led by a religious figure, the Ayatollah Khomeini, whose view of the ends of society was based on establishing a version of the Islamic way of life. Through propaganda and repression, often with popular support, the government imposed some striking new laws that banned many forms of music, closed movie theaters, and required women to appear in public with long dresses covering their entire body and much of the head and face. The curriculum of all courses in school in history, government, and law were completely changed to reflect Islamic principles. Almost no major aspect of the daily lives of Iranians was left untouched by the new government.

Efforts to use political authority directly to form or mold a people, even against its will, are not unusual. History is filled with attempts by constitution makers to shape a particular kind of human being. Indeed, this understanding of government's role was once the predominant view. A model for this way of thinking was the constitution of the ancient Greek city state of Sparta, which has been widely discussed by political theorists. Established by one of the most renowned of all founders, Lycurgus, the Spartan constitution was designed to create the ideal citizen-soldier. To encourage more perfect physical specimens, Spartan practices carefully regulated the training of youth, prescribed the diet of the citizens, and even established rules for sexual relations and breeding. To prevent any corruption of the people's morals, contacts with foreigners were strictly limited and economic activity was tightly regulated. All of society was organized to encourage a sense of duty and of devotion to the state. The Spartan constitution was in one sense a great success, as Sparta was able to maintain its independence for hundreds of years and to remain one of the most powerful states of ancient Greece.

This general understanding of the role of government prevailed in many areas of America before the founding. (America, recall, began to be settled by Europeans in the 1500s, and even though these colonies were part of Great Britain they often exercised extensive control over their own domestic laws.) In the seventeenth and eighteenth centuries, some of the New England colonial settlements used public authority to promote Christian virtue and ideals. Connecticut and Massachusetts defined what was orthodox religious belief, required church attendance, forbade premarital sexual relations, and even regulated the length of people's hair. Nathaniel Hawthorne's classic novel *The Scarlet Letter* provides a striking picture of the rigid code of behavior that these theocratic republics required of their citizens.

Some contemporary political scientists define politics as "who gets what, when, and how," that is, as a competition over physical resources and economic goods.4 Although much ordinary political activity and debate revolves around economic issues, such as the levels of taxation and the amounts of public subsidies for housing or for college tuition, these concerns should not make us forget the more fundamental role of politics as a way of influencing the overall character and quality of life in society. Indeed, far more than many suppose, many of these so-called economic contests in fact are not about economics alone, but involve concerns over the way of life of society. It is this aspect that a constitutional perspective always keeps in sight.

Where do we turn to find a statement of America's fundamental ends? It is here that Americans look back to the Declaration and the Constitution and find the basic goals of liberty, self-government, equality, and citizenship. These form a large part of the "core" or "creed" of the American constitution—the beliefs that have united Americans, in the Declaration's words, as "one people" despite the size and diversity of the population. It is to these ends that we now turn.

Liberty

Modern-day Americans no doubt find the idea of using political authority directly to form a people, in the fashion that existed in Sparta, not only unacceptable but difficult even to comprehend. Government, they believe, should not dictate the goals or aims of individuals. The Declaration establishes the legitimate end of society: to secure certain "unalienable rights," which include "life, liberty, and the pursuit of happiness." By making the protection of individual rights central to the role of government, the Declaration implies that public authority should for the most part remove itself from imposing a specific end or way of life on its citizens. Citizens may pursue their happiness as they see fit, which leaves the determination of many questions of the best way of life chiefly to the private sphere—to the influence of the family, religious institutions, the "culture" as it develops, and ultimately to each person's individual choice.

Although liberty is clearly a fundamental end of society, the founders did not interpret it as a generalized right to "do one's own thing" that exempts all individual behavior from government regulation. Nor did they think that a whole theory of government can be constructed from the idea of rights, according to which government may only act when the exercise of rights by some directly conflicts with the exercise of rights by others. Some may prefer a minimalist government of this sort, but it is not the kind of government required by the founders' understanding of liberty. Government—meaning here not just the federal government, but government on all levels—could do more than ban actions involving a physical interference with the practice of others' rights. Government may act in many areas to secure general benefits, from building highways, to assisting the poor, to providing public education. It can protect basic community values, as in laws that outlaw prostitution, ban obscenity, and in certain cases even prevent individuals from practices deemed harmful to their own well-being, such as the use of certain drugs.

What then does protecting liberty and securing rights mean? The answer, as we shall see throughout this book, is not simple. For the moment we can say that it has meant, in the first

BOX 1.1

The Debate Over Laws Banning Obscenity

The continuing differences over the meaning of liberalism are illustrated in the following arguments about the legality and wisdom of laws that would limit materials deemed to be obscene:

Governmental control of ideas or personal preferences is alien to a democracy. . . . The only completely democratic way to control publications which arouse mere thoughts or feelings is through nongovernmental censorship by public opinion (Judge Jerome Frank, concurring in *U.S. v. Roth*, 1956).

The ultimate evils include influences upon the cultural and moral environment of a people and, hence, upon mind and character. . . . By means of laws against the more extreme forms of obscenity, we are reminded, and we remind ourselves, that "We, the People" have an ethical order and moral limits (Harry Clor, *Censorship and Freedom of Expression*.)

place, strong protection for a core of fundamental rights. These rights consist of rights specified in the Constitution and many state constitutions—included generally are the rights of free speech, free press, and the free exercise of religion—and some rights that have been recognized as inherent, such as a freedom of movement. Disputes of course arise about the precise meaning of these rights as well as which are in fact fundamental or inherent, as, for example, in the current debate over a proclaimed right of abortion. Second, a government that secures liberty also protects many other matters that involve claims of right, such as a right of privacy and a right to acquire and dispose of property. These rights, however, cannot be protected by simple or absolute injunctions. They need to be put into effect by various laws and also weighed in relationship to other rights claims and to other ends.

A government that secures rights thus does not mean a government that recognizes a legal claim to "do one's own thing." There is no doubt a presumption that government should not usually intervene in areas of personal choice or in spheres being handled well enough by the interaction of individuals and private groups. But for the founders—and still for most Americans today—a government that protects rights possesses broad powers to act at its discretion in a large number of areas.

The task of protecting rights does, however, place important restraints on the authority of government relative to what governments had claimed before. Government now gets out of the business of imposing orthodox views in the moral and philosophic realms. Public authority, whatever its other obligations, secures the setting in which the pursuit of happiness takes place, but it does not seek directly to define the content of happiness.

This understanding of the role of government is known as *liberalism* or *liberal* government, as that word is used in the term *liberal democracy*. Liberal here means government that aims to protect rights and which, in that sense, is limited. (The word liberal, as we shall see, is often used in a different sense in contemporary politics.[5]) Some of the important premises of liberalism were set out in the seventeenth and eighteenth centuries by several political theorists who had a great influence on America's founders, among them John Locke (1632–1704), Charles de Montesquieu (1689–1775), and Adam Smith (1723–1790). These theorists argued that government should relinquish the responsibility of saving souls—a responsibility, incidentally, that many governments had used to pursue tyrannical ends. Government should also withdraw from directly controlling large parts of the economy, a role it had often exercised not just to try to promote economic activity but to increase political control. Instead, modern government should act to ensure a sphere of free action for the individual.

The implications for government of securing liberty was well-stated by a famous nineteenth-century historian of liberty, Lord Acton:

By liberty, I mean the assurance that every man shall be protected in doing what he believes his duty against the influence of authority and majorities, custom and opinion. The state is competent to assign duties and draw the line between good and evil only in its immediate sphere. Beyond the limits of things necessary for its well-being, it can only give indirect help to fight the battle of life by promoting the influences which prevail against temptation—religion, education and the distribution of wealth.[6]

Notice Acton did not say that liberal governments must abandon all consideration of the quality of life or the kinds of human beings society should promote. But there were now to be strong limitations on government's responsibility in this area and on the kinds of actions government might legitimately take to address its concerns.

Among the opponents of the Constitution, a number questioned whether it was wise for government to give up its role of directly forming virtuous citizens. They argued that in a government in which the people would hold the ultimate source of power strict controls were necessary to build good citizens. If citizens were selfish, popular government would degenerate into a struggle among groups seeking their own narrow ends. Limited government, with its protection for commerce and property, would encourage "luxuriousness," "corruption," and "voluptuousness." Government should thus ban luxury items, as such commerce would "corrupt our manners."[7] (Today, this would be equivalent to government prohibiting the purchase of sports cars, yachts, and videotape recorders on the grounds that the desire for these items encouraged materialism.) Although defeated in the contest over the Constitution, these opponents expressed concerns that were also held by the founders. Indeed, it would be an error to conclude that the founders or Americans thereafter abandoned efforts to promote citizenship or to cultivate an admirable way of life. With the ratification of the Constitution, the terms of the debate about defining a good way of life shifted. The permissible forms of governmental intervention were greatly reduced, but there was no intent to eliminate all governmental support of important community values, especially at the state and local levels.

Self-Government

A second fundamental end of American society is self-government. Legitimate government, according to the Declaration, must derive its power "from the consent of the governed." No power external to the people—be it a monarch asserting divine right, or an ordained class of clerics asserting a religious title to govern—has a legitimate claim to rule. The principle of government by the consent of the governed would not sanction either a personal dictatorship or communist regimes in which the leader or party claims knowledge of the laws of history and thus what is best for people in the long run.

Governments established by the consent of the governed can differ in form. It is possible, for example, for a people to consent to a system that includes a qualified monarchy. In the United States, however, this principle led quite naturally to an insistence on a popular form of government—what we today call a "democracy." Only a government that derived its power and authority from what *The Federalist* called "the great body of the people," rather than a particular class, family, or group, was acceptable. No other kind of government was compatible with the "genius of the American people," "the fundamental principles of the Revolution," or Americans' determination to "rest all our political experiments on the capacity of mankind for self-government." (*Federalist* 39)

To be sure, there was a lack of precision, indeed probably a deliberate vagueness, in the expression the "great body of the people." For many practical reasons, the definition of citizenship as it related to voting was left largely to the states. Certain parts of the people in America were fully excluded from citizenship, such as slaves and Indians; women rarely had the suffrage; and voting privileges even among white males carried some property qualifications. But whatever the restrictions and practices of the time, American politics has developed in accord with the logical meaning of self-government as the inclusion of all adult citizens.

Self-government is usually understood in America in a much broader sense than popular government at the national level. The views of some of the opponents of the Constitution are instructive on this point. Many were against creating any kind of strong national government, no matter how democratic its forms and arrangements, on the ground that a government so far away from home could never realize self-government in a meaningful or robust sense. Genuine self-government was possible only in smaller communities where individuals could actually take part in political life. Although this position was rejected in its strong form by the founders, its basic sentiment finds expression in our constitutional framework in the division of power among different levels of government: the federal or national government, the fifty states, and the thousands of counties, townships, and cities.

This division of authority is supported by the structural arrangement of the Constitution that we know today as *federalism*. Federalism refers to a system in which two levels of government, national and state, each have recognized powers and prerogatives that are set out in the fundamental law (the Constitution). The federal or national government is limited to certain enumerated, though very broad, ends, while the remainder of power remains with the states as determined by their own constitutions. This arrangement is supported by a widespread belief, which carries the principle of self-government even further, that political decision making should be kept close to home, where the opportunities for citizen participation are most meaningful. Thomas Jefferson called for at least four different levels of government: the national government, the state government, the county, and finally the township or "ward," which would be "a small republic in itself" in which each citizen could transact in person a great portion of his duties.[8]

Today, the national government is far more active and has assumed more responsibilities than it did two hundred years ago. And, as we shall see, many people today prefer rule by the national government to that of state and local governments, which they charge are unresponsive. Yet it is still the case that large numbers of Americans resist federal interventions in the name of maintaining opportunities for self-government at lower levels. Even though the governments of many states as well as some large urban areas can themselves seem far away from home, the dispersal of power in the United States means that many citizens can hold office and have access to officeholders. There are today over half a million elected officials in the United States, only 537 of whom hold office at the national level! Serving on a town council or a local school board provides the chance for citizens not just to vote, but also to make actual decisions that affect the character of their communities.

Interestingly, Americans use the same word, freedom or liberty, to refer to both of the fundamental ends we have discussed thus far: individual rights and self-government. "Free persons" are those who possess rights and a "free people" is one that practices self-government. These two ends usually reinforce each other. Self-government eliminates a source of arbitrary government deriving from the unchecked rule of a single person or a small clique. But self-government does not always lead to the protection of rights and in fact sometimes can endanger people's liberties. Self-government is thus no automatic solution to securing rights. Majorities can play the part of the tyrant. Majorities before the Civil War voted at the state levels to enslave the black minority; and after the Civil War states and localities persisted in forcing black people into segregated parks, schools, and housing. Conflicts between self-government and liberty have been evident in other areas as well.

Unlike certain enthusiasts of democratic government who denied this tension, the founders thought that constructing a popular government that would also secure rights presented one of the most formidable challenges they faced. Their solution—actually, their various solutions— often moved in the direction of limiting the degree of immediate popular control over political decisions. Rights in some cases were better secured by relying on the government furthest away from home (the national government), not the states or localities. Within the national government, some decisions were given to courts with judges appointed for life, and arrangements were introduced for the government to slow down or resist pressures of public opinion to be transferred into public policy. The founders favored self-government, but self-government was not defined as the most democratic arrangement. The founders called their more tempered scheme a "republic" or a "representative democracy."

Equality

A third end of the American constitution is equality. According to the Declaration of Independence, "all men are created equal," and leaders and citizens have spoken ever since of the centrality of equality to the American creed. Yet the meaning of equality has been subject to extraordinary controversy, especially when applied to the realm of economics and ideas about governmental redistribution of wealth.

Let us begin by looking at the core of the idea as it was understood at the founding. Equality for the founders provided the framework and justification for self-government and liberty. Equality in the first sense meant that whatever differences existed among persons, these did not give anyone (or any group) a title to be their masters or to rule them without their consent. According to Thomas Jefferson, who drafted the Declaration, "Whatever be [people's] degree of talent, it is no measure of their rights. Because Sir Isaac Newton was superior to others in understanding, he was not therefore lord of the person or property of others." Equality for the founders therefore required a society without legal classes, and the Constitution bans both the federal government and the states from granting any titles of nobility. Equality in the other sense meant, citing Jefferson again, "the equality of every citizen in his person and property."[9] This was equality in liberty. All persons—and not just one class of them—had claim to the protection of the same basic rights.

Because political principles inevitably influence practices in other realms, the idea that people are fundamental equals has had profound consequences for manners and behavior in everyday life in America. Many Americans, for example, are in jobs where they must serve others, but they do not think of themselves—nor are they generally treated by others—as members of

a "servant class" that must defer to its superiors. European observers have always been struck by the absence of class feelings in America. The following description by Werner Sombart, a German sociologist who visited the United States in the early twentieth century, is typical:

> The whole of public life has a more democratic style. The worker is not being reminded at every step that he belongs to a "lower" class. . . . The bowing and scraping before the "upper classes," which produces such an unpleasant impression in Europe, is completely unknown.[10]

There have, of course, been glaring exceptions to realizing equality. For years slavery made a mockery of this end, and for long periods there has been severe legal discrimination against blacks, Asians, and Indians. Women were not guaranteed the vote until 1919 and have faced discriminatory legislation. For individuals in certain groups, therefore, equality has been more a standard for which they have had to struggle than a reality in their everyday lives. Yet equality—not inequality—has been the principle to which one could publicly appeal. Abraham Lincoln saw the principle of equality as establishing "the *right*, so that *enforcement* of it might follow as fast as circumstances should permit. They [the founders] meant to set up a standard maxim for society . . ."[11]

Equality understood as the equal right of persons to enjoy the protection of their liberty means there will be a good deal of inequality in society. A right can often be thought of as providing an opportunity to enjoy or acquire something. Because people's abilities differ (some, for example, have great athletic skills, others little) and because their inclinations vary (some prefer more leisure, others like to work), the results will also be different. Equality in the possession of rights is therefore another way of acknowledging the legitimacy of certain inequalities. "The first object of government" according to The Federalist, is the protection of the diversity in human faculties or capacities "from which different degrees and kinds of property results." (Federalist 10)

Political Equality Nothing in the Declaration stated the idea of equality, but did not spell out every respect in which people possess equal rights. One of the early issues the nation faced was whether equality presumed a right to vote. The Constitution bars property or religious qualifications for *holding* federal office, but it leaves the determination of voting requirements to the states. Although the suffrage from the beginning was fairly widespread (among the white male population), nearly all of the states initially had some qualification for voting based on property ownership or on some other method of demonstrating a stake in the community. Almost immediately, however, people began to demand the vote as an elementary right of citizenship, not only to protect their interests, but also to lay claim to their essential equality with others. By the 1830s most states had extended the suffrage to all free white males.

The expansion of the suffrage to nearly all adults has involved a long and complex process. No single provision in the Constitution positively guarantees the vote to all citizens, but a right to vote is now protected by a series of Constitutional amendments that ban states from limiting the suffrage on the grounds of race, sex, the payment of any poll tax, or age above eighteen years. In addition, a number of Supreme Court decisions and important pieces of federal legislation, such as the Voting Rights Act of 1965, recognize and protect the right to vote.

Economic Equality Nothing in the Declaration is said about ensuring economic equality, and unlike the revolutions in the Soviet Union in 1917 or Cuba in the 1950s, the distribution of wealth was not an important issue in 1776. Still, the general equality of rights was known to have definite implications for the economic sphere, as it would eliminate the kinds of economic inequalities found in Europe that were based on legally-protected class privileges. Equal rights would promote economic mobility and lead to a greater degree of material equality among the various strata of society. Still, there was never any doubt that property relations in an economic system based on equal rights would produce economic disparities. As Alexander Hamilton noted at the Convention, "an inequality would exist as long as liberty existed, and it would unavoidably result from that liberty itself."[12]

A concern for the degree of economic inequality has nevertheless been a constant issue in American politics and in fact has been a persistent constitutional question. Disputes over the distribution of wealth were common in the nineteenth century. A major contention was that policies of the federal government artificially produced a wealthy class. For Thomas Jefferson and Andrew Jackson, the economic system if left to its own devices would produce an acceptable allocation of wealth in society; it was government interference in economic matters that created privileges leading to great inequalities. In the twentieth century, those concerned with economic inequality emphasize a different argument. They contend that in a modern economy the free working of the economic system fails to provide for a fair allocation of wealth or to insure a tolerable level of security. Government must now take positive steps to correct the defects of the economic system. According to President Franklin Roosevelt, who was president during the Great Depression of the 1930s, "political rights have proved inadequate to assure us equality in the pursuit of happiness . . . true, individual freedom cannot exist without economic security and independence."

Roosevelt's statement helped lay the foundation for what is known as the welfare state. The welfare state is a general name given to the idea that government, by positive action and programs, should provide citizens with a certain level of welfare and economic security. Economic equality is not an explicit goal, but equalizing conditions in some sense is. At the least, there is an effort to help bring the bottom closer to middle. A welfare state thus differs from *socialism*, which is based on the ideas that the wealth of society is owned in the first instance by society as a whole, not separately by the individuals who comprise it, and that government should distribute the wealth with a high priority for achieving economic equality. In contrast to many European nations, socialism has never had much appeal in America. Yet many in America regard the degree of economic inequality as a question that merits careful attention and some measure of direct political supervision. Whenever tax laws and social policies are debated, many insist that a main objective should be to narrow economic differences among segments of the population.

Enforcing Equality   Aside from basic welfare state measures (unemployment insurance, social security, and welfare), the main efforts to secure equality in the middle of the twentieth century related to the elimination of discrimination. Laws and court decisions were enacted that sought to reduce or ban practices of government and larger private institutions that supported discrimination by race and sex. (Some of the most egregious examples were state and local laws or practices that enforced segregation by race in public parks and schools or that effectively barred black participation in electoral politics.) Most of these practices were banned by the 1970s.

Efforts at enforcing equality then entered a new stage, which raises some of the constitutional issues of the current decade. To alter societal practices, programs were advocated and adopted that sought to secure certain specific results in university admissions, jobs, promotions, and political representation for persons from groups subject to past discrimination. These affirmative action or quota policies began now to recognize the idea of group, as distinct from individual, rights in the case of certain designated minority groups. Insofar as government enforced such policies, it also involved a major increase of government monitoring and intervention in areas previously untouched by government rules or regulations. Some of the major constitutional controversies of the 1990s, raised in court cases, laws, and state referenda, have involved the legitimacy of such group affirmative action policies.   .

Citizenship

A final end of society is to foster the human attributes that produce good citizenship and promote a high quality of life. The founders knew good citizenship to be essential, as it would be citizens who were responsible for performing many of the tasks that enable free government to operate, such as voting, serving on juries, and being part of the militias. The preamble to the Constitution points to the aim of the quality of life by speaking of securing "the blessings of liberty." Attention therefore had to be given to what would help assure these human attributes.

Yet, as noted earlier, how this goal was defined and carried out differed from traditional ideas which held that government had the job to save people's souls and must do so by a constant monitoring of citizens. The founders acknowledged the need for good citizenship, but they were looking for a new model for encouraging it that was consistent with a government committed to protecting personal liberty.

No definitions of good citizenship or a good person are stated in the Constitution. Such a statement went beyond the kind of legal language—the preamble excepted—that was characteristic of the Constitution and of most formal law under a limited government. Conceptions of good citizenship and a good person were rather part of an intended set of general ideas or a creed that American constitution makers wished to promote. This creed would then inform people and government officials when making public policy. On such matters, of course, there are likely to be important differences of opinion, and this was true among the founders. But some common threads were evident. Most founders emphasized the importance of individuals who took great pride in fending for themselves and who exercised the qualities of independence, self-reliance, the use of reason, and a prudent form of patriotism, based on a pride in the political system and on belief in republican principles. These may seem like rather empty statements. But in fact many before had argued that the mass of people could only be governed by superstition and that society could only be held together by common prejudice. America's founders, by contrast, emphasize individual energy and enterprise and holding society together by a rational acknowledgment of its benefits, both political and economic.

The assumption of limited government is that good citizenship and decent human beings will develop in sufficient measure in a free society without the direct and constant supervision of governmental authority. These human attributes obviously need guidance and direction, most of which is to come from private institutions such as families, civic associations, and churches. Government also has a role to play, in part by protecting and encouraging these private institutions, but also in promoting certain activities itself. In the founding era, the national government's part in this area was indirect and limited, with state and local governments having the main responsibility for governmental action. These governments did so by prohibiting certain actions through their police powers and by taking positive steps to help build an enlightened citizenry. One function that developed was public assistance to promote education. Thomas Jefferson, for example, urged a system of universal public education in Virginia, noting that as the people are "the ultimate guardians of their own liberty," they must know the elementary lessons of history to be in a position to protect their rights: "to render the people safe, their minds must be improved."[13] Higher or university education was also part of his plan, and it was advocated not just to promote learning for its own sake, but also to help educate those who would most likely be called on to serve in public life.

A constitution that protects personal liberty never has meant that government is indifferent to the "way of life" of the people. Government policies, by lending support or providing incentives for certain activities, help fashion the general context in which rights are exercised and affect the basic way of life that develops. It is interesting to observe how this concern over the way of life enters into policies that might seem on their face to be about something quite different. Early debates on the tariff present an example. Tariffs encouraged the development of manufacturing and thus assisted the growth of cities. For Alexander Hamilton, urbanization would add to diversity and afford the opportunity for greater human development. For Thomas Jefferson, by contrast, the tariff would undermine the necessary qualities of good citizenship, which depended on the existence of hardy yeoman farmers. A congressman following Jefferson's view argued that a nation of city dwellers would be "distorted and decrepit as respects both bodily and mental endowments."[14]

With government today touching so many aspects of people's lives, modern governmental policies now have a greater impact on basic aspects of citizenship and character. The "moral" dimension of such policies is increasingly under debate in the various discussions of government's role in reducing drug use, regulating pornography on the Internet, policing the content of films and recordings, and controlling gambling. As William Bennett, the drug "czar" in 1990, stated, "A true friend of freedom understands that government has a responsibility to craft and uphold laws that help educate citizens about right and wrong."[15] But the question of how citizenship and the quality of life are affected by government goes well beyond the effects of these specific, character-related policies. Many contend that the most important consequences of government on citizenship and character come from much larger government programs where the effects on character are unintended or hidden—for example, from social and welfare programs which (some charge) undermine citizenship and character by fostering attitudes of dependence on government.

It is appropriate to conclude this section by noting some of the general features of liberalism's impact on the quality of life in society. Limited government, we said, means that government desists from establishing orthodox moral beliefs and directly defining a right way of life. A liberal constitution thus tends to appear publicly neutral about many aspects of the way of life in society, which produces distinct consequences when compared with the effects of other constitutions.

As one might expect, a liberal society promotes a wide diversity in lifestyles, from libertarian "swingers" to ascetic members of religious sects whose lives are devoted to otherworldly concerns. Travel the length of the United States, or visit almost any one of its large cities, and you see many different subcultures and lifestyles. This diversity provides the room in which individuals can pursue not just differences, but excellence in the realms of arts, philosophy, and pure science. By protecting freedom, government supports a society that allows free inquiry and that is dynamic, innovative, and resourceful.

Yet, if liberty produces diversity, some worry that by allowing people to pursue their individual ends, there is the risk of encouraging self-interestedness and an excessive emphasis on commercialism and physical gratification. This danger was discussed by the nineteenth century political theorist Alexis de Tocqueville, who in his classic work, *Democracy in America,* identified the "taste for well-being" as the "most striking and unalterable characteristics of democratic ages."[16] Unchecked, materialism could lead to both a growing apathy in political affairs and a decline in the level of culture. Modern critics of liberalism have gone further and speak of a moral and spiritual vacuum amid an ever-growing abundance of material goods.

The founders were aware that a significant degree of self-interested behavior would be a characteristic of a society based on liberty. They were not seeking the perfection of human beings, realizing that the power to seek such perfection could lead to enormous abuse and tyranny. And while self-interested behavior could clearly result in excesses, against which some measure might need to be taken, it also has the effect of releasing human energy that contributes to dynamism and economic growth. The founders, according to one commentator, "understood that the business of most Americans was going to be business, and they had no snobbish disdain for such activity."[17] Accepting the connection between liberty and self-interest, the founders sought to construct a society and government that did not rely entirely on "moral and religious motives," but that balanced "rival interests" to promote the public good. (*Federalist* 10 and 51) The founders made cool and realistic estimates of the sources of human behavior, taking into account people's passions as well as their reason. They did not assume, in utopian fashion, that "men were angels," but they were mindful of the higher qualities that were needed in the American citizenry to sustain the system. (*Federalist* 51)

The Role of Government in Society

The second question any constitution maker must ask is what role government should play in society. In some nations, government extends into almost every sphere, whether it be the economy, the arts, or the dissemination of information. For years, the communist government in the Soviet Union owned all the major industries, controlled the labor unions, decided what was taught in the schools (no private schools were allowed), and directly ran all the television and radio stations as well as the newspapers. Such systems aimed for a near total control of society by the state—hence the term "totalitarian" government.[18]

The definition of the ends of society discussed above has clear implications for the role of government. A government that secures liberty is limited in its scope; it is only one part of a society that includes other semiautonomous parts or systems. The cultivation of the arts, the dissemination of information, and the direction of business enterprises are left primarily in private hands that are sometimes regulated and aided, but not controlled, by government. A crucial distinction thus exists under liberal theory between "government" (the officers and offices of the state and its legal machinery) and "civil society" (the various institutions, interactions, and systems that develop outside of government supervision). In a liberal system there is a presumption against bringing more aspects of civil society under governmental control or influence, on the grounds that this interference restricts liberty and risks creating a center of power so large and formidable that it overwhelms the capacity of any element of society to offer resistance.

Yet to say government should be limited does not provide a complete theory of the proper scope of government. Securing rights sets boundaries beyond which government may not go, but it does not tell us what powers government needs. This question was one America's constitution makers had to confront. The founders, in fact, worried that an exclusive focus on the theme of securing rights would lead people to deny to government the requisite "firmness and efficiency." (*Federalist* 1) Government needs an adequate sum of power. It needs it in the first place to protect liberty, which requires order, the defense of nation, and the authority to define the concrete meaning of many rights. Government also is instituted to perform other desirable functions for the common good, including promoting commerce, coining money, and a host of other functions. Granting broad powers to government admittedly poses dangers, but running this risk is necessary: "a power to advance the public happiness involves a discretion which may be misapplied and abused." (*Federalist* 41) Of course, to grant government a power does not mean that it must use that power to the fullest extent, but only that it is available.

Discussing the role of government role in the United States is complicated by the issue of federalism. Debates over limited government sometimes end by confusing the question of how much power government at all levels should have with how much power the *federal* government should have. There have been many who wish to limit the scope of the national government while calling for extensive powers for states and local government. The discussion of federalism is clearly important, because significant consequences follow from which level of government exercises which powers. To account adequately for the role of government, two different dimensions of the question need to be kept in mind: the powers and limits of the federal government, and the power and limits of government at any level.

The federal government was originally conceived as a government of broad but enumerated powers. These included such things as conducting diplomacy with foreign nations, establishing the armed services, and regulating interstate commerce and commerce with foreign nations. For most of the nineteenth century—with some major exceptions relating to the Civil War and its aftermath—most government activities that directly touched people's lives on a daily basis—education, police protection, road building, and the like—were performed by state and local governments. In the twentieth century, the federal government has assumed more tasks and responsibilities in numerous areas, ranging from regulating aspects of the economy, to providing social security and medical care, to playing an important role in housing grants and education. The list of activities now performed by the national government, in fact, can go on and on. The federal government operates today under few of the restrictions that once made it a government of enumerated powers that was limited in its relationship to the states. It does more by itself (like owning and operating Amtrak); more to aid non-governmental institutions (major private universities receive large parts of their funds directly or indirectly from the federal govern-

ment); more to regulate and control what goes on in the economic sphere (auto companies must produce a fleet of cars that average a certain number of miles per gallon of gasoline); and more in combination with state and local governments (such as providing funds for public education).

One indication of the expanded role of the federal government can be seen from how much it spends relative to the total spending in the nation as a whole. In 1880, federal expenditures represented about 2.6 percent of the gross national product. (The gross national product—abbreviated GNP—represents the total value of goods and services produced by a nation during a given year.) In 2000, federal expenditures accounted for 30 percent of the GNP.

The growth in the role of the federal government does not mean that states and localities do less than they once did. State and local governmental activity and spending have also increased greatly in this century, and in certain key areas—health care, industrial policy, and environmental regulation and welfare—important new initiatives have taken place at the state level.

Combining the activities of the national and state and local governments, it is clear that one of the notable constitutional changes in the twentieth century has been the general growth in government's role in society. Together the combined spending for government spending now accounts for nearly 40 percent of the GNP. Government growth has not occurred in every area, and in certain areas—for example, state regulations on the hours businesses may operate—government control has diminished. Overall, however, more elements of society are touched today by government regulation or depend on government funds than was the case fifty years ago.

Yet when compared with the size and scope of government in many of the other developed nations, government in the United States is far more limited. Nor does it follow that because government expanded so rapidly over the past half century that it will continue to do so in the future. Indeed, during the past twenty years, there has been growing public resistance to an expanding role for government and especially for the federal government. The debate over the

---

BOX 1.2

The Expansion of the Role of the Federal Government

Today, you can hardly turn around without bumping into some federal restraint or requirement. It wasn't always so; there was a time you could embark on almost any venture without encountering a single federal constraint. Now, however, if you should take it into your head, say, to manufacture and market a new product, you would probably run into statutes and administrative regulations on labor relations, occupational safety, product safety, and air purity. Your advertising would probably fall within the jurisdiction of the Federal Trade Commission. The Department of Justice would be interested in your relations with your competitors. Should you want to raise capital by the sale of stocks or bonds, you would fall under the Securities and Exchange Commission. You would need export licenses from the Department of Commerce to sell your product in some areas of the world. Federal prohibitions against race, age, and sex discrimination in hiring and promotion would apply to you. If you were to extend credit to your customers, you might fall under truth-in-lending laws. You would have to file sundry reports for tax, social security, pension, and census purposes. In some fields—communication, transportation, energy, insurance, and banking, for instance—restrictions and oversight are especially stringent. But firms of all kinds, large and small, are subject to diverse federal requirements. You can't just start and run a business without reference to federal specifications and officials.

Source: Herbert Kaufman, *Red Tape* (Washington, D.C.: Brookings Institution, 1977) pp. 5–6.

wisdom of "Big Government" has become a central constitutional controversy of our time.

The Concept of Power Under a Limited Government

"Power" is a word always used in discussions of politics, but often without much precision. Usually, it refers to control that *government* exercises and to the influence that groups or individuals have on what *government* does. But some conceive of it in broader terms as the capacity of any agency or institution—governmental or non- governmental—to affect the lives of others and control access to resources. Using for the moment this broader definition, the place of government itself as a source of power in society can be considered.

In a limited government, a great deal of the power in society remains in private hands. Thus private universities determine their own admission policies and thereby exercise an important kind of power over access to careers such as law and medicine. Or business corporations make decisions that can have an enormous impact on people's lives, as in cases when a corporation decides to close down a factory in a small town. Examples of the exercise of such "private" or non-governmental power could be multiplied across many areas of American life.

Critics of the system of limited government have tended to rely on the concept of "private" power to expose and attack the real character of power in American society. They contend that the line that separates private from public control has been unjustly drawn to exclude from political consideration whole areas of power that favor the interests of the wealthy and privileged. Even if all existing governmental power were to be made strictly subject to popular control, they argue, our constitution as a whole would still be highly undemocratic, because so little power in society is in fact public (or political). To promote a genuinely just or democratic society, public authority must extend its reach into previously private areas and establish new standards to promote equality.

Defenders of limited government respond that the exercise of power in social and economic spheres is, as a general rule, better left in private hands. This arrangement not only protects the freedom of individuals, but also avoids a huge concentration of power in government. If ever most power in society were transferred to government, government would become nearly impossible to restrain. Furthermore, all contro-

---

BOX 1.3

Modern Liberalism and Conservatism

The Republican party's conservative view of the role of government is set forth in the following passage from the 1980 Republican platform:

> For too many years, the political debate in America has been conducted in terms set by the Democrats. They believe that every time new problems arise beyond the power of men and women as individuals to solve, it becomes the duty of government to solve them, as if there were never any alternative. Republicans disagree and have always taken the side of the individual, whose freedoms are threatened by the big government that Democratic idea has spawned. Our case for the individual is stronger than ever. A defense of the individual against government was never more needed. And we will continue to mount it.

On the other hand, Samuel Beer describes the New Deal liberalism of Franklin Roosevelt and the Democratic party in the 1930s, which continues to represent the core ideas of many liberals today:

> Roosevelt called not only for a centralization of government, but also for a nationalization of politics . . . He exhorted voters and citizens to turn to Washington as the center of power on which to exert their pressures and project their expectations. . . . A principle and reiterated theme . . . of his administration was to assure the people that the federal government could solve their problems.

Source: Samuel Beer, "In Search of a New Public Philosophy," in Anthony King (ed.), *The New American Political System* (Washington, D.C.: American Enterprise Institute, 1978), p. 8.

versies would become political conflicts, burdening government with more responsibility than it could effectively handle. Finally, government decisions in certain spheres, especially economic matters, often produce inefficient results. For defenders of limited government, then, the dividing line between public and private spheres is one of the keys to maintaining liberty.

Perspectives on the Role of Modern Government

Government in the twentieth century expanded for a number of reasons. Conditions became more complex and interrelated, requiring more government activity to accomplish objectives that were more simply managed in the past. People accepted the basic idea of the welfare state and came to expect government to provide security for medical treatment and retirement and to supply more services, from job training to subsidies for artists and opera companies. Finally, a part of the public sought to bring more aspects of society under public authority in order to eliminate what they consider an unjust distribution of

resources. With growing demands for equality, the scope of government necessarily increased.

The controversy over the size of government has been the central constitutional conflict of American politics since the time of the New Deal in the 1930s. It has served to define the two major contemporary public philosophies (or "ideologies"): (modern) liberalism and (modern) conservatism. Modern-day liberals, who are found mostly within the Democratic party, have generally supported an expansion of the role of government, especially the role of the federal government, contending that more government is needed to protect the individual's economic security and promote greater equality. Conservatives, who are most often associated with the Republican party, have generally opposed the growth of government, especially on the national level. Although conservatives are not perfectly clear about just how much they would like to reduce government (just as liberals are not clear about just how far they would like to extend it), they contend that too much government threatens basic liberties and jeopardizes economic well-being.

Proponents of both of these public philosophies claim to be the heirs of eighteenth-century liberalism. But each interprets the requirements of liberalism for modern times in a different way. Modern liberals argue that positive government, while conflicting somewhat with the form of earlier liberalism, best realizes its ends. The situation in modern economies, with large concentrations of power in private corporations, requires more government today than was once the case. Conservatives (some of whom, incidentally, still call themselves liberals) stress their links with classical liberal ideas and claim that their ideas best promote the classical liberal goals of equal opportunity, limited government, and individual freedom.

The Organization of Institutions and the Distribution of Political Power

The third question a constitution maker must ask is who should govern and how political power should be distributed within the government. The Declaration speaks of the right of the people "to institute new government, laying its foundation on such principles, and organizing its power in such form" as will produce the people's safety and happiness. The task of devising the actual structure of government fell to the authors of the different state constitutions and to the founders at the Convention in 1787.

The constitution maker's job in organizing the form of government is to determine who holds the reins of power and makes authoritative decisions. This question had traditionally been approached by deciding which persons or social class should govern. Thus, where a single person or family governs, the constitution is a monarchy or, in the absence of law, a tyranny. Where a small class or limited number of individuals governs, the constitution is an aristocracy (rule by the most able) or an oligarchy (rule by the wealthy). Where the citizens as a whole govern the constitution is a democracy. A mixture of these constitutions, exclusive of a tyranny, is known as a "mixed regime."

People today still distinguish constitutions in the first instance by asking who rules. Thus everyone knew a change had taken place in the states of Eastern Europe in 1989–90 when the communist party officials, who had ruled these nations without elections, were thrown out of power and replaced by leaders chosen in popular elections. Yet important as it is to investigate who governs, this question does not fully define how power is distributed in a representative democracy. Political power in a representative government is held not merely by a specific group or social class, but also by laws and by institutions. The founders sought to modify the impact of who governs by adopting a written constitution and by creating a government in which institutions have authority to operate in some measure on their own. In addition, therefore, to inquiring into *who* governs, we must also ask *what* governs.

A Written Constitution

A major innovation of the founding was to base government on a *written* law that spells out the government's powers and limits. Prior to the American founding, most rulers and governments exercised power without being subject to the control of a single written document. In a system based on a written constitution, power is given to government in the form of a written and legal trust or agreement. This arrangement establishes two sources of authority: the "fundamental law" (The Constitution), which sets the terms of the agreement under which government exercises its powers, and the government, which acts pursuant to the fundamental law. The Constitution "is paramount to government." (*Federalist* 53) This theoretical claim is backed by the practical measure that the Constitution cannot be altered by the government, but only by a distinct procedure: the amendment process that is spelled out in Article V of the Constitution. (The Constitution has been amended only twenty-seven times, with the first ten of these amendments, known as the Bill of Rights, ratified together in 1791.)

What kind of document is the Constitution? When many think today of the Constitution, they have in mind chiefly a list of specific rights that are adjudicated in highly publicized Supreme Court cases. Yet the core of the Constitution is not a list of specific rights, but a scheme that distributes and arranges political power. The Constitution defines the sum of powers of the federal government and places restrictions on both the federal government and the states; and it determines the basic framework of the government, sketching the powers and basic structure of each office or institution.

Insofar as the Constitution governs the nation, determining who governs requires looking at how the Constitution was originally approved and how it may be amended. The Constitution was ratified from 1787 to 1789 by special conventions in the states, which were quite democratic bodies by the standards of the time. (Slaves did not vote for the delegates to these conventions, and women voted only in one or two states.) Amendments to the Constitution may be passed in one of four different ways, but—with one exception—they have followed the route of being proposed by a two-thirds majority in both houses of Congress and then approved by the legislatures of three fourths of the states. Neither the president nor members of the judicial branch have an official role. Only legislators or special representatives of the people are involved. The ratification and amending process, according to the founders, represent a more direct expression of the "consent of the governed." The people, as the "pure original fountain of all authority," establish a Constitution and through it remain the "master," while the government is the "servant." (*Federalist* 22 and 78)

The idea that the Constitution rests more directly on the people's will than an act by the current government is an extraordinary claim. It says that what the American people did in 1789 and what they did over the years in the various amendments is somehow more truly representative of the people than what government officials just elected might wish to do. Nearly all Americans, however, accept this claim. A belief that the Constitution is in fact the fundamental law, which is known as constitutionalism, is one of the fundamental aspects of our form of government. Constitutionalism means that there are two separate levels of rule and that the people, insofar as they participate in ruling, wear two different hats. When acting as agents in the amending process, the people take part in the solemn Constitutional function of deciding the general powers, limits, and structure of the government. When acting in more ordinary ways in the election process, the people help to shape the general policies of government.

Does this formal supremacy of the Constitution over the government actually hold in practice? Is it not possible for the "servant"—that is, the government—to ignore the Constitution and proceed (perhaps with popular consent) in a way that violates or distorts the Constitution's plain intent? There have been instances in which this has occurred, and some cases no doubt in which the Constitution has been effectively altered without an amendment. (Deciding when this has occurred is controversial, because no one admits to this behavior.) Overall, however, clear violations of the Constitution have been rare. Allowing for the fact that the Constitution can reasonably be interpreted in different ways, we find that the Constitution manages to set the broad outlines of the structure of the government. Time and again, presidents and members of Congress have had to set aside actions they might have wanted to take because they conflicted with the Constitution.

Constitutionalism as a living principle also helps explain the extraordinary power of the judicial branch in American politics. The Supreme Court, although itself one of the institutions of government, has come generally to be recognized as the final interpreter of the meaning of the Constitution. Speaking for the Constitution (and thus, in a sense, for the people), the Supreme Court is now an immensely powerful body—indeed, many worry, too powerful. If Americans did not believe in the authority of a written constitution, they would not accept placing so much power in the hands of nine unelected officials.

Representative Government and Separation of Powers

The American political system is a *representative* government, meaning a government exercised by elected or appointed officials in designated offices. The principal institutions outlined in the Constitution are the Congress, the presidency, and the judiciary. Officials of these offices hold the immediate power of the federal government.

Recognizing the significance of this simple fact explains why it is necessary to speak not only of *who* governs but of *what* governs. If the government were a pure democracy, decisions would be made not by representatives, but by the people voting directly on laws and policies—by means, perhaps, of votes taken in referendums or by the use of computer consoles in the home. Similarly, if the government were an oligarchy, political decisions would be made directly by business leaders and the rich—say by a council of the heads of the largest 500 corporations plus members of the wealthiest families.

The fact of the matter, however, is that the power to govern is given in the first instance to the officials (the president, members of Congress, the judges) who possess a certain amount of autonomy and who operate in institutions designed to promote certain qualities in governing. These institutions must therefore be considered in part on their own terms and not simply as substitutes for forces in society. Government, in other words, is in some measure an independent force that is supposed to deliberate and reach judgments about the public good.

Because institutions govern, much of the debate in American politics on how political power should be distributed has focused on the relative power of three branches of government. These debates, of course, sometimes reflect claims of who should govern. For example, when the Supreme Court in the 1930s declared unconstitutional much of President Roosevelt's New Deal program, the President attacked the Court as an oligarchic institution and sought to bring it into line with the people's wishes by expanding the number of judges on the Court. But this famous incident, known as the Court-packing plan, also demonstrates the importance of the forms of government (what governs). Roosevelt's plan was blocked when many Americans rallied to the Court's defense, including a large number who opposed its decisions, because they thought that an independent judiciary was essential to the preservation of the Constitution.

The Constitution's division of power among the branches of the government is based on the general principle known as the separation of powers, which was an idea of political science developed initially by John Locke and Charles Montesquieu. This principle holds that political power should be separated and divided among different institutions of government in order to guard against the possibility of its abuse. As the founders stated: "The accumulation of all powers, legislative, executive, and judiciary, in the same hands, whether of one, a few, or many, and whether hereditary, self-appointed, or elective, may justly be pronounced the very definition of tyranny." (*Federalist* 47) Notice that this principle rests chiefly not on who governs, but on how power is distributed. By the same token, many critics of the Constitution attack it because they claim that the separation of powers produces government that is weak, divided, and incapable of systematic policy innovation. Debates over political power in the United States have thus partly been transformed from arguments over who governs (the allocation of power among different segments of society) into controversies over the role of the different institutions.

Who Governs?

In the final analysis, however, a constitution is broadly characterized by who governs or exercises the major influence on the governing institutions. The institutions of the United States government, while they are intended to have in some measure a will of their own, do not function in isolation from society. Officials are selected in certain ways and operate under certain expectations about whose interests they are to serve.

A constitution maker establishes the rules and arrangements that determine "who governs"— that is, which groups or segments of society will influence the operation of these institutions. The relevant factors here include the practices and provisions respecting such matters as who is eligible for office who may vote, how candidates are nominated and elected, how campaigns are funded, who has standing to sue before the courts, and who is in a position to obtain access to a legislator or member of the executive branch. Examining these factors will be a major part of this book. Many of them have undergone considerable change since 1789, and they must be analyzed not just on the level of the written Constitution, but across a whole range of federal and state laws, institutional practices, and public doctrines. But the exploration of these issues should not prevent us from restating the basic conclusion that the United States government was intended to be—and is—a government in which the people have the decisive say on the direction of our governing institutions. Time and again at the Constitutional Convention, delegates noted that the new government would be popular. Even those who had reservations (and there were a few) recognized that the nation was about to embark on an experiment in popular government.

One often hears this form of government referred to today as a "democracy," although a pure democracy is strictly speaking a system in which the people rule directly without the intermediary of representative institutions. In light of this fact, it is more correct to characterize the United States government as a species of popular government known as a "representative democracy" or a "republic." Because our government is popular, does it then follow that it must be as responsive as possible to the majority? The answer, quite clearly, is no. Forms of government differ not only in kind, as in the distinction between a monarchy and a representative democracy, but also, within each kind, by degree. Popular governments, for example, can vary in how much and how quickly they are designed to respond immediately to public opinion, and how much discretion they give to the officers and institutions.

The Constitution as originally ratified contained many qualifications on immediate popular influence. It provided for an indirect election of the president and the Senate, a fairly long term (six years) for those chosen for the Senate, and a nonelective judiciary. The founders justified these qualifications on the grounds that they would improve the quality of governmental decisions and lessen the danger that a majority itself, under certain circumstances, might threaten the rights of a minority. It is a measure of the founders' confidence in the people's judgment that they openly argued that the "the cool deliberate sense of the community," not "every sudden breeze of passion" or "every transient impulse" or every "momentary inclination," should ultimately prevail. (*Federalist* 63, 71, and 78)

American history has been filled with constitutional debates over the degree to which the popular will should influence government. Generally speaking, there has been a growth in popular influence, brought about sometimes by formal amendments to the Constitution and sometimes by changes in laws and practices. The suffrage, as noted, has been secured for all adults; the selection of the president since the 1830s has been by the vote of the public; political parties developed in the nineteenth century to facilitate popular rule, and introduction of primary elections in the twentieth century brought popular influence more directly into the nomination of party candidates; and senators since 1913 have been selected by direct popular vote.

Yet limits on popular rule have also developed, some perhaps without forethought. Large bureaucracies and independent regulatory commissions now exercise considerable decision-making authority, removing questions, such as the control of the supply of money, from popular influence. The judiciary has greatly broadened the range of issues subject to its jurisdiction, often assuming authority that once was exercised by state legislatures and local governments. Finally, some contend that many important practices in the electoral process, involving how incumbents may use their office to secure support and campaigns are financed, make our system far less democratic than many think.

Once the constitution makers have decided on the basic type of government, they must determine its exact character and form. It is here, in fact, that most of the real work of constitution making takes place. Questions of degree—of how much popular government—are not secondary or incidental matters, but become the core of the practical study of the constitution of a country. The study of degree is a question not just of knowing how much influence the people have, but of trying to determine when, where, and in what ways increasing or decreasing that influence will tend to preserve the constitution and to promote more deliberate government. It is a study of quality and not just quantity.

Four Models of Political Analysis

Up to this point, we have discussed who governs without using any technical vocabulary. Yet because of the centrality of this question, analysts have tried to develop models specifying the different possible elements of society that exercise influence on our government. These models are: elitism, bureaucratic rule, pluralism, and majoritarianism. The first two taken in a strong sense conflict with the claim made that the American constitution is in fact a representative democracy, while the latter two are compatible with it. All four of the models can nevertheless be helpful in providing insights into how the political system works, as a government that is in the main a representative democracy may contain certain nondemocratic elements.

Elitism This view holds that the decisive influence in the United States is exercised by a relatively small number of individuals. In one sense, of course, a representative government is by definition a government by an elite inasmuch as only the small number of officials in the government actually make authoritative decisions. Furthermore, the aim of many of the Constitution's institutional arrangements was not to secure the selection of average or mediocre individuals, but so far as possible highly qualified persons, who possess "the most wisdom to discern, and most virtue to pursue, the common good of society." (*Federalist* 57) In this sense, elitism is not just consistent with representative government, but is one of the founders' ideals.

Most references to elitism, however, have a different meaning in mind, in which the exercise of power is by a specific group with an identifiable interest that is distinct from that of the public at large. One such group, certain analysts claim, is the wealthy and the heads of big businesses. The United States, in this view, is governed by "a ruling class" or an "establishment" that exercises power first by keeping government authority out of domains in which the establishment already exercises its private power, and second by having disproportionate influence within the limited sphere in which government does operate. Government may not literally be "bought," but politicians greatly favor the wealthy, who achieve influence through well-financed lobbying efforts, campaign contributions, favors (legal and illegal), and an established network of social contacts. According to the elite model, then, while the government may look from the outside to be a representative democracy, behind the scenes it is largely controlled by the few and in the interests of the few.

Bureaucratic Rule This model holds that government power is dominated by public bureaucracies—that is, by the agencies charged with administering the government. Although the aims of these agencies are certainly not hostile to those of the public, public bureaucracies nevertheless develop their own interests (often protecting their own turf). Elected officials sit atop this structure, trying to control it but in reality are often controlled by it. The tasks of governing today are so complex that elected officials and politicians have no choice but to turn much of the operating authority over to the bureaucracies, which slowly accumulate more power. Presidents and cabinet members come and go (often rather quickly), but the officials in the bureaucracy remain. As one assistant to two secretaries of defense remarked: "The bureaucracy knows deep in its heart that it can outlast almost any secretary of defense."

Bureaucracies, of course, have competing interests. Thus, the State Department may sometimes be at odds with the Defense Department, or the different services of the Defense Department (the Army, Navy, Air Force, and Marines) may sometimes be at odds with each other. Agencies struggle for influence among themselves and seek to dominate policymaking by forging alliances and by drumming up support from clients that depend on their goodwill. The conflict among bureaucracies generates a distinct kind of politics. As described by Henry Kissinger: "In bureaucratic societies policy emerges from a compromise (among bureaucratic agencies) which often produces the least common denominator, and it is implemented by individuals whose reputation is made by administering the status quo."[19] Bureaucratic politics in this sense conflicts not only with popular rule, but with energetic and imaginative leadership of any kind.

BOX 1.4

Four Models of the Dominant Influence of Who Governs

I. An elitist interpretation of the American political system

Our government represents the privileged few rather than the needy many. . . . Elections, political parties and the right to speak out are seldom effective measures against the influences of corporate wealth. (Michael Parenti)

II. A bureaucratic interpretation of the American political system

David Brinkley, a leading journalist at ABC, provided one of the best anecdotal statements of the bureaucratic model.

This town [Washington, D.C.] is sort of like a great big steamboat that keeps going its way regardless of which way the wind blows, or how elections go, or how the current goes; it keeps going, and it might move one degree in one direction, but it essentially keeps going the same direction. It goes on grinding out paper, spending money, hiring people, getting bigger and bigger and more troublesome all the time, and nothing seems to affect it. Presidents don't affect it. Every President I have known has complained about the fantastically cumbersome size of this establishment here. As far back as Harry Truman, I was covering the White House and Truman said, "I thought I was the President, but when it comes to these bureaucrats I can't make 'em do a damn thing."

III. A pluralist interpretation of the American political system

Pluralism is the least precise of the four models of American politics, and its definition often varies according to the author employing the term. A leading political scientist, Nelson Polsby, has sought to provide an illustrative list of pluralism's major characteristics:

Dispersion of power among many rather than a few participants in decision making; competition or conflict among political leaders; . . . bargaining rather than hierarchical decision making; elections in which suffrage is relatively widespread as a major determinant of participation in key decisions; bases of influence over decisions relatively dispersed rather than closely held.

IV. A majoritarian interpretation of the American political system

In America the people appoint both those who make the laws and those who execute them. . . . So direction really comes through the people, and though the form of government is representative, it is clear that the opinions, prejudices, interests, and even passions of the people can find no lasting obstacles preventing them from being manifest in the daily conduct of society. In the United States, as in all countries where the people reign, the majority rules in the name of the people. (Alexis de Tocqueville)

Sources: Michael Parenti, *Democracy for the Few* (New York: St. Martin's, 1980), p.2; Nelson Polsby, *Community Power and Political Theory* (New Haven, Conn.: Yale University Press, 1980), p. 154; Alexis de Tocqueville, *Democracy in America*, J. P. Mayor, ed. (New York Anchor, 1968), p. 173.

The model of bureaucratic influence was first suggested by Max Weber (1864–1920), a German sociologist who pioneered the study of bureaucracy. For Weber, bureaucratization is the overwhelming fact of modern social organization, both public and private: "The future" he wrote, "belongs to bureaucratization." Important functions, he believed, would come to be performed less by people working as individuals and more by officials operating in complex organizations. Even those working within the bureaucracies cannot really master these organizations, which take on virtually a life of their own. Power lies with the human cogs (the bureaucrats) enmeshed in an uncontrollable machine (the bureaucracy). It is the behavior of these organizations that must be understood.

Pluralism   This model holds that the major influence on government derives from numerous organized groups representing a broad spectrum of different interests in American society.

Included among these groups are those that aim to protect bread and butter interests (business groups, labor groups, agricultural groups), and those that promote different causes or objectives (civil rights groups, environmental groups, and good government groups). Significant groups can usually "make themselves heard at some crucial stage in the process of decision."20 Governing involves the formation of coalitions among these groups in a bargaining process. In our system of separation of power, in which many hurdles must be overcome before a new policy is adopted, important groups are often in a position to block initiatives they dislike. Policymaking according to the pluralist model is very slow and requires a large degree of consensus.

Pluralism sounds like—and is—a model of government that reflects the interests of broad segments of the public. Yet pluralism does not perfectly mirror those interests. Some interests, like big labor or big business, are in a position to organize with relative ease, while other potential interests, like the poor or like consumers in general, lack comparable means or have less incentive to create viable and effective organizations. Moreover, because group influence is related not just to the number of persons for whom an organization claims to speak, but also to the capacity and skill of the organization, some interests may fare much better (or worse) than one would expect on the basis of their general weight in society. Finally, the leaders of powerful interest groups do not always represent the wishes of their constituents, but may often speak for themselves or for what helps their organization (but not its constituents).

Those who subscribe to a pluralist model all agree that the influence of groups does not perfectly represent all social interests. But they disagree about the degree and character of this distortion. Some hold that the interests that are effectively represented greatly favor the wealthy and the privileged, so much so that pluralism is not really a popular model of government but a form of elitism. Others say that pluralism gives a voice to most of the important interests and constitutes a reasonable, although far from perfect, way for them to press their claims. There is no systematic exclusion of groups, and differences in the strength of groups often derive as much from the intensity of people's views as from their status or wealth.

Analysts also disagree in their evaluation of pluralism. Some criticize a pluralist system because (as just noted) it overrepresents the privileged; or because it enables major groups to block enactment of measures they dislike; or because it concentrates attention on bargains among specific interests rather than on deliberation about the broader, general interest. Others defend a pluralist model as a reasonably fair and efficient way by which the interests in a complex modern society can be represented. Government, they go on, should take account not just of citizens' preferences, but of the intensity of their feelings as well; strong opposition by an important interest in society should often prevail even in the face of a mild preference from a majority. Finally, the overall interest of society is often best discovered by a process of practical accommodations among concrete interests rather than by debates about abstract theories of the general interest.

Majoritarianism This model holds that the decisive influence on our institutions derives from the public at large, and in particular from the majority of the citizens. The people's views hold great weight because of the almost universal acceptance of the idea that the people's will should be carefully considered and the people's interest served. In Abraham Lincoln's famous phrase, America is a government "of the people, by the people, and for the people." This principle finds practical expression and reinforcement in many institutional arrangements. The public exercises its influence by popular elections of the major officers of the government, relying often on the assistance of political parties to help organize national majorities. Majoritarianism also works, a bit more vaguely, through the "instrument" of public opinion, to which politicians—in part because of their interest in reelection—are usually quite attentive. Knowing that they must obtain the votes of a majority to win office, politicians will do either what the majority wants or else what they believe a majority can be persuaded to accept. (Between these two conceptions of majoritarianism, obviously, there is a very important difference.)

A majoritarian model does not mean that a majority exists on every issue. Public opinion studies confirm that on many questions there is no meaningful division of opinion in the public at large and that for many problems there is no majority position about which policy to adopt. Nor does a majoritarian model necessarily hold that, even where there is a majority preference, the government always follows that preference. (Some might prefer this would be the case, but few maintain that it is always so.) A more usual version of majoritarianism as a descriptive account states that on important issues and choices on which the public focuses, the will of the people is in the end usually the most decisive influence.

As analysts often use one of these four models—elitism, bureaucratic rule, pluralism, and majoritarianism—to describe the basic distribution of power in the United States, we need to indicate how we shall employ them in this text. First, because the American constitution is a representative democracy, the models that best help to characterize the American system are pluralism and majoritarianism. Elements of these two models, often mixed together in complex ways, shape most the major political processes in our system. Aspects of pluralism are present in the openness to interest groups and in the institutional arrangements that provide many points of access to groups in the policy process, while the majoritarian idea is present in the basic democratic principle of majority rule and in key elements of the electoral system. Both of these models also rest on ideas that have had support of important constitution makers and that enjoy a considerable degree of public acceptance.

Second, neither pluralism nor majoritarianism accounts fully for the distribution of power in our system because the government itself acts in some measure as an independent source of authority. We shall therefore speak of these models as helpful descriptions of major influences that operate on the government rather than as direct accounts of how power is exercised.

Finally, even though the two non-popular models—elitism and bureaucratic rule—do not capture the basic character of our government,

they nevertheless often help describe influences that operate on government in certain areas and at certain times. (Incidentally, analysts who favor these two models almost never recommend them as prescriptions for how the American system ought to operate.) All four of the models are therefore helpful as analytic tools and will be used in this book. Indeed, no single model absolutely depicts reality; actual political processes frequently involve elements of different models operating with different relative weights. On balance, however, the pluralist and majoritarian models are predominant.

Security and the Promotion of Purpose in the World

The final question a constitution maker must address is how the nation can protect its security and promote its interests and purposes in a world of states that have conflicting interests and sometimes hostile intentions. "To provide for the common defense," as the preamble to the Constitution puts it, is clearly one of the chief ends of society. But we single it out for separate treatment because it raises different kinds of considerations than those involved with the ends of liberty, self-government, equality, and good citizenship, which are selected because they are desirable in themselves for our domestic way of life. But in security affairs and foreign policy, the focus is different. The question is often not what we might prefer but what we may need to do in order to ensure the nation's independence and promote its interests.

In the realm of foreign affairs, the constitution maker must take into account some cruel and unpleasant realities that result from what other nations may do.

"Necessity" in Constitution Making

In the beginning of *The Federalist*, Publius wonders whether mankind is capable of establishing good government from "reflection and choice," or whether it must always depend on "accident and force." In the founder's view, "reflection and choice" meant republican government, where the people are sovereign and not dependent on the accident of a benevolent monarch or aristocracy. "Accident and force" were seen as necessities that limited republican choice. But foreign actions that limit choice, which we would like to wish away, are brought into the Constitution to be dealt with by the president. While the president and Congress may cooperate on domestic affairs, the executive was created to handle the actions of other nations that we would not choose, and which would otherwise disrupt republican deliberation. For example, the terrorist attacks of September, 11 2001 illustrate necessity, or the force of events beyond our control.

The basic decision facing the nation was whether to remain essentially a confederation of independent states, or to form a genuine union under a strong national government. However appealing (to some) might be the idea of living in a smaller and independent state, the founders argued that this choice would result in control or conquest by larger European powers. Union offered the "best security that can be devised against hostilities from abroad," as well as against the prospect of frequent conflict between the states. (*Federalist* 3)

The importance of security was reflected not only in the question of whether to form a national government but also in the decisions about what powers that government should have and how its offices should be organized. Many opponents of the Constitution—fearful (as all were) of the great dangers of a large standing army—wanted limits to be placed on the size of the armed forces in peace time. The founders did not deny the danger but replied that, as "it is impossible to foresee or to define the extent and variety of national emergencies," no one could know how many troops might be needed in the future to defend the nation and deter aggression. (*Federalist* 23) The Constitution accordingly provides the national government with an unlimited power to provide for the nation's defense—"to raise and support armies [and] to provide and maintain a navy." (Article I section 8) On the arrangement of offices, the Constitution provides for a single executive (a President), who is commander-in-chief and has broad powers to conduct foreign policy. Again opponents of the Constitution objected, complaining that too much power was vested in one individual. The

founders responded that the conduct of foreign and defense affairs required a government able to act on occasion with "secrecy and dispatch [quickness]"—qualities that are associated with command decisions made by a single individual. (*Federalist* 70) What is characteristic of these arguments is a certain logic that considers not just what we want in some perfect world, but what we must consider in the actual world in which we live. By recognizing these needs, we can realistically accommodate ourselves to them in a way that maintains the chosen form of government.

The formation of the union in 1789 enabled the United States to achieve the security from European powers. Indeed, with no nation in this hemisphere being a serious match for American power, Americans in the nineteenth century could profit from the advantages of geography and largely ignore foreign threats. In the twentieth century the United States became a major power that was involved in two world wars and that for the last half century has maintained far-flung alliances that commit us to the defense of scores of nations all over the globe. Security concerns in part dictated this new role. Changes in military technology—airplanes, missiles, nuclear weapons—reduced the value of geographic position. The emergence of new and aggressive ideologies in this century, in the form of fascism and communism, brought unprecedented threats to America and its allies. From the end of World War II until the 1990s, America assumed the major burden of defense of the non-communist world against the threat of the communist system backed by the power of the Soviet Union. With the collapse of the Soviet Union and the end of the Cold War, America has emerged as the world's dominant power.

Being a world power has added a new dimension to the government: a large permanent military and intelligence establishment. Military spending in peacetime grew enormously after World War II, although it has leveled off since the end of the Cold War. New institutions for gathering intelligence and conducting covert activities, such as the Central Intelligence Agency (CIA), were established during this period, and creating conflict between the usual norm of openness in a representative government and the need for strict secrecy in intelligence matters. Conducting an active foreign policy, often with military involvements, also led to major conflicts between the president and Congress, as these two institutions sought to define their respective roles in this new environment. Finding the proper balance between the executive and Congress in national security matters has proven one of the central most controversial, constitutional issues of recent times.

Purposes in Foreign Affairs

The conduct of foreign affairs is not governed entirely by considerations of security. Within their limits, some nations may also seek to promote certain political and moral goals and try to shape the future course of history. Such matters cannot be fixed definitively in fundamental law, but constitution makers may nevertheless try to set some of the basic goals, in the form of principles or ideas, that will influence future action.

From the beginning, many Americans argued that this nation had a special responsibility to help spread the "light" of republican government in the world. The source of this idea might be traced partly to the Declaration of Independence, where the principles of liberty and self-government are grounded not in a mere preference of Americans, but in "the laws of nature." These principles must therefore be valid in some sense for all peoples. In addition, as the world's first representative democracy, the United States felt a special proprietary (and practical) interest in having other nations adopt a liberal democratic form.

In any case, spreading republican government has consistently been a theme of American politics, even at moments when it has had little significance for concrete policy. But how this goal should be pursued has been a matter of much disagreement. For some it has meant a careful realism in which America limits its role in accord with the constraints of its position and power; for others an isolationist posture in which America avoids tarnishing republican ideals by withdrawing from an involvement in international politics; and for others still a more vigorous internationalism that obliges us to take positive steps to "make the world safe for democracy" and to pro-

mote human rights. Whatever the form, however, a commitment to encouraging liberty and democracy in the world has been an influential force in American politics and an important element of our constitution.

Conclusion

In this chapter, we have looked at politics from the perspective of a constitution maker, posing the four basic questions that are involved in any rational attempt to found a government. In the context of American politics, these questions provide a way to think about the fundamental issues that confronted the founders. These same issues, in different forms, still confront us today. Each generation, within the circle traced out for it by its predecessors, has the task of preserving the constitution. Making constitutional choices cannot be avoided. Learning to think in constitutional terms, therefore, should help citizens to deal with the constitutional decisions they will face in their own time.

Chapter 1 Notes

1. Samuel Huntington, *The Politics of Disharmony* (Cambridge: Harvard University Press, 1981), p. 29.
2. Max Farrand, The Records of the Federal Convention of 1787, vol. 1 (New Haven: Yale University Press, 1911), p. 424 (June 26).
3. Bunker Hill Address, June 17, 1825.
4. Harold D. Lasswell, *Politics: Who Gets What, When, How* (New York: McGraw Hill, 1936).
5. In the contemporary use of the term, liberalism refers to the active use of government to promote economic security and provide welfare benefits. How and why the term came to have this second meaning is described below.
6. John Acton, *The History of Freedom and Other Essays* (London: Macmillan, 1907) pp. 3–4. In the words of one political theorist, Isaiah Berlin, liberty means "a certain minimum area of personal freedom which on no account must be violated." Isiah Berlin, *Four Essays on Liberty* (London: Oxford University Press, 1969), p. 124.
7. Max Farrand, *The Records of the Federal Convention*, vol. 2, pp. 344, 606.
8. Letter to Joseph Cabell, Feb. 2, 1816; and to Major John Cartwright, June 5, 1824.
9. Letter to Samuel Kercheval, July 12, 1816; Letter to Henri George, February 25, 1809.
10. Werner Sombart, *Why Is There No Socialism in the United States?* (White Plains, N. Y.: Sharpe, 1976), p. 110.

11. Speech on the Dred Scott decision, June 26, 1857.
12. See Max Farrand, *The Records of the Federal Convention*, vol. 1 (June 29).
13. Thomas Jefferson, *Notes on the State of Virginia*, Query 14.
14. Dall Forsythe, *Taxation and Political Change in the Young Nation* (New York: Columbia University Press, 1977), p. 73.
15. *The Wall Street Journal*, "A Response to Milton Friedman," Sept. 29, 1989, p. A22.
16. Alexis de Tocqueville, *Democracy in America*, J. P. Mayer, ed. (New York: Doubleday, 1968), p. 448.
17. Thomas West, "The Rule of Law in *The Federalist*," in Charles Kesler, ed., *Saving the Revolution* (New York: Free Press, 1987), p. 165.
18. An authoritarian government, distinguished by some analysts from a totalitarian government, limits by repressive measures many forms of political dissent, but stops short of attempting to remake the entire culture or way of life.
19. Henry Kissinger, "Domestic Structure and Foreign Policy," in *Daedalus*, vol. 95, no. 2 (1966), p. 524.
20. Robert Dahl, *Preface to Democratic Theory* (Chicago: University of Chicago Press, 1956), p. 137.

2

The Founding

CHAPTER CONTENTS

Do the Declaration of Independence and the Constitution hold any importance for Americans today? After all, these two pieces of eighteenth-century parchment were written in a very different age and under very different circumstances. Two centuries ago, the United States was a mostly rural nation of scarcely more than 3 million inhabitants strung along the eastern seaboard of North America; now it is a commercial and industrial nation with over a quarter of a billion citizens, occupying much of the continent. Then, the free population of the United States was descended largely from the stock of the British Isles, distinctions of family and class still carried great weight (although hereditary aristocracies had been left behind in Europe), and one-fourth of the inhabitants were black slaves; now, the United States is a country of great ethnic and social diversity, aristocratic distinctions and customs are all but unknown, and the descendants of the black slaves are free citizens (although racial tensions persist). Then, the world stood in the infancy of modern science; now, modern communications and machinery have remade the globe. Then, wars were fought with musket and cannon; now, we command missiles and nuclear weapons.

Clearly, a great gulf exists between the founding era and our own. Nevertheless, the Declaration and the Constitution remain the two main pillars on which our political system rests. They were written under different circumstances, but their authors intended them to embody certain enduring principles. These documents are essential sources—though by no means the only ones—for understanding American politics today. The study of the founding, which is the focus of this chapter, presents a rare opportunity to observe constitution makers grappling with the fundamental problems of forming a new government.

The Declaration of Independence

The principles of the Declaration of Independence have occupied a central place in American politics from the beginning of the republic. The Declaration's prominence resulted in some measure from the willingness of those who signed the document to make sacrifices for the principles it embodies. Among the signatories were John Adams, Thomas Jefferson, and Benjamin Franklin. Of the fifty-six men who signed, nine would die during the Revolutionary struggle, five would be captured by the enemy, and seventeen would lose their property. These sacrifices gave meaning to their pledge to risk their "lives," "fortunes," and "sacred honor."

Yet the enduring quality of the Declaration has probably owed even more to its contents. The Declaration transcended the particular facts of the eighteenth-century struggle, justifying the war on the basis of underlying principles of political life derived from the "laws of nature and of nature's God." This standard, in the philosophy of the Declaration, remains constant and true, notwithstanding any changes of place or circumstance. The appeal to these principles has helped the Declaration achieve its global influence.

The message of the Declaration is not extreme. It certainly does not encourage acts of revolution on superficial grounds. It acknowledges, for instance, that "governments long established should not be changed for light and transient causes." Yet if the Declaration is cautious in defense of revolt, in its appeal to "nature" as the ultimate justification it is truly revolutionary. The Congress of the new United States government was not obliged to raise the issue of independence to the level of universal principle stated in the Declaration. Legally speaking, Congress had already settled the matter on July 2, 1776, by adopting Richard Henry Lee's resolution declaring the colonies "independent States." But Congress chose to go further and endorse a broader justification for independence.

This new justification reflected a gradual but profound shift in American thought in the decade before the Revolution. As the Crown and Parliament had attempted to tighten their grip on the colonies through a series of unpopular laws and policies, such as the Stamp Act (1765), the ties of affection and goodwill that had existed between the colonies and Britain loosened. Americans began to base their understanding of liberty not on the "rights of Englishmen," but on *natural* rights. And here they drew inspiration from a rather surprising source: English political thinkers, most notably John Locke (1632–1704). In his famous *Second Treatise on*

Government (1690), Locke argued that human beings in a "state of nature" possessed equal natural rights to life, liberty, and property. Government is formed when individuals contract among themselves to provide greater security for these rights. If a government persistently threatens these rights, then people have the right to take matters into their own hands and resist the tyranny. Locke's ideas, and even some of his key phrases (altered only slightly), reappeared almost a century later in the Declaration.

The growing disaffection among the colonists with British policies enabled them to see more clearly the inadequacy of the British system of government, with its undemocratic features of monarchy and nobility. In rejecting Britain, the colonists began to search not only for a new foundation of rights, but also for new principles on which to erect a government. All these changes in opinion had actually begun to take place before the Revolution, so much so that Jefferson later would note that the ideas in the Declaration were not original to him, but represented the "sentiments of the day, whether expressed in conversation, in letters, printed essays, or the elementary books of public right."[1]

We have repeatedly referred to the novel and revolutionary principles embodied in the colonists' appeal to "nature" and to "self-evident truths." These principles discussed in Chapter 1 consist of equality, the possession of certain "unalienable rights" (such as "life, liberty, and the pursuit of happiness"), a government established with the "consent of the governed," and a commitment to foster the kind of citizenship that would sustain the system. Clearly, however, most societies in the world were not then—and are not today—established on such principles. What then could it mean to say that these principles are based on the "laws of nature" and represent "self-evident truths"? If the principles are natural, why are they not recognized and embodied in every society? Were those who believed in such doctrines merely naive or ill-informed?

The notion that Thomas Jefferson or John Adams never considered these problems is itself ill-informed. They did. Their view was not that all people perfectly understood the laws of nature or perceived the self-evident truths. They realized that false doctrines had been propagated to keep people in submission and that many cultures had not yet developed a capacity for abstract political thinking. But they were convinced nevertheless that there were certain principles of nature to which people could appeal as they became more enlightened. As Jefferson wrote, "All eyes are opened, or opening, to the rights of man. The general spread of the light of science has already laid open to every view the palpable truth that the mass of mankind has not been born with saddles on their backs, nor a favored few booted and spurred, ready to ride them legitimately."[2] Unless duped by myth or brainwashed by propaganda—by doctrines such as the divine right of monarchs, racial inferiority or superiority, and historical determinism—a people can be awakened to see the palpable truths expressed in the Declaration. While Jefferson may have been too optimistic in expecting that other peoples would quickly embrace those truths, in no sense can it be said that the standards of the Declaration are naive or have become outmoded. In the struggle of groups within the United States for their rights, in the assertions of freedom by many former colonial countries, and in the resistance of many to brutal tyrannies, appeals to nature—or something like it—continue to be heard. Indeed, the events of the past decade in Eastern Europe stand as an eloquent testimony to the power of these ideas. The entire Soviet empire began to crumble in 1989 as people rejected Marxist-Leninist ideology. The truths of the Declaration appeared as self-evident to the people in Prague or Warsaw in 1989 as they did to the American patriots in 1776.

The relationship between the founders' ideas in the Declaration and their practice was not, of course, without tensions, especially on the question of equality. Abigail Adams complained to her husband John, just weeks before the vote on independence, that "whilst you are proclaiming peace and good-will to men, emancipating all nations, you insist upon retaining an absolute power over wives."[3] Looming above all else was slavery, which most of the signers of the document knew full well to be incompatible with the principle of equality. This included Jefferson and Washington, who both owned slaves but who called for the abolition of slavery. Their expectation in 1776 was that a majority of slave holders might agree to a plan of emancipation, as slavery became less viable economically and less tenable morally and politically. Their hope proved to be without foundation, and the founding generation was unable to develop a solution—or even take steps toward a solution—to this gravest of problems. The responsibility for redeeming the founding principles has thus rested not just with the founders themselves but with subsequent generations as well.

The Articles of Confederation

The Second Continental Congress that approved the Declaration could scarcely be called a formal government. It was a council of the different colonies formed by delegates selected by revolutionary "second" governments that sprang up in the colonies beside the legal colonial institutions. Americans had had practically no experience with any form of continental union. Britain had ruled the colonies as separate entities, and, with the exception of the New England Confederacy (1634–1694) and a conference at Albany (1754), united intercolonial activity had been almost nonexistent.

The pressures of the revolutionary situation made it necessary to establish some form of national government. Accordingly, soon after appointing the committee to draft the Declaration, the Second Continental Congress formed another committee to prepare a "form of confederation" as an official government. The contractual character of the Congress as a meeting of separate colonies shaped the understanding that the ratification of any new government would require the consent of all the colonies. The committee preparing the Articles of Confederation reported a draft after only one month of deliberation. The proposal proved controversial and was not ratified by all the states until 1781, near the end of the Revolutionary War. For most of the war, the Second Continental Congress simply acted as the government, informally implementing most aspects of the proposed new charter.

The Government of the Articles

The government of the Articles in 1781 faced a very difficult situation. Six years of war had exhausted the nation, and many communities lay devastated. A large national debt had been incurred. The paper money used to finance the Revolutionary War was all but worthless. And the public and most political leaders had settled into a pattern in which they looked to the individual states as the centers of political activity. During the years that the proposed government of the Articles awaited final approval, the former colonies wrote constitutions for themselves, each establishing a separate republic. A union of all Americans existed in some degree in the minds and hearts of the people, but it seemed secondary to their attachment to the separate republics.

The government established under the Articles of Confederation vested all the powers of the national government in a Congress of the states. There was no regular national judiciary and only the merest shadow of an executive power. Each state had one vote in Congress, regardless of its size. Important measures required the votes of nine of the thirteen states to pass, while amendments to the Articles required the unanimous consent of all the states. This structure suggested a very weak government.

A look at the powers of Congress, however, indicates that its objectives went far beyond a mere league for defense. The Articles gave Congress the authority to make war and peace, enter into treaties and alliances, manage trade with the Indians, and borrow money and regulate coinage. The states were forbidden to make treaties or exchange diplomatic representatives with foreign nations, and any alliances or treaties between the states themselves required Congress's consent. On paper the powers of the national government seemed considerable; in practice they often proved impossible to exercise. There was a glaring disproportion between the stated aims of the government and its capacity to carry them into effect.

Weaknesses of the Articles

Among the problems with the Articles, the gravest was that the government had to exercise authority through the states and not directly on the individual citizen. Where the laws of a government apply to individuals, the government can require individuals to comply with its laws by its own officials or courts; the individual is no match for the authority of the government. But where the laws apply to a state, compliance must be secured by making sure that a state government carries out the commands. In the event that a state refuses to carry out a law or implements it slowly or halfheartedly, the central government is placed in a hazardous position. It can, presumably, threaten the entire power of a state, thus raising the normal task of law enforcement virtually to the threshold of a potential civil war. Since in practice it is unlikely that a national government will be either willing or able to take matters to this extreme limit, the result is that the states often go their own way. This is what occurred under the Articles. Many states either ignored laws passed by Congress or else complied with them when and to the extent they pleased.

This weakness was especially evident in military affairs. Congress under the Articles could raise an army only by requisitioning troops from the states, which frequently failed to send the soldiers, even during the Revolutionary War. After the war, the situation became even worse, and Congress could do little or nothing in the 1780s to protect settlers in the West from British- and Spanish-inspired Indian raids. Similarly, Congress could raise funds only by assessing the states rather than individual citizens. Again, noncompliance was frequent. In 1786 Congress's total revenue was equal to less than one-third of that year's interest on the national debt.[4] Efforts to secure a more adequate source of funding by a tax on imports required an amendment to the Articles. But under the unanimous-consent provision a single state could block any change, and on two occasions one state—first Rhode Island and then New York—did so. The national government thus lacked the essential tools of force and finance.

In addition, the government of the Articles lacked even on paper one very important power: the authority to regulate commerce between the states and with foreign nations. Without this authority, the states were individually permitted to impose tariffs and erect trade barriers against other states as well as foreign nations. This competition retarded the development of the American economy and threatened to fulfill one Englishman's prophecy that Americans would remain a "disunited people till the end of time, suspicious and distrustful of each other, [fragmented into] little commonwealths or principalities, with no center of union and no common interest."[5]

At the root of these problems was the guarantee in Article II that each state would retain "its sovereignty, freedom, and independence." This assertion of state sovereignty conflicted directly with some of the stated objectives of the Articles, which sought the blessings of a national union. It also prevented the formation of anything resembling a strong executive force, which was essential to the effective operation of such a union.

The record under the Articles was not, of course, entirely one of failure. The nation fought the Revolutionary War to a victorious finish, obtained a favorable peace settlement, and resolved the problem of the Western territories with the passage of the Northwest Ordinance (1787). But the successes of the Articles came in spite of, rather than because of, the structure of the government. The threat of defeat by the British during the war forced what little cooperation there was among the states. With the war over, the government, with its clash of contradictory and irreconcilable principles, left little confidence in its ability to handle future problems. George Washington summed up the feeling of many when he described the Articles as a "half-starved, limping government, always moving upon crutches and tottering at every step."[6]

The Crisis in the States

The failure of the Articles was not the only cause, however, behind the growing movement to establish a new national government. Of equal concern was the increasing unrest in many of the states. This unrest occurred in the form of frequent changes of laws, weak administration, and above all of measures that threatened the sanctity of property rights. The effect was to undermine public confidence in these governments and to lead many to wonder whether popular governments could ever be instituted in a way that was consistent with good government.

The problems of the state governments became evident in the inability or unwillingness of some states to adopt sound measures of public finance during the difficult economic times of the 1780s. Pressured by depressed segments of the population, many states pumped excessive amounts of paper money into their economies, thus deflating the value of the currency. Creditors were often forced to accept this currency as payment of their loans. In Rhode Island, for example, the situation became so bad that creditors sought to hide from debtors in order to escape being paid back in the worthless money which the state had created.

In some states whose legislatures resisted popular demands for inflated currency, events took a more violent turn. In New Hampshire, the state militia had to repel an armed mob that converged on the legislative meeting house in Exeter. More violent still was Shays' Rebellion in Massachusetts in the summer and fall of 1786. There, crowds of disgruntled citizens descended on state courts to stop foreclosure proceedings initiated by creditors. Soon an outright rebellion erupted under the leadership of Captain Daniel Shays, an embittered Revolutionary War veteran. When the governor asked Congress to send troops to put down the rebellion, Congress was unable to raise the necessary money. Since the state militia was nonexistent, private funds had to be raised to hire an army that marched on Springfield and dispersed the rebels—but not before news of the revolt in Massachusetts, the cradle of the Revolution, had shocked many sober-minded Americans into assessing carefully the state of affairs in the country. "Was it to be supposed," Madison asked at the Convention, "that republican liberty could long exist under the abuses of it practiced in . . . the States?"

Although much variety existed among the state constitutions, in general they reflected the influence of highly democratic theories. Property restrictions were in force on voting, but the suf-frage for white males was by all past standards very broad. More important, most of the states followed the democratic doctrine of the era which called for vesting most of the power in the legislative branch and jealously limiting the powers of the executive and judiciary. These structures of government were generally supported by theories emphasizing the power of the people acting through highly responsive representatives to work its immediate will. The states, as Thomas Jefferson worried, were threatened by the emergence of legislative despotisms: "All the powers of government, legislative, executive, and judiciary, result to the legislative body. . . . An *elective despotism* was not the one we fought for." The instability in the states left many to wonder whether republican governments could ever be firm enough to protect basic liberties and resist unjust demands.

The movement to form a new national government, accordingly, had a twofold objective: to correct the defects of the Articles by creating a national government capable of effectively exercising new national powers; and to construct a national government that could counteract the instability of measures in the states by taking certain key powers out of the hands of the state governments altogether or by constraining or regulating state practices.

The effort to establish a new national government was not a movement against popular rule. Rather, it was a movement to make popular government work and to find, in Madison's words, "a republican remedy to the diseases most incident to republican government." This remedy required modifications in the prevailing idea about how best to construct popular governments. Those who took the lead in forming the new government were frank in acknowledging, that a stable and effective republican system needed far more energy and firmness in administration and more restraints on transferring immediate popular impulses into law than had been the case in most of the state governments. Saving republican government necessitated a rethinking of its form and structure.

The Road to the Convention

The idea to change the Articles grew directly out of a meeting of a small group of men at George Washington's home at Mount Vernon in 1785. James Madison, a participant at that meeting, shortly afterwards arranged to have the Virginia General Assembly invite all the states to hold a commercial convention in Annapolis, Maryland, in September of 1786. The strategy was clear: to develop a mechanism that could provide an impetus for a complete restructuring of the national government. Only five states sent delegates to Annapolis, but the meeting passed a resolution calling for a new convention to meet in Philadelphia in May of the following year to devise ways of making the national government "adequate to the exigencies of the Union."7

Congress later endorsed the idea of a convention, but "for the sole and express purpose of revising the Articles of Confederation." Thus the Philadelphia Convention had two possible mandates, an informal one that opened the possibility for creating an entirely new kind of government and an official one that limited its task to revising the existing one. In choosing the first and more radical alternative, as it quickly did, the Convention put itself on a potential collision course with Congress and with those who would later argue that the Convention had exceeded its authority. The risk was one the founders thought they must take. As in the case of the Revolution in 1776, on truly grave occasions, in Madison's words, the "forms of government ought to give way to substance: the safety and happiness of the people are the objects to which all political institutions aim, and to which all such institutions should be sacrificed."8 The Philadelphia Convention was not, to be sure, engaging in an act of revolution, but only proposing a new form of government that the people would then have to ratify. Still, the method of ratification was wholly outside the provisions of the existing government, and there is no question that the founders were pressuring the existing government to give up on itself.

Currents of Opinion in 1787

Most leaders in the United States at the beginning of 1787 believed that the government established by the Articles of Confederation needed to be revised in some way. But no firm consensus existed about how it should be changed, and by no means did everyone think that the nation required an entirely new form of government. Opinion was fragmented. Later in the year, after the Constitution had been formally proposed, opinion crystallized under two different labels: the Federalists, who supported the Constitution, and the Antifederalists, who opposed it. Yet because the Antifederalists were an opposition group, they never had to achieve complete unity among themselves and ended by attacking the Constitution from a number of different and conflicting viewpoints.

At the risk of imposing more order on the situation than may have actually existed, it will be helpful to identify two main currents of thought in the nation at the time. One is the *small republic* position, which became a key element in the thought of the Antifederalists; the other was the *nationalist* position, which formed the core of the thought of the Federalists. Both positions were represented at the Convention, although most of the delegates had nationalist leanings and the small republic advocates soon felt isolated. Some of them, like Robert Yates and John Lansing, Jr., of New York, left the Convention; others, like George Mason of Virginia, refused in the end to endorse the plan.

The Small Republic Position

Advocates of the small republic position favored, if not the exact government of the Articles, then something close to it. They proposed at most a modification, not an abandonment, of the existing government. Their view was based on the contention that a true republican form of government could not exist in a large, unitary state. Republican governments could only be established in smaller communities with a relatively homogeneous population. It followed that the only form of national government consistent with republicanism was a confederation, in which most of the governing power was kept close to home and in which only a very limited amount of authority, necessary for security against external threats, was assigned to the national government. Any strong national government, even one organized in theory in a highly democratic way, over time would become despotic. A large and powerful national government was simply incompatible with republicanism and freedom. As one small republic spokesman observed, "You might as well attempt to rule Hell by prayer."[9]

The advocates of a small republic offered three main arguments to support their view. First, a republic required that the obedience of the people to the laws be voluntary, which would be possible only if the people had confidence in their government. But large states, in which the government is both literally and figuratively at a considerable distance from the people, could not secure the people's close sympathy or attachment. In the view of one small republic defender, people "will have no confidence in their legislature, suspect them of ambitious views, be jealous of every measure they adopt, and will not support the laws they pass."[10] In order to enforce its laws, the national government would require a large standing army. Force, not persuasion, would be the method of governance, and a large national government would therefore inevitably become a despotic state.

Second, republican government required a strict responsiveness of the government to the people. Representatives had to mirror the characteristics of their constituents and to be held on a short leash. In practice, this meant a large number of representatives from small districts who would stand for reelection at short intervals. Small republic advocates helped popularize the idea that "where annual elections end, tyranny begins." Representatives "should be a true picture of the people; possess the knowledge of their circumstances and their wants; sympathize in all their distresses, and be disposed to seek their true interests."[11] This type of representation was not possible in large states, where representatives would necessarily be chosen in large and diverse electoral districts and would be drawn mostly from an educated segment of the population. The representatives would form an interest of their own apart from that of the citizens. No matter what the form of government might be on paper, in practice its spirit would soon become despotic.

Finally, small republic advocates argued that the citizenry must be molded or shaped to have certain distinct personal qualities, which they called "civic virtue." Because republican government means government by the people, the people must be disposed to seek the common good rather than their personal interest. Virtue, for small republic theorists, meant "the love of one's country and the love of equality."[12] Moreover, to avoid the problem of one part of the community exploiting another, the populace should possess a certain similarity in wealth, education, and religious views. Diversity was a curse. Promoting virtue and maintaining homogeneity were possible only within the scope of a small republic. The small republic was seen as a school of citizenship as much as a method for governing. A large state, with boundless possibilities of growth and movement, would introduce distinctions of wealth and position and would create temptations to give up the sturdy life of the true citizen. Large states cultivate a taste for luxury, expand passions, and throw together under one government people of vastly different manners and morals. In a large state, according to small republic advocates, "indolence will increase. . . . The springs of honesty will gradually grow lax, and chaste and severe manners be succeeded by those that are dissolute and vicious."[13]

These three arguments led small republic advocates, as noted, to oppose the idea of a genuine national government and to support the government of the Articles, with perhaps a few modifications. A confederation was the best way to solve the problem posed by the small republic: almost all the real governing would take place in the states (conceived as small republics), while the central government would handle the very few common problems like defense. After the Constitution was proposed, however, the small republic advocates were inevitably drawn into a discussion of the kind of national government they would favor if they had to accept one. Their views on this score represented many of their criticisms of the specific character of the Constitution. A national government, they contended, should be granted the minimum of powers needed; these powers should be hedged in with the maximum of restrictions and limitations; there should not be a single strong executive officer, but perhaps an executive commission; the number of representatives should be very large, and elections for the House should be held each year.

The Nationalist Position

The nationalist position, advocated by such men as Hamilton, Madison, and Washington, was based on very different views. The nationalists contended that a strong national government, one that acted directly on individuals, was needed both to achieve security and to establish a safe and stable republican order. A strong national government was both necessary and desirable.

The main aspects of the nationalists' critique of the small republic position have already been suggested in the discussion of the Articles. First, a confederal form of government lacked the energy and cohesiveness to provide for the nation's defense and to conduct a stable foreign policy. Second, small republics had in reality failed to protect the liberties of individuals. In spite of claims that democracy always protected rights, experience in the states, according to Madison, demonstrated conclusively the "necessity of providing more effectually for the security of private rights."[14] Any form of government, including a democratic form, could endanger individual liberties, and small republics had in fact proven themselves highly inclined to do so. Finally, the nationalists pointed to important flaws or contradictions in the small republic position. Thus, some of the states—such as Pennsylvania, Virginia, and New York—were already so large that it no longer made sense to consider them under the theories of the small republic model. And the strict social controls required to shape a virtuous citizenry and a homogeneous populace were incompatible with the freedom of individuals to "pursue happiness" in their own way.

For the nationalists to point up defects in the small republic argument was one thing; for them to show the superiority of their own position was something else. The nationalists favored a strong central government in which the authority of the states would be subordinate to the national government and in which certain powers formerly exercised by the states would be taken over by the national government. (There was even some sentiment among a few nationalists for abolishing existing state identities.) But what of the small republic advocates' claim that a powerful government in a large territory could not remain republican, but must in the end become despotic?

The nationalists, surprisingly, did not dispute the contention that certain supports previously thought indispensable for republican government would be diminished or lost in a large nation. Representatives would be unable to mirror perfectly the populace, and the national government could not serve as an intimate "school of citizenship." But in a strikingly innovative argument, the nationalists claimed that a republican form of government could be made to work, and work even more effectively, without certain features that small republic defenders deemed essential.

The nationalists' response will be presented in more detail as we discuss the founders' decisions at the Convention. But the outline of their position can be briefly summarized here. First, a national government that proved its efficacy in administering wise national policies could win the people's respect and confidence. People might not feel quite as close to this government as to that of a tiny republic. But as the advantages bestowed by union became clear, the public would accept its claim to their obedience without the need of any more force than moderate government by its nature requires.

Second, a strong national government could be constructed that was accountable to the people, but that would have a degree of freedom from the immediate constraints of public opinion. This greater discretion for the government would be a benefit rather than a defect. Representatives would be able to make up their own minds after deliberating on the best policies, and the government would have some time to demonstrate the efficacy of its course of action.

Finally, a republican government could operate without the kind of stifling classic civic virtue and homogeneity in the populace that small

---

BOX 2.1

A Contemporary Looks at His Fellow Delegates

William Pierce, a delegate to the Convention from Georgia, observed his fellow delegates with a keen eye and made sketches of their characters. The following are some of his observations:

Gouverneur Morris (of Pennsylvania)—"One of those Genius's in whom every species of talents combine to render him conspicuous and flourishing in public debate:—he winds through all the mazes of rhetoric, and throws around him such a glare that he charms, captivates, and leads away the senses of all who hear him. . . . But with all these powers he is fickle and inconstant,—never pursuing one train of thinking, nor ever regular. . . . This Gentleman is about 38 years old, he has been unfortunate in losing one of his Legs, and getting all the flesh taken off his right arm by a scald, when a youth."

James Madison (of Virginia)—"Every Person seems to acknowledge his greatness. He blends together the profound politician, with the Scholar. In the management of every great question he evidently took the lead in the Convention. From a spirit of industry and application which he possesses in a most eminent degree, he always comes forward the best informed Man of any point in debate. . . . Mr. Madison is about 37 years of age, a Gentleman of great modesty,—with a remarkable sweet temper."

James McClurg (of Virginia)—"He attempted once or twice to speak, but with no great success."

---

republic proponents had demanded. To be sure, a certain kind of citizenship was essential, and governments at all levels, especially local governments, would have to promote it. Republican government called for qualities of citizenship "in a higher degree than any other form." (*Federalist* 55) But in a system in which securing liberty was a central end, an exclusive reliance on moral or religious motives to support the system was not possible. Modern citizenship could rest on different principles that did not seek to repress all self-interested passions, but to deflect them from doing harm and channel them into serving the public good. The role of the national government should be regarded more as one of regulating conduct than directly molding character.

Looking back on the conflict between the small republic advocates and the nationalists, Americans today are apt to think of the small republic position as slightly foreign. The American tradition, after all, has been shaped largely—though not entirely—by the principles of the nationalists. But to understand the founding, it is essential to recall that in 1787 it was the nationalist position that appeared untested and new. Americans to that point had thought chiefly in terms of a confederation, and the dominant view in political theory held that a large state and a republican form of government were incompati-

ble. In all of history, in fact, no example existed of a republic that covered an extended territory. If there was one point on which small republic proponents and the nationalists agreed, it was that the nationalists' position was a "novelty in the political world." (*Federalist* 14) The small republic advocates deplored the "phrenzy of innovation" sweeping the nation and appealed to the "ancient and established usage of the commonwealth."[15] Nationalists sought to turn this criticism into an advantage. While counseling a "decent regard to the opinions of former times," The Federalist appealed to Americans' boldness, urging them not to "suffer a blind veneration for antiquity, for customs or for names." (*Federalist* 14)

The Constitutional Convention

Throughout history most governments have been established during periods of revolution or violence, and their forms have generally been dictated by whoever has the greatest force. America's experience was more fortunate. The Convention met in peacetime, and even though the problems under the existing government were grave, the nation was not under the immediate threat of armed insurrection or disintegration. The delegates were therefore in a position

BOX 2.1 (cont.)

Alexander Hamilton (of New York)—"Deservedly celebrated for his talents . . . Hamilton requires time to think,—he enquires into every part of his subject with the searchings of phylosophy, and when he comes forward he comes highly charged with interesting matter, there is no skimming over the surface of a subject with him, he must sink to the bottom to see what foundation it rests on. . . . He is about 33 years old, of small stature, and lean. His manners are tintured with stiffness, and sometimes with a degree of vanity that is highly disagreeable."

James Wilson (of Pennsylvania)—"He has joined to a fine genius all that can set him off and show him to advantage. He is well acquainted with Man, and understands all the passions that influence him. Government seems to have been his peculiar Study, all the political institutions of the World he knows in detail, and can trace the causes and effects of every revolution from the earliest stages of the Grecian commonwealth down to the present time. No man is more clear, copious, and comprehensive than Mr. Wilson, yet he is no great Orator. He draws the attention not by the charm of his eloquence, but by the force of his reasoning. He is about 45 years old."

Roger Sherman (of Connecticut)—"He is awkward, unmeaning, and unaccountably strange in his manner. But in his train of thinking there is something regular, deep and comprehensive; yet the oddity of his address, the vulgarisms that accompany his public speaking, and that strange New England cant which runs through his public as well as his private speaking makes everything that is connected with him grotesque and laughable;—and yet he deserves infinite praise,—no Man has a better Heart or a clearer Head."

Source: Max Farrand, ed., *The Records of the Federal Convention of 1787*, vol. 3 (New Haven, Conn.: Yale University Press, 1966), pp. 87–97.

to make significant choices about the new government. They came to Philadelphia with a willingness to discuss alternative plans and to make compromises for the sake of reaching agreement. Even so, the differences that emerged were so great that the Convention at one point nearly broke up, with delegates threatening that the unresolved issues might have to be settled by force among the states.

The work of the Convention was facilitated by a set of procedural rules adopted in the first days that were designed to allow the delegates to deliberate and change their minds without posing risks to their political careers. Thus, the delegates rejected the idea of recording individual votes on the grounds that "changes of opinion would be frequent," and they decided to keep the meetings of the Convention closed to the public and the press.[16] The delegates wanted to give themselves the latitude to consider various proposals and voice opinions without fear that these would be published and used against them by political opponents. Most of the delegates, in fact, did at one point or another change their minds on important issues, which might never

have happened if they had been compelled to stake out their positions publicly.

Our knowledge of what went on at the Convention comes mostly from a record kept by James Madison, which he allowed to be published only after his death in 1836. (Madison was the last of the major founders to die, and his decision to withhold publication of the Notes—despite entreaties and strong political pressures to do so earlier—was designed to keep to the pledge of secrecy agreed to at the Convention.) In an age before tape recorders and typewriters, the Notes required a truly massive effort on Madison's part, all the more so because he was simultaneously playing a leading role in the Convention. While the other founders were relaxing in the taverns in Philadelphia, Madison was diligently recopying his daily notes. Madison later admitted to a friend that the "labor of writing out the debates . . . almost killed [me]." He persisted in this task because he foresaw the potential value of a record "on which would be staked the happiness of a young people great even in its infancy, and possibly the cause of liberty throughout the world."[17]

The Delegates

The fifty-five delegates who attended the Convention—only thirty of whom participated regularly in the proceedings—constituted an unusually talented group. They came from all the states of the union except Rhode Island, which refused to send a delegation because of the opposition in the state government to any change in the Articles. Some delegates were merely respectable members of their communities, but many were highly intelligent, well-read, thoughtful, and experienced. Several delegates prepared for the Convention by historical and philosophical studies; Madison, for example, wrote out a history of the fate of past confederations and arrived in Philadelphia with a stack of books to aid him in his learned discourses. Nearly all the delegates could boast of having extensive political experience. Twenty-one had fought in the Revolutionary War, six had signed the Declaration of Independence, forty-six had served in colonial or state legislatures, thirty-nine had served in Congress, and seven had been state governors.

For all this experience, however, the delegates as a group were strikingly young. George Washington was by then an elderly 55, but Hamilton was only 32, Madison 36, and Gouverneur Morris 35. At 81, the venerable but frail Benjamin Franklin was by far the oldest member of the Convention.

A few famous leaders of the Revolution were conspicuously absent. The two leading intellectual figures of the Revolution—Thomas Jefferson and John Adams—were serving as ministers in Europe; the great patriot Samuel Adams was ill; and one of America's most renowned rhetoricians, the fiery and tempestuous Patrick Henry, refused to attend, claiming that he "smelt a rat" in Philadelphia.[18] (Henry later attacked the Constitution in a famous exchange with James Madison at the Virginia ratifying convention.) Some historians have speculated that the absence of these figures—in particular, the commanding minds of Jefferson and Adams—might have a been a blessing in disguise; it seems highly doubtful whether the shy James Madison could have played so prominent a role in the proceed-

ings if these two men had been at the Convention.

Besides their extensive experience in politics, most of the delegates at the Convention had substantial business and propertied interests. This fact, together with the founders' concern for protecting property, led many at the time to charge that the delegates were attempting to establish a government for a propertied elite. More than a century later, the Constitution again came under attack for elitism by progressive reformers. A well-known historian, Charles Beard, developed this line of argument into a full-scale economic account of the founding.[19] Beard contended that those who had designed the Constitution and fought for its ratification made up an urban and mercantile elite that was seeking to profit economically from the new government. The struggle over the Constitution, according to Beard, was an economic battle between the oligarchically minded founders on the one hand, and the mass of simple farmers on the other. The founders managed to win the struggle and institute a nondemocratic system because of their superior organization and restrictions on the suffrage.

Beard's thesis, which projected an elitist interpretation back onto the origins of American politics, initially found a large and sympathetic audience. Yet subsequent research has done much to call it into question. By one account, more than one-fourth of the delegates "had important economic interests that were adversely affected, directly and immediately, by the Constitution."[20] Moreover, in the ratification debate, people of all classes could be found on both sides of the question, indicating that economic interests were not the only question or were viewed in very different ways.

There is little doubt that economic issues were at stake in the struggle and that many consulted their interests; and there is even less doubt that the founders sought the backing of propertied segments of the population. Indeed, the founders never denied, but on the contrary openly asserted, the importance of protecting property both as an element of liberty and as a necessity for promoting economic prosperity and development. Thus, merely because the founders sought to protect property is no proof of the contention that they were motivated chiefly by a desire to protect their own economic interests. Some at the Convention surely worried about their economic well-being, but the dominant concerns were political. It is unlikely that many of those who had jeopardized their interests in the Revolutionary War a decade earlier would suddenly turn into petty calculators of economic gain. If self-interest played a role, it may well have been personal pride of a different sort: the glory and fame that would redound to those who established the first successful modern republic.

The Choices of the Convention

The delegates faced an enormous task. They had to decide whether merely to revise the Articles (as they had been authorized to do by the Continental Congress) or to devise an entirely new national government (as many of the delegates had all along intended). They had to decide on the form of government and the role that the people would play in it. And they had to decide on an array of issues related to the great problem of slavery.

To complicate their task, the founders could look to no single political system, past or present, as a perfect model for a new American government. Some founders expressed admiration for certain aspects of the government of Great Britain, but nearly all realized that the English constitution, with its hereditary monarchy and aristocratic traditions, was wholly unsuited to the American context. The state governments, while having many admirable features, in the main furnished examples of democratic excesses to be avoided. Nor did previous republics in other nations offer much guidance. "It is impossible to read the history of the petty republics of Greece and Italy," Hamilton observed, "without feeling sensations of horror and disgust at the distractions with which they were continually agitated." (*Federalist* 9) In trying to remedy the defects of past republics and compensate for the inadequacies of the states, the founders would have to ground the American Constitution on new principles. They were sailing in part on uncharted seas, the first to attempt a modern republic in an extended territory.

A National versus a Confederal System

Certainly the most important question facing the Convention—and the one first debated—was whether to abandon the Articles and form a national government. Realizing that the manner in which an issue is initially formulated greatly influences the outcome, James Madison decided it was best to present at the outset an entirely new scheme of government based on national principles. Introduced by Governor Edmund Randolph on behalf of the Virginia delegation, but drafted primarily by Madison, the proposal for a national government became known as the "Virginia Plan." It called for a "strong consolidated union" that would act directly on individuals rather on state governments. The national government, divided into three branches, would have extensive powers on all questions on which the states were not competent to act. In an extraordinary provision of national power, the legislature would be able to veto any laws passed by the states. The legislature would consist of two houses, the first or "lower" house chosen by the people and the second or "upper" house elected by the lower house, without regard to representation of the states.

This striking plan caught the opponents of a strong union off guard. After fighting a rear-guard action for two weeks the opposition finally offered a counterproposal. Presented by William Paterson of New Jersey and known as the "New Jersey Plan," the scheme called for a series of amendments to the Articles of Confederation that would have strengthened the power of Congress to raise money, and added a federal judiciary and an executive council empowered to use force to compel compliance with the Confederation's laws. Clearly, the New Jersey Plan had moved in the direction of a stronger national government than under the Articles, but the proposal remained essentially confederal in character. Congress would consist of representatives chosen by the state legislatures, not the people directly; national laws would apply only to states, not to individuals; and the powers of the general government would be severely limited. The plan had the backing of those opposed in principle to a strong national government, and it also drew support on practical grounds from some

Born into a wealthy New York family in 1752, Gouverneur Morris was one of Pennsylvania's delegates to the Constitutional Convention in 1787. A champion of a strong national government, Morris favored a congressional veto over state laws, a council of revision, and direct election of the president. (Photo provided by the National Portrait Gallery, Smithsonian Institution. Used with permission.

Born in Boston in 1706, Benjamin Franklin is one of the most well known of all American patriots. He was an inventor, a journalist, a scientist, an author, and a diplomat. He died in 1790. (Photo provided by the National Portrait Gallery, Smithsonian Institution. Used with permission.)

small-state delegates worried that the national government proposed under the Virginia Plan would allow the larger states to dominate the new government.

The New Jersey Plan was vigorously opposed by the nationally minded delegates. It was decisively defeated when the convention voted seven states to three in favor of the Virginia Plan. Now the Convention had finally resolved against any purely confederal plan, although in the meantime certain nationalist ideas—like a congressional veto on all state laws or a reorganization of state boundaries—had been discarded. But the question of the kind of representation for the states inside of a new national government remained unresolved. The battle lines were immediately redrawn for the fiercest struggle at the convention. The nationally minded delegates, having won the vote on the Virginia Plan, pressed ahead for a bicameral legislature in which representation in both the House and the Senate would be based on population. The

opposition now dug in, arguing that each state should have the same number of votes in Congress. The Convention decided that representation in the House would be based on population, but after extensive debate they could not agree on the principle of representation for the Senate. Here the Convention deadlocked.

At this critical point, with tempers rising and the late June heat soaring, the Connecticut delegates, Dr. William Johnson and Oliver Ellsworth, stepped in. Johnson proposed to combine the principles of representing the nation by population and by states. Instead of the two ideas "being opposed to each other [they] ought to be combined; . . . in one branch, the people ought to be represented; in the other, the States." Ellsworth concurred: "We were partly national; partly federal . . . on this middle ground a compromise would take place."[21] This plan, known as the "Great Compromise" or "Connecticut Compromise," was approved by a committee appointed over the Fourth of July holiday. The committee submitted its plan to the Convention, and it was narrowly adopted. The committee's plan created a House of Representatives, apportioned roughly on the basis of population, whose members would be elected by the voting public. The Senate would consist of two senators from each state, chosen by the state legislatures. The plan also called for a single, independent executive and a judicial branch.

Many important choices still had to be made, and there remained many points on which the delegates would continue to disagree. But with the single greatest hurdle cleared, the Convention was able to resolve the other problems without the looming threat that the delegates might walk out. The Convention was thus saved by the willingness of members to compromise. Still, it leaves a false impression to suggest that the Constitution was merely a bundle of deals, or, as one commentator has put it, a "patchwork sewn together . . . by a group of extremely talented democratic politicians."[22]

The Convention did, of course, involve much give-and-take, tactical maneuvering, and plain old-fashioned bargaining. But even in the instance of the Connecticut Compromise, there was first a decision on the fundamental principle of establishing a strong national government, which carried the day, and only then a compromise on the question of the nature of representation within that government. Looking at the Convention as a whole, moreover, one finds that the majority adhered to certain fixed principles— liberty and self-government, for example, and even the structural principle of separation of powers—which set boundaries to the debate and limits on compromise. Without an underlying theoretical agreement, no workable compromises were possible.

The Sectional Problem and Slavery

In addition to the great question of the character of the union, which divided small and large states, there was the problem of conflicting interests between sections of the nation, particularly between the North and the South. The South was primarily agricultural, while the North had developed a significant commercial component to its economy. This difference led to jockeying between the sections on several economic issues, including whether the national government should have a power to tax exports (which the South opposed) and whether the power to regulate internal commerce should require a two-thirds majority of Congress (which the South favored). These issues were dealt with in a series of compromises that illustrated the Convention's skill at averting deadlock: The South won the first, but lost the second.

By far the most important sectional question, however, had to do with slavery. Slavery came up on a number of issues. The Convention agreed that any "direct taxes" levied by government should be apportioned among the states according to population. The problem lay in defining "population." If the definition included slaves, the Southern states would have to bear a larger tax burden. Consequently, Southern delegates demanded that slaves be given less weight than free citizens for purposes of taxation. On the other hand, if slaves were counted as full members of the population for purposes of deciding on representation in the population-based House of Representatives, the Southerners (and the slave interest) would control nearly half the seats. The North accordingly wanted slaves to have less weight than free citizens for the purpose of determining representation. From these conflicting sectional views emerged the "Three-Fifths Compromise," which followed a formula already in use under the Articles. It stated that for purposes of both taxation and representation, five slaves would count as the equivalent of three free persons.

A second slavery-related compromise is reflected in Article IV, section 2 of the Constitution, which in effect required the extradition of fugitive slaves from one state back to their owners in another state. The third compromise dealt with the slave trade. Southern delegates worried that Congress, having been empowered to regulate commerce, might interfere with the importation of slaves from Africa. The result was a provision (Article I, section 9) that forbade Congress to outlaw the trade for twenty years.

Many at the Convention deplored the great evil of slavery and saw clearly its inconsistency with the principle of equality. Gouverneur Morris, for example, spoke of the injustice of "the mere distinction of color" being made the ground for "the most oppressive dominion ever exercised by man over man." Even some Southern delegates like George Mason, himself the owner of 200 slaves, lamented the existence of this "national sin" and would have approved a national power to prevent its increase. Yet even if those opposed to slavery had been disposed to take action against it, they were in no position to do so. The Southern states as a whole were not then prepared to give to the national government the power to regulate slavery or even to limit the slave trade. And they found allies among Northern delegates favoring a looser confederation. As Connecticut's Oliver Ellsworth stated: "The morality or wisdom of slavery are considerations belonging to the states themselves." Any attempt to force the issue of abolition might have destroyed any chance for union while leaving slavery still intact. The Convention chose instead to form the union and compromise on the slave question, with the hope—which had some foundation at the time in the deteriorating economic rationale of slavery—that the states on their own might soon move toward abolition.[23]

Some have attacked the founders for making any kind of compromises at all on this issue. Certainly, many founders were only too aware that slavery was a deep flaw in the new republic, though not one the Constitution had created. So unwilling were many of the founders to sanctify slavery that the word itself never appears in the Constitution, but is always referred to indirectly by various verbal constructions. Some see this as mere hypocrisy, although others view it as an attempt "to avoid giving federal legal sanction to the institution, leaving it to exist as the creature of state law alone."[24] Whether anything more could have been done at the Convention by those opposed to slavery is a different question. In any event, the inability to come to a permanent solution to the problem of slavery did eventually prove to be the flaw that led to the Civil War and nearly destroyed the Union.

The Basic Principles of the Constitution

As we noted in Chapter 1, the constitution of any society refers in the most fundamental sense to how that society is constituted—to its basic ends or goals, the scope of governmental authority, the distribution of power and the arrangement of institutions, and the basic provisions for security and defense. The written document the founders proposed, the Constitution of the United States, deals in some way with all of these issues. It notes in the Preamble the goals, among which are providing defense and domestic tranquility, establishing justice and securing the blessings of liberty. As an actual body of law, however, it does not consist of long statements of philosophical principles. It is concerned for the most part with outlining the scope of governmental authority and establishing the basic arrangement and powers of the governing institutions. In analyzing the basic principles of the Constitution, we shall accordingly emphasize questions related to the powers and the structure of the government, noting how this framework is designed to secure the basic ends of society.

The Scope of Government: A Strong but Limited National Government

Americans after the Revolution understandably were highly suspicious of strong government, especially government far away from home. For many, a distrust of central authority had been a major lesson of the colonial experience. After all, had not the government of Great Britain used its extensive powers to subvert basic liberties? And could not a strong American government do the same?

The authors of the Constitution shared this concern against government, but only up to a point. Their experience with the state governments and with the weakness of the Articles taught them another lesson: the need for union and for strength and vigor in government. Whereas opponents of the Constitution spoke constantly of guarding people's liberties against a new and powerful government, the founders spoke of the need to provide government with the necessary amount of energy and stability. Without an effective government, they argued, liberty itself was at risk. "Vigor of government," *The Federalist* notes, "is essential to the security of liberty." (*Federalist* 1) Moreover, strong government is needed to promote other important objectives, from providing an adequate defense to encouraging a vigorous economy. For the founders, accordingly, the question of establishing good government involved striking a proper balance between protection against government and grants of power to government.

The founders, no less than the opponents of the Constitution, opposed unlimited government. But in drawing the limits of national governmental power, the opponents of the Constitution would have been much more stingy. They wanted to keep more powers under the control of the states, deny more specific powers to the national government, and tie more strings to the exercise of national powers.

Although the Constitution contains many important limitations of power on the national government, it is generally favorable to national authority. It *transferred* important powers from the states to the central government—for example, the powers to coin money and print paper currency. (These powers were shifted to the national government, not only because of the need for uniform currency, but because the states had exercised them unwisely.) Moreover, it avoided placing narrow restrictions on the exercise of the granted powers. For instance, the government has the power to "raise and support armies" and to "provide and maintain a navy"; contrary to the demands of opponents, there is no limit on how large the armed forces should be or how much money could be spent on them. "Every power," according to *The Federalist*, "ought to be in proportion to its object." (*Federalist* 30) Because it is impossible to know in advance what size army or navy is needed to provide security—this will depend on circumstances and the nature of the threat—it is foolish to attempt to limit these powers in a written constitution.

The national government while strong was also to be limited. The Constitution withholds power in two ways: by certain specific prohibitions—for example, no ex post facto laws or no taxes on exports; and by the general idea that the national government is one of enumerated powers—that is, that the government does not possess any and all powers, but only those powers granted to it (which, to be sure, are rather broad). By current standards, the original list of enumerated powers of the national government may not appear so extensive. The Constitution has been amended to give the national government more powers than it had in 1787, and it is now interpreted—some say stretched beyond its natural meaning—to allow for a very generous exercise of national power.

Thus today we find the federal government directly or indirectly playing an important role in providing health benefits, setting speed limits on the highways, and even establishing the legal drinking age. Since the 1930s and especially since the 1960s, many contend that there is almost no limit to the exercise of national power, so long as a national majority wants some policy and so long as it is not expressly prohibited by the Constitution. But to understand the conditions out of which the Constitution emerged, it is necessary to recall that the founders were claiming more power for the government than most Americans at the time were initially disposed to grant.

Given that the national government was to be so strong, how could it be controlled? What could prevent it from seizing powers not granted to it, or from exercising its broad powers in a way that would threaten people's liberties? These were among the most important questions debated at the convention and discussed during the struggle over ratification.

The founders responded to these concerns with three major arguments. First, people could rely on the goodwill of governing officials, and in any case most officials were responsible to the public by elections. The national government was not an alien force detached from the people, but a government chosen by the great body of the people. Second, there were written provisions in the Constitution specifying the powers and limitations of the government; these provisions were legally binding, and the Supreme Court would be able to enforce them. Finally, and perhaps most important, the structure of the government itself was designed to be a guarantee against the abuse of power. The institutions of government were to be so arranged and the powers so balanced that governing officials would be highly unlikely to threaten people's liberties. Thus, while the power of the government as a whole would be formidable, its structure would create powerful barriers to despotism and help preserve a constitutional balance.

We shall turn in a moment to the structural features of the Constitution that contribute to controlling the government. First, however, we must inquire into who was intended to rule and whether it was in fact possible to establish a popular form of government in a large territory.

The Distribution of Power: Who Rules?

Did the Constitution establish a democratic system? The answer is not as straightforward as one might think. Part of the problem comes from a certain confusion in how we use the term "democracy" and from differences in its meaning today as compared to 1787. It will help initially to present the issue here as it was seen by the founders. At the Constitutional Convention and in *The Federalist,* the founders constantly drew a distinction between a "democracy" or a "pure democracy" on the one hand and a "republic" or "representative democracy" on the other. By a "pure democracy," they meant what we would call a direct democracy—a form of government in which the people themselves assemble and vote directly on the policies and the actions to be pursued. (Not even the smaller states ever realized this objective.) By a "republic" or representative democracy, they meant a system in which the people do not govern directly, but turn power over to representatives who are chosen directly or indirectly by the public. Madison defined a modern republic as a "government which derives all its power directly or indirectly from the great body of the people, and is administered by persons holding their offices during pleasure for a limited period, or during good behavior." (*Federalist* 39)

Democracies and republics are both species of popular government, because the ultimate power in both systems lies with the great body of the people, not with one particular class or element of society. But there are important differences between them in the kinds of government they produce. Democracies, the founders argued, could not be relied upon to protect liberties. The democracies of ancient Greece tended to degenerate into the rule of mobs, in which the passions of the people, not their better judg-

ment, posed a constant threat to the well-being of society. A modern republic, by contrast, allowed the sense of the majority to govern, but held out the possibility of being able to protect the rights of minorities and to supply effective government. Power was vested not immediately in the people, but in governmental institutions that would have a certain degree of independence and discretion.

Unlike many opponents of the Constitution, who saw no tension between popular government and the protection of rights, the founders warned of the great dangers posed by "majority faction." A "faction," as the founders used the term, referred to a group of people seeking to advance its own interest at the expense of other citizens or of the permanent interests of the nation. In a popular form of government, whether a democracy or a republic, a majority faction could seize control of the government under the principle of majority rule and threaten the rights and interests of others. A republic, however, offered two important advantages over a democracy in controlling the threat of majority faction: government is in the hands of representatives, who might possess broader and more disinterested views than the people at large; and republics can be large and encompass a great number of diverse interests or factions, making it unlikely that any one faction could itself become a majority. Let us consider further these two points.

Representation   A representative is someone authorized to speak for someone else. The Constitution established a government in which all power was held by representatives—either elected officials or officials chosen by the elected officials. The people possess no direct, formal power in their collective capacity, but must have their will expressed in and through representatives operating in established institutions. Under the Constitution, the people directly chose the members of the House and indirectly selected the president and the members of the Senate. (Today, senators are directly elected, and the president—in all but a technical sense—is chosen by the voters.) Supreme Court justices are appointed by the president and confirmed with the advice and consent of the Senate.

BOX 2.2

The Federalist Papers

In the fall of 1787 Alexander Hamilton enlisted the aid of James Madison and John Jay to write a series of articles for New York newspapers explaining and defending the proposed Constitution. Together, these politically seasoned and reflective republicans wrote eighty-five articles, which collectively became known as *The Federalist Papers* or just *The Federalist.* Although written in haste to aid in the ratification fight in New York, *The Federalist* constitutes the best explanation and defense of the Constitution ever written, as well as the most profound examination of republican government ever produced in the United States.

The authors originally kept their identities secret, publishing the papers under the pen name of "Publius." The original Publius, a statesman of ancient Rome, had been instrumental in establishing the Roman republic and in alerting its citizenry to dangers to freedom that lurked within it. The authors of *The Federalist* apparently saw themselves as playing a similar role as both founders and educators of the American republic. Today we know that Hamilton wrote fifty-one of the papers, Madison twenty-six, and Jay five, and Hamilton and Madison wrote three jointly.

The two most famous of the papers, *Federalist* 10 and *Federalist* 51 (both written by Madison), address the problems of "majority faction" and abuse of power by government officials.

Representation, according to the founders, offered a way to improve the decisions of government. People would not select carbon copies of themselves, but individuals more knowledgeable and experienced in governing. Furthermore, representatives would operate in institutions designed to promote deliberative decision making. Representatives would spend a large part of their time weighing arguments and considering information about which most citizens might be only dimly aware. Representation, then, is a way to "refine and enlarge" the public views. (*Federalist* 10) Representation must be sufficiently broad-based to reflect the sense of the community, but not so large as to preclude the establishment of deliberative assemblies. (If the size of a representative body is in the thousands, true deliberation becomes impossible.) The founders' plans for effective representation, therefore, depend on a number of factors that we shall examine in this book: the availability and willingness of capable people to run for office, the intelligence of the voters, and the character of electoral campaigns.

A Large Republic Representation, however, is only part of the solution to the threat of majority faction. Representatives, too, can be captured by factions and made to serve their interests. Exactly this had occurred in some small states under the Articles of Confederation. Indeed, factional rule seemed a likely consequence of government, in small republics, which tend to share the defects of direct democracies. A corrective, according to the founders, can be in "extending the sphere" and creating a republican government in a larger territory. Let us, then, turn to the famous argument for a large republic.

Almost everyone agreed that a large nation, with its greater resources and population, was better able to defend its citizens from foreign threats. Yet large nations, most believed, could not support a popular form of government. The founders rejected this view and argued that a large republic was not only possible, but also that it could offer better protection against majority faction. This argument began with the realistic premise that wherever liberty exists, factions inevitably follow: "Liberty is to faction what air is to fire." (*Federalist* 10) Liberty creates factions because it allows individuals to pursue happiness in their own way and to develop their own talents; differences of opinion and differences in the amount and type of property result. Individuals then form into different groups or factions, seeking to protect and promote their distinct interests.

The founders conceded that it might be possible to eliminate factions by imposing the same opinions and by dividing property equally among the citizens. This solution was one that some democracies and small republics had attempted in earlier eras, though with only limited success. The problem with this "cure," however, was that in trying to eliminate factions, it eliminated liberty as well. If securing liberty was one the chief aims of political life, it followed that factions had to be tolerated. The small republic advocates in the United States were unwilling to face up to this reality. They wanted liberty, but—following at times the old theory of republicanism—they continued to call for a stringent kind of civic virtue.

Given that liberty was a fundamental aim of political life and that factions would inevitably accompany it, the founders turned away from the idea of eliminating the causes of faction and looked for ways of controlling their effects. Here the superiority of a large republic over a small one became apparent. A small republic would have a relatively simple economy with people constantly in contact with one another; in this setting, it was likely that a faction would constitute a majority of the populace and seize control of the government. If, for example, the majority were made up of farmers and the farmers fell into debt, they could—as in the case of Rhode Island—quickly organize and pursue their advantage at the expense of their creditors. The same thing could occur in the case of conflict between two religious sects. By contrast, in a large republic that contains a major commercial component, there is a multiplicity of economic interests, religious groups, and local attachments. The number and diversity of these interests makes it unlikely that any one of them will constitute a majority; and even where a potential majority might exist, it takes much longer for any group to realize its situation and organize effectively. In a large republic, accordingly, a single-interest majority is far less likely to occur than in a small republic.

Majorities in large republics must therefore form in different ways than in small republics. Representatives who might initially be disposed to pursue factional aims, but who now find that they are unable to do so, may join together with other representatives to form a coalition. Each party to the coalition will have to make adjust-ments and bargains. These coalitions will tend to be more moderate and less enduring than a simple factional majority. Another possibility is that the factional positions will create an initial stalemate; the only possibility for action will be for representatives to abandon their factional aims and join together on a principle of "justice and the general good." (*Federalist* 51)

The large republic solution to majority factions was especially important in the economic realm. Divisions between the rich and poor had destroyed many ancient republics, and class divisions were similarly threatening the stability of some of the smaller states. The multiplicity of economic interests in a large commercial republic, the founders reasoned, held out the prospect that majorities would form that cut across the great divide of rich and poor. Competition among interest groups would replace the class struggle. By combining the refinement of the public views afforded by the principle of representation with the multiplicity of interests found in a large republic, the founders thought that the nation would be free of the rule by majority factions that had destroyed so many republics in the past.

There are two interesting points to observe about the large republic argument. One is that pluralism, or the competition and interplay of interest groups, becomes an accepted and legitimate element of governance. Interest groups are not suppressed, but tolerated and in some measure welcomed. According to *Federalist* 10: "The regulation of these various and interfering interests forms the principal task of modern legislation and involves the spirit of party and faction in the necessary and ordinary operations of government." Much of American politics is—and was intended to be—an adjustment and bargaining process among important societal interests, often economic ones. In this process, there is an essential role for politicians and institutional arrangements that help broker various interests and facilitate coalition making. Second, the large-republic argument rests on a realistic view of human nature. It does not envision a utopian scheme of suppressing factions, but recognizes that in a large commercial republic people will often be disposed to pursue their self-interest. Properly arranged, this pursuit of self-interest need not lead to rule by factional majorities, but to a moderate form of democratic politics.

The argument for a large republic with a multiplicity of interests was strikingly new, bold, and inventive. It is one of the founders' great contributions to political theory. Partly for this reason, many interpreters present this argument as a full description of the foundation of American government. But this view is misleading. The founders regarded a multiplicity of interests in a large republic as only a part, albeit a very important one, of their full theory. It takes nothing away from the significance of this argument to remind ourselves here of its place inside of that fuller theory.

Recall, first, that avoiding majority faction was not the founders' only objective in constructing good government. They also stressed the need for energetic government. This point is important to note here because solving the problem of majority faction by a multiplicity of interests relies on a process of bargaining among groups, which can entail a blocking governmental action. Energetic government, by contrast, emphasizes the importance of a capacity for governmental initiative, which is needed not only to take advantage of changing situations, but also to remedy long-standing ills in society. A process of bargaining can work tolerably well to avoid majority tyranny where it is not already part of the status quo, but it cannot respond well to the great moral and political crises that have faced the country, such as the battles over slavery and civil rights. The two objectives noted here—preventing the formation of unjust majorities and giving broad scope to governmental action—require different and not perfectly compatible properties in government; the founders looked for ways of "mingling them together in their due proportions." (*Federalist* 37) The brokering element of politics would take place initially in the House, while the president (and sometimes the Senate) would supply energy and long-range planning.

Second, recall that the founders never conceived that a large republic was the only or the full solution to the problem of majority faction. While the large republic argument offers a more or less mechanical solution to avoiding majority factions, it would be a misreading of the

founders' view of government to claim that they relied only on mechanical solutions and saw no need for good citizenship. On the contrary, they made clear that the scheme of fostering competing interests must operate in a system in which the public is committed to certain basic principles and in which the resolution of many important issues would require qualities on the part of citizens and leaders whose actions were able to transcend mere interest and to conduct political affairs at a higher level. Although the founders recognized a need for this kind of politics, some interpreters criticize them for not providing an adequate foundation for it. Their task, in any case, was to establish a government that provided a solid grounding for a stable political order. They could not reasonably have been expected to foresee every major problem of American politics.

The question with which we began this section was that of who ultimately rules under the Constitution. We have now seen that the founders sought to establish—and indeed were among the first who believed one could establish—a republican form of government in a large territory. This government was popular in the sense that it clearly rested on "the great body of the people." Yet the weight of the people in the operation of the government would be felt differently than in a pure democracy or small republic. In a large republic, very often there would be no clear and visible majorities, majorities would have to be put together. Far from being a defect, this situation gave greater latitude and discretion to representatives. The arrangement of institutions was designed to foster and take advantage of this latitude in order to promote deliberative decision making and energetic government. The spirit or tone of the Constitution was in no sense populist; in the words of *The Federalist,* it was the "deliberate sense of the community" that should govern, not every "breeze of passion" or "transient impulse" felt by the public. This did not mean that the will of the great body of the people should not prevail; it did mean, however, that more latitude and discretion should lie with government than in a small republic where decisions were driven by claims of simple majority rule.

We have spoken until now of rule by "the great body of the people" without defining that phrase in any detail. The new national government would rest on the foundation of popular rule to a degree no less than that of the governments in the states, which were then considered to be republics and which generally enjoyed a fairly widespread suffrage. The Constitution left the thorny problem of defining the suffrage to the individual states, requiring only that a state could not set qualifications for voting for the House of Representatives that were more restrictive than those it used for determining voting in its own most popular assembly. But it is important to remember that some states at the time had property qualifications for the vote; that slaves were denied all the privileges of citizenship, including of course the suffrage; that Indians were then mostly foreign peoples outside the community; and that in all but one or two states women did not vote.[25]

The Arrangement of Institutions: Complex Government

The Constitution was intended both to prevent tyranny—tyranny by the many as well as by the few—and to promote effective government. To achieve both of these aims required establishing a complex plan of government in which different parts promote different and sometimes partially conflicting qualities. The framework of government created by the Constitution is thus anything but simple. It includes such structural features as separation of powers, checks and balances, bicameralism, and federalism.

Many opponents of the Constitution decried its complexity and called for a simpler plan that would come closer to vesting all political power in one elected assembly. But such a system, according to the founders, could not meet all the aims of good government. It should come as no great surprise, then, that America's system of government is more difficult to understand than that of most other nations. Nor is it any surprise that the Constitution has been attacked from very different sides. Some have complained that the national government is too strong and energetic (this was the view of many of the original opponents of the Constitution), while others criticize the national government for its inefficiency and inability to promote rational and

coordinated policies (this view is held by many observers today who favor a movement toward a parliamentary-type system).

Separation of Powers The founders created a structure of government characterized by a division of power into three separate branches. The theory that informs this division, which is known as the doctrine of the separation of powers, begins with the premise that there are three primary powers involved in the task of governing: making laws (the legislative power); enforcing laws and administering the government (the executive power); and determining criminal and civil penalties and interpreting laws including the Constitution (the judicial power). The Constitution places each of these powers largely, although not exclusively, in a separate branch of government: the legislative function is given to Congress, the executive function to the president, and the judicial function to the courts. This distribution of power is reflected in the opening sentence of each of the first three articles to the Constitution: "all legislative powers herein granted shall be vested in a Congress of the United States" (Article 1); "the executive power shall be vested in a President of the United States" (Article 2); and "the judicial power shall be vested in one supreme Court, and in such inferior Courts as the Congress may from time to ordain and establish" (Article 3).

Two questions immediately arise from the Constitution's allocation of powers: Why did the founders choose to assign the different powers for the most part to different institutions? And then why did they provide for powers to be shared in some degree by different institutions?

Let us consider first the reasons for assigning the powers to separate institutions. Separating the powers in different branches, the founders argued, is a convenient way to reduce the chance of despotic government. Under this arrangement no single institution possesses a monopoly of power, and the other institutions are in a position to watch and resist an institution having despotic designs. Moreover, the specific way powers are divided makes individuals more secure in their personal liberty. Those who make or execute the laws do not have the power to carry out the punishment of individuals, which is

Table 2.1
Major Constitutional Offices

	House of Representatives	Senate	Executive	Supreme Court
Membership	Number determined by Congress (currently 435), apportioned by population with at least one for each state	Two from each state	One president One Vice-President	Number to be determined by Congress (currently nine)
Method of selection	By the people	Originally by the state legislatures; after the Seventeenth Amendment (1913), by the people	Electoral college; if no majority there, House of Representatives chooses from among top three	Nominated by the President; confirmed by the Senate
Minimum age	25 years old	30 years old	35 years old	None
Other qualifications	Must have been a citizen for seven years and an inhabitant of the state from which elected	Must have been a citizen for nine years and an inhabitant of the state from which elected	Must be a natural-born citizen and a resident of the United States for fourteen years	None
Term of office	Two years	Six years, with one-third of members elected every second year	Four years: originally indefinitely reeligible, but as a result of Twenty-Second Amendment (1951) restricted to two terms	During good behavior

a judicial function. The separation of the power of punishing from the power to execute or legislate was widely regarded as one of the great bulwarks in the defense of individual liberties.

Assigning the different powers of government to different branches also means that each branch can then be designed to perform its particular function well. Lawmaking, executing, and judging are different kinds of functions requiring different skills and attributes. The task of making laws requires a body that enjoys the public's confidence and that can represent the nation's different views and opinions. Speed of decision is usually not as important as broad representation and deliberation. An assembly is the best institution to perform this function.

By contrast, the task of executing the law and acting with discretion for the nation's good in foreign affairs sometimes requires energy, secrecy, and speed of decision making. These qualities make unity of command imperative and suggest the need for an office headed by a single individual. The importance of unity of command is most evident in crisis situations or in military operations where delay or deadlock can prove fatal. For example, when President George H. Bush decided to send American troops to invade Panama in 1989, he was able to move quickly and secretly. If the matter had been debated in Congress, there would have been prolonged exchanges, and security leaks might well have occurred.

Finally, the tasks of making judgments in criminal and civil cases and of interpreting the law require an independence from immediate electoral and popular pressures and a special knowledge of the Constitution. In the Supreme Court the founders established an institution that would interpret and protect the law without fear of immediate reprisals. Confirmation of judges by the Senate after nomination by the president would help ensure the selection of individuals possessing the special qualification of legal competence, while life tenure would free the courts from the usual pressures of democratic representation.

Checks and Balances Having decided on the wisdom of vesting the greater part of each power in a different institution, the founders then proceeded to mix and blend certain aspects of these powers among the institutions. For example, the president has a major share of the legislative power through the provision of a qualified veto of all bills passed by the legislature; the legislature, in turn, has part of the executive function in its responsibility to confirm executive appointments. In other words, the founders did not favor a pure separation of powers. They considered such a position to be not only dogmatic, but also contrary to the views of theorists (such as Montesquieu) who had suggested the general idea of a separation of powers. Where there were good reasons to mix and blend powers among the institutions, the founders did so.

One reason for blending powers, curiously enough, was to help maintain the independence of each branch and thus over time to maintain a separation in practice. The founders were concerned that one of the branches might overawe the others and eventually pull all power into its own hands. Merely calling for a separation in a written Constitution was inadequate, for a piece of parchment cannot by itself restrain the drive for power of headstrong individuals. Each institution must be given the means to protect its prerogatives against possible assaults by the other institutions.

The Constitution secures this independence by a number of means, including independent electoral bases for the president and Congress, life tenure for the judges, and a ban on reducing the salaries of the president or the Supreme Court justices while the same persons hold office. One of the most effective ways to provide for each institution's independence, however, is to give it a share in the power of the other institutions which would enable it to protect itself. Madison explained at the Convention that the idea was to "add a defensive power to each [institution] which should maintain the theory [of separation of powers] in practice. . . . We erected effectual barriers for keeping them [the departments of government] separate."[26] Seen in this light, the president's veto is a way to guard the executive power against encroachments by the legislature; the Senate's role of advice and consent in the treaty making process is a way of protecting the legislature against an overly ambitious president; and judicial review is a way for the Court to protect its own prerogatives against the other branches.

Another reason the founders shared certain powers was that, in some instances, a sharing would result in better or safer government. The most important example is the lawmaking power, where the president is given an ongoing role, both in stopping legislation through the veto power and in suggesting new policies through the power to give information on the state of the union and make recommendations to Congress. This arrangement was designed to provide yet another check against majority faction and to allow for the introduction of a broader, national view of affairs, which the president can sometimes provide. Another example is the war-making power, which was generally regarded as a power that was executive in nature. The Constitution gives the power to declare war to the Congress, and not the president, because this power was deemed too dangerous to give to

BOX 2.3

On the Origin of the Term "Federalism"

The choice of terminology during the ratification debate amounted to an important victory for the Federalists. Before 1787, the terms "federal" and "confederal" were synonymous. Strictly speaking, a federal system was a decentralized, confederate government like that of the Articles. In adopting the name of *Federalists* and forcing their rivals to accept the name of *Antifederalists,* proponents of the Constitution appropriated a term already in wide use, but gave it their own novel meaning: the modern sense of "federal," which refers to a government that is neither entirely unitary nor entirely confederal, but a mixture of the two. The Antifederalists were forced to accept a label which made them appear opposed to the very form of government they advocated. The term "federal government" today means the national government, but "federalism" refers to the division of power between the national government and the states.

one person and because any major war would need the support of the legislature.

Underlying the effective operation of this system is the same realistic understanding of human nature that was evident in the solution to the problem of factions. The motives on which the founders relied to maintain the separation of powers included not only a concern for the public good, but also the interest of officials to protect the power of their own institution. Politicians normally want to exercise more power, and this motive, properly channeled, can be used to fortify their resolve and promote the public interest. In the words of *The Federalist:* "Ambition must be made to counteract ambition." (*Federalist* 51)

To summarize, the allocation of power in the national government is based first on placing separate powers in different branches and second on strategically mixing elements of those powers among the branches. This system provides a great degree of security against arbitrary government. It also possesses some elements of efficiency, for each institution is specifically designed to carry out its particular task in an effective way.

Yet there is no denying that this system also pays a price in terms of its efficiency. For most major policies to be implemented, there must be cooperation among these different institutions. In the case of any domestic policy, whether it originates with the president or within the Congress, in the end there must be support from both institutions for any law to be enacted (except in the rare case where there is sufficient

congressional support to override a presidential veto). The judiciary, too, will normally at least have to accept the constitutionality of any measure that is adopted. In foreign affairs, the president may be able to carry out certain quick emergency actions and diplomatic initiatives on his own, but any long-range program will require congressional support. The problem in policymaking is thus that any policy must clear a number of different hurdles (president, Senate, House, and the Court). The difficulty in achieving cooperation is, as we shall see, one of the ongoing challenges in the conduct of American politics. What is clear, however, is that some degree of conflict among the institutions is an inevitable byproduct of this system, with its separation of powers and further checks and balances. If this is a problem in the system, it was one that the founders in some measure foresaw and were willing to endure for the sake of preventing despotic government.

Bicameralism From observing the experience of the state governments, the founders were clearly worried most about the tendency of the legislature to gather all governmental power into its hands. This tendency was backed by the legislature's claim, expressed often by its lower house, to speak directly and immediately for the people. To restrain the legislature, but also to help shape the way it exercised power, the founders favored a bicameral legislature—that is, a legislature of two houses. In this system, both the Senate and the House of Representatives must concur in the passage of any piece of legislation. This system creates an internal balance inside the legislature itself. The Senate, whose members were elected indirectly until 1913 and serve a six-year term, was designed to serve as a kind of "upper house" that could check the possible instability and populist demands of the House. In addition to providing some representation for the states, the Senate was set up so that it would generally provide more stability and offer greater knowledge and experience in the conduct of affairs than the House. For these reasons, too, the Senate was given the role of assisting in the executive-type functions of confirming presidential appointments and ratifying treaties.

Federalism The dominant spirit of the founders was nationalist in the sense that they wanted to replace the existing confederation with a genuine national government. Exactly what role the states were to play within this new framework, however, was uncertain at the outset of the Convention. But by the end of the Convention, after all the compromises had been struck, it became clear that there was a large and important place for state governments operating inside of a strong national government. The national government was intended to be strong but limited to certain broad ends. Beyond these limited ends, decision-making power would reside with the states. Moreover, in the Senate the states were partly represented in the national government *as* states—or at any rate their equality was partly acknowledged.

The Constitution created what we know today as a federal system, even though the founders did not use that term in the sense we do today. By federalism now one means a system of two levels of government (the central government and the states or provinces) in which the central government is fully sovereign within its sphere and in which the states or provinces are recognized as distinct governments under the Constitution. Almost every country has a division of power of some kind between the central government and governments at lower levels (counties or cities). But where that relationship has no protection in the fundamental law and can be altered at any time by ordinary statute, there is no federal arrangement. Under a federal

arrangement, states possess a residuum of power—advocates sometimes like to call it sovereignty—and retain a large sphere of independent action. They may have their own identities, their own governments (sometimes with their own constitutions), and their own means of raising revenues—all of these, of course, being consistent with certain restrictions and requirements from the national government.

A federal arrangement serves a number of functions. One is to serve as a counterweight or check to the central government, standing up against if it should overstep its rightful powers. (For many in the United States prior to the Civil War, the idea of states being a check or rallying point included vague notions that the states might offer noncompliance or resistance to the national government.) Another function of federalism is to make government more democratic or popular. The decentralization of authority enables each state to develop policies according to the standards of local majorities, and it allows for a much greater degree of political participation in decision making than if all laws were passed by the central government. Finally, federalism can aid in maintaining the nation's diversity and in some ways even in increasing the effectiveness of the government. Federalism relieves the central government from performing a whole range of functions on which it might be unwise to impose a uniform principle. The central government in America does not have to worry (directly) about how to run schools or how to police neighborhoods—these are matters for state and local governments. The states can also experiment with different responses to political problems, serving as laboratories for good public policy.

Ratification

Political life always faces the great challenge of reconciling wisdom with consent—of somehow getting people to accept good laws. Other constitution makers, the founders observed, had been able to engineer consent for their governments by "mixing a portion of violence with the authority of superstition." (*Federalist* 38) Neither of these means, however, was sought by, or available to, America's founders. They had to win consent for the Constitution by a process of public persuasion.

Almost as much as the content of the Constitution itself, the way in which it was ratified helped secure a firm foundation for the new republic. As Alexis de Tocqueville remarked about the two-year-long ratification process:

> That which is new in the history of societies is to see a great people, warned by its lawgivers that the wheels of government are stopping, turn its attention on itself without haste or fear, sound the depth of the ill, and then wait for two years to find the remedy at leisure, and then finally, when the remedy has been indicated, submit to it voluntarily without its costing humanity a single tear or drop of blood.[27]

The founders, of course, paid careful attention to the practical problems of securing consent, as they had no wish to make the task any more difficult than was necessary. They defined their own method for ratification, bypassing completely the amendment process of the Articles that required unanimous consent of all the state governments. The Constitution was offered as an entirely new government that would go into effect after being ratified by conventions in nine of the states. The Congress of the Articles silently acquiesced in this plan by forwarding the Constitution to the states for their consideration, though without ever endorsing it. No more, perhaps, could have been asked of a government that was itself being asked to sacrifice its own existence.

The plan of ratifying by special conventions in the states, rather than by votes of the existing state governments, was appealing on several counts. Conventions were the most democratic method known at the time and were thus the best instruments for instituting a government by consent. Moreover, because the new government reduced the power and authority of the state governments, to have given the decision to state officials would probably have doomed the whole enterprise. Ratifying by state legislatures would also have implied that the new government was a compact among the several state governments, rather than a national government resting ultimately on "we the people." Finally, declaring that the new government would begin after nine states ratified it gave the Constitution

a reasonable chance of being adopted. No state refusing to ratify was compelled to join the union, but in a practical sense many of the smaller states would have lacked the means to stay outside of a new government.

The Debate on Ratification

The process of ratifying the Constitution produced a sober and exhaustive discussion of the nation's political principles. Virtually every point contested at the Convention was reopened for debate. Both proponents and opponents of the Constitution could boast of some very formidable political leaders. Besides most of the delegates to the Convention, friends of the Constitution—who by now were calling themselves "Federalists"—included John Adams, John Marshall, and, with notable reservations, Thomas Jefferson. The opponents, who came to be known as "Antifederalists" (see Box 2.3), included such figures as George Clinton of New York and Richard Henry Lee and Patrick Henry of Virginia. Joining them were George Mason, Elbridge Gerry, and Edmund Randolph, all of whom had attended the Convention but refused to sign the Constitution.

In the ratifying conventions and in numerous newspaper articles and pamphlets published during this period, opponents levied a wide array of criticisms against the Constitution, some petty and some to the point. It was argued, among other things, that under the new government the president might become a monarch; that the states would forfeit their sovereignty; that the Supreme Court would become an all-powerful governing council; that the people could ill afford to pay taxes to both state and national governments; that a standing army would oppress the citizenry; that the Constitution gave too much protection to the institution of slavery (in part a Quaker criticism), or too little (the criticism of some Southern planters); and that it contained too few safeguards for religious freedom (a Baptist concern). Small republic themes were well summed up by Patrick Henry, who attacked the Constitution as a government hostile to the "spirit of republicanism" that would create "one great, consolidated, national government" that would crush the states.[28] The

Table 2.2
Methods of Amending the Constitution

Article V of the Constitution specifies two methods of proposing amendments: a two-thirds vote of both houses of Congress or a national convention called by Congress "on the application of" two-thirds of the state legislatures. It further specifies two methods of ratifying amendments: approval by three-fourths of the state legislatures or by ratifying conventions in three-fourths of the states; in either case Congress chooses the methods of ratifying. To date, all amendments have been proposed by Congress, and all except the Twenty-First, which repealed the Eighteenth (Prohibition) Amendment, have been ratified by the state legislatures.

Step 1:

Amendments may be PROPOSED:

(a) By a two-thirds vote of both houses of Congress

or

(b) By a national constitutional convention requested by legislatures of two-thirds of the states

Amendments may be RATIFIED:

(a) By legislatures of three-fourths of the states

or

(b) By conventions called for the purpose in three-fourths of the states

founders did not insist that their plan was perfect, but that it was "the best that the present views and circumstances of the country will permit." (Federalist 85)

Even so, ratifying the Constitution proved to be extremely difficult, and a successful outcome was far from being a certainty. It was necessary not just to acquire the support of nine states, but as a practical matter to win approval of the major states (Massachusetts, New York, Pennsylvania, and Virginia). In Pennsylvania, the legislature could only call a convention after a mob forced the attendance of Antifederalists who had been boycotting the session in order to prevent a quorum. In New York, ratification came about through the brilliant maneuvering of Alexander Hamilton, but by only three votes, and only after New York City threatened to secede if ratification failed. The story in several other states was similar. Finally, however, on June 21, 1788, New Hampshire became the ninth state to ratify, and the Constitution became law. By 1790, even contrary-minded Rhode Island had joined the union.

The Bill of Rights

The difficult campaign for ratification would almost certainly have been lost if the Federalists had not agreed to one more implicit compromise: the addition of a bill of rights. The Constitution contained a procedure for amendment (see Table 2.2), although few of the founders at the convention anticipated any major additions at the outset. But as the ratification debate proceeded, support for a bill of rights gained ground; and some state conventions agreed to ratify the Constitution only after they had recommended adding a set of amendments. An understanding that a bill of rights would be passed thus became the last agreement on the road to building the new government.

The omission of a bill of rights in the Constitution strikes many today as strange. But the Federalists had reasons for opposing a bill of rights. They argued that the Constitution itself already protected certain key rights, such as the explicit ban against bills of attainder and ex post facto laws (see Box 2.4). (This was true, but the Antifederalists replied that it was no reason not to provide explicit protection for other basic rights, such as free speech.) The Federalists also argued that to list things the national govern-

---

BOX 2.4

Civil Liberties Guaranteed in the Constitution before the Addition of a Bill of Rights

Opponents of the proposed Constitution complained that it lacked a bill of rights. Yet, as the Federalists pointed out, the new plan of government did include some provisions for the protection of personal liberties. These provisions are listed below in the order of their appearance in the Constitution:

1 Writs of habeas corpus may not be suspended unless, during rebellion or invasion, the "public safety may require it."
2 No bill of attainder may be passed by Congress or the states.
3 No one may hold a title of nobility.
4 No ex post facto law may be passed by Congress or the states.
5 Laws "impairing the obligation of contracts" may not be passed by the states.
6 Citizens accused of crimes are to be tried by jury "except in cases of impeachment."
7 Citizens of each state must possess "all privileges and immunities of citizens in the several states."
8 No one may be compelled to pass a religious test as a condition for holding federal office.

---

ment could not do might inadvertently imply that it was not a government of limited or enumerated powers. (The Antifederalists brushed this objection aside by contending that exclusions of specific powers did not imply a grant of total power.) Finally, the Federalists were concerned that a bill of rights might compromise energetic government. As rights could never be absolute, in the course of time the government would have to decide when and how they would be modified in particular circumstances. Putting rights in a Constitution might make these deliberations more difficult; and appearing to provide protection for things that could not absolutely be protected would undermine respect for the Constitution. (The Antifederalists answered that providing explicit protection for key rights would add to their safety over the long run.)

In the end, the Antifederalists' argument prevailed, and the decision to add the Bill of Rights was a victory for them and a sure sign that the open and free method of ratification had produced effects of its own (see Box 2.5). At the same time, much of the credit for the Bill of Rights belongs to the Federalists, especially James Madison. Madison accepted that a bill of rights was part of the agreement for ratification and perhaps came around to the view that it could be a helpful safeguard to liberty. But it had to be the proper kind of bill of rights.

In the first session of Congress, Madison and his allies proposed twelve amendments, ten of which were approved and later became known as the Bill of Rights. The debate over these amendments rekindled the Federalist-Antifederalist dispute, as each side had a different understanding about what a bill of rights should be. The impetus for the bill of rights had come from Antifederalists who were fearful of the national government. For them, the best way to protect liberty was to hedge in the power of the national government by adding to the powers and protection of the state governments; a bill of rights was a way of chipping away at the powers of the national government in relationship to the states.[29] For Madison and the Federalist majority in Congress, however, the aim was not to rewrite the Constitutional balance of power between the national government and the states, but to enhance protection for individual rights.

The Bill of Rights in its final form was intended mainly to protect citizens' rights against abuse by the national government, not by the state governments. This emphasis follows from Antifederalist concerns about the threat to liberty posed by the power of the national government. The First Amendment, for example, begins by declaring that "Congress shall make no law respecting an establishment of religion." Nothing is said in this amendment about the lim-

---

BOX 2.5

The Bill of Rights (Amendments I-X, Ratified 1791)

Positive rights

Amendment I: Freedom of religion, speech, press, and assembly; right to petition government for redress of grievances.

Amendment II: Right to bear arms.

Amendment III: No quartering of troops in private homes in peacetime.

Amendment IX: Rights not enumerated in Constitution are retained by the people.

Amendment X: Powers not delegated to the United States or denied to the states are reserved to the states or to the people.

Procedural rights

Amendment IV: No unreasonable searches or seizures.

Amendment V: Grand jury indictment required in serious criminal cases; no double jeopardy (standing trial twice for the same offense); no compelling of persons to testify against themselves; no taking of life, liberty, or property without due process of law.

Amendment VI: Right to a speedy and public trial by jury in criminal cases; right to legal counsel in criminal cases.

Amendment VII: Right to trial by jury in civil suits exceeding $20 in value.

Amendment VIII: No excessive bail or fines; no cruel and unusual punishment.

The Bill of Rights provides positive and procedural rights. Positive rights define the domain of individual or state freedom. Procedural rights protect citizens from illegal or arbitrary action by government. Speaking for the Supreme Court in *Barron v. Baltimore* (1833), Chief Justice John Marshall ruled that the Bill of Rights limits only the powers of the federal government, not the states; relying on the Fourteenth Amendment, the Court in this century has applied most of these limits to state governments as well.

---

its imposed on state legislatures. The protection of people's rights from state governments was certainly not a responsibility Antifederalists wanted to turn over to the national government or the federal judiciary. The protection of these rights was left to the individual states themselves—according to their own constitutions. Beginning with the decision in *Gitlow v. New York* (1925), however, the Supreme Court has used the "due process" clause in the Fourteenth Amendment (1868) to bring in or incorporate most of the guarantees enumerated in the Bill of Rights to protect citizens against actions by all levels of government, national or state.

Conclusion

The two basic documents of the American founding are the Declaration of Independence and the Constitution. Many have charged that the two documents are inconsistent with one another, the Declaration speaking in a hopeful and democratic voice, the Constitution in a harsh and reactionary one.[30] While there are differences in tone between the two documents, the authors of the Constitution never doubted that it was consistent with the Declaration. The two documents, of course, had different purposes. The Declaration set forth some of the most cherished principles of legitimate government in declaring why America was separating from Great Britain; it was never meant to specify the arrangements of a particular structure of government.

The Constitution represented one possibility for how the principles could be embodied in a particular government. Other forms of government, such as the Articles, were also arguably faithful, at least in intention, to the Declaration. The challenge the founders faced at the Convention was to devise a structure of government that met the principles of the Declaration and that also was strong and energetic enough to provide for effective government. Among the possible choices, the founders were at least hopeful that they had found a workable framework. Its form was popular or republican, the only kind of government, in Madison's words, consistent with the "fundamental principles of the Revolution." (*Federalist* 39) And the system was further designed to fulfill the Declaration's goals of ensuring equality and protecting liberty, with the glaring exceptions of those still excluded from a full place in the community. The consistency between the Declaration and the Constitution on these basic principles was probably what John Quincy Adams had in mind when he proclaimed both to be "parts of one consistent whole, founded upon one and the same theory of government."[31]

The Convention of 1787 continued the work of 1776 and established the structure of the government. But not all questions about America's Constitution were definitively resolved by the founding generation, either in 1776 or in 1787. Studying the founding is the best place to begin to understand constitution making, but we must also look at the constitutional decisions of Americans after the founding generation.

Chapter 2 Notes

1. Paul Leicester Ford, ed., *The Works of Thomas Jefferson*, vol. 12 (New York: Putnam, 1904), p. 409.
2. Paul Leicester Ford, ed., *The Works of Thomas Jefferson*, vol. 12, p. 477.
3. Abigail Adams, *Letters of Abigail Adams*, vol. 1, 2nd ed. (Boston: Little, Brown, 1840), p. 98.
4. Clinton Rossiter, *1787: The Grand Convention* (New York: Macmillan, 1966), p. 49.
5. Richard Hofstadter et al., *The American Republic,* vol. 1, 2nd ed. (Englewood Cliffs, N.J.: Prentice-Hall, 1970), p. 226.
6. Richard Hofstadter et al., *The American Republic,* vol. 1, 2nd ed., p. 239.
7. Max Farrand, *The Framing of the Constitution of the United States* (New Haven, Conn.: Yale University Press, 1913), p. 10.
8. *Federalist* 40 and *Federalist* 43. The same points were made at the Convention.
9. Clinton Rossiter, *1787: The Grand Convention,* 1966, p. 284.
10. Herbert J. Storing, *What the Anti-Federalists Were For* (Chicago: University of Chicago Press, 1981), p. 16.
11. Herbert J. Storing, *What the Anti-Federalists Were For,* p. 17.
12. Montesquieu, *The Spirit of the Laws,* translated by Thomas Nugent (New York: Hafner Publishing Company, 1975), p. lxxi.
13. Herbert Storing, *What the Anti-Federalists Were For,* p. 20.
14. Max Farrand, ed., *The Records of the Federal Convention of 1787,* vol. 1, p. 51.
15. Herbert Storing, *What the Anti-Federalists Were Fo*r, p. 7.
16. Max Farrand, ed., *The Records of the Federal Convention of 1787,* vol. 1, p. 10.
17. Max Farrand, *The Framing of the Constitution of the United States,* p. 60; Max Farrand, ed., *The Records of the Federal Convention of 1787,* vol. 3, p. 550.
18. Max Farrand, *The Framing of the Constitution of the United States,* p. 15.
19. Charles Beard, *An Economic Interpretation of the Constitution* (New York: Macmillan, 1913).
20. Forrest McDonald, *We the People: The Economic Origins of the Constitution* (Chicago: University of Chicago Press, 1958), p. 349.
21. Max Farrand, *The Records of the Federal Convention of 1787,* vol. 1, pp. 461–62, 468.
22. John P. Roche, "The Founding Fathers: A Reform Caucus in Action," *American Political Science Review,* vol. 55, 1961, p. 815.
23. James Madison, *Notes of the Federal Convention,* Adrienne Koch, ed. (New York: Norton, 1969), p. 77 (June 6), pp. 503–04 (August 21, 22).
24. Don Fehrenbacher, "The Federal Government & Slavery," Bicentennial Essay Number 1 (Claremont, Calif.: The Claremont Institute, 1984), p. 6.
25. In New Jersey women in some counties voted up until 1807. For a discussion of the founders' view of the suffrage, see Thomas G. West, *Vindicating the Founders* (Latham: Rowman & Littlefield, 1997).
26. Max Farrand, ed., *The Records of the Federal Convention of 1787,* vol. 2, p. 77 (July 21).
27. Alexis de Tocqueville, *Democracy in America,* J. P. Mayer, ed. (Garden City, N.Y.: Doubleday, 1968), p. 113.
28. Clifton Rossiter, *The Grand Convention,* pp. 283–284.
29. For instance, in what is now the Tenth Amendment, they attempted to have the word "expressly" inserted after "delegated" in the clause that guaranteed to the states the "powers not delegated to the United States by the Constitution, nor prohibited by it to the States." Madison objected to the addition of this single word on the grounds that governments must necessarily possess implied as well as expressed powers; otherwise, the Constitution would have to "recount every minutia."
30. Charles Beard, *An Economic Interpretation of the Constitution.*
31. Mortimer J. Adler and Wayne Moquin, eds., *The Revolutionary Years* (Chicago: Encyclopaedia Britannica, 1976), p. 315.

3

Constitutional Development

CHAPTER CONTENTS

Although the Constitution written in 1787 continues powerfully to shape our political life, many significant changes have occurred in the basic elements of our political system since that time. Some of these changes have come through Constitutional amendment (slavery was abolished by the Thirteenth Amendment, women were guaranteed the right to vote by the Nineteenth). Some have come through new interpretations of the Constitution (legal segregation of the races was abolished in 1954 through a new interpretation of the Fourteenth Amendment). Some have come from federal laws of extraordinarily important character (such as the Civil Rights Act of 1964). And finally, some have come about through the development or decay of institutions and practices (such as the rise of political parties).

Just as John Adams noted that the real American revolution had been the change in people's opinions, so, too, subsequent changes in the Constitution, laws, and practices of the country have rested upon shifts in people's attitudes and beliefs.

In each of the great controversies that have punctuated American political life, there has been a tendency for one or both parties to draw upon the sources of the founding, interpreting the Constitution and the Declaration of Independence to support their position. Jefferson, the author of the Declaration, was himself the leader of one of the parties in the first great controversy under the Constitution, which took place between the Federalist and the Republican parties in the 1790s and early 1800s. Jefferson believed that his opponents, the Federalists, had betrayed the principles of the Revolution and were seeking to transform the Constitution into a system of rule by a propertied oligarchy. Later, in the 1820s and 1830s, the Jacksonians saw themselves as the heirs of Jefferson, struggling against the economic power of those who relied on a great government corporation (the National Bank) to maintain their privileges. Abraham Lincoln in the 1850s and 1860s appealed over and over to the principles of the Declaration of Independence in resisting the spread of slavery. Progressives in the late nineteenth and early twentieth centuries sought to reform the Constitution and rescue the political system from corruption and decay. Finally, in the 1930s Franklin Roosevelt understood the New Deal as a great renewal of Jefferson's struggle against the "economic royalists" who formed a privileged elite.

This symbolic struggle reflects the fact that American politics have always involved disputes over principles as well as immediate struggles for advantage and power. The Declaration has been central to America's great political controversies because it is the most eloquent and authoritative statement of the purposes of government and of the standard of justice upon which the United States was founded. The Constitution contains the fundamental law governing its institutions. Those who would change the government have usually found it necessary either to show how the change is consistent with the common understanding of the Declaration and the Constitution or to bring about a new understanding of their meaning.

In this chapter we shall examine some of the fundamental changes in the opinions and sentiments of Americans since the founding. We shall see how these shifts in belief have resulted in changes in the Constitution and its interpretation and have brought about political and other changes that have had important effects on our constitutional system. We shall focus our discussion on the differing answers given to three of the four fundamental questions of politics: (1) that changes have occurred in the ends and purposes of society—in people's understanding of liberty, equality, self-government, and citizenship? (2) What changes have been brought about in the scope of government, in the tasks it is expected to perform, and in the relationship between the state and national governments? (3) Finally, what changes have occurred in the organization of the institutions of government and the distribution of power? (Matters relating to national security and America's role in the world will be discussed in Chapter 17.) In examining these questions we will see how citizens have continually been called upon to adopt the perspective of a constitution maker.

Federalists versus Republicans

The first great controversy under the Constitution resulted in the formation of the first American political party, founded by Jefferson and Madison in the 1790s and known as the "Republican party" (later the "Democratic-Republican party"). The party of their opponents, led by Hamilton and Adams, became known as the "Federalist party." The quarrel between these parties developed during the 1790s over a number of important issues, both domestic and foreign. It began with opposition to the financial policies Hamilton developed as secretary of the treasury under Washington. The partisan quarrel was heated by varying reactions to events surrounding the French Revolution and the subsequent war between France and England. Federalists and Republicans denounced each other as "Anglomen" and "Gallomen" or "monarchists" and "Jacobins" (a revolutionary French society favoring a radical form of democracy). The passage of the Alien and Sedition Acts in 1798 (acts which limited the right to criticize the government) brought the dispute to a head and led to the subsequent victory of Jefferson in the presidential election of 1800. Although the quarrel continued, the Federalists, defeated in the congressional elections of 1800 as well, never again won a national election and, as a party, soon faded forever from American politics.

The Ends of Society: The Character of a Free People

Both Republicans and Federalists accepted the basic idea of liberalism (a limited government that protects rights), movingly expressed by Jefferson in his first inaugural address:

> All, too, will bear in mind this sacred principle, that though the will of the majority is in all cases to prevail, that will to be rightful must be reasonable; that the minority possess their equal rights, which equal law must protect, and to violate would be oppression.[1]

The two parties disagreed, however, on the kind of society and economy that should be fostered to fulfill this objective. Hamilton used his position as secretary of the treasury under Washington to formulate policies that would encourage the development of commerce and industry and create economic interests that would tie people to the national government. His policies were designed to create a diversity of economic interests which would check each other, provide an outlet for the ambitious, and leave scope for governmental discretion and leadership. A strong commercial economy, he believed, would not only ensure a powerful and thus independent nation, but it would also provide the soundest protection for individual rights and give great scope for individual ambition.

The Republicans, on the other hand, thought that the key to successful republican government was to be found in a majority so educated and informed as not to desire to oppress minorities. Some Republicans, for example, believed that the country should be based on an agricultural, not a diversified, commercial economy. Cities and commerce, they thought, bred citizens with selfish habits and produced people more interested in manipulating others than in cooperating with them. Hamilton's policies fostered inequality and encouraged the kinds of people—speculators, stockjobbers, people out for a fast buck—who would corrupt government and undermine republicanism. Independent farming, on the other hand, taught personal self-reliance and self-discipline, as well as encouraged a "quiet life, and orderly conduct, both public and private." These were the qualities needed for good citizenship. Instead of relying upon the diversity of interest groups in a commercial society to check each other, the Republicans sought to foster one interest, the agricultural, as the source of sound republican opinion that could guide and check the government. "When we get piled upon one another in large cities, as in Europe," Jefferson said, "we shall become corrupt as in Europe, and go to eating one another as they do there."[2]

If under today's circumstances a nation composed mainly of independent farmers is impossible, the Jeffersonian view may nevertheless remind us of the importance of the qualities of citizenship needed in a republican form of government. While this concern is certainly not absent from the Federalist view, the Jeffersonians gave it powerful expression and helped lay

---

BOX 3.1

Jefferson and Hamilton on National Character

What kind of people Americans were to become was one of the issues which divided Alexander Hamilton and Thomas Jefferson. Each recognized that the way people lived and made their living would affect their habits of mind and qualities of character. Jefferson favored encouraging agriculture; Hamilton manufacturing. The effect each thought his policy would have on Americans is shown in the following quotations:

Jefferson

. . . Those who labour in the earth are the chosen people of God, if ever he had a chosen people, whose breast he has made his peculiar deposit for substantial and genuine virtue. . . . Corruption of morals in the mass of cultivators is a phenomenon of which no age nor nation has furnished an example. It is the mark set on those, who, not looking up to heaven, to their own toil and industry, as does the husbandman, for their subsistence, depend for it on the casualties and caprice of customers. Dependence begets subservience and venality, suffocates the germ of virtue, and prepares fit tools for the designs of ambition. . . . Let our workshops remain in Europe.

Hamilton

It is a just observation, that minds of the strongest and most active powers for their proper objects fall below mediocrity and labour without effect, if confined to uncongenial pursuits. And it is thence to be inferred, that the results of human exertion may be immensely increased by diversifying its objects. When all the different kinds of industry obtain in a community, each individual can find his proper element, and can call into activity the whole vigour of his nature. And the community is benefitted by the services of its respective members, in the manner, in which each can serve it with most effect. . . .

Sources: Thomas Jefferson, *The Writings of Thomas Jefferson,* Andrew A. Lipscomb, ed., vol.2 (Washington, D.C.: Thomas Jefferson Memorial ASsociation, 1904), pp. 229–230; Alexander Hamilton, *The Papers of Alexander Hamilton*, Harold C. Syrett, ed., vo. 10 (New York: Columbia University Press, 1966), pp. 255–256.

the foundation for such ideas as universal public education (see Box 3.1).

The Scope of Government

The Federalists favored a construction of the Constitution that gave broad authority to the national government. Not only was the national government more remote from the voters and hence less susceptible to majority tyranny, but a broad understanding of its powers enabled it to be used to foster commercial development and provide for a strong national defense. In *McCulloch v. Maryland* (1819) the Supreme Court under Chief Justice John Marshall (a Federalist) upheld the Constitutionality of a national bank while striking down a state law which levied taxes on the bank. While acknowledging that the Constitution did not explicitly give Congress a specific power to establish a bank, Marshall's decision for the Court found this to be an acceptable means of carrying out the financial responsibilities assigned to Congress by the Constitution. The government, in the Federalist's view, should be conceived as having broad discretion over the means to achieve the basic Constitutional ends. The Constitution should be read as a document that not only limits, but that grants powers to government. This is what Marshall meant by his famous phrase in *McCulloch:* "We must never forget it is a Constitution we are expounding."

The Republicans, on the other hand, thought the Constitution ought to be interpreted narrowly in order to restrict the powers of the national government and strengthen those of the states. Not only were the state governments closer to the people, but a less active national government would better serve the cause of protecting the agricultural interests. In response to the Alien and Sedition Acts, which allowed the federal government to punish those who attacked the government in the press and to deport non-citizens holding certain views, Madison and Jefferson wrote resolutions passed by the legislatures of Virginia and Kentucky which put forth the view that the states had a right not to obey a national law they thought unconstitutional. Madison and Jefferson were both concerned about the threat to individual rights that was posed by the Alien and Sedition Acts, but they were even more concerned with the power it gave to the federal government.

As in many cases in American politics, the Republican-Federalist quarrel over the proper scope of the national government also reflected differing opinions about substantive policy. A strong national government for the Federalists was not only good in itself but also beneficial as a means to commercial development, just as a weaker national government to the Republicans was not only good in itself but also conducive to the end of protecting agriculture. The context of politics seldom provides an opportunity for considering questions concerning the power and structure of government apart from the policies that will be advanced or hindered.

Organization and Distribution of Power

The many disputes between the Republicans and Federalists reflected a fundamental disagreement about the organization of governmental power, both in the relationship between voters and their representatives and in the distribution of power between the branches of government.

Representation Jefferson said that the difference between his party and Hamilton's was that the Republicans trusted the people while the Federalists feared them. While this statement was a partisan exaggeration, it contained a germ of truth. The Republicans wanted a government much more directly responsive to people's opinions than the Federalists did. The Federalists thought that good government required decisions that were not immediately popular, and they preferred representatives to be relatively free from the pressure of popular opinion. Sound financial policies required a government that could make and carry out unpopular decisions. Similarly, in foreign affairs unpopular decisions might also be required. For example, the Federalists supported neutrality in the war between France and England in the late 1790s in

spite of the fact that England had recently been the country's enemy and the sympathy and gratitude of the people were naturally attached to the country's former ally, France.

In order to make it possible for representatives to support such unpopular decisions, the Federalists thought that voters should select representatives on the basis of their reputation and accomplishments and judge them on the results of their policies, but not bind the representatives to their own opinions of what should be done. By fostering the growth of commerce and industry they hoped to create such a diversity of interests that the opinions of no one group would predominate, giving greater discretion to the deliberation of elected officials.

The Republicans, on the other hand, thought that representatives should be tied more closely to popular opinion. As Jefferson put it:

> The further the departure from direct and constant control by the citizens, the less has the government of the ingredient of republicanism; . . . it must be agreed that our governments have much less of republicanism than ought to be expected; in other words, that the people have less regular control over their agents, than their rights and their interests require.[3]

Jefferson thought that Hamilton's policies as secretary of the treasury created a corrupt union of bankers, bondholders, and governmental officials that threatened to make a mockery of republican government. Only the American people at the ballot box could prevent representatives from developing into a self-interested class that would advance its own welfare at the expense of the public.

Jefferson and other political leaders, including now James Madison, created the Republican party in order to bring public opinion to bear on the government. They saw the party as a means by which the majority could be mobilized to resist the dangers of self-interested minorities and be given a greater hand in shaping the direction of the government. The political party was in fact a new political instrument that simplified matters for voters and allowed citizens in different districts to vote for the same national principles. Party competition created the possibility for the victorious party to speak of a national majority, not only in Congress but also for the presidency.

The victory of Thomas Jefferson and for his Republican-Democratic party in 1800 stands as one of the most important events not only in American history, but also in the history of modern democracy. It marks the first time that an opposition party took control of government not by force, but by means of a popular election. Jefferson saw his victory in 1800 as a revolution as great as that of 1776 because it showed that the people could check their representatives when they threatened to undermine republicanism and could peacefully decide a great national dispute.

The Balance of Institutional Power The Federalists favored a strong presidency and lent their support as well to the development of a more powerful Supreme Court. These two branches of government, apart from being capable on occasion of resisting oppressive majorities and protecting property, helped provide for the two great governmental qualities of energy and stability.

In the case of the presidency, the Federalists clearly saw that institution as having a strong independent source of authority—the "executive power" noted in Article II of the Constitution—to take the initiative in the conduct of foreign affairs; and under Washington's presidency, Alexander Hamilton, who served as secretary of the treasury, was constantly involved in preparing major bills to propose to Congress and in setting the basic agenda of congressional debate. The Republicans objected to this kind of power in the presidency and accused the Federalists of seeking to transform the presidency into a kind of American monarchy. Republicans regarded the Congress, not the presidency, as the normal source for initiative in government, and even when Jefferson took the lead (as he often did), he did so not directly but by calling on certain friends in Congress to speak for the Administration.

Although the Constitution had not explicitly granted the Supreme Court the right to declare laws of Congress unconstitutional, the Federalists favored this power of "judicial review." The Republicans, on the other hand, opposed it or at any rate sought to closely check it. Jefferson argued that each branch of government had the right to decide for itself whether its actions were Constitutional or not, and he thought that judicial review undermined democratic control and threatened to create a judicial despotism. Supreme power, according to the Republicans, ought to reside in Congress as the branch most representative of the people.

These opinions concerning the distribution of power were bound up with the views of the Federalists and the Republicans concerning the ends of society, a point vividly illustrated by Jefferson's actions as president. When Jefferson had the possibility of securing the Louisiana Purchase for the United States, he was willing to go beyond the Constitutional authority of the government (as he understood it) in order to acquire new land for an expanding agriculture and greater security for trade in agricultural produce down the Mississippi River. Congressional predominance within a restrained national government was meant to serve a certain end; when that end could be served by strong presidential action, Jefferson was willing to take it.

The result of the Republican triumph of 1800 was not a complete victory for the Republican view of the proper balance among governmental institutions. John Marshall, a leading Federalist, had been appointed Chief Justice by the outgoing President Adams. By the time of his death thirty-five years later, he had been able to forge the Supreme Court into a powerful political force, with the nearly undisputed right to declare laws of Congress unconstitutional. The case in which Marshall established this right—*Marbury v. Madison* (1803)—is one of the great cases in American law.

Moreover, although Jefferson had advocated a deferential executive, and put forward this view as president, some of his conduct in the office provided precedents for a stronger presidency. Through his role as head of the Republican party, he actively led the legislature and, as already mentioned, was willing to go beyond his Constitutional authority (as he saw it) to secure the Louisiana Purchase for the United States. The strong presidency implied by such actions was gradually to find a Jeffersonian justification. The turning of presidential elections into party conflicts led the way toward seeing the presidency not as an undemocratic check upon democratic legislatures, but as a fully democratic office which could reflect the most significant political judgments of the voters.

In opposing the restrictions on speech and press of the Alien and Sedition Acts on the grounds that they usurped powers rightfully found in the states, the Republicans raised an issue that was to beset American politics through the Civil War and beyond. As sectionalism hardened and the issue of slavery grew more divisive, the question of the power of the states to resist acts of the national government became a question of life or death for the American union.

Although it proved difficult to maintain the United States as an agricultural country, and many Republicans, including Jefferson himself, came to modify their views, the issue raised by the Republican-Federalist conflict over the ends of society continues to this day. Jefferson and the Republican party directly raised the question of virtue (or citizenship) and its link to republican government. To what degree does republican government rest upon the public-spirited qualities of its citizens, and what can be done consistent with the principles of liberalism to foster those qualities? The Republicans always expressed grave doubts that republican government could be maintained by the mechanical "auxiliary precautions" discussed in *The Federalist*, including pluralism fostered by a diverse economic life and institutions capable of resisting popular passions.

Jacksonian Democracy

After the War of 1812, politics settled into an "era of good feelings" in which the old quarrel between Federalists and Republicans seemed to come to an end. Within the overwhelmingly predominant Republican party a politics of personal rivalry developed, largely divorced from the stirring issues of the recent past. But new and even more momentous issues soon arose. In 1824 the presidential election was thrown into the House of Representatives. John Quincy Adams emerged as the victor despite the fact that Andrew Jackson had received more popular and electoral votes. The supporters of Jackson charged that the election had been "stolen" by the maneuverings of Adams in the House. Beginning with this charge,

Elected in 1828 as the seventh president of the United States, Andrew Jackson is most commonly identified with the egalitarian and populist Impulses that defined his presidency. His veto of the National Bank's recharter in 1832 was motivated by his antipathy toward economic elites and his glorification of the common hardworking physical laborer. The modern two-party system was also institutionalized during his tenure. (National Portrait Gallery, Smithsonian Institution; Gift of Mr. William H. Lively, Mrs. Mary Lively Hoffman, and Dr. Charles J. Lively. Used with permission.)

a political movement developed behind Jackson that swept him into the presidency in 1828.

The Ends of Society: Equality and Democratic Voting

Andrew Jackson's name has come to symbolize the growing sway of equality, both social and political, in the United States at that time. With him the West, without the more aristocratic habits and traditions of the east, came to power. Jackson was from Tennessee (all previous presidents had come from either Massachusetts or Virginia). But what did this growing equality mean for the character of political and social life? Did it mean the "reign of King Mob," as Justice Story of the Supreme Court thought it meant? Would the country, like a mob, be governed by the passions and impulses of the major-

BOX 3.2

Education and Self-Government

With the spread of democratic voting, the movement for free public education grew. The connection between voting and education is expressed by one of the leaders in the fight for public education, Horace Mann:

> But, in the possession of this attribute of intelligence, elective legislators will never far surpass their electors. . . . It is not more certain that a wise and enlightened constituency will refuse to invest a reckless and profligate man with office, or discard him if accidentally chosen, than it is that a foolish or immoral constituency will discard or eject a wise man. This law of assimilation between the choosers and the chosen results, not only from the fact that the voter originally selects his representative according to the affinities of good or of ill, of wisdom or of folly, which exist between them, but if the legislator enacts or favors a law which is too wise for the constituent to understand, or too just for him to approve, the next election will set him aside. . . . The establishment of a republican government, without self-appointed and efficient means for the universal education of the people, is the most rash and foolhardy experiment ever tried by man (Mann, 1867:688).

Source: Horace Mann, "The Importance of Universal Free Public Education," *Lectures and Annual Reports on Education,* Mary Mann, ed. (Cambridge, Mass.: Harvard University Press, 1867).

ity, unguided by thoughtfulness and reason, perhaps resulting in the destruction of minority rights and constitutional government?

To the Jacksonians their movement was a rekindling of the cause championed first by Jefferson. The great issue was the "war against the Monster Bank"—the Bank of the United States. The Jacksonians characterized the fight over the bank as a great struggle between the "people" and "aristocratic privilege and plutocratic corruption." The Bank fostered trades "which seek wealth without labor, employing the stratagems of speculative maneuver, privilege grabbing, and monetary manipulation" which nurtured "defective morals, habits, and character." In contrast, republican simplicity and responsibility were to be found in planters, farmers, mechanics, and laborers who performed some "immediate, responsible function in the production of goods."4

It was to give these people and their way of life political power that Jackson fought the elections of 1828 and forged a powerful political coalition through the Democratic party. These ends also fostered a rapid extension of the suffrage in the states. Universal adult suffrage is a relatively recent development in the United States that did not become a reality until the

1960s. Nevertheless, with the exception of women and blacks, the United States led the modern world in extending the right of suffrage to the broad mass of the people. Indeed, the United States is the only one of the major industrial nations to have granted the suffrage to the mass of people (including workers) *before* the industrial revolution of mid- and late-nineteenth century; this fact is seen as an important factor in explaining why large socialist or communist parties never emerged in the United States, as workers here were not struggling to achieve the right to vote at the same time that they were seeking social and economic protections. The Constitution, although it did not require a democratic electorate by present-day standards, nonetheless allowed for the rapid extension of suffrage that took place after Jackson's election.

At the time of the founding, all the states had restrictions of some kind on voting. In addition to the limitation to white males over 21 years of age, the states restricted voting to those holding property or showing some evidence of being stable members of the community. These qualifications were based on the idea that citizens should have at least some stake in the community before being entitled to vote. While property and acreage qualifications in some states greatly limited the franchise, in others the requirement for voting was merely to be a "taxpaying citizen," which embraced most free and permanent members of the community. Even with these restrictions, however, the state legislatures of the time were considered by both friends and foes of the Constitution to be highly democratic bodies, a fact which calls into question the claims of some that the founders had wanted to establish a propertied oligarchy. Indeed, the federal Constitution, unlike the constitutions of most of the states, required no property qualification for holding office.

After the ratification of the Constitution, the movement within the states quickly grew for the expansion of the suffrage. New states joining the union adopted either the taxpaying qualification or else the even more liberal residency requirement. (These new states, free of the established classes and traditions of most of the older ones, became an important source of pressure to democratize the regime.) The older states, stimulated by the national currents of democratic opinion that swept across the nation with Jefferson's election in 1800 and Andrew Jackson's election in 1828, began to reduce or remove their restrictions. By 1840, only two states—Virginia and Louisiana—still had property qualifications, and those restrictions were abolished by the 1850s. Just as important, after 1832, only one state (South Carolina) chose its presidential electors by means other than popular election. Thus by the 1830s, universal white manhood suffrage was in existence throughout nearly all the nation for both congressional and presidential elections.

The Scope of Government: States' Rights

For many of the same reasons that moved the Jeffersonian Republicans, the Jacksonians favored interpreting narrowly the powers of the national government. In the fight over rechartering the Bank of the United States, Jackson upheld "strict construction" of the Constitution (the view that the powers granted the government ought to be interpreted "strictly" or narrowly). In disagreement with Marshall's view in *McCulloch v. Maryland* (1819), Jackson believed

creation of the bank to be an unconstitutional exercise of Congress's powers.

Yet Jackson also opposed the growing belief that the states were superior in authority to the national government. A tariff law passed in 1828 had placed higher duties on imported raw materials than on manufactured goods, to the disadvantage of the South, which was less industrialized than the North. In opposing this tariff South Carolina set forth the doctrine of "nullification." This doctrine held that the states, not the American people, had created the union and were still sovereign. Each state, acting through convention, had the right to judge the constitutionality of the actions of the federal government. If it found the national government acting unconstitutionally, it had the right to prevent the enforcement of the federal law in its territory. When a new tariff was passed in 1832 with many of the objectionable features of the tariff of 1828, South Carolina held a convention, declared the tariff unconstitutional, prohibited federal officers from collecting customs duties within the state, and threatened secession if force were used against it.

Andrew Jackson, although he strongly believed in the power of the states, was adamantly opposed to disunion. He denied that a state had the right to secede and took strong actions to enforce the federal law. Before the issue reached a military showdown, Congress passed a compromise tariff and South Carolina repealed its nullification ordinance. The union had been upheld, but South Carolina's position had been maintained by a determined stand. Jackson saw what lay ahead. The "next pretext [for disunion]," he predicted, "will be the Negro, or slavery, question."

The Organization and Distribution of Power: Parties and the President as Popular Leader

The election of 1824 was the last time that a presidential election has been thrown into the House of Representatives. This is largely because of the development of the two-party system under Jackson, which has worked to ensure that one of the candidates would receive a majority of the electoral votes. This strengthened the presidency by diminishing the possibility that the election would be disputed or perceived as illegitimate. At the same time, the development of parties created a new role for the president as party leader. The Democratic party, which could trace its origins back to the Jeffersonian Republican party, changed its name to reflect the democratic spirit of the movement it represented. Its opponent, shortly to be known as the Whig party, emerged in the 1830s and challenged the Democrat's idea of a strong presidency while also calling for a stronger role for the national government. The electoral system that developed in the 1830s established the basic pattern of conflict—competition between two major parties, with occasional entries of significant third parties—that has persisted to the present day.

The Jackson administration also saw the development of the "spoils system." Under this system most national employees were dismissed when a new president was elected. The president would then fill the offices with personal friends. The system threw open federal employment to large numbers of new people, democratizing the executive branch and bringing in fresh blood. But these people were also frequently chosen for their political loyalties rather than their competence in their official duties.

The Jacksonian era shows that powerful forces of democracy could find scope under and give shape to the Constitution. By extending the suffrage, developing political parties, and providing a focus for change in the presidency, the country's basic political institutions remained intact while serving new goals and concerns.

Slavery and the Civil War

The events and debates that led to the election of Lincoln to the presidency and brought on the Civil War more sharply reveal the character of the constitution (with a small c) formed from 1776–1789 and its inner tensions than any other episode in American politics. The existence of slavery within a republic which proclaimed the equal rights of all was a great injustice in itself and opened free government to the charge of hypocrisy. A nation which proclaimed the equality of all people, but tolerated—and verged on

One of the most influential men in nineteenth-century American politics, John C. Calhoun (1782–1850) served as vice president, secretary of state, and senator from South Carolina. Calhoun defended the principle of "states rights" and the merits of the slave-plantation system. (National Portrait Gallery, Smithsonian Institution; transfer from the National Gallery of Art; gift of Andrew W. Mellon, 1942. Used with permission.)

endorsing—slavery was a nation at war in its soul—in Lincoln's words a "house divided against itself." The attempt to extend slavery led Americans to examine more profoundly than ever before or since the fundamental meaning of liberty, self-government, equality, and citizenship.

The Character of American Slavery

In treating people as property, slavery denies human beings the freedom to decide for themselves and to exercise those rights which characterize them as human beings. There was an additional feature of slavery as found in the United States that compounded the evil. Slavery was based on race: only blacks were slaves. In the ancient world where slavery flourished, individual slaves might be freed, and they and their descendants could soon disappear into the general free population. But in the United States, racial prejudice supported slavery, and slavery supported racial prejudice. To justify slavery on the basis of race, many whites contended that the black race itself was inferior to other races. Freed slaves could therefore never simply disappear into the general population; the badge of servitude could be seen in the color of their skin. The prejudice against slaves combined with racial prejudice made the life of the freed scarcely more hopeful, and often harder, than that of the enslaved. But even this dim avenue of escape from slavery, the granting of freedom, was largely cut off by the time of the Civil War. In the decades before the war, the laws of the slave states were gradually toughened to make it difficult or impossible to free a slave. The principle of slavery in the United States by the time of the Civil War was that people who belonged to a particular group (i.e., the black race), irrespective of individual characteristics, were permanently to be slaves.

Yet finding a solution to the problem of American slavery was incredibly difficult for the statesmen of the time. Hundreds of thousands of people had an economic interest in slavery. Just as important, whites were afraid to free the slaves, who in many areas were a majority. Racial prejudice, fears, and loyalty to one's state swelled the ranks of those opposed to its abolition. In addition, most blacks were uneducated and unpracticed in the exercise of freedom and self-government. If blacks became free and voting citizens, the opponents of emancipation argued, would they not be prey to the manipulations of unscrupulous politicians or turn on the whites who had enslaved them? Many who sympathized with the plight of the slaves nevertheless believed that large-scale emancipation might have tragic and disastrous consequences for both black and white. Speaking of the problem of slavery, Jefferson wrote that he trembled for his country when he reflected that God is just and that "his justice cannot sleep forever." Yet recognizing the absence of an easy solution to the problem, he also observed, "We have the wolf by the ears and we cannot let him go."[5]

The Extension of Slavery

By the 1850s the situation was more difficult than in Jefferson's day because of the increase in the number of slaves. Forty percent of the population of the southern states was black, and in large areas blacks were in the majority. Not only did slaves constitute a great share of the wealth of the dominant class in the South, but the advocates of slavery viewed the numbers of slaves and their condition as a threat requiring that slavery be extended into the lands to the west. It was this issue which brought on the Civil War.

The admission of new states carved from the territories in the west offered the possibility (or the threat) that either the slave states or the free states might be able to assume a commanding position in the federal union and then use the power of the national government to attack the institutions of the minority states.

Self-Government and Popular Sovereignty

The smoldering dispute over the western territories had been temporarily dampened by two famous compromises during the first half of the century. The Missouri Compromise of 1820 divided the territory of the Louisiana Purchase into slave and free by prohibiting slavery north of the present state of Missouri, and the Compromise of 1850 settled the disposition of the territories of the southwest acquired from Mexico. But the moral questions at the base of the conflict failed to be resolved by the normal art of compromise, or "bargaining." After 1850 Stephen Douglas, a senator from Illinois, took the lead in trying to find a program and principles that would settle the slavery issue. The formula that Senator Douglas advanced was "popular sovereignty." According to this doctrine, the most fundamental principle of American republican government is that the majority in each state should be able to do whatever it wants. Congress should not attempt to legislate with respect to slavery in the territories; the people of each territory should decide for themselves whether they want slavery or not and, when they come to apply for admission to the union, decide whether the new state should be slave or free. In this way Douglas hoped to remove the slavery

BOX 3.3

Slavery and Free Government

The depth of the dispute which led to the Civil War can be seen in these quotations from John C. Calhoun and Abraham Lincoln. Calhoun argues that it is possible to have freedom only by making some people slaves. Lincoln claims the freedom of one requires the freedom of all.

Calhoun

I fearlessly assert that the existing relation between the two races in the South, against which these blind fanatics are waging war, forms the most solid and durable foundation on which to rear free and stable political institutions. . . . There is and always has been in an advanced stage of wealth and civilization, a conflict between labor and capital. The condition of society in the South exempts us from the disorders and dangers resulting from this conflict; and which explains why it is that the political condition of the slaveholding States has been so much more stable and quiet than that of the North.

Lincoln

I can not but hate [the view that regards slavery as a matter of indifference]. I hate it because of the monstrous injustice of slavery itself. I hate it because it deprives our republican example of its just influence in the world . . . and especially because it forces so many really good men among ourselves into an open war with the . . . Declaration of Independence. . . . insisting that there is no right principle of action but *self-interest*.

Sources: John C. Calhoun, *The Works of John C. Calhoun,* Richard K. Cralle, ed., vol. 2 (New York: Russell and Russell, 1968), p. 632; Abraham Lincoln, *The Collected Works of Abraham Lincoln,* Roy P. Basler, ed., vol. 2 (New Brunswick, N.J.: Rutgers University Press, 1953), p. 255.

issue from national politics. He would gain the North's consent because economic and geographic factors would probably keep slavery out of the new territories by making it unprofitable. The South's consent would be gained because it would at least have the chance to extend slavery and would be reassured by the principle that slavery was a question of states' rights.[6]

In 1854 Douglas secured the application of his doctrine to the Nebraska Territory (the present states of Kansas and Nebraska), thereby repealing the Missouri Compromise, which had forbidden slavery north of the present state of Missouri. The country was sharply split during the debate and the passage of the Kansas-Nebraska Act. Party lines adjusted themselves upon the single issue of extension of slavery. The Democratic party became the party of extension, losing some supporters and picking up others. The Whig party disappeared altogether, its northern members joining with "anti-Nebraska" Democrats to form the new Republican party.

Abraham Lincoln rose to national prominence and the presidency as a leader in the fight against the repeal of the Missouri compromise and the idea of "popular sovereignty." Through the Lincoln-Douglas debates, held as Lincoln and Douglas challenged each other for the Senate seat from Illinois in 1858, Lincoln became the chief spokesman of the Republicans. Although Douglas won the seat, Lincoln went on to win the Republican nomination for president in 1860. Lincoln and his Republican followers maintained that the repeal of the Missouri Compromise and the doctrine of popular sovereignty threatened a revolution of such disastrous proportions for the United States that it was better to risk war than to let that revolution come to pass. What was that revolution, and on what grounds did Lincoln resist it?

The Principle of Equality

As president, Lincoln denied the right of the South to secede from the union and led the nation in war in order to preserve the union. But

The Lincoln-Douglas debates took place during the Illinois senatorial campaign in 1858. Although Abraham Lincoln lost the election to Stephen Douglas, his performance won him broad acclaim and paved the way to his nomination for president by the Republican Party in 1860. (Courtesy of Illinois State Historical Library. Used with permission).

Lincoln believed the union to be more than the simple attachment of the various states to each other. He prized the Constitution, but did not believe the union to have been formed by the Constitution. In the Gettysburg Address, as elsewhere, he identified the nation as having been born in 1776, the date of the Declaration of Independence. The union in its deepest sense, as Lincoln saw it, was a union of people "dedicated to the proposition that all men are created equal." Lincoln interpreted this to mean all Americans, regardless of race. But in the 1850s, Lincoln worried that a new idea, in favor of inequality and slavery, might replace the old one as the central sentiment of public opinion. It was to save the old opinion, as he believed it had been formed by the Declaration, that conflict must be risked.

Americans, of course, had never lived up to their creed; slavery was still in existence in the 1860s. But now there was a worse possibility; that Americans would resolve the tension between their declared beliefs and the existence of slavery by changing their declared beliefs. There were a few who simply maintained that the equality of humans, whether white or black, was a "self-evident lie." But it was difficult to attack the Declaration of Independence so directly. The subtler attack was to interpret the Declaration in such a way as to deny the manifest implication of its words. Douglas, who never explicitly endorsed slavery, nevertheless maintained that the majority had the right to have slaves if it wished. He argued that the famous phrase of the Declaration meant "all men of English descent" or "all white men." The evidence for this was the argument that the great founders would have been hypocrites if they had meant "all humans" by the phrase "all men," for they did not free their slaves. (Lincoln's reply was that they did not make all white people or people of English descent immediately equal either.)

Douglas's view was later endorsed by the Supreme Court and by Chief Justice Taney in the case of *Dred Scott v. Sanford* 1857). By this argument one could uphold slavery without having to attack the Declaration and the prestige of its authors. Contrary to Lincoln's view that all human beings possessed certain natural rights, including the right of self-government, the Court, along with Douglas, said that white men could rightly subject blacks to slavery.

Serving as Chief Justice of the Supreme Court from 1835 until his death in 1864, Roger B. Taney defended the states' role in our governmental system. He is most often remembered for his fatal judgment in the case of *Dred Scott v. Sanford* (1857), which made slavery legal in the U.S. territories. (Photo provided by the Library of Congress.)

Liberty and Self-Government

In advancing the doctrine of popular sovereignty, Douglas espoused an interpretation of American principles that can recur and has continually recurred in politics down to today. Liberty, he argued, meant the right of the majority to do whatever it likes. Unrestrained majority rule thus seems to be the first principle of a free society. Lincoln argued that it was not. No vote can rightfully deny individuals their equal rights to their liberty. Lincoln posed the problem in this way.

> The shepherd drives the wolf from the sheep's throat, for which the sheep thanks the shepherd as a liberator while the wolf denounces him for the same act as the destroyer of liberty, especially as the sheep was a black one.[7]

Whose definition is correct? It is the sheep's definition that Lincoln takes to be the true one. This becomes evident when people see that equality is the ground of liberty. The majority can rightfully rule because among equals the decision is rightfully made by the majority. If individuals or majorities deny the equality of others, they undermine the basis for their own rights. No one person or no number of people has the right to undermine the principle of human equality.

To uphold the equal rights of all was the duty of Americans, Lincoln thought. They owed it not only to themselves because it was the very foundation of their own politics, but also to the rest of humanity. Lincoln's speeches are suffused with the sense that the world is observing and depending upon the fate of the American experiment in self-government. As he said at Gettysburg, only the resolve of the American people could determine that "government of the people, by the people, and for the people shall not perish from the earth."

This politics of uncompromising principle seems distant from the pluralistic style of politics contemplated by *Federalist* 10 that places an emphasis on bargaining among different economic interests. Yet Madison clearly understood that the politics of pluralism presupposes the answer to the prior question of who is to be recognized as a citizen. The politics of bargaining cannot by itself resolve such matters of principle, which must be addressed on a different plane and by different means. It is apparent, however, that a politics of high principle can degenerate into fanaticism and become terrifying. The fanatic's refrain is that, "We know the right course, and we will force society to follow it, even if we must destroy everyone's liberty and many people's lives to get them in line."

It was Lincoln's conviction that the politics of pluralism is proper only within the context of a fundamental commitment to the principle of human equality. Otherwise compromises might be made at the expense of the rights of others. Lincoln was willing to make certain compromises with slavery in practice as long as it did not erode the conviction in people's minds that slavery was an evil. Lincoln thought that if people believed that slavery was *wrong*, however much they might compromise with it out *of necessity*, the day would come when there would be an opportunity for abolishing it. There were many abolitionists, among them the great Frederick

Douglass, who would push Lincoln and the public in that direction.

Politics is the art of compromise, but it is also the art of knowing when it is proper to compromise. The basic principles of free government ought never to be compromised, Lincoln thought, but as long as those principles were not threatened, compromises might be made with existing prejudices and evils without giving up the end one seeks. Indeed, such compromises might even be required if government by consent is to be maintained.

Results of the Civil War: Citizenship and Voting

The Civil War resulted in the abolition of slavery and the establishment of the principle that blacks and former slaves, as well as whites, could be citizens of the United States. These two great outcomes were enshrined in the Thirteenth and Fourteenth Amendments to the Constitution. The war also established that individual states did not have the right to withdraw from the union—it was not the states but the people who stood as the foundation of the union. Yet ridding the country of slavery did not rid the country of racial prejudice. Not only did differences between the races and racial prejudice result in difficult social relations between blacks and whites, but new laws were erected on the ruins of slavery to grant to blacks only a second-class citizenship. "Jim Crow" laws segregating the races were passed and justified under the banner of "separate but equal." But "separate" was in fact never "equal."

The third Constitutional amendment arising from the Civil War, the Fifteenth, ratified in 1870, prohibited the federal government or the states from denying the vote to anyone "on account of race, color, or previous condition of servitude." The Amendment, it should be stressed, did not remove from the states their discretion to establish qualifications for voting, but simply barred them from enforcing restrictions on racial grounds. The intent, nevertheless, was clearly to enfranchise black citizens. However, that intent was soon subverted in many southern states by a number of techniques including the use of allegedly "neutral" qualifications which in fact were designed to exclude black voters. (Similar techniques were employed in other localities to exclude either blacks or Asians.) The adoption of these legal ploys, accepted after the 1870s by a nation weary of conflict, meant that for almost a century the "right" of blacks to vote in many southern states was a mere promise on paper, honored more in the breach than in the observance.

The crudest method used to deter blacks from voting in the South was intimidation. As the white population regained control of the state governments in the South following Reconstruction, criminal acts committed against blacks who attempted to vote often went unpunished. In effect, local police authorities were in complicity with "private" vigilante groups, like the Ku Klux Klan, that systematically sought to prevent black voting through threats and violence. Although the federal government passed legislation in the 1870s to protect citizens in the act of voting, the Supreme Court disallowed federal prosecution of these criminal acts on the grounds that they were the activity not of the "state" but of private individuals, notwithstanding the fact that the states sometimes did little to protect their citizens. Thereafter, blacks who attempted to vote in some areas were subject for many years to every manner of harassment, physical intimidation, and, in some instances, lynchings.

By the end of the 1870s the nation and the Republican party had lost their fervor on the issue of race and black equality. This change of political climate gave southern states the latitude to adopt a series of laws which had the effect of excluding most blacks from voting by "legal" methods. Beginning in the 1890s, most southern states passed laws requiring the payment of a poll tax and the passage of literacy tests in order to vote. Since most former slaves were poor and uneducated, these laws effectively deprived most blacks of the franchise, which they had generally enjoyed, despite recent obstacles from the era of Reconstruction. For blacks who could pay the poll tax and who were literate, local registrars frequently applied literacy tests in blatantly discriminatory ways, demanding impossible "tests" of black citizens wishing to vote.

Led by Mississippi, some states also employed "character tests" that again were subject to

Born in 1818, Frederick Douglass was the most important black American leader of the nineteenth century. His three autobiographies, written after he escaped from slavery at the age of 20, are classic narratives that capture the evils and injustices of slavery. He became one of the foremost abolitionists of his time. His actions helped bring about the Emancipation Proclamation of January 1, 1863, in which President Lincoln freed all slaves in the Confederate states. (Left photo: National Portrait Gallery, Smithsonian Institution; Gift of an anonymous donor. Right photo: National Portrait Gallery, Smithsonian Institution; Gift of Mrs. Chester E. King. Used with permission.)

biased enforcement by registration officials. To ensure that poor and illiterate whites were not similarly excluded, a number of states passed so-called "grandfather laws" that exempted from the poll taxes and the literacy tests all those whose ancestors had voted before the end of the Civil War when blacks, of course, had been unable to vote. (In some states, however, poor whites were effectively disenfranchised along with blacks—in part, it appears, in order that the wealthier whites could maintain control of the state government and prevent any alliance from developing between poor whites and blacks.) Finally, in many southern states, the Democratic party, using its status as a private association, excluded all participation by black citizens in its activities; and most states soon passed "reform" primary laws which enforced the party's "private" restriction of the votes to white citizens. Since nearly everyone elected to office in the South was a Democrat, the device of the "white primary" excluded blacks from any real influence, even where they were permitted to vote in the general election.

The result of all these restrictions was nothing less than the disenfranchisement of blacks throughout most of the South. Furthermore, because the great majority of blacks in the nation then lived in the South—the great migration of blacks to the north and west did not begin on a large scale until the 1940s—the black population in America was virtually without influence within the American electorate. By the simplest standards of representative democracy, the American regime was clearly defective. Although some improvements were made in small steps over a long period of time, it was not until the 1960s that a major transformation of this situation took place.

The Progressives

The Civil War set off a booming industrial development. Government sought to aid this development, and the Supreme Court found support for many of the principles of laissez-faire capitalism in its interpretation of the Constitution. The unrestrained development of large corporations raised the question whether the inequality of private wealth threatened to undermine the republican character of the United States. The "populism" of the late nineteenth century was the last attempt to meet this threat by means of an agrarian-based solution. The "progressive" movement, while sharing many of the ideas of the populists, accepted the industrial development of the United States and tried to find a response within the framework of industrial society. As finally shaped by the presidencies of Theodore Roosevelt and Woodrow Wilson, this movement sought to bring about major changes in the American constitutional system.

The Ends of Society: Democratic Equality and National Unity

The massive immigration of the nineteenth century had created a vast, heterogeneous population increasingly crowded into cities, and the growth of corporate wealth had created new centers of power. The progressives thought that it was necessary to create unity out of this new diversity, to remedy the scandalous working conditions in the burgeoning factories, and to restore democratic equality in the face of concentrated private wealth and power. While the emphasis upon equality in the ideas of the progressives was by no means new to American politics as we have seen, the thought that this required the reshaping of economic and social life within the context of industrialism was.

The Scope of Government: Increased Power and Representation

In the eyes of the reformers, these goals required an expansion of the scope and power of the national government to control private power and a better way to make that government express the unity and will of the people. As Theodore Roosevelt put the new ideal, "The people . . . have but one instrument which they can effectively use against the colossal combinations of business—and that instrument is the government of the United States."[8] Increased governmental power was used to break up trusts (supercorporations controlling a single industry in order to eliminate competition and set prices),

to reform banking (the Federal Reserve system was established in 1913), to guarantee the right to organize unions (in the Clayton Antitrust Act of 1914), and to bring about many other social and economic reforms.

The Organization and Distribution of Power: The President as Popular Leader

In order to increase the power of government and use it in the proper way, the progressives as finally led by Woodrow Wilson thought that governmental power should be more unified in the hands of the president. The Constitutional separation of powers, according to Wilson, did not provide an effective government for the twentieth century. Instead of creating a government capable of representing the people and promoting the energetic leadership necessary to meet the danger of concentrated corporate power and special interests, it merely made for stalemate. Each branch could stand in the way of the others, preventing progressive legislation from being formed and implemented:

> As at present constituted, the federal government lacks strength because its powers are divided, lacks promptness because its authorities are multiplied, lacks wieldiness because its responsibility is indistinct and its action without competent direction.[9]

This political stalemate allowed the special interests to thrive. Political parties only compounded the difficulties. They were largely controlled by political bosses who, operating out of the public limelight, created unholy alliances and corrupt deals with the special interests, to the detriment of the public good. The government of the Constitution was a rudderless government that allowed the selfish sharks of commerce to rule society.

Wilson originally favored the creation of a "cabinet" form of government like that of Great Britain. Under the cabinet form, legislative and executive power are united and concentrated in a prime minister chosen by the legislature. But later Wilson came to believe that the defects of the Constitution could be overcome without major changes to it by reinterpreting the political system. In particular, the president's connection to the people could be exploited to bring about a stronger presidency and a greater concentration of political power. The president provided the key both for increasing the power of the government and for making it represent the general interest rather than special interests.

In place of the traditional system of checks and balances with a weak president, Wilson favored a government that would above all encourage strong political leadership. Leadership was the ability to marshall public opinion behind progressive policies. It required two things lacking in the Constitutional scheme: power and unitary direction. Power in modern democracies, Wilson felt, is to be found in the ability to move the people. Public opinion must provide the driving force for government.

The older view had not denied great importance to public opinion. We have seen that both Jefferson and Lincoln believed that behind the laws and the Constitution stood a set of public beliefs that made the right kind of laws possible. At critical junctures, both believed, public opinion might have to be marshalled to keep the laws and the Constitution on the proper track. Wilson radicalized this view. Public opinion could not only be a check on the government, it could be the regular authorizing and moving force. Officials could be directly empowered by the people to the extent that they could tap deep public sentiment in their policies.

Wilson viewed the power of the people as immense, but also diffuse. To give unity and direction to their power, he argued, it must be concentrated in one person. The only office in the American system capable of concentrating this power was that of the president. The chief quality necessary for the sort of president that Wilson desired was that of popular leadership. The president must be capable of articulating the unconscious aspirations of the people, thus attracting and concentrating their power. The president must become, as Franklin Roosevelt was later to say, the "moral trumpet" of the nation. Such a president, empowered by the backing of the people, could lead Congress and even force it in the desired direction if it resisted.

Wilson did not believe that to enhance the power of the people and concentrate it in one person was dangerous to liberty. Outstanding leaders would be attracted to the power and opportunities the new presidency offered. The dangers of demagogues, leaders who would serve selfish interests under the cover of flattery of the people, were much exaggerated. As Wilson put it:

> There is no permanent place in democratic leadership except for him who "hath clean hands and a pure heart." If other men come temporarily to power among us, it is because we cut our leadership up into so many little parts and do not subject any one man to the purifying influences of centered responsibility.[10]

Checks and balances could be partly overcome by the ability of a leader to move mass opinion.

Wilson, and the progressives generally, favored Constitutional and political reforms that would help to bring about this new power for public opinion and the presidency. They favored changes that would increase the direct power of the people and that would concentrate power within the government in the hands of the president. The Seventeenth Amendment to the Constitution, providing for direct election of senators, was supported by the progressives and was ratified in 1913. By this means the Senate was brought under greater popular control and made more subject to a president backed by public opinion. On the state level the power of the people was enhanced by such measures as *the initiative* (the procedure by which citizens can propose a law by petition and ensure its submission to the electorate), the *referendum* (the submission of a proposed measure to direct popular vote), and the *recall* (the power of the people to remove an incumbent from office by means of popular vote).

To destroy the power of party bosses, the progressives advocated primaries as the proper mode of nominating candidates. Presidential primaries, Wilson thought, would both free presidents from the control of bosses and also enable the executive to claim a popular mandate for a general direction of public policy. The president would become able to dictate to the party and would no longer have to court party bosses. When the Senate threatened not to ratify the treaty for the League of Nations after World War I, Wilson toured the country in order to arouse public opinion to force the Senate to acquiesce. Although he failed, he introduced a mode of dealing with Congress that presidents have used ever since.

Wilson did not completely succeed in achieving the aims of his reforms. Separation of powers continues to be a major feature of American constitutionalism and determinant of policy. But his new view of the presidency also remains, sometimes in uneasy tension with the separation of powers. Wilson's partial victory altered the shape of twentieth-century American politics.

The Extension of the Vote to Women

Another important constitutional change which occurred during the presidency of Woodrow Wilson was the extension of the vote to women. The movement for women's suffrage had much support from the progressives as a democratic reform. But the movement predated the progressives and had other roots, which is why we single it out for special attention. It had begun in the 1830s and was linked indirectly to the abolitionist movement. Both appealed to the same principle: citizenship implied the right of equal treatment before the law for every group. After the Civil War, suffragists under the leadership of Susan B. Anthony advocated the right of women to vote under the Fourteenth Amendment, which granted citizenship to all born and naturalized Americans and called for equal protection of the laws. Citizenship, however, was not understood by the authors of the Amendment, nor Americans generally, to include the right to vote. Susan Anthony, after trying to vote, was arrested in 1872 in Rochester, New York, and convicted of the crime of "voting without a lawful right to vote."

Suffragists thereafter pursued a dual strategy of pushing for acknowledgment of their right to vote from the states and attempting to amend the Constitution to guarantee a federal right of suffrage. The women's movement made some progress at the state level in the late nineteenth century, when four western states granted women the full right to vote in all elections: Wyoming (1870), Idaho (1870), Utah (1876), and Colorado (1888). Elsewhere, however, the movement met stiff resistance. During the pro-

Susan B. Anthony was instrumental in defining and advancing the cause for equal rights for women. She died in 1906, fourteen years before the ratification of the Nineteenth Amendment, which guaranteed women the right to vote. (Photo provided by the National Portrait Gallery, Smithsonian Institution. Used with permission.)

gressive era, additional gains were made in several states, but the main effort by the movement was now directed at obtaining a Constitutional amendment forbidding denial of the right to vote on the grounds of sex. At first, many Democrats in Congress, following President Wilson's lead, refused to vote approval. But suffragists, using Wilson's own World War I rhetoric of "making the world safe for democracy," eventually won his endorsement in 1918. Congressional approval followed shortly thereafter. In 1920, the Nineteenth Amendment was ratified, denying any state the authority to abridge the right to vote on account of sex.

In the elections immediately following the passage of the Nineteenth Amendment, turnout of women was low (about one-third of all those eligible). Over time, however, beliefs and practices changed, and today women and men turn out to vote at approximately the same rates.

Supporters of women's suffrage originally included not only those favoring in principle the right of women to vote but also many who believed that adding women to the electorate would increase support for certain programs and policies such as prohibition, increased expenditures on education, and world disarmament. Some utopians went so far as to think that granting women the vote would "abolish poverty, protect family life, and raise educational and cultural standards." In fact, no dramatic changes resulted immediately from extending suffrage to women. Men and women differ marginally in their opinions in some areas—for example, men have shown a greater willingness to favor the use of force in the solution of certain international and domestic problems—and these differences have had some impact on voting behavior. In general, however, women and men vote in much the same ways, and the major factors that influence their votes are related not to gender but to other determinants that affect both sexes in the same fashion.

The New Deal

Franklin Roosevelt became president in 1932 in the midst of an economic crisis unparalleled in the nation's history. The great depression not only ruined businesses and put millions out of work but also threatened to arouse class antagonisms to such a point that fascism or communism might find fertile ground. Roosevelt tried simultaneously to meet both the economic and the political threats. His solution to these simultaneous crises has become known as the "welfare state." There have been two main thrusts toward the welfare state, the first under Roosevelt's "New Deal," the second under President Lyndon Johnson's "Great Society." While the two movements viewed the ends of society in the same way, the Great Society involved an even larger role for government and provided for a somewhat different distribution of power within the national government. We shall examine these two movements separately.

The Ends of Society: The New Deal Critique of Free Enterprise

The pursuit of private wealth free from government control was justified by the defenders of free enterprise by means of the idea of the "invisible hand." If people were left free to pursue their private profit, the argument ran, the public good would also be served (quite unintentionally and hence invisibly). In developing a business that produced wealth for the owner, other people would be given jobs, new goods would be produced for consumers, and the wealth of society as a whole would be increased. Grocers, the defenders reasoned, provide us with food, not because they love us but because they desire to make money.

Supporters of the New Deal denied that this invisible hand worked. The frantic pursuit of wealth had resulted not in general prosperity but in the great depression. Private interest was not automatically converted into public benefit. It might be true, Roosevelt conceded, that the development of modern industrial society would have been impossible without unleashing private entrepreneurs. Creating an economic order capable of raising the standard of living for everyone required, in Roosevelt's words,

> the use of the talents of men of tremendous will and ambition, since by no other force would the problems of financing and engineering and new developments be brought to a consummation. . . . The financiers who pushed the railroads to the Pacific were always ruthless, often wasteful, and frequently corrupt; but they did build railroads, and we have them today.[11]

By the 1930s, however, the industrial plant was built. The task now, Roosevelt argued, was not "producing more goods. It is the soberer, less dramatic business of administering resources and plants already in hand. . . . of distributing wealth and products more equitably."[12]

Roosevelt taught a new understanding of the ends of society. Government must protect the rights of the Declaration, but those rights were not what the advocates of laissez-faire thought them to be. The right to life must be understood to include the "right to make a comfortable living," and it must be understood that the para-

BOX 3.4

The Foundations of the Welfare State

The issues involved in the extension of governmental regulation of the economy and provision of economic security were not restricted solely to economic issues. Part of the debate concerned the issue of the effects of a welfare state upon individual character. Consider these opinions of presidents Herbert Hoover and Franklin Roosevelt:

Hoover

This is not an issue as to whether people shall go hungry or cold in the United States. It is solely a question of the best method by which hunger and cold shall be prevented. It is a question as to whether the American people on one hand will maintain the spirit of charity and mutual self help through voluntary giving and the responsibility of local government. . . . If we break down this sense of responsibility of individual generosity to individual and mutual self help in the country in times of national difficulty . . . we have not only impaired something infinitely valuable in the life of the American people but have struck at the roots of self-government.

Roosevelt

Those words "freedom" and "opportunity" do not mean a license to climb upwards by pushing other people down. Any paternalistic system which tries to provide for security for everyone from above only calls for an impossible task and a regimentation utterly uncongenial to the spirit of our people. But Government cooperation to help make the system of free enterprise work, to provide that minimum security without which the competitive system cannot function, to restrain the kind of individual action which in the past has been harmful to the community—that kind of governmental cooperation is entirely consistent with the best tradition of America.

Sources: Herbert Hoover, *The State Papers and Other Public Writings of Herbert Hoover*, William Starr Myers, ed., vol. 2 (Doran, New York: Doubleday, 1934), p. 424; Morton J. Frisch and Richard G. Stevens, eds., The *Political Thought of American Statesmen* (Itasca, Ill.: Peacock, 1973), pp. 307–308.

mount property right is the right to be secured against the burdens of sickness and unemployment and the disabilities of childhood and old age. Instead of the spirit of private competition and advantage, Roosevelt sought to cultivate the spirit of reciprocal self-denial for the common good among businesspeople as well as others. If business should lack that spirit, the "government must be swift to enter and protect the public welfare."[13]

There is another way to conceive of Roosevelt's new understanding of the ends of society and the role of government. Roosevelt in enunciating his four freedoms spoke of a "freedom *from* want" and "freedom *from* fear." The idea here is not that of a freedom from a specific action of government that threatens to abridge one's liberty—for example, a law that forbids a citizen to express certain political or religious views. Instead, it is freedom from a certain condition (want or fear). It is obvious that realizing this kind of freedom does not merely require

government to desist from acting, but on the contrary now more or less requires that government act, in new and more extensive ways, to ensure that citizens are free from these conditions. Roosevelt's idea of freedom opened the way to a new and "positive" understanding of the role of government, which has given rise to the great modern debate between liberals (the defenders of "positive government") and conservatives, who have worried about the consequences of too much government and the threat it poses to individual liberty.

The Scope of Government: Economic Security and the Welfare State

The New Deal did not seek to destroy the free enterprise system. It did not favor socialism: it did not seek to have business owned by the government, except in unusual circumstances. Nor were the advocates of the New Deal much attracted to the "trust-busting" approach earlier favored by the progressives. The progressives sought to break up large corporations in order to restore economic competition in the face of monopoly power. New Dealers wanted, not to preserve the competitive spirit of traditional capitalism, but to transform that spirit into one of cooperation between business, labor, and government in the service of public goals.

The public goal to be served was that of the "welfare state." The welfare state is a state in which the government assumes responsibility for guaranteeing the economic security of its citizens. Before the New Deal, it had not been regarded as the government's business to provide for economic security. At most, it was thought the government's business to keep open the opportunities whereby individuals might provide for their own security. But now, as Roosevelt put it, it would become the aim of government to move toward "greater security for the average man than he has ever known before in the history of America." According to one of Roosevelt's advisors, Samuel Beer: "Before Roosevelt the issue of national action to sustain and direct the economy did not arise . . . the question of 'government management of the economy' . . . was simply not on the agenda."[14] If the government before the 1930s could be held responsible for the sin of committing an error that allegedly made the economy falter, it would now be held responsible for the sin of failing to take the necessary steps to make the economy work well. This greater security was to be achieved essentially by three means: governmental regulation of economic enterprise, social security, and income redistribution.

The Regulation of Economic Enterprise   Because the New Deal sought to transform the spirit of private economic enterprise, the essential aim of the vastly expanded governmental regulation of business and labor that came out of the New Deal was to infuse private enterprise with public goals. This was possible, the New Dealers thought, if economic life were organized. While the private interests of individuals might frequently be in conflict with the public good, the interests of groups (such as labor unions and trade associations) were much closer to the public interest. When management and labor sat down together at the bargaining table, they would come to realize that they essentially shared the same interests. The general prosperity of the industry would mean general prosperity for the workers as well. Early in his administration, Roosevelt seemed to have the hope that the transformation of the spirit of economic enterprise could come about without much permanent governmental regulation of business, but later he came to believe that it required the imposition of public goals by government. Government, labor, and business would cooperate, but government would set the basic public goals to be reached.

A good recent example of governmental regulation made in the New Deal spirit is the laws and regulations specifying that only automobiles getting a certain number of miles per gallon can be built. This does not make the government the owner of the automobile companies, but it imposes an explicit purpose—energy saving—upon a private economic activity by means of governmental regulation.

Social Security   The New Deal saw that the goal of economic security for all could not be reached simply by the government's taking responsibility for a prosperous economy and by its infusing private enterprise with public purposes. There were many people who could not participate in the active life of the economy and who would not share in its fruits. Parentless children, old people, victims of accidents, the physically or mentally disabled—all could be guaranteed economic security only by some other means.

Before the 1930s, these people were considered the concern of the states and private charity, not of the national government. Back in 1854, President Franklin Pierce had vetoed a bill to provide federal money for the construction of mental hospitals. His reason had been that this would provide an opening wedge for federal intrusion into the welfare field: "It cannot be questioned," he claimed "that if Congress has the power to make provision for the indigent insane . . . it has the same power to make provision for the indigent who are not insane, and thus to transfer to the Federal government the charge of all the poor in the States."[15]

But Congress in 1935 enacted a series of measures providing pensions for the aged; unemployment insurance; benefits to the blind, to dependent mothers, and to crippled children; and appropriations for public health work. These constituted the foundations of the idea of the welfare state, which is now in considerable degree the responsibility of the federal government.

Redistribution of Wealth In seeking security for the average American, the New Deal necessarily also sought a greater equality of wealth and power. Although its primary goal was not to distribute wealth more equally, programs such as the social security system worked to bring about some amelioration of extreme inequalities. Roosevelt extolled the average person who sought "good health, good food, good education, good working conditions and the opportunity for normal recreation and occasional travel." By means of greater economic equality, the New Deal sought to bring about a stronger national unity.

The impulse of the New Deal has been the primary source of change in our politics from the 1930s into the 1970s. Only in the last twenty years has the New Deal agenda no longer simply dominated. The persistence of the issues of the New Deal is due in part to the fact that its aims could not be achieved once and for all. What constitutes economic security depends on the level of economic development. There is no definite quantity of economic well-being one can achieve and then have security. Hence the goal of economic security is constantly moving ahead even as people move to achieve it. It has often been said that today's liberal is tomorrow's conservative. Conservatives were originally simply opponents of the New Deal, but later conservatives became opponents of new manifestations of the New Deal, having accepted its earlier stages.

The friends of the New Deal have been called "liberals" because the New Deal saw economic security as essential to liberty. If people did not have good jobs and were not protected against the potential disasters of life, how could they be free? Liberty means something only to those who are able to make use of it. Economic security establishes the condition under which liberty

will be useful to everyone. Without this condition, people may become willing to give up liberty for the sake of the satisfaction of their wants. "Freedom from want" is the condition of all other freedoms.

The opponents of the New Deal responded that if one makes economic security and equality and principal aims of government, human liberty may be forgotten in the search for a better-regulated economic life with its emphasis on health, welfare, and freedom from want. People may become willing to turn over all the difficult choices of their lives to a government that cares for their every want. Such people may be economically secure, but they will not be free human beings.

To reach the aim of economic security for all, the New Deal broke down the previous line between private economic activity and government. Government, business, and labor were to become partners in creating and equalizing wealth. This new view was resisted not only by the Republican party but initially also by the Supreme Court, which declared major aspects of the New Deal unconstitutional. President Roosevelt tried but failed to "pack" the Court with new appointees who would support his program. However, the Court reversed its position in *West Coast Hotel v. Parrish* (1937), upholding for the first time a statute imposing major regulations on business activity (here a minimum wage law for women and children). The decision in *Wickard v. Filburn* (1942), which held that production of grain even for a farmer's own use could be regulated by Congress as interstate commerce, finally acknowledged a virtually unlimited power in the national government to regulate economic life.

The Organization and Distribution of Power: A Strengthened Presidency

At the same time that the scope of government was increasing, the shift of power within the national government toward the presidency (as originally desired by the progressives) was receiving new impetus. Representation, too, was understood by the New Dealers in essentially the same terms as it had been by the progressives. The government, and particularly the presi-

Martin Luther King, Jr., the leader of the civil rights movement of the 1960s, played a decisive role in ending segregation in the South and in promoting the historic civil rights legislation of 1964 and 1965. King was assassinated in 1968. (Copyright Washington Post; Reprinted by permission of D.C. Public Library.)

dency, increasingly found its practical authority in its ability to portray itself as the leader of a great popular movement and national community. The increased role of the government in regulating economic life also led to an increase in both the size and the power of the bureaucracy.

The Great Society

The 1960s witnessed a continuation and development of the ideas of the New Deal, with a new focus. In particular the Great Society programs of President Lyndon Johnson and the views of the Supreme Court under Chief Justice Earl Warren led to a new and expanded view of the importance of achieving equality of opportunity.

The Scope of Government: Protecting Civil Rights and Promoting Equality

The "Great Society" continued the effort of the New Deal to use governmental power to ensure greater welfare and regulate the economy. At the same time it saw new scope for the govern-

ment in protecting civil rights and promoting equality of opportunity for all Americans. The ambitions of the "Great Society" were immense, as indicated by the very choice of the name itself. In the speech in which he adopted that name, Johnson spoke as follows:

> The Great Society rests on abundance and liberty for all . . . but that is just the beginning. The Great Society is a place where every child can find knowledge to enrich his mind . . . where leisure is a welcome chance to build and reflect . . . where the city of man serves not only the needs of the body and the demands of commerce, but the desire for beauty and the hunger for community . . . .[16]

The Great Society may not have rested on a new principle of government from the New Deal, but it certainly represented a change in the degree of involvement of the federal government in society. Federal government spending began to rise dramatically. Just as important, the character of the involvement changed. Instead of proceeding by payments to individuals or to other levels of government, as the New Deal had done, the Great Society required the establishment of scores of specific programs, each of which had its own administrative structure. The degree of federal bureaucratic involvement in the lives of Americans thus rapidly expanded. The expansive attitude toward policymaking that lay behind the Great Society is explained by Harry McPherson, one of Johnson's top advisers:

> But a new philosophy of government had emerged since New Deal days. In essence it held that our problems were more of the spirit than of the flesh. People were suffering from a sense of alienation from one another, of anomie, of powerlessness. This affected the well-to-do as much as it did the poor. Middle-class women, bored and friendless in the suburban afternoons; fathers, working at "meaningless" jobs, or slumped before the television set; sons and daughters desperate for "relevance"—all were in need of community, beauty, and purpose, all were guilty because so many others were deprived while they, rich beyond their ancestors' dreams, were depressed. What would change all this was a creative public effort: for the middle class, new parks, conservation, the removal of billboards

and junk, adult education, consumer protection, better television, aid to the arts; for the poor, jobs, training, Head Start, decent housing, medical care, civil rights; for both, and for bridging the gap between them, VISTA, the Teacher Corps, the community action agencies, mass transportation, model cities.[17]

One of the major achievements of the Great Society was to complete the extension of voting rights that had begun as far back as the presidency of Andrew Jackson. As we have noted, there were some small steps taken to extend the votes to blacks during the first half of the twentieth century. The Supreme Court struck down the "grandfather clause" in 1915, the white primary in 1944, and some of the most discriminatory applications of the literacy tests in 1949. Some states also took certain remedial steps on their own, especially after 1940. So the situation for black voters was by no means equally bleak in all the southern states. But the major transformation in southern politics had to await the 1960s and was accomplished by means of national intervention into the states' traditional role in defining qualifications for voting.

With pressure from the civil rights movement in the 1960s, the federal government finally began to move in earnest to topple the entire legal structure that supported discriminatory voting laws and practices. In 1963, the Twenty-Fourth Amendment, which banned the use of poll taxes for federal elections, was ratified. Two years later, the Supreme Court extended this ban to state elections. In 1965, the federal government passed the landmark Voting Rights Act that barred the use of literacy tests and permitted federal authorities, at the attorney general's discretion, to order registration in states and counties where less than half of the voting-age population was registered or had voted in the last election.

These measures, in combination with the changing attitudes resulting from the civil rights movement, had very impressive results. Immediately, the level of black voting rose dramatically in the South. In 1940, only 5 percent of voting-age blacks were registered; by 1966, that figure had risen to 45 percent and by 1976 to 63 percent, nearly the same as the figure for white voters. For the first time since Reconstruction,

black politicians were elected to many state and local offices, and black voters played a pivotal role in determining election results. Many white politicians who previously had spurned black support now began to court it. The Voting Rights Act of 1965 itself was passed partly because Democrats saw that black voters had held the balance of power in the Kennedy-Nixon presidential contest of 1960 and wished to consolidate this vote for their party. Although acquisition of the right to vote by no means proved a panacea for civil rights problems, it at least enabled blacks to assert their interests within the normal coalition-building processes of a representative system.

Suffrage was further extended by the Twenty-Third Amendment, which in 1961 gave electoral vote representation to Washington, D. C.; and by the Twenty-Sixth Amendment, which in 1971 gave the right to vote to all persons over 18 years of age. (Most states before this Amendment set the voting age at 21.) The Twenty-Sixth Amendment was ratified during the Vietnam War, when 18-year olds were being drafted for military service and were fighting and dying in southeast Asia. The chief argument put forward by proponents of the Amendment rested on this simple theme: "If you're old enough to fight, you're old enough to vote." Although some analysts expected the inclusion of younger voters to move the nation dramatically to the left, no such result has occurred. Young people do not vote exactly like the rest of the electorate, but the differences are variable and are likely to shift as each new group passes through this age bracket. Moreover, younger people turn out to vote at a significantly lower rate than the rest of the electorate, which dilutes the strength of whatever peculiar attributes they possess as a group. Their lower turnout rate is attributable mostly to the fact that many young people have not yet settled into a community and developed the habit of participation in citizenship.

Today, then, citizenship is understood to include the right to vote for almost all adults; and no distinction, such as was made in the past, now exists between citizenship that guarantees an individual equal protection under existing civil law and a fuller notion of citizenship that entitles one to the privilege of voting. Indeed, in an important Supreme Court decision of the 1960s, *Wesberry v. Sanders* (1964), the Court argued the position that the exercise of the franchise is necessary for the full enjoyment of other rights.

> No right is more precious in a free country than that of having a voice in the election of those who make the laws under which . . . we must live. Other rights are illusionary if the right to vote is undermined.

Given this understanding of the franchise, it is not surprising that the federal government has now undertaken much of the task of protecting it. Although one can find a few persons who still advocate limiting the franchise by a minimum literacy criterion, Americans on the whole have now rejected this view and have adopted the simpler and more democratic concept of universal adult suffrage. Implicit in this extension of the franchise is the idea that whatever else the vote may be—such as a method for expression of policy—it is at least an instrument of self-protection through which individuals and groups can assert their interests in the electoral process.

Simultaneously the national government came to be used to protect other civil rights of Americans. Beginning in 1925, but proceeding most rapidly under Chief Justice Warren in the 1960s, the Supreme Court came to regard most of the protections of the Bill of Rights as applying to state as well as national governments. The result was a great extension of the use of federal power to achieve the protection of civil rights.

The Organization and Distribution of Powers: The Role of the Courts

The Great Society continued the New Deal emphasis upon the presidency, with Lyndon Johnson taking a vigorous lead in advancing its programs. As government supervision of social and economic life became more complex and detailed, the role of the bureaucracy also expanded. At the same time, the Supreme Court achieved new power within the system, deciding many issues previously thought to be the responsibility of the legislative or executive branches.

Beginning with *Brown v. Board of Education* in 1954, the Court began to adopt a broader view of its role within the government. It saw itself as a body with the ability and the right to step into matters previously thought to belong to the legislative branch, especially when Congress did not take the steps the Court thought the good of the country required (such as desegregating the schools). It moved to regulate the electoral process, to desegregate many areas of social life, to promote equality, to reform the criminal justice system, and to change the laws regulating families and the relations between the sexes. In short, the Court has taken an active hand in shaping most of the major political and social transformations in the United States in the past quarter century.

President Johnson, in one of his speeches in 1965, uttered a phrase that many later began to associate with policies of the federal courts of the 1960s and early 1970s. Johnson stated: "We seek not just equality as a right and theory but equality as a fact and result."[18] This rather vague formulation seemed to point to new kinds of enforcement of civil rights that would assign or redistribute benefits in the name of attempting to insure an equality of result. It was this general idea that seemed to lead to large scale school busing and then certain kinds of affirmative action programs, which were by no means an invention only of the federal courts.

Reagan through Bush

The election of Ronald Reagan in 1980 brought a major change in some of the reigning ideas about the ends and scope of the federal government. If Reagan did not succeed in "dismantling" the government, he did nevertheless raise profound doubts about the ideas of the New Deal and the Great Society. This liberal public philosophy had held sway in American politics since the 1930s, with Republicans arguing for going slower than the Democrats wished, but not disputing the general direction. After the 1980 election, however, it was the Republicans who proposed a new course for the nation and the Democrats who found themselves in the position of objecting to what someone else had proposed. As President Reagan noted in a news conference in 1983: "Very few of you have realized that for the last three years, unlike the last fifty, there haven't been arguments going on in Washington about whether or not and what to spend additional money on. The arguments have been on where do we cut."[19]

The Ends of Society

Two great domestic disputes of the early 1980s particularly involved an understanding of the proper ends of society. One was over economic policy, the other over the treatment of minorities. The economic policies of the Great Society rested on the assumption that there would be continued economic growth in the United States and that the challenge facing government was to control swings in the economy and to provide security for all through the proper distribution of the national wealth. But the steady growth the economy enjoyed came to a halt in the 1970s. The issue of the *production* of wealth assumed a new priority over the *distribution* of wealth.

Faced with a stagnant economy and high inflation, Ronald Reagan suggested a new economic program, "Reaganomics," that included lower marginal tax rates, a slowed rate of growth in domestic federal spending, and reduced governmental regulation of private business. In the Republicans' view these policies would give a new dignity and higher rewards to those who work and produce, which would in turn stimulate the economy. The Democrats, in resisting this program, argued that it would merely give more wealth to those already rich, and that it would foster a selfish, uncaring society. Reagan's supply-side theory held that the key to promoting economic growth was to increase incentives to produce, which could only be done by cutting the amount of nonproductive expenditures—in other words, the size of government expenditures—and by reducing the marginal tax rates. The novel element of this theory was its assertion that a decrease in marginal tax rates was more important in the short run than balancing the budget, because any effort to balance the budget at current (or a higher) level of government expenditures would reduce growth.

As for the policies for minorities, although legal segregation of the races had been ended by the 1970s, inequalities between the races continued to persist. The problem of how to address these inequalities created new disputes. Inequalities involving other groups—women, hispanics, and others—also received new attention. "Affirmative action"—the position that minorities should be given special preference in order to overcome the effects of past discrimination—gained increased support as a response to this situation, creating a potentially deep split over the meaning of justice in the United States. Is a just society to be defined by the equality in status of various groups within it, or by the degree to which it treats persons as individuals entitled to the same benefits or burdens regardless of the group to which they belong? While the Reagan administration did not entirely reject the principle of affirmative action, it moved to reduce the scope of some affirmative action programs.

In 1992 Bill Clinton broke the Republicans' three-term hold on the presidency. But he campaigned on a different program than previous Democrats, calling himself a "New Democrat" who would operate from the center of the political spectrum. But soon after assuming the presidency, Clinton made a clear shift away from the centrist stance in the attempt to satisfy his electoral base. During his first two years in office, he espoused liberal policies of raising taxes on the top brackets of income and of making health care into a government responsibility. After a strong reaction to his health program and a Republican victory in both houses of Congress in the 1994 elections, Clinton began to move toward the center. In his support for such things as middle-class tax cuts, balanced budgets, and welfare reform, President Clinton appeared much more conservative. By his second term, it was hard to determine whether the Clinton presidency was a reaction against, or a continuation of, the "Reagan Revolution."

Just as Clinton campaigned as a "New Democrat" in 2000, George W. Bush campaigned as a "compassionate conservative." Bush's theme was not tied to any particular intellectual or political constituency, and so it had a certain amount of flexibility in its meaning. Nevertheless, compassionate conservatism was based on a belief that government should aim more at helping individuals facing particular problems than at transferring resources to groups that were considered in need. As Bush said in his "Duty of

Hope" speech delivered in Indianapolis on July 22, 1999:

> In every instance where my administration sees a responsibility to help people, we will look first to faith-based organizations, charities and community groups that have shown their ability to save and change lives … We will rally the armies of compassion in our communities to fight a very different war against poverty and hopelessness, a daily battle waged house to house and heart by heart. This will not be the failed compassion of distant bureaucracies. On the contrary, it will be government that serves those who are serving their neighbors…[20]

The ideals of compassionate conservatism were reflected in Bush's proposals for renewed community and national service and in the "faith-based initiative" to allow government to support faith-based groups providing social services. It was the response to terrorist attacks, however, that dominated Bush's agenda soon after he took office.

The Scope of Government

Will the country continue to expand the scope of government into more aspects of life, or will it move toward reducing the scope of government? Ronald Reagan came into office believing that the government was trying to do too many things and that greater scope should be given to private initiative. In his view, the federal government was simply not equipped to handle all of the demands placed upon it under the governing philosophy inspired by the Great Society. In a radio address in 1984, the President elaborated on this point, linking it to his view of the original intentions of the policy capacities of the federal government:

> [The Founding Fathers] knew well that if too much power and authority were vested in the central government, even if intended for a noble purpose, not only would liberty be threatened but it just wouldn't work. . . . I think during the last decade and before, we've gotten a taste of just what [they were] warning us about. So much power had centralized in Washington that frustration and stagnation ruled the day.[21]

This view confirmed Reagan's pledge four years earlier, made at the time of his inauguration in 1981: "It will be my intention to curb the size and influence of the federal establishment and to demand recognition of the distinction between powers granted to the federal government and those reserved to the states or to the people."[22] Under Reagan the number of government regulations was reduced substantially and the rate of growth of the federal government in domestic affairs—although it did not stop—slowed considerably.

Opposition to this trend developed, however, and by the beginning of the 1990s the nation seemed prepared to add to the responsibilities of the federal government, although with a bit more caution than in the 1960s. President Clinton tried to promote a considerably more active role for the federal government in stimulating economic development, providing national health care, and guiding the direction of social policies. But the Republican victory in the 1994 Congressional revived the sentiment that government needed to be reduced in size and scope. President Clinton seemed half to acknowledge this sentiment with his claim in his 1996 State of the Union Message that "the era of Big Government is over." His reelection in 1996 together with a Republican Congress suggested that Americans neither wanted government expanded nor contracted. The extent and character of new federal involvement in society remains one of the major questions of American domestic politics in the 21st Century.

The Organization and Distribution of Power

Two decades ago many political scientists would have confidently predicted that power would continue to gravitate to the presidency as it had done since the advent of the New Deal. However, political events have a way of upsetting confident predictions, and today the future strength of the branches seems much less certain. As a result of the Vietnam War and Watergate, as well as changes in American political parties, much power returned to Congress in the 1970s. Congress asserted new control not only over domestic issues but even over foreign policy issues traditionally thought to be the particular province of the president.

The 1980s opened with a show of presidential strength. During the first two years of his administration, Ronald Reagan was able to get much of what he wanted from Congress, even though it was partly controlled by the opposition party. The idea that the presidency was an institution in crisis, incapable of providing any kind of political leadership, began to fade. Although the direction of domestic politics remains very much in question because of the divided party control in government over the past decade (the presidency being in the hands of the Republicans and one or both houses of Congress in the hands of the Democrats) there has been a renewed confidence in the presidency as an institution of government and a recognition—as in the case of the war on terrorism after September 11, 2001—that certain delicate acts of diplomacy can only be carried out by the president.

The power of the courts, enormous in recent decades, has also been challenged. Will objections to the use of judicial power by the federal courts lead to a lesser role for the judiciary? The Reagan and Bush administrations have made more conservative appointments to the courts, and up to this point at least the new direction of the Court in many areas appears to be to leave more decisions in society to the "political" institutions in the states and in the federal government. President Clinton's first two appointments did not reverse this trend. The kind of broad activism exercised by the courts during the era of the Warren Court now seems over.

Conclusion

American politics today seems fluid and undetermined in many ways—as it has often been in the past. Today, as in former times, Americans are faced with choices concerning the ends society should serve, the scope that government should have, and the way power is to be organized and distributed. In looking at the alternatives Americans have faced in the past and at the choices they have made, we can see that each generation faces anew the challenge of constitution making—shaping, accepting, or questioning the understandings and choices it has inherited.

Court Cases

Brown v. Board of Education of Topeka, 347 U.S. 483 (1954).

Dred Scott v. Sanford, 19 How. 393 (1857).

Marbury v. Madison, 1 Cranch 137 (1803).

McCulloch v. Maryland, 17 U.S. 316 (1819).

Wesberry v. Sanders, 376 U.S. 1 (1964).

Wickard et al. v. Filburn, 317 U.S. 111 (1942).

Chapter 3 Notes

1. Thomas Jefferson, *The Writings of Thomas Jefferson,* Andrew A. Lipscomb, ed., vol. 3 (Washington, D.C.: Thomas Jefferson Memorial Association, 1904), p. 318.
2. Thomas Jefferson, *The Writings of Thomas Jefferson,* vol. 6, pp. 392–393.
3. Thomas Jefferson, *The Writings of Thomas Jefferson,* vol. 15, pp. 20, 22.
4. Marvin Meyers, *The Jacksonian Persuasion,* (Stanford, Calif.: Stanford University Press, 1957), pp. 7 and 15.
5. Thomas Jefferson, *The Writings of Thomas Jefferson,* vol. 2, p. 227.
6. Harry V. Jaffa, *Crisis of the House Divided* (Garden City, N. Y.: Doubleday, 1959).
7. Abraham Lincoln, *The Collected Works of Abraham Lincoln,* Roy P. Basler, ed., vol. 7 (New Brunswick, N.J.: Rutgers University Press, 1953) p. 302.
8. William A. Schambra, "The Roots of the American Public Philosophy," *The Public Interest,* 67, Spring, 1982, p. 42.
9. Woodrow Wilson, *Congressional Government* (Cleveland and New York: Meridian, 1956), p. 206.
10. Woodrow Wilson, "The Nature of Democracy in the United States," *Political Thought of American Statesmen,* Morton J. Frisch and Richard G. Stevens, eds. (Itasca, Ill.: Peacock, 1973), p. 284.
11. Franklin Roosevelt, "Commonwealth Club Address, 1932," *The People Shall Judge,* (Chicago and London: University of Chicago Press, 1949), p. 452.
12. Franklin Roosevelt, "Commonwealth Club Address, 1932," *The People Shall Judge,* pp. 454–455.
13. Franklin Roosevelt, "Commonwealth Club Address, 1932," *The People Shall Judge,* p. 456.
14. Samuel Beer, "In Search of a New Public Philosophy," *The New American Political System,* Anthony King, ed. (Washington, D.C.: American Enterprise Institute, 1979), p. 7.
15. John E. Tropman, "American Welfare Strategies: Three Programs under the Social Security Act," *Policy Sciences,* vol. 8, no. 1, 1977, p. 37.
16. Rowland Evans and Robert Novak, *Lyndon B. Johnson: The Exercise of Power* (New York: New American Library, 1966), pp. 424–34.
17. Harry McPherson, *A Political Education* (Boston: Atlantic Monthly Press, 1972), pp. 301–302.

18. Speech at Howard University, June 1965. *Public Papers of the Presidents: Lyndon B. Johnson, 1965,* vol. 2 (Government Printing Office, 1966), p. 636.

19. *Weekly Compilation of Presidential Documents,* vol. 20, no. 12, March 12, 1984, p. 400.

20. George W. Bush, Duty of Hope Speech, Indianapolis, July 22, 1999. Also see James W. Ceaser and Andrew E. Busch, "The Politics of the Perfect Tie," in the *Perfect Tie* (Lanham, MD.: Rowan and Little Publishers, 2001), pp. 17–47.

21. Radio Address to the Nation, February 25, 1984, *Weekly Compilation of Presidential Documents*, vol. 20, no. 9, March 5, 1984.

22. "Inaugural Address of President Ronald Reagan," *Weekly Compilation of Presidential Documents*, vol. 17, no. 4, January 26, 1981.

4

Federalism

CHAPTER CONTENTS

One of the most notable characteristics of American government is the way in which power is deliberately divided to prevent an excessive concentration of authority at any one point. This allocation of power manifests itself in two major ways. First, within the national government, there are multiple checks and balances built around a separation of powers among the executive, legislative, and judicial branches. Second, there is a division of power between the national government and the states that we call "federalism." This system combines a central government that deals with the needs of the nation as a whole with fifty separate state governments that can provide meaningful self-government at a lower level.

Federalism was perhaps the most unique innovation of the founders. Prior to the writing of the Constitution, political theorists had recognized two forms of arranging power among governmental units: a "unitary" or "national" government, in which all power was invested in a central government; and a "confederal" or "federal" government, in which sovereign power was held by the individual governments which agreed to act together for some purposes in the form of a voluntary league (such as the American Articles of Confederation from 1781 until 1789). The founders devised an alternative system, what Madison called a "compound republic" and what is known today as federalism. (A few of the founders began to employ the term "federal" in this new sense, but this usage only became widespread in the nineteenth century.[1])

The new arrangement consisted of a division between the central (or "national" or "federal") government and the states in which the existence and viability of the states were Constitutionally sanctioned. While the central government was to be supreme in its own sphere, it was also to be a government of enumerated powers in which all powers not given to it were reserved to the states. In establishing this new form of government, the founders broke a deadlock over the tricky question of how it was possible to divide up "sovereignty," which until then had been considered an absolute property of one government. They did so by holding that sovereignty rests not in any government but in the people themselves, who through a written constitution may assign

functions to different levels of government.[2] This said, however, it remains that the classical attributes of sovereignty as understood in international relations—the power to make war, to sign treaties, to regulate commerce—were vested chiefly in the national government.

The introduction of this new form of federalism resulted from some very difficult decisions made at the Constitutional Convention. No one came into the Convention with a plan for federalism along the lines that finally emerged. The initial proposals reflected the ideas of the nationalists on the one hand and those who feared a strong central government on the other. The nationalists would have given the central government greater authority in relation to the states—and the opponents of a strong national government would have given the states more power and more influence over the central government—than the Constitution finally granted. American federalism was thus constructed during the Convention—in part through deliberation about what would best fit the American people and in part through sheer compromise between the two groups. As such, federalism has always been a somewhat nebulous concept, and it is difficult to say exactly what it is or what it was meant to be. Thus a principle that was so innovative—and that is still such a central element of our system—is also one that cannot be clearly defined. The dispute over the division of power between the national and state governments has been a constant theme of American history, leading in its most tragic case to the Civil War.

At the end of the 1970s, many had begun to conclude that this dispute over power between the national and state governments had reached an end. The states seemed on their way to extinction, if not in a technical legal sense (since their existence is protected by the Constitution), then as functioning political units possessing any real power. Even in the field of elementary and secondary education, traditionally a quintessential state and local function, officials expressed fears of a "federal takeover."[3] After decades of decline the remaining powers of the state governments were being swallowed up inexorably by the federal government. While some cheered the decline of the states as a necessary condition for the triumph of an activist national government, others worried about the consequences of the breakdown of one of the fundamental founding principles.

By the 1990s, worries about the irrelevance of the states had subsided. These concerns were replaced by amazement at the recovery of the states—not quite in their earlier sense as units jealously seeking to deny powers to the central government, but rather as units willing to take the initiative in new areas and to tackle certain problems before the central government acts. Federalism has proved to be more dynamic than many had believed, and it is clear that the debate over the relationship between the states and the central government will be a part of our nation's political discourse for a long time to come.

A Multitude of Governments

While a few matters such as national defense and foreign policy are handled almost entirely by the central government, virtually all others involve the actions of state and local government in some fashion. State governments play a major role in such tasks as handling highway networks, providing social services to citizens running park systems, encouraging industrial development, and setting the rates we pay for insurance. Local governments directly affect citizens almost every day. Police officers walking the beat, school board members deciding which textbooks to authorize for use in social studies classes, zoning officials deciding on the density of suburban housing development, sanitation workers clearing city streets of refuse, and public health experts checking patients for venereal disease— all these represent the activities of officials tending to some of the varied responsibilities of American local governments.

Strictly speaking, federalism refers only to relations between the national government and the states. No other governmental entities are recognized in the Constitution. Yet the spirit of federalism goes well beyond this, ultimately resting on the more general idea of decentralization and self-government at the local level. Thus, to understand the true nature and importance of federalism, we need to look for a moment at all of the subnational levels of government.

The States

The Constitution, as the fundamental law of the land, created two separate—though partly interdependent—levels of government: the national, or federal level, on the one hand, and the states on the other. Although not the nearly autonomous entities they were under the Articles of Confederation, the states were intended to be governments of substantial strength. Federalism in this sense was a new system at the time of the founding, but in the years since many other nations have adopted variants of a federal design, including Canada, Switzerland, Germany, and Australia. American federalism has been one of the major contributions this country has made to the structure of governance in the modern world.

All fifty states have their own written constitutions. All organize themselves according to an allocation of power among three major branches: executive, legislative, and judicial. Nevertheless, the formal structures of the states vary significantly. Some, like New York, have chief executives (governors) with great formal authority; others, like Mississippi, give the legislature more control. One state, Nebraska, has organized its legislature into a unicameral, or one-house, body. Some state legislatures are professional and in session for much of each year while others only meet every other year. The judicial branch imposes capital punishment in some states, such as Texas, but is not permitted to in others like Massachusetts. Elected officials are constrained by term limits in some states but in others can serve indefinitely. Finally, a number of states have provisions for, and regularly make use of, a process known as the initiative and referendum, whereby citizens may bypass the legislature and vote directly for legislation on state ballots. Oregon and California, for example, have laws making it easy to put referendum issues on the ballot. As a result, significant legislation has been enacted by the voters in these and other states dealing with issues such as medical marijuana and assisted suicide. Other states, like Virginia, rarely use the referendum, if ever.

The politics and interests of the states are impressively varied as well. There are one-party Democratic strongholds like Alabama, where conservative interests and agricultural organizations are frequently in control; two-party competitive states with strong labor union influence, like Michigan; traditional Republican, religious states like Utah, a bastion of the Mormons; and the diverse, fragmented, weak-party politics of California. (California, with its 34 million inhabitants is by far the nation's largest state and possesses by itself an economy that would rank seventh in size among the nations of the world, larger than Italy, Spain, or Canada.)

All of the states have created or acknowledged the existence of a great many other governments. There are in fact some 83,000 local governments of one sort or another that inhabit the American political landscape. There are so many, and they exist in such variety and complexity, that the U.S. Census Bureau periodically counts and classifies them—just as it does people, businesses, and houses with indoor plumbing! What are these other governments?

Counties

First there are the counties, known as "parishes" in Louisiana and "boroughs" in Alaska. These units, numbering more than 3,000, serve most of the land area and population of the United States. A couple of New England states, the District of Columbia, and selected portions of a few other states (such as the "independent cities" of Virginia) have no county government. But for most Americans, counties are governments of some significance.

Originally, counties were created as arms of state authority at the local level and until recognition of urban and regional problems in the 1960s and 1970s, rarely represented local interests in any systematic fashion.[4] However, especially in urban areas, counties have now acquired substantially more authority. Many of them now provide a full range of local services such as public health, libraries, sanitation, and recreation, in addition to more traditional county duties such as highway maintenance and law enforcement. In some states, especially in the more heavily populated regions, a few counties have even been given a "home rule" charter and consequently are able to pass local laws and raise revenue without seeking approval from the state

government. Counties are on the rise as a form of local government because they are often the one government capable of serving the entire metropolitan area for urban centers. Counties have also served as a base for powerful suburban populations seeking influence over units larger than their own municipality.

Counties, like all local units of government, have different legal status than the national government or the states. The latter two levels of government have Constitutional standing and thus neither can eliminate or totally ignore the interests of the other. By contrast, local governments, no matter how important, are technically creatures of the states, and their authority to act can be determined by state law. (Politically, of course, many local governments have deep roots and support and cannot be threatened by the states.) Although some local governments look to Washington for support and seek to gain a certain amount of freedom from this lesser status, the dependent nature of local governments in relation to the states remains an essential fact in state and local politics.

Municipalities

Municipalities are the cities and villages of the United States—from the giant megalopolises like Los Angeles and New York City, to small cities like Charlottesville, Virginia, and Claremont, California, to tiny villages like Gambier, Ohio. These are the political subdivisions incorporated by the state to "provide general local government for a specific population concentration in a defined area."[5] Whereas counties were originally meant to serve state interests, municipalities have been "created mainly for the interest, advantage, and convenience of the locality and its people."[6]

Traditionally, municipalities have been the most independent unit of local governments. Even so, their independence has been strictly limited by state legislative action and judicial interpretation. The major principle restricting municipal autonomy is known as "Dillon's rule," named after the pronouncement of a judge in the state of Iowa in 1872. Relied on by most American courts, Dillon's rule states that municipalities have only the powers expressly delegated to them by the states. Although many states now grant their largest cities a measure of self-sufficiency through home rule, the relations between states and municipalities have been stormy throughout American history. Traditionally, states have tended to keep a fairly close watch on their major cities, while urban political leaders have sought to widen their own scope of authority.

Although technically falling under a different legal status, the town or township in the New England states is the most important unit of local government in that region and has assumed the role played by the municipality throughout the rest of the country. The New England towns represent the model (or the ideal) of local self-government. There, townmeetings antedated the states themselves and are classic examples of early American efforts at democracy.[7]

School Districts and Special Districts

To complicate matters even more, there are at least two other levels of local government worth noting. The first is the school district, which number some 15,000 unique school systems and whose sole purpose is to run public school systems. (School districts are separate governments in most states, although in certain cities they are an agency of the city government.) The number of these districts is evidence of the long-held view that education is primarily a duty of local government; their separate status is a testimony to the strength of educational interests and professionals who have long sought to keep education beyond the conflicts of the rest of local government. Of course, creating school districts does not really remove education from politics. School administrators fully recognize how much they must become involved in politics, not only in interacting with their own communities, but also in dealing with the state and federal governments.

The other "level" of local government is the special district, which is sometimes also referred to as a "commission" or an "authority." These are limited-purpose units that have responsibility for a particular function such as ensuring fire protection in rural regions, supplying water in cities, running park systems and hospitals, and even operating cemeteries and controlling mosquitoes. If you live in or near a large city, your mass transit system may be governed by a special district. If you live in a rural area, a water conservation district may be making important decisions. Special districts allow people to match the jurisdiction of a local government to the problem that needs to be solved, such as pollution in a common river basin. These units often possess a political advantage as well, since they may provide a service for which users can be charged directly, such as fees for sewage collection. More than other governmental forms, the 25,000 special districts probably typify Americans' pragmatic adaptation of their public institutions to the needs of different people at different times.

Critics of these governments raise some of the same questions often at the core of controversy in other debates over the distribution of power in the United States. Many complain about the independence of these governments and their officials from electoral constraints and control of mayors; others argue that the crazy-quilt pattern of many duplicating and overlapping jurisdictions in the same region impairs efficiency. How many police departments, some wonder, does a single urban area need?

Whatever the complaints, however, special districts have displayed impressive persistence and will have a significant role to play in the future. These units of government, along with the more well-known units of cities and states, remain in continual interaction with each other. The pattern and network of interaction with these governments and the national government is what is commonly referred to as intergovernmental relations. If the Constitution prescribed neatly divided spheres of authority for the states and the national government, how is it that today virtually all American governments must deal with each other so frequently and on so many matters? To answer this most important political issue of the present, we must look briefly at the development of intergovernmental relations in American history.

The Development of American Federalism

Much of the debate at the Constitutional Convention revolved around determining the role of the states in relation to the national government. Those favoring a strong central government claimed that it was essential to the protection of rights, successful commerce, and good government; those favoring strong states rested their case on the importance of self-government and the protection of local diversity. The Convention nearly broke up over this question, as delegates on both sides initially stated their cases in a way that threatened to exclude the position of the other. Some nationalists proposed abolishing the existing state governments, while some advocates of strong states wanted merely to patch up the government of the Articles and maintain the states in their existing power. Cooler heads began to look for a middle ground that would provide, in the words of one delegate, a "considerable, though subordinate jurisdiction" of the states inside "the general sovereignty and jurisdiction . . . of the national government."[8]

The framework the founders finally devised envisioned the protection of federalism by three mechanisms: (1) a legal allocation of power between the national and state governments, (2) a structural design that would protect each level of government, and (3) a reliance on political factors that could be counted on to maintain a balance between the two levels of government. Let us look at each of these.

First, the Constitution recognizes two levels of government, national and state, and allocates power in a way that implies a division of responsibilities between the two governments. The major instrument for this allocation is the enumeration of Congress's powers contained in Article I, which gives Congress some eighteen basic powers. The dominant understanding of this enumeration is that the national government is limited to specific powers listed in the Constitution. This enumeration of national powers, which courts could presumably help enforce, could act as a significant defense for the states. As *The Federalist* notes, "the powers of the [national] government extend to certain enumerated powers only, and leave to the states a resid-

uary and inviolable sovereignty over all other objects."[9] This general understanding was underscored, no doubt because of anti-federalist fears that it might be ignored, in the Tenth Amendment, added as part of the Bill of Rights in 1791, which declares the "powers not delegated to the United States by the Constitution, nor prohibited by it to the States, are reserved to the States respectively, or to the people."

Nevertheless, the powers granted to the national government under the enumeration were generous, so much so that opponents of the Constitution during the ratification debates predicted—perhaps deliberately exaggerating—that "the state governments must be annihilated or continue to exist for no purpose."[10] Not only were some of the specific grants of power impressive, such as regulating interstate commerce and coining money, but the national government was also given the general power "to make all laws which shall be necessary and proper" to carry out its specific powers and to collect taxes to "provide for the . . . general Welfare of the United States" (Article I, Section 8). With such carefully chosen and ambiguous phrases, it is no wonder that reasonable people have differed over the years on just what the national government is allowed to do (see Box 4.1). In addition, national law is clearly declared to be superior to state law. The Constitution, all federal law, and all treaties are the "the supreme law of the land" and take precedence over "anything in the constitution or laws of any state" (Article VI).

The second level of defense for federalism is found in the structure of the government. The Constitution arranged the institutions and selection of officials so that the states have certain means for protecting their interests inside the national government. For example, state legislatures were responsible for selecting United States Senators and for determining the manner of selecting electors for the selection of the president. The states also have a significant role in the process of amending the Constitution. These powers meant, as Madison pointed out, that "the state governments may be regarded as constituent and essential parts of the federal government." (*Federalist* 45) Examined from the other side, the federal government had means to pro-

---

BOX 4.1

Powers in the Federal System

Express powers are those explicitly granted to the national government by the Constitution. The power to declare war is an express power of Congress.

Implied powers are those not explicitly granted to the national government but reasonably suggested from the express powers. Regulating television is not mentioned in the Constitution but is implied by the express power of Congress to regulate interstate commerce.

Concurrent powers are those shared at both national and state levels, such as the power to tax.

Reserved powers are those left to the states to exercise. The Constitution does not list the reserved powers, but leaves the states all powers granted neither to the national government nor directly to the people themselves. An example is the power to set policy to promote public safety.

Denied powers are those prohibited to one or both levels of government. The power to establish an official religion is denied to the national government. A power to grant titles of nobility or to pass ex post facto laws or bills of attainder are denied to both the federal government and the states.

---

tect its interests against the states. In addition to its extensive grant of powers, it had, for example the authority to create a national court system that would be able to enforce national law directly on citizens.

Third, and finally, the founders relied on substantial political defenses for federalism. These political supports derived in part from the existing sentiments of the people, which were characterized by a strong affection to their states. Moreover, in much the same way that the founders expected that "ambition would counteract ambition" to defend the separation of powers within the national government, so too they expected that political officials in state governments (governors, legislators, and mayors) would be jealous of the national government's prerogatives and would not tamely permit any state usurpation of authority. So strong was the attachment of the people to the states that the founders observed, without ever condoning it, that the state governments might be able to rely on an implicit threat of physical resistance under extreme circumstances to check the power of the central government.[11] On the other side, the national government would enjoy the developing attachment of people to the whole nation and would profit from the pride people would feel in viewing the success of an effective new government. Furthermore, national officials would have a strong interest in defending the powers

and prerogatives of a government from which their own authority and status derived.

Thus both governments would have the power and political will to defend themselves. These structural and political forces, along with the legal allocation of powers, would work to maintain a balance between the two levels of government. Yet even the most optimistic of the founders realized just how difficult maintaining a satisfactory balance would be. Their concerns, as the nation's history reveals, were not misplaced.

The Early Years

Exactly how the two levels of government were to deal with each other was not (and indeed could not be) perfectly clear from the Constitution. The relationship between the two levels of government was something that would be determined in part by precedent and practice under the new system. The basic pattern, however, that the founders seemed to expect was that of two levels of government operating side by side, but mainly in different spheres—the national government handling certain issues, the states taking care of others. While there would be occasions for overlap, thereby inviting cooperation or conflict, the usual situation would be characterized by one of the two governments operating independently on distinct matters.

Shortly after the founding, the idea emerged that the spirit if not the letter of the Constitution required that a responsibility or function be placed under the control of either one level of government or the other, but not both. (This idea has sometimes been referred to in the literature of political science as "dual federalism.") This view could serve in theory to favor either a much stronger national government or much stronger states. In practice, due to the fairly narrow construction of the federal government's enumerated powers, it tended to operate in favor of those who wanted stronger states. Because the states were already involved in most areas of governmental activity, the idea of separate spheres was employed as an argument to deny that the national government should enter, even in a supplemental way, in areas such as economic development, education, and other social policies. Where the states acted, the national government should abstain.

This position was advocated by the Republican-Democratic party, which was founded by Thomas Jefferson and James Madison in the 1790s. One of the clearest statements of this principle was made by Madison, when as president he vetoed legislation in 1817 that would have established federal financing of construction for internal transportation improvements such as roads and canals. In his veto message, Madison argued that such a power was not among the expressly enumerated powers of the national government and could not be "deduced from any part of it without an inadmissible latitude of construction"; moreover, because these improvements have traditionally been the responsibility of the states, and because "the permanent success of the Constitution depends on a definite partition of powers between the Federal and State Governments," the federal government should not act.[12] President Andrew Jackson continued in the same line, vetoing a bill for reestablishing the National Bank in 1832 in part because it intruded on state functions. The institution of slavery was also seen as a policy within the province of the states and defended by reference to states' rights.

Yet the actual pattern of intergovernmental relations in the nineteenth century was not nearly as neat as this idea of separate spheres or dual federalism would suggest.[13] Not even Republican-Democratic presidents always remained pure in practice, and the opposition party (first the Federalists and later the Whigs) advocated much greater involvement of the national government in economic development. National-state relations had a degree of overlap and interdependence. At times these relationships were characterized by suspicious antagonism, but at other times state governments and the central government successfully cooperated to achieve common objectives. Intergovernmental cooperation took place during the last century on a wide variety of construction, finance, and education projects, and technical assistance by the federal government to the states was commonplace.

Despite such examples of federal-state-local partnership, however, the dominant theme of intergovernmental relations throughout the first half or more of the nation's existence was one in which the national government and the states each performed separate functions without hindrance. This relation stemmed from the nature of problems and tasks that government faced, the understanding of the doctrine of the national government as a government of enumerated powers, and finally from the idea that separate spheres of action was the proper Constitutional arrangement.

The Civil War

The clearest and most dramatic clash between the federal government and states occurred in the Civil War. Eleven southern states tried to secede from the Union, claiming that a right to unilaterally nullify federal law and secede was inherent in the nature of the Constitutional "compact" among the states. This notion had its roots as far back as the Virginia and Kentucky Resolutions of 1798, which did not mention secession but clearly did assert the right and duty of states to serve as rallying points to resist encroachments from the national government. This in turn was an extrapolation of the founders' observation (and fear) that people might turn to the states in response to claims that the national government threatened to overreach its power.

The victory of the Union fundamentally changed national-state relations forever. Most obviously, it settled that the states were subordinate entities in the American scheme of government. The concept of states as sovereign bodies that had created the "compact" of the Constitution, and were thus ultimately superior to the national government and able to withdraw from it, was dead. So too was the idea that the states might in the extreme act as a focus of armed resistance (although milder versions of the states invoking their sovereignty to refuse to carry out national policies remained until the 1960s). As one newspaper editorialized in 1865, "The territorial, political, and historical oneness of the nation is now ratified by the blood of thousands of her sons."[14]

The adoption of the Thirteenth, Fourteenth, and Fifteenth Amendments (the "Civil War Amendments") extended the reach of the federal government into areas that had previously been reserved to the states. The Thirteenth Amendment abolished slavery, the Fourteenth Amendment prevented states from denying any citizen equal protection under the law, and the Fifteenth Amendment prohibited states from denying anyone the vote on the basis of race. Many legislators at the time thought that these amendments granted the national government a broad new power to deal with race relations by legislation. Thus in 1875, Congress enacted a civil rights act that banned segregation in all public facilities (boats, parks, theaters, and places of public amusement). Yet the nationalist sweep of these amendments and laws was dramatically limited by the Supreme Court. In one of its most momentous decisions, *The Civil Rights Cases* (1883), the Supreme Court declared this legislation to be unconstitutional on the grounds that the Fourteenth Amendment was limited to preventing the *states* in their official capacity from acts or statutes that denied equal protection of the laws; the amendment, in the Court's view, did not confer on the national government a positive power to act on individuals. Such a power, the Court argued, would "make Congress take the place of the state legislatures and supersede them . . . and would establish a [federal] code of municipal law regulative of all private rights between man and man in society."[15]

This decision—and others along the same lines—meant that the national government could not by statute directly protect black citizens from discrimination. The state governments, by turning a blind eye (as many did), allowed practices of racial discrimination and segregation to continue or develop. This legal situation remained largely in effect until the Civil Rights Movement of the 1950s and 60s, when other means were found to give the national government power to legislate in this area. Ironically, while the Fourteenth Amendment has not been used as the major Constitutional justification for this power, it has become, as noted earlier, the major vehicle through which the federal courts now exercise their greatest scrutiny over state governments, including the area of race relations. It has been through the Fourteenth Amendment that most of the federal bill of rights have been "incorporated" to protect individuals against the states, and today federal courts interpret the ban against states' denying equal protection of the laws in a way that subjects thousands of state and local laws and practices to close judicial scrutiny.

Another unrelated development in federalism during the Civil War period must be mentioned. It was in 1862 that the first significant federal grants—land grants—were established. The national government at the time owned huge tracts of land in the midwestern states carved out by westward expansion. (It still owns major areas of land in many of the Western states). The government gave lands to the states to sell for certain broadly designated purposes, such as constructing roads, developing educational systems, and creating welfare programs. The Morrill Act of 1862, for instance, provided federal land grants for establishing colleges of agriculture and the mechanical arts. Many of the major public universities in the midwest had their origin in this act, such as Michigan State University, the University of Wisconsin, the University of Nebraska, and Ohio State University. These early grants, unlike most federal grants operating today, required little extra attention on the part of the states, as the administrative requirements were quite limited.

The Turn of the Century

A growing influence of the national government, very often at the expense of the states, came about in a series of different steps that began during the late nineteenth century. The increased federal role and the shift toward interdependence between the federal government and the states were the result of several factors: changing public views about the governmental arrangements that could best serve the public, an acceptance of a broader role for government in the society, a recognition of the complexity of modern problems, and altered financial circumstances. The terms of the Constitutional bargain, at least as they had been understood through most of the nineteenth century, began to be altered. Not only would the role of the federal government be greater, but also the two governments could not always act in distinct spheres. More and more, the two governments would be acting on the same issues and would have to develop means to work together.

During the late nineteenth century and the progressive period, political forces pressed for national government activity in policy fields previously either left to the states or avoided by government altogether, such as economic regulation, highway construction, and conservation. The Interstate Commerce Commission (1887), the Pure Food and Drug and Meat Inspection Acts (1906), and the Federal Trade Commission (1914) began regulating commercial activities that had either been unregulated entirely or regulated by the states. Supporters of these federal efforts had two major arguments: some states had no regulation at all, thus endangering the safety and health of their citizens, and those states that did regulate differed wildly in their requirements, thus making it difficult to conduct business equitably across state lines. President Theodore Roosevelt established a National Conservation Commission in 1908 to conduct a systematic study of the nation's mineral, water, forest, and soil resources with the assistance of local conservation commissions in 41 states. And, in 1916, Congress passed the Federal Road Act, which gave the states matching funds at a 1:1 ratio to pave rural dirt roads used by the U.S. Postal Service, on the condition that states create

ate highway departments to oversee and audit these projects (this program accounted for more than three-quarters of all intergovernmental aid in the years prior to the New Deal).

Support for these programs, and for intergovernmental cooperation, came not only from the public but increasingly from interest groups that hoped to benefit from large new expenditures or involvement by the national government. It was around the turn of the century that large-scale, national interest groups first formed permanent organizations.[16] These interests were joined by rapidly professionalizing federal and state bureaucracies that also saw advantages to more intergovernmental involvement. Political pressures quite similar to these help to account for more recent intergovernmental programs as well.

Yet the federal government would not have been able to extend its role in domestic policy-making nearly as much as it did without the ratification of the Sixteenth Amendment in 1913 which authorized a federal income tax. It is difficult to overestimate the importance of this event for the later development of federalism. A national income tax, especially a "progressive" and "elastic" income tax—that is, one that taxes higher incomes at a greater rate than lower ones and that more than keeps pace with economic growth—eventually gave the federal government the means to generate funds and to increase its revenue without continually having to enact tax increases. The power to levy an income tax put vast new financial resources at the disposal of the federal government, without which the expansion of federal programs into areas traditionally reserved to the states would have been impossible.

Finally, the beginning of the twentieth century saw the final breakdown of one of the last structural defenses of federalism, the election of Senators by state legislatures. The selection of presidential electors, which were originally made by the state legislatures in some states, had for more than a half century been conducted directly by the people; and the electors in any case had long since lost any personal discretion in their votes. As for Senators, their election in many states had been increasingly subject to de facto direct election, either through the practice of turning state legislative races into surrogate Senate elections or through statewide "advisory" referenda. In 1913, the Seventeenth Amendment was added to the Constitution, making direct election of Senators official and universal.[17]

The New Deal

The trend toward greater involvement of the federal government in domestic policy matters increased dramatically during the Great Depression. State and local governments were unable to cope with the severe economic pressures that resulted from the virtual collapse of the economy, and they were thus unable to meet what had previously been considered state and local responsibilities, especially in the area of social welfare. People turned to the national government to start large-scale federal programs in traditionally state and local areas of activity. During a two-year period (1933–1935), federal laws were passed creating new grants for the distribution of surplus farm products to the poor, free school lunches, child welfare, maternal and children's health and crippled children's services, old-age assistance, aid to dependent children, aid to the blind, general health services, emergency highway expenditures, and emergency work relief.[18] In addition, the federal government adopted major new programs regulating certain prices, limiting production of farm products, and protecting workers organized in labor unions.

In the early 1930s the Supreme Court declared some of the New Deal Programs unconstitutional on the grounds that they did not rest on any enumerated power of the national government. By the end of the decade, however, after much turmoil and controversy, the Court altered its course and began to interpret federal authority more broadly. The combination of determination by the president and Congress to act, and (after 1937) the willingness by the Supreme Court not to interfere, led to the virtual collapse of the notion of a limited national government of enumerated powers.

The method by which some of these programs were to be carried out also differed from traditional ideas of how federalism was supposed to operate. While these programs were established by national legislation, they were carried out and significantly influenced by the states. The national government now committed itself deeply and permanently to intergovernmental programs. The older idea that each government should act in a separate sphere ("dual federalism") had clearly been replaced by something else, as federal dollars increased by tenfold for intergovernmental programs within a decade and as national economic regulation (such as the introduction of the minimum wage) soared. In many respects, regarding both federalism and governmental power in general, the national government in 1940 was not what it had been in 1930, even though no Constitutional amendment respecting the general powers of government had been adopted. To this day scholars differ over whether this change represented only a new and maximal use of existing federal powers or whether the Constitution was in effect altered by being ignored.

The provision of federal grants to the states and localities, which was virtually nonexistent before the New Deal, began to grow steadily thereafter and soared after the adoption of the Great Society program until the Reagan presidency (see Table 4.1). Federal grants, which are the principal mechanism by which the federal government deals with these other governments, are transfers of resources—now usually money—from the national government to other lower levels of government. Their purpose may be broad (for instance, to help cope with education or social services), in which case the transfer is known as a "block grant," or they may be directed to a specific aim (for instance, to eliminate rats in urban sewer systems), in which case the transfer is known as a "categorical grant." Additionally, grants that are allocated on the basis of a calculable formula (for example, aid to combat unemployment based on the population of the state and the unemployment statistics) are known as "formula grants," while those given by federal agencies on a discretionary basis to local governments making application (for example, a grant from the Department of Housing and Urban Development to build a specific housing project in the city of St. Louis) are known as "project grants."

Table 4.1
Federal Grant Outlays in Current and Constant (1992) Dollars, 1960–2000

	Current Dollars (billions)	Constant Dollars (billions)
1960	7.0	33.4
1965	10.9	45.8
1970	24.1	86.9
1975	49.8	126.6
1980	91.5	155.3
1985	105.9	135.6
1990	135.3	144.3
1995	225.0	209.3
2000	284.6	262.5

Source: Budget of the United States Government, 1998, Historical Tables.

Grants have another characteristic. They come with strings attached. The federal government specifies conditions that must be met before the funds are given. Usually these conditions are linked closely to the purpose of the grant. For example, funds provided for interstate highways require that the roads be constructed to a certain thickness from approved materials and that the exit and entrance ramps must meet detailed standards. In some cases, however, grants are conditioned on compliance with some rule that is only indirectly related to the grant's main purpose. For example, continuing in the case of highway funds, while the federal government has no direct power over the age at which people may begin to drink alcohol, federal rules for granting highway funding have prescribed that no one be able to buy alcohol under the age of twenty-one. Technically, then, the federal government does not legislate the drinking age; it says only that if a state wants to keep its federal highway funds, it must meet a certain standard.

The Constitutionality of the use of grants as a tool in intergovernmental relations was tested before the Supreme Court as early as 1923, in regard to a federal statute that granted funds to states to establish programs to reduce infant mortality and protect the health of mothers and infants. The Court indicated that it would not ban such statutes, which opened the door to the whole revolution in federalism.[19] The Court's decisions in 1923 were based more on technical grounds (who could sue), but in subsequent cases it has made clear that as long as acceptance of these grants (and the conditions) is voluntary as far as the state or local governments are concerned, they are constitutional. In a challenge by the state of South Dakota to the aforementioned 1984 federal law that conditioned a state's receipt of federal highway funds on passing state laws to set the legal drinking age at 21, the Court declared that "objectives not thought to be within Article I's enumerated legislative fields may nevertheless be attained through the use of the spending power and the conditional grant of federal funds."[20] Congress has not sought to condition funds on matters that bear no relation to the grants, but the federal government's discretion in this area seems to be nearly as large as it wishes to make it.

Federal grants have therefore become a major tool of federal influence on state practices, for despite the Court's assessment that states can withhold participation in any grant program that seemed unpalatable, the political truth is usually very different. Understandably, officials representing governments that are offered federal grants have great difficulty rejecting assistance to solve pressing problems. Potential recipients have usually felt compelled to accept the aid, and thus the accompanying strings. This arrangement has often worked to erode the position and influence of the states in the American federal system.

During the last few decades nearly every governmental task has been spread across governmental levels in intricate, complex patterns. Government programs now typically involve two or more levels, each working as parts of a detailed whole. Take any domestic policy areas, and one often finds that more than one level of government is involved in providing a service and running (directly or indirectly) a program. For example, Washington, D.C.'s Metropolitan Area Transportation Authority, which runs the mass transit in and around the nation's capital, involves and receives support from the federal government, the District of Columbia, the states of Maryland and Virginia, and the cities of Falls Church and Alexandria, Virginia. Another example might be in the realm of education, in which the federal government's program to educate disadvantaged children (called "compensatory education") provides federal dollars to Local Educational Agencies ("LEAs," or school boards), whose use of this money is approved and monitored by State Educational Agencies ("SEAs," or State departments of education).

The degree of influence or power that each level of government exercises depends upon the programs in question and, at least partly, on the amount of funds each level of government is supplying. There are no hard and fast rules to measure exactly the relative power of the different governments, and they themselves are often in the position of negotiating among themselves on their relationship. Thus instead of the relations between the federal government and the states being characterized by distinct separate spheres and responsibilities, we have the federal government acting together with the states and local governments in the same sphere.

The Great Society and Its Aftermath

Federalism was again transformed, although along the same lines initiated by the New Deal, during the administration of Lyndon Johnson. The first element of this change came in the area of civil rights. Major federal legislative action was taken to protect the civil rights of blacks, thereby establishing new protection for individuals under federal law and requiring close new federal supervision of many state and local activities. The Civil Rights Act of 1964 banned segregation in all public accommodations (hotels, restaurants, public transportation), and thus in effect finally accomplished what the Civil Rights Acts of nearly a century earlier had attempted.[21] The Voting Rights Act of 1965 prohibited certain state practices, such as literacy tests, in order to ensure the possibility of electoral participation by blacks, and mandated that Federal Marshals be present in certain (mostly southern) areas to observe the election process and enforce the law.

The second element of the transformation was Johnson's "Great Society" program, which led to an explosion in federal intergovernmental grants. Federal efforts to combat rural poverty, to improve education, to solve the urban crisis, and to accommodate the demands being voiced by the politically, socially, and economically disadvantaged resulted in many new federal programs, again in spheres that were formerly the domain of lower levels of government. The programs, while very appealing to social activists, often proved threatening to parts of the state and local establishment. Indeed, some grant programs actually seemed to have been designed to undermine existing local or state political systems. One of the grant programs from this period, the Community Action Program, distributed funds to local organizations of poor people, sometimes even challenging the activities of local governments that seemed to be working contrary to the group's interests.[22] The Community Action Program stimulated a storm of controversy, was revised, and ultimately was terminated in 1974 (though some of its functions were transferred to a different agency).

In 1964, there were 51 different grants-in-aid, which may seem like a rather healthy number; but by 1967, there were 379. The number contin-

---

BOX 4.2

Intergovernmental Complexity: Fifty-Two Programs for Fire-Fighters

The sometimes bewildering complexity of the intergovernmental system is illustrated by the example of federal aid available to state and local governments for fire prevention and control. Despite the fact that fighting fires would seem to be a preeminently local activity—one with which the national government would not be involved—as of 1980 there were fifty-two federal grant programs in operation to assist other American governments in some phase of this activity. All federal departments but two (Defense and State), plus more than ten other agencies, are somehow involved in this network. It is no wonder that state and local officials find the pattern unwieldy and difficult to understand.

The U.S. Forest Service in the Department of Agriculture, for instance, supervises aid for cooperative federal-state forest fire control, research on the subject, and protection of rural communities from fires. Another bureau in the same department (the Science and Education Administration) helps states perform research on a similar subject. A third unit in Agriculture, the Soil Conservation Service, gives grants to help indirectly through a program aimed at resource conservation. The Public Health Service in the Department of Health and Human Services, meanwhile, administers a number of intergovernmental programs designed to educate people about safety, perform research on eliminating safety hazards, train workers in on-the-job fire prevention, educate emergency personnel, and improve medical services for fire victims. The Department of Housing and Urban Development works with local governments to upgrade building safety. The Bureau of Mines in the Interior Department aims at preventing coal mine fires—and so does the Mine Safety and Health Administration in the Department of Labor, with a different program. There is even a special federal agency, the U.S. Fire Administration, to handle additional grants and to coordinate all the others, although it really has no means to encourage other units to go along. Furthermore, according to the Advisory Commission on Intergovernmental Relations,

> Eight agencies make loans of money or equipment that can be used to improve fire protection. Five collect data related to fire incidence, injuries, and losses, and many provide some kind of technical assistance and information available to those who request it.

These programs have different standards for eligibility, different strings attached, and different matching and administrative requirements.

---

ued to climb after Johnson left office—to 550 in 1974, for instance—but the acceleration was at its peak in the late 1960s.[23] Today, no one, including government officials, really has a clear count on the number and size of all these federal programs. President Johnson called his era a time of "creative federalism," and it certainly did not lack for major intergovernmental experiments.

Almost all the new programs were categorical ones, and most were project-funded rather than formula-funded. These arrangements assured that the money was being used for nationally approved purposes, but it also meant that recipient governments were increasingly tied to a long list of federal priorities and that state and local political leaders had less control over their own governments' actions (see Box 4.2). At the same time, many of the new programs provided a very

high donor-to-recipient matching—that is, the federal government offered to pay most of the money—so it became even more difficult for recipients to decline participation. Over this period, federal aid accounted for a larger and larger share of state budgets.

Federal assistance going directly to local governments, especially cities, also grew greatly during this period. Urban leaders increasingly turned to Washington for a more sympathetic hearing than they had often received from their states. State government officials came to view the direct federal-local interdependence with mixed feelings. On the one hand, they could hardly complain about federal help for their own citizens. Yet on the other, many state officials would have preferred to have a hand in decisions about how the money would be spent and the programs run. State officials thus sometimes saw these developments as threatening, with the federal government and the local governments, which were, after all, state creations, teaming up to combat the priorities of the states.

In the aftermath of the Great Society, during the 1970s, there was a political reaction against some of these programs and some effort made to bolster the role of state and local governments. President Nixon came to office calling for a "new American revolution" and a "new federalism." He sought to increase the strength of the general-purpose political leaders—governors, mayors, county commissioners—relative to the functional specialists such as welfare administrators, highway bureaucrats, and state education officials. Some categorical grants were combined into block grants, so that recipient governments would have more ability to make their own decisions.[24] Nixon also won creation of a federal program called general revenue sharing that transferred money to state and local governments by formula with very few strings attached, the aim again being to allow state and local political leaders to assert their own priorities, instead of merely using their governments to carry out federal policies.

Yet the changes during the 1970s proved to be only marginal. The national government remained as heavily committed as before, and the interdependence among the various governments increased. Most old grants were left unchanged, while the new block grants proved to be politically vulnerable.[25] Moreover, more new grants were born than old ones were killed. Federal regulation expanded yet further in areas such as the environment and workplace safety, continuing to "pre-empt" state regulation; and the federal courts became increasingly active not only in overturning state and local laws but in mandating remedies.

By the time President Reagan took the oath of office in 1981, the federal government was providing in excess of one-quarter of state and local revenues, more than $80 billion, and was involved in literally hundreds of intergovernmental programs. It seemed to be an open question whether the states were viable political entities or were on the road to becoming mere administrative units of the national government. This state of affairs came about in no small part

because the three original defenses for the states under the federal scheme had ceased functioning in an effective way.

The legal defense, a national government of enumerated powers, had fallen by the wayside in part through amendments to the Constitution and in part through a much looser interpretation of the federal government's original enumerated powers that emerged from the New Deal. By 1985, the Supreme Court in *Garcia v. San Antonio Metropolitan Transit Authority* came very close to forswearing any responsibility for protecting federalism. The structural defense also grew weaker, as Senators were subject to direct election. As the states lost structural power, the federal government gained it, most notably through the adoption of the income tax; this added to the states' decline by giving the federal government a major advantage in the resources available to it.

Finally, the political defense also seemed to be weakening. Federal grants had transformed state and local officials from jealous defenders of their prerogatives against the federal government into advocates of more federal programs. The attachment of the people to states and local governments also waned, as state and local governments often showed themselves to be amateurish and incapable of dealing with a wide range of new economic and social problems. The rise of an activist national government also occurred when the call for "states rights" was being used as a mask for segregation, which in the end discredited still further public support for the federal principle. None of the three defenses of federalism seemed adequate to the task.

The States Make a Comeback: Federalism from the 1980s to the Present

Within a decade, this gloomy assessment of the role of the states had to be reconsidered. By the beginning of the 1990s, it was clear that the states had made a comeback in the 1980s. This resurgence displayed itself in many ways. States were at the forefront of many policy fields; for instance, major federal welfare reform legislation that passed in 1988 was modelled after similar legislation in California and Massachusetts.

The Federal government was looking to the states to solve some of the nation's most pressing problems, like education and transportation. And, while far from consistent in this regard, the Supreme Court seemed increasingly willing to protect the right of states to make laws without interference from the judiciary (like permitting some restrictions on abortion). The federal government was responsible for a smaller percentage of state and local budgets (down from its high point of 27 percent in 1978 to about 17 percent in 1988); most states were fiscally healthy while the federal government was running large deficits. According to some observers, the states—not the federal government—was where the action was by the end of the 1980s. How did this happen?

Little has changed legally or structurally to revive the states; a full-fledged revival of the idea of enumerated powers as a limiting doctrine on national power did not occur. Much, however, had changed politically. Part of this change resulted from President Reagan's own views about the role of the national government and the importance of federalism. Reagan reopened national debate on at least three basic constitutional questions we discussed in the opening chapter. He argued that the role of government generally in society should be reduced; that the institutions of state and local government could, more appropriately than the federal government, handle much of the public's business (thus addressing the question of who should rule); and that the intergovernmental system had shifted too much toward interdependence and striving for equality across the states and should be changed to revitalize diversity and local liberty.[26]

On the specific question of federalism, Reagan, perhaps more than any recent chief executive, was committed to rebuilding vigorous state governments. In 1982 he proposed to redefine national-state relations by reducing federal control over certain joint programs, by returning to the states some programs in their entirety, and by carving out well-defined substantive policy areas reserved for each level of government. This plan encountered major opposition from many local officials, who worried about their role under a state-centered intergovernmental system, and from many state leaders as well, who worried about losing federal support for their own states and about a reduction of aid to some of the nation's poorest and weakest states. Reagan's ambitious package was derailed, revised, and scaled down—a process that indicated the limits to how far Americans were prepared to return to an "older" idea of federalism. But it remained a symbol of the administration's desire to reinvigorate federalism, and in 1987 Reagan issued an executive order requiring executive agencies to take "federalism principles" into account and to prepare "federalism assessment" reports describing the impact of proposed agency actions on the federal system.[27] Furthermore, Reagan took special care to appoint federal judges who were philosophically compatible with his conception of the Constitution, including his views on federalism.

What President Reagan might have done for the state governments, however, was less important than what he did to the federal government. As a firm believer in limiting the role of the national government, he fought successfully for spending restraint in many of the social welfare areas that the national government had only recently entered, and for a major tax cut in 1981 which restrained the growth of federal revenues for the rest of the decade. While overall federal spending and revenue continued to rise, it did so at a slower rate than before and was concentrated in areas of past activity. For the first time in decades, no new major social programs emanated from Washington. This permitted a major policy vacuum to develop, which the states were willing and able to fill. The federal deficits of the 1980s were a sign that Washington was overextended. Regardless of the legal or structural defenses for federalism, the states proved indispensable in practical terms. State governments may always "help fill the federal government's performance gaps," but in times of a large federal deficit the gaps may be more frequent and wider than before.[28]

As a result, states became major innovators in areas such as welfare reform, education reform, growth management, and health.[29] They also accepted (or were given) the primary burden for emerging problems like homelessness and child care, and took up the challenge of economic, environmental, and worker and consumer safety regulation with such vigor that many businesses were actually asking Washington to step in and give them relief by issuing centralized (and less stringent) regulations.[30] Cecil D. Andrus, who was both a Secretary of the Interior in the Carter administration and a Governor of Idaho, remarked in the 1980s that there was "no question I have more influence on the direction the country's going—not just my state—as a governor than I did in the Cabinet."[31] Finally, in response to a Supreme Court that had become noticeably less activist, some state supreme courts began to rely on provisions of their own state constitutions to judge state legislation, and began handing down rulings which extended individual rights beyond the boundaries established by the Supreme Court.[32] To cite one example, the state supreme court in Florida used a clause in that state's constitution guaranteeing a "right to privacy" to overturn a state law requiring parental notification in the event of an abortion performed on a minor.

The political situation of the 1980s featuring retrenchment by an overextended national government, thus presented the states with opportunities for rejuvenation. Most states and more than 100 cities established their own offices in Washington, which are almost like miniature versions of embassies that gather information and bargain in a type of intergovernmental diplomacy.[33] Moreover, state and local officials became increasingly well-organized, ambitious, and capable of influencing national policy. Organizations of governments were created such as the National Governors' Association, the National Conference of State Legislatures, the Council of State Governments, the U.S. Conference of Mayors, and the National League of Cities. These organizations, which represent general units of government, have Washington offices, keep members informed about what the national government is doing, and convey the position of local governments to federal officials. A large group of governors or mayors rarely agree on much; but when they do, their point of view is likely to be influential. For instance, not only did Congress draw its inspiration for the 1988 federal welfare reform from state legislation, but the National Governors Conference was actively involved in the drafting of the fed-

eral bill and in forging the Congressional coalition on its behalf.[34]

At the same time that state and local office-holders were regaining a certain degree of their predisposition to guard their positions, a shift occurred in the way the people viewed both the states and the national government. Some of the problems that afflicted the national government during the 1970s—such as the Vietnam War, the Watergate scandal and resignation of President Nixon, the mismanagement of the economy in the late 1970s, and the perceived failure of many Great Society programs—resulted in an increasing public disillusionment with the federal government. Simultaneously, the states were growing in competence and respectability. With some exceptions, state governments have made major reforms over the last three decades that have substantially improved their efficiency and professionalism. These reforms have included such things as constitutional revision, to streamline what were often long and detailed documents; reorganization of the executive branch to consolidate departments and to place more power in the hands of the governor and less in the hands of independent commissions; reduction in the number of elected executive officers (like treasurer, secretary of state, and superintendent of education); and a replacement of political patronage with civil service merit systems for selecting state employees. Additionally, the prestige and power of the office of governor has been upgraded in most states by increasing the staff assigned to the governor, placing responsibility for central budget preparation in the governor's hands, and expanding the power of the governor to veto legislation and issue executive orders.

Likewise, legislative capabilities have improved: more state legislatures meet at least annually and more meet year-around, legislative staffing has also improved, and legislators have assumed greater responsibility for the oversight of state government. Both governors' and legislators' salaries have been increased. And the longstanding stalemate between urban-based governors and rural-based legislators has been broken in more than a few states by the effects of federally-mandated decennial reapportionment of legislative districts; now the constituency which votes for the governor will be (in aggregate) approximately the same one that elects the legislature. (It is, of course, ironic that this federal requirement, which was criticized as an attack on federalism when it was pronounced by the Supreme Court in 1962, may have served in the long run to strengthen it.) Not all of these reforms, of course, have been implemented by all states, and some states have implemented hardly any. Nevertheless, taken as a whole, state governments have become vastly more professional, more competent, more creative, and less corrupt than they were even twenty years ago. In short, there is a "new breed" of governor and legislator, and they have largely succeeded in regaining the confidence of the people.[35] In 1972, citizens believed that they got more for their money at the federal level than at the state level by a margin of 39 to 18 percent (with 26 percent saying that local governments provided more for the money). By 1984, this had been reversed—27 percent said the state governments were more efficient, 35 percent said local governments, and only 24 percent said the federal government.[36]

Finally, while many Americans had always believed in decentralized government, and in fact feared concentration of power in Washington, they had also been repelled by the abuses of civil rights that had occurred under the cover of "states' rights." When desegregation finally prevailed, and the civil rights battles of the 1960s began to fade, it became more possible for Americans to judge the question of federalism on its philosophical and practical merits. Calls for greater power in the hands of the states were not automatically suspect, nor could those who wanted to centralize power in Washington necessarily justify further centralization by reference to civil rights (though this tactic was not completely foresworn).[37]

In short, the political defense of federalism was reinvigorated in the 1980s. This shift can be accounted for by changed political circumstances in Washington, renewed efforts by state and local officials to be a major force, and the revived affection of the people for their states, which the founders saw as so crucial. This is not to say that the states became more powerful than the national government, or that they became as powerful as they once were. They did not. Their improved position, though real, was also very relative to their status in the preceding decades.

Since the 1980s the trend toward devolution has subsided. The central government has made important gains since the Reagan presidency. Several federal programs have been enacted that expand the federal government's reach into areas that were once the responsibility of the states. In the process, the states have often seen their influence reduced and, in some cases, have been left with huge costs as a result of accommodating the new federal measures. For instance, the Americans with Disabilities Act, passed under George H. Bush, and George W. Bush's education plan both intrude into local prerogatives. In addition, environmental regulations passed under President Clinton have limited the states' control of their natural resources.

While the federal government has seen its power expanded in these significant ways, the states have also continued to gain power in some areas. The states were aided by welfare reform measures passed during the Clinton administration. These reforms gave the states significant flexibility in administering welfare programs to its citizens. Additionally, the Supreme Court gave the states a victory in *U.S. v. Lopez* in 1995. By striking down a federal law that bans the possession of hand guns near or in schools, the Court set a limit on the reach of the Commerce Clause and thus reserved this area of responsibility to the states.

It is, of course, far from clear whether the comeback by the states will last, or what forms it may take in the future. Most legal and structural defenses are no longer available, and what changed political circumstances can give, can later be taken away. Yet the states have retained control over at least one major factor in their comeback: their own competence, and by extension the trust the people are willing to place in them.

Policy Dilemmas of Federalism

Constitutional questions of federalism are of particular interest today given the current balance between the national government and the states. Several federalism issues significantly affect the lives of Americans and indicate that the nature of American federalism remains to be settled.

Social Issues

Among the most divisive issues in American politics today are the so-called "social issues," which include such inflammatory matters as school prayer, a right to die, and restrictions on abortion. While the content of these debates receives most of the attention, it is often intertwined with questions about the role of the federal government versus state and local governments. This is because many of these issues became controversial national issues only when the Supreme Court intervened and overturned a state or local law.

Abortion policy is an example. In 1973 only four states permitted "abortion on demand." State laws restricting or regulating abortion were often over one hundred years old. Under pressure from both women's rights activists and steadily changing social mores, enough states had loosened their restrictions that a trend toward liberalization was evident. The process of change was nevertheless slower than proponents desired and was spread very unevenly across the states. Pro-choice activists took their case to the courts, and in January 1973, the U.S. Supreme Court in *Roe v. Wade* ruled that laws restricting abortion in the first three months of pregnancy were unconstitutional. While the Court acknowledged that the states may have a "legitimate interest" in protecting potential life, it ruled that the mother's right to terminate her pregnancy is contained within a "right to privacy" implied (though not stated) in the Fourteenth Amendment which overrides such state interest, at least in the earlier stages of pregnancy. This decision had the effect of disallowing 46 state laws, and mandating, for all practical purposes, a uniform national policy of abortion on demand.

Pro-choice activists were pleased by this result, which obviated the need for further lobbying of the statehouses. But *Roe v. Wade* also had an unforeseen effect; by taking the issue out of the legislatures, where laws were being slowly, moderately, but steadily liberalized in what seemed to be the development of an incipient political consensus, the Court succeeded in polarizing the issue and energizing the pro-life movement. That movement took its battle back to the states (as well as to Congress), showing in certain respects the dynamism of the federal system. Rather than simply accepting what Justice Byron White had called in his dissent of *Roe* an "exercise of raw judicial power," many state legislatures resisted *Roe* by chipping away at its edges: prohibiting the use of public funds for abortion, requiring parental notification or consent for abortions performed on minors, and requiring that women seeking abortions be informed of all other options and of the possible side-effects of the procedure. Beginning in 1989, the Supreme Court modified its position and permitted states to proceed with some of these regulations of abortion (in *Webster v. Reproductive Health Services of Missouri*, 1989 and *Planned Parenthood v. Casey*, 1992). Debates continue in many states about what sorts of measures can be adopted and which ones are permissible under the Court's understanding of the Constitution.

Side by side with questions of policy (permitting or restricting abortion?) are questions of who should decide (the federal courts or the state legislatures?) and whether having a uniform national policy is more important than permitting the law to reflect the values and beliefs of diverse local majorities. It is this mix of problems which will continue to prove so explosive in the debate over abortion and the other "social issues."

Judicial Power

A related question is how far federal courts should go in interjecting themselves into state and local affairs. It is clearly the duty of federal courts to overturn state or local actions that they deem unconstitutional or that conflict with federal statutes. The founders regarded this power in the judiciary as essential if the national government was to be sufficiently strong.[38] The Constitution is the "supreme law of the land," and ever since *McCulloch v. Maryland* in 1819, the Supreme Court has asserted its right to uphold it against the states. There have been scores of cases in which the federal judiciary has protected Constitutional freedoms against state abuse—for example, *Brown v. Board of Education of Topeka, Kansas*, in which the Court in 1954 ordered school desegregation.

Two grounds for criticism of the federal courts have emerged in recent years, however, from supporters of federalism: first, that federal courts have taken advantage of their expanded scope of inquiry to overturn state and local laws that are not clearly unconstitutional, but that merely conflict with the policy preferences of certain judges; and second that federal judges have overstepped their bounds and gone from constitutional interpretation to usurpation of legislative and executive functions at the state and local level.

What is clear is that the degree of federal judicial supervision of the normal activities of state and local governments, has increased enormously. It is commonplace today for any major piece of state legislation touching on rights or equal protection to be challenged one way or another in federal courts. In recent years many federal judges have not only overturned state or local actions, but ordered particular policies as remedies; some have gone even further, taking control of implementation of these policies. School desegregation cases are one example. In cities such as Boston, Detroit, and Denver, federal judges have literally taken over nominal operation of the school systems to ensure implementation of their desegregation plans. In another instance, Federal judge Frank Johnson ordered the state of Alabama to make a series of specific improvements to its mental health facilities, and implied that he might seize Alabama state lands and sell them to pay for the improvements if the state did not provide the necessary funds on its own. And in Kansas City, Missouri, a federal judge used his power to order a local tax increase to pay for a school program that he deemed Constitutionally necessary.[39]

Actions like these by the federal courts have met with the approval of citizens who favor activism on behalf of what they consider to be Constitutional issues of civil and individual rights, and with outrage by citizens who believe that federalism and localism are under attack by an unelected and unaccountable judiciary. The role of the federal judiciary in our federal system is one of the most highly contested institutional issues in contemporary politics.

Federal Mandates

When the federal government makes its grants conditional on certain actions of the recipient government, these conditions are called "mandates." There are many kinds of federal mandates, such as requirements that federally supported transportation facilities be accessible to the handicapped, that construction projects not damage the environment, and that state and local hiring practices meet federal guidelines. All mandates, of course, represent efforts by the national government to have its goals achieved through other governments. Mandates may be an expected part of an intergovernmental bargain, but too many of them are certain to cause political controversy. Between 1956 and 1960, the federal government imposed only four new mandates, whereas in a brief two-year period between 1976 and 1978, 413 were created.[40] More recently, the Congressional Budget Office estimated that federal regulations imposed on local governments between 1983 and 1990 cost up to $12.7 billion. The National Association of Towns and Townships estimated the cost of the four year period between 1994 and 1998 to be $54 billion.

Cost is not the only issue. Recent mandates have increasingly tended to become quite broad and only indirectly related to the purpose of the grant. For example, federal highway funds can now be denied to states that do not have a minimum drinking age of 21 (on the argument that drunk driving affects safety on federal highways) and states that have failed to meet pollution standards set forth in the Clean Air Act (on the argument that air pollution is largely produced by vehicles traveling on federal highways). In neither case are the conditions directly related to federal highway construction or maintenance. Furthermore, in many cases (such as mandates requiring handicapped access to public buildings), the mandate is tremendously expensive to implement—and Congress does not supply the necessary funds, but merely threatens to cut off funds to the original project if the conditions are not met.

State and local officials have become more and more alarmed at the increase of these mandates. In 1994 Republicans included as part of their "platform" for the congressional election a pledge to end further unfunded mandates to state and local governments. The legislation Congress passed in 1995 has done far less than this—how it will work is still unclear—but it at least offers procedural means by which the issue of the cost of any federal mandate should become part of any congressional debate. All proposed mandates of any size must now have cost estimates made by the Congressional Budget Office, and members have ways of objecting to the implementation of new mandates. Political conflicts like these are the inevitable consequence when different governments have to deal with each other so extensively, as is demonstrated by the fact that states themselves impose as many or more mandates on their local governments as the federal government does.

The outlines of the conflict are clear. Grants are funds given by the national government, and mandates can ensure that those funds are used according to its intentions; this seems only reasonable. Further, mandates are one of the most effective tools the national government possesses to pursue national objectives. But mandates can also be arbitrary, made without regard to the actual conditions that state and local governments face and without deference to reasonable claims for the autonomy of those governments. Mandates can smack of centralized high-handedness, and—especially when largely unrelated to the actual grant—can impose unfair burdens on state and local governments and taxpayers.

The Supreme Court has generally upheld such mandates as Constitutional. But in a recent case, *Printz v. United States* (1997), the Court held that a portion of the Brady Act which directed state and local law enforcement officers to conduct background checks on gun purchasers was unconstitutional, because the federal government simply commandeered state and local executive officials and assigned them a federal administrative function. As Justice Scalia remarked, "Such commands are fundamentally incompatible with our constitutional system of dual sovereignty." Still, it is highly unlikely that the Court alone will go much further in limiting the federal government. Accordingly, a defense of the prerogatives of state and local governments can not be based on a strategy that relies primarily on the courts to limit the reach of federal power. The Constitutional question in this area will be decided largely in the political process—by the skill of state and local governments in protecting themselves through negotiation with the national government and through the willingness of voters to elect representatives who give some weight to the claims of federalism.

The Central Question

The above examples are instances of specific dilemmas facing the federal system. Some may be resolved, or at least mitigated, in a relatively short period of time, while others are likely to remain, or even intensify, for a long time. But we should be careful not to confuse specific policy questions with the sum total of federalism. The ultimate question for federalism lies not in any particular area of policy, but—as for the last 200 years—in the relationship between the national government and the states. Is federalism as a principle worth defending, or is it an anachronism that stifles national progress? Is decentralized government good or bad? In the debate over this fundamental constitutional question, there are arguments that can be made on both sides.

Advantages of Vigorous State Governments

Safeguard of Liberty A major argument for maintaining strong states is that decentralized government, along with the separation of powers, is a major safeguard against the emergence of a tyrannical concentration of power. As Madison said in a famous passage from *Federalist 51*:

> In the compound republic of America, the power surrendered by the people is first divided between two distinct governments, and then the portion allotted to each subdivided among distinct and separate departments. Hence a double security arises to the rights of the people. The different governments will control each other, at the same time that it will be controlled by itself.

While the possibility that the states might physically resist central authority is now ended, strong state governments provide an alternative source of power and influence to central authority in Washington.

Proximity to the People State and local governments are in many respects closer to the people than the national government. For a country of 250 million, there are 537 elected officials at the national level; each member of the U.S. House of Representatives represents a district of over half a million people. Yet there are over 500,000 state and local officeholders. While a few states like California have legislative districts almost as large as Congressional districts, most state legislators represent districts that are much, much smaller than their federal counterparts (for instance, Georgia, with districts of 30,000, or in the extreme case, New Hampshire, with districts of only 2,500!). Furthermore, despite the increased professionalization, state legislators and local officials often have other jobs in the community as well and fit the mold of the "citizen politician" much more than U.S. Representatives or Senators. Finally, the seats of state and local government are physically closer to the people than is Washington, D.C., making government more accessible. Local government is, in many ways, the epitome of democratic self-government.

For many of the same reasons, state and local governments promote political participation and enhance qualities of citizenship among the people. The 500,000 state and local officeholders are able to participate in decisions having a real impact on their communities; the hundreds of thousands of citizens each year who are called to local jury duty likewise have the opportunity actually to participate in the process of governing. And, unlike the federal government, numerous states and local jurisdictions have provisions for citizen-initiated referenda and recall elections. While voter turnout on the average is far lower for state and local elections than for national elections, the tasks citizens perform in state and local government generally provide opportunities for far more significant forms of participation.

Diversity Governments below the national level are capable of instituting a variety of policies that are appropriate to the diversity of circumstances which exist in a country as large as the United States. For example, it is doubtful that a single national policy on education would be equally appropriate to an inner-city school in Boston, a suburban school outside of Houston, and a one-room schoolhouse in Alaska. Much the same could be said about any national policy for providing police protection or housing.

Decentralization can therefore result in more effective policies that can be tailored more closely to fit local circumstances. Effectiveness aside, citizens of varying locales hold a wide array of beliefs and values, and a system of federalism permits the values of local majorities to be reflected in policy. Thus, New Yorkers would not be forced to live under the same pornography laws as citizens of Utah. This arrangement has the advantage both of permitting the maximum freedom for communities to define their own standards and of reducing the strains that would result if a single standard on every question were dictated from Washington.

Innovation Closely related to the ability of state and local governments to better meet local circumstances is the ability of those governments to test solutions to a variety of social and economic problems. Thus the states act as "laboratories," from which other states and the federal government can draw lessons. One example is that of welfare reform, where over two-thirds of states are experimenting with some form of "workfare" program that required welfare recipients to work. These state programs ultimately served as models for federal welfare legislation. This is by no means an isolated, modern case. The defense of the idea of the states as laboratories goes back to Madison himself, who counted as a chief advantage of federalism "the many opportunities and chances [it affords] in the local legislatures for salutary innovations by some which may be adopted by others; or for important experiments, which, if unsuccessful, will be of limited injury."[41]

National Effectiveness Strong states in certain ways can actually make the federal government more effective. States provide relief to the national government by handling functions which, if they had to be decided in Washington, would overload the "circuits" of the Congress, presidents, and courts and would overwhelm the federal bureaucracy. Moreover, the states provide a training ground for national officeholders; a little over half of all members of the U.S. House of Representatives today once were state legislators, and 16 out of our nation's 41 presidents were governors first, most recently Bill Clinton and George W. Bush.

Advantages of Centralization

Just Government States may be more susceptible to tyranny of the majority than the national government. The heart of this argument can be found in *Federalist* 10, which defended the creation of a relatively strong national government by maintaining that a "large republic" would contain such a diversity of factions that they would be unable to unite in permanent majorities to oppress the minority. This situation contrasted with that in "small republics" (read states) that contained far fewer factions and thus were more likely to fall under the sway of a factional majority.

This argument in *Federalist* 10 was not one against the existence of states (which are an important part of the diversity of the large republic), but against states having too much power uncontrolled by a higher level of government. One of the principal reasons in the movement for the Constitution was a fear that many states were endangering the rights of their people and therefore needed to be restrained by a more moderate national government. As recently as the 1960s, the federal government could point to the systematic mistreatment of black citizens in many states. Ultimately, civil rights were protected only after the federal government stepped in and took the issue out of the state's hands.

Equality A more centralized system of government fosters greater equality. In a centralized system there would be one law applied to all citizens within the nation, rather than a myriad of differing state and local ordinances. One of the arguments in defense of *Roe v. Wade* has been that it ensured a single nationwide standard of abortion law. Likewise, proponents of greater centralization have urged that the federal government institute a single national standard for chartering corporations, which is currently handled by the states, in the belief that competition and innovation among states may lead to inadequate regulation as states try to attract businesses.[42] In terms of social welfare policy, a centralized system could ensure equal treatment of those receiving aid, unlike today when Aid to Families with Dependent Children payments range from $114 per month in Alabama to $580 a month in California. A more powerful national government might be able to pursue policies consciously designed to equalize various regions of the country.

Competence When the founders established the "compound republic," they expected that the national government would attract public servants of a higher quality than those in the states.[43] Even with the recent rise in competence in the states, the level of competence of state bureaucracies does not, in general, match that of the federal government. Certain programs can accordingly be far better managed by the federal government, and there are often instances in which citizens prefer the federal government to step in to handle certain problems.

Scope of Problems Issues requiring governmental attention have changed dramatically in the last 200 years—and even the last 50 years. The advent of new communications and transportation technologies have made the nation (and the world) much smaller, leading to greater interconnectedness among the states and among the nations of the world. For example, pollution and other environmental problems do not always stop at the boundaries of local jurisdictions. Interstate commerce has vastly expanded. The fact that so many problems are now of national or international scope means that states or localities acting alone may be insufficient.

Policy Activism Those who favor active governmental intervention in social or economic questions may oppose a federal system because of its fragmentation of power. It is easier to gain passage of a program once, at the federal level, than to attempt to have the same program approved by fifty different state governments or innumerable local governments. The difficulty in successfully lobbying fifty statehouses has been one of the driving forces behind the expansion of federal grant mandates. One sign of the revival of the states in the 1980s as centers of significant policymaking is that lobbying undertaken at the state level by various interest groups has increased substantially. Such was not the preference of many interest groups, which still see Washington as "policy maker of first resort," but was a pragmatic response to the decline of activist government at the national level.[44]

National Unity Finally, proponents of a centralized system can point to the disruption and chaos that can occur if local governments become too powerful or important. Our own Civil War is perhaps the most extreme example of this danger, but contemporary problems in Canada's federal system—where Quebec is agitating for greater autonomy even at the risk of the breakup of Canada as a nation—shows that even today, decentralized systems carry within them the latent potential for centrifugal forces to spin out of control. Such a breakdown of national unity could endanger not only domestic tranquility but the nation's security in the world. In this sense, a strong central government is urged not in spite of the local diversity of America but because of it, as one of the few forces that can provide a common point of reference for all Americans.

It is impossible to weigh with precision all the advantages and disadvantages of centralization and arrive at a commonly accepted appraisal. There is something to be said on both sides. Federalism fits the logic of this analysis, for it is not an "either-or" proposition. There are degrees of centralization or decentralization, and not only does federalism contain elements of each, but it is flexible enough to move in one direction or another to achieve particular advantages in different area. There is nevertheless a limit beyond which centralization (or decentralization) may go, after which the state (or federal) government loses its ability to deal effectively with the other government and its capacity to protect its interests over the long run. It is at this point that fed-

eralism itself as a constitutional doctrine is threatened.

Conclusion

There are some 83,000 different governments in the United States today, ranging from the federal government to the tiniest village or school district. These governments have become tied together by fiscal, political, and administrative forces made possible, but no less controversial, by the founders' constitutional framework. Since the time of the founders, when the Constitution established a federal system of national and state governments, Americans have struggled with the issues of intergovernmental relations: how our governments deal with each other, which ones have responsibilities and jurisdiction over which sort of problems, and how conflicts among them are resolved.

The founders foresaw three major defenses for the federal system: legal, in the constitutional enumeration of the powers of the national government; structural, in the constitutional role given to the states in several areas; and political, in the ambition of state and local officials and the affection of the people for the governments closest to them.

In the earliest years of the republic, these defenses of a federal system worked, no doubt too well, to the advantage of the states. The notion of two governments operating in separate spheres dominated thinking about intergovernmental relations, beyond what many of the founders themselves seemed to have in mind. The national government's role, especially, was quite limited. The Civil War, apart from adjusting certain powers of the national government, put to an end any idea of the nation as a mere confederation. The twentieth century has seen the rise of the national government on a grand scale, along with the beginning of a breakdown of key elements of the defense of the states role in the federal system. National influence has particularly accelerated during periods of crisis or unusual policy initiatives such as the New Deal and Great Society years.

Today, the primary defense remaining for the states is neither legal (with the faltering of the doctrine of enumerated powers) nor structural (with direct election of U.S. Senators), but political. Insofar as the states improved their position in the 1980s, they were able to do so because of changed political circumstances in Washington that favored decentralized government and because of a renewed political vigor in the states themselves. Since the 1980s however, devolution has slowed. It remains to be seen whether the states will be able to secure their gains or whether their resurgence will prove transient.

The arguments in favor of increased centralization are part of a long tradition; indeed, our federal system is the result of a constitutional arrangement that sought greater, not less, centralization than had been present in the prior Articles of Confederation. Yet the original design also provided for a strong role for the states. The guarantee that it provides against tyrannical concentration of power, the protection of diversity and local self-government, the possibilities for citizen participation, and the examples of innovation that have come from the states have all been fundamental advantages of a federal system for the last 200 years.

Because the Constitution guarantees the existence of the states, some sort of federal arrangement will always exist. But whether that arrangement is built around the actual spirit of federalism—a national government supreme in its own sphere but limited in its scope and respectful of the legitimate prerogatives of viable states—or around a spirit that accepts no limits to national action and treats the states only as administrative units, depends on more than the Constitution. It depends also on which tools we use to build and maintain federalism, and on how skillful we are at using those tools. A political defense of federalism will require continued attention by citizens to the issues of federalism, a willingness by our elected leaders and unelected administrators in Washington to exercise forbearance in their relations with lower levels of government, and vigor and competence by our elected leaders in state and local government. It may also be the case that a truly successful defense of federalism over the long term may require us to reinvigorate some of the legal or structural defenses that have fallen into disuse, particularly the notion of enumerated powers, despite the inherent difficulty in defining them.

The challenge of how to run a compound republic in an era of interdependence will be a major question occupying citizens and political leaders in the years—and, undoubtedly, decades—ahead.

Chapter 4 Notes

1. See Martin Diamond, "What the Founders Meant by Federalism," in Robert A. Goldwin, ed., *A Nation of States* (Chicago: Rand McNally, 1961).
2. For instance, see Madison's *Notes,* June 6 and June 20. Speeches by James Wilson.
3. See Joseph Cronin, "The Federal Takeover: Should the Junior Partner Run the Firm?" in *Federalism at the Crossroads* (Washington, D.C.: George Washington University Press, 1976).
4. Susan W. Torrence, *Grass Roots Government* (Washington D.C.: Luce, 1974), pp. 6–7, 10–19.
5. U.S. Bureau of Census, *1977 Census of Governments* (Washington, D.C.: U.S. Government Printing Office, 1977), p. 2.
6. Ohio Supreme Court, 1857, quoted in Susan W. Torrence, *Grass Roots Government,* p. 6.
7. Other states besides New England also have created townships, but these units for the most part are mere subdivisions of rural counties and perform few functions.
8. Madison's *Notes,* June 21. Speech by Doctor Johnson, spelling modernized.
9. Federalist 39. There are many other statements in *The Federalist* to the same effect, although it should be noted that the authors were making every effort to allay fears that the national government might threaten the states.
10. Letter from the Federal Farmer, October 9, 1987 included in Ralph Ketcham, ed., *The Anti-Federalist Papers and the Constitutional Convention Debates* (New York: NAL Penguin, Inc., 1986), p. 268.
11. Federalist 17 and 28.
12. Veto message on the Bonus Bill March 3, 1817. In James Richardson, ed., *A Compilation of the Messages of the Presidents, 1789–1797,* vol. 1, pp. 584–85.
13. David B. Walker, *Toward a Functioning Federalism* (Cambridge, Mass.: Winthrop, 1981), p. 50.
14. Cited in Eric Foner, Reconstruction: America's Unfinished Revolution 1863–67 (New York: Harper and Row, 1988), p. 24.
15. The Civil Rights Cases 1883, 109 U.S.3. Majority opinion by Justice Bradley.
16. James Q. Wilson, *Political Organizations* (New York: Basic Books, 1973), pp. 143–4.
17. William H. Riker, "The Senate and American Federalism," *American Political Science Review,* vol. 49, no. 3 (June 1955).
18. Daniel J. Elazar, *The American Partnership: Intergovernmental Cooperation in the Nineteenth Century* (Chicago: University of Chicago Press, 1962).
19. Massachusetts v. Mellon *and Frothingham v. Mellon.*

20. South Dakota v. Dole (1987).

21. The federal power to reach these issues in the Civil Rights Act of 1964 was claimed under the commerce power, not primarily the fourteenth amendment. This legislation was upheld by the Supreme Court in 1964 in the cases of *Katzenbach v. McClung* and *Heart of Atlanta Motel v. United States.* In *Katzenbach,* the Court ruled that the interstate commerce power was sufficient to force a restaurant to serve blacks, since the restaurant had purchased 46 percent of its meat from a local supplier who had procured it from out of state.

22. Daniel P. Moynihan, *Maximum Feasible Misunderstanding: Community Action and the War on Poverty* (New York: Basic Books, 1969).

23. Advisory Commission on Intergovernmental Relations, *The Federal Role in the Federal System: The Dynamics of Growth—A Crisis of Confidence and Competence,* Report A-3077, July 1980.

24. Harold L. Bunce, "The Community Development Block Grant Formula: An Evaluation," *Urban Affairs Quarterly,* vol. 14, no. 4, 1979; see also Bernard J. Frieden and Marshall Kaplan, *The Politics of Neglect: Urban Aid from Model Cities to Revenue Sharing* (Cambridge, Mass.: M.I.T. Press, 1975).

25. Leonard Robins, "The Impact of Converting Categorical into Block Grants: The Lessons from the 314(d) Block Grant in the Partnership for Health Act," *Publius,* vol. 6, no. 1, 1976. General revenue sharing was really only a relatively minor part of the federal aid many governments received, and thus did not fundamentally emancipate the recipients from federal oversight. In addition, those governments, especially small local ones, which had not been receiving much support from the national government before the onset of revenue sharing were more rather than less reliant on the feds for what they did.

26. Richard S. Williamson, *Federalism in Perspective: A Republican Monograph* (Washington, D.C.: 1982).

27. Executive Order 12612 of October 26, 1987: Federalism. *Federal Register,* vol. 52, no. 210.

28. Martha Derthick, "The Enduring Features of American Federalism," *The Brookings Review,* Summer 1989, p. 38.

29. Richard P. Nathan, "Federalism, the `Great Composition,'" in Anthony King, ed., *The New American Political System,* 2nd ed., (Washington, D.C.: American Enterprise Institute, 1990), pp. 242–243.

30. Susan Bartlett Foote, "Administrative Preemption: An Experiment in Regulatory Federalism," *Virginia Law Review* 70:1429 (1984).

31. David S. Broder, "Nation's Capital in Eclipse as Pride and Power Slip Away," *Washington Post,* February 18, 1990.

32. Shirley S. Abrahamson and Diane S. Gutman, "New Federalism: State Constitutions and State Courts," in Burke Marshall, ed., A *Workable Government?* (New York: Norton, 1987).

33. National Journal, Sept. 6, 1981, pp. 1485–1487.

34. Julie Rovner, "Welfare Reform: The Issue That Bubbled Up from the States to Capitol Hill," *Governing,* December 1988.

35. Larry J. Sabato, *Goodbye to Good-time Charlie* (Washington, D.C.: Congressional Quarterly Press, 1983).

36. Changing Public Attitudes on Governments and *Taxes* (Washington, D.C.: Advisory Commission on Intergovernmental Affairs, 1984), p. 1.

37. See Martha Derthick, "American Federalism: Madison's Middle Ground," *Public Administration Review,* vol. 47, no. 1, January–February 1987, p. 72.

38. Federalist 80; *Federalist* 81.

39. For detailed discussion of several such instances, see Philip J. Cooper, *Hard Judicial Choices* (New York: Oxford University Press, 1988).

40. Catherine H. Lovell, *Federal and State Mandating on Local Governments: Exploration of Issues and Impacts,* final report to the National Science Foundation, June 20, 1979, p. 72; Catherine H. Lovell and Charles Tobin, "The Mandate Issue," *Public Administration Review,* vol. 41, no. 3, 1981.

41. Letter to Edward Livingston, July 10, 1822.

42. William L. Cary, "Federalism and Corporate Law: Reflections Upon Delaware," *The Yale Law Journal,* March 1974.

43. Federalist 10; also *Federalist* 27.

44. The Transformation in American Politics: Implications for Federalism (Washington, D.C.: Advisory Commission on Intergovernmental Relations, 1986), pp. 234–243; "Lobbyists File in with Welcome Mats as State Capitols take Bigger Role," *Wall Street Journal,* May 30, 1990, p. A14.

Part Two

The Public and the Government: Intermediary Institutions and Electoral Politics

5

Public Opinion

CHAPTER CONTENTS

When public opinion decides that something has to change, it changes. This was the explanation given by Congressman Jim Jones from Oklahoma following the enactment of Ronald Reagan's first budget in 1981, which called for a sharp reduction in projected federal spending. Although many in Washington had earlier doubted such cuts were possible, President Reagan managed to awaken a tremendous degree of support for his basic proposal. With public opinion on his side, the President succeeded, for better or worse, in accomplishing the "impossible."

But did this vote prove Congressman Jones correct when he claimed that public opinion, what the public thinks about the issues, "decided" public policy? Only partly. Not all major policy changes stem from shifts in public opinion, and on some occasions policy changes may be initiated without majority support. In fact, at the very same time that President Reagan was pushing for his budget reductions, he was also calling for a controversial tax-cut that most Americans at the time, according to opinion polls, did not support.

The relationship between government and public opinion is a complex one. One aspect of the American system recognizes and approves government's responsiveness to public opinion. As a form of popular government, a representative system is supposed to be sensitive to the public's wishes. Elections and frequent contacts between the public and its representatives are designed to guarantee that responsiveness. But representative government is also based on the premise that elected officials are entitled not only to attempt to persuade public opinion to their point of view, but also to exercise their own discretion and to act on specific occasions contrary to public demands. As Edmund Burke pointed out, "Your representative owes you, not his industry only, but his judgment; and he betrays, instead of serving you, if he sacrifices it to your opinion." A Congress or president that always followed public opinion would probably earn the contempt of the American people. Americans tend to look upon those who rely upon the public opinion polls to guide policy as being without moral purpose and easily swayed. Also, Republican government implies a guarantee of the sanctity of certain fundamental rights, which government is obliged to protect, regardless of public opinion.

There is, then, a built-in tension in America's system of government between a "democratic" idea that emphasizes a more rapid transfer of the public will into public policy and what is sometimes called a "representative" idea, which stresses discretion for elected officials and a degree of insulation from the pressures of public opinion. These two ideas have often been at odds in attempts to shape the character of our political institutions. The founders, while recognizing a place for the democratic idea, emphasized the representative idea, which they wove into the fabric of the Constitution. Since the founding, more weight has been given, at least in theory, to the democratic idea, especially in the influential twentieth-century movements of Progressivism (1908–1916) and Reform (1968–1976). Today, the national government retains its strongly representative character: all political power is vested in elected or appointed officials and no federal government decision is made directly by the public. Many state governments, by contrast, make extensive use of the initiative and referendum.

In this chapter, we shall look at how public opinion is measured and survey public attitudes on some of the major dimensions of political life. We shall then turn to the question of how opinions are formed and conclude by discussing the role that public opinion plays—and should play—in a representative system of government. This last question returns us to the fundamental constitutional question of who governs.

Measuring Public Opinion

Americans are probably the most polled people in the world. A week does not pass without the news media reporting on one or another public opinion poll. These surveys are supposed to inform Americans about public opinion on a variety of public questions, be it what people think of potential candidates for the presidency, the public's support for putting or maintaining troops in a foreign country, or people's views on a constitutional question such as a "right to die." Polls have become so much a part of modern politics that many equate the concept of public opinion with what is reported in polls.

Yet polling as we know it today was a twentieth century development. It came into use in the 1930s, and valid scientific national samples were not commonly used until the 1950s. To identify public opinion only with what is measured in polls would lead to the untenable conclusion that public opinion did not exist before the advent of modern polling. In fact, not only did earlier politicians speak regularly of public opinion, but many of the classic treatments of the subject—by Alexis de Tocqueville, James Bryce, and Walter Lippmann—were written before modern polling was developed.

Public opinion in earlier times was assessed by means other than polls, and these techniques still remain important today. Politicians constantly gauge public opinion in their contacts with citizens, in their interpretation of election results, and, at the outer limits, in their sense of what the community either demands or will not tolerate. One campaign worker noted that the Congressman he worked for counted how many people waved to him and how many gave him a "thumbs down" sign as he walked down Main Street as an indicator of his level of support in a certain community. These methods, unscientific as they may be, remain highly useful, sometimes far more so than polls, because they focus on opinion not merely as an abstract response to a hypothetical question but as an actual or potential force that can come into play in political life. The older conception of public opinion conceived of it as a demand for action emerging from the public or as a likely reaction that would emerge if a certain policy or law were adopted. Many are the members of Congress who still prefer to think of public opinion in these terms and who prefer to assess it by relying on their contacts with constituents and community leaders.

Polling represents one way of discovering public opinion. It is a technique that has brought new range and much greater accuracy to the study of the topic. But pollsters are among the first to acknowledge that certain dimensions of public opinion can only be studied by other techniques, such as in-depth interviews, focus groups (a small group of people invited to discuss issues), or observations of political behavior.

What these latter techniques lack in "science," they sometimes make up for in depth and richness. To talk with citizens on the street corner or to see them, angry or enthusiastic, at a rally or a convention may provide a "feel" for the nuances or intensity of opinion that no poll can offer.

Not only are there limits to what polls can study, but polls can also at times be misleading. Polling is not itself a science, but a human activity based on certain scientific (mathematical) principles. Without going into all its techniques here, it is important at least to be familiar with the basic principles of polling and with a few issues concerning the use and abuse of polls.

"How can pollsters claim to know what the public thinks when they have never asked me or anyone I know?" This question has probably occurred to many people, because, despite all the reports of what the public is thinking, very few people are actually polled on any particular issue. Polls are based on the statistical principle known as sampling, according to which the characteristics of an entire population can be known by surveying a relatively small number of randomly selected cases. Take a barrel, for example, that is filled with twenty-five thousand marbles, 60 percent of which are black and 40 percent white. Shake the barrel (to ensure that the marbles are all mixed up) and then pull out a sample of 500 marbles. In 95 out of 100 such drawings, the percentage of black balls and white balls in the sample will be within 3 percent of the actual total in the barrel, that is, between 57 and 63 percent black marbles and 37 and 43 percent white marbles. Increase the size of the sample of marbles drawn—say to six hundred—and your chances of error and range of error will diminish, but not by very much.

With a few technical adjustments, the same basic principle is employed in opinion polls. Most national polls contact no more than 1,500 people. This is enough for most purposes, although conclusions from these samples about the opinions of subgroups in the population (southerners, old people, blacks, etc.) will be subject to greater error. Contacting more people, if the sample is not random, will not improve the accuracy of the poll. The classic case that illustrates this point occurred during the 1936 election. The *Literary Digest* conducted a poll with a huge sample of over 2 million people, drawing the names randomly from telephone books and automobile registrations. The poll predicted a sweeping victory (57 percent to 43 percent) for Alf Landon over Franklin Roosevelt. The actual result was a landslide for Roosevelt, with 61 percent of the vote. What happened? The answer today is obvious. The random sample was not really a random selection of the whole population. In 1936, many poor people had neither telephones nor cars, so that the sample was heavily skewed in the direction of wealthier persons. It was also subject to *selection bias*, because the survey was mailed and therefore relied on self-motivated individuals, usually with strong opinion, to return the survey. Only 22% of those who were sent surveys responded. Since class voting proved so important in 1936—as it had not been, incidentally, in several previous elections, when the *Literary Digest* poll proved quite accurate—the 1936 results were wrong by more than 19 percent.

Even when the samples are truly random, however, polls can be inaccurate. One set of problems derives from the fact that people are not marbles. On occasion, those interviewed may conceal their opinions or give false responses, either deliberately or unconsciously. We know, for example, that the number of people who claim in polls to vote exceeds the number who actually turn out to vote. Many people no doubt feel embarrassed to admit, even to a pollster, their failure to be good citizens. For reasons of mistrust or suspicion of pollsters, or uneasiness of admitting to holding an unpopular or socially undesirable opinion, people sometimes hide or distort their views. This distortion occurs more in some circumstances than others, more among some groups than others, and more in certain countries than others. Thus, polls in the United States after the terrorist attacks of September 11, 2001 showed that a significant majority of people claimed to have voted for President Bush in the last election when he actually received only 48% of the votes cast. In short, the accuracy of polling is affected substantially by the subculture and culture in which the polls are conducted.

A second set of problems relates to the way questions are worded. A poll (at best) gives evidence of opinion about the question asked, not necessarily about the issue itself. For example, two leading polling firms sought during the same week in 1993 to determine the public's view on the participation of homosexuals in the military, which became a major national issue at the beginning of the first Clinton administration. The *Los Angeles Times* asked the following question, "Do you approve or disapprove of allowing openly homosexual men and women to serve in the armed forces of the United States?" The position opposing participation had a slight edge (47%) over the position favoring participation (45%). *Time/CNN* put the question another way, "Do you think that gays and lesbians should be banned from the military or not?" In this instance, the position favoring allowing homosexuals in the military ("not banning") had a clear majority (57%) as against 37% opposing their participation. Clearly, what was reported as majority "opinion" in this case depended on how the question was posed.[1] Ambiguous results of this kind are not infrequent. Responses also vary because of the tone of the interviewer, the setting or method of surveying, and the perceived social desirability of the answers. Carefully worded questions and evidence from a number of polls can, of course, provide a much surer indication of opinion. But it is always wise to remain skeptical of assertions of what "the public thinks" about an issue without knowing exactly what question was asked.

A third set of problems relates not so much to the accuracy of polls but to what it is that they are actually measuring. Are all opinions measured by polls "real" opinions? Polls that pose questions on matters that at the moment are hypothetical may accurately give the public's response, but that response might be quite different under circumstances when the issue became a real matter of debate. For instance, people may say that they support "universal" healthcare but change their mind when they realize that this might raise their taxes. Another factor, which applies especially to primaries, is that many voters are tentative in their decisions ("soft" in pollsters' jargon) or are waiting until the last moment to make up their minds. In this situation, the poll itself may not be inaccurate, but rather the situation is in flux. Often, polls

TABLE 5.1
Final Poll Results: Election of 2000

Polling Firm	Gore	Bush	Nader
ACTUAL RESULTS	*48*	*48*	*3*
Zogby	48	46	5
CBS	45	44	4
CNN/USA Today/Gallup	48	46	4
NBC/Wall Street Journal	44	47	3
ABC/Washington Post	45	48	3
FOX/Opinion Dynamics	43	43	3
Rasmussen	49	40	4

Source: www.pollingreport.com; www.ncpp.org

report "opinions" about matters that citizens may have only casually considered. In this case, the reported opinion in effect becomes a response that is created or generated by the poll.

For the opinion measured in most polls, it is well to recall that there is no objective or external test of their validity. Polls that measure the public's view on a question such as Social Security reform, for example, deal with matters on which there is no public vote. Confirmation of a poll's accuracy in such cases can only come from repeated results in a number of different polls. For only one type of poll, in fact, is there regularly a genuine "test" of poll results: an election poll.

Despite these obstacles, the major American polling firms have had a fairly good record of accurately stating the range of the vote in presidential elections. For example, in sixteen presidential elections since 1936, the differences between Gallup's final pre-election survey figures and the actual election results was 2.2 percent and, since 1960, only 1.5 percent (See Table 5.1). Polling organizations consider the problems discussed here and more news organizations now employ established procedures for reporting poll results, such as citing the question asked and reminding the audience of the margin of error.

(Consider that in close elections, like the election of 2000, the margin of error in the polls is sometimes larger than the distance between the candidates.) But it is still possible for polls to be inaccurate or misleading, and it is up to those who read these polls to be on guard against facile generalizations of what the public supposedly thinks. Strictly speaking, no poll is a prediction; it is only a measurement of the state of public sentiment at a given moment. It is good only for the day on which it is taken.

Polls have provided those who study politics with a better understanding of public opinion and how it influences public policy. How polls are used by political actors is a different matter. Polls would seem to offer the clear benefit that politicians can, where they wish, take into consideration public feeling without the danger of completely misperceiving it or speaking only for those who clamor the loudest. For this reason most major political leaders regularly consult polls in order to keep informed about trends in the public's thinking. (Presidents Carter, Reagan, and Clinton made use of their campaign pollsters as political advisors.) Yet polls also present a certain danger. Politicians are more tempted to follow public opinion instead of exercising independent judgment. Especially in political campaigns, many worry that candidates today craft images of themselves and gear their messages to fit what pollsters find the people want.

Polls have also affected the general character of democratic politics. They not only measure public opinion, but also increase its influence on the governing process. The very fact that people can claim to know with some accuracy what the public is thinking alters political calculations. To take one example, the daily readings of opinion in the aftermath of the terrorist attacks at the World Trade Center showed strong support for President Bush and clearly strengthened the President's hand in dealing with Congress and foreign nations. Of course, politicians still can act contrary to majority sentiment, and there is probably a tendency in news accounts to overestimate the influence of polls on decision making. Those in high positions know perfectly well that they will be judged by the public not by how popular a policy is at the moment, but on how well it will prove to work by the time of the next election. Still, polling has likely narrowed somewhat public officials' assessment of the discretion they can normally exercise.

Constitutional Opinion

Public opinion may be defined in the broadest sense as the opinions people hold respecting politics and government, in particular opinions held strongly enough that they either are (or could become) the basis for political action. The last element has been added to emphasize the idea that public opinion should be thought of not as a fiction measured by a poll, but as something real that could potentially be brought to bear in political life.

Public opinion exists in relation to attitudes people hold on three levels of politically relevant beliefs: (1) fundamental constitutional questions, (2) the general direction of governmental policy, and (3) specific policy issues of the day and opinions about politicians in office or running for office.

The first and deepest level is "constitutional opinion," which some scholars call "political culture."[2] Opinion here deals with the public's views on the nature of the political order—questions about the ends of society and the best form of government—and on basic premises about human reality insofar as they impinge on politics, such as views about religion and about the sources of validation of truth and error.

The study of constitutional opinion is nothing new. The founders were attentive to its significance because they knew popular government rested ultimately on opinion. In drafting the Declaration, Jefferson consciously sought to give expression to the deepest sentiments of the "American mind," so that the document could serve as a point of reference of the nation's guiding principles. The authors of the Constitution were even more explicit. Because "all governments rest on opinion," it was essential to inculcate a degree of reverence for the principles and formal arrangements of the system: "the most rational government will not find it a superfluous advantage to have the prejudices of the community on its side." (*Federalist* 49)

Because constitutional opinions deal with the animating ideas of the system, they affect not just a single issue, but a whole range of policies. Struggles to maintain or transform constitutional opinion therefore make up some of the most critical moments in American history. It was Abraham Lincoln who best explained the importance of constitutional opinion in 1858:

> In this and like communities, public sentiment is everything. With public sentiment, nothing can fail; without it nothing can succeed. Consequently, he who molds public sentiment goes deeper than he who enacts statutes or pronounces decisions. He makes statutes and decisions possible or impossible to be executed.[3]

Despite its importance, constitutional opinion is generally ignored in polls and in most discussions of public opinion. The reason is that there is not much open controversy in the United States about these opinions. Americans since the founding have—with a few notable exceptions—shared a basic commitment to the general principles of liberty, equality, the rule of law, and a republican form of government. It is thus only by comparing American constitutional opinion with that of other nations that it is possible to see some of its characteristics. And one of the leading characteristics is, in fact, precisely the high degree of consensus that has prevailed on the most important questions. European observers over the years have referred to this as a leading element of American difference or exceptionalism. While the United States in the nineteenth century was steadily developing democratic traditions, many European nations remained bitterly divided between supporters of monarchy and republicanism; and well into this century, European democracies were subject to challenges by fascist parties on the right and communist parties on the left. By contrast, America's two major parties have agreed on the basic nature of the political order and have largely confined their disputes to matters of policy, with elections focusing on different ways of promoting widely shared political values.

The existence of a consensus on constitutional issues is all the more striking in light of the diversity of the American population, which is made up of citizens from different ethnic, religious, and racial backgrounds. Although these differences have been the source of many tensions and divisions, they have not—with the exception of a few in the American Indian community—resulted in demands for separate nations, such as one finds in Canada with the tensions between the French and English-speaking populations. The agreement on basic political beliefs has been a bond of unity that has gone deeper than any physical differences.

Scholars have speculated about the causes of this political consensus. One factor is certainly America's unique historical experience. As a new nation settled mostly by Europeans from the middle ranks of society, Americans never had the problems of eliminating established feudal classes of nobles and serfs. Geographical and economic factors have also played a role. An abundance of land contributed to a sense of independence among early settlers, who knew they could escape menial jobs in the cities and eventually purchase land of their own. Throughout the nineteenth century, the frontier tradition contributed to the democratization of the nation by providing new opportunities for people in new communities. America's level of economic growth in the late nineteenth and early twentieth centuries, which was higher than that of any other nation, also helped to moderate the con-

flicts among economic classes that plagued most European nations. Still, it is easy sometimes to be too mechanical about explanations and to reduce a political achievement to certain economic factors. Some of the advantages just cited, such as abundant land and good resources, existed in other nations, like Argentina, but did not produce political consensus. And the economic growth that undoubtedly has contributed to greater political consensus has itself been partly a consequence of that consensus.

Although America has enjoyed an exceptional degree of consensus by comparison to many other nations, this should not obscure the important conflicts that do exist in American politics. Opinion has been widely supportive of certain general principles, but Americans have sometimes interpreted these principles in different and conflicting ways. In addition, the United States has had unique problems related to the heritage of slavery that no other Western nation has faced. It is in these respects—rather than in the outright rejection of fundamental principles—that the American consensus has been threatened and at certain points broken.

Liberty

Liberty means the protection of certain basic rights, such as freedom of speech and association and the free exercise of religion. Americans support these rights in the abstract by overwhelming margins, although this support has often been coupled with reservations about granting the full exercise of these rights to persons in groups that many fear or dislike, such as homosexuals, communists, and racists. Attitudes of intolerance as measured by polls do not actually mean people would act in practice to deny the exercise of a right, but there have clearly been times when majorities have sought to jeopardize minority rights. Surveys on civil liberties taken in the period from 1950–1980 indicated that political leaders and more highly educated members of society were more likely to support the application of general rights in particular instances, from which some concluded that the protection of liberties has depended on a minority that often restrains an intolerant majority. This argument, while perhaps exaggerated today, indicates the importance of constitutional safeguards and of restraints by representative institutions in providing protection for fundamental liberties above what majorities might spontaneously offer.[4]

Liberty for Americans consists not only in the protection of rights of expression, but also of basic economic rights, including the right to hold and dispense property. Associated with the right of property is the existence of economic inequality, which results in part from different skills at acquiring property and different inclinations toward making money. As noted in *The Federalist*: "From the protection of different and unequal faculties of acquiring property, the possession of different degrees and kinds of property immediately results." (*Federalist* 10) When asked specifically, "Which is more important— (a) insuring that each individual has as much opportunity as possible even if it means some people enjoy far more success than others, or (b) insuring greater equality of income even if that limits individual opportunity," three quarters of Americans (73%) favored more opportunity and 18 percent favored greater equality (9 percent did not express an opinion).[5]

Property rights require detailed definition and regulation by law, which means that opinions about specific concepts are often unclear. But Americans do tend to distinguish between an individual's right to hold and dispense property and that of legally created entities, such as business corporations. Americans hold that the large impact of corporations means that they may need to be treated differently from individuals, with their property claims regulated more closely. In fact, there is a long tradition of mistrust of large corporations that dates back to at least as far as Andrew Jackson's attack on the "monster" Bank of the United States as a symbol of undemocratic corporate power. Similar attacks against corporate power surfaced during the Populist era in the 1890s, during the Depression in the 1930s, in the 1970s (during the energy crisis) against the large oil companies, and in the 1990s in President Clinton's campaigns against pharmaceutical companies and tobacco companies.

A right to acquire and dispense property is at the core of the free enterprise or capitalist sys-

tem. Under this system ownership of the means of production is largely in the hands of private entities (individuals, partnerships, and corporations), and economic inequalities (at least up to a point) are viewed as necessary and justifiable. In a socialist system, by contrast, the government often owns the major corporations and means of production; and while private property and income differences may be permitted, socialist ideology places a premium on government policies that seek to create greater equality in income and property.

The economic system is of constitutional significance not just because of the importance of economics but also because of the connections that exist between the economic system and the protection of other political rights. Many argue that a free enterprise system is a necessary, although not sufficient, condition for maintaining liberty. It supports liberty both because the right to acquire property is itself an important liberty and because private ownership limits the power of the government over the economic system. Private property is a check on political power. Americans generally favor a free enterprise system and today strongly oppose the nationalization of key industries or overt steps in the direction of socialism. Americans' support for elements of the free enterprise system becomes especially clear when compared with opinions in many of the western democracies. Americans are far less disposed than the people in Great Britain, Canada, Sweden, Italy, and Germany to consider it the government's responsibility to redistribute wealth and far more disposed to think that one's success is determined by forces within one's own control.[6]

Americans' views of the economic system are not, however, fully captured by the choice between a free enterprise system and socialism. Americans accept the need for government regulation and control of business within a free enterprise system. In addition, the public fully endorses the idea that government has an obligation to provide certain benefits, such as universal education and medical care for the indigent and the aged. Public opinion accordingly does not support the notion of the minimalist state in which the government's role is limited solely to supervising an unbridled economic competition

TABLE 5.2
Opinions on the Character of the Nation's Political Economy

Question: (Agree/Disagree) The private business system in the United States works better than any other system yet devised for industrial countries.

Agree Private Business System Works Best	Disagree	Don't Know
79%	9%	12%

Question: Is a free market economy essential to freedom or not?

Free Market is Essential	Not Essential	Not Sure
59%	17%	24%

Question: In the future, do you think there should be more government regulation of business, less government regulation, or about the same amount there is now?

"It depends."	More Government Regulation	Same	Less
12%	26%	30%	32%

Source: Civic Service, Inc., 1981; *Cambridge Reports,* 1979; Lou Harris and Associates, 1979.

among private parties. Opinion favors a modified free enterprise system that includes elements of a welfare state, although the degree of government intervention within this broad consensus remains perhaps the major point of dispute between our political parties today (see Table 5.2).

Equality

Given that most Americans favor a free enterprise system, their idea of equality does not mean a guarantee of equal economic outcomes. In what sense, then, do Americans conceive of equality? As noted in Chapter 1, equality has meant an absence of special legal prerogatives for any groups and a belief in the equal dignity of each individual. This basic idea, while elusive, is essential for understanding American political culture and distinguishing it from that of many other societies, where feelings of superiority and inferiority among classes still prevail. A study of American workers using the in-depth interview technique captured this notion:

> Woodside, a Protestant policeman . . . says that men are equal "not financially, not in influence, but equal to one another as to being a person."

Being a person, then, is enough to qualify for equal claim of some undefined kind. . . . And when Sokolsky, a machine operator and part-time janitor, says in an interview, "the rich guy—because he's got money he's no better than I am. I mean that's the way I feel . . ." he's saying, in effect, to his prosperous older brother and snobbish wife, "Don't look down on me," and to the world at large, "I may be small, but I will protect my self-esteem."[7]

The concept of equality implies the existence of the same rights and privileges before the law for each person and—more broadly—the absence of prejudices that bar an individual's advancement in society on grounds unrelated to competence or merit. This last notion refers to the individual's general chances in society and depends not only on laws but also on practices and attitudes. Thus, individuals may be legally entitled to run for office without regard to their race or sex, but if people will not vote for them because they are black or female, legal protection is not enough to ensure full equality. The civil rights movement in the 1960s, which helped transform the legal framework of society, was almost as important for the changes it helped to initiate in relation to opinions about equality

TABLE 5.3
Attitudes on Equality

Question: Do you think white students and Negro students should go to the same schools or to separate schools? (Opinion of white respondents.)

Pro-integration Response

1956	51%
1968	73%
1980	89%
1984	90%
1994	88%

Substance of Question: If your party nominated a well-qualified woman or black for president, would you vote for him or her?

	Would Vote For Woman	**Would Vote For Black**
1937	31%	(not asked)
1958	58%	42%
1969	59%	77%
1982	86%	86%

Sources: National Opinion Research Center, general surveys, 1956–1980; surveys by Gallup Organization; October–November 1984.

(see Table 5.3). In Americans' own beliefs about the realization of equality today, a large number (about 40%) think that blacks and women do not yet today have an equal chance to succeed—and this opinion is held more strongly among persons from these groups.[8]

Although belief in the general principle of equality has been a fundamental point of consensus, there have been major political differences recently on the question of group rights and affirmative action. The issue here has sometimes been posed in terms of whether the injustices done to individuals of a certain group (blacks, Hispanics, and women) can be righted or corrected by bestowing advantages on other individuals in that group. On this question Americans are divided, and a strong current of opinion in recent years has pushed toward an ending of affirmative action policies.

The Constitution and Republican Government

Another element of constitutional opinion is respect for the written Constitution as the highest legal source of authority. Inculcation of this kind of opinion was a direct objective of the founders, who argued that a "reverence for the laws" was an advantage that even the most rational government would find helpful. (*Federalist* 49) This view gives rise to the potential for two different kinds of opinion on the same issue: an "ordinary" opinion that reflects what people initially prefer, and an opinion based on how the Constitution is understood or interpreted. An interpretation of the Constitution may be invoked to limit or set aside ordinary opinion, as when Congress rejects a demand for action on the grounds that it would be unconstitutional or when the Supreme Court voids a law on the grounds that it violates the Constitution.

When the Supreme Court voids a law or action on the grounds that it conflicts with the Constitution—a practice known as "judicial review"—we are presented with the most striking test of the strength of the opinion supporting the Constitution. The Court in effect is telling the people: "You may think you want to have such and such a law, but in reality you don't, because this law is contrary to the Constitution which you support and uphold above all other laws." Although people may not always be convinced that the courts have correctly interpreted the Constitution, in modern times they have generally stood by the idea that the independence of the Supreme Court must be preserved and that the Court has a special role to play in interpreting the Constitution. In the words of one scholar, "When all is said and done, the Supreme Court's power stems . . . from the fact that its pronouncements are perceived as 'the law' in a nation that believes in obeying the law—and not only `the law' but `the constitutional law' in a nation that believes that the Constitution is a higher and better law."9

Support for the Constitution and the Supreme Court became clear in a dramatic contest in the 1930s, after the Supreme Court declared unconstitutional some of the key programs of President Roosevelt's plan to fight the Depression. Roosevelt was incensed by the Court's actions, and after the 1936 election he proposed a plan to enlarge the Court, with the aim of changing its membership to endorse his programs. Although Americans agreed by a margin of 59 to 41 percent that the Court "should be more liberal in reviewing New Deal measures," they rejected decisively (62 to 38 percent) Roosevelt's court-packing plan. It was seen as an attack on judicial independence and thus on the integrity of the Constitutional framework itself.10

Americans strongly support the basic form of government as outlined in the Constitution and as it has evolved over the past two hundred years. Although polls sometimes show majorities to support specific constitutional amendments, there is an overwhelming belief in the fundamental legitimacy of the system and a positive attitude toward the basic norms of democratic politics. A famous study done in the early 1960s that compared fundamental political beliefs among the populations of five democratic nations found that Americans possessed more pride in their institutions and a greater sense of

their ability to influence events than the citizens in the other nations. Americans' positive evaluation of their basic form of government remain.11

Beginning in the late 1960s, however, polls began to detect sharp increases in various measures of mistrust and dissatisfaction about government. Americans had growing doubts about the performance of political institutions and felt less in control of events. The federal government was increasingly perceived as something beyond people's control—as "the government" rather than "our government." This growth of mistrust and the loss of a sense of efficacy ceased temporarily in the 1980s only to resume again at the beginning of the 1990s. Looking over the whole period, the change has been dramatic: in 1964, nearly 78 percent of the population felt it could "trust the government Washington to do what is right"; in 1994 the figure was 21 percent.12 Analysts variously labeled this view as a growing "cynicism" or "alienation," a phenomenon which resembled Lord Bryce's great concern, more than a century ago, that in a democracy people might develop a sort of "fatalism" and come to feel a "sense of the insignificance of individual effort, the belief that the affairs of men are swayed by large forces whose movement may be studied but cannot be turned."13 This feeling, Bryce worried, could lead to an erosion of people's confidence in democratic government. Until now the expressions of dissatisfaction have been with the performance of institutions and political leaders rather than with the system itself, but some worry that opinions about the system may eventually be affected.

Dissatisfaction with governmental performance has had several causes. In the earlier period it derived from some clear shocks, scandals, and reversals, including the assassinations of major leaders (John and Robert Kennedy and Martin Luther King), the urban riots of the mid-1960s, the Vietnam War, the Watergate scandal, and the forced resignation of President Nixon. Subsequently, poll results reflected the public's view that the federal government had become too big and powerful while still being unable to resolve many of the nation's social problems. The trend toward increased distrust also occurred as television became the public's major source of political information. Television brings political problems more directly into people's homes, emphasizing drama, conflict, and feelings of crisis.

World Views

Constitutional opinion refers not only to clear political opinions about the fundamental questions of politics but also to underlying public beliefs of what shapes reality. Such beliefs naturally affect the context in which political action occurs. People in any society tend to have certain views that make them, in some degree, different from people in other societies. The differences enable one to speak (very broadly) of an Iranian, a French, and an American "culture" or national character.

Cultural elements change gradually in response to developments in society, although on rare occasions, such as moments of revolution or national trauma, they can undergo major adjustments. The general idea of culture, however, is that of a deep-seated set of attitudes that tends to persist and to resist quick or easy change.

Religion

The United States was settled in large part by religious groups, such as the Pilgrims and Quakers, who came to the new world to practice their religion free from persecution. America was the "New Jerusalem" or the "Heavenly City." From the beginning, religion has been an important part of America's culture. The dominant religious ideas historically have been viewed as supporting the basic American beliefs in liberty, equality, and a republican form of government. What has been called the "Judeo-Christian" heritage—and is now extended to Islam—has played a crucial role in the development of American institutions. Although the United States has experienced a secularizing within one segment of its population in the 1960s and 1970s, the importance Americans ascribe to religion in their own lives stands far above that of any of the other developed liberal democracies (see Table 5.4).

While the American religious tradition is strong, its links to political opinions have tended to be indirect. Unlike many other nations, the United States has had no major political party with avowedly religious connections, such as the Christian Democratic Party in Germany and Italy. The First Amendment, which protects the free exercise of religion and bans the establishment of a state religion, has had the effect of promoting the general idea of separation of church and state. Most Americans believe that it is inappropriate for religious institutions to intervene *directly* in political affairs and that the clergy and churches should generally avoid taking sides on purely partisan issues, at least on church time.

But the line between political and religious issues is obviously not clear-cut. When religious leaders identify issues that they judge to have profound religious import, such as civil rights, abortion, or obscenity, they often take a stand, even where such matters embroil them deeply in political controversies. Religious groups such as the Moral Majority and the Christian Coalition have launched very successful grassroots lobbying and campaign efforts over the past twenty years. As American politics in the last decade has focused more intensely on questions of character and values, religious leaders have more often emphasized the connections between religious and political questions. While most Americans claim to judge political matters independently of church *authority*, the voice of religious leaders carries some weight on some issues; and independent of the authority of the church or the clergy, a large majority attests to the importance that religion plays in making up their minds on many questions, including many that fall into the political arena.

In a nation of great diversity of religious traditions and a multiplicity of sects, religious beliefs by no means lead to a unanimity of political views. There are denominations and religious associations that tend to espouse liberal causes and others that tend to favor conservative causes. There is no question, however, that over the past two decades the sharp growth of the Christian Evangelical movement has added to and helped shape the conservative movement in American politics. A large majority of white Protestant evangelicals identify with conservative causes, and organizations like the Christian

TABLE 5.4
Importance of Religious Beliefs in Several Countries

Citizens of the different countries described their religious beliefs in the following manner:

Country	Religious	Not Religious	Atheist	Don't Know
United States	82%	15%	1%	2%
Sweden	29%	56%	7%	9%
France	48%	36%	11%	5%
W. Germany	54%	27%	2%	17%
Britain	55%	37%	4%	4%
Spain	64%	27%	4%	5%
Canada	69%	26%	3%	2%
Mexico	72%	22%	2%	4%

Source: *World Values Survey, 1990–1993*, Inter-University Consortium for Political and Social Research.

Coalition have become important participants in the political process.

To say that religious belief is stronger in America than in most other western democracies does not mean that all are believers or that religion is always a source of consensus in American politics. In America, as elsewhere in Europe, there has been a decline in religious belief and influence among some segments of the population. As one measure, the number of those who reported never attending religious services or attending only once a year doubled from 1967 (12%) to 1993 (24%).[14] What has been occurring therefore is the development of different tendencies in different segments of the population. One segment of America has moved away from religious thinking and has embraced a more secular outlook. Another segment has become more orthodox in religious matters and has seen a greater connection between religion and issues in their daily lives, some political ones included. The difference between these two basic orientations has led to what some call a "culture war," which shows up today in American politics on a wide range of issues, from school choice, to abortion, to the meaning of "family values." The line of division between these two orientations is not always clear and shifts from issue to issue, but the differences between them have had a major impact on the debates of contemporary America politics.

The Culture of Capitalism

Americans' belief in liberty, including economic competition in a free market system, frees people's acquisitive instincts and exercises a profound impact on the general tone of society. It leads to a strong passion for moneymaking and to a heavy emphasis on commercial values, which permeate such realms as entertainment, sports and even the arts. The freeing of the acquisitive instinct also puts a premium on innovation, mobility, and change, as sectors of the economy constantly adapt in an effort to find more efficient ways of producing goods and services.

The culture of capitalism has undergone significant transformations. For much of the nineteenth century the commercial spirit was coupled with religious beliefs that emphasized the virtues of hard work, personal self-control, savings, and the deferral of personal gratification. Capitalism in the main was therefore compatible with, and even reinforced, a stern and moralistic tone in society, sometimes known as "the Protestant ethic," that linked the activity of moneymaking to thrift, order, and traditional values. In the last half of the twentieth century, with greater affluence in society and with the advent of mass commercial advertising (with all the images it purveys), far more emphasis is placed on consumption, immediate gratification, and self-expression. The motto "show me the money" expresses the selfish and hedonistic tone of modern commercial society, which has broken down the sterner ethic of earlier capitalism.

Many are reacting against these tendencies, although in different ways that define new divisions of opinion. Some are looking to revive traditional moral and religious views as the only genuine antidote to consumerism. Others are searching for ways to go "beyond" commercial values to a new, anti-commercial, humanist ethic often linked to modern environmental movements.

Pragmatism and Rationalism

"Americans," Tocqueville once wrote, "treat tradition as valuable for information only" and "seek by themselves and in themselves for the only reason for things, looking for results without getting entangled in the means towards them."[15] Tocqueville here identified an important feature of American culture—a marked strain of anti-traditionalism and pragmatism. Outside the realms of basic political and religious beliefs, Americans are known to be an open and experimental people, trusting less in schools of philosophy and tradition than in practical science and in what works.

The anti-traditionalist strain of American culture is reflected in a suspicion of displays of pomp and deference (as distinct from respect) to those in authority. In 1789, John Adams pressed for a formal title for the president other than the simple "Mr. President." His choice: "His Highness the President of the United States and Protector of the Rights of the Same." Many in Congress found the title offensive, not to say ridiculous. Opponents of Adams, who was then

vice president, jokingly proposed for the Vice president the titles of "His Superfluous Excellency" or "His Rotund Highness." In 1973 President Nixon, after observing royal guards on a trip to Europe, ordered White House guards to dress in fancy costumes with decorated caps. The idea of American police officers wearing feathered caps was greeted in Washington with a mixture of amazement and derision. While Americans are respectful of high public offices and public ceremonies, they refuse to tolerate any appearance that political leadership derives its authority from on high.

General Opinions on Government Policy

A second level of public opinion comprises basic views on the general role and direction of government—for example, whether the federal government should expand or reduce its activities, whether more or less power should be held by national government or the states, and what posture the United States should adopt in international affairs. Opinion on this level is less stable than constitutional opinion, and struggles to win majorities make up some of the major contests in American political life. Differences of opinion on this level are often given expression by our political parties, and in modern politics these differences are frequently discussed under the labels of "liberalism" and "conservatism."

Political Parties and Partisanship

Parties have been the traditional vehicles for expressing positions about the general direction of policy. To have identified oneself as a Federalist or a Republican in 1800, or a Democrat or Republican in 1880, would have been the best way to characterize one's basic position. Political parties not only express general opinions, but they also help to form them. Once citizens identify with a party and develop ties to it, the parties are in a position—in some measure—to shape the opinions of their followers.

Yet the major parties clearly are not always perfect instruments for expressing positions. Because they include groups with diverse and partially conflicting policy views, they often try to blur or mute certain differences. Citizens therefore often use other instruments, such as factional groups within the parties, third parties, interest groups, mass movements, and the press to express and try to shape basic policy views. During the last half century, moreover, the whole system of "intermediary" agencies that affect the formation of public opinion has changed. The parties have lost influence in structuring opinion to interest groups, individual candidates, and especially to the mass media. These other institutions are less stable than parties, with the result that there is today probably more volatility in public attitudes than in the past.

Liberalism and Conservatism

The terms currently employed to identify general opinions about government are "liberalism" and "conservatism." These terms have become so commonplace that it may be surprising to learn that they were not used in their present sense until the 1930s, when it became apparent that the party labels were not adequate to express the major division in the country about the role of government. President Roosevelt adopted "liberalism" to refer to his view of the positive and active role for the federal government, which he sought to distinguish from the view of limited government held not only by most Republicans but by many Democrats as well. Roosevelt's opponents were labeled "conservatives."

Since the 1930s we have thus had four terms to identify basic political tendencies—the two party labels (Democratic and Republican) and the two position labels (liberal and conservative). These two sets of labels overlap to a great extent, with Republicans being conservative and Democrats liberal. But the fit is far from perfect. There is a part of the Democratic party that is not liberal and a part of the Republican party that is not conservative. The size of each of these groups was once very large, as the Democrats in particular had an entire wing of the party, found largely in the South, that was conservative. In the last decade the followings of the two parties have become more consistent, but there remain significant numbers of moderates inside of each party. Various candidates try to make inroads in

just these groups. Ronald Reagan, for example, was famous for appealing to conservative Democrats, who came for a time to be known as "Reagan Democrats," while Bill Clinton tried to appeal to more moderate Republicans.

Political analysts sometimes identify liberalism and conservatism as "ideologies." This use of the term should, however, be distinguished from the more usual one, which refers to a comprehensive system of belief, like communism or Nazism, that offers an "all inclusive representation of the history of the world, of the past, the present and the future, of what is and what must be."[16] Clearly, "conservatism" and "liberalism" in America are not opinions in this sense. They refer generally to positions about the role of government and the policies it should pursue. Originally, as noted, they were used to define differing views of government's role in economic and welfare policy. Since the 1930s, they have also been employed to identify views in two other areas: social and cultural issues and issues of national security and foreign affairs. Below we survey these three dimensions.

Economic and Welfare Issues   Differences on economic and welfare issues make up an important and enduring line of division between liberals and conservatives. In his acceptance speech for the Democratic nomination in 1932, President Roosevelt called on the Democratic party to become "the bearer of liberalism" and to bring a "new deal for the American people." Liberalism thereafter came to refer to an active use of national power to intervene in the economy, establish welfare and security programs, and help labor unions in relation to business. In the 1960s liberalism was extended under Lyndon Johnson's "Great Society" to include federal programs to assist the cities and the poor. In addition, liberals have been the strongest supporters of federal civil rights legislation and of programs of affirmative action.

Conservatism was the term political commentators used to identify the opposition to Roosevelt's New Deal policies. Initially, Republican leaders like President Hoover rejected this label and described themselves as "true liberals," meaning (in an older sense of the term) the opponents of big government. But the next generation of Republican leaders, beginning with Barry Goldwater and later Ronald Reagan, embraced the term and made it into the dominant public philosophy of the Republican party. Conservatism opposes a large central government that is active in the areas of domestic and welfare. "Big Government," as conservatives call it, is a threat to personal liberty and an invitation to collectivism. Whereas liberals have tended to see the economic system in more collective terms— for example, liberals in the early 1980s became fascinated with the idea of "an industrial policy" to guide economic development—conservatives stress the value of the free market system and of economic individualism. On civil rights legislation, conservatives have insisted on preserving the idea of individual rights and have opposed plans and remedies that embody notions of group rights.

Reinforcing these positions are different views about what government can accomplish by collective programs. Liberals emphasize what government—especially the federal government—can achieve through direct programs. Conservatives contend that big government creates large and inefficient bureaucracies and leads to unhealthy dependencies of citizens on government. These differences of opinion were evident in the debate in 1993 over President Clinton's national health care proposal. Liberals supported it, arguing that it would make health care available to everyone. Conservatives opposed it, contending that it would create a bureaucratic nightmare and destroy the quality of American health care.

Social and Cultural Issues Liberalism and conservatism refer here to attitudes about government's role—often the role of state and local governments—in protecting order and in maintaining moral values and community standards. This dimension of opinion, which was subordinate in national politics in the 1930s and 1940s to economic questions, grew in importance beginning in the late 1960s with mounting concern over increases in crime, the use of drugs, the production of pornography, a general attack on "traditional values," and the establishment of a national right to an abortion.

Liberalism in this domain refers traditionally to beliefs that favor the extension of free expression and that support each individual's right to experiment in matters of lifestyle, free of any attempts on the part of government to promote certain moral values. Liberals accordingly opposed (for a time) legislation banning pornography and any measures for sanctioned prayer in the public schools. Liberals also favored promoting the idea of abortion as an unqualified right. Finally, liberals, at least in the 1960s, were also more apt to explain the origin of crime in terms of social causes like poverty rather than to place the burden of responsibility on the individual.

Conservatism has supported some use of government power, usually on the state and local level, to foster certain community values. Conservatives have favored prayer or a moment of silence in schools, have worked in behalf of anti-pornography statutes, and have held much stricter attitudes about crime and punishment, including support for the death penalty. Thus in the 1988 presidential campaign, candidate George H. Bush contrasted his views on crime with the "liberal" views of Michael Dukakis, who opposed the death penalty and who as governor of Massachusetts had supported a controversial program of furloughs for convicted felons.

Some of these culture issues were brought into American national politics as a result of Supreme Court decisions. From the 1960s into the 1980s, the Court issued many decisions based on interpretations of Constitutional rights that conservatives argued reflected liberal ideology. The role of the courts and theories of Constitutional interpretation became a heated political issue dividing liberals and conservatives. Ronald Reagan in his 1980 campaign pledged to appoint justices who would adopt a restrained position and who supported a theory of judicial interpretation based on what conservatives called original intent. The nomination of justices in the 1980s became occasions for debate of these issues, and the bitter Senate struggles over President Reagan's nomination of Robert Bork in 1987 (who was not confirmed) and President Bush's nomination of Clarence Thomas in 1991 (who was confirmed) marked the rancorous divisions between liberals and conservatives. In the election of 2000, George W. Bush made judicial ideology an issue saying he would "put competent judges on the bench, people who will strictly interpret the Constitution and will not use the bench to write social policy."

Looking at these first two dimensions of liberalism and conservatism, it is clear that there are tensions within each position. Conservatives speak of limited government, but they mean primarily limitations in the economic sphere. On social issues, many conservatives favor certain uses of government power to support what they see as basic community values. Liberals, on the other hand, speak of a guiding role for government in economic and welfare issues, but they have opposed certain kinds of state intervention on social and cultural issues. These internal tensions create problems, especially on the conservative side, where some conservatives hold the limitation of government to be the fundamental principle and thus are uneasy with government support of community values.

Issues of National Security and Foreign Policy
The divisions between liberals and conservatives on this dimension have changed over the past half century, and today the beliefs that separate them have become unclear. From the onset of World War II until the escalation of the Vietnam War in 1965, liberals advocated an active, "interventionist" role for the United States in world affairs. Liberal internationalism was directed initially against Fascism and Nazism, but after World War II it was expanded under President Truman to include a steadfast resistance to the spread of communism. Liberal presidents (Truman, Kennedy, and Johnson) led the United States into two wars against communist forces: the Korean War and the Vietnam War.

During the Vietnam War, however, most liberals changed position, as the anti-war movement captured the liberal wing of the Democratic party after 1968 and rejected Lyndon Johnson. Liberalism in the 1970s and 1980s came to be associated with the view that the United States was spending too much on national defense, that it was too preoccupied with an inordinate fear of communism, and that it has been too ready to rely on military interventions.

Conservatives before World War II held an isolationist position and sought to prevent the United States from active involvement in world affairs. But with the attack on Pearl Harbor, conservatives joined in the support of the war effort. After World War II, conservatives again sought to avoid major foreign commitments and involvement in foreign alliances. But during the 1950s conservatives changed to a more activist posture, becoming proponents of the internationalist position. They argued that the United States and its allies were threatened by communism and by the Soviet Union (which President Reagan in 1983 called an "evil empire"), that a higher level of spending on national defense was necessary, and that the use of military force was sometimes required.

Today, however, the lines between the two are confused. Conservatives approach foreign affairs with a somewhat more nationalist perspective than liberals, but this leads some conservatives today to adopt a more isolationist position and others to adopt a position of strong American world leadership in the post-Cold War world. Liberals are also divided, prepared to support some internationalist positions but still seeking greater cuts than conservatives in military spending.

The Meaning of Liberalism and Conservatism
These, then, are the three dimensions—economic/welfare, social/cultural, and defense/security—that define liberalism and conservatism, with the defense/security dimension becoming less important. Among political activists and elites, these three dimensions have been linked, meaning those who classify themselves as liberal or conservative tend to be liberal and conservative on all three. But this tendency is far from absolute, and even where it applies people assign different priorities to different dimensions.

Whether it is logical to group these three dimensions into a single package is disputed. It is clear, however, that the average citizen feels no hesitation in picking and choosing among the three dimensions. For the great majority of citizens, the linkage among these dimensions is quite weak. This fact has played a major role in American electoral politics in recent history. Republican candidates appeal to conservatives

TABLE 5.5
Self Identification as Liberal and Conservative, 1976–2000

	Liberal	Moderate	Conservative	No Opinion
1976	21	41	26	12
1980	19	40	30	11
1982	17	40	33	11
1986	20	45	28	7
1992	19	41	34	6
1996	17	45	34	4
2000	21	50	29	--

Source: Gallup Reports: *New York Times*/CBS News Surveys.

throughout the electorate, attempting in particular to lure Democrats and independents who are conservative on certain social-cultural and national security issues into their camp. (This was the centerpiece of the presidential campaigns of Ronald Reagan and George Bush.) Democrats do the opposite, seeking to win moderate Republicans by making somewhat more liberal appeals on certain social issues, especially on the issue of abortion. President Clinton had success with this approach in his 1996 campaign.

The meaning of liberalism and conservatism is partly relative, shifting somewhat with the times. Conservatives in the 1930s rejected certain kinds of federal intervention—such as social security and unemployment insurance—that they accept today. Liberals today are apt to be much more cautious than in the 1960s in opposing longer prison terms or capital punishment. Liberalism and conservatism thus are terms used to indicate a tendency of opinion in relationship to the status quo. Positions can change and evolve. What is conservative or liberal depends in part on the views adopted by leaders who have been traditionally identified with a particular ideology. For example, conservative doctrine in foreign affairs changed dramatically toward internationalism in the 1950s, while liberal doctrine changed just as strikingly against containment after the Vietnam War. Neither viewpoint is fixed in stone. Conservatism and liberalism are imprecise terms, so

much so that some doubt whether they are useful at all. Still, people do refer to them, and as long as these terms are employed carefully they can assist in identifying the general opinions about the direction of government policy for many in American society.

Levels of Ideological Thinking and Recent Trends

Most people today are acquainted with the terms, know roughly what they mean, and are willing to provide an answer when asked to categorize themselves as liberal, moderate, or conservative. These responses provide a rough indication of the general leanings of the American public. They show a nation that over the last thirty years has become more conservative in its self description, but in which the largest group is the moderates. The movement of American politics over the last thirty years has roughly tracked this shift away from liberalism, at least as this can be seen from the labels politicians adopt for themselves. In the 1960s, many Democratic candidates embraced the label of "liberal," while recent Democratic presidential candidates—Michael Dukakis in 1988 and Bill Clinton in 1992 and 1996—have sought to avoid it.

But do most people actually think in these terms and organize their political responses to particular issues on the basis of these (or any other) general ideological categories? That is, do they tend to think, I am liberal, and as a liberal I am obliged to oppose legislation that calls for the death penalty? The answer is only to a rather limited extent. The reason is not just the imprecision in the meaning of these terms, but also that many in the public do not appear to view the political world primarily in such general ideological terms. They may view politics more in terms of general concerns, for example the performance of the economy or the prestige of America, making some overall judgment about whether a party or president has handled things well in the recent period. Or they may be single issue voters concerned about a particular issue relevant to them or a group with which they identify, but fail to fit this concern into a general ideological framework. Or the public may judge the political world more in terms of their trust or assessment of different personalities and individuals. Many Americans, in short, view the political world not in an ideological way, but in concrete terms—in terms of parties, personalities, and subjective measures of performance and in terms of certain specific issues that impinge on them and occupy their attention, be it inflation, a war, or government benefits.[17]

Even so, it would be a mistake to underestimate the importance of ideological thinking. The political activists—those, for example, who hold positions as elected officials, interest-group leaders, and party officials—do use ideological categories in thinking about politics, even though many take different stands on the three dimensions noted above. Because of the impact of activists on political life, American politics is more influenced by ideological considerations than an analysis of mass opinion would suggest.

Opinions on Specific Issues and Personalities

When most people think of public opinion today, they probably have in mind what we have called the third level of opinion: the public's views on specific issues and personalities. Polls are conducted to find out what people consider to be the important issues of the day, to determine how they stand on those issues, to see what they think of the performance of their president, and, natu-

rally, to chart opinions about prospective candidates for public office, especially for the presidency.

Unlike constitutional and ideological opinions, which tend to be relatively stable, opinions on specific issues and personalities are frequently volatile, shifting with changes in the political environment and sometimes even with daily events. During presidential campaigns, for example, a mistake committed by a candidate or an especially strong or weak showing in a primary can lead to large changes in opinion. For presidents, a well-handled crisis can boost support and reverse a declining trend of popularity. President George W. Bush's approval ratings shot up dramatically after the terrorist attacks of September 11, 2001, reaching one of the highest levels of any modern president (92%) due to his handling of the crisis.

In thinking about public opinion on this level, distinctions must be made about different kinds and attributes of opinions. Not all opinions measured in polls are equally meaningful. Some represent a momentary and unformed response—"sudden breezes of passion"—while others testify to a more settled conviction—the "deliberate sense of the community." (*Federalist* 71) It is important to know not only the overall distribution of opinion on an issue—that is, people's position about what should or should not be done—but also the intensity of feeling within the population and within different subgroups. For many purposes intensity is more important than distribution, because people are likely to act or vote on the basis of matters on which they have strong views. One also should consider the stability of opinion—that is, the extent to which people have made up their minds and are no longer changing from one position to another. Finally, it is necessary to explore latent opinion, meaning opinion that is not now active or visible, but that very quickly could become so if certain actions were taken.

Some issues, such as the Vietnam War, are of intense concern to many people and after a certain time evoke a stable distribution of opinion. By 1972, most people had made up their minds about the war and could not easily have their opinions changed. Divisions on issues on which opinion is intense and stable are potential national voting issues that can influence how large numbers of people cast their ballot. There are other issues on which there may be much intensity of feeling, but no clear distribution of opinion. During periods of high inflation or high unemployment, there is often a strong sentiment that "something should be done" to handle the problem, but what people want done may be vague or inconsistent; people seem in such instances to wait to see how leaders act and then judge by the general criterion of "whether it worked." An instability of opinion was manifest during the buildup to the Gulf War in 1991. At each stage—before beginning the war and then before launching the ground offensive—public opinion only barely supported President Bush's policies. But after the War, when the public judged the policies to have worked, there was strong backing for the policy and tremendous support for the President. Where opinion has not firmly crystallized, it can be shaped by the outcome of events and easily changed. Any president who would seek only to follow public opinion would be pursuing a very short-sighted strategy.

There are always certain issues that are of relatively little concern to most citizens but which are highly important to specific groups, such as the level of agricultural benefits for the farming population or the subsidies for supporting clean energy sources for environmentalists. Citizens in these "issue publics" respond with a great deal of intensity on a particular issue. In addition, political leaders are always considering latent opinions, which they know might quickly become intense, stable, and perhaps unfavorable. In 1993, for example, President Clinton quickly backed off from any suggestion of allowing gays to serve openly in the military for fear of a hostile public response.

Effects of Public Opinion

From the viewpoint of political leaders, public opinion can operate either as a resource or a constraint. It is a resource because it can be called on by political leaders attempting to pursue certain policies. Theodore Roosevelt called the presidency the "bully pulpit," because presidents had the ability to speak directly to the people. This is what presidents do, for example,

when they appear on television and attempt to mobilize opinion to support a given policy. An active and intense majority opinion in favor of a position "works" in two ways: first, a favorable opinion is recognized as having some claim on government, and second, politicians calculate the possible electoral consequences of thwarting a popular opinion. The significance of this "force" became apparent during the Gulf War. After the war began, public opinion moved to support it at a very high level. This support was evident not only from polls, but from the flags and ribbons that millions of Americans displayed. It provided President Bush a freer hand in his decisions.

Opinion may also act as a constraint on leaders, who have a policy they might like to pursue but know they cannot. For example, President Nixon was unable in 1973 to enforce the Paris Peace Accords for the Vietnam War through further bombings. The public had turned against the war (and the President) in a way that made the resumption of bombing impossible. Of course, the leeway presidents have is subject in part to their capacity to persuade the public. As Theodore Roosevelt once remarked, "I did not divine what the people were going to think. I simply made up my mind what they ought to think and then did my best to get them to think it."[18] When presidents can succeed in persuading the public, they can often get their way. But the sources of opposition to presidents are also quite formidable.

Opinion Formation and Change

How do opinions come into being and change? If social scientists could answer this question, they would hold the key to understanding not only the behavior of contemporary societies but also the movement of history over the past few centuries. Not surprisingly, social scientists have no such kind of knowledge and at best have been able to identify some of the major sources of opinion formation and to indicate their importance in certain circumstances. Below we survey some of these findings.

Opinion Formation in Free Societies

The most important factor affecting opinion formation is the nature of the political regime. Political scientists sometimes classify governments by distinguishing between those that rule by force, holding the public down against its will, and those that have the active consent of the governed. This distinction is useful as a first step, but it ignores that some totalitarian systems, without forsaking the use of terror and force, have sought to engineer consent by total social control that included staging rallies, dictating what is taught in the schools, and deciding the content of all news and art. By contrast, a central characteristic of liberal democracy is its plurality of opinion-forming agencies and an absence of anything approaching a governmental monopoly over the formation of opinion. Free societies do, of course, exercise some influence or control over certain opinion-forming agencies. In some nations, the government owns some of the major television channels and has exercised considerable influence over television news coverage. But in all free societies, the written press is independent of the government and the tradition of vigorous criticism is strong. Again, all liberal democracies use the primary education systems in some degree to instill favorable opinions about the basic regime. Thus public schools in the United States generally accept the teaching of the American political tradition as part of their mission, and few school boards would tolerate, let alone encourage, hostile treatments of basic American principles. Civic education is a logical part of any system whose people believe in it and want to see it perpetuated. Still, a civic education that allows for inquiry and challenges is a far cry from rigid indoctrination.

Accepting these qualifications, liberal democracy is characterized by numerous opinion-forming agencies that are free of government control and that are often highly critical of the government. The existence of this plurality makes the formulation of a single, comprehensive theory of opinion formation all the more difficult. Liberty itself breeds diversity: "As long as the reason of man continues fallible, and he is at liberty to exercise it, different opinions will be formed." (*Federalist* 10)

Opinion-Forming Agencies

Family The learning of political opinions occurs through a process known as political socialization. The most important institution in this process is the family, which shapes an individual's earliest opinions. Although the family has lost some ground as a socializing agency over the past half century because of competition from the media and mass culture, it remains the first place to look in understanding the development of opinion. The family's influence is greater in promoting basic world views and ideology than in forming specific political opinions. Parents are more likely to pass on their religious views and their attitudes toward authority than their position about how to deal with inflation or reform welfare. Partisan leanings (Democratic and Republican) are also often transmitted from one generation to the next, but this tendency has been diminishing and obviously does not work where the parents themselves have different positions (which is increasingly the case).

Although the family's influence is strong, individuals often "unlearn" what they have imbibed as children as they come into contact with other views and experience events for themselves. A diverse modern society provides many opportunities for such challenges, and children are no doubt freer from their parents' influence than ever before. Family socialization thus has an important bearing on opinions, but it is far from being decisive.

Primary and Secondary Education Education is another major socializing institution. It plays an important role in teaching children about basic constitutional values, and primary schools have historically sought to inculcate a positive view of the political system. Most schools do not seek directly to influence opinion on specific policy issues, but the curricula in subjects such as social studies, history, or sex education may have an indirect impact on students' views.

Generalizations about the public school curricula are difficult to make because the authority for deciding what is taught lies not with a single federal agency but with hundreds of different state and local school boards. The content therefore tends to reflect the views of different communities, although professional educators have a great deal of influence. Not surprisingly the political struggles over local schools are often the most intensely contested of all local issues. Community groups seek to influence the curricula, especially on matters touching on morality and religion.

Parents may also choose to send their children to private schools, the greater part of which have a religious orientation. (Currently, 15 percent of the nation's primary school children attend private schools.)[19] George W. Bush has pushed for school vouchers, which would allow the government to partially subsidize this private education. The growth in recent years of private (and religious) education, or even home schooling, has been only in part a reaction to concerns about the quality of public education. It has more to do with the content of the education, as parents are generally trying to keep the orientation of the schools in harmony with the basic beliefs of the family.

Because of its importance as a socializing agency, private education has been one of the great points of conflict in American politics. For a time in this country, from the 1880s until the 1920s, some states sought to discourage or ban private education and compel attendance at public schools, often with the intent of preventing attendance at Catholic educational institutions. In a major case, *Pierce v. Society of Sisters* (1925), the Supreme Court declared unconstitutional an Oregon law banning private education, on the grounds that the child was not "the mere creature of the state" and that the state had no power to "standardize its children."[20]

While the Constitutional question of the permissibility of private education has been settled, the policy question of whether to give more encouragement to private education is one of the major issues in contemporary politics. Conservatives have been calling for vouchers or for tuition tax credits for parents who wish to send their children to private schools, which would clearly increase the number of children attending private schools. Liberals have opposed these plans, stressing the benefits of the secular public schools and the opportunities they afford for children to be exposed to a more diverse environment. They also argue that any voucher plan would violate the First Amendment's ban on establishing a religion and would decrease the proportion of federal money contributed to public schools.

Higher Education Higher education has had an important impact on ideological opinion and opinions on specific issues. Many students encounter a new environment away from home, where they are introduced to new influences from ideas that circulate in university communities. Colleges and universities differ greatly in their orientation. A religious, fundamentalist-supported university, such as Oral Roberts University, has a quite different atmosphere from a secular state campus such as the University of California at Berkeley. But overall the ideas that dominate in the national intellectual community tend also to permeate the college campuses, at least when speaking of the four-year residential communities.

Beginning in the 1950s, the intellectual community in the United States has developed a predominantly liberal cast of mind. The result has been that university education has exercised a strong liberalizing influence. This influence was most noticeable during the late 1960s and early 1970s, when college campuses were seething with political activity, much of it directed against the Vietnam War. Universities became the centers of the so-called "counterculture," in which many traditional beliefs were either held up to ridicule (such as individual economic achievement) or alleged to be shams (such as claims that the United States was protecting the free world). Liberal dominance continues in the universities today, but conservative voices have grown stronger on many college campuses over the last decade.

Reference Groups Another important influence on opinion is the reference group, meaning a group with which one identifies because of a shared characteristic (race, religion, or ethnicity) or a more organized group that one joins (such as a labor union, a church group, or an environmental organization). Persons of the same group may have had certain shared experiences that cause them to see the world in similar ways, and they often look to recognized group leaders for cues on political matters. Opinion is therefore in some degree mediated by these groups and their leaders. Reference groups will be discussed in greater detail in Chapter 9.

Class Many theorists assign economic class—a kind of reference group—a central role in explaining opinion formation. The best known of these theorists was Karl Marx (1818–1883), who argued that political opinions derive chiefly from people's position in the economic system. Marx went on to predict a polarization of modern capitalist society into two classes—the bourgeoisie, or capitalist, class (consisting of those owning the means of production) and the proletariat, or laborers (consisting of those toiling in the factories). This polarization would spawn class-based parties deriving from the antagonistic economic interests of these two classes. Capitalists would espouse some variant of liberal democracy, which would serve to protect their property rights and advantaged position, while the proletariat would eventually form a revolutionary party calling for the abolition of business property and the formation of communist society.

Unlike most European nations, American politics has been largely free of class-based parties. Party struggles have, of course, involved elements of conflict between rich and poor and owners and workers. Franklin Roosevelt's 1936 presidential campaign stressed class divisions to an extent unprecedented in American history, in part reflecting the tensions between labor and capital that had been growing for many years and that were sharpened by the Depression. But class-based appeals, even during the Depression, had to compete with divisions based on other differences (ethnicity, religion, and geography) and with competing responses to international affairs. For the most part in American history, the political divisions deriving from class have been less important than those deriving from these other sources. Class-based opinions today are evident on certain issues, but recent voting patterns reveal the (relatively) modest influence of class in presidential elections. As a general rule citizens at the lower end of the income scale tend to support Democratic candidates while those at the upper end are more favorable to Republicans.

Why has class played only a relatively modest role in American history, and why has the American working class never developed a working-class consciousness comparable to that found in many European nations? One explanation is found in the founders' theory of economic pluralism, which in a sense anticipated Marx's ideas. It contended that the political division between rich and poor could be avoided in a large commercial society having a variety of economic groups—farmers, various manufacturers, and different commercial interests. Individuals would favor their group's particular interest rather than the interest of a class as a whole. Owners and workers from one sector of the economy would often join together in coalitions against owners and workers from rival sectors of the economy. But as the strong class basis of voting that emerged during the Depression years demonstrated, the continued impoverishment of the American worker could well have led to permanent class-based party division in the United States. The remarkable economic success that followed World War II prevented this result, and the concept of class as Marx originally conceived it lost much of its meaning. Far from being exploited and growing poorer and poorer, blue-collar workers began to earn relatively good wages and to become property owners in their own right. The entrance of the worker into the middle class, with a strong stake in protecting the system, put an end to the development of any kind of revolutionary-minded workers' party that made up a majority of the population.

The nature of the modern economy that developed also went beyond classical Marxist theory. The economy in the late 1960s entered a post-industrial stage in which the growth sectors are no longer in areas of heavy industry such as steel, but in service sectors, such as white-collar professions and government work, and high-technology fields. The nature of wealth has also changed from a reliance on ownership (which of course still remains important) to a reliance on high salaries found among members of a "new class" of technicians, experts, and professionals. Few of these persons are classic owners of capital, in the sense of owning their own businesses. Their opinions are shaped less by their place in the economic order than by the intellectual ideas to which they are exposed. A large portion of the activists on both the liberal and the conservative side of the political spectrum are drawn from this very same strata of the educated upper middle class.

But the economy never stands still, and some analysts argue that under the impact of globalization it is entering yet a new phase in which the gaps between skilled and unskilled workers are destined now to grow permanently larger. This, they argue, may eventually spawn a new kind of class-based politics. While there are definitely signs in this decade showing that the top part of income earners are moving further ahead relative to the bottom part, it is too soon yet to see these trends as shaping opinions. In any case, the large mass of Americans remain in what they consider to be the middle-class of society.

Ideas   Thus far, we have looked at opinions as shaped by one's upbringing or position in the economic and social structure. But where do families and reference groups get their opinions in the first place? In part, no doubt from a common experience. Yet they also take their cues from the opinions of group leaders, who in turn derive some of their views—especially newer ones—from general ideas produced by intellectuals. Leaders mediate between the existing views within a group and "new" ideas that come from religious and secular thinkers. It is, furthermore, in the character of modern society that individuals tend to be shaped less than before by the views of a single group. People today often have contacts with several groups, and systems of mass communication expose people directly to a variety of arguments and ideas expressed in the press, in journals and by commentators and politicians.

Ideas and arguments, then, powerfully affect public opinion, both as they are mediated through groups and as they are evaluated directly by individuals. According to John Maynard Keynes, the famous British economist of the last generation:

> The ideas of economists and political philosophers, both when they are right and when they are wrong, are more powerful than is commonly understood. Indeed the world is ruled by little else. Practical men, who believe themselves to be quite exempt from any intellectual influences, are usually the slaves of some defunct economist. Madmen in authority, who hear voices in the air, are distilling their frenzy from some academic scribbler of a few years back. I am sure that the power of vested interests is vastly exaggerated compared with the gradual encroachment of ideas.[21]

This claim may appear surprising, for few consider intellectuals as being among the power brokers of society. Rarely do they hold elective office, although more and more have been given appointments to office. Their influence derives not from holding power but from influencing those who hold power. Politicians and journalists seldom initiate broad new theories, but instead receive them once or twice removed from scholars and intellectuals, who thus constitute one of the chief sources of opinion formation and change. The influence of ideas on opinion became evident in the 1970s. The public philosophy of liberalism that had dominated American national politics since the New Deal came under increasing attack from a group of "neoconservative" thinkers. This new wave of thought altered the climate of intellectual opinion on both domestic and foreign affairs and prepared the way for the acceptance of Ronald Reagan. Similar kinds of intellectual debates were important to the process of opinion formation in the past. The ground for both the Progressivism and the New Deal was prepared in each case by formidable intellectual movements.

Ideas, then, have power, which explains why those concerned with shaping elite and mass opinion today spend money sponsoring scholarly research institutes and supporting intellectual journals of opinion. In Washington today, there are large and prestigious "think tanks," such as the Brookings Institution, the Urban Institute, the American Enterprise Institute, and the Heritage Foundation, that sponsor or employ prominent intellectuals writing about public affairs.

Theories of why certain ideas take hold at certain times have remained at best highly speculative. All one can really say is that ideas constitute an important autonomous source of influence on opinion formation. A critical discussion of ideas can thus itself have major consequences on the political process. This is one of the reasons that this book has emphasized the role of ideas in shaping constitutional development, and it is for this reason as well that students need to consider carefully the basic concepts of our constitutional system. The ideas that win acceptance from today's thinkers may well become the foundation of tomorrow's public opinion.

The Media

Opinion formation and change are strongly influenced by the communications system in society, so much so that some today contend the communications system is the most important of all influences on society.[22] Although it is likely that such theories of determinism from communications are overstated (just as Marx's theory of determinism from economics was overstated), it is clear that changes in the communication system can profoundly effect both the nature and strength of public opinion.

Before the advent of the printing press in the fifteenth century, only a limited number of people had access to written material. Public opinion, to the extent that it existed at all, could be more easily influenced by established authorities and institutions, such as the church. The newspaper, which developed in the eighteenth century, initially gave greater weight to a new group of intellectuals operating independently of the church. Newspapers initially were not money-making ventures and therefore required political sponsors. American newspapers in the early nineteenth century were nearly all founded and supported by the political parties. Newspapers were mouthpieces for the political parties, and political news was presented in a partisan perspective.

Toward the latter part of the nineteenth century, the first money-making newspapers—the "penny press"—developed and were able to operate free of financial support from the parties. These newspapers reached a large portion of the public. But to sell papers, the editors often presented the news in a sensational fashion. It has plausibly been argued, for example, that the government was virtually pushed into making war on Spain in 1898 because of the pressure of public opinion whipped up by "yellow journalism." It was not really until the early twentieth century that the responsible modern newspaper emerged, in which news was reported subject to general rules of the journalistic profession. A newspaper, in this modern view, should provide a nonpartisan account of events. Of course the news consists of more than merely a factual presentation of what happened—it may be an analysis of what is going on—but the journalist is supposed to avoid expressing partisan or personal views, which are saved for the editorial pages and the opinion columns.

Scholars today are more cognizant of the impact of communications because most have lived through major communications revolutions—the advent of radio in the 1920s, television in the 1950s, and the internet in the 1990s—comparable in importance to the advent of the printing press. The electronic media have made it possible for the entire nation to be tied together in one communications network, which in turn is immediately in touch with much of the rest of the world. One effect has been a nationalizing (and internationalizing) of the entire process of opinion formation, since everyone sees the same events at the same time. Americans (and much of the world) watched together on television the terrorist attacks on the World Trade Center and the Pentagon.

The electronics revolution has affected the representative tone of the government by bringing leaders and the public into more direct—although not necessarily more genuine—contact. The founders had relied on a large nation with a slow communication system as one way of reducing mass pressure on government and giving officials greater discretion. Today, more pressure forms from "below"—that is, in the spontaneous reaction of people to events—while political leaders from "above" seek to address the public directly in an effort to build support for their policies. Television, in almost the literal meaning of the word, is a medium—something which stands in between the mass public on the one hand and those attempting to shape and influence public opinion on the other. It has changed the way that groups and individuals attempt to persuade the public and has altered the relationship among various elements of the body politic.

The Impact of Entertainment on Public Opinion

Most viewers watch television to be entertained, and normally only a small portion of the twenty-one hours per week that the average adult devotes to TV goes to news or political programs. Television thus exercises most of its impact on cultural and moral views, whether it be in the form of influencing attitudes about violence, sexual morality, or material consumption. This impact may be especially strong in the case of children, who are now partly socialized—no one can quite say how much—by television.

The belief that television forms such opinions has led various groups to seek controls or restraints on the content of television programming and commercials. These pressures have increased over the past twenty years because of the changed character of programming. One study that surveyed the content of television entertainment concluded that in the 1950s and early 1960s program entertainment emphasized traditional moral and cultural values, whereas after the mid-1960s it gave more attention to sex and violence and to liberal and experimental lifestyles.[23] In response some groups have pressured the television networks to reduce the amount of explicit violence and sex on television, with some instances of success. Others have voiced concerns about the character of commercial advertising, especially for children's programs. In the Children's Television Act of 1990, Congress gave the authority to the Federal Communications Commission (FCC) to limit advertising on television programs for children and set standards to improve the educational quality of these programs. The FCC has since taken steps to implement these objectives.

Efforts to influence the character of programming have been partly overtaken by the development of cable television. Up until the 1970s, everyone watching television was the captive of one of the three networks, which were the only channels available. The content of the programming was thus the choice of the networks as much as the public. Cable television has given viewers more choice of programming. A viewer's situation reflects that of a consumer entering a book store, in which the selection is more the result of what each individual wants than what the owner offers. Today, cable systems in many major markets provide between forty and fifty channels, with future possibilities for more than a hundred different stations. The word "narrowcast" rather than "broadcast" describes the strategy of many stations to appeal to specific groups.[24] Today, for example, there is a Christian Broadcasting Network, Black Entertainment Television, a Spanish International Network, several all-news networks, MTV, and, for the genuine addicts of public affairs, two Cable-Satellite Public Affairs Networks (C-SPAN).

Political Information and News

Television coverage of the news and politics is now the major source of political information for most Americans. But this development by no means eliminates the importance of the nation's principal newspapers and weekly magazines. Papers like *The New York Times*, *The Washington Post*, and *The Wall Street Journal* and magazines like *Newsweek* and *Time* are widely read by those active in politics. The reports found in the print media are closely followed by those in the electronic media, and the print media often set the agenda for television news.

The change from a public influenced by the print media to one influenced primarily by the electronic media has many implications. One derives from the different legal status of the two media. The print media were—and remain—entirely private, beyond the regulation of the government. Newspapers can take whatever stand they wish, print the kind of stories they want, and can refuse any kind of advertising. Television stations and networks, while privately owned, are regulated in important ways by the government on the grounds that they occupy a limited space on "public" air waves. Stations must be granted licenses by the Federal Communications Commission, a process which some have asserted is a means by which government can control the media. But the major impact of the federal regulatory process has been that it minimizes overt political bias in political communications. Television stations can take editorial stands, but they are obliged to follow certain rules that include: the equal-time rule, which gives a candidate for political office the right to the same time as an opponent (free time as well as the right to buy the same time for advertisements); the personal-attack rule, which gives individuals or groups a right to reply if they are attacked on the air; and the political editorial rule, which gives candidates a right to reply to an endorsement of another candidate.

This legal framework of television was established at an earlier time when only a few channels existed. It was intended to protect the viewer rather than the provider (the network). It is thus quite different from the legal structure governing newspapers, where it is the provider who receives nearly absolute protection. As the technology of television produces a much larger number of channels, some of the previous legal doctrines are coming into question. But the traditions of television news journalism grew up under the old system, and the major networks claim that objectivity and balance are the main objectives of news presentation.

The latest technological revolution in communications has come in the form of the Internet, which allows for a large number of producers of information at the same time that it provides almost complete choice to the consumer. The number of Americans who receive their political information from this source is growing rapidly, although it is still much smaller than that of the printed press or television. But this may change, as more and more candidates, parties and interest groups see the internet as an efficient way to disseminate political information. In 2000, John McCain caused a media stir by allowing visitors to his campaign website to donate money to his campaign.

Communication of political information on television is presented to the American public through at least four different "channels": (1) political advertising, (2) direct coverage of speeches and political events, (3) interview and discussion programs, and (4) news coverage. Each of these channels has distinct properties.

Political Advertising Advertising is used mostly by groups and individuals during election campaigns to persuade the public to vote for or against a candidate, party, or issue on the ballot. Television stations have no say on the content of a candidates' advertisements and (unlike newspapers) must accept to run them. Political advertising is often criticized for its effect of trivializing politics by bringing it down to the same level as selling deodorant or soda pop. The quick thirty-second spots, with their frequent attempts to find a clever image or a catchy line, have degenerated into what some call "sound-bite" politics that lack any real effort at serious argument or deliberation.

Despite the trivial or negative character of much advertising, ads often do contain important information. Recent evidence has shown that negative ads can activate voters, making them more likely to vote. A candidate can state positions on issues in a brief ad, which may serve to remind voters of positions that have been developed at further length in another context. There is much discussion and criticism of ads, but ads will remain—for better or worse—an important way of conveying political information.

Direct Coverage Direct coverage of events, such as presidential addresses, news conferences, and campaign debates, allows political leaders to have unmediated contact with the public and to present their views in an extended fashion. The presidency has profited most from this opportunity, because the president is a single individual whose personality and policies are certain to be of deep interest to the American public. Difficult as it is to conceive, most citizens never heard their presidents speak until Calvin Coolidge and never saw them "live" until Dwight Eisenhower. But the advantages a president gains by television are offset by certain costs. The media's intense focus on the presidency occurs not just when things go well, but when things go poorly. Expectations grow that presidents should have some plan to fix things and that they should address the nation whenever there is a major problem—even when they may have little or nothing to say.

Access to television is governed by laws and by precedents worked out over the years between the networks and government. Although the networks retain the option of refusing the president time for an address, they seldom do so. To balance the time given to the president, the networks now generally offer the opposition party time to respond to presidential addresses. The question of access has been resolved to the satisfaction of most major politicians, but complaints are still heard from third-party candidates, who have usually been excluded from presidential debates. (Ross Perot, a major independent candidate, participated in the presidential debates in 1992, but was left out in 1996, as was Ralph Nader in 2000.)

Interview and Discussion Programs Direct coverage in a slightly different form is found in programs like *Meet the Press* in which leaders and public figures present their views in response to reporters' questions. Shows like *Crossfire* and *Nightline* have added the dimension of give-and-take between advocates of different viewpoints, leading to extensive dialogue and often heated debates. Such programs allow viewpoints to be expressed vigorously, at the same time that they supply the "discipline" of forcing individuals to confront objections and different arguments. Political pundits also have a large impact on the political debate. Radio and TV commentators such as Rush Limbaugh and Bill O'Reilly are heard and watched by millions of Americans, and the influence of these and other shows is considerable.

A recent development in direct media coverage has been the appearance of presidential candidates on softer, "infotainment" talk-shows. Ross Perot in 1992 virtually declared his candidacy on the *Larry King Live* show, while candidate Bill Clinton did a famous saxophone gig, in sunglasses, on the *Arsenio Hall* show. In 2000, both Al Gore and George W. Bush appeared on the highly rated *Oprah Winfrey* show to appeal to her audience. These shows have given candidates an extraordinary opportunity to speak directly to the American people in a fairly relaxed environment. They have been criticized, however, for allowing the candidates to escape the more vigorous style of questioning of the professional journalists' interview programs.

News Television news coverage is the most important source of political information for Americans and also the most controversial channel of communication. Television journalists and editors must decide what is newsworthy and how the news should be presented. Their decisions can have an important effect on how the public views events and a tremendous impact on the course of political campaigns. A great deal of analysis has therefore been devoted to discovering how these journalists make their selections about news. Journalists themselves will say that it is based on the standards and practices of their profession. Others add that the selections are also influenced by the pressures of competition for ratings and, whether consciously or unconsciously, by the political views of the reporters and the news bureaus.

Practices of reporting over the last generation, in both the print and the electronic media, have undergone a major change. The value of objectivity remains supreme, but how reporters conceive the meaning of objectivity has shifted. Since the 1970s more journalists have adopted an investigative and adversarial relationship to their subjects, attempting to uncover a lie or scandal hidden beneath official sources and comments. This attitude was fueled first by government and press relations during the Vietnam War, when official government sources continually sought to present the news in a favorable light by distorting the truth, and then by Watergate, when President Nixon consistently lied about his relationship to the cover-up of the break-in at the Democratic campaign headquarters. Journalists have had reason for their suspicions, as government officials often attempt to "manage" or "spin" accounts in a way that, at a minimum, presents matters in the least unfavorable light and, at a maximum, involves outright distortion. On the other hand, many officials complain that journalism today all too frequently rushes to disseminate hearsay evidence that casts doubts on the statements or interpretations of politicians. In seeking to uncover the "real" story, these critics argue, journalists exaggerate and distort matters. There is a common feeling among government officials that they are getting a "bad" press. All recent presidents at one time or another have complained bitterly about the press coverage of their administrations, and frequently with some justification.

Competition and the desire to make the news interesting can also lead to distortions. The news, especially television news, is a highly competitive business, and the networks and sponsors inevitably seek to attract large audiences. There is therefore pressure to cover stories in a dramatic way and to focus on "interesting" items, often those involving conflict. (It is more visually stimulating to show a cut from a rally or demonstration than to cover a candidate's speech or to give the statistical background on a problem.) What journalists select as news naturally influences the behavior of those seeking access to the news. Political campaigns, for example, will seek to provide interesting "visuals" for the evening news, and candidates will learn to speak in sound bites rather than in longer, developed paragraphs. News reporting also focuses on the drama of events, rather than on the substance. In the coverage of presidential races, television journalism has tended to play up the "horse race" among the candidates rather than to focus on what they are actually saying.[25]

The preeminence of television as the source of news has profoundly affected the entire political process. Groups that once had little access to the American system can now gain public attention by staging dramatic events that capture the eye of television journalists. Not surprisingly, demonstrations (and perhaps terrorist acts as well) have become more frequent in a media age, as these are obvious ways of gaining attention and creating interesting news. Television may also have contributed to certain institutional changes, such as the weakening of the power of party organizations, because television enables candidates to appeal directly to the public. Television contributed to the importance of presidential primaries over party conventions as the mechanism for selecting presidential nominees. In general, the activities and institutions that can be portrayed on television have tended to gain power at the expense of those which cannot. At the same time, the critical attention sometimes focused on the most visible institutions may have made people more cynical about them. At the very least, the sheer amount of media coverage, offered in ways that seems to impose demands and to magnify errors, makes governing more difficult. As one political scientist has observed, "The media accelerate political consciousness and feed on impatience for quick results, no matter how complex the problems; they want things solved in 60 minutes."[26]

Finally, there is the problem of journalistic bias. Like other people, journalists have their own political viewpoints, and these color to some extent the way in which they present the news. A concentration of bias in favor of one viewpoint can pose serious problems of objectivity in political communication. In the late 1960s, conservatives complained that the major media were dominated by a "liberal establishment" that slanted the news against conservative positions. One point is clear: whether journalists let their bias show or not, they are decidedly more liberal than the American population at large. In 1985 only 23 percent of the American people considered themselves liberal compared to 55 percent of journalists; 56 percent of the public had a favorable view of President Reagan compared to 30 percent of journalists.[27]

Given the character of the American system of government and the great protections afforded to the news profession under the First Amendment, it is inevitable that there will be tensions between politicians and the press, and equally inevitable that there will be occasional journalistic excesses. Politicians and governing officials prefer a favorable press, or at any rate a press that takes into account the difficulties and uncertainties that go into making any decision. Journalists, often suspicious of official explanations, have their own incentives to cover events in a more dramatic fashion and also to concentrate on failures more than successes. Within bounds, the tension between the two is healthy for democratic politics.

Public Opinion and Public Policy

Having examined the concept of public opinion, we should now realize that the simple question—does public opinion govern?—has no simple answer. Public opinion exists on at least three different levels, and on each level its nature and influence differ.

The Role of Public Opinion

On the constitutional level, public opinion has an influence that is pervasive, yet—because it is so often broadly accepted—invisible. It sets the broad boundaries of acceptable public discourse. Dominant opinions about liberty or equality may be challenged by radical groups like the Communist party or the Ku Klux Klan, but these views are for the most part simply ignored. Only on rare occasions do constitutional issues become a subject of major, sustained controversy in the United States. At such moments, such as the period before the Civil War or during the civil rights struggle, political leaders raise issues of constitutional principle and place themselves "ahead" of current standards in an attempt to lead public opinion in new directions.

Politicians at other times may adopt a long-term "educative" strategy in an attempt to change constitutional opinion. But their ability to push policies at odds with dominant opinion is limited, at least in the short run. Statesmen must act within the realm of the possible. Thus even as Lincoln was fighting for the idea of equality in opposing slavery, he was not prepared to call for social equality of the races. As he explained, "A universal feeling, whether well or ill-founded, cannot be safely disregarded."[28] Constrained by such "universal feelings," the role of the statesman is necessarily different from that of the activist.

On the level of general opinion toward government policy, we observed that while most Americans may not think systematically in ideological terms, citizens nevertheless can be placed roughly on a spectrum of general policy opinion. There are certainly positions which, if broached by leaders, would evoke powerful opposition. New departures from general policy by political leaders, it seems, may not have the immediate support of a majority, but there often exists at least a general willingness to try something new. Thus in 1932, when Roosevelt was elected president, it was unlikely that a majority would have backed the new liberal principles on which he began to act. But it is clear that support for the principle of limited government had weakened as a result of the Depression and that the public was willing to embark on a new experiment. By the same token, in 1980 it was questionable whether a majority in the public was in favor of President Reagan's conservative principles. Again, however, it was clear that by the late

1970s there had been a significant loss of confidence in "big government" and a willingness among a much greater number than before to try new approaches. An election victory, for whatever reasons, coupled with a significant movement of ideological opinion, can provide a strong-willed president with the necessary leeway to attempt a new departure. If the policies prove to be successful, a president can change the basic policy or ideological disposition of the majority.

Opinions on specific policies and issues are sometimes taken very seriously and sometimes discounted. On certain issues, such as the Vietnam War, opinion is intense and pushes itself into the policymaking process by way of electoral pressures. Political leaders may be forced to change or accommodate their positions under the threat of being replaced. The reverse situation is found where leaders might like to act differently but are aware that the level of opinion needed to support their policies would not be forthcoming. President Roosevelt, for example, wanted to involve the nation more actively in the fight against Nazi Germany in the 1930s but was unable to buck the strong isolationist sentiment at the time. He therefore had to bide his time and wait for an event that would change public opinion, which came dramatically with the Japanese surprise attack on Pearl Harbor in 1941.

Potential national voting issues such as the Vietnam War are more the exception than the rule. The public frequently wants to see an issue addressed (like inflation or unemployment), but it has no one particular means specifically in mind. In many instances the policies of government are at odds with what the majority wants (as measured in opinion polls). These may be matters on which people do not have strong feelings or have not had time to organize. Politicians in these instances have the leeway to act at their discretion. Moreover, in many instances majority opinion may be much less important to politicians than intense and well-organized minority opinions. The majority may be largely indifferent, whereas for various minorities the policies may well constitute a voting issue.

Limitations on the Influence of Public Opinion

Why is it that on some issues of public policy majority opinion does not have its way? The most important reason is the most obvious one: public opinion in our representative system is not legally or Constitutionally empowered to govern. Authority is in the hands of officials who are not required to follow popular opinion, and in fact many elements of the system are designed precisely to guard against the necessity of quick transfers of public sentiment into official policy.

Yet the system is essentially popular. The selection of most officers by election provides a vehicle by which public opinion in certain cases can be translated into public policy. People can elect politicians who are in sympathy with their views and turn out of office those who are not (with the exception of federal judges). Elections stand at the base of power of the government, and it follows that a strong and persistent majority must, over time, have its way. In fact, there are few conflicts between this kind of majority and governmental policy, because the government will normally evolve to reflect such opinions.

Where, however, something less than a strong and persistent majority exists, the mechanism of popular election does not produce—and was not designed to produce—a strict correspondence between majority opinion and policy. Consider the following three points about elections. First, when voters cast their ballots for a candidate, they do not—indeed cannot—express their views on every issue. Voting decisions boil down to a choice among candidates offering a "package" of policy views, and voters can choose only the entire package. Where there is no one dominant issue, elections cannot ensure that a candidate supports what the majority wants on any particular matter; in fact, candidates often win support by taking stands on a series of issues that minorities favor with much intensity.

Second, when people vote, they often consider not only the candidates' issue positions, but also their character, their performance in office, and their party affiliation. In many elections, the candidates' effort to win the public's trust is just as important as their being strictly in accord with

the public on many policy issues. Elections are not simply mechanisms for registering policy preferences, but devices by which people select those whose judgment and character they respect.

Finally, public opinion—considered as the views of all adults in the nation—is not exactly the opinion that is registered in the electoral process. Turnout in some elections can be quite low, and it is with the voting public that politicians must be concerned. Furthermore, an election itself is the last act of the electoral process, and in order to compete effectively, candidates must raise funds and secure the help of volunteers. Thus it is the views of potential contributors and activists that often count for more than those of ordinary citizens. Electoral calculations, therefore, do not always confirm the results of general opinion polls.

Beyond the issue of electoral considerations, it would be false to assume that politicians think always and only of reelection. They often deliberate about what they think will work best, apart from what the public wants (today) and occasionally at some risk to their electoral chances. Especially in the case of presidents, it is often clearly not in their interest to follow public opinion in the short-run. In the end, when seeking reelection, presidents are judged by how well their policies appear to have worked, not by how popular they were at the moment they were adopted. Furthermore, most presidents are concerned not just with popularity, but with their place in history. This "love of fame" can lead presidents to take risks for policies they believe will ultimately prove their worth.

Conclusion

Institutions and laws can be arranged to give more or less weight to public opinion in the governing process. Realizing this fact, constitution makers have tried to adjust institutional arrangements to reflect their understanding of the proper influence of public opinion. The founders, while recognizing the legitimacy of public opinion as expressed (indirectly) through elections, placed limits on its influence by such means as long terms of office, indirect elections, the separation of powers, and the inculcation of the norm that officials should deliberate and exercise their own discretion. Developments since the founding have provided greater weight for public opinion in many areas. Not only have theorists accorded it greater legitimacy, but changes in the electoral process have increased its influence. So too has the development of polling and the frequent reporting on pubic opinion. At the same time, the growing power of courts and bureaucracies has tended to diminish the influence of opinion.

Although most citizens are sympathetic to majoritarian arguments favoring greater influence for public opinion, it is important to recall some of the reasons for limitations to this influence. Many recognize the importance of taking into account, up to a point, the intensity of minority sentiments, which is a pluralist rather than a strict majoritarian concern. Many would also see the need for the "representative" elements of deliberation and statesmanship as well as the need to protect certain rights against momentary majorities. All these concerns require according some discretion for governing officials from the immediate dictates of public opinion. Determining the balance between the proper influence for public opinion and the necessary discretion for representative institutions remains one of the main challenges of modern constitution makers.

One way to think about the proper role of public opinion is to consider the merits of a proposal to increase its weight in our political system. The proposal, which had considerable support in the Senate in the 1970s, is for a Constitutional amendment to establish a national initiative and referendum, thereby enabling voters in certain areas to make final policy without needing a law passed by Congress. (Many states currently have such a provision in their constitutions, and in some states, such as California and Oregon, it is frequently employed.) This proposal could be modernized and extended by a procedure that would allow for regularly scheduled referenda on national issues to be conducted by people voting at home through two-way television hookups and computers. The public could listen to the debates of their "representatives" after which they could then register their preferences and decide the issue.

This last idea, which may soon be feasible, represents a logical extension of the principle that public opinion should govern. Given communications technology today, representative government is no longer a necessity imposed by the fact that the public as a whole cannot assemble in one place and vote. If, therefore, Americans are to continue to choose a representative system, it cannot be merely the result of a concession to physical limitations; rather it must be because of the recognition that, while majority opinion on particular issues has a legitimate role to play, it is not finally equipped to govern directly. In part, this recognition might be based on the constraint that the people "assembled" through television or computer hookups cannot make the same adjustments and compromises that are possible in a political assembly. For the most part, however, the choice to support a representative system must be based on an appreciation that elected officials operating in a setting that allows for deliberation are better-suited than the public to make day-to-day political decisions. To make such a claim is neither to insult the public nor to put elected officials on a pedestal. It is merely to assert that in a representative system the public and officials have different roles to play.

Chapter 5 Notes

1. The *Los Angeles Times* poll was taken between January 14–17, 1993 (1,733 persons were polled), and *Time/CNN* was taken on January 13–14 (n = 1,000).
2. Gabriel Almond and Sydney Verba, *The Civic Culture* (Princeton, N.J.: Princeton, 1963).
3. Robert W. Johannsen, *The Lincoln-Douglas Debates* (New York: Oxford, 1965), pp. 64–65.
4. See Herbert J. McCloskey and Alida Brill, *Dimensions of Tolerance*, (New York: Russell Sage, 1983).
5. Roper Survey of August–September, 1994, reported in *The Public Perspective*, April/May 1995, p.19.
6. Time Mirror Surveys 1991, reported in *Public Perspective*, April/May 1995, p.20.
7. Robert Lane, *Political Life* (Glencoe, Ill.: Free Press, 1959), p. 41.
8. Survey by Roper Center, August–September 1994. Reported in *Public Perspective*, April/May 1995, p.18.
9. Martin Shapiro, "The Supreme Court: From Warren to Burger," in Anthony King, ed., *The New American Political System* (Washington, D.C.: American Enterprise Institute, 1978), p. 195.
10. *Public Opinion*, June 1981.

11. Gabriel Almond and Sydney Verba, *The Civic Culture*; Sydney Verba et al., *The Changing American Voter* (Cambridge, Mass.: Harvard University Press, 1973); *Public Opinion*, February–March 1978, p. 35.
12. Data from the American National Election Studies of the Inter-University Consortium for Political and Social Research.
13. James Bryce, *The American Commonwealth*, vol. 2 (New York: Macmillan, 1889), p. 32.
14. Survey by the National Opinion Research Center. Reported in *The Public Perspective*, September/October, 1994.
15. Alexis de Tocqueville, Democracy in America, J. P. Mayer, ed., George Lawrence, trans. (Garden City, N.Y.: Doubleday [Anchor], 1968), p. 429.
16. Raymond Aron, *Democratie et Totalitarisme* (Saint-Amand, France: Gallimard, 1965), p. 53.
17. V. O. Key, *The Responsible Electorate* (Cambridge, Mass.: Harvard University Press, 1966); Gerald Pomper, *Voter's Choice* (New York: Dodd, Mead, 1975).
18. Charles W. Kegley, Jr. and Eugene R. Wittkopf, *American Foreign Policy: Pattern and Process* (New York: St. Martins, 1982), p. 288.
19. *Statistical Abstract of the United States*, 1989, p. 124.
20. *Pierce v. Society of Sisters*, 268 U.S. 510 (1925), p. 535.
21. John Maynard Keynes, *The General Theory of Employment and Money* (New York: Harcourt, Brace, Jovanovich, 1936), p. 383.
22. Marshall McLuhan, *Understanding Media: The Extensions of Man* (New York: McGraw-Hill, 1966).
23. Michael Robinson, "Television and American Politics, 1952–1976," *Public Interest*, Summer 1977, pp. 3–39.
24. Austin Ranney, "Broadcasting, Narrowcasting, and Politics" in Anthony King, ed., *The New American Political System*, 2nd ed. (Washington, D.C.: American Enterprise Institute Press, 1990), pp. 175–201.
25. Doris Graber, *Mass Media and American Politics* (Washington, D.C.: Congressional Quarterly Press, 1980).
26. David Broder, "Second-Year Slump," *Washington Post*, April 4, 1982, p. 1.
27. *Public Opinion*, August–September 1985, pp. 6–11 and 58–59.
28. Robert W. Johannsen, *The Lincoln-Douglas Debates*, p. 51.

6

Political Parties

CHAPTER CONTENTS

In 1844, the first message ever sent by telegraph—from Baltimore, Maryland to Washington, D.C.—slowly ticked out the news that James K. Polk had been nominated by the Democratic party as its candidate for the presidency. On receiving this news, Democrats in Washington ran jubilantly through the streets shouting, "Hurrah for Polk," only pausing now and then to inquire of each other, "Who is James Polk?" Today, by contrast, when a presidential candidate is nominated, few find cause for celebration merely because their *party* has chosen a nominee. Americans today are much more likely to take interest in the *individuals* who are running for office. The party label is important, but no longer decisive.

This change is one example of the diminished hold of political parties over the American electorate. This decline is evident in a number of areas. A century ago, the press routinely branded the few voters who considered themselves independents as "oddballs"; today, almost 40 percent of the voters call themselves "independents" without feeling the least sense of inferiority. A century ago, party organizations chose the party's nominees for all elective offices through a system of party conventions; today, most candidates are nominated in primary elections in which the individual candidates present themselves directly to the voters. (In presidential nominating contests, party conventions still make the final choice, but most of the delegates are chosen in primaries.) A century ago, the nation's major newspapers were all associated with one or the other of the political parties and presented highly partisan accounts of events; today, candidates for federal offices contact the voters largely through the newspapers and television, which provide news on a nonpartisan basis and which feature paid advertisements that focus more on the candidates' individual qualities than on their party identification.

Less than two decades ago, many were predicting an imminent collapse of our traditional party system. No such thing has occurred, and as we shall see, in certain respects political parties have even gained ground. The current situation, accordingly, cannot be summed up by a single slogan. American parties have declined in strength relative to the position they once held, and electoral competition today focuses much more on the individual candidates rather than the party labels. But the major parties are still alive, and almost all office holders are elected under their labels.

Does it matter if parties decline? Some think it a positive development, arguing that electoral procedures have become more democratic, while others see it as a loss for our system that has made effective governance all the more difficult. Parties are complex institutions that affect the political system at almost every point, and important choices will have to be made about the future of parties. To help with this task, we shall begin by defining what a party is and then analyze the functions constitution makers have assigned to parties throughout our history. We shall then turn to how parties have been regulated by law, how they have been organized, what forces in the country they have represented, and what role they have played in structuring relations between Congress and the president.

What Are Political Parties?

Eighteenth century British politician and philosopher Edmund Burke considered a party to be a group united by common political interests in service to the national interest. According to Burke, the aggregation of people in support of common political interests promoted the public good and corrected the factious nature of unaffiliated or independent politicians. The founders initially held a different view about parties, regarding them as organizations that inflated the tendency for faction by multiplying the selfish or uninformed interests of individuals. Hence, during the drafting and ratification of the Constitution, parties were discouraged as dangerous and prone to promoting majority tyranny.

As parties have changed greatly from one generation to the next, any definition tailored to fit them all would have to adopt the lowest common denominator. A party in this minimal sense is an organization that competes for political power under a specific label. But this definition, while technically correct, tells us very little about the life and spirit of a party. A much better way to

BOX 6.1

Theories of Political Parties

Edmund Burke thought of party as a necessary and virtuous combination of political interests and opinions in the national interest. The Founders disagreed and considered parties to be factious and a chief causes of majority tyranny.

> They [the Whigs] believed that no men could act with effect, who did not act in concert; that no men could act in concert, who did not act in confidence; that no men could act with confidence, who were not bound together by common opinions, common affections, and common interests…. Party is a body of men united, for promoting by their joint endeavors the national interest, upon some particular principle in which they are all agreed.

—Edmund Burke, "Thoughts on the Cause of the Present Discontents," 1780.

> Let me warn you in the most solemn manner against the baneful effects of the spirit of party generally… It serves always to distract the public councils and enfeeble the public administration. It agitates the community with ill-founded jealousies and false alarms, kindles the animosity of one part against another, foments occasionally riot and insurrection…. A fire not to be quenched, it demands a uniform vigilance to prevent its bursting into a flame, lest, instead of warming, it should consume.

—George Washington, Farewell Address, 1796.

> I never submitted the whole system of my opinions to the creed of any party of men whatever in religion, in philosophy, in politics, or in any thing else where I was capable of thinking for myself. Such an addiction is the last degradation of a free and moral agent. If I could not go to heaven but with a party, I would not go there at all.

—Thomas Jefferson, Letter to Francis Hopkinson, 1789.

proceed is to analyze a party in the process of formation and then look at the parties as we find them today as established institutions. We can then combine elements of the two conceptions to arrive at a more satisfactory definition.

Imagine, then, that you wished to establish a new political party. Most likely, this would occur under circumstances in which you were convinced that important policies being followed by elected officials were wrong and that no existing party adequately reflected your views. Finding others in sympathy with your position, including perhaps a few elected officials, you would join together and form an association. The association would adopt a name, agree on rules by which to conduct its internal business, and proceed to nominate candidates for various offices and support them in their election campaigns. The final objective would be to win power and enact the party's program.

Notice certain points that emerge from considering a party in the process of formation. In the first place, a party is not an "official" public institution, but a semi-private association of citizens and leaders who come together on their own to win political power. Parties stand between the people and the official institutions of government, serving as intermediary bodies that link citizens and their opinions to the government. Second, parties are highly "democratic" in the sense that they give many citizens an influence on the government that goes beyond merely voting for or writing to elected officials. The party cuts across electoral districts and potentially organizes a nationwide, self-governing association. Parties ensure that candidates will be fielded for office, that citizens will be exhorted to exercise their right to vote, and that policy will be formed and debated in the public sphere. Ultimately, parties provide a vital link between the people and their government, creating a system for the promotion of citizenship that was not supplied by the Constitution.

The Democratic and Republican parties are much more than temporary private associations, and have been sustained over their long history by motivations other than simply the agreed-upon political goals. The Democratic party, which was organized in the 1820s and can perhaps trace its origins to the 1790s, is America's oldest political party; the Republican party, formed in the 1850s, has existed for nearly 150 years. As long-standing bodies, these (once) private associations have become virtually accepted elements of the political system. Congress is organized along party lines, party channels are part of the folkways in Washington, party mechanisms are the accepted means of nominating candidates for federal offices, and the laws of the states and the federal government implicitly recognize and regulate the conduct of these two parties.

Because of their longevity, widespread acceptance, and legal status, our two major parties can be considered semiofficial institutions of our political system. It is not surprising that parties, as the accepted gatekeepers for acquiring political power, have over the years attracted candidates and supporters for reasons other than promoting a larger political purpose. People have joined parties to win power or obtain government jobs, so that at certain times, when these motives have predominated, parties have lost all but the slightest connection with achieving political principles. We have, then, two conceptions of a political party, one deriving from the party in the process of formation as an association of like-minded citizens and the other deriving from the specific characteristics of our two major parties, which have become semi-official institutions. Both conceptions are needed to understand parties. Our major parties began as purposive associations of (relatively) like-minded individuals; and, while at some times they have lost a sense of purpose or have been paralyzed by internal disagreement, they have nonetheless been periodically renewed as bodies of common purpose.

The party, in the comprehensive sense just defined, includes many elements. At the core are the officials of the party organization (national party chairs, state party chairs, and local precinct leaders) and its elected officials (presidents, members of Congress, governors, and mayors). Next are the party workers, whether paid or volunteer, who perform the work of the party, ranging from polling to calling and reminding people to vote on election day. Further removed are the party members, official or unofficial, who attend meetings and lend occasional support. Finally, at the periphery, there are the voters who identify with the party and vote regularly in its primaries, or at least support most of its nominees in the general election. In this chapter we shall be concerned chiefly with the organization and structure of the parties, saving the treatment of the behavior of voters for Chapter 8.

Political parties strive to fulfill their own goals. But in doing so they affect the performance of many key activities in politics. At the governing level, parties build coalitions out of diverse interests in the nation and influence how relations among leaders are coordinated under a system of separation of powers and federalism. By observing how parties affect the performance of these functions and how these functions are altered by changes in the character of the parties, a constitution maker can begin to make some of the judgments necessary for deciding the proper role and structure of the party system.

The Development of Political Parties

What accounts for the role and strength of an institution in any given historical period? Besides the Constitution and legal powers, one of the most important factors is the prevailing doctrine of what a given institution's role should be. Such doctrines are the products of ideas and historical experience. In the case of the three principal institutions—the presidency, the Congress, and the Supreme Court—the ideas have been strongly influenced by the founders' thought and the Constitution. Influences from other sources have also been important, but the fact that these institutions all derive power from the Constitution has shaped and limited the doctrinal debate.

Political parties present a different case, as they are never mentioned in the Constitution and lack a permanent foundation in fundamental law. The case for political parties was not made until nearly forty years after the founding. Lacking an anchor of authority in the Constitution, doctrines about political parties have been more easily changed than those of the other institutions. Parties originally were considered dangerous and nearly illegitimate. By the mid-nineteenth century, they were universally accepted and recognized as vital to the effective operation of our government. In this century, the parties have been scorned and attacked in their existing form, though often idealized in some possible forms which they *might* assume. Our parties have to some extent been what we have wanted them to be, and their current status of relative weakness reflects a low estimate of—or perhaps a confusion about—the role they should play.

The Founders and the Case for a Nonpartisan System

The founders opposed national political parties, preferring instead a nonpartisan system in which candidates would compete for office on the basis of their individual qualifications and political beliefs. The founders wanted no formal associational links between candidates for the presidency, the House, and the Senate; no permanent national political organization of citizens for nominating candidates; and no labels dividing the population into opposing camps.

Nominating candidates is one of the most important functions performed by political parties; and the founders—at least in the case of the presidency—established a formal constitutional alternative to party nominations. The original plan for the electoral college was to select the president in a nonpartisan fashion by elevating individuals of outstanding national reputation.

The nonpartisan character of the founders' intentions becomes even more strikingly evident when one considers that the vice president was selected not as a candidate on a ticket with the president but as the runner-up in the total of electoral votes. This arrangement, defensible in a system without parties, is untenable in a system with them. In 2000, for example, it would have produced George W. Bush as president with Al Gore as vice-president. In fact, a result no less strange occurred in 1796 when John Adams, a Federalist, was elected president and Thomas Jefferson, the opposition leader, became vice president. By 1804, the Twelfth Amendment was adopted, which implicitly acknowledged the existence of political parties and provided for separate balloting by the electors for president and vice president.*

Why did the founders oppose party competition? Their hostility to parties was based first on their fear that parties tended to be factious in nature, promoting particular goals over the public good. Madison in *Federalist* 10 barely distinguishes between a faction and a party. He observed that this perceived tendency of "the spirit of party and faction" to promote polices "adverse to the rights of other citizens, or to the permanent and aggregate interests of the community" presented a threat to democratic regimes. In addition to promoting policies adverse to the public good, the founders thought that parties would stir up unnecessary and dangerous divisions, "agitating the community," as George Washington argued in his Farewell Address of 1796, "with ill-founded jealousies and false alarm." The proper way to express conflict was through elections of individual officers and not through party organization. In fact, something of the same mistrust of parties exists today, as indicated by the appeals of leaders, often in moments of crisis, to put "petty" partisan concerns aside and consider the true national interest.

---

* The original system for the electoral college was extremely complex. Each elector had two votes for president. The candidate receiving the most votes, provided the number constituted a majority of all the electors, would be president; the runner-up would be vice president. In the event that no candidate received a majority, the House would select the president from among the top five electoral vote recipients. (In the event of a tie for first place among candidates receiving a majority, as occurred in 1800, the House would also make the decision by choosing among those tied.) When the House voted, each state delegation—not each member—would have one vote, and a majority of the votes of all the states was required for election.

The Twelfth Amendment (1804), which still governs the Constitutional rules, provides for separate elections for president and vice president, with each elector having one vote for each office. In the event that no candidate for president receives more than a majority of electors' votes, as occurred in 1824, the House decides among the top three recipients of electoral votes by the same state voting system described above.

Second, the founders worried that permanent national parties would conflict with the intended roles of the presidency and the Congress. A president elected as the head of a party might have to defer to partisan demands rather than exercise personal judgment and might lose the intangible claim of being "president of all the people." As President Taft once explained, "It seems to me impossible to be a strict party man and serve the whole country impartially."[1] In the case of Congress, the founders feared that parties would prevent deliberation. Representatives would meet in party caucus, decide on a party position, and then vote automatically as a bloc in formal congressional sessions. Congress would cease to be a forum for serious debate and would instead merely register predetermined party positions.

Finally, some founders feared that powerful parties would introduce too popular an influence on the political system, undermining its representative character. Parties are instruments for bringing representative institutions closer to the people by linking elements of the public with the elected officials. Certain founders saw dangers in this link, especially if it resulted in elections that would bind both the president and Congress to a party program backed by a national majority. Elections, as the founders understood them, should not closely tie down the decisions of the government, but should instead indicate in a general way what the public wants.

Even though the founders opposed political parties, they never considered introducing a constitutional ban against them. Under a system that guaranteed political liberty, government could not prevent people from combining into peaceful associations to influence the selection of public officials. What the founders hoped was that national parties could be avoided because the government could function without them and because most people would believe that parties were dangerous.

Plainly, the founders' expectation that the United States would be a nonpartisan regime proved incorrect. Yet we should not conclude that the emergence of parties totally transformed the political system. Parties have clearly modified the original constitutional design, but they have just as clearly been shaped by it. They never assumed the rigid form that founders feared. In fact, many scholars believe that the way in which parties eventually developed served to promote many of the founders' most important goals.

The Formation of Parties and the Case for Party Competition

The transformation from the founders' nonpartisan system to a system of party competition occurred in two phases: during the Jeffersonian era, when parties formed temporarily but were not widely regarded as permanent or legitimate institutions; and during the Jacksonian era, when parties were reestablished and eventually accepted as legitimate and normal components of the political system. In the first phase, political leaders made use of political parties but never really embraced the concept of permanent party competition. After the crucial election of 1800, in which Jefferson's party won control of the presidency and both houses of Congress, the Federalist party went into a rapid decline, and by 1816 it had dwindled to a tiny regional party that could no longer offer candidates for the presidency. Thereafter, in the period known as the "era of good feelings" (1817–1824), the political system had effectively returned to a nonpartisan—though Jeffersonian—footing, and most of the leading politicians of the period were as firm in their denunciation of the evils of party competition as the founders had been in the early 1790s.

The task of reestabliblishing parties and transforming the public's perception of them was undertaken by Martin Van Buren in the 1820s. Van Buren, then a senator from New York, proposed viewing parties in a way different from the founders—"in a sincerer and wiser spirit [that] recognizes their necessity and gives them the credit they deserve."[2]

As the focal point for his analysis of parties, Van Buren looked at the presidential election of 1824, a nonpartisan contest between four major candidates, none of whom could win an electoral majority. According to Van Buren, the experience of 1824 pointed to three problems with the existing nonpartisan system. First, without party nominations to mark the beginning of the race, the activity of governing was distracted and agitated by an open campaign begun some two years in advance of the election. Second, with nothing to restrain or moderate the positions of the candidates, the campaign itself featured dangerous appeals stimulating sectional animosities and popular appetites for charismatic leaders. Finally, with so many contenders allowed to enter the race, the possibility that any candidate would capture a national majority was small, and the incentive for the candidates was therefore to establish a firm base of support in a particular region or with a particular constituency. As suggested by the controversial selection of John Quincy Adams for president by the House of Representatives in 1824, which Jackson claimed had robbed him of the office, no one was satisfied with a system that allowed the House to decide the presidential contest.

Van Buren also thought that the era of nonpartisan politics led to a breakdown in coordination between the presidency and Congress. Without parties, there was no common program or coordination between the two institutions and no mechanism for helping to push through a legislative agenda. The policymaking process tended to lose focus, and the government lacked the necessary energy to follow a coherent line.

The Theory of Party Competition   All these problems led Van Buren to the conclusion that if parties were not reestablished, the stability of the political system itself would be threatened. Van Buren accordingly set forth the basic case for party competition that remains today the classic defense of reasonably strong political parties. It consisted of four points:

First, party competition would prevent the election from being decided by the House because the nominees of a major party would have the broad support of a large segment of the people, enabling them to win a majority in the electoral college. (With minor parties, it is still possible for the election to go to the House, but since 1824 this has not happened.)

Second, party competition limits the appeals of candidates to the safer issues backed by the broad parties and their general principles. Narrow demagogic appeals or sectional pleas would be avoided. The parties in effect would be placed "above" the individual candidacies, forcing pres-

A leading figure in New York state politics, Martin Van Buren (1782–1862) went on to become the eighth President of the United States. His argument for a strong, perpetual two-party system was his most enduring political contribution. (Photo provided by the National Portrait Gallery, Smithsonian Institution; gift of Mrs. Robert Timpson. Used with permission.)

idential aspirants to adopt a general set of party principles rather than appeal to momentary issues of the candidate's own devising. (The parties have, in fact, tended to avoid such appeals, with the notable exception of the period before and after the Civil War.)

Third, under party competition, voters can more easily grasp what elections are all about, because parties, more than individual candidates, have a long history and set of principles that most voters come to know and understand. Nonpartisan competition gives an advantage to narrow interest groups able to push a particular candidate in the short term without the great body of people knowing what that candidate's sympathies are.

Fourth, party competition would provide a greater degree of coordination between the president and Congress than that provided in a nonpartisan system. Van Buren's intention was not that parties would override the Constitutional separation of powers, but that they would help smooth the relationship between the executive and the legislative branches, at least when both were controlled by the same party.

Of course, these benefits of party competition were dependent upon the existence of a certain kind of party. If the parties formed on the basis of radically different ideas about the first principles of government—for example, one favoring communism and the other monarchy—the solution would not work. Van Buren's entire plan for party competition rested on the presupposition that parties would not disagree on first principles, but rather would be limited in their conflict to secondary issues about how to achieve certain commonly accepted goals. While believing in the principles of their own party, party leaders would no longer attempt to eliminate the opposition; they would instead respect its right to exist and learn to accept and tolerate the doctrine of permanent competition between political parties faithful to the principles of the Constitution.

Van Buren's conception of parties was based on the view that they would not simply reflect political divisions but also to a certain extent manage and moderate them, screening out those of the most dangerous kind. Yet this view posed a problem: What would happen if the two major parties ignored or closed out a substantial body of opinion? Van Buren addressed this question when considering third or minor parties. Originally, he had assumed that the norm of American politics would be competition between two parties. And, in fact, many of the benefits he outlined would be threatened if competition among three or four parties became the usual practice. Nevertheless, as he argued in 1848, when he headed a third-party ticket for the Free-Soil party, there are dangers if the norm of two-party competition becomes so rigid that it excludes minor parties. Groups advocating new ideas might be denied access to the political process. Van Buren therefore allowed that the party system should be open to change, either by replacing one of the major parties (as it can be argued the Republicans did to the Whigs after 1852) or by forcing a majority party to change its position for fear of being replaced (as the Populist party did to the Democratic party in 1896). Under this solution, the electoral process is dominated by two parties without denying minor parties access to the system. Uncontrolled political change

through electoral politics is not encouraged—since starting a new party is difficult—but neither is it completely foreclosed.

The Establishment of Permanent Party Competition Articulating a theory of party competition was one thing; getting it accepted in the 1820s, when most leaders regarded parties as undesirable, was something very different. Van Buren had to persuade politicians that submitting to party regularity and tolerating a permanent opposition were legitimate codes of political conduct, and he had to convince the American people that joining or identifying with a political party was not a violation of good citizenship.

Van Buren accomplished this feat by using a most unexpected method. He persuaded Andrew Jackson, who previously had opposed party competition, to associate himself with the new Democratic party in return for its support in the election of 1828. Jackson was such a controversial figure at the time that his presence by itself helped to draw a partisan division with a new opposition party, which would soon adopt the name "Whig." This partisan division was solidified in the great struggle over the chartering of the National Bank in 1832, and by 1840 both sides had accepted the idea of permanent party competition.

The Consequences of Party Competition The advent of party competition altered American politics. Parties assumed control of the conduct of political campaigns. They recruited and nominated candidates, created strong partisan feelings in the electorate, and exercised control over the dissemination of news by the creation of party-run newspapers. Party competition also stimulated political interest within the electorate and contributed to the extension of the suffrage, as the parties vied to mobilize new segments of the public. Finally, parties changed the governing process by introducing a new, extra-Constitutional institution that helped bridge the separation of powers and tie national politics to state politics.

While these changes were significant, they were not revolutionary. They took their place within the basic constitutional structure, modifying it but not overturning it. In fact, as different

Party competition spawned popular political campaigns with rallies, torchlight parades, and numerous party banners and insignia. (Photos provided by the National Portrait Gallery, Smithsonian Institution. Used with permission.)

as the "form" of partisan competition was from the founders' goal of nonpartisanship, the effects of partisan competition frequently were in line with the founders' objectives. Van Buren, like the founders, sought stable competition in an electoral process that regulated the ambitions of politicians and promoted moderate majorities; and while Van Buren clearly favored a democratic system of choosing the president, democracy was not the only objective he valued. Like the founders, he thought that the electoral system should operate to prevent dangerous divisions and promote candidates having the support of broad coalitions. While the electoral process, in Van Buren's view, was responsible for expressing divisions, electoral choice should be structured to express them in a responsible way. One of Van Buren's main arguments, in fact, was that the nonpartisan electoral system that had emerged in the 1820s did not promote the founders' own goal of political stability.

Because of the many similarities between the goals of the founders and those of Martin Van Buren, many later analysts of American politics have tended to see the party system as virtually a part of the basic constitutional design. The main

feature of Van Buren's model of parties—governing with the aid of broad and moderate majorities—promoted the Madisonian goal of safe majority coalitions. Yet parties on occasions, as in 1800, 1856–1860, and 1932–1936, have also served as vehicles for national majorities that have reinterpreted the American constitutional order in ways that their opponents have viewed as dangerous and extreme. Parties, in other words, have performed the dual function—at different moments—of maintaining continuity and promoting change. As agents of change that emerge in part from the mass public, parties have added a distinctly new element to the original political system as conceived by the founders.

The Attack on Parties: The Nineteenth-Century Reformers

All in all, Van Buren had accomplished a remarkable feat of constitution making. But the results were not without defects, which became more apparent as time went on. After the Civil War, critics began to attack the party system on interrelated grounds: that the major parties no

BOX 6.2

A Progressive's Views on Party Nominations

Put aside the caucus and convention. They have been and will continue to be prostituted to the service of corrupt organization. . . . Substitute for both the caucus and the convention a primary election . . . where the citizen may cast his vote directly to nominate the candidate of the party with which he affiliates. . . . The nomination of the party will not be the result of compromise or impulse, or evil design . . . but the candidates of the majority, honestly and fairly nominated.—Senator Robert La Follette

Source: Robert La Follette, *Autobiography,* (Madison, Wis.: R. M. La Follette, 1913), pp. 197–198.

longer stood for any important principles, and that they stayed in existence only for the corrupt purpose of securing public service jobs for their members.

Critics may have exaggerated the absence of party principles during the late nineteenth century, but there can be no disputing the importance for the parties of what one analyst called "the hunting for office." Party patronage, simply defined, is a system in which the victorious party distributes jobs in the public service to faithful party workers. Personal qualifications for these jobs are sometimes ignored, and continuity in administrative service often takes a backseat to responsiveness to the party majority.

Patronage was crucial to the operation of the parties, and it changed the nature and tone of public administration. Before the 1820s, government employment at the national level had been, except at the top political levels, mostly a career occupation. President Jackson began to change this practice when he proclaimed the principle of rotation in government service and begin to fire and hire employees at his own discretion. For Jackson, the main goals were to make the public service more democratic and ensure its responsiveness to those in power. But this change soon opened the doors to mass party patronage. When an administration of a new party came to power, it dismissed the existing employees and hired new workers faithful to the party. All this was done under a motto coined by Senator Marcy in 1832: "To the victor belong the spoils." Hence another name for the mass use of patronage—the "spoils system."

Patronage became so widespread after the Civil War that a group of intellectuals, journalists, and working politicians—known as "reformers"—insisted that the parties had lost their rightful character. Instead of being organizations devoted to principle, which incidentally awarded jobs to their adherents, they had become organizations of office seekers which incidentally proclaimed a concern with principles. Patronage undermined the efficiency of the public service by driving away anyone who wanted a serious career, and it degraded the entire system of politics by giving effective control of the nomination of candidates to political organizations that were unconcerned with matters of policy and principle. As a cure, reformers proposed placing government jobs beyond the reach of partisan politics by making all hiring decisions subject to merit standards. According to one reformer, "the nation might then see the correction of corruption in politics and the restoration of political parties to their true function, which is the maintenance and enforcement of national policies."[3]

Known as "civil service reform," the proposal for merit hiring made great headway in the federal bureaucracy after President Garfield was assassinated by an unsuccessful government office seeker in 1881. The Pendleton Act of 1883 began a long process of federal civil service reforms that gradually reduced party influence by establishing a bipartisan Civil Service Commission that based federal employment on competitive examinations. Later, in 1939, Congress passed the Hatch Act, which forbade most forms of partisan activity by federal employees, thus further separating government employment from partisan politics. The Hatch Act was later partially repealed under President Clinton in 1993 as part of the Federal Employees Political

Activities Act to give federal employees greater ability to participate in politics. At the state and local levels, the success of reformers during the nineteenth century was much more limited. Some states and localities preferred not to adopt civil service reforms, while others passed weak laws and did little to enforce them. Thus, while parties lost most of their source of national patronage, they retained for a time much patronage at the state and local levels. Today, however, the parties' patronage power has been severely limited by state and local laws passed in this century, by some federal grant-in-aid requirements mandating state and local merit systems, and by recent federal court decisions.[4]

The Progressive Attack on Parties

The attack on parties assumed more far-reaching proportions during the "progressive era" (1908–1916). The Progressives rejected the reformers' view that parties could be saved merely by changing the rules for employment in the public service. The abuses and deficiencies of the parties, the progressives believed, were too deep-seated to be cured by such mild reform. The parties were corrupt, wedded to old and outmoded ideas, parochial, and unable to offer new ideas to solve the problems of a rapidly industrializing national economy. There was no way to proceed other than by attacking and destroying the existing party organizations.

Some Progressives also had in mind the positive goal of instituting a more popular or democratic method of selecting candidates. The existing system of nominations by the party organizations, they argued, took from the people their right to a free choice of public officials. The Progressives' ideal was a rational and public-spirited electorate that would select candidates without the interference of party bosses and without any old-fashioned attachment to party labels. Exactly how this would work in practice, however, was a matter of dispute between two strains of progressive thought.

One group favored the gradual elimination of parties and the establishment of a democratic, nonpartisan system. Adherents of this group led the movement for a legal ban on party activity from local elections. For higher offices they favored primaries open to all voters. This group extended its attack upon parties to an attack on representative institutions, advocating in the name of democracy the referendum, the recall, and direct popular election of judges. This "populist" understanding of nonpartisanship obviously rested on a different view than the founders' nonpartisan system.

A second group of Progressives had a different conception of the role of parties, though the difference has turned out to be much greater in theory than in practice. Like the first group, these Progressives advocated primaries as a way of destroying traditional parties. But instead of a nonpartisan system, this group favored rebuilding new and more powerful parties that would be democratic and operate as cohesive units at the governing level. Some Progressives went so far as to claim that the doctrine of separation of powers was outmoded. What the nation needed were strong national parties that would allow the majority party to govern without the impediments of checks and balances. The check on power should come from democratic elections, not separate institutions contending with each other. Early in his academic career, Woodrow Wilson, in his book *Congressional Government*, suggested the person and duties of the presidency could be folded into the Congress in a parliamentary style of government. Advocates of this doctrine of "pure" party government, modeled after the British parliamentary system, never succeeded in winning much popular support for their views.

Both strains of progressivism agreed on the need for a more democratic electoral process. The nineteenth-century system had favored nominations made by party leaders, after which the voters would choose from among the party nominees at the general election. The standard of legitimacy for electoral politics had been that of *interparty* democracy. The Progressives considered this insufficient and, where they still tolerated parties, called for the additional criterion of *intraparty* democracy—democracy within the parties—enforced through state-run primaries, in which individual leaders competed for nominations.

Instead of putting the party "above" the presidential aspirant as a means of limiting the appeals of candidates to safe principles, as Van Buren had wanted, the Progressives favored placing the individual candidate "above" the party and having the party take shape around the principles of the nominees. Only in this way could the stimulus of new programs and new ideas that the country needed be attained. Woodrow Wilson best encapsulated this formula: "No leaders, no principles; no principles, no parties."[5] The Progressives went a long way toward establishing the idea of presidents as popular leaders who commanded their parties and the nation through their ability to shape public opinion.

Progressive thought on political parties left a confused legacy. By all accounts the progressives succeeded in giving traditional parties a bad name, though they never managed to destroy them. The Progressives criticized parties—and not without justification—for being closed, selfish, boss-ridden, and obsolete in their principles. They went on to deplore what many considered to be the virtues of traditional partisanship—the spirit of compromise within party counsels, the warm enthusiasm of voters for party traditions, and the willingness of elected officials to accept some party discipline from traditional organizations. But having attacked parties for all their supposed faults, the Progressives were divided on what should take their place. Where they favored strong parties—as many did—they failed to establish any method for securing them, leaving the nation instead with a set of norms and laws that in fact have weakened the parties.

Modern Reformers (1968–2000)

The Progressives had a great impact on the legal status of parties. They transformed the method of nominations for senators and House members, though they did not completely eliminate the party organizations' influence. In the case of the nomination of the president, the Progressives had less success. After failing in 1913 to pass federal legislation establishing national presidential primaries, they turned to the states and persuaded many of them to adopt primary elections to select delegates to the national conventions (or at least to register the voters' presidential preferences). Yet most delegates contin-

ued to be selected in party-run caucuses in which the organizational regulars dominated. Thus, as late as 1968, aspirants for the presidency did not necessarily have to enter primaries to win the nomination, although participation in some primaries was the usual practice.

The modern reform movement arose in reaction to this one remaining vestige of "traditional" organizational control. The immediate impetus came in 1968, when Hubert Humphrey was nominated at the riot-torn Democratic convention in Chicago. Humphrey had not entered any primaries, and his nomination was likened by many in Chicago to the kind of corruption and back-room management that the Progressives had deplored. Large public protests took place during the convention, fueled by the supporters of the candidates who opposed the Vietnam war. (One of these candidates had been Senator Robert Kennedy, who was assassinated shortly before at a victory party following the California presidential primary.) The disappointed followers of these reform candidates insisted on wholesale changes in the presidential nomination process that would eliminate the influence of party organizations and increase the power of the rank and file voter. To accomplish this goal, reformers alternatively proposed a national primary, more state primaries, and "open" caucus procedures in those states still using party-run selection processes.

Like the Progressives, these new reformers held ambivalent views about parties. Some opposed parties altogether, preferring a democratic form of nonpartisan politics that focused on competition between individual leaders. Others wanted to strengthen the parties and place them on a new footing, although they could not say exactly how and were convinced that all the prerogatives of the existing party organizations must first be destroyed.

The most important structural change of the reform era has been the decline in the number of party-run selection procedures in favor of primaries. In 2000, forty-one states held presidential primaries for at least one party and selected over eighty percent of the delegates. In presidential nominations, parties have tended to become merely labels under which individual aspirants compete for public support, often

TABLE 6.1
Development of Methods of Nomination and Election for Federal Office

Office	Original Practice	Nineteenth-Century Practice	Twentieth-Century Practice
House			
Nomination	Nonpartisan; no regular nominating agency	Party nominations, by local party conventions	Nominations by primaries in most states
Final election	By voters, in districts or by state general tickets	Requirements of single member districts by federal law of 1842	Requirements of equal population of congressional districts in
Senate			
Nominations	Nonpartisan; no regular nominations agency	Party nominations, mostly by state party conventions	Nomination by primaries in most states
Final election	By state legislatures	By state legislatures	Direct, popular election of senators, Seventeenth Amendment, 1913
President			
Nominations	Nonpartisan	Party nomination by caucus of members of Congress, 1800–1816; party nomination by convention, beginning 1832	Selection of some convention delegates by primaries (1912–1968); selection of most convention delegates by primaries, 1972
Final election	By electors, acting at their own discretion, chosen in manner determined by states; some chosen by legislatures other by the people	Separate election of president and vice president, Twelfth Amendment; by 1840s, electors bound to candidates and chosen by popular election within states, mostly by winner-take-all	No new developments

from independents and members of the other party. Nevertheless, because the electorate voting in each party's primaries is different, the parties still retain very different characters.

Beginning in 1980, many party leaders, especially in the Democratic party where the reforms had gone furthest, attempted to restore some prerogatives to the party organizations. They were concerned about the absence of party pro-

fessionals at the conventions, which had led to chaotic platform fights and weakened any sense of collective responsibility between the presidential candidate and the other major party leaders. Also, as the grassroots party activists that participated in nominating conventions became more radical, delegates were selected who were at odds with the larger American electorate. Party leaders in this movement called for a renewed look at the role of the party organizations and a greater say for party officials in the selection of the presidential candidates.

So far, the postreform movement has had a limited, but by no means negligible, impact on the party system. More attention has been paid in recent years to upgrading the technical capacities of both national political parties. And in 1984 the national Democratic party added 561 new delegates ("superdelegates") drawn from among party leaders and elected officials (members of Congress, chairs of state parties, and mayors of large cities). These delegates were chosen outside of the primary process and were not officially bound to any candidate. Although this contingent made up only 14 percent of all the delegates to the 1984 Democratic party convention, it marked a first step in an effort to "reform the reforms" and return more power to party organizations and elected officials.

American Parties and the Law

The doctrines discussed above about parties refer to general ideas about the parties' role and function in American politics. They tend to be embodied and reflected in state and federal legislation that deals with parties. The parties began, from a legal standpoint, as virtually private organizations; in the late nineteenth century, they begin to be regulated and more or less "incorporated" into public law with the intent of limiting their influence; and finally, very recently, there has been some effort to free them—at least in some realms—from strict legal control.

The Parties as Private Associations (1790s–1860s)

As the existence of parties was never intended by the founders, it is not surprising that when parties developed they were entirely private associations, unregulated by federal or state law. Parties were simply groups of citizens coming together voluntarily to accomplish a purpose. As one political scientist remarked: "It was no more illegal to commit fraud in a party caucus than it would be to do so in the election of officers of a drinking club."[6] The states in this period limited their role in the electoral process to supplying

the ballot boxes and counting the ballots. What happened before the election, regarding nominating and campaigning, were entirely private matters.

The nomination of candidates was carried out primarily in party meetings called "conventions," for which delegates were selected in party-run procedures. The process usually began with open meetings for party members in local districts and precincts, where delegates were chosen to attend city or county conventions. The degree of procedural fairness at this initial stage varied from area to area, ranging from the corrupt to the perfectly democratic. In general, in areas where party organizations were strong, they dominated this stage, making sure that the meetings endorsed the decisions of the party leaders.

The local meetings chose the delegates to attend city or county conventions, where local candidates (for mayor, for state legislatures and often for the House) were nominated and where delegates were chosen for the state conventions. The state conventions, in turn, nominated statewide candidates (governors and senators) and selected delegates to the national conventions. The state and national conventions were dominated by blocs of delegates managed by powerful party leaders who negotiated among each other.

The general elections were held under state auspices. The states provided the voting place (where balloting was conducted openly before election officials) and counted the votes. In theory, it was up to the citizens to make up their own ballots, writing on a piece of paper their preferred candidates and thus both nominating and electing in the same act. In practice, however, the parties had already nominated a slate of candidates in advance of the election and were able to carry the elections for their candidates by publicizing their nominees and by providing the voters with colorful "tickets" on which the names of the candidates were already printed. These tickets were distributed to the party faithful, usually just outside the voting area. Most voters simply deposited them in the ballot box, the colors allowing party officials to see which party people were supporting. For all practical purposes, the parties printed the ballots.

The Regulation of State Parties (1860s–2000)

Although parties were private associations in a legal sense, they performed crucial public functions, such as nominating candidates, organizing and funding election campaigns, and even staffing most government jobs. After the Civil War, when reformers' objections to parties began to grow, there were increasing demands for the states to take steps to regulate parties and control their operations. This process of legal "incorporation" gained momentum at the turn of the century, as each step in the legal regulation of parties led to new demands to resolve remaining problems by further regulation.

The initial state statutes dealing with parties were designed to ensure against fraud, intimidation, and coercion in the parties' internal proceedings. They helped end certain gross abuses without interfering very much with legitimate party activities. They also established the principle, after many challenges in various state courts, that parties could be regulated by state law because of their direct effects on the political system. Parties might have begun as private associations, but their importance now justified their treatment as quasi-public bodies.

During the progressive era, state regulations became far more intrusive and strict. Some states regulated every aspect of party behavior, from the election of party officers to the internal organization of the party machinery. In a few cases regulation become so burdensome that the real organizations of local parties convened "unofficially" in order to escape the detailed rules imposed on them. The situation in the nation today remains highly uneven. Some states have had—and continue to have—very extensive regulation, while others have scarcely any regulation whatsoever.

The legal situation of state parties in the South presented a special case. After the Civil War until the 1950s, the Democratic party in most areas in the South was the only party able to win office, as Republicans were identified with civil rights for blacks. Many Democratic parties in the southern states relied on their "private" status to ban participation by black citizens, which effectively eliminated whatever influence the few black voters could exercise. State primaries in many southern states permitted the parties to discriminate under the fiction that the parties were private associations. In 1944, the Supreme Court declared such primaries unconstitutional in the case of *Smith v. Allwright.* Since the 1960s both national parties have taken steps to ensure that parties in their internal operations do not discriminate on racial grounds

In contrast to the state parties, the national party organizations have never been directly regulated by federal statute. The freedom from direct legislation that national parties have enjoyed has been important. Since the 1970s, the national parties have used this freedom to enact party rules for selecting delegates to their national party conventions, which has forced a change in the entire delegate selection process. These rules have sometimes conflicted with state laws for delegate selection, but the Supreme Court has upheld the parties' right to set their own qualifications for seating national delegates.[7] Because the states want their delegations to be accredited to vote at the conventions, they have usually complied thus far with national party rules. On the other hand, state parties have begun to resist attempts by the national committees to control party rules.

The Australian Ballot (1888–1900)

Another important change in the legal status of parties resulted from the adoption of the Australian ballot, a reform enacted in most states between 1888 and 1900. This change, modeled on the Ballot Law of 1856 in Australia, provided for secret voting on ballots printed by the states. Secrecy was designed, among other things, to put an end to the practice of buying votes. If those buying votes could no longer see how citizens voted, they would be unable to guarantee their investment.

Once the states began printing the ballots, they had to determine how candidates would qualify for having their names appear on the ballot. In nearly all states, access was automatically given to the candidates of parties who had received a specified minimum of votes in the last elections. For new parties, however, another method of qualification was necessary, and most states adopted laws requiring candidates to submit petitions by a specific date bearing the signatures of a certain number of citizens. These requirements were justifiable for administrative reasons, but by the 1920s the leaders of the major parties in some states had also managed to use these devices to limit competition and to keep certain "undesirable" parties, like the Socialists, off the ballot. The laws required large numbers of signatures (in some cases 10 percent of the electorate) and early filing deadlines (in some cases five months in advance of the election).

The presidential campaigns of Robert La Follette for the Progressive party, George Wallace in 1968 for the American Independent party, and Ross Perot in 1992 and 1996 were hampered by these obstacles. Some candidates challenged the constitutionality of these laws in federal court and succeeded in easing (though not eliminating) the restrictions of ballot access for new parties. Although legal obstacles for new parties still remain, especially for state and local elections, federal court decisions have brought much greater protection for third parties and independent candidates.

State ballots created another set of controversies regarding the format of the ballot. Almost all states print the candidates' party affiliations on the ballot, but the ways in which the states display the party labels differ. There are two basic ballot forms: the party-column, or "Indiana," ballot; and the office-bloc, or "Massachusetts," ballot. The party-column ballot lists the candidates down a series of columns or rows, each column containing candidates from the same party. This arrangement is favorable to party voting because it enables the voter to go quickly down the column and vote for all the candidates of that party, sometimes even by a single vote at the top of the column (a "straight-ticket" vote).

The office-bloc ballot lists the candidates under each separate office. No single mark can cast a ballot for the entire party slate, and the voter must go through each office to identify the party's candidates. This system is more favorable

to "split-ticket" voting (voting for candidates from different parties). Progressives favored the office-bloc over the party-column ballot in order to discourage "blind" partisan voting.

Split-ticket voting in the nineteenth century was rare. Partisan feelings ran strong, and the parties, which printed most of the ballots, naturally listed only their own nominees. When the states began printing the ballots, split-ticket voting became much easier. Between 1890 and 1920 split-ticket voting increased greatly but then leveled off. It began to rise again after the 1950s. This more recent increase has been a result, not of any legal change in the ballot, but of the voters' greater willingness to disregard party labels and focus on individual candidates rather than party affiliations.

Primaries

As legally private associations, nineteenth-century parties performed the function of nominating candidates according to their own internally established processes. The adoption of primary laws, first urged by the Progressives, removed this function from the private control of parties and gave it to the states. A primary is an election run by the state or under its auspices that determines the official nominees of the party; it may be distinguished from the caucus or convention, which is composed of party members under the rules and procedures of the party itself. Primaries are now used in nearly all the states to nominate candidates for the House, the Senate, and most state and local offices. For the presidency there is no national primary, but in most states the delegates to the national conventions are chosen in state-run primaries and are normally bound by state laws for a specified number of ballots at the convention. Of all the legal regulations affecting political parties, the primary laws have without question been the most significant. The reason is easily stated: "He who can make the nominations is the owner of the party."[8]

The passage of primary laws did not immediately undercut the ability of all party organizations to control the nominating process, because some organizations were powerful enough to control the primaries. In a few places, party organizations still retain this capacity. For the most part, however, primary laws, together with the weakening of the party organizations and the rise of the mass media campaigns, have removed control of nominations from the parties. Primaries have created a situation in which no group "owns" the party. Rather, individuals build their own personal organizations, bargain with special interest groups, and devise programs and media strategies in an effort to win the primary and capture the party banner. The regular party organizations often have little or no influence in this process. As a consequence, fewer political activists have found it worth their while to join party organizations. Instead, political activists today are often attracted to the personal campaign organizations of individual candidates or to organized groups such as the National Rifle Association or the Sierra Club.

Once states adopted primaries, a new legal question immediately arose: Which voters would be allowed to participate? Previously, the parties as private associations had the power to decide who could take part in the nominating process—a situation that still holds in some states not using primaries. In most states, however, the state law determines who may participate. In some states, like Wisconsin, no barrier is placed in the way of primary participation. Voters can take part in whichever party's primary they prefer, without regard to their party registration or affiliation. Such primaries, held in eight states, are known as open primaries.[9] Three states—California, Alaska and Washington—go a step further and give citizens a combined ballot, allowing them to vote for the candidates of either party for any office. This is known as a blanket primary. The constitutionally of the blanket primary has been challenged on the grounds that it allows persons of one party to vote for the other party and thus violates a political party's right to free association as guaranteed by the First Amendment. This matter is still under litigation and the future of the blanket primary remains in question.

In twenty-six states, the law requires voters to indicate or establish a party preference in order to vote in a given primary. These elections are considered closed primaries. In many such cases, however, the primaries are closed more in name than in fact. In some states—as in Virginia—there is no official registration by party, which makes it impossible to determine who is a "valid" member. In other states—such as Indiana and Illinois—there is party registration, but voters can declare their party preference at the primary election itself, making the restriction of party membership very weak. Only in those states which require a person to be registered in the party before the primary election is there a significant attempt to restrict primary voting to party membership. However, the federal courts have limited preregistration requirements to no more than ninety days. As judged by historical standards, today's definition of party membership is not very restrictive.

Primaries have been one of the most important factors in undermining the strength of political parties. They are consistent with the anti-party strain in American political culture, and they seem to realize Americans' desire for a democratic electoral process. Yet, they have also produced many questionable effects, including long and drawn-out campaigns, divisiveness within the parties, and a weakening of party discipline. Their claim to being exercises in pure democracy is also questionable, given the low turnout rates in many primary elections. The debate on the merits of primaries is likely to continue, although most Americans seem wedded to the primary system for most offices.

Campaign Finance Legislation (1971–2002)

The reform era of the 1970s led also to the enactment of a goal once championed by the progressives: stringent regulation of campaign financing for all federal election campaigns, including public financing for presidential elections and contribution limitations not only for individuals and groups but for parties as well. The details of this complex legislation are discussed in the next chapter, and here only its general effect on the role of the parties will be discussed.

The major significance of this legislation is that it has legally defined the center of the modern campaign as the individual's own candidate organization. Political parties are limited by law in how much direct support they can provide for their own candidates. In the case of congressional campaigns, although the amount that national and state parties can contribute is not insignificant, it is still far below what parties would be capable of providing. The parties have thus been transformed into a kind of interest group, albeit an important one, with respect to their own candidates. The relationship between party and candidate in the conduct of the campaign has been dramatically reversed from what it had been in the nineteenth century. Due to exceptions in campaign financing laws, the parties by 1990 managed to escape some of these restrictions by becoming the chief collectors of campaign funds for distribution to federal candidates. The recent Bipartisan Campaign Reform Act, signed into law by President Bush in 2002, contracted this ability of national parties to exert influence on elections by ending their ability to accept unlimited funds from individuals or corporations known as soft money.

Another major effect of the legislation, largely unforeseen, has been the encouragement of new organizations, known as "political action committees" (PACs), which have served as partial competitors of parties. These committees contribute money to campaigns and spend independently on behalf of candidates. Examples of PACS range from Americans for a Republican Majority (ARMPAC) and the National Organization for Women (NOW/PAC) to the Snack Food Association (SNACKPAC). The committees, often formed on the basis of ideological positions or as support for single-interest groups, now wield important control over the financing of congressional campaigns and try to pressure candidates to support their positions. They have thus complicated the moderating and consensus-forming functions once performed by political parties, and the best one can hope for is a solution in which so many competing interests flourish that none becomes too significant.

Party Organization

Doctrines about parties help form people's expectations of their proper role, while legal rules codify certain aspects of party behavior and create part of the environment in which parties operate. In the final analysis, however, the character of our parties is shaped by their organizations—by how parties arrange their own affairs and by the activities of those who work on their behalf.

Any discussion of party organization must take great care to distinguish between their "textbook" organization and the real power relations within the organization. In a textbook chart (which the parties themselves, incidentally, never publish), the parties appear to be organized on a hierarchic basis, with the power flowing down from the national level through the state party organizations to the local level and finally to the neighborhood precinct captains. In practice, however, the various levels of organization—national, state, and local—operate with a great deal of autonomy. For the most part, the organizational strength of American parties is found at the state and local levels, and the national parties are in many respects confederations of the state and local parties, although the national parties have asserted a much greater role in the last decade and a half.

As we look in this section at the form and power of these party organizations, it is important to keep in mind that they now play a different and more limited role than they did in the past. Functions have been stripped from the organizations, and certain new technological developments in communications (especially television) have made them less important in reaching voters and winning elections.

The National Parties

The impetus for the formation of parties in the 1790s came from a division on national issues, and the party organizations were built from the top down. This pattern was partially reversed when parties were reestablished between 1824 and 1840. Although the struggle over the presidency and the National Bank galvanized the new party division, the national organizations were created by linking together existing state party organizations that had operated during the era of nonpartisan politics. Much of the organizational strength of our parties originally existed—and has since remained—at the state and local levels.

TABLE 6.2
Party Organization in America

Party Levels	Party Components	Major Elected Officials as Party Spokespersons
National parties	National convention National committee National party chair National party headquarters and staff Congressional party campaign organizations	President Party leadership in Congress
State parties	State convention State committee State party chair State professional staff	Governor Party leadership in state legislatures
Local parties	Local conventions (county, city, ward) Local committees Local chairpersons Ward or district leaders Precinct captains Regular participants and workers	Mayors Members of Congress Local politicians

For much of their history, the national parties functioned only during the period of the presidential election campaign. In between, the national organizations existed on paper only. Today, however, both national parties maintain permanent staffs, remain continuously in operation, and raise and distribute some funds for their candidates. The national organizations have become more important in relation to their state and local affiliates than they have ever been.

The formal structure of the national party has changed very little since the middle of the nineteenth century. Then, as now, each party had a national committee, a national party chair, and a national party convention, which is the supreme rule-making body for the party as a whole. Both parties added campaign committees for House elections after the Civil War and for Senate elections after the ratification of the direct-election amendment for senators in 1913. These organs constitute the official parts of the party's formal organization. But it is necessary also to include the party's major elected officials—the congressional party leaders and the president—who,

while not official party officers, often wield the most power.

National Committees The national committees of the Democratic and Republican parties are made up of members selected by the parties in each of the fifty states, the District of Columbia, Puerto Rico, and various territories. The national committees have certain functions to perform related to calling conventions and carrying out business assigned to them by the national conventions.

Generally speaking, however, the national committees are not very powerful bodies. "A national committee," a journalist once noted, "never nominated anybody, never elected anybody, [and] never established party policy."[10] Indeed, one of the most important formal powers of the national committee—choosing the party chair—is often accorded in practice to the president or to the presidential nominee, with the national committee usually merely ratifying the choice. Only when the chair of the party out of power resigns, or where there is division in the out party after its presidential candidate has been defeated in an election, will the national committee actually make the choice.

Since the mid-1970s there has been a quiet transformation of the role of the national party, in which modern techniques of fund raising and campaign training have strengthened the national party despite other tendencies operating in the opposite direction. Under National Committee Chairman William Brock (1976–81), the national Republican party adapted the technique of direct mail fundraising (pioneered by the presidential campaigns of Barry Goldwater, George Wallace, and George McGovern) for use by the political party as an institution. Republicans built on Goldwater's lists to become the most successful direct mail fundraising enterprise in American politics.

Republicans used their funds in four ways: to provide direct aid to party candidates, first for federal and later for state and local offices; to help rebuild lower-level party units; to create in-house capacities for polling, media production, research, and campaign training; and to communicate general party positions directly to the public. The Democrats began their national party-building a few years later, and by the election of 1996 the Democratic National Committee had largely eliminated the Republican's advantage. Both national committees are continuing their efforts to play a greater role in politics and elections. Although their functions remain relatively limited, the cumulative impact of their efforts can be important. Elections are frequently won at the margins.

The National Chair and National Staff The national chairs run the national headquarters, help to raise funds and decide how they are spent, and occasionally "represent" the party, when the opposition controls the presidency. The last task is one that party chairs generally handle with considerable care, as they by no means are regarded as the party's exclusive official spokesperson. Indeed, for the out party, no one really speaks authoritatively for the party's policies. The "titular" leader—that is, the party's last nominee—has only limited influence. Various party figures, including on occasion the chair but more often congressional leaders and presidential aspirants, vie to play the role of party

spokesperson. In the United States, in contrast to Great Britain and Canada, there is no designated opposition leader or shadow Cabinet.

The national party staff, which is responsible to the party chair, performs such functions as data collection, fund raising, training of candidates and party members in modern campaign techniques, and preparation of party literature. The national party chair is also sometimes designated as the official head of the nominee's presidential campaign, though this title is now often ceremonial. Formerly, national chairs actually performed this role, but with the development of extensive preconvention campaigns, the candidates already possess their own personal organizations whose leaders enjoy their full confidence. The national chair is thus left with the secondary role of coordinating the activities of the regular organization with those of the candidate's own personal organization.

The national party chair, when working under an incumbent president, serves very much at the president's pleasure. Some recent presidents have kept the chair on a short leash. When the national Republican chairman Robert Dole attempted to put some distance between the national party and President Nixon during the Watergate crisis, be was summoned by the President to Camp David and dismissed. As Dole later quipped, "I had a nice chat with the president, while the other fellows went out to get the rope."[11] Democratic party chair Don Fowler, who served under President Clinton from 1994–1996, admitted to taking direct orders on most fundraising decisions from the political operatives in the White House. The chair of the out party has much more room in which to operate, not having an immediate boss to accommodate in the person of the president of the United States.

Congressional Campaign Committees Both parties have their own congressional campaign committees for each house of the Congress. They consist of members of Congress and have small, permanent staffs. These committees are independent of the national committees, although they often coordinate activities with them.

Their role is to help their party in Congress, especially the incumbents. The committees raise and distribute funds, conduct research, help to devise campaign strategies, and provide other services such as writing speeches and preparing position papers. The chairs of these committees can become very powerful members of Congress, as they are at the center of an activity dear to incumbents: fund raising. Even though the committees can give only a limited amount of money, the chairs "know where the money is" and can direct it towards favored members.

National Conventions and Party Commissions

The supreme authority of each national party is vested ultimately in its national convention, which meets every fourth year to select the party's nominee and write the party's platform. The national conventions are made up of delegates from the states and territories, selected in accordance with rules devised by the national parties, the laws of the states, and the rules of the state parties.

The conventions today are huge bodies, in 2000 comprising 4,336 votes for the Democratic party and 2,066 votes for the Republican Party. These figures actually understate the number of delegates, since both parties have alternative delegates. With the number of observers and journalists in attendance, the national conventions are indeed huge and sometimes confusing (or confused) assemblies. The size of the conventions has increased dramatically since 1952, when the convention vote total for the Democratic party was 1,230 and that of the Republican party 1,206.

In addition to nominating the candidates, approving the party platforms, and ratifying the nominee's choice for vice president, the conventions make the final decision about the party's rules. One of the most important party rules in American history was the Democratic party's requirement, in effect from 1832 until 1936, that presidential nominees be chosen by a two-thirds vote of the convention delegates. This rule gave the South a virtual veto over the party's nominee. After the rule was abolished to allow nominees to be selected with only a simple majority of votes, the center of gravity of the national party moved to the urban areas of the nation and the party's presidential nominees have tended to represent its liberal constituency. The Republicans have always chosen their nominee by a simple majority.

The most significant development in the history of rule making by national parties occurred in the Democratic party after 1968. The 1968 convention approved a party commission—later known as the McGovern-Fraser Commission—to rewrite the rules of delegate selection for the next convention. Similar party commissions were established by the Democrats after each subsequent presidential election. These commissions for the first time devised a body of national rules for regulating the selection of delegates to national conventions. Previously, the national parties had been content to accept the methods of delegate selection provided for by state law or by rules of the state parties.

It was through the first three of these commissions that the modern reformers were able to "legislate" rules that undermined much of the power of traditional party organization in certain states. Included in these rules were provisions that required open and highly publicized caucus meetings, banned the automatic selection of delegates by virtue of their position (for example, governors or state party chairs), and mandated the selection of delegates in proportion to the preferences of the voters or caucus participants. Another effect of these reforms, perhaps not entirely foreseen, was to induce states to adopt primaries in place of caucuses. With more than forty states now holding presidential primaries, presidential nominations are in effect made by popular vote before the convention ever meets. The convention merely ratifies the determined choice and does not, as it ordinarily did in the past, serve as a decision-making body having discretion over which candidate to select as the party's nominee. Only in the event that none of the candidates should emerge from the primaries with a majority of the delegates would a convention today actually deliberate and choose the nominee. Clearly, then, the party organizations have lost a great deal of power in the presidential nominating process.

The reform commissions present an interesting paradox in the history of American political parties. They represent one of the few instances in which the national party has dictated structure and procedures to state and local parties, and in this sense a claim can be made that they have significantly strengthened the national parties. This new authority was used between 1968 and 1980 to remove control from the state party organizations and turn the nomination decision into an electoral contest between the various presidential aspirants. After 1980, however, many party officials began to use this same rule-making authority to restore certain prerogatives to the party organizations, such as creation of the "superdelegates." But, national parties have recently experienced difficultly in altering their rules at the expense of state parties. For example, attempts by the Republican National Committee in 2000 to alter the calendar for the presidential primaries was rejected by large states who feared losing their influence in the nomination process.

The President   Although not a part of the official hierarchy of the party, the president inevitably is the head of the party during his tenure. Some presidents relish this role and have attempted to build up their party, both as a source of support for their own programs and as a legacy for the future. President Reagan, for example, showed considerable interest in party-building. Other presidents, however, have largely ignored party affairs and have sought to present themselves as chiefly nonpartisan figures. President Carter, for example, did little to build the Democratic party, and President Eisenhower largely preferred to take a stance above partisan conflicts.

Presidents may avoid building the party apparatus, but they cannot fully escape being associated with the electoral fate of their party's elected officials. They are virtually compelled to campaign for members of Congress from their own party in midterm elections. A president's power is typically gauged in part by the perception of the strength of his party and how his party has done in the most recent congressional election. As others in the party depend in part on the president for their electoral fate, so he has depended on them for his own capacity to govern. It is in ways like this that the American

political party takes on a reality not evident from observing the legal forms of our government.

Federalism and Party Organization

An issue of great significance is the extent to which national party organs can directly control local party decisions on nominations. It is by means of such control that many European parties are able to solidify national party discipline. In the United States, the national chairs and staff have seldom attempted to exercise such power openly, although recently the Republican National Committee and campaign committees have taken a more active role in selected local races. At least two presidents—Woodrow Wilson in 1918 and Franklin Roosevelt in 1938—intervened in the primary campaigns of certain members of Congress in an effort to defeat candidates who did not support the "national" party program as determined by the President (see Box 6-3). These efforts have never met with much success, largely because the voters and the state parties do not accept the propriety of a national party figure dictating local decisions. In this sense, federalism has become a "norm"; and it is generally accepted that the national party organization and the president should help out only "after" the local nomination decision has been made, not before. Because of primary laws and other developments, no party organization—national or local—is in a position to control most nomination races. Ultimately, then, hierarchic parties do not exist in the United States, because they are in tension with the constitutional principle that the states and localities should determine the character of their own representation.

State and Local Party Organizations

Much of the strength of party organizations exists at the state and local levels. By a "party organization" we mean a group of persons, whether consisting of employees or volunteers, who can be called on to perform activities on a regular basis on behalf of the party—that is, on behalf of all or most of its candidates and the organization itself. Among the activities performed by party organizations are recruiting

BOX 6.3

The President and the Political Party

One of the most powerful national party chairmen in history, James A. Farley, advised his chief, President Roosevelt, not to undertake his effort to "purge" thirteen anti-New Deal Democrats in the 1938 primaries. Roosevelt's effort was largely unsuccessful, and Farley later wrote about the incident:

> I knew from the beginning that the purge could lead to nothing but misfortune, because in pursuing his course of vengeance Roosevelt violated a cardinal political creed which demanded that he keep out of local matters. Sound doctrine is sound politics. When Roosevelt began neglecting the rules of the game, I lost faith in him. I trace all the woes of the Democratic party, directly or indirectly, to this interference in purely local affairs. In any political entity voters naturally and rightfully resent the unwarranted invasion of outsiders.

Source: James A. Farley, *Jim Farley's Story: The Roosevelt Years* (New York: McGraw-Hill, 1948), pp. 146–147.

candidates, identifying potential voters, distributing campaign materials, raising money, organizing local party activities, and engaging in a wide range of detailed work needed to keep an organization operating.

The strength and character of American political parties vary greatly from state to state. In some states, the state chair and party staff run highly efficient organizations with computerized mailing lists, telephone banks, and training resources for the candidates. In other states, the organization is run virtually out of the trunk of the party chair's automobile. Many state parties have made efforts to upgrade their procedures by adopting the new techniques of campaign management. At the local level, where the final and crucial activities of talking to voters and getting them to the polls take place, the strength of the parties varies even more. In some localities, the parties have hundreds of people who can be relied on to do at least some work; in other locations, party organizations hardly function or exist only on paper.

What is it that induces people, other than salaried party officials, to join a party organization? Although motives are seldom unmixed, and organizations never fit perfectly into any one model, we can distinguish three major types of party organizations: the machine, and the ideological or policy-oriented organization.[12]

The Machine A political machine is an organization that sustains itself by offering tangible benefits, usually jobs, to its members and which is frequently controlled at the local level by a single leader, or "boss," who may or may not be an elected official. Machines were the predominant organizational form in many large urban areas from the middle of the nineteenth century until the middle of this century. They have died out in most cities and can be found today in pale versions of their classic form only in relatively few places, such as Chicago.

The "classic" machine operated by giving government jobs to the party's faithful; in return, the party faithful worked for the party's ticket and donated money—often deducted from pay envelopes as a "tax"—to pay for the organization's activities. In the late nineteenth century in Pennsylvania, the Republican state committee amazingly maintained a payroll of some 20,000 full- or part-time party workers at an annual cost of about $24 million. Federal employees were also appointed to help the party keep power. In Indiana, a state well known in the nineteenth century for its rough-and-tumble politics, it was said that the postmaster general was "appointed not to see that the mails were carried, but that Indiana was carried."[13]

The machines, of course, could not offer a job to everyone and therefore had to devise ways of appealing to a majority of the voters. To accomplish this, they relied in particular on the work of their local precinct captains, who either were on the government payroll in jobs that took no time or else were paid directly from the party's cof-

BOX 6.4

The Views of a Machine Politician

Plunkitt of Tammany Hall, a book written by the ward boss and later United States senator from New York, George Washington Plunkitt, captures the flavor of party work by a precinct captain in New York City at the turn of the century:

> If a family is burned out I don't ask whether they are Republicans or Democrats, and I don't refer them to the Charity Organization Society, which would investigate their case in a month or two and decide they were worthy of help about the time they are dead from starvation. I just get quarters for them, buy them clothes, if their clothes were burned up, and fix them up till they get runnin' again. It's philanthropy, but it's politics, too—mighty good politics. Who can tell how many votes one of these fires bring me? The poor are the most grateful people in the world, and, let me tell you, they have more friends in their neighborhoods than the rich have in theirs. . . .

> There's only one way to hold a district: you must study human nature and act accordin'. You can't study human nature in a book. . . . If you have been to college, so much the worse for you.

Today, machines are much less in evidence; still, in many states and localities party patronage remains an important source of maintaining party organizational strength. In suburban Nassau County in the state of New York, for example, the Republican organization still exercises extensive control over the choice of 17,000 public employees.

Source: William L. Riordan, *Plunkitt Tammany Hall (New York:* Dutton, 1963), pp. 28, 25.

fers. The precinct captains "hung around" their neighborhoods, befriending voters and offering them small favors. Precinct captains often served their local constituents as welfare agents, helping people to get settled and coming to their aid in time of need (see Box 6.4).

Machines are remembered today as a part of American folklore; they are feared but admired, somewhat like the "outlaws" of the Wild West. Some analysts celebrate machines for their role in stimulating voters' participation, in serving as welfare agencies in an era before the welfare state, and in providing an avenue of advancement for poorer ethnic politicians. Though based largely on self-interest, machines (according to their defenders) also promoted the public interest. Finally, for national politics, the machines brought an element of non-ideological pragmatism to bear on the choice of presidential nominees, as the bosses were interested in candidates likely to be elected.

Reformers have always stressed the negative aspects of the machines, such as the corruption and the trading of jobs and favors for votes. Reformers have never denied that machines are democratic in the sense that they stimulate pop-

ular participation in politics. Turnout in areas where machines exist has typically been much higher than one would expect, controlling for all other factors. But reformers argue that the quality of participation must also be considered, and by this standard machines are undesirable. Political participation, according to the reformers, should follow not from self-interest but from a concern with public policy.

The reasons for the decline of machines are not difficult to identify. Civil service reform has taken away much of the available political patronage, and recently the courts have ruled that political authorities may not dismiss any but the highest of government officials for "political" reasons.[14] In effect, patronage is now unconstitutional. The immigrant groups on which machines depended for so much of their support in the northern and Midwestern cities have declined as a percentage of these cities' population. The welfare state, which provides citizens with services by legal entitlement, has ended any role for the party as a welfare agency. Finally, the political culture is now dominated by reform ideas that are inhospitable to machines. Even where they still exist, machines attempt to hide their true character and present themselves in a reformist light.

Ideological and Policy-Oriented Organizations
Many people join party organizations because they want to further a cause or a set of policies in which they believe. Most third parties, which have never controlled very much patronage, have relied on members devoted to their cause. The antislavery parties before the Civil War, the agrarian and prohibition parties in the late nineteenth century, and the socialist and libertarian parties in this century have all relied on a core of "true believers" to run and maintain the organizations. The major parties also have always had members who have been motivated chiefly by policy concerns, and this proportion has increased in periods when the parties have adopted clear positions on the issues as one or both parties have done in 1860, 1896, 1936, and 1980.

In recent years, some party organizations have drawn increasingly from policy-oriented activists as patronage resources have dried up. These activists—sometimes called "amateurs" by political analysts—look to political activity not for material rewards or as a social outlet, but rather, in the progressive vein, as an opportunity for promoting policy ends. Generally speaking, amateurs are less willing to compromise about selecting "electable" candidates than party members drawn in by other motives. They tend to be not only ideologues, whether liberal or conservative, but ideologues for whom purity of commitment rather than flexibility is considered the supreme political virtue. Yet as some of these people become involved in party activities and assume positions of responsibility, they moderate their "purity" somewhat and adopt more flexible positions.

The three organizational types discussed above are abstract models. No organization consists entirely of persons animated by the same motives, and few individuals are moved by only one consideration. Thus, while machine politicians may have been primarily concerned with jobs and winning elections, they were by no means completely unmindful of policy positions. Likewise, modern policy activists, though always speaking in terms of policy commitments, frequently have their eye on government jobs or preferments of some kind.

Candidate-Centered Politics and Its Consequences

Today, much of the organizational activity in political campaigns is carried on not by the regular party organizations, but by personal organizations attached to the candidates and by political associations and interest groups that agree to support a particular candidate. With nominations now made in primaries that the party organizations do not control, each candidate must build his or her own organization in an effort to capture the party label. After succeeding, the candidate will then usually maintain this organization for the general election campaign, accepting as much help from the regular organization as it can provide. This individualistic ("candidate-centered") style of politics has also been facilitated by the modern mass media. Candidates in large constituencies can now be seen directly on television and do not require large organizations to contact the voters. Candidates can rely initially on a small group of pollsters and media consultants, hoping that as their appeal grows they will be able to obtain more and more organizational support.

From the presidential level down to the congressional and local races, it is the candidates' personal campaign organizations that dominate the political scene today—as far, that is, as organization itself counts in political campaigns. In some ways, the system of primaries and individual organizations seems the very embodiment of democratic fairness. Yet critics point to the difficulties it creates for candidates and elected officials. First, the candidates of the same party have no common responsibility to any core organizations. As fellow party members they may share many of the same views, but no supplementary bonds deriving from reliance on an organization hold them together. Second, in the absence of party organizations, the candidates are left in an exposed position before the voters. They must devise their own electoral strategies, which in a competitive situation can encourage empty image appeals or demagogic issue campaigns. Third, and somewhat paradoxically, without parties standing as a buffer between individual candidates and the electorate, the candidates may be more indebted to the policy-oriented groups, such as Common Cause or the Christian Coalition, with which they must frequently deal in order to obtain money, receive organizational support, and win votes.

Perhaps the most alarming aspect of this system is its impact not on the candidates but on the citizenry. Party organizations traditionally taught local leaders the values of compromise and conciliation necessary for establishing enduring party coalitions. By contrast, the individual campaign organizations and the separate policy interest groups encourage participants to assert only what is in the interest of their candidate or their own particular cause. Ultimately, the kind of majorities envisioned by Madison and Van Buren depend on the capacity of people to practice the art of coalition building. It is this capacity that would be threatened by a further decline of the power of party organizations relative to personal organizations.[15]

Party Competition and Party Coalitions

Even without centralized and hierarchic national party organizations, American parties have managed to acquire a semblance of unity in their ideas and programs. The reason is that in the final analysis, the parties become identified with a general public philosophy articulated at the national level in presidential elections (by the party platform and by the presidential candidates) and in the process of governing (by congressional leaders and especially by the president). These public philosophies, such as welfare state liberalism for Democrats since 1932 or the "new" conservatism for Republicans since 1980, create national party "images" which permeate the nation and penetrate into the states and localities, where the voters and local organizations tend to adopt them. In the words of one political scientist: "The fact that our parties have been organized mainly in state and local units should not lead us to forget that the electoral alignments producing their support, initially and to a large extent subsequently too, have been national and specifically presidential."[16]

This process of national penetration, however, represents a tendency and not an iron law. The national principles are often articulated in broad enough terms to allow most party members to believe that there is a rough consistency between their position and that of the president. In some cases, however, accidents of geography or strategy can lead to the inclusion within the party of candidates or groups that do not fit with the national party image. These differences are made possible by the decentralized character of American party structure, which enables state and local parties and voters to nominate the kinds of candidates they prefer for Congress and for all state and local offices. The results can play havoc with party discipline. From the 1930s through the present era, the national Democratic party has been characterized by its support of welfare state liberalism; but in some districts, especially in the South, the Democratic party has for many years sent members to Congress who are conservative and who vote regularly with the majority of the Republicans.

Such geographical centers of support for alternative views do not always serve to protect "old" ideas that have no chance of gaining a national majority. On the contrary, they often become bases for creating and sustaining new conceptions of a party's national position. Thus, over the last generation it was Republicans in the far west who generated much of the initial support for the new conservatism of Ronald Reagan, which in the end won control from a more traditional form of conservatism that prevailed in the midwest and east. At times the geographical and ideological struggles of a party's factions may be so intense and evenly balanced that the party cannot be said to stand for any one point of view; the party is in a state of confusion or turmoil in which its public philosophy is itself the chief point at issue. Many Democrats have voiced fears that their party has been in that situation for at least the last decade.

Critical Realignments

In their quest for political power, the two major parties must seek the support of a majority of the electorate. This process usually leads them to cast a broad net that appeals to a variety of different constituencies. By the standards of most other democratic nations, American political parties tend to be far less ideological, although as other nations have developed two-party systems, their parties have become more "American" in style. Still, American political parties do have different centers of gravity, and at certain moments they embody very different ideas of how the nation should be governed. Even though parties generally have the pragmatic goal of holding power, they have always been influenced by persons who have sought power to promote certain ideas and who at times have been willing to risk defeat for the sake of promoting their principles.

New public philosophies emerge, but only infrequently. Only in a few elections is the nation presented a new or fundamental choice; in many elections the differences between the parties are relatively minor. Ironically, one of the reasons for this similarity is the decisiveness of the outcome of elections in which a fundamental choice has been offered. As it has happened, a party's victory in a decisive election establishes that a majority in the nation favors its public philosophy. The defeated party then faces the choice either of adhering to a public philosophy that has been rejected (and facing continual defeat) or else moving in the direction of the majority party (and thus having some prospect for success). Not surprisingly, it usually chooses the second alternative, thus minimizing ideological conflict.

Political scientists call these decisive elections "critical realignments." A critical realignment, more precisely, is an election (or a sequence of two elections) in which a large number of voters change their party preference, or in which new voters entering the electorate identify with one of the parties to a much greater extent than the rest of the electorate. ("Party preference" here refers not to a formal legal designation, but to a voter's feeling of identity for a particular party.) This process of change usually results in a net shift in the relative strength between the two parties. Critical realignments are generally periods in which major changes in public opinion take place and in which the people adopt a new governing public philosophy that has been articulated by one of the parties. It is at these moments that the parties take on new images in the minds of most voters. These images may last for up to a generation, until a new set of issues arises and another realignment occurs.

Realigning periods have usually left one of the parties in a dominant position for a period of time. Of course, the fact that one of the parties has more adherents does not mean that it wins every election. Elections that are won by the smaller party (known as "deviating elections") occur because party adherents do not always vote for the party with which they identify. Certain voters, while maintaining their partisan identification, cast their ballot for candidates of the other party because of temporary or short-term factors, perhaps because they disapprove of the recent performance of their party or find a particular candidate from the other party to be especially attractive. Alternatively, deviations may occur because independents vote decisively for one party, thereby tilting the balance in its favor. Thus, to say that a party is the dominant or majority party in a particular historical era means, not that it will always win, but only that it enjoys an advantage if "all other things are equal," which of course they never are in politics. Each election has its own features, and critical realignments merely set the broad contours within which the particular struggle of each campaign is waged.

Over the course of American history, there have been five realignments associated with the "critical" periods of change discussed in Chapter 3: 1796–1800, 1828–1832, 1856–1860, 1896, and 1932–1936. In the first period (1796–1800), the Jeffersonian Democratic-Republicans displaced the Federalists as the majority party and established the dominant public philosophy of limited government in the name of agrarian values. The election sequence of 1828–1832 saw the Democratic party, which declared itself the heir of the Jeffersonians, argue against using federal power for developing the nation, contending that federal programs, like the National Bank, created monopoly privileges and advantages for the wealthier classes. The opposition party, initially called the National-Republicans and later the Whigs, favored a broad-based program of federal aid (internal improvements or the "American plan") to promote national economic development.

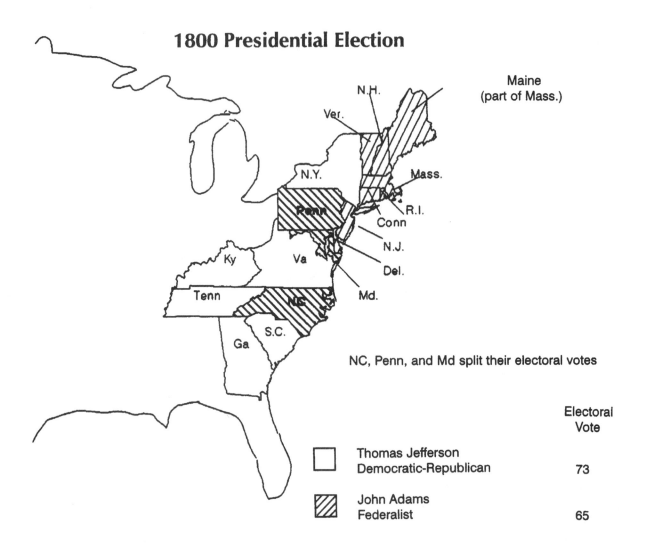

FIGURE 6.1 The election of 1800. From 1800 to 1826, the Republican Democrats won every presidential election and controlled both houses of Congress in every session. So complete was their dominance that after 1816, during the so-called "era of good feelings," the Federalist Party ceased to offer opposition in the presidential contest and collapsed as a national party.

The Whig party disintegrated after 1852 in the struggle over slavery. The Republican party arose as a new party in the mid-1850s to prevent the spread of slavery into the territories and to reclaim the principles of the Declaration of Independence. In the election of 1860, Abraham Lincoln won less than 40 percent of the popular vote but nonetheless received a clear majority of the electoral vote. After the Civil War, the Republican party, relying on its support for the union and continually reminding voters of the Democrats' betrayal, dominated the national political arena for the next two decades.

By the 1880s, as the southern states returned to the union under Democratic party control, the Republicans began to lose their majority. The two parties appeared to be equally balanced. The election of 1896 solidified rather than reversed the Republicans' advantage. It aligned the electorate in favor of the previous majority. The election focused on economic and cultural issues. The Republicans under William McKinley favored sound money and steady industrial

1828 Presidential Election

Maryland and New York split their electoral votes between Adams and Jackson

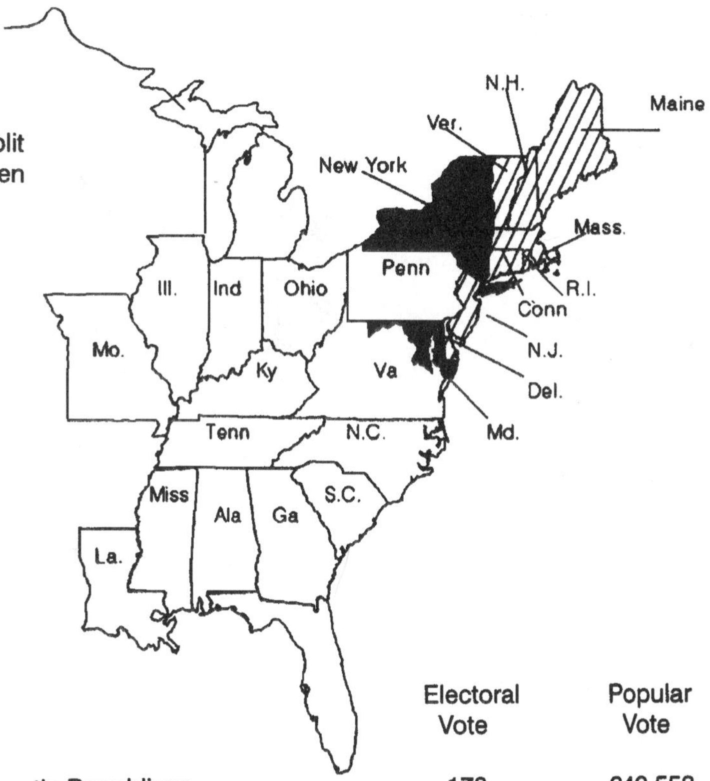

	Electoral Vote	Popular Vote	Percent
☐ Jackson—Democratic-Republican	178	642,553	55.9
▨ Adams—National Republican	83	500,897	43.6

FIGURE 6.2 The election of 1828. During the 32-year period from 1828 to 1860, the division of popular support between the parties was very close, but the Democrats had a slight edge. The Democrats won six of eight presidential contests and controlled the House for all but six years and the Senate for all but four years.

development, while the Democrats under William Jennings Bryan adopted a populist and agrarian program, favoring free silver (cheaper money) and extensive government regulation of industrial development. The Republicans remained firmly in control of the government until the Depression, with the exception of two terms during which Woodrow Wilson was president (1913–1921).

The last decisive realignment took place in 1932–1936, as Franklin Roosevelt led the Democratic party to two sweeping victories and articulated the new Democratic public philosophy of welfare state liberalism. Reversing their traditional Jeffersonian hostility to a strong central government, the Democrats now favored more federal government intervention in the economy. The Republicans became wary of federal solutions to social and economic problems and feared the growth of a large federal bureaucracy. In the elections of 1932 and 1936, Roosevelt helped forge the New Deal coalition of union

1860 Presidential Election

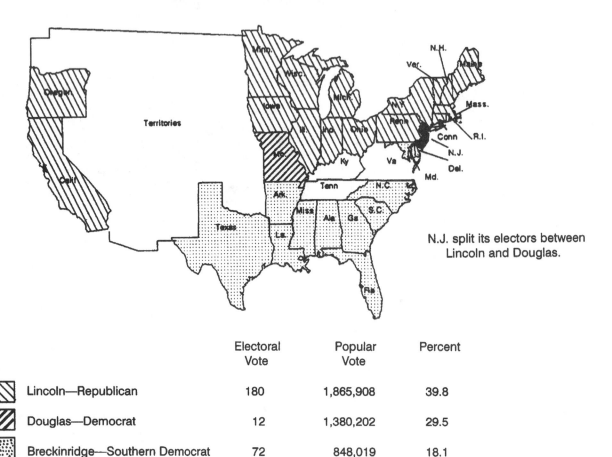

N.J. split its electors between Lincoln and Douglas.

		Electoral Vote	Popular Vote	Percent
▨	Lincoln—Republican	180	1,865,908	39.8
▨	Douglas—Democrat	12	1,380,202	29.5
▦	Breckinridge—Southern Democrat	72	848,019	18.1
☐	Bell—Constitutional Union	39	590,901	12.6

FIGURE 6.3 The election of 1860. During the 36-year period from 1860 to 1896, the Republicans won seven of the nine presidential contests and controlled the Senate for all but four years. Republicans had a majority in the House for 20 years, but the Democrats were regularly in command after 1880.

members, workers and minority groups that moved the electoral center of gravity of the party from the South to the urban areas—although the South continued to vote Democratic in most presidential elections and to send a majority of Democrats to the Congress.

The New Deal coalition dominated American politics from 1932 until the late 1960s. Throughout this period, the Democrats held a substantial margin over Republicans in partisan adherents, and could normally count on the backing of their supporters. Democrats were stronger among workers, minorities, and southerners. Republicans were stronger among professionals, business groups, and, to a lesser extent, farmers. Both parties had a broad spectrum of opinion within their ranks, but of the two, the Democratic party was substantially more diverse (and disunited). The center of gravity of the Democratic party was liberal and that of the Republican party conservative, but Democrats had a substantially larger share of voters outside of the party's own mainstream. As a result, in Congress the effective majority on many issues was often a

1896 Presidential Election

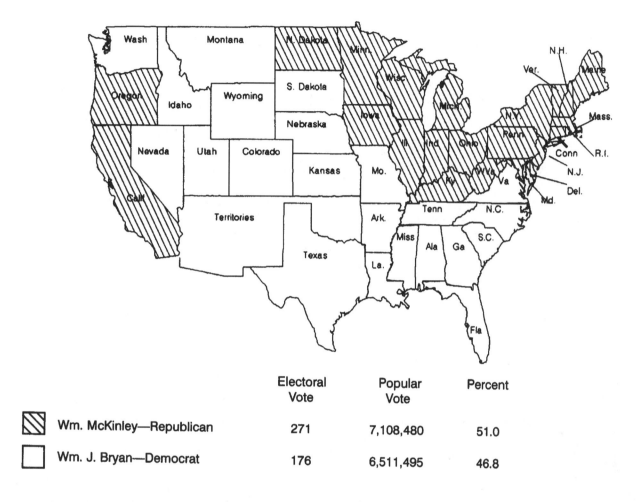

	Electoral Vote	Popular Vote	Percent
Wm. McKinley—Republican	271	7,108,480	51.0
Wm. J. Bryan—Democrat	176	6,511,495	46.8

FIGURE 6.4 The election of 1896. During the 36-year period from 1896 until 1932, the Republicans won six of eight presidential contests and controlled the House for all but 10 years and the Senate for all but six years.

coalition of Republicans and conservative Democrats.

A Modern Realignment?

Over the past forty years, there have been two major changes in the structure of the electorate, but clearly no full partisan realignment. The first is that the electorate has shifted away from the clear ascendancy that the Democrats held in the 1960s. Today, Republicans and Democrats are as close to parity as they have ever been. Repub-

licans in 1994 were stronger at the subpresidential level—among governors, in the statehouses, and of course in Congress—than they had been in many decades. But genuine realignment depends on their capturing simultaneous control of both the political branches of the national government. For a short while in 2001, Republicans barely held on to control of both Congress and the Presidency, but lost it when Republican Senator James Jeffords of Vermont defected to the Democrat Senate Caucus. In the wake of the 2000 election, partisanship is divided evenly

1932 Presidential Election

	Electoral Vote	Popular Vote	Percent
☐ F.D. Roosevelt—Democrat	472	22,825,016	57.4
▨ Herbert Hoover—Republican	59	15,758,397	30.6

FIGURE 6.5 The election of 1932. During the 36-year period from 1932 to 1968, the Democrats controlled the presidency for six of eight terms, the House for all but four years, and the Senate for all but two years.

across the country, with neither party having a clear advantage.

The second change has been an increasing "dealignment" in the electorate. Voters care less about parties than they used to, and campaigns emphasize the individual candidate rather than the party. A large segment of the American electorate, perhaps well over a third, will float from party to party, changing its preference according to a judgment of how well affairs have been managed and how it evaluates issues of the day.

Critical Realignments and Who Governs

The American system, we have said, is a popular form of government in which a majoritarian influence plays the major role. This does not mean that the public makes every major decision before elected officials take action or that it determines every turn or adjustment of public policy. Rather, it means that the voting public, whether by signaling its intentions in advance or by retrospective approval, can set the major outlines of policy. Such choices are made to some extent in every presidential election. But in many

2000 Presidential Election

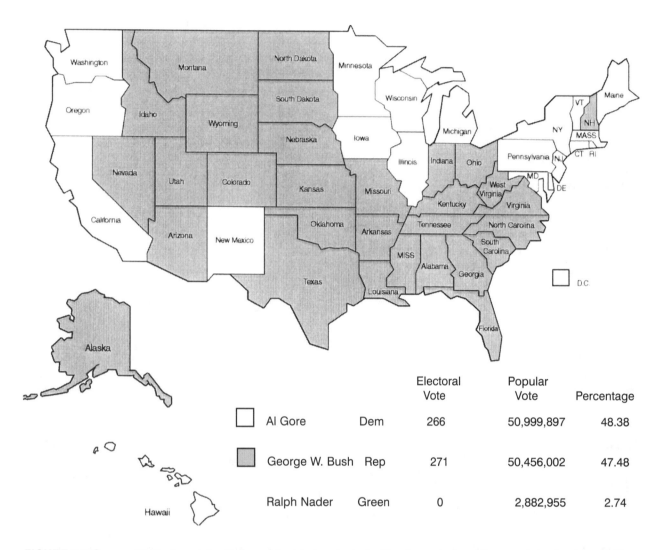

			Electoral Vote	Popular Vote	Percentage
☐	Al Gore	Dem	266	50,999,897	48.38
▨	George W. Bush	Rep	271	50,456,002	47.48
	Ralph Nader	Green	0	2,882,955	2.74

FIGURE 6.6 George W. Bush was the first president to be elected without a majority of the popular vote since 1888.

elections, the lines drawn between the parties are unclear, and the issues are not yet ripe for decision. In certain elections, however, the public is presented with distinct choices that set the policymaking agenda for an entire era. The choice, as seen by the voters, may be as clear-cut as being for or against slavery or for or against the development of a welfare state. In these elections, the public is a decisive influence on the governing institutions.

No doubt the wishes of the public could be registered without political parties. But parties, with all their imperfections, have facilitated pop-ular influence on the government. They have provided a degree of continuity from one election to another, and they have connected, to a limited extent, basic public philosophies with a common party label and with an organizational structure that exists throughout most of the nation. Realignments in particular have offered powerful "majoritarian" mechanisms for ensuring popular control of the government and for facilitating presidential leadership. No president having in mind a dramatic shift in the nation's politics can hope to accomplish every goal in one or even two terms. To fix an imprint indelibly on public policy, a president must ordinarily find a way to keep power, so to speak, after leaving office. Realignment offers the means. It allows a president to articulate a new majority public philosophy that sets the boundaries for future policymaking; and it bequeaths to the president's successors the political support in the form of a majority party status that can accomplish the long process of passing the many laws that transform a set of ideas into a working framework of public policy.

Minor Parties

The United States, it has been said, has a "two and one-half party system," the "half" being what we have referred to as a "minor" or "third" party. Minor or third parties in American history have come in a variety of sizes and forms. Paradoxically, those that have endured longest, like the Communist party, have exercised little influence, whereas some that have been short-lived, like the Populist party of the 1890s, have had a significant impact. With the exception of the Republican party at its inception, however, no third party has ever won the presidency or come even close to controlling either house of Congress.

Many have wondered why the United States has never developed sustained competition among more than two major parties. Part of the explanation lies with the acceptance of the doctrine of two-party competition as the norm of political life. But important institutional factors also support two-party competition. American elections take place in single-member districts in which the victor is decided by a plurality vote, which is the electoral arrangement considered most helpful to a two-party system. If congressional seats were chosen in multimember districts with proportional representation (which is the system used in some democratic regimes), a third party receiving 15 or 20 percent of the vote would win a substantial number of seats and would have a greater incentive to maintain its separate identity and avoid accommodation with a major party. Moreover, the presidential race, itself a "winner take all" contest, further discourages minor-party challenges. The desire to have a say in choosing the president leads many

potential third-party groups to form coalitions with one of the major parties.

In the final analysis, however, these structural explanations depend on the willingness of major political forces in America to enter into workable coalitions that can appeal to a majority. This willingness in turn reflects the fact that almost all Americans share a general commitment to the basic ends of the political system and that their differences can therefore usually be accommodated within one of two parties. Where political forces disagree on fundamental ends, coalitions among them are rare and unstable.

If two-party competition has been the norm, minor parties have nevertheless occasionally offered strong competition. Victory is not necessary for third parties to exert influence. Their greatest effect has come from pressuring the major parties to make changes in response to the threat that they might lose votes or be replaced. The role of minor parties, therefore, cannot be assessed by looking simply at their electoral performance. Especially in periods preceding realignments, third parties have been influential in bringing into the electoral arena the new issues over which the major parties subsequently divided. Thus, the antislavery parties in 1840 and 1848 served as forerunners of the Republican party, and the parties of agrarian discontent between 1880 and 1892 embodied positions that were adopted by the Democratic party in 1896 and later included in the policy proposals of the Progressives. More recently, George Wallace's American Independent party of 1968 pressured the Republican party under Richard Nixon to move to the right, at least in its rhetoric, in an effort to co-opt Wallace's support.

Minor parties have also served as a vehicle for a faction within a major party to test its political influence. A faction that feels it has been shut out or denied its rightful place may attempt (or threaten) a third-party challenge. Its objective may be not to win but to prevent its own party from winning by draining away critically needed votes. If that attempt is successful, the major party may then accommodate the faction in the next election on more favorable terms. The Progressives in 1912 succeeded partly by this strategy, while the States' Rights party in 1948—a disgruntled southern offshoot from the Democratic party—tried but failed.

In recent years—1976, 1980 and 1992—a new type of minor party, the independent candidacy, has emerged. In 1980, John Anderson offered himself not as the head of a new-issue constituency, like the Free-Soilers or the Populists, or as the leader of a bolting faction, like the States' Rights party, but as an alternative candidate better qualified than the major parties' nominees. In 1992, Ross Perot also ran as an independent, stressing his ability to end gridlock in Washington and to resolve critical national problems, especially the budget deficit. (Perot ran again in 1996, this time as nominee of the Reform party, a partisan vehicle largely of his creating.) This kind of candidacy would have been impossible without the modern media, which enables individuals to present their case directly to the American people. An important third-party effort in congressional elections, however, remains unlikely. The reason is that the primary system now allows factional candidates the chance to win the nomination of a major party, which is a prize too valuable to forsake for a mere gesture of protest.

Do minor parties play a constructive role? There is no simple answer. On the one hand they pose the risk of promoting narrow factional candidacies that are radical or demagogic in their appeals. At least two examples bear out this concern: the American or "Know-Nothing" party of 1856 which appealed blatantly to prejudice against Catholics, and the American Independent party of 1968 which had clear racist overtones. On the other hand, minor parties serve as potential checks on the major parties when these parties lose contact with the voters or refuse to offer alternatives on significant issues. Entering the presidential race periodically, minor parties can help to keep the major parties responsive and ensure that the electoral process remains open to new ideas.

The lesson to draw from this historical record appears to be that the electoral system should remain open to third parties, but not encourage them. Legislation that directly discriminates against third parties, such as unreasonably long filing periods, probably goes further than desirable in foreclosing competition from third parties. But changes in the political system that weaken the major parties and provide encouragement for third parties need to be closely scrutinized. If the case for a two-and-one-half-party system is sound, legislators must keep a careful watch on all proposals that affect the delicate balance between encouraging minor parties and maintaining the major ones.

Parties in Government

Parties are not merely electoral organizations. Once elected, governing officials continue to wear their party hats, and there is some expectation that fellow party members will work together in some fashion to promote their goals. Yet parties in the American system are only one influence at work on elected officials, and the degree of party unity in American politics is a disappointment to those who measure our parties by the standards of parliamentary systems.

The United States is the only major democracy today in which the notion of party representation has not displaced the classical idea of representation, according to which elected officials represent their constituencies as well as their own views of the public good. Elected officials in America have pressures and duties that invariably conflict with their party loyalty. A president is not merely a Democrat or a Republican, but the president in some sense of all the people. A member of Congress is not merely a partisan, but the representative of a particular district or state. Moreover, both the president and the members of Congress have their own institutions to defend, and our system was established with the expectation that some measure of conflict would be the norm in the relationship between these two institutions. The most telling point of all, however, is that the American people do not believe their elected officials should place party loyalties above all other considerations.

The different alternatives for party involvement in the functioning of government range from complete dominance by parties ("pure" party government) to no involvement by parties whatsoever (nonpartisan government).

TABLE 6.3
New and Minor Parties in American Presidential Elections Since 1828*

Year	Party	Candidate	Percent of vote	Electoral votes	Description
1832	Anti-Mason	William Wirt	8.0	7	A party that opposed the influence of the Society of the Masons.
1848	Free Soil	Martin Van Buren	10.1	0	A party that opposed the extension of slavery into the southwest territories; a part of the antislavery movement.
1856	American or Know-Nothing	Millard Fillmore	21.4	8	A strongly nativist party that opposed the immigration of foreigners and that favored limiting public offices to native-born Americans only.
1856	Republican	John C. Fremont	33.1	114	A party that opposed slavery and its expansion to the territories; replaced Whigs as the second major party.
1892	Populist	James Weaver	8.5	22	An agrarian protest party that sought to regulate railroads and banks.
1912	Progressive or "Bull Moose"	Teddy Roosevelt	27.4	88	A section of the Republican party that favored progressive measures including reforms such as expanded suffrage and antimonopoly laws. Received more votes in 1912 than the Republicans.
1912	Socialist	Eugene Debs	6.0	0	A workers' party with the goal of ending economic classes. Sought income tax.
1924	Progressive	Robert La Follette	16.6	13	A party that continued the earlier progressive label and favored strong action to control or break up corporate monopolies.
1948	States Rights or Dixiecrat	Strom Thurmond	2.4	39	A conservative faction of the Dixiecrat Democratic party from the south that opposed Truman's civil rights program. The party sought to protect segregation.
1968	American Independent	George Wallace	13.5	46	A protest party against Democratic Independent Great Society programs that fed on frustrations with civil rights activism, urban riots, and antiwar demonstrations.

TABLE 6.3 (cont.)
New and Minor Parties in American Presidential Elections Since 1828*

Year	Party	Candidate	Percent of vote	Electoral votes	Description
1980	Independent	John Anderson	7.0	0	A challenge to the adequacy of both parties; it stressed the qualifications of its candidate more than it did any program.
1992	Independent	Ross Perot	19	0	A populist style candidacy by a billionaire who pledged to end the gridlock in Washington, stressing his ability to reduce the deficit.
1996	Reform	Ross Perot	8	0	Pledged to eliminate deficit and clean up campaign finance abuses.
2000	Green	Ralph Nadar	2.7	0	Emphasized environmental protection and attacked the influence of corporate money on politics.

*New or minor parties that either carried one state or more in the electoral vote or received more than 6 percent of the popular vote. The election of 1860, where the parties were split, is excluded.

"Pure" Party Government

Under the party government model, favored by many progressives and some contemporary political scientists, the political party acts as a cohesive unit with both the president and the members of Congress from the same party adhering strictly to a common program. In effect, separation of powers gives way to party government, and voters, in deciding on their representatives, choose a national party program. Proponents of this model contend that it would give more energy to government and enable presidents (or parties) to put their programs into law without running into opposition from a fully independent legislative branch. As examples of moments when government "works" on a model resembling party government, adherents point to the first administrations of Jefferson, Wilson, and Franklin Roosevelt.

Obviously, this system could produce the desired form of majority government only if the presidency and Congress were controlled by the same party. Often this is not the case, especially in recent times, when Republicans captured the presidency for five of six terms between 1968 and 1988 but never had control of both houses of Congress. In addition, party government would require the parties in Congress to enforce by disciplinary measures a party line on all members of Congress, something which they have been reluctant to do. Adherents of party government argue, however, that if their scheme were somehow to become the accepted norm, split government would become a rarity. Yet most proponents now acknowledge that merely adopting a norm of party government puts the cart before the horse. Parties cannot be so radically changed without first changing the Constitution. Accordingly, advocates of party government favor Constitutional amendments that would make all congressional terms, senatorial and House, four years in length, and would require voters to choose presidential and congressional candidates from the same party.

TABLE 6.4
Partisan Unity and Division in the Presidency and Congress, 1801–2002

Years president's party has a majority, percent of time

Years	In *both* houses of Congress	In *one* house of Congress	In *neither* house of Congress
1801–1828	93%	0%	7%
1829–1860	63%	25%	13%
1861–1896	61%	28%	11%
1897–1932	83%	11%	5%
1933–1968	78%	9%	22%
1969–2002*	18%	23%	59%

* Counts Senate as Democratic after switch of Jeffords from Republican to Independent in 2001.

Nonpartisan Government

Under a nonpartisan model, favored by the founders, neither Congress nor the president would be "party" bodies. Congressional majorities would form on each issue, with the coalition varying according to the type of issue in question. The president would be identified with no preexisting organization and could accordingly make accommodations with Congress on a case-by-case basis. No doubt temporary blocs and working alliances in Congress would emerge, but without the sustaining force of a party label they would probably change with its shifting membership. This model existed in practice only during the First Congress in 1789 and during the period from roughly 1818 to 1824. In the latter period, Martin Van Buren argued that effective cooperation between the president and Congress had become impossible.

American Constitutional Government

American parties have operated in practice somewhere between these two models, being closer at some periods to party government and at others, despite the existence of party labels, to nonpartisan government. Given our system of government, this in-between status hardly comes as a surprise. By permitting parties, the system allows for whatever coordination the parties on their own can achieve. Yet, unlike a parlimentary regime, it does not encourage party cohesiveness. The government does not fall when legislative members of the executive's party break ranks and the president's party loses a vote. Party members tend to share certain views and to act together, but the federal structure of representation and the separation of powers allow for disagreements.

Obviously, in this system there is a great deal of room between stronger and weaker parties—between parties that move closer to the pole of party government and parties that, while maintaining their names, scarcely serve to guide or discipline their members. Whether parties move closer to the one pole or the other makes a great deal of difference for the operation of the government, and it is on the issue of more or less party-related behavior that much institutional debate has taken place. Over American history, the cohesiveness of parties has varied greatly.

From the 1920s through the 1980s, roll-call votes in Congress indicated that party unity markedly declined. The reasons for this decline are various: within Congress, power became more dispersed, and party leaders have had less leverage over their members; in the nomination of presidential candidates, fewer institutional connections exist between congressional leaders and presidential nominees, and presidential election results have had a diminishing impact on the outcome of congressional races. During this era, however, there were notable periods of unity for the Democrats after the elections of 1932 and 1964 and for the Republicans after the elections of 1980 and 1994. Unity in both parties was on the upswing over the last decade. Since the 1990s, partisanship has become more polarized as the moderate and liberal wing of the Republican party has grown smaller, and the conservative wing of the Democratic party has diminished.

Conclusion

Political parties must be understood in two different ways. They are associations of citizens for promoting a general set of principles and policies, and they are structures and organizations influenced by various legal arrangements and incentives for participation. As associations for promoting principles, parties throughout American history have alternated between strength and weakness—between bodies that vigorously present clear goals and bodies that flounder about as loose coalitions in search of a purpose. As structures and organizations, parties have been undergoing a marked decline in strength for most of this century, although recently there have been signs of resurgence.

A clear sense of purpose can hold a party together as a cohesive and powerful instrument even with a weak organizational structure. But American parties tend to possess this firmness of purpose for only relatively brief periods. If a strong commitment to a common goal is the only thing American parties rely on to hold themselves together, it is unlikely that they will operate effectively most of the time. To play an influential role as instruments for accommodating broad coalitions with a general sense of direc-

tion, they need a structure strong enough to carry them through "normal" times.

In considering the place of parties in our scheme of government, the constitution maker must look well beyond the founding. The founders opposed political parties, although they largely had in mind different kinds of parties from those which subsequently developed. The case for political parties was made by thinkers and political leaders after the founding, in part to realize certain of the founders' goals and in part to correct or "amend" the original constitutional system. Adding parties was seen as a means of providing for more democratic influence on the government, for controlling the ambitions of factions, for building coalitions, and for establishing links among elected officials in a system of separation of powers and federalism. Other intermediary institutions—personal campaign organizations, interest groups, and the media—either do not perform these functions at all or do so not nearly as well as parties. A decline of party influence beyond a certain point thus means the political system as a whole suffers.

There is, to be sure, no possibility of returning to the style of party politics of a previous era. The practical question today is whether certain steps could be taken, consistent with modern conditions, to restore some of the functions to political parties—supposing, of course, that this objective is desirable. Whether this restoration can be accomplished should become clearer after analyzing how campaigns and elections are conducted—the subject of the next chapter.

Chapter 6 Notes

1. Joseph E. Kallenbach, *The American Chief Executive* (New York: Harper and Row, 1966), p. 286.
2. Martin Van Buren, *Inquiry Into the Origin and Course of Political Parties in the United States* (New York: Hurd and Houghton, 1867), pp. 3–4.
3. George William Curtis, *Harper's Weekly,* November 12, 1887, p. 813.
4. The most important of these court decisions were *Elrod v. Burns* (1976) and *Rutan v. Republican Party of Illinois* (1990), in which the Court held that it was "unconstitutional to hire, promote, or transfer most public employees based on party affiliation." "Patronage System Dealt Setback," *CQ Weekly Report,* June 23, 1990, p. 1973.

5. Woodrow Wilson, "College and State," in *The Public Papers of Woodrow Wilson,* Ray Stannard Baker and William E. Dodd, eds., vol. I (New York: Harper, 1925), p. 37.

6. V. O. Key, *Parties, Politics and Pressure Groups,* 5th ed. (New York: Crowell, 1964), p. 375.

7. *Cousins v Wigoda* 1975.

8. E. E. Schattschnieider, *Party Government (New* York: Rinehart, 1942), p. 64.

9. Not all of these states, however, hold open primaries in presidential nominating contests. National Democratic party rules strongly discourage the use of open primaries.

10. Hugh A. Bone, *American Politics and the Party System,* 3rd ed. (New York: McGraw Hill, 1965), p. 202.

11. *Washington Post*, January 20, 1973.

12. James Q. Wilson, *Political Organizations (New* York: Basic Books, 1973).

13. Morton Keller, *Affairs of State* (Cambridge, Mass.: Harvard University Press, 1977), p. 256.

14. *Elrod v. Bums (1976); Rutan v. Republican Party of Illinois (1990).*

15. Wilson Carey McWilliams, "The Meaning of the Election," in Gerald Pomper, ed., *The Election of* 1980 (Chatham, New Jersey: Chatham House, 1981).

16. Leon D. Epstein, "Presidential Parties and the Nominating Process," a paper prepared for a Wilson Center Colloquium, May 13, 1980, p. 17.

7

Campaigns and Elections

CHAPTER CONTENTS

For most Americans, elections—above all, presidential elections—are the most interesting and riveting of all political events. They contain all the elements of the human drama, from the tragic and the noble, to the pathetic and the ridiculous. In the past three decades, Americans have witnessed the assassination of one candidate (Senator Robert Kennedy in 1968) and the shooting and paralysis of another (Governor George Wallace in 1972). They have seen a leading contender (Governor Bill Clinton in 1992) appear on *60 Minutes* with his wife in order to explain their marital problems—and then go on to win the Democratic nomination and the presidency. Finally, in 2000, they witnessed the most improbable of all results: an election that ended in a virtual tie, in which a swing of fewer than 250 votes in the official count of one state (Florida), would have changed the winner from George W. Bush to Al Gore. The 2000 election was also disputed. Challenges over the counting of ballots in Florida made their way up and down state and federal courts, and it was not until six weeks past election day, after the Supreme Court issued its highly controversial decision of *Bush v. Gore*, that Americans knew who their next president would be.

An electoral campaign represents the kind of contest that everyone readily understands. It is a race in which in the end there is only one winner. Given the drama of campaigns, it is tempting to focus on the most exciting aspects, emphasizing, as the media often do, the "horse race" aspects. Yet students of politics must also pay attention to the underlying factors that help explain how campaigns operate. As any lover of sports knows, games are played according to certain rules and norms, a change in any one of which can affect how the game is played and who wins. The same is true of the electoral process. It is important, therefore, to study some of the most important rules and norms of electoral politics and observe how they have developed and how they operate today. From the perspective of the constitution maker, it is necessary as well to ask not only how these rules affect which candidates win or lose, but also how they influence the operation of the government and the behavior of elected officials.

Presidential Selection: General Considerations

No part of the political system has been subjected to greater change in recent times than our method of selecting a president. Since the 1960s, the nominating process has been transformed from a system that relied on party conventions to make the choice of nominees to one that relies chiefly on primary elections; financing for campaigns has been changed from a largely unregulated system based on private funding to a partly regulated one based on a mix of private and public funding; and campaigning has changed from a system in which the candidates contact citizens in rallies or meetings to one in which they rely heavily on mass media. Finally, though no changes have been made, amendments have been proposed to alter the Electoral College and to replace it with a form of direct elections. Many of the arrangements and issues in the presidential selection system remain controversial, and changes will almost certainly be made in some areas in the near future.

Eligibility: Legal Qualifications and Norms

Age and Residence Who runs for president of the United States? The field of potential candidates is limited in the first instance by certain Constitutional standards of eligibility. Article II of the Constitution requires that the president be at least 35 years old and a natural-born citizen. The age requirement hardly seems restrictive, as few voters today would probably even consider someone younger than 35. The youngest person ever elected president was John F. Kennedy at 43, and the average age of an incoming president has been 54. At 69 years old, Ronald Reagan in 1980 was the oldest person ever to be elected president. This preference for individuals over 40 follows from the general pattern of political careers and perhaps from voters' natural inclinations. In part, however, it reflects the "conditioning" imposed by the Constitution, which establishes age qualifications for all federal elective offices. The founders' intention for the presidency was to limit consideration to persons of maturity and, ordinarily at least, some experience in public affairs.

Requiring the president to be a natural-born citizen (and a resident for fourteen years before election) might be considered unfair to those who are excluded. These requirements, however, illustrate the founders' concern with structuring electoral rules with a view to governing. The founders reasoned that the nation's highest office had to be above even the slightest suspicion that a president's deepest loyalty might be to another nation; this concern took precedence over any theoretical right of an individual to become president. Henry Kissinger, the famous German-born foreign policy advisor to Presidents Nixon and Ford, is a recent example of a person whose political career may have been affected by this provision.

The Constitution imposes no religious, racial, sexual, or economic qualifications for holding office. Of course, legal qualifications set only the outside limits for consideration. Until well into this century, the party politicians who controlled the nominating process employed certain "unwritten laws" or norms in judging electability. For example, at the turn of the century, it was generally held that only white, Protestant males—preferably of English stock—were electable. Democrats challenged the religious barrier in 1928 when they nominated a Catholic candidate, Al Smith. Smith lost the election to Herbert Hoover, with the religious question playing an important role for many voters. In 1960, Democrats nominated a Catholic for a second time, John F. Kennedy, who won a narrow victory over Richard Nixon. Religion was again an important factor, helping Kennedy with some voters and hurting him with others. One remarkable result of Kennedy's election has been that since 1960 Catholicism has never been considered a disqualifying factor.

Today, there might still be resistance to the nomination of certain candidates because of their race, religion, or sex. But poll surveys indicate that such resistance is weakening among the voters. This trend has been illustrated in a number of ways. Democratic presidential nominee Walter Mondale chose a woman, Geraldine Ferraro, as his running mate in 1984, and in 1984 and 1988 the civil-rights leader, Jesse Jackson, was a major candidate in the Democratic nominating race. In 1996 retired Joint Chiefs of Staff Chairman Colin Powell, an African American and the son of immigrants, was the preferred choice of a majority of voters in many opinion polls, until he decided not to seek the office. In 2000, Senator Joseph Lieberman, an orthodox Jew, was nominated as the vice presidential candidate for the Democratic Party. The informal norms that limit the choice of presidential candidates, while they have certainly not all been eliminated, are much less restrictive than they once were. Gone are the days when only a WASP (White Anglo-Saxon Protestant) need apply.

Term Limitation A second Constitutional qualification on eligibility was not adopted until 1951, when the Twenty-Second Amendment was passed, limiting a president to no more than two elected terms (or ten years, in the event of a vice presidential accession). The exclusion is perpetual, meaning that the person cannot step down for a term and then run again, as is the case for governors in some states, such as Ohio and North Carolina. This amendment was passed in reaction to the four consecutive elections of Franklin D. Roosevelt from 1932 through 1944. Before Roosevelt and dating all the way back to George Washington, who retired after his second term, a tradition developed that a president would serve no more than two terms. But as an unwritten rule, this tradition was never considered completely binding. Some presidents either genuinely contemplated a third term or deliberately refused to remove themselves from consideration until the last moment, probably to protect their power while still in office.

The question of presidential term limitations was debated during the Convention in 1787, but ultimately rejected. Among other things, the founders thought it unwise for the nation to deny itself the services of a particular individual during a period of crisis. Alexander Hamilton famously argued this point in *The Federalist* (#72): "There is no nation which has not, at one period or another, experienced an absolute necessity of the services of particular men in particular situations, perhaps it would not be too strong to say, to the preservation of its political existence." Supporters of Franklin Roosevelt used this argument in 1940 and 1944, when he ran for his third and fourth terms amidst the international crisis of World War II.

The argument in favor of a limitation rests on the idea that a republican system should not have to rely on the abilities of any one individual. To permit someone to serve for too long risks transforming a republic, in spirit if not in letter, into a kind of elective monarchy, in which the people identify the government, not with its laws and institutions, but with the personality of a single leader. As the Republican Party Platform of 1940 argued, a term limitations amendment was needed to protect "against the overthrow of the American system of government."

The Twenty-Second Amendment has had other consequences besides just exclusion from office. Calculations of who will hold power in the future inevitably influence the willingness of officials to follow a president, making it more likely that presidents in their second term will face more resistance from some in Congress and the bureaucracy. A president serving a second term is sometimes referred to today by the expressive phrase of a "lame duck." Presidents may attempt to deal with this status by adopting a hurried approach to the making of policy, attempting to make a mark before the effectiveness of their powers begins to wane.

Screening and Selecting Candidates

Within the broad boundaries of eligibility marked out by laws and norms, a mechanism must exist to survey the possible candidates and then limit the field to a manageable number. The founders assigned this task to the electors, who they thought would be in a good position to decide among the nation's leading figures. Since the advent of political parties in the early nineteenth century, however, the choice has been carried out under a two-step process: a nominating stage, in which the major parties narrow down the number of candidates to two (with an occasional serious third-party contender); and a general election, in which the public, voting within the fifty states, selects electors bound to the candidates, who in turn officially choose the president.

The number of people actually considered in this process is rather limited. No one would—or perhaps should—expect the parties to conduct a talent search at election time to discover some unknown leader. Electoral institutions are ideally designed to select candidates with the combination of skills, experience, and political support needed to meet the burdens of what is probably the world's most demanding political office. Both political considerations and common sense suggest that the field of candidates should be confined to prominent persons with known political skills. It is hardly surprising, therefore, to find that our majority-party nominees have mostly been politicians of some kind—vice presidents, governors, and senators.

Nevertheless, compared with Great Britain, where the prime minister is almost always drawn from existing leaders of the parliamentary party, the pool of potential candidates in the United States is much broader. American parties have on occasion gone outside the usual sphere of politicians—to generals like Ulysses S. Grant or Dwight D. Eisenhower, to Supreme Court justices like Charles Evans Hughes (the Republican nominee in 1916), and to businessmen like Wendell Wilkie (the Republican nominee in 1940). Nor does a candidate need to be a leading member of Congress or highly experienced in national politics. For example, a rather obscure ex-governor of Georgia, Jimmy Carter, won the presidency in 1976; and a number of candidates have been chosen without ever having held an elective office or in the federal government: Reagan, Clinton, and George W. Bush all came from the ranks of state governors. There is, of course, no single path to the presidency. It is, however, worth noting that of the major party candidates from 1968 thru 2000 (excluding incumbents), five last held the office of Vice-President (Nixon, Hubert Humphrey, Mondale, George H. Bush, and Gore); two of Senator (McGovern and Dole); and five of Governor (the four mentioned above plus Michael Dukakis).

The Nominating Stage

Candidates today frequently enter the nomination race for reasons other than that of winning their party's nomination: to publicize a cause, to gain recognition for a future race, and to stake a claim for being considered as a vice-presidential nominee. Serious presidential aspirants, however, enter the nominating phase with two basic objectives: to obtain enough delegates to win the nomination and to do so in a way that minimizes creating party disunity, which can diminish the chance of victory in the general election. These two objectives are often in tension, and candidates often find that they must put first things first and secure their own nomination before anything else. George W. Bush's 2000 campaign illustrates this necessity. Bush began as the clear front-runner and initially sought to run as a consensus candidate for the whole party. But after he lost early primaries to Senator John McCain, he had to take the gloves off and attack McCain, which risked dividing the Republican Party and driving away moderate Republican and independent voters.

The nature of the current nominating process, consisting as it does of open contests among various contenders, often leads to an airing of divisions among different elements of the party. Elections are frequently about drawing lines, and attacks made publicly on opponents during primary campaigns can make the subsequent process of healing party rifts very difficult. President Ford in 1976 and President Carter in 1980 both blamed their losses in the general election in large part on the difficult nomination campaigns they had to wage, Ford against Reagan and Carter against Senator Edward Kennedy. On the positive side, however, this process forces candidates to make some difficult choices, and voters get to see them performing under trying circumstances.

Nominating Systems: A Historical Glance

Earlier methods of nomination sometimes posed fewer problems for party unity, though they raised difficulties of other kinds. The first system of nominating candidates (1800–1816) was by a vote of the party's membership in Congress (the congressional caucus). This system was never fully "institutionalized," meaning it was never completely accepted as the legitimate way to select nominees. Early on it became a focal point of controversy. Critics charged that it was undemocratic-they began to refer to it derisively as

"King Caucus"—and that it compromised the president's independence from Congress, threatening the separation of powers. In 1812, for example, President James Madison was pressured by members of his party in Congress to agree to declare war against Great Britain as a condition for his renomination for a second term. By 1824, when there was only one national political party (the Democratic-Republican Party), the caucus met to select a nominee, William H. Crawford. But many members of the party in Congress boycotted the event, and rival contenders, among them John Quincy Adams and Andrew Jackson, simply ignored its decision and went on to run for the presidency. Adams was eventually elected in a highly disputed contest that was decided by the House of Representatives. "King Caucus" had been deposed.

The Pure Convention System (1832–1908) Following the reestablishment of party competition after 1828, the parties devised a new system of nomination. It was a national party convention made up of delegates selected in the states according to procedures determined by each state party organization. In 1832 the Democrats held the first major party convention in Baltimore to re-nominate Andrew Jackson as presidential nominee and nominate Martin Van Buren for the vice-presidency. By 1840 both major parties (the Democrats and the Whigs) were wedded to the convention system. Party conventions have been with us ever since.

The convention method initially satisfied the calls for a more democratic system at the same time that it insured presidential independence of Congress. The system also transferred the decision-making power from national party figures in Washington to state party leaders, who generally were the major players at the Conventions. The two parties used roughly the same methods of selecting delegates, relying on the different practices of parties in different states and regions. In some cases, the selection was highly democratic and participatory; in other cases, it was pretty much dictated by state or local party figures. There was, however, one important difference between the processes of the two parties. The Democratic Party in 1836 adopted a rule that required a two-thirds vote of the convention to receive the nomination. This rule, which lasted until 1936, gave an effective veto over the nominee to the states of any region of the nation.

With the choice of the nominees now often in the hands of the party leaders at the convention, contenders for the presidency could do no better than to campaign by positioning themselves so as to be on good terms with party leaders and acceptable to a widespread following within the party. Actually, "campaigning" is the wrong term to use. Standard practice in the nineteenth century was for the party to seek out the candidate, not the candidate to seek out the party. Candidates were supposed to make a pretense of appearing reluctant to seek office. The Democratic nominee in 1868, Horatio Seymour, was heard to exclaim to a friend upon learning of his nomination, "Pity me, Harvey, pity me"; Seymour was spared the full burden by losing the election to General Grant.

The "courtship" between the candidates and the party was conducted according to customs that today seem very quaint. Candidates known to be genuine possibilities for nomination did not attend the conventions, but stayed home. (In point of fact, however, some candidates stayed in frequent contact with their lieutenants at the convention.) After the convention made its choice, a delegation was sent to inform the candidate of his nomination. The candidate would receive the delegation at his home, listen to its request, and then agree to accept the proffered honor. Candidates today might occasionally yearn for the dignity of this process.

The Mixed System (1912–1968) An important change in the nominating system began to take place in 1912, when a large number of states passed laws for the selection of delegates to the conventions by primary elections. With the advent of these primaries, some candidates began to campaign openly for the nomination, much as they do today. In 1912 Teddy Roosevelt competed in primaries across the country, delivering scores of speeches and attending hundreds of rallies. Yet because the majority of the delegates were not yet selected or bound in primary contests, candidates could still opt to follow the old "inside" method of appealing to party leaders and to delegates chosen by party-run caucuses. Neither Adlai Stevenson in 1952 nor Hubert Humphrey in 1968 entered any primaries, yet both won the Democratic Party's nomination.

Most candidates, however, did enter at least some of the primaries, and the nominees generally had won support from primary states and from party leaders in caucus states. The nomination process in this period is best described as a "mixed system" in which there was a balance between the older method of selection by party leaders and the new method of popular choice by the voters. Democrats also dropped their two-thirds rule for nomination, adopting a simple majority system after 1936.

The Primary System (1972 to the Present) After 1968, a large number of states shifted from caucuses to primaries as the method of selecting delegates, and by 1976 the balance for the system had tipped decisively in favor of presidential primaries. Presidential nominations are now determined by popular direct elections that are conducted in separate states.

Delegates today are chosen by two basic processes: primaries and caucuses. In addition, in the Democratic Party, some office-holders and party officials (governors, party chairs and mayors of larger cities) are chosen automatically because of their positions, and some members of Congress are selected by meetings of the Democratic congressional caucus for each chamber. Of these methods, primaries, as just noted, are by far the most important, accounting for the selection of more than eighty percent of the delegates. The selection of delegates in caucus states has been transformed as a result of the predominance of primaries to almost "copy" primaries: instead of choosing unbound delegates (as they did in the past), caucus states today tend to pick delegates committed to particular candidates, as everyone is aware that the winner will normally be determined before the conventions meet. One state that has used the caucus method—Iowa—has managed to carve out an important role for itself since 1976 because it has been among the first of the scheduled contests. (Other states—Louisiana and Alaska—have tried to move in front, but have yet to be given much attention by the candidates.)

TABLE 7.1
Presidential Primaries, 1912–2000*

	Democratic		Republican	
	Number of primaries	Percent of total delegates chosen in primaries	Number of primaries	Percent of total delegates chosen in primaries
1912	12	33	13	42
1916	20	54	20	59
1932	16	40	14	38
1960	16	38	15	39
1968	17	37	16	34
1972	22	65	21	57
1980	29	71	33	76
1988	34	67	35	77
1992	36	67	37	80
1996	34	74	44	85
2000	40	85	44	90

*Because of legal complexity, these figures are approximate.

The predominance of primaries also helps account for the different character of the modern campaign when compared to what took place under the mixed system. Candidates today cannot rely, as they once did, on party leaders and traditional party organizations to secure them the nomination. They must go out and win over the voters. While endorsements by major party figures can help somewhat—George W. Bush in 2000 had the support of almost all of the Republican governors—ultimately a candidate can prevail only by an appeal to the rank and file in the party.

Candidates today press their courtship of the voters with an openness and aggressiveness that would have shocked nineteenth-century political sensibilities. With the first real contest for delegates coming now in the winter of the election year, and with a long time needed to organize a campaign and raise funds, candidates usually make an official declaration of their candidacy in the year preceding the general election. "Outsiders," that is, candidates who are not initially considered to have much chance may start even earlier, announcing two years before the general election. The candidates then begin traveling around the country, pressing their case with the voters and appealing to the party activists. No wonder that some analysts now speak of the "continuous campaign."

The Campaign Organization

In launching a campaign, a candidate must first assemble the professional core of a personal electoral organization, which will include the functions of campaign management, fund-raising, press relations, polling, speech writing and media consulting (ad preparation). Pollsters and media consultants sometimes now have firms of their own and are hired by the candidates. The fact that many of these functions are now performed by these specialists, rather than by traditional party leaders, speaks volumes about the nature of modern nomination campaigns, which are less efforts in coalition building among party leaders and more exercises in mass communication and persuasion.

The main advisers, along with the candidate, devise the basic plan for the campaign. The plan, which evolves with circumstances, outlines at each point the themes and issues the candidate will stress, the priorities for the candidate's time, and the allocation of campaign resources. In 2000, the Bush campaign early on sought to discourage too many entrants by accumulating endorsements from other important Republicans and by raising huge sums of money. Bush also adopted a centrist policy, based on the theme of "compassionate conservatism," which was designed to appeal down the road to independents and Democrats. Republicans definitely considered themselves underdogs going into the race, and the Bush campaign plan always tried to keep its focus on the final election. Al Gore in 2000 was known for changing his plan, which was both a strength and weakness of the campaign. Gore was willing to alter strategies and change personnel until he found a successful approach, but this gave his campaign a reputation for inconsistency.

Each of the advisers performs a certain role. The campaign managers (sometimes the function is shared by two persons), in addition to overall management responsibility, helps put together the candidate's personal organization, which consists of paid regional or state coordinators plus a volunteer staff in most states. The use of the term "manager" is revealing. Like the baseball manager, the position often receives much of the credit for the candidate's success and much of the blame for failure. Managers can also be dismissed. Ronald Reagan, whose nomination bid in 1980 started slowly with a loss in the Iowa caucuses, dismissed his manager, John Sears, and Al Gore twice shook up his campaign team in 2000. George W. Bush had Don Evans (the official campaign manager) and Karl Rove (his chief political strategist) as two of his chief advisors; both—and this is not unusual—took positions in the administration, Evans as Secretary of Commerce and Rove as a senior advisor on the White House staff.

A campaign's pollsters perform a quite different function from pollsters syndicated in newspapers, who usually focus on the "horse race" aspect of the contest, i.e., which candidate is up and which down. A campaign pollster, especially for a candidate who is still relatively unknown, is more interested in discovering what a candidate can do to improve his or her standing. The pollster attempts to learn what themes the candidate might be able to use most effectively in the campaign and what strengths and weaknesses other candidates, especially the leading contenders, possess. As the campaign gets under way, polls can assist in deciding whether a strategy is working and how the candidate might best expend additional resources. In a sea of uncertainty, which is the condition of political campaigns, pollsters can at least profess to having "hard evidence," which can help in deliberations on strategy. Richard Wirthlin, Reagan's pollster in 1980, proved to be a highly influential figure in the campaign and helped to pioneer Reagan's famous appeal to "Reagan Democrats." After testing certain themes with voters in the early primaries, he found that Reagan had "a very unique appeal to blue collar workers . . . . We determined [that] the emphasis on the family and the neighborhood and values generally and an appeal for hope were very, very strong thematic elements that had good impact not only in solidifying that early support, but also in building a base for a strong run for the presidency in November."[1]

Media and advertising consultants plan and help to produce the candidate's advertising campaign. Much effort goes into devising the best way to display the candidate's personality, to present the campaign's themes and issues, and to raise questions about opponents. Although media ads are widely criticized for being empty—for trying to market candidates like brands of soap—they do provide valuable information about the candidates' positions. Even ads that attack opponents, which sometimes degrade a campaign, are often quite helpful in pointing out important differences. The problem with attack ads in primaries is more practical than ethical. Negative ads create resentment on the

---

BOX 7.1

Campaign Pollsters

Polls are of obvious value to candidates devising their strategy and tactics, but Robert M. Teeter, President Ford's pollster in 1976, warned that opinion surveys should be kept in perspective.

> Too many people have the idea that our job is to find the hidden lever to move all the voters. There's an incorrect public perception that they (polls) can measure everything to a precise degree. Polls should provide some guidance on what candidates ought to talk about or how they should frame their presentations—but I don't think polls should ever override good judgment or replace people's brains.

Source: *National Journal*, May 1, 1976, pp. 574–579.

part of candidates and voters whose support is necessary for building party unity.

A large share of the campaign budget today, usually well over one half, is spent on television and radio advertising. Yet, for all the money spent, paid advertising is not nearly as important as the "free" time that candidates receive from the media in the form of news coverage, interviews, and debates. Some studies have suggested that ads may have little effect in presidential elections, either during the primaries or during the general election campaign. Of course, no major candidate has been willing to test this theory by forgoing an advertising campaign. In addition, a small effect in politics can make a big difference; in a large filed of candidates, it is frequently the case that only a few percentage points will separate a first from a second or a second from a third place finish. Finally, part of the reason why ads may not seem to count very much is that in the end, rival advertising may often cancel itself out. Media consultants today are aware of the limits of paid advertising, and they direct much of their attention to the themes and images projected during the campaign as a whole. Advertising is no longer separate from the rest of the campaign, but is integrated, almost daily, into plans of what the candidate will be emphasizing.

If a campaign is to have any prospect of success, the professional campaign staff must be supplemented by organizations of unpaid volunteers. Professional staff make the key strategic decisions, such as where to allocate the candidate's time and resources, while the volunteer organization tends to be given the more mundane tasks of telephoning voters, setting up meetings, and getting supporters to the polls. Most volunteers participate, not because they expect a job in Washington, but because they believe in the candidate and the cause. In some cases candidates receive the help or endorsement of organizations, such as a labor union or the Christian Coalition, which can supply many helpers. (Motives of volunteers, of course, are often mixed, and a few may have an eye on working their way up in local circles in preparation for running for office.) Volunteer organizations are particularly important in caucus states, such as Iowa, where participation is generally very low, and in smaller primary states, where a large percentage of voters can be contacted personally.

Candidates seeking to build an effective volunteer organization must be especially solicitous of the activist portion of their party, from which volunteers tend to come. Volunteers are often strongly committed to a particular cause or ideological viewpoint—this is why they participate. In some years this has created problems for the candidate. A candidate may need the support of committed activists in order to get the campaign off the ground, but as the campaign begins to achieve success the candidate may seek a broader base by making more moderate appeals. Early organizational volunteers may resist this movement and pressure the candidate to remain true to earlier commitments. This situation can prove damaging, as in 1972, when George McGovern tried to moderate some of his views on the Vietnam War only to find his early volun-

BOX 7.2

Media Consultants

Campaigning for federal office is now done mainly through television. The reliance on television means an increased role for the media consultant, whose job it is to make the candidate seem more attractive to the public than his or her opponent. Because of costs and restrictions imposed by the broadcasting industry, consultants normally attempt to get their message across in a thirty-to-sixty-second ad. This, combined with the fact that, as one top consultant put it, "TV is basically a visual, entertainment medium," means consultants must emphasize a "look" a "quality," a quick overall impression.

The consultant Robert Goodman claims that he managed to get Malcom Wallop of Wyoming elected to the Senate in 1976 because he put a white hat on the Republican candidate and, to the beat of sweeping music, had him lead a hoarse caravan to Washington; Ray Strother, a consultant who handles only Democratic candidates, says he tries for the "soft look"; and Roy Pfautch, president of the American Association of Political Consultants, claims that the key is to get across a "subliminal message."

While some consultants are concerned by the extent of their influence, the costliness of their product, and the shallowness of their message, many openly relish their assumed power and talk in terms of creating or controlling a candidate. Whether consultants are actually as influential as they sometimes claim, however, is very questionable. First, opposing consultants probably neutralize one another in many campaigns; second, the cause and effect relationship between seeing an ad and voting for a candidate is uncertain; and finally, every campaign is a sea of uncertainty in which events, personalities, and ideas affect people in unpredictable ways.

Source: *Washington Post*, June 5, 1982.

teers threatening to turn against him at the convention.

The Three Phases of the Pre-Convention Contest

The modern nomination campaign goes through three rough stages: the so-called "invisible primary" in the year before the primaries; the actual campaign in the primary and caucus contests; and the new interregnum period, running from the selection of the nominee until the party conventions. The term invisible primary was once quite descriptive, but has recently become something of a misnomer. Campaigning in the year before the primaries once took place largely out of sight; but this is no longer the case. By the late summer of the pre-election year, reporters are already focusing on the candidates and closely covering their activities, even if most Americans still show little interest. This period looms all the more important today because of the compression of the primary season, in which

more and more contests have been scheduled right at the outset.

Candidate activity during the invisible primary consists of soliciting endorsements, setting up volunteer organizations, competing in occasional straw polls of state parties, and, of course, raising money. Primary campaigns need a lot of money, and much of it is required right at the beginning. The raising of money is important in itself, but it is also taken as an indicator of support. If a candidate cannot raise money, it is a sign to the media and to other professionals that the campaign may not be viable. Candidates who find that they are not making much headway, whether in winning endorsements or raising money, may quit the race before it actually begins. In the Republican contest in 2000, some of the more prominent contenders, including Elizabeth Dole and Dan Quayle, pulled out during this period.

News columnists and leading journalists also begin to play an important role in this period. Even if their stories are not widely read at this point by the casual reader, other professionals and journalists pay close attention. These early stories begin to create the preconceptions (or, as some analysts say, the "frames") in which the candidates will subsequently be analyzed. Thus journalists began writing stories early on about whether George W. Bush had the intellectual weight and experience to be president. This "frame" continued throughout the entire campaign, and Bush continually had to try to live down this image.

The candidates in this period also engage in a good deal of intensive one-on-one campaigning in Iowa and New Hampshire. Finishing "closer than expected" in an early contest does not assure a candidate of the nomination, but it immediately draws attention to the campaign and raises a candidate's status from that of an also-ran, lost in the pack, to that of a genuine contender. One of the best barometers for predicting the results of primary contests is to look at how the candidate did in the previous contests. To win, it helps to have won. Much of the campaigning at the initial stage is an exercise in village politics, not mass politics. This is especially the case for the challengers and outsiders, who must make some kind of impressive display in these early contests to stay in the race. After these events, the campaign will quickly shift to election days with huge numbers of voters in many different states. The candidates now will spend less time in any one state and contact most voters either through advertising or through news coverage of their campaign appearances.

The second phase in the process is the actual campaign for the selection of delegates in the primaries and caucuses. Since the emergence of the modern system after 1968, this phase has changed importantly in relation to the timing and scheduling of the contests. The selection of delegates traditionally took place over a four-month period that began in the winter of the election year, with contests in Iowa (the first caucus) and New Hampshire (the first primary), and extended until early June. Primaries were spread out over this period, such that, in 1976, it was not until some two and one half-months into the process (mid-April) that more than half of all the delegates had been chosen. This arrangement had a certain "rhythm" to it. It slowly narrowed the field, as candidates who fared poorly early in the season and could not rebound would drop out or suspended their campaigns. Voters in subsequent primaries could focus on a more manageable number of candidates, with time to adjust to the new situation.

The problems in this arrangement were two-fold: first, states holding the earliest contests-Iowa and New Hampshire—had an undue advantage, if not in picking the nominee, at least in narrowing the field; and second, states coming near or at the end found that the nomination choice had been made before their primary was held. California, which normally held its primary in June, was among the states whose voters felt disenfranchised in the process. This situation was inherently unstable, and a predictable reaction began to set in. States began moving their primaries closer to the start of the process ("front-loading" as it was called); the more they did so, the more that some of those further back felt the need to try to move theirs forward as well. Front-loading was in full swing by 1988, when a large group of Southern states in 1988 created a huge regional primary ("Super Tuesday") shortly after New Hampshire, with the goal of gaining more say over the nomination choice. Other states followed in 1992, and the race was on. The national parties made some efforts to control or regulate this process, but other than allowing an advantaged spot at the front for Iowa and New Hampshire these attempts have proven largely ineffective. On the Republican side in 2000, over two-thirds of the delegates had been chosen within the month following the first primary contest. The race was over by the middle of March.

Entering 2004 the system will allow Iowa and New Hampshire to come at or near the beginning, but all other efforts to halt front-loading have, for the time being, ceased. After New Hampshire the selection of delegates will come in a torrent, and by the middle of March more than three-quarters of the delegates will have been chosen and, except for the possibility of a deadlock, the nominees will likely have been selected. The decisive part of the campaign will take place on three or four election days in the first month. The system now is geared to produce a result very quickly.

This early selection has created a new, third phase in the pre-convention campaign: the "interregnum." As long as this new schedule, or something resembling it, continues, the nominees will be selected some five months before their formal anointment at the conventions and eight months before the final election. This period is one in which the victorious nominees attempt to patch up their relations with others in the party and in which they begin to focus attention on the opponent. This period actually marks the early start of the final election campaign, although it is still limited somewhat by the fact that the candidates have not been officially nominated and by the tradition of beginning the real campaign after the conventions. But how long this tradition will remain is now very much in question. In both 1996 and 2000, the campaigns began running national advertising early in the summer, a practice that seems likely to continue, if not expand, in the future.

Candidate Strategies

Despite the sophisticated technology of modern campaigns, devising a campaign strategy is far from being an exact science. Each campaign is distinct, having its own issues, strategic setting, and cast of characters. Knowledge of previous campaigns is helpful for intelligent planning—all the great election strategists have been close students of past campaigns—but anyone who attempts merely to copy the strategy of the last campaign runs the risk, like a general who tries to fight the last war, of being surprised by a new strategy. Each election year has brought alterations in some of the rules and new developments in electoral technologies. The campaign of 2000, for example, saw the intensification of front-loading and the first significant uses of the Internet.

Nomination campaigns can be divided into two basic groups: those in which the president is seeking re-nomination, and those in which the president is not a candidate. In the first case, there is sometimes no real campaign at all, as the president goes unchallenged. This was the case with President Clinton in 1996 and President Reagan in 1984. But a number of recent incumbents have faced opposition (usually from only one challenger): President Johnson from Senator Eugene McCarthy in 1968, which led Johnson to drop out of the race; President Ford from Reagan in 1976; President Carter from Edward Kennedy in 1980; and President George H. Bush from Patrick Buchanan in 1992. The incumbent's record is always an important issue in these races, and some who vote for the challenger may not be supporting him as much as sending a message of protest to the incumbent. Challengers have the luxury of being able to criticize without having to take responsibility for running the country. Incumbents, however, enjoy most of the strategic advantages. A sitting president with a lead has the option of ignoring the challenger, adopting the so-called "Rose Garden strategy" of remaining at the White House rather than going out on the campaign trail. Incumbents can also command the media's attention. A press conference, an announcement, or a speech will be covered as a regular presidential activity, even though its purpose and effect may be political. Finally, incumbents can act, while challengers can only talk. Still, a challenger who can win enough support to force a president into an open campaign has won a considerable political point; and no one can know when an incumbent's support might begin suddenly to dissolve, as Lyndon Johnson's did in 1968.

In the case where no incumbent is running, there is always competition, usually from a number of candidates. At the beginning of the campaign there is often a front-runner whose previous reputation and initial standing in the polls put him ahead of the others. (This was the position of Reagan in 1980, Mondale in 1984, George H. Bush and Gary Hart in 1988, and George W. Bush and Al Gore in 2000.) The front-runner position has many obvious advantages; the perception that one is likely to be the winner helps that candidate raise money, win endorsements, and attract volunteers. But front-runner status carries one major disadvantage. Front-runners become the objects of intense media scrutiny, with reporters digging into their record and history. Prior to the 1988 election, Senator Gary Hart was discovered to have been involved in an extra-marital affair that he had denied, and he temporarily left the race. In the 2000 election, a great deal of attention was paid to George W. Bush's background, with questions raised about his early use of alcohol and drugs.

As the list of front-runners mentioned shows, most of them do in fact survive and go on to win the nomination. But the road is often so rocky and filled with so many hazards along the way that no one can say with any assurance that the front-runner has an easy time of it. An upset is always possible. In fact, some of the front-runners noted were on the ropes and had to stage strong comebacks to win the nomination. This was the case with both nominees in 2000. Al Gore fell behind the self-styled outsider, Bill Bradley, in many polls of New Hampshire voters, and a Bradley victory in that state could well have sent Gore's campaign into a tailspin. Bush was trounced by McCain in New Hampshire, and a McCain victory in South Carolina might have spelled the end to Bush's quest.

There is in addition a natural tendency to look for drama in the race, which can leave a front-runner prey to the desire to see an established figure toppled by an underdog. For months everything looks under control, with the front-runner safely ahead, and then things may seem to turn somewhat. Fascination with the "new" candidate unexpectedly "coming on" makes for a powerful story. One need only look at the media attention given to John McCain after his New Hampshire victory in 2000 to appreciate this phenomenon. As far back as 1972, Senator George McGovern's media consultant, Charles Guggenheim, remarked on this fact:

> There's a phenomenon in American politics (in primaries) which television has emphasized: men who have no record are often more appealing than men who have a record; . . . TV dramatizes this political virginity. Before there was television an unknown couldn't run at all because he couldn't get the exposure. With television, he can become known in a very short time.[2]

Candidates in nomination races base their appeals on one or more of the following four elements: (1) the record of the incumbent (when running), (2) positions on issues and ideological stances, (3) themes or moods (for example, the call for honesty or "straight talk"), and (4) personal qualifications and character. These elements are woven into campaign strategies, and their relative emphasis helps to define the character of each race. A contest in which the leading contenders emphasize and differ not only on important issues but on fundamental principles can make the race into an ideological contest. In 1972, for example, Democrats faced a fundamental ideological choice between George McGovern on the left and George Wallace on the right. In 1992 and 1996, Pat Buchanan offered a right-wing populist challenge to the mainstream of the Republican Party. (Buchanan left the party in 2000 to run as the Reform Party nominee). Ideological differences are often absent from primary campaigns—after all, the candidates are all from the same party—and even the differences on the issue may be small. Such, for example, was the case in the Democratic race in 200 between Gore and Bradley. These campaigns will then stress general themes and the candidates' qualifications and character.

Candidates communicate their appeals through a number of different channels: speeches, television advertisements, interviews, and position papers. As the campaign progresses, the candidates may shift their emphasis from a greater to a lesser reliance on issues (or vice versa). Campaigns develop and take on a dynamic character of their own, although in the last two contests, everything has been compressed into a much briefer time span. Anyone who expects campaigns to be high-minded seminars in which the candidates continually offer new positions on every subject is likely to be disappointed. Major candidates will usually be pressed into defining their views on most important topics, but they will not spend their time elaborating the nuances of public policy. Candidates during campaigns are pushed to the limits of physical endurance. Moving from one city to another with little rest or time for reflection, their effort is directed at delivering a basic message that promotes their central theme and their positions on a few key issues. Most candidates, in fact, repeat the same presentation to every audience, which can make reporters covering the campaign grow weary with boredom. Reporters look for news in developments unrelated to the candidate's message, even though most people hearing the speech for the first time may find it new and fresh.

Finally, political campaigns are affected not just by the candidates' deliberate strategies but by unplanned events. Over the course of their travels, candidates are barraged by thousands of questions, give scores of interviews, and are asked to comment on news events, often with little or no time to prepare responses. Not everything can be programmed or planned. A blunder can destroy a campaign, especially in the primaries where candidates are attempting to establish their personal credibility and where voters can easily turn to other candidates as suitable alternatives. When Senator Edmund Muskie broke down in tears during the 1972 Democratic race, or Senator Bob Dole snapped in anger at George H. Bush on national television after the New Hampshire primary in 1988, their prospects were damaged. The possibility of a fatal slip is much greater nowadays because reporters following the candidates are always looking for the exceptional story that can make or break a campaign. Blunders have been nearly as decisive as the overall campaign strategy in determining the outcome of nominating contests.

To speak of candidates developing strategies in conjunction with pollsters and advertising consultants may convey the impression that candidates are without principles, changing their positions, like chameleons changing their color, with shifting popular moods. This conclusion, however, would be unduly cynical. Most politicians running for the presidency have long records of public service and have been identified with certain issues and principles. Often they have strong convictions. Within the framework of these constraints, they will of course try to tailor their appeals in the interest of winning, but this is quite a different matter from being putty in the hands of slick media advisers.

Instances, of course, might be cited of campaigns that have very nearly fit the advertising model consisting of candidates who pander to images of what the public wants at a given moment. Deplorable as these are, however, it is important not to fall into the opposite trap of identifying healthy nominating campaigns with those that emphasize issues. Issue campaigns, too, can be dangerous when conducted on dem-agogic grounds that appeal, whether cynically or sincerely, to people's hatreds, fears, or unfounded hopes; and they can split a party when the candidate's position represents only one of its factions, as occurred in 1964 when the Republicans chose Barry Goldwater and in 1972 when the Democrats chose George McGovern.

The main question in judging the campaign process, however, is not whether one can find a specific instance of an empty ad campaign or a demagogic appeal. These will occur under any democratic electoral system. Rather, the issue is rather whether the nominating system on balance encourages or discourages campaigns that trivialize politics or that reward extremism, and whether it promotes well-qualified candidates who have a broad base of support. This is the perspective from which the constitution maker should judge electoral institutions.

Media Influence

Modern campaigns cannot be discussed without taking into account the role of the media. A large part of the campaign today is conducted in and through the media. Even when candidates are meeting and talking with real audiences, their true audience is often people at home who might catch a snippet of what was said on the evening news. Candidates vie for media attention, arrange their schedules to conform to media deadlines, and seek to fashion a positive media image. The role of the media is pervasive.

One part of what the media covers is under the control or near control of the candidates. This is the part that consists of their television ads and what they may say on an interview show, in a debate, or in a televised speech. The other part is what journalists and commentators select as the story of the campaign. Much of what the American people see and know of the candidates, and what they experience of the campaign, come filtered through the choices of these journalists. What they choose to emphasize, what they consider to be newsworthy, and what biases they may have will affect how the American people see the campaign. Collectively and over time, the journalistic community has a way of framing some of the big questions or standards of the campaign. It has been said, too, that the very essence of news reporting is to search out the unusual rather than the routine. Journalists don't like to simply report what the candidates are saying, especially if they have heard it before. They are looking for an interesting story. Bad news is more interesting than good news. Journalists will often pounce on a story, especially one that may raise questions about the candidates, in a competition that has been likened to a "feeding frenzy."[3]

An important source of the media's influence during the primaries rests on the fact that the voters' decision in these elections is influenced by their perception of a candidate's chances of winning the nomination. This perception is based largely on the objective performance of candidates in primary contests, which the media cannot affect. Extremely poor showings will be enough to convince voters that a candidate is finished, while very strong showings will indicate viability. But in between these extremes, people's perceptions can be affected by how well candidates do in relation to some vague standard of what is "expected" of them. A candidate who does better than expected conveys the impression of coming on, while one who does more poorly, even if he or she may have done fairly well in absolute terms, loses some glamour. Obviously, the criterion of "what is expected" is in some degree a judgment made by reporters in the media, not a fact in any objective sense. Just one of many noteworthy examples of this phenomenon occurred in 1996, when Patrick Buchanan finished a surprisingly strong second behind Bob Dole in the Iowa Republican caucuses and was treated by the media as a rising contender, which helped him ride to victory in the New Hampshire primary. The opposite occurred in 2000 when Senator Bill Bradley lost narrowly to Vice President Gore in New Hampshire, but was then deemed to be finished. Reporters quickly lost interest in Bradley's campaign. Front-loading of the primaries has reduced the number of occasions for the press to interpret results, but perhaps increased the importance of each one.

Journalists have been strongly criticized for how they cover campaigns, and much of it is justified. Yet this criticism in some measure misses the larger point. Journalists in doing their jobs inevitably emphasize aspects of the campaign that are interesting and newsworthy. The items on which they focus (and which therefore play some role in people's decisions) make up a different set of considerations than the ones that party leaders would raise if they still had control of the nominating decision. The criteria of news organizations are different, ultimately, from those normally employed by politicians. Even with "perfect" reporting—which no one can quite define—the media would still exert enormous influence on the current nominating decision because of the arrangement of the current system. It is one in which the media must inevitably play an important role.[4]

The Conventions

Depending on one's taste, the national party convention may be judged either the most absurd or the most ingenious of all political institutions. From its inception, the convention has been the largest of formal political gatherings in America and certainly the most boisterous. Where else can adults get together and yell, shout, march around, blow balloons and horns, and have this behavior considered almost "normal"? And where else can so many people from the same party come together, build personal contacts, forge alliances, and enjoy the spirit of indulging in pure partisan raillery? The famous essayist H. L. Mencken described it best: "There is something about a national convention that makes it as fascinating as a revival or a hanging. It is vulgar, it is ugly, it is stupid, it is tedious, it's hard upon the cerebral centers. . . . and yet it is somehow charming."

Modern conventions, however, have lost much of their influence, if not their charm. Fifty years ago a textbook treatment of nominations would have had relatively little to say about primaries, but a great deal to say about conventions. Today, the emphasis must be just the reverse. The reason is obvious: nomination decisions were once made at the conventions, while today conventions merely ratify a decision that is made months in advance. The special vocabulary once used to describe convention politics has now virtually vanished, and a new one, derived from primary contests, has taken its place.

Words such as "stampede" (the sudden transfer of delegates to one of the candidates) and "dark horse" (a candidate with little initial support or prominence who is nonetheless a possible choice as a compromise on a later ballot) have been replaced by terms such as "momentum" (the enthusiasm engendered by a strong primary showing that will carry over to the next set of primaries) and "outsider" (a candidate with few party connections who nonetheless hopes to win public favor).

The transformation in the role of the convention can be seen in the function of the delegate. Formerly, delegates were agents who had discretion and could move on their own, or, more frequently at the direction of party power brokers who controlled large blocs of delegates. The nomination decision was made at the convention itself, sometimes after a number of ballots. Woodrow Wilson in 1912 was not nominated until the 46th ballot, while John W. Davis, the Democratic nominee of 1924, owns the record for having to wait until the 103rd ballot in a process that lasted almost two weeks! The last multi-balloted convention took place in 1952, when the Democratic nominee Adlai Stevenson was chosen on the third ballot. Since then, every nomination has been made on the first ballot, and the results since at least 1976 have been known in advance. Delegates today are generally bound by the selection process to a specific candidate, and the convention merely records these results. Only in the event of a deadlock, in which no single candidate wins a majority of the delegates in the primaries, would the decision revert to the delegates, either at the convention itself or more likely in informal contacts before it convened.

It is no small irony that the convention began to lose its effective power at just about the same time it became directly accessible to the American public through television. Advance knowledge of the winner removes the central element of drama of the convention, and an event that goes on for four days in which the outcome is known can make for some pretty tiresome television. The major commercial networks—and until about 1980 these were the only channels in existence—all used to cover the conventions in their entirety, "gavel to gavel" as the saying went. Anyone seeking entertainment was in for a bad week. But since 1984, the commercial networks, facing a loss of viewers to the new channels and realizing the lesser importance of conventions, cut back on their coverage and today show only parts of the proceedings. The conventions in turn schedule the parts they want Americans to see most at the time when the networks are on.

The party convention's main purpose today is not to make major decisions, certainly not decisions about the candidates, but to present a picture of the party and candidate to the American people. Modern conventions when successful, at least from the nominee's perspective, are affairs in which the nominee's team controls almost everything that goes on, down to approving the texts of most of the speeches. The 2000 Republican convention at Philadelphia, at which George W. Bush was nominated, took this process to its logical conclusion. Nearly everything was scripted, from the entertainment to the speeches, with each night having its carefully predetermined "theme." (Generally, the Republican Party in 2000 was trying to present itself as a warmer and more compassionate party, open to the concerns of minority groups and women.) Nevertheless, there remains the great interest and drama in the speeches of the vice-presidential and presidential nominees, in which both the delegates and American people get a chance to take the measure of the candidates and to focus on the major themes of the campaign.

It is certainly not always the case, however, that the nominee can fully control the convention. If there are divisions in the party and if the defeated candidates control enough delegates, contrary views may be heard, as occurred with a speech given by Pat Buchanan to the 1992 Republican convention. Of course, some disagreement can be helpful—it makes things look less staged—but genuine discord can hurt the nominee. Nominees accordingly attempt to reach agreements with their rivals before the convention, offering concessions and favorable exposure in return for putting on a display of respect and harmony.

The Platform

The party convention has other formal functions, including voting on major national party rules and approving the party platform. But again its actual role has tended to atrophy or diminish. Until recently the party platform, which is the party's official statement of principles and pledges, was put together right before the convention, and delegates from different segments of the party often disputed different sections or "planks." Contentious issues were then brought to the convention floor itself, where they were vigorously debated and resolved in spirited and contentious votes. This role is by no means excluded today; but it is very much in the victorious candidate's interest to attempt to resolve the major issues beforehand, so that the convention presents a picture of harmony. The platform writing process today begins far in advance of the convention, and a strong nominee can pretty much expect to get his way on most items.

The party platform itself is much less important than it was once was. Formerly, the platform was the principal document of the campaign. Its purpose was to both inform the people of where the party stood and to attract votes (which sometimes meant obscuring the party's position). Before 1912, when candidates did not ordinarily give campaign speeches, the platform was the single best statement of the party's position, even if the candidate might now and again indicate disagreement with a particular plank. Although electoral documents were clearly meant to help win elections, platforms were generally taken seriously by the parties as commitments for governing.[5] Over time, however, the platform became less important. Once a brief document, platforms grew into book-length statements that addressed in great detail positions on most areas of public policy; occasionally parts were included to placate parts of the party rather than to state its real positions. Bob Dole, the Republican nominee in 1996, reportedly joked that he had not even read the party platform.

But the more important point is that another vehicle has developed to take the place of the platform: the nominee's acceptance speech, which is now the highlight of the convention and provides the best statement of the basic themes of the campaign. The first candidate to deliver an acceptance speech was Franklin Roosevelt in 1932, who broke with the tradition of waiting to be informed at home of the convention's decision. Since then, the acceptance speech has grown in importance, and the media in the weeks before the convention hardly tire of billing it a "make or break speech" for the candidates. George H. Bush's vigorous 1988 acceptance speech was viewed by many as the turning point in his campaign, while both Walter Mondale in 1984 (who promised to raise taxes) and Barry Goldwater in 1964 (who said that "extremism in the defense of liberty is no vice") may have doomed their subsequent campaigns, which were already in trouble, with these ill-advised statements.

Voters today focus more on the candidates' own rhetoric than on the platforms to learn about the candidates' intentions, and candidates feel bound more by their own words than by their party's statements. Of course, candidates today may have to break a promise made in their acceptance speech, just as candidates previously might go back on a statement in the platform. But there is sometimes a price to be paid. George H. Bush, in his aforementioned 1988 acceptance speech, had uttered as one of his most important lines: "Read my lips, no new taxes." He did, however, agree to a major tax hike in 1990, and this reversal without an adequate explanation clearly hurt him in his 1992 campaign loss to Bill Clinton.

Vice Presidential Nominations

The convention also has the formal authority to nominate the vice-presidential candidate. Until the middle of the last century, the convention's role in this decision had to be taken into account, although the nominee's preference weighed very heavily. But in recent years, the real decision for the vice presidential choice is made solely by the presidential nominee. Until the 1980s the tendency of the nominees—incumbents excepted—was to wait until the convention to name their running mate. They did so in order not to appear presumptuous (after all, they had yet to be officially nominated) and to maintain an element of suspense for the convention. But the nominees now have dispensed with this formality and name their vice-presidential choice shortly before the convention.

In traditional political calculations, vice-presidential candidates were selected with an eye to balancing the ticket, which meant choosing a candidate with a different base of strength and support within the party; for example, a southerner (like Jimmy Carter) may look for a northerner (like Walter Mondale), or a conservative (like Ronald Reagan) may look for a moderate (like George H. Bush). This was helpful in uniting the party and thus improving the chances of victory.

Balance, however, must itself be balanced with compatibility: presidential candidates would appear simply opportunistic and lose credibility if they chose candidates who differed significantly on major issues. Some element of balancing is always going on, but recently balance within the party has not been as important as seeking a vice-presidential candidate who is a strong figure and a competent campaigner. Vice-presidential candidates receive a great deal of public scrutiny during the campaign, and if they fail as spokespersons it can hurt the nominee's chances. It was on the strength of Al Gore's solid record in the Senate and perceived appeal to the electorate, rather than traditional notions of ideological or geographic balance, that Bill Clinton chose him as his running mate in 1992. (Clinton was from Arkansas, Gore from Tennessee, and both were moderate Democrats). In 2000, George W. Bush selected Richard Cheney less for any kind of traditional balance than for his reputation as a mature and skilled leader, which he had earned as Secretary of Defense during the Gulf War in 1990–91.

The right to name the vice-presidential nominee is obviously a formidable power, as many vice-presidents will go on to become their party's presidential nominee. Included in this group are Richard Nixon (Eisenhower's vice-president), Hubert Humphrey (Johnson's vice-president), Walter Mondale (Carter's), George H. Bush (Reagan's), and Al Gore (Clinton's). These men might have been able to win the nomination on

their own, but their chances were dramatically improved by having been vice-presidents.

The Current Nominating System: Evaluation and Proposed Changes

The nomination process is the stage that narrows the field of potential candidates to the two major contenders. It is clearly an important constitutional institution, even if its major elements are governed mainly by state laws and party rules. The nomination process has gone through four major changes since the founding, most recently after 1968 with the emergence of nomination by presidential primaries.

The idea of selecting presidential nominees by primaries was initially very controversial, and some concerns remain today. Advocates of the primary system praised its democratic character and its openness to a variety of different candidates. They argued that it was now possible for insurgent candidates and outsiders to raise new issues in the presidential campaign and to emerge as players in the nomination decision, if not occasionally to win a nomination. The people under this system would not be limited to the kind of compromise candidates traditionally favored by party leaders. Critics responded that too much emphasis was being placed on the abstract value of democratic participation to the exclusion of considerations such as ensuring the experience and high quality of the nominees, creating and maintaining harmony within the parties, and restricting the nomination process to a reasonable length of time. The nomination process was thought of as an end in itself, not as a means to ensuring sound governance. Finally, critics doubted whether the system would ever come close to being as democratic as many hoped, because of such issues as the scheduling of primaries, the degree of media influence, and the role of money.

Assessing these arguments is difficult, since institutional arrangements are by no means the only factor that contributes to nomination outcomes. On the question of the character of the nominees under the current system, nearly all seem to be the sort that would have been selected under the older system. (Jimmy Carter, who came from the "outside" in 1976 to capture the nomination, is a likely exception.) On the other hand, it is clear that many candidates have been in the mix and played a role in influencing the decision, who would almost certainly have had no major voice before, among them Jesse Jackson, Pat Robertson, and Patrick Buchanan. In some instances, this openness put enormous strains on party unity, although it can also be said to have forced certain issues in the party to be discussed and aired. Finally, the current system has greatly lengthened the active phase of the nominating process, increasing the period when elections and the prospect of changing power are uppermost in people's minds. This long election process, many agree, unsettles matters and can drain the presidency of its effective authority.

However one may judge this debate, the current system by now seems to have become institutionalized in its major principle of the use of presidential primaries. But important issues remain about how this general principle will be put into effect. There has been much instability in the nomination process since 1972, with significant changes in almost every election year in either the method of selecting delegates or the scheduling of primaries. Each set of changes in turn breeds calls for still more changes. Some are content to leave things as they are, or at any rate to leave choices in the hands of the same authorities (chiefly the state governments and the parties); others believe that it is time to seek to "rationalize" the process in some way by inviting the federal government to legislate a comprehensive system, perhaps in the form of a rotating series of regional primaries or a national primary. But one thing is clear. The debate of the structure of the current primary system is sure to continue.

Campaign Financing

Few issues have generated more controversy over the years than how to finance campaigns, which are hugely expensive enterprises, growing more costly by the year. Candidates for office must have money to pay a staff, move themselves and others around their district or the country, conduct polls, produce advertisements, and buy media time. In addition, the political parties and candidates have an enormous stake in seeking out citizens likely to vote for them and then getting them to the polls on Election Day. All this costs money as well.

The money to pay for campaigns must come from somewhere—and therein, of course, is the problem. Funding raises a number of concerns: that giving money will lead to outright corruption or at least a granting of undue influence to contributors; that vast differences in funding among candidates competing for the same office will allow the best-funded candidates to "buy" elections; that candidates (including office holders) will have to spend an inordinate amount of their time and energy in the task of fund raising; and—pointing in a different direction—that attempts to limit and regulate campaign funding impinge on the right of individuals and groups to "speak" (which today effectively entails spending money) in behalf of or against any position, candidate, or party.

The Development of Campaign Finance Regulation

Prior to the 1972 election, campaigns were financed from private sources. Funding was largely unregulated, except for a ban on loans or direct contributions from business corporations and labor unions. Money was raised by the parties (national, state, and local) and by the candidates' personal organizations. In presidential campaigns, the importance of fundraising grew in the 1960s, as the candidates became more active in the pre-convention period and as costs increased with the advent of television advertising. Funds for election campaigns were raised from a variety of sources, including small contributions, benefits held by celebrity performers, personal spending by the candidates themselves, and huge individual contributions from so-called "fat cats. (Richard Nixon's friend, W. Clement Stone, donated $18 million to his campaign in 1968.)

The increased cost of campaigns, together with growing fears that large donations could buy influence, led to demands for more extensive regulation. These demands reached a crescendo after the 1972 presidential election, in which President Nixon's campaign accepted millions of dollars of illegal contributions from business corporations and in which the Nixon campaign ordered its infamous break-in of the Democratic campaign headquarters in Washington's Watergate hotel in search of information and documents. Although the break-in was not directly a finance scandal, "Watergate" became the generic symbol for political corruption of all kinds and created a climate in the nation and in Congress for extensive campaign finance reform.

In 1974 Congress passed a sweeping law that sought to impose limits on campaign contributions and spending and that provided for public funding for presidential elections. The law was challenged before the Supreme Court in the case of *Buckley v. Valeo* (1976), and important parts of the law were declared unconstitutional, chiefly for violating the First Amendment protection of free speech. A framework for campaign regulation that reflected no one's clear intention emerged from this mix of decisions by different institutions. It established three different funding systems: one for presidential nomination campaigns, one for presidential general elections, and one for congressional elections. For presidential primaries, there would be a mixture of private funding and (optional) matching public funds; if public funding was accepted, there would be a cap on overall campaign spending. For the presidential general election, there would be almost complete public funding for the major parties, which, if accepted, would set the cap for spending for the election campaign. Finally, for congressional races, there would be no public funding or limits on overall spending; but strict limits were placed on the amount any contributor or group could give to a campaign.

Viewed from the standpoint of contributors, the new system imposed limits on how much an individual or a registered group (called a "political action committee" or PAC) was permitted to give both to a single candidate and to all campaigns or parties in any given two-year period. Parties, too, were limited in what they could give to a campaign. All political contributions, whether to a campaign, a party, or a political action committee, had to be disclosed to the Federal Election Commission and thus made public.

There were, however, exceptions or exemptions to this regulative scheme. Expenditures of individuals and groups that were uncoordinated with the campaigns were left uncontrolled. This exemption, which the Supreme Court made to accommodate the First Amendment protection of free speech, meant that a person or group could spend any amount of money on any election, so long as it was not planned with the candidates' campaigns. Another exception, again required by the Court to protect free speech, allowed candidates to spend as much of their own personal money as they wished on their own campaigns in races in which no public funding was accepted. Finally, the Federal Election Committee began to allow state and local parties to spend additional monies on party building activities and plans for voter registration. Some of this money—called "soft money"—could be collected under state laws where there were no limits on campaign contribution.

The campaign finance system, like so many reforms, led to a number of results that few originally foresaw. Some of these posed new problems. One effect was to simulate a growth in political action committees (PACs), which became especially important in congressional campaigns. The limits on personal contributions were so stringent that candidates began looking to these groups, and more and more of them formed to meet the demand. Funding sources became more group-driven and professional. A second effect was a greater advantage for the self-financed wealthy candidate. Personal wealth was always an asset, but it became even more so under this system, as candidates without personal wealth had to raise money in small sums from many individuals while wealthy candidates could simply write a check. Finally, an incumbent president who faced no competition in the primaries could still collect his share of public matching funds, which he could then spend against the nominee of the other party, thus giving the incumbent an additional advantage.

Whatever problems there might be with this system, it could be said initially to have "functioned," in the strict sense that it regulated and controlled most of the funding for political campaigns. Most of the money that was collected and spent up until the 1990s passed through the campaign organizations of the candidates, which were designed to be the major actors in the process. Yet by the election of 1996 and certainly by 2000, there was widespread agreement that much of the system had broken down. While candidates continued to raise and spend money under all of the existing limitations, thus respecting the letter of the law, more and more of the actual fundraising and spending on campaigns simply started going around the candidates' organizations. Funds were now being raised and spent by independent organizations and by parties under the form of "soft money." The "soft money" exception was gradually expanded to include spending for virtually all of the normal elements of campaigning, including advertising. There were no limits on the amounts of contributions for soft money contributors, and funds were sought from corporations and unions as well as individuals. The system had broken down, and politicians began raising and spending money without limit.

To illustrate how matters operated in the general election campaign of 2000, each of the two parties was given around $70 million in public funding under the campaign finance law to conduct its campaign. But instead of this amount being a ceiling, as had been intended, it now become a floor. On top of the public funding, the two parties raised and spent (combined) another $80 million in soft money, while independent groups added another $16 million. Soft money and independent spending were also becoming a much larger factor in spending in congressional races.

For those opposed to a system of campaign finance regulation, other than the public disclosure requirement, its breakdown was not unwelcome. They argued, in fact, that it was the original attempts to limit contributions and spending by candidate campaigns that had created many of the problems, pushing funding into soft money contributions and into expenditures by independent groups. In any case, said these critics, the expansion of soft money expenditures helped to build up the role of political parties, which was seen as a positive development. Moreover, spending more money on campaigns is not a bad, but a good, thing. It helps to educate voters and to increase voter turnout. Finally-and

here perhaps is their nub of the argument—all schemes of finance regulation interfere with the right of free speech and association as protected by the First Amendment.

Many political leaders, however, argued that the regulation system had to be fixed. The champions of a reform initiative were Senators John McCain and Russell Feingold. Over much opposition, they managed to persuade Congress in 2002 to enact a new campaign finance law, known popularly as the McCain-Feingold Bill, which President Bush signed into law. This legislation, which is to go into effect in 2003, bans most soft money from federal election campaigns and tries to funnel most spending back through the candidates' campaigns, in part by increasing the amount that individuals may contribute to campaigns. In addition, the legislation imposes certain reporting requirements on independent groups, which must now make known large expenditures that are made on behalf of any candidate. Finally, in cases in which a congressional candidate is facing a candidate spending huge amounts of his personal funds, the "poorer" candidate will be able to raise money in larger chunks than the law ordinarily allows. Otherwise, however, the basic structure of the campaign finance scheme established in 1974 remains intact.

How this legislation will actually work will not be known until the 2004 election. In the meantime, the law faces a test in the Supreme Court challenging a number of its key provisions. New ways are already being sought to work "around" the restrictions.

Funding in Presidential Nomination Campaigns

We consider at this point only the issues for funding in presidential nomination campaigns. During the nomination stage, as noted, the candidates raise money on their own and then have the option of accepting matching public funds, in which case they must accept a spending limit. Most of the candidates thus far have accepted matching public funds. This system does not guarantee equality in spending—it can magnify differences—but it allows candidates who raise some money to increase their funds. If the main concern is to give candidates "enough" money to run a campaign, the matching public funds may have helped.

Three important candidates have thus far decided not to accept matching public funds: John Connally in 1980, Steve Forbes in 1996 and 2000, and George W. Bush in 2000. Forbes did so in order to spend a huge amount of his private wealth, which he did in both of his campaigns. Bush did so in 2000 because he was able to raise so much money that he did not wish to be limited by the spending ceiling. (The ceiling for those who accepted public funding in 2000 was $46 million dollars, whereas Bush raised $94 million.) Bush was the first candidate to have foregone matching funds during the primary period that went on to win the nomination.

All the rules aside, the old question remains: can money "buy" presidential nominations? Obviously, it is much better to have money than to be without it; but spending more money certainly is not a sufficient explanation of success. There are stunning examples that prove this point. Going back to the 1980 campaign, John Connally raised an enormous amount of money early in the race; but the effort netted him only one delegate, facetiously labeled "the $13 million delegate." In 1996 Steve Forbes, using some $42 million of his own money, won just one primary and collected only 70 delegates before quitting the race. It is true that the candidates who raise the most money during the invisible primary have fared very well and have generally gone on to win the nomination. But the money they have raised is more a result of the support they enjoy than a cause of their success.

Despite the provision for matching public funds, some candidates find it difficult early on to raise enough money to make their campaigns viable. Candidates may therefore pull out before ever beginning the campaign. Contribution limits here may hurt. The task of raising "enough" money to mount a serious race is daunting, especially where there may be so many other candidates vying for funds from the same sources. Candidates who end up withdrawing usually include those who would have faced a huge uphill battle in any case, and the excuse that they could not raise the funds to continue can provide a graceful way of exiting a race. Finally, it is

clear that success can bring money—and fast. John McCain ran his race on very limited funds in 2000 until his breakthrough victory in New Hampshire; at that point money started pouring into the campaign by checks and through the Internet. At least for the month of March, McCain had sufficient funding to continue his challenge to Bush.

The General Election Campaign

Imagine that you have campaigned for over a year, participated in over thirty primaries, delivered hundreds of speeches, and shaken thousands of hands—and then you wake up one morning only to say, "Now the real campaign begins." This is the enviable—or perhaps unenviable—position of the victors of the nomination contests: all they have earned for their labor is the right to wage another campaign.

Victory in the general election is achieved by winning a majority of the electoral votes. From the moment of the nomination until the eve of the final election on the Tuesday after the first Monday in November, the candidates expend every effort to obtain the magic number of 270 electoral votes. Because electoral votes are awarded on a state-by-state basis, with the candidate who wins a statewide plurality receiving (in all but two states) all the state's electoral votes, candidates gear their campaigns to fifty separate races. Although it is unlikely for a candidate to win the presidency while losing the popular vote, the 2000 election campaign reminded everyone that this outcome is indeed possible. In any case, the strategies of the campaign have always focused first on winning the necessary electoral votes, not on gaining a national plurality.

The Primaries versus the General Election

General election campaigns differ in many respects from nomination campaigns. Recall that in primary campaigns a candidate, while seeking to defeat all opponents, also has to keep in mind how (if possible) to mollify them and bring them back into the fold to support the ticket. This imperative normally imposes a degree of restraint. In final election campaigns, by contrast, all the chips are on the table, and fewer political advantages are to be gained by holding back or pulling any punches. Presidential elections often have a harsher undertone than primaries, although one check on overtly bad behavior is close scrutiny and the possibility that it may backfire.

General election campaigns also differ from nomination campaigns in that the contests are now *between parties*. Voters are selecting not just an individual but the nominee, often now called the "standard bearer," of a party having a long history and record. Despite a decline in partisan identification in the last half century, well over a majority of voters still retains a standing preference for one of the major parties. Candidates in the general election campaign not only on the basis of the four elements noted above—the incumbent's record (when running), stands on issues and ideology, general political themes, and personal qualifications—but also on the basis of the records, reputations and public philosophies of their political party.

Last, the choice in the general election is narrowed to two, or at most three, significant candidates. The candidates are much better known to the voters than during primary contests, where some of the aspirants are "new" faces to most Americans. With fewer candidates and with the "stabilizing" effect of party identification, final election campaigns tend to be somewhat less volatile than primary campaigns. More voters have already all but made up their minds before the campaign begins, barring, of course, some wholly unexpected development. Still, many voters decide during the campaign, and as partisan attachment in the last half-century declines, the percentage of voters able to be influenced by the campaign has increased. Some 40 percent of the voters ordinarily report making their decision at the time of the conventions or afterwards.

Do campaigns matter? Obviously, they are important events quite apart from any effect of changing people's minds. People get involved in politics more so during campaigns than at any other time; they listen to what political leaders are saying and engage more in political discussions and activity themselves. But do campaigns matter in the precise sense of changing people's intentions to vote and therefore affecting the outcome? The argument that campaigns often do not change that many votes is not the shocking claim that it might at first seem. It would be strange, in fact, if all waited until the campaign began before making up their minds. After all, people know what the basic conditions are in the country; they likely have an opinion of the performance of the incumbent president or his party; and they often know which party they favor. It is no surprise, then, that so many voters all but decide how they will vote before the candidates begin their massive efforts to try to win voters to their side.

Yet even if large numbers of voters make up their minds before the race, there are ordinarily more than enough persuadable voters to change the outcome of most races. Election experts have developed models that "predict" how these undecided voters will vote, based on the reasonable assumption that voters tend to return to power candidates from the incumbent party if the economic conditions are good, and to throw out the incumbent party if conditions are poor. These models have proven quite accurate, but sometimes they can be simply wrong. For instance, all of the models predicted a solid Gore victory in 2000.

One remarkable aspect of American presidential election is that the outcome of so many races remains genuinely in doubt up to the last moment. The elections of 1960, 1968, 1976, and 1980 and 2000 were all considered by pollsters to be too close to call up to the very end, although Reagan's victory in 1980 turned out to be substantial. The closeness of so many campaigns adds to their excitement; and it provides confirmation of what the candidates already know: campaigns count.

The Character of the Campaign

The presidential campaign is an extra-constitutional development that has evolved into its current form as a result of changes in norms, traditions, and technology. The founders' plan to avoid long popular campaigns gave way by the 1830s to the party-run campaigns, with their mass rallies, slogans, and torchlight parades. Campaigns provided the electorate with theater, spectacle, and the thrill of involvement in a major national event.

Table 7.2
Presidential Election Results Ranked by the Closeness of the Popular Vote, 1868–2000

Election	Winning Candidate and Political Party	Losing Candidate	Winner's Percent of Popular Vote	Popular Vote Margin of Difference	Electoral College Vote Vote % for the winner
Near Dead Heats					
1876	Hayes (R)	Tilden	47.95	-3.02	50.1
1888	Harrison (R)	**Cleveland**	47.82	-0.80	58.1
2000	G.W. Bush (R)	Gore	47.81	-0.45	50.5
1880	Garfield (R)	Hancock	48.27	0.02	58.0
1960	Kennedy (D)	Nixon	49.72	0.17	58.0
1884	Cleveland (D)	Blaine	48.50	0.25	54.6
1968	Nixon (R)	Humphrey	43.42	0.70	61.2
1976	Carter (D)	**Ford**	50.06	2.06	55.2
Close Contests					
1892	Cleveland (D)	**Harrison**	46.05	3.09	65.6
1916	**Wilson** (D)	Hughes	49.24	3.13	52.2
1896	McKinley (R)	Bryan	51.01	4.28	60.6
1948	**Truman** (D)	Dewey	49.55	4.48	61.6
1868	Grant (R)	Seymour	52.66	5.32	72.8
Moderately Competitive					
1992	Clinton (D)	**Bush**	43.01	5.56	68.7
1900	**McKinley** (R)	Bryan	51.67	6.16	65.3
1944	**F. Roosevelt** (D)	Dewey	53.39	7.50	81.4
1988	Bush (R)	Dukakis	53.37	7.72	79.2
1908	Taft (R)	Bryan	51.58	8.53	66.5
1996	**Clinton** (D)	Dole	49.24	8.53	70.4
1980	Reagan (R)	**Carter**	50.75	9.74	90.9
1940	**F. Roosevelt** (D)	Willkie	54.74	9.95	84.6
1952	Eisenhower (R)	Stevenson	55.13	10.75	83.2
1872	**Grant** (R)	Greeley	55.63	11.80	78.1
Landslides					
1912*	Wilson (D)	**Taft**	41.84	14.45	83.2
1956	**Eisenhower** (R)	Stevenson	57.38	15.43	86.2
1928	Hoover (R)	Smith	58.24	17.46	83.6
1984	**Reagan** (R)	Mondale	58.77	17.74	97.6
1932	F. Roosevelt (D)	**Hoover**	57.42	17.78	88.9
1904	**T. Roosevelt** (R)	Parker	56.41	18.81	70.6
1964	**Johnson** (D)	Goldwater	61.05	22.57	90.3
1972	**Nixon** (R)	McGovern	60.69	23.16	96.8
1936	**F. Roosevelt** (D)	Landon	60.80	24.26	98.5
1924	**Coolidge** (R)	Davis	54.03	25.19	73.8
1920	Harding (R)	Cox	60.34	26.22	76.1

Comments: Bolded candidates are incumbents who sought reelection. In 1876, 1888, and 2000, the margins are negative numbers, indicating that the candidates who received majorities of Electoral College votes in these elections did not win pluralities of the popular vote. The vote totals of 1876 are disputed.

*In 1912, the Progressive candidate Teddy Roosevelt finished ahead of the Republican candidate William Taft. Roosevelt had 27.39% of the popular vote and Taft 23.18.

Nineteenth century presidential campaigns were famous for their highly participatory character. But in a bow to older norms, the candidates themselves seldom directly campaigned. Campaigns were run for the candidate by the party. The candidates' positions were the positions enunciated in the platforms, voters were contacted by the party organizations, funding was handled by the parties, and debates about the candidates' merits were conducted through party-run newspapers. The candidates entered personally into the campaign by their letters of acceptance of their party's nomination and through occasional communications to citizens or to newspapers. The first candidate to campaign in earnest for the presidency was Stephen Douglas in 1860. His experiment was not repeated in any extensive way until William Jennings Bryan went on the campaign trail in 1896; despite logging thousands of miles and delivering hundreds of speeches, all without the benefit of electronic amplifiers, Bryan lost the race to William McKinley, who conducted a "front-porch campaign," staying at home and from time to time stepping out on his porch to deliver some harmless messages of welcome to the thousands who came to visit. Woodrow Wilson in 1912 may be counted as the first successful candidate to have waged a modern campaign.

Today, in contrast, candidates crisscross the country at a dizzying pace, making one speech after another and responding to questions on the issues of the day. Voters are contacted largely through television—by means of campaign advertisements, news coverage, direct coverage of speeches, debates, and interviews. The organization of the campaign relies in part on the pre-existing apparatus of the national and state parties, but it is headed up by the candidate's personal organization created during the nominating phase.

Campaigns at this point are all that the candidates have; whether behind or ahead, the stakes are too great to leave anything undone. Candidates who realize they are likely to lose—like Barry Goldwater in 1964, George McGovern in 1972, and Walter Mondale in 1984—live in hopes of an unexpected turn of events; and candidates aware that they are likely to win—like Lyndon Johnson in 1964, Richard Nixon in 1972,

and Ronald Reagan in 1984—begin to think of increasing the margin of victory. A landslide will give a president a stronger claim to possessing a mandate, which can enhance the likelihood of getting his programs enacted.

Each campaign is a story unto itself, with its own special characteristics and decisive events. The most important general distinction to be made among presidential campaigns is whether or not an incumbent is running. If an incumbent is running, no matter what strategies the candidates may adopt, the election turns in large measure on the public's judgment of the president's performance and on whether things are thought to be "going well" in the country. The election is in large measure a referendum. Since 1868, incumbents have been involved in more than half of all of the elections (twenty one of thirty-four), of which they have won two-thirds (fourteen).

The other category of presidential election is a contest for an open seat, when no incumbent is running, such as in 2000 or 1988. Candidates in this case stand a bit more on their own. But even here an indirect incumbency factor still exists because the candidate of the party holding the presidency is held partly accountable for the performance of the incumbent. The connection is somewhat closer if the candidate is the vice-president of the incumbent's administration, such as George H. Bush in 1988 or Al Gore in 2000. Thus, in almost every presidential election, voters take the measure not only of the issues, themes, and qualifications of the candidates, but also of whether a change is needed from the policies of the incumbent or the incumbent's party. Campaigns look backward as well as forward.

Modern campaigns have developed a certain tempo and they center on a few key events. The first is the nominating convention itself. Millions, as noted, watch or see parts of the convention acceptance speech, which sets the themes of the campaign. Next come the face-to-face television debates. Debates were held for the first time in 1960 and then not again until 1976; since then they have been held in every election, and the practice now seems to be part of the system. The idea of a "shoot-out" between the candidates generates a tremendous amount of attention, so much so that some wonder whether too much emphasis is placed on debate performance. Some of the debates have been rather tepid affairs, with the candidates giving carefully rehearsed answers and attempting—understandably—to guard against making the big blunder. Yet blunders there have been. In 1976 President Gerald Ford made a comment about Poland being free of communist dominance, which he failed to correct. The error cost Ford dearly, compromising his reputation as the experienced statesman facing a newcomer. Perhaps the most crucial blunder to date came in the 2000 election, in the first presidential debate. Al Gore embellished a couple of stories, which unfortunately for him fit precisely the main concern that journalists had voiced before the debate. Gore apologized and then seemed overly restrained in the second debate. During this period, Gore slipped from being ahead in the polls to trailing George W. Bush.

Debates thus far have often provided an opportunity to help the candidate initially perceived as having less experience: John Kennedy (in 1960), Jimmy Carter (in 1976), Ronald Reagan (in 1980) and perhaps Bill Clinton but certainly Ross Perot (in 1992). By putting the less experienced individual in a forum on an equal footing with the more seasoned candidate, the debates allow the less experienced candidate—when they can hold their own—to neutralize the charges that they might not be ready to meet the demands of the office.

The final important moment of the campaign comes, at least when the race is considered too close to call, in the last few days. The remaining undecided voters are taking their last look, and the campaign is devoting every resource to fire up the faithful to turn out to vote. The pace of the campaign becomes feverish, with the candidates criss-crossing the nation in an effort to touch down in as many media markets as possible in the states still up for grabs. The candidates at this point, usually sleepless and hoarse, are either energized or haunted by the old adage: "every vote counts." The near tie in Florida in 2000 proved that that this was just about right.

Campaign strategies involve hundreds of different decisions that are based on a combination of geographical considerations and the targeting of key groups. As the campaign goes on, candidates narrow their attention and focus on the voters whom they perceive have not yet made up their minds, which becomes an increasingly narrow share of the electorate. Of course, those who have decided must still be kept enthusiastic—in campaign parlance this is known as "keeping the base energized"—as the turnout rate among supporters can be the key to victory.

A general rule of campaign strategy is to attempt to control the terrain on which the campaign is fought. Both sides vie to make the factors on which their candidate is strongest—and the opponent weakest—the focal point of the campaign. For example, a candidate whose personal experience is highly regarded in comparison to the opponent's will try to focus attention on this factor, as President George H. Bush sought to do against Bill Clinton in 1992. An opponent, sensing the possibility of convincing the electorate on certain key issues, may seek to make issues the focal point, which was Clinton's response to Bush in 1992, when Clinton's campaign reminded Americans that the major issue was the condition of the economy. Often, therefore, the candidates are not talking at each other, but past each other. Still, when a candidate's appeals begin to work, his opponent must try to meet the challenge, if only to blunt the criticisms.

Campaign Financing in General Elections

Money is a valuable asset in all elections, but it is probably of less importance, relatively speaking, in presidential contests than in other campaigns. By the time the presidential campaign begins most voters know a great deal about the candidates, and there is an enormous amount of coverage of the campaign in the press. But even though advertising arguably counts less in presidential contests, so much is at stake that fundraising is at its most intense and the dollar amounts collected the largest. Moreover, concerns about fundraising at this level have provided much of the stimulus for reform of the whole finance system. Such was the case after the Watergate affair in 1972, and much of the momentum for reform of the current system came from the scandals of the Clinton campaign in 1996.

Before the 1974 campaign finance legislation, spending and funding had been entirely private and largely unregulated. Between 1932 and 1972, Republican presidential candidates regularly outspent Democrats, although Republicans lost more races than they won. Still, many regarded the money advantage of Republicans as a great inequity and an impediment to genuinely democratic elections. The campaign finance legislation of 1974 sought to eliminate all problems of financing for the general election campaign by a sweeping provision that provided for full public funding. If the candidates accepted this funding—and all have—the intent was that the public funds, which were the same for both parties, would be the ceiling for all spending. This system worked in roughly this sense for three or four elections. By 1988, however, soft money was being collected and spent above the publicly-provided amount, and by 1996 and 2000 the public funding was clearly serving as just a base for further campaign fundraising by both parties. The McCain-Feingold bill passed in 2002 seeks to restore the basic idea of a publicly funded general election campaign, with only small supplemental amounts added on top.

A difficulty with all public funding plans is the question of how to treat minor parties. Obviously, a new party entering the race cannot just be given huge sums of money, or else everyone would suddenly be running for president. The finance legislation has tried to deal with this issue by giving funding before the election only to parties that received more than five percent in the last election. (The amount is pro-rated on the basis of the share of its vote.) In addition, for the current election, if a minor party receives more than five percent for the first time, it will be given its share of funding after the election, which can help with paying back loans and other expenses. Thus in 2000, the Green Party under Ralph Nader was struggling to reach 5 percent, both to help with the expenses of 2000 and to provide advance funding for 2004.

Given the short-lived nature of some of the minor parties in the United States, this legislation can produce some strange effects. It can keep a party alive after it has effectively died out. Such was the case with the Reform Party under Ross Perot, which won eight percent of the vote in 1996 and qualified for $12.6 million for the 2000 campaign. The party was kept alive by the interest candidates had in using this money. After numerous splits and legal contests, what was left of the Reform Party nominated Patrick Buchanan in 2000, who received less than a half a percent of the popular vote.

The Electoral College: Evaluation and Proposed Reforms

The most controversial structural feature of the presidential election is the electoral college system. The system as it operates today involves provisions of the Constitution, state laws, and practice. The Constitution assigns to each state a number of electoral votes equal to the sum of its senators and representatives, plus three votes to Washington, D.C. (the Twenty-Third Amendment). This comes to a total of 538 votes. An absolute majority (270 votes) is needed for election. If no candidate receives a majority-which could result from a 269–269 tie in a two person race, or from a third candidate receiving a share of the vote—the election for president goes to the House of Representatives, where the decision is made by an unusual process. Each state delegation casts one vote, with an absolute majority of states (26) required for election.

When voters cast their ballots in the general election, they are not, as many think, voting directly for the candidates, but for a slate of electors within each state that is pledged to vote for a particular candidate. State law determines how the electoral votes will be allocated. For many years, all of the states awarded their electors on a winner-take-all basis, meaning that the candidate who received the most votes in the state received all of the states' electoral votes. Two states today, Maine (since 1972) and Nebraska (since 1992), award the electors by a different system, under which the popular vote winner in each congressional district receives one electoral vote and the statewide winner receives two votes. Several other states have seriously considered adopting this system in the last twenty years.

TABLE 7.3   Electoral Votes of the States

1988	1996	2004
California (47)	California (54)	California (55)
New York (36)	New York (33)	Texas (34)
Texas (29)	Texas (32)	New York (34)
Pennsylvania (25)	Florida (25)	Florida (27)
Illinois (24)	Pennsylvania (23)	Pennsylvania (21)
Ohio (23)	Illinois (22)	Illinois (21)
Florida (21)	Ohio (21)	Ohio (20)
Michigan (20)	Michigan (18)	Michigan (17)
New Jersey (16)	New Jersey (15)	New Jersey (15)
Massachusetts (13)	North Carolina (14)	North Carolina (15)
North Carolina (13)	Georgia (13)	Georgia (15)
Indiana (12)	Virginia (13)	Virginia (13)
Georgia (12)	Indiana (12)	Massachusetts (12)
Virginia (12)	Massachusetts (12)	Indiana (11)
Missouri (11)	Missouri (11)	Missouri (11)
Tennessee (11)	Tennessee (11)	Tennessee (11)
Wisconsin (11)	Wisconsin (11)	Washington (11)
Louisiana (10)	Washington (11)	Wisconsin (10)
Maryland (10)	Maryland (10)	Maryland (10)
Minnesota (10)	Minnesota (10)	Minnesota (10)
Washington (10)	Alabama (9)	Arizona (10)
Alabama (9)	Louisiana (9)	Alabama (9)
Kentucky (9)	Arizona (8)	Louisiana (9)
Colorado (8)	Colorado (8)	Colorado (9)
Connecticut (8)	Connecticut (8)	South Carolina (8)
Iowa (8)	Kentucky (8)	Kentucky (8)
Oklahoma (8)	Oklahoma (8)	Connecticut (7)
South Carolina (8)	South Carolina (8)	Iowa (7)
Arizona (7)	Iowa (7)	Oklahoma (7)
Kansas (7)	Mississippi (7)	Oregon (7)
Mississippi (7)	Oregon (7)	Mississippi (6)
Oregon (7)	Arkansas (6)	Arkansas (6)
Arkansas (6)	Kansas (6)	Kansas (6)
West Virginia (6)	Nebraska (5)	Nebraska (5)
Nebraska (5)	New Mexico (5)	New Mexico (5)
New Mexico (5)	Utah (5)	Nevada (5)
Utah (5)	West Virginia (5)	Utah (5)
Hawaii (4)	Hawaii (4)	West Virginia (5)
Idaho (4)	Idaho (4)	Hawaii (4)
Maine (4)	Maine (4)	Idaho (4)
Montana (4)	New Hampshire (4)	Maine (4)
New Hampshire (4)	Nevada (4)	New Hampshire (4)
Nevada (4)	Rhode Island (4)	Rhode Island (4)
Rhode Island (4)	Alaska (3)	Alaska (3)
Alaska (3)	Delaware (3)	Delaware (3)
Delaware (3)	D.C. (3)	D.C. (3)
D. C. (3)	Montana (3)	Montana (3)
North Dakota (3)	North Dakota (3)	North Dakota (3)
South Dakota (3)	South Dakota (3)	South Dakota (3)
Vermont (3)	Vermont (3)	Vermont (3)
Wyoming (3)	Wyoming (3)	Wyoming (3)

Critics of the electoral college system attack it on two grounds. First, they point out that the Constitution allows the electors to vote as they please, despite their pledges or what state laws require. Known as the problem of the "faithless elector," this aspect of the system temporarily became an issue in 2000, when it was widely rumored that, during the period of the post election dispute, the Gore campaign was seeking to induce some Bush electors to change their votes. Gore ultimately renounced this strategy. In practice, faithlessness has been rare and has never affected the outcome of an election. The positive side of keeping the elector as a real person is that unforeseen events, such as a revelation of corruption, might occur in the period between the election (early November) and the casting of the electoral votes (mid-December) in which the discretion of live human beings would be welcome.

The more substantial objection centers on the fact that it is possible for a candidate to receive a nationwide plurality in the popular vote and yet lose the electoral vote and not be chosen president. This result may take place when a candidate wins some states by a large margin and loses other by narrower margins. The minority president problem has occurred unambiguously in only two instances, 1888, when Grover Cleveland, the Democratic candidate, received 90,000 votes more than his Republican opponent, Benjamin Harrison, but lost decisively in the electoral vote, 233 to 168, and 2000, when Al Gore received about a half-million more votes than George W. Bush, but narrowly lost the electoral vote 271-267. In three other cases—1824, 1876, and 1960—an argument can be made that the plurality winner of the popular vote did not become president, but these cases are far from being clear-cut.

A number of plans have been suggested to alter the system. One has been to try to get states to adopt the Maine-Nebraska system (which they are free to do on their own), or to pass an amendment to the Constitution that would require states to adopt this system. Whether or not this change is advisable on other grounds, it does not fully solve the problem of the "minority" president. A calculation of the results in 2000, assuming this plan had been used nation-wide, would have given Bush an electoral college victory of 282-256 (Bush won 222 congressional districts, plus thirty states). In addition, this plan would introduce considerations of presidential politics into the drawing of congressional district boundaries.

The most frequently suggested alternative is to replace the electoral college with a direct national election, in which the winner of the national popular vote would become president. In order to prevent the possibility of electing a president with a low percentage of votes in a large field, advocates generally add the further provision that in the event that no candidate receives more than 40 percent of the national popular vote, a second runoff election would be held between the two candidates who received the most votes in the first round.

Defenders of the current system concede that the choice of a "minority" president poses a problem, although the nation has survived this result without having any great crisis. They see certain merits in the current plan and in any case believe it to be preferable to any of the proposed alternatives. First, the current system provides an important support for federalism because it makes candidates and strategists think in terms of separate states and increases the importance of working through existing state party organizations. Second, it minimizes the danger of having a long drawn-out dispute in a close election like that of 1960, when Kennedy and Nixon were separated by less than two-tenths of a percentage point (if that). Under a direct-election plan, a recount would require every ballot in the nation be recounted, a process in which there is always a certain percentage of error. Under the present system, on the other hand, recounts are limited to states that are closely contested and where the number of electoral votes might sway the national outcome. This rare event, of course, occurred in 2000 in the case of Florida, which was so close that the national election remained disputed while the votes were recast. Yet the national result in 2000 was close enough that under a direct election plan, there would no doubt have been a national recount.

Finally, defenders of the current system argue that the direct-election plan is fraught with serious difficulties. Because of the runoff provision, third parties might have a greater incentive to compete, as they can tell supporters that their votes will not necessarily be wasted; a substantial vote for minor parties might throw the election into a run-off, during which time the minor parties might enter into alliances or bargains with the major parties. The unpredictability of this aspect of the direct-election plan has led many people to favor the present system, even with its possible flaws. The dangers of the present system are at least known and manageable, while those that might result from a new system are unknown and largely incalculable.

Immediately after the 2000 election, a number of major political leaders called for an amendment to change the electoral college system. Surprisingly, this appeal did not gain much ground, and no congressional hearings were held on the issue. The absence of a strong movement for change reflected in part recognition by many lawmakers of the difficulty that would be involved in winning such an amendment. Amendments require the consent of three-quarters of the states, and many of the smaller states that enjoy an advantage under this system would be unlikely to support a change. More importantly, however, there has been no great popular demand for an amendment. Many view the current system as embodying important qualities that merit its continuation.

Congressional Elections

Moving from presidential to congressional contests is a bit like changing accommodations from a first-class hotel to a slightly run-down roadside inn. It is not just that presidential candidates have someone else to carry their luggage; it is also that presidential campaigns seem so much more glamorous. In presidential contests, the candidates (at least while they are enjoying some success) are followed by a retine of aides, harassed constantly by journalists seeking interviews, and cheered (or jeered) by large audiences. In congressional contests, especially those for the House, candidates often move around their districts in relative obscurity, soliciting media coverage and looking for gatherings of people willing to tolerate an intrusion.

Contests for the presidency and Congress could hardly be more different. These differences flow not only from the character of the constituencies but also from the nature of the offices in question. In the case of the presidency, the constituency spans a vast and heterogeneous nation and the office is one of an executive responsible for running foreign affairs and a domestic administration. In the case of Congress, while a few constituencies (such as a Senate seat from California) are almost as diversified as the nation itself, many districts are relatively homogeneous (such as a rural House district in Kansas). The officers being chosen are not executives, but representatives; they are selected not so much on the basis of how they can "run things" (governors are closer to presidents in that respect), but on the basis of how well people think they represent the particular district or region, with domestic considerations usually ranking supreme.

But even with these vast differences, a combined analysis of some campaign elements was, until recently, possible: financing was governed by roughly the same rules, party organizations played an important role in determining the nominees, and voting behavior was strongly influenced by partisan identification. Over the past fifty years, however, many points of similarity between presidential and congressional elections have diminished. They operate under separate rules for financing. Party strength and party voting, which are weaker in both processes, have led to a dramatic strengthening of incumbents' position in the case of members of Congress, while no such effect has been evident in the case of presidential contests.

General Features and Constitutional Provisions

The Constitutional separation of powers both depends on, and contributes to, the character of the nation's electoral process. The United States government differs from parliamentary systems in no small part because the choice of members of Congress is distinct, both in law and fact, from the selection of the executive. Congressional elections are independent of the elections for the president. This feature allows Congress to register its own expression of the national will. In fact, every second congressional election—the one in the midterm of the president's four-year tenure—takes place in the absence of a presidential race. In the public's understanding, members of Congress are not merely appendages of the President or of their national political party; they are representatives of their districts and individuals selected to exercise their personal judgment and discretion.

Take, for instance, the election results in 2000 from the state of North Dakota—a small state with only one representative in the House. Voters selected George W. Bush, the Republican, over Al Gore, the Democrat, by a nearly two to one majority (61 percent to 33 percent), at the same time that they were re-electing their popular Democratic Senator, Kent Conrad, by nearly the same rate over his Republican challenger (61 to 39). A Democrat incumbent won the House seat by a slightly narrower majority (54 percent to 45 percent), while in the race for Governor, the Republican beat the Democrat by the same margin. Thus in four different statewide races on the same day, the same electorate chose two Democrats and two Republicans. There were many citizens who voted either all Democratic or all Republican. But enough voters were looking at something else—the particular persons involved or the different characters of the office (executive and legislative)—to account for the great variety of outcomes for the two parties. Results along these lines are not so unusual and could be found in many states.

To be sure, the emergence of political parties modified the nonpartisan system that the founders had in mind. A common label for presidential and congressional elections allows people, to some extent, to express a common opinion on national party programs. But the influence of common national party programs on presidential and congressional voting is limited and variable. Voters can—and increasingly do—vote for a presidential candidate from one party and congressional candidates from another. Voters can—and do—modify presidential interpretations of the public will by changes in the mid-term elections. And voters within each state and district can—and do—define their local parties in different ways. And yet, in certain elections in American history, enough voters can choose to make use of the party label to send a general national message about which party they want to see in control in Washington.

Terms   Whereas presidents now are limited by the Constitution to two terms, members of Congress may serve without limit. Since the last century, more members seek reelection, and more are reelected. The high reelection rate of incumbents is one of the most striking features about the modern Congress. Representatives now serve an average of nearly four and one half terms (as opposed to about two before the Civil War), and senators now serve nearly two terms (as opposed to one before the Civil War). Since 1950 incumbent representatives have won over 90 percent of their races, a figure that rose to over 98 percent in 1986 and 1988; the record of incumbent senators has been more erratic, but still impressive (see Table 7.4).

The founders would certainly have been surprised at the average length of service in the House. Unlimited re-eligibility for the president was originally designed in part to provide stability in the government, as a counterweight to the expected turbulence of the House. Of course, the stability of an institution depends on more than the number of years served; but changes in average tenure, up for the Congress and down for the presidency, have changed the character of executive-legislative relations. The House is no longer a body made up mostly of amateur legislators serving in Washington only for brief stints. For many representatives today, serving in Congress has become a career. The Senate, with its six-year term and system of staggered elections (one-third of the Senate being reelected every two years), was designed by the founders to be the more stable body. Because of its longer terms, the Senate, even with lower rates of incumbent victories, has less change of personnel than the House.

In the 1990s a large and important popular movement formed with the aim of limiting the number of terms of members of Congress and of state legislatures. The case in favor of limits was nicely stated by Representative Charles Canady from Florida: "Congress has become too much like a permanent class of professional legislators who can use the powers of the federal government to perpetuate their own careers." Opponents decried the limitation on voter choice and the likelihood that the nation would be deprived of the services of some of its greatest and most experienced legislators.

The Term Limits Movement, as it is called, worked at first through state legislatures. Twenty states passed legislation restricting the number of terms of senators and representatives. This approach was challenged in the courts. In *U.S. Term Limits v. Thornton* (1995), the Supreme Court by a 5-4 majority declared state laws limiting the terms of members of Congress to be unconstitutional. "Allowing individual States to craft their own qualifications for Congress," the Court argued, "would erode the structure envisioned by the Framers," and create a "patchwork" of different laws. The states have no such authority under the Constitution, and neither for that matter does Congress. Term limits could only be enacted by a Constitutional amendment. This decision probably had greater consequences on the character of Congress than any Court case in American history. Although House Republicans endorsed the idea of a constitutional amendment in an election document in 1994, *The Contract with America*, the plan never received anything near the two-thirds majority of the House (part of the requirement of the amendment process) and made no headway in the Senate. Passage of such an amendment is today considered highly unlikely.

Many states in this period also placed term limits of varying lengths on their state legislatures. Today such limits remain in effect for seventeen states, including California. These changes were not affected by the Supreme Court decision, which applied only to national, not state, offices. Term limits in these states are likely to have an indirect effect on Congress. State legislators form the most significant group of challengers for representatives in the House; as they begin to be forced to leave their state legislatures, they may be more likely to challenge incumbents.

Size of Congress The provisions for the size and districting of the Senate are set by the Constitution and are self-executing: each state, no matter what its population, has two senators. But in the case of the House, the matter is not so simple. The Constitution provides for the apportionment of representatives among the states on the basis of population, with each state having at least one representative. The first House, as determined by the Constitution, had only 65 members. The overall number after that point was to be decided by statute. The early practice was to increase quickly the number of representatives to accommodate the growth in population and the addition of new states. In 1833 there were 240 members and by 1911 there were 433. No states experienced a reduction in their representation. This practice had to stop at some point if the House was to maintain any semblance of being a deliberative body. Congress in 1911 finally adopted a law that limited the number of representatives to 435, which works out today to districts of approximately 650,000 people.

Under this limit, a gain in representation for one state must now be made up by a loss from another. Each census accordingly brings the agony for some states of having districts eliminated. Over the last two censuses (1990 and 2000), the big losers have been New York with a loss of 5 seats (3 in 1990, 2 in 2000), Pennsylvania 4 seats (2 in 1990, 2 in 2000), and Michigan, Ohio and Illinois 3 seats each (2 in 1990, 1 in 2000). The big winners were California with a gain of 8 seats (7 in 1990, 1 in 2000), Florida 6 seats, (4 in 1990, 2 in 2000), Texas 5 seats (3 in 1990, 2 in 2000), and Georgia and Arizona 3 seats each (1 in 1990, 2 in 2000). These figures illustrate the huge shift in relative population in the United States over the last thirty years from the "Rust Belt" (the Northeast and Midwest) to the "Sun Belt" (the Southwest and the South).

Apportionment of House Districts The founders probably intended that House seats would be apportioned into single-member districts of roughly equal population, although no provision to this effect was put into the Constitution. The Constitution allows Congress to decide questions of apportionment, if Congress chooses to exercise this authority; otherwise, the matter is left to the states. Congress originally took no position on apportionment, and some states opted to select representatives on a statewide basis, which enabled the majority party within the state to win all the seats. Congress ended this practice in 1842 by a law that required states to elect representatives in single-member districts.

Congress did not act, however, to guarantee equal population among the districts. Some state legislatures proceeded to draw district lines (or not redraw them) so as to create (or allow) differences in population among the districts. Malapportionment became especially pronounced in the middle of the twentieth century, following some of the dramatic population shifts from rural to urban areas. States that left district lines where they had been ended up with situations in which rural areas were overrepresented and urban districts underrepresented. For example, in Georgia in 1960, one rural district had 272,000 people, while a district that included a part of Atlanta and its suburbs had more than three times as many (823,000). Representatives in the House, many of whom were the beneficiaries of this system, were reluctant to pass legislation to correct the problem. Nor were many state legislatures willing to do so, as they had the same rural bias.

Remedy was sought in the courts. After resisting for many years to enter into this "political thicket," the Supreme Court took the jump during the 1960s. In the decision of *Baker v. Carr* (1962), the Court established the principle of districts of equal population for state legislatures, arguing that the "debasement" of the vote for citizens in larger districts violated the Fourteenth Amendment's equal protection clause. Two years later, in the case of *Wesberry v. Sanders*, the Court extended this principle to congressional districts, holding that the constitutional provision in Article I that apportions representatives among the states "according to their respective numbers" means that "one man's vote in a congressional election is to be worth as much as another's." As a result, after each census every state must review its district lines to ensure equality in population for all legislative districts.

These decisions have certainly not put an end to political maneuvering. Equal districts can still be drawn with a political purpose in mind. Politics are inseparable from the process of apportionment. The drawing of district lines for political purposes is called "gerrymandering," a name derived from a particularly ingeniously shaped district conceived by Elbridge Gerry in Massachusetts in 1812. While the Court's apportionment decisions ban one of the most flagrant kinds of gerrymandering, they increase the occasions for engaging in the practice it, as states now are obliged to readjust district lines every decade. (Formerly, many states avoided these battles by simply leaving boundaries in place for several decades.)

States use various methods to draw up district plans. Ultimately, however, the political forces that control a state's government at the time of reapportionment have the greatest say. This is one reason why the national parties now pay more attention to state legislative and gubernatorial contests, for the control of the House of Representatives may depend on redistricting decisions in the states. The two main political interests that state parties seek to promote are the protection of seats of incumbents from their party and the maximization of the number of seats for the party. The two interests are partly in conflict. Incumbents prefer seats that are as safe as possible, which means packing as many partisans as can be found into their districts—which of course leaves fewer partisans to be spread out in other districts. State legislatures try to balance these competing interests, but it has been a general rule that they "err" in favor of protecting incumbents.

State governments have the chief responsibility for drawing district lines, but they face many more restrictions than they did in the past. State plans must now conform to the Constitution (as it has been interpreted by the courts) and to certain federal statutes. The states are banned from creating districts of unequal size, from drawing district lines designed to discriminate against minorities, and—although this has thus far proven unenforceable—from creating an apportionment scheme that aims too blatantly to disadvantage voters of either political party. In addition, under some parts of federal civil rights legislation, states have had to take steps to ensure that certain districts have a majority of black or Hispanic voters. With all these rules and restrictions, it is no surprise that redistricting plans are often contested in the courts, and many states have been forced to alter or throw out their laws. In addition to being the most intense of all political processes, redistricting has become something of a paradise for litigants.

Nominations

The first major hurdle in winning a House or Senate seat is nomination by a major party. Significant third-party activity at the congressional level, once a fairly frequent occurrence, is now rare, in part because of the open character of the current system of party nominations. Individuals on occasion can, however, win running as independents.

Party nominations in the nineteenth century were made by conventions of the political parties, which often were controlled by party officials. This practice may have had a modest effect in promoting party discipline in Congress, although the highest level of party control came from the state parties. Today, nominations for members of Congress are made in almost all states by primaries, not conventions.[6] Primary laws vary enormously among the states, in timing (some are in the spring or early summer, others in the late summer just months before the election), in who can participate (some are closed to declared party members, others open to any voter), and in their number (some are plurality winners, while others require a run-off primary if no one receives over 50 percent of the vote). The predominance of primaries as the system of nomination means that congressional candidates are not under the control of party organizations, as no party organization can deliver a nomination. Congressional candidates tend to be individual entrepreneurs, dependent mostly on their own reputations, organizations, and strategies. Local parties sometimes play a role in recruiting candidates, and recently even the national parties have played an active role in some districts. The closeness of the balance between the parties in Washington in the last decade has meant that party control of the House and Senate may depend on the outcome of a handful of races. But in the end, most candidacies still result from the self-initiation of individuals and the encouragement of interest groups within the constituencies.

Voter turnout in congressional primaries is typically low, especially in House races. In many districts, as few as 25,000 votes can secure a primary victory, although a hotly contested primary can sometimes generate a large turnout, especially for a race in a party that enjoys a huge advantage in a district. Under these circumstances, it is clear why incumbents, when they run, enjoy such an advantage. They begin with name recognition and an edge (usually) in raising funds. Important benefits also come just from being in office. These include a record of constituency services provided to many voters; a large staff that contacts citizens and (indirectly) helps with the campaign; free mailing to constituents in between elections; and "credit-taking" for government projects that they may or may not have played a role in securing for the district. By such means, members of Congress try to build a core constituency of supporters whom they can rely on to defeat any primary challenge.

As a result, incumbents often face no, or only token, competition in primaries. Serious competitors planning a political career will ordinarily think hard before risking a challenge to an incumbent, as no politician can afford to go too often to the well with supporters and keep coming up dry. Competitors will therefore pick their spots. Obviously, some incumbents reach a point where they are known to be vulnerable. Scandal is one reason. Congressman Gary Condit, a seven-term incumbent from California, was perfectly safe in his district until his name became connected in 2001 with a young Washington intern, Chandra Levy, who disappeared (and was later discovered dead). Condit was immediately challenged in the primary and suffered a decisive defeat.

The success rate of incumbents is indeed impressive. Since the mid-1950s, less than 2 percent of all incumbents in the House and Senate have been defeated in primary contests. (See Tables 7.4 and 7.5) These figures both slightly overstate and understate the incumbents' advantages. They overstate it because not all of the retirements are truly voluntary; some incumbents, knowing they will face stiff competition in a primary, may take the opportunity to retire.

The figures are slightly understated in that a few incumbents in the House running in the first contest after redistricting (such as 2002) are not really defending "their" districts; they may have been placed into a district that has been considerably altered, and on a few occasions, where the state has lost a seat, two incumbents have been thrown into the same district.

Competition in primary contests is greater for the party that is challenging an incumbent. And competition generally increases to its highest level in contests for an "open" seat, meaning a seat in which no incumbent is running. In this instance, at least if the district is competitive between the parties, candidates are attracted into both parties' primaries, as political aspirants in both parties now see a better chance of winning a seat. The competition in Senate primaries is often highly interesting, as Senate races sometimes attract individuals of considerable reputation and stature.

Candidates campaigning in primaries face great challenges. In most districts, as noted, the party organizations play little or no role in the nominating stage, remaining neutral among the candidates. Candidates are thus on their own. They must devise a way to appeal to the small and relatively highly motivated segment of the electorate that turns out to vote in primary elections. Along with personal followings based on some knowledge of them as individuals, candidates often rely on the support of interest groups in building a constituency.

General Elections

Congressional elections have long confounded foreign analysts of American politics. The reason is as simple as it is complex: when citizens vote for members of Congress, they are not simply casting a vote on a national idea or party program (as usually occurs in parliamentary systems); they are also deciding which *individual*, with his or her particular reputation and particular stand on the issues, should serve as their senator or representative. National trends play a role and sometimes an important one, but they are always reflected through the particular forces working in each race.

No simple dimension of electoral behavior can therefore explain the outcome of congressional elections. Four broad factors come into play in voters' choice in congressional races: (1) the candidates' personal qualities and (if they are incumbents) their record in office; (2) the candidates' issue stands; (3) the candidates' party (which usually tells something about their positions on issues, but does not define it entirely); and (4) voter judgments of national trends—in presidential election years, often of the presidential candidates, and in midterm elections, of how well the incumbent president is doing.

The first two factors have become relatively more important today because of the weakening of strict partisan voting patterns. Voters are looking today at the *individuals* who are running. As a result, congressional races now tend to be fought out in different ways in each state and district. This does not mean that the contests are more isolated than in the past from issues of national politics—the opposite is probably true—but that voters look at how these issues are developed by the candidates running in their district. The increased importance of voters' judgments on individuals may be one reason for the greater success of incumbents; personal reputation counts for more when fewer voters are deciding on grounds of pure partisanship. Of course, in many districts the incumbent is from the party with the greater number of supporters of that party; this fact makes it difficult to determine whether success is due to incumbency or to party affiliation. But the importance of incumbency is suggested by cases in which a representative manages to win in a district having a normal plurality for the opposition party; afterwards, the incumbent is very difficult to replace and usually is able to attract enough independents and members from the other party to hold on to the seat.

Although the incumbents' rate of victory is impressive—less so for the Senate than for the House—it does not follow that they generally think of themselves as being safe or beyond accountability to their constituents. They tend to run scared. Members of Congress, Richard Fenno has observed, operate with "a terrific sense of uncertainty . . . and perceive troubles

TABLE 7.4
The Advantage of Incumbency in the House, 1946–2000

| | | House | | |
| | | Defeat | | |
Year	Seeking reelection	Primary	General	Percent reelected
1946	398	18	52	82.4
1948	400	15	68	79.2
1950	400	6	32	90.5
1966	411	8	41	88.1
1968	409	4	9	96.8
1970	401	10	12	94.5
1972	390	12	13	93.6
1974	391	8	40	87.7
1976	384	3	13	95.8
1978	382	5	19	93.7
1980	398	6	31	90.7
1982	381	2	29	91.9
1984	409	3	16	95.4
1986	393	2	6	98.0
1988	408	1	6	98.5
1990	408	1	15	96.1
1992	368	19	24	88.0
1994	386	4	33	90.4
1996	382	2	21	94.0
1998	402	1	6	98.2
2000	401	3	6	97.8

where the most imaginative outside observer could not possibly perceive, conjure or hallucinate them." Nor are they being simply paranoid. With the number of independents in the electorate, incumbents, even when they win by wide margins, may reasonably conclude that their support is not all that firm. In fact, incumbents may be reelected so often in large part because they are so solicitous of their constituents and so careful in staying in tune with them. Members of Congress perform an enormous amount of constituency service for voters in their districts, which can earn them the reputation of being almost nonpartisan representatives. While voters often express a negative or cynical view of Congress as an institution, they frequently exempt their own representatives or senator, who is seen as different and working for the good of his or her constituents. Members of Congress have even been known to run for Congress by running against it—a nice trick that involves criticizing the institution as a whole while exempting oneself for any of the blame.

TABLE 7.5
The Advantage of Incumbency in the Senate, 1946–2000

Year	Seeking reelection	Senate Defeated Primary	Senate Defeated General	Percent reelected
1946	30	6	7	51.7
1948	25	2	8	60.0
1950	32	5	5	68.8
1952	31	2	9	64.5
1954	32	2	6	75.0
1956	29	0	4	86.2
1958	28	0	10	64.3
1960	29	0	1	96.6
1962	35	1	5	82.9
1964	33	1	4	84.8
1966	32	3	1	87.5
1968	28	4	4	71.4
1970	31	1	6	77.4
1972	27	2	5	74.1
1974	27	2	2	85.2
1976	25	0	9	64.0
1978	25	3	7	60.0
1980	29	4	9	55.2
1982	30	0	2	93.3
1984	29	0	3	89.6
1986	28	0	7	75.0
1988	27	0	4	85.2
1990	32	0	1	96.9
1992	28	1	4	82.1
1994	26	0	2	92.3
1996	21	1	1	90.5
1998	30	0	3	90.0
2000	29	0	6	79.3

Incumbent reelection rates fell somewhat in 1992 and 1994, partly as a result of a partisan swing in favor of Republicans but partly also in response to a sharp rise of anti-incumbent sentiment (See Table 7.4). Suddenly, in district after district, incumbency was no longer the advantage it had once been, especially for Democrats who had been the dominant party in Congress, especially in the House, for almost a half century. The anti-incumbent sentiment was real and powerful, but after a few years—and with a transfer of party control to the Republicans both the House and Senate in 1994—the discontent began to abate. By 1996, incumbent re-election rate surged to 94 percent, and many fewer members of Congress mentioned the issue of term limits.

In all but unusual election years, there are today a fairly limited number of House and Senate seats that are considered to be genuinely competitive. These contests are concentrated among the open seats, but in every year there will also be a certain percentage of incumbents—usually higher in the Senate than the House—who are considered vulnerable. Throughout the summer and fall, election analysts in both parties continually assess and reassess the races that are still in play, as it is on this basis that the national parties will decide where to put additional resources to assist their candidates.

Even though congressional elections have a strongly local element to them, they are also, of course, contests between two national parties for control of the majorities in Congress. Congressional elections can set national agendas or help to undo them. The swings of enough voters in enough districts can on occasion send very important national messages. One important connection of congressional elections to the national party comes in the form of the influence of the presidential election on congressional races. This element of congressional voting can be examined first by looking at the so-called "coattail" effect that was once so pronounced. Under this effect, voters in presidential election years favoring a candidate for president would tend to vote for members of Congress from the same party. A popular presidential candidate would consequently bring in ("on his coattails")

a gain for his party in Congress (and almost always a majority in the House). This result created an important link between the president and members of Congress from his own party, who were likely to think that their fortunes depended on the president's success.

Since 1960, however, the coattail effect has greatly diminished. Naturally, candidates for Congress prefer to have a strong presidential candidate at the head of their ticket. But the overall impact of the presidential race on congressional elections can now be small. To take some striking examples, when Presidents Nixon and Reagan won their landslide 49 state victories in 1972 and 1984, the Democrats captured a solid majority in the House. When George H. Bush won his substantial victory in 1988, Republicans actually lost seats in Congress. Likewise, Democrats lost seats in 1992 when Bill Clinton captured the White House, and Republicans lost seats in 2000 when George W. Bush was elected, although in both of these cases the victorious presidential candidates did not run very strongly in the national vote contest. Voters clearly find it easier today to "separate" their votes for President and Congress. Finally, in a new development, there was even evidence in the last decades of many citizens voting consciously in such a way as to try to assure that a different party would be in control of the two branches. Many voters actually prefer "divided government."

In midterm elections, national trends come into play in the net swing in the number of seats between the parties. As a rough benchmark against which to measure these swings, past electoral performance has established that it is "normal" for the president's party to lose a handful of seats in the midterm election in the House and Senate. The reasons for this result are probably that frustrations accumulate as things do not go as well for the president as many hoped and that some of the voters who were brought in to support the president's party by the presidential campaign stay home or return to their own party. In any case, when the president's party loses a few seats, no judgments are usually drawn one way or the other. But when there are significant deviations from this norm, voters can be seen to be sending a message about national politics.

Table 7.6
President's Party Seat Shift in Midterm Elections, 1894-1998

Year	House	Senate
1894	-116*	-5*
1898	-21	+7
1902	-16**	+2
1906	-28	+3
1910	-57*	-10
1914	-59	+5
1918	-19*	-6*
1922	-75	-8
1926	-10	-6
1930	-49*	-8
1934	+9	+10
1938	-71	-6
1942	-55	-9
1946	-55*	-12*
1950	-29	-6
1954	-18*	-1*
1958	-48	-13
1962	-4	+3
1966	-47	-4
1970	-12	+2
1974	-48	-5
1978	-15	-3
1982	-26	+1
1986	-5	-8*
1990	-8	-1
1994	-52*	-8*
1998	+5	0

* Loss of Party Control

** Because of an increase in the size of the House, Theodore Roosevelt's Republicans gained 9 seats at the same time Democrats were gaining 25, representing a net loss of 16 for the president's party.

If the president's party loses a large number of seats, it is generally taken as a signal that the public has lost confidence in the president's leadership and wishes to see a different program. Thus, Republicans lost forty-eight seats in the 1974 election following the Watergate crisis and the resignation of Richard Nixon. The most striking recent example occurred in 1994, when the Democrats lost fifty-two seats in the House and eight in the Senate, surrendering the majority inside both chambers. The election provoked

a huge change in Washington, as President Clinton was forced to alter many of his policies, and the new Speaker of the House, Newt Gingrich, emerged temporarily as the dominant figure in national policymaking.

The opposite signal occurs when the President's party manages to beat the norm and actually gain seats. Indeed, this result in the case of the House occurred only two times in twentieth century, in 1934 under Franklin Roosevelt, when the voters were signaling that they favored the New Deal program, and in 1998 under President Bill Clinton. The latter case shows how a midterm contest can indicate voters' position on a national issue. The year began with the accusation of the affair between President Clinton and Monica Lewinsky, which the President for a long time publicly denied. The scandal led many to think that Republicans would gain an unusually large number of seats, a result that might well have led Democrats in Congress to demand the President's resignation. As Republicans began calls for impeachment, it became clear that the midterm election was to be a kind of referendum on impeachment. Not only did the Republicans fail to win even the usual number of seats, but they actually lost five seats in the House. The election did not stop the House from voting for an impeachment of the President, but the vote was almost exclusively on party lines; and the election results made it highly unlikely that the Senate would vote to convict him. The outcome also discredited the Speaker of the House, Newt Gingrich, who resigned as Speaker and retired from Congress.

Financing in Congressional Elections

Money is vital to conducting effective congressional campaigns. Although its importance is often exaggerated relative to other factors, such as organization and strategy, it clearly counts for a great deal. Moreover, because of differences in the laws and in the nature of the races, funding has a greater relative impact on the outcome of congressional races than presidential campaigns.

The campaign finance legislation of 1974 limited what individuals and groups (including national and state parties) could contribute to congressional campaigns. (Individuals spending on their own campaigns, however, faced no limits.) Unlike presidential campaigns, no overall spending limits existed for campaigns as a whole, and there was no public funding. All funds were raised privately. As a result, the amounts spent on various congressional campaigns varied greatly, and these differences had an important bearing on the results.

This system functioned in its own way for much of the period, although with many complaints and problems. But by the middle of the last decade, it too had begun to break down. As in presidential contests, money began to be raised and spent outside of the candidates' campaign organization by independent groups and by parties in the form of "soft money." The McCain Feingold bill of 2002 attempts to address this breakdown. It keeps the system of private funding without any spending limits, but it seeks to eliminate all soft money. It also increases what individuals may give to congressional campaigns. (The new limit is $2,000 per candidate per election, which will increase with the cost of living; contribution limitations by PACS stay at $5,000 per candidate per election and will remain fixed.) The great question for 2004 and beyond is whether these new efforts to funnel campaign spending back through the candidates' campaigns will work.

Money, it was said, is so important in congressional races because it can help to buy exposure and recognition. In many primary races and House general elections, candidates face a great problem in just getting themselves known. (Senate general elections generally receive a great deal of media coverage and free exposure, which makes them a bit more like presidential contests and gives more equality to challengers of incumbents than is the case in the House.)

There are two types of candidates for whom achieving name recognition is not a major problem: incumbents (people cannot always remember the name of their members of Congress, but they can usually recognize them on the ballot) and persons who already have huge public reputations, derived from holding other offices or from activities outside of politics. A perfect example was Hillary Clinton, when she ran for the Senate in New York. On a lesser scale are prominent athletes, like J. C. Watts, the college football star from Oklahoma who was widely recognized in his first race for the House.

The question of financing in races involving incumbents deserves special comment. Incumbents usually find it much easier to raise funds than challengers do, in part because it is known that they are likely to win, which is an important consideration for many of the individuals and especially the groups who give money. (Groups are rarely buying a vote, but rather access or the likelihood that they will get a hearing from an elected official.) Campaign spending by incumbents, however, is usually not worth as much as it is for challengers, who are the ones who need to spend money in order to overcome the incumbents' advantages. Challengers will therefore have to spend a great deal of money—and often outspend the incumbent—in order to have a serious chance of winning. The level of spending in a race therefore tends to be set by the challenger. When a challenger is capable of mounting a serious campaign, the incumbent will be forced into a major fund-raising effort. Incumbents can almost always raise what they need to conduct a major campaign. What they would prefer, of course, is to discourage a serious challenge altogether by convincing everyone in the district that they are invulnerable.

In regard to the sources of funds for congressional campaigns, the 1974 finance legislation had two effects. First, by the strict limitations imposed on individual contributions, the law stimulated the emergence of political action committees. These "professional" givers, formed around groups, grew in significance and importance after 1974. Their growth meant that a greater share of funding in congressional races was coming from sources outside the state and district. The McCain-Feingold bill will not change the race for money, but, as noted, it bans the soft money, and it increases the importance of individual contributions relative to PAC contributions by upping the limit on the former while holding the line on the latter.

Second, the 1974 campaign finance legislation gave individual wealthy candidates a greater advantage than they once had by allowing them to spend without limit while the less fortunate opponent could not rely on wealthy friends to counterbalance these expenditures. Wealthy individuals have been attracted to public office, especially to the Senate. The 2000 race of Senator John Corzine of New Jersey set all records and may not be surpassed for years to come. Corzine spent about $60 million dollars of his own money in competing for that seat, in which he outspent his Republican rival by a factor of 10. McCain-Feingold has tried to deal with this kind of problem by relaxing the contribution limits of individuals who are faced by candidates spending so much of their personal money.

Nearly everyone who has studied financing legislation for congressional elections has come away dissatisfied. The agreement that something is wrong has not translated into any agreement about what would be better. The McCain-Feingold bill marks an attempt to return to the system of the 1980s, with some adjustments. Even if it works, many troubling elements will remain in place. The race for money will continue, and candidates and office holders will have to spend a great deal of time raising it. Many have wanted not merely to fix the system of regulation, but also to introduce public financing for congressional campaigns. Such a system, if it were ever adopted, would eliminate differences in campaign spending and advantages of wealth. Yet it would not necessarily be fair, if by "fair" one includes the concept of a good chance for challengers to unseat incumbents. Where incumbents and challengers spend equal but modest amounts, incumbents have the advantage of greater visibility and recognition. But the debate on public funding for congressional elections has now been put off for a number of years, at least until the current campaign reforms can be assessed.

Conclusion

The electoral process is an intricate maze of provisions coming from the Constitution (including Court interpretations), federal and state laws, party rules, and traditions and norms. Together, these make up a central "institution" of our political system that helps determine who governs and how power is distributed. It does so by influencing the type of people who are attracted and elevated to public office, the nature of the

campaigns, and the kinds of choices offered to the public.

A striking fact about the electoral process during the last century has been the institutional weakening of political parties. Nominations are now more open to outsiders, and campaigns rely more on the particular appeals of the candidates. The system is more individualistic and candidate-centered than it was in 1900. Parties have had to learn to operate in this new environment, putting together as best they can their coalitions and programs. The transfer of power from party leaders to the public appears to make the system more democratic, in form, if not always in reality. It has created a new style and character to politics that has demanded tremendous adjustments and created new kinds of problems and challenges, from co-coordinating the actions of politicians to controlling the influence of money in political campaigns. Of course, the political parties are still very much in business, and it remains an important question whether they will preserve their position in the political system.

Chapter 7 Notes

1. Jonathan Moore, ed., *The Campaign for President: 1980 in Retrospect* (Cambridge, Mass.: Ballinger, 1981), p. 40.
2. Lewis W. Wolfson, "The Media Masters," *Washington Post*, Feb. 20, 1972, p. 15, Potomac supplement.
3. See Larry Sabato, *Feeding Frenzy*, (New York: Free Press, 1991).
4. For an argument of this thesis, see Thomas Patterson Out of Order (New York: Knopf, 1993).
5. Researchers who have analyzed the relationship between platform pledges and party performance have generally concluded that the platforms used to present fairly serious statements of intention; and in elections when the parties have been opposed to each other on fundamental issues, these differences have been clearly reflected in the language of the platforms. See Gerald Pomper, with Susan Lederman, *Elections America: Control and Influence in Democratic Politics*, 2nd ed. (New York: Longmans, 1980).
6. In Virginia, the major parties may opt for conventions rather than primaries. In a few states, among them Connecticut and Utah, party conventions are held before the primaries. Louisiana follows a unique system without any party primaries. All candidates who qualify appear on the ballot on Election Day; a candidate receiving more than 50 percent of the vote is declared the winner. If no one received 50 percent, a runoff is held between the top two vote recipients.

8

Voting Behavior and Political Participation

CHAPTER CONTENTS

As defined in *The Federalist*, a representative government (or a republic) is a "government which derives all of its powers directly or indirectly from the great body of the people, and is administered by persons holding their offices . . . for a limited period or during good behavior." (No. 39) Such a government, in the founders' view, could rest on the will of the public, but could also be fashioned to permit certain institutions to operate at a distance from immediate public pressure. A mix of "direct" and "indirect" elements would best promote the public good.

The chief mechanism of direct popular influence on government is an election. Originally, the House was the only body whose members were elected directly by the people. Today, not only members of the House, but also Senators and (in practice) the president are chosen directly by the people. The electorate thus has a greater influence on the operation of the government than under the original Constitutional design. It is not by the vote alone, however, that citizens influence governing officials. They do so by other modes of participation, such as contacting members of Congress, contributing money to candidates and political parties, and attending mass rallies to demonstrate for a position they support.

In this chapter we look at the American citizen as a voter and political participant. This investigation should contribute to an assessment of some of the institutional changes in the electoral process discussed in the previous chapters as well as shed light on the fundamental constitutional question of who rules in the United States.

Voter Turnout

The mass of American males, with the exception of those in certain minority groups, have had the right to vote longer than the citizens of any other nation. Yet voter turnout rates—never as high as those in most other established democracies—have fallen since 1960 (see Table 8.1 and 8.2). In 2000, presidential election turnout was only 51 percent of the eligible electorate, and turnout in years with no presidential election is routinely lower.

These facts have led some to question not only the health, but even the existence of genuine democratic decision making in the United States. In this view, low voter turnout indicates at best mass indifference to the political system, at worst an alienation that could be mobilized in behalf of a radical political alternative not currently represented by the two major parties. Of course, anyone looking at Tables 8.1 and 8.2 will be concerned. But whether one should draw the dire conclusion that democracy is threatened is another question that can only be answered after further consideration of nonvoters and the reasons for nonvoting.

General Factors Affecting Turnout

Whether an individual turns out to vote first depends on the legal right to vote, the franchise, and its protection in practice from intimidation or harassment. Exclusions of these kinds were common in several states, most in the South, and continued in some cases well into the 1960s. African American citizens and, for a time, Asians were systematically kept from voting by various legal subterfuges, such as poll taxes, and violence from vigilante groups such as the Ku Klux Klan. Since the Civil Rights movement of the 1950s and 60s, restrictions on voting have been reduced or removed, which should have resulted in greater rates of participation. Another factor that should lead to increased participation, the average level of education, has increased since the 1960s. Yet turnout has declined.

The explanation for low voter turnout and possible decreased participation thus no longer lies with a denial of the right of suffrage. Three other factors need to be examined: (1) the legal and administrative regulation of voting, such as registration requirements; (2) the health of civic institutions, such as political parties, that mobilize the electorate; and (3) citizens' attitudes about voting, for example the extent to which people regard voting as a duty or think that elections can make a difference.

Table 8.1
Voting Participation in Various Democracies

Country	Election Year	Voter Turnout
Australia	1996	93%
New Zealand	1993	85%
Sweden	1991	85%
Italy	1996	83%
Finland	1994	82%
Israel	1996	80%
France	1995	80%
Germany	1994	79%
Great Britain	1992	78%
Norway	1993	75%
Canada	1993	71%
Ireland	1992	69%
Japan	1993	67%
United States	1996	49%
Switzerland	1995	42%

Source: Various election reports in *Electoral Studies*

The United States and Other Nations

Comparing turnout rates among democratic nations is not the simple exercise it may seem. National elections mean different things in different countries. In a centralized system like Great Britain, the choice of the prime minister decides where almost all the political power is vested. In the United States, by contrast, power is more decentralized, and sometimes the most important election for some people is at the state or local level. Furthermore, because of the federal system and the use of primaries in nominating candidates in the United States, there are more elections here than in many other democratic countries. Typically, important elections in the United States are held in three out of every four years, often with primaries in advance of the general election. Some voters turn out to vote in state or local elections, but then may miss the national election. Despite the cross-national differences, voter turnout is declining in many democratic nations, suggesting that there are larger issues at work other than simply the peculiarities of U.S. election law. Partisanship, or the number of people who have a fairly strong identification with a political party, has declined in many coun-

tries and may be a source of the decline in turnout.[1] Another cause may be that younger generations around the world are more inclined to participate in unconventional ways such as boycotts, demonstrations, and unofficial strikes.[2]

Voter turnout in the United States is nevertheless still lower than in most other established democracies. One factor that accounts for this difference is the system of legal regulation of voting. In a few nations with high turnout rates—Australia, Italy, and Belgium—voting is compulsory. Although the penalties imposed are minimal, the principle that citizens are legally required to vote has a significant effect. In some countries, elections take place on a weekend or holiday, whereas in the United States they are held on a working day (Tuesday)—although businesses now often allow time to vote. Moreover, many states have begun to allow voting by mail in a two week period before the final election day. Finally, in many nations the burden of registering voters is assumed by the state, whereas in the United States it falls on the individual citizen. The extent of that burden varies among states and localities; in some cases voters may register by mail or even when they vote (Minnesota and Wisconsin), while in other states voters must register in person in advance of the election, sometimes in inconvenient places. Self-registration poses an obstacle to voting, and if all states adopted one of the easier forms of registration, turnout might increase in the range of 8 to 10 percent.[3]

These differences in legal regulations may help explain why turnout in the United States is lower than in some other nations. But they do not tell us which legal changes, if any, should be adopted to increase voter turnout. After considering some of these measures, many people may conclude that it is better on balance to live with the "problem" of lower turnout than to adopt some of the legal solutions employed in other nations. As for compulsory voting, the right to vote, as Americans see it, includes the right not to vote. Registration laws have already been eased considerably in recent years, not just by the actions of the states but by the National Voter Registration Act, more commonly known as "motor-voter," that was signed into law by

TABLE 8.2
Percentage of Eligible Voters Participating in National Elections*

Year	Percentage of Eligible Voters Who Voted
1840–1872 (average)	77%
1876–1900 (average)	79%
1904–1916 (average)	63%
1920–1932 (average)	48%
1940	59%
1952	62%
1960	63%
1964	62%
1968	61%
1972	56%
1976	54%
1980	53%
1984	53%
1988	50%
1992	56%
1996	49%
2000	51%

*Percentages are based on estimates of potential eligible voters. Women are excluded in years before state laws or the Nineteenth Amendment accorded them the right to vote. Eighteen years are excluded before state laws or the Twenty-Sixth Amendment accorded them the right to vote. Other adjustments have been made.

Source: *Historical Abstract of the United States, Colonial Times to 1970*; Congressional Research Service.

1993. This law enables citizens to register to vote when they obtain a driver's license.

Other recent efforts to increase turnout include early voting in person and voting by mail. All mail voting in Oregon seemed to increase turnout by 10 percentage points, controlling for other factors, but this practice is probably not wise for states with a history of ballot fraud.[4] Legal regulations partially explain low turnout in the United States, but it is not clear that they tell the whole story.

It may be that the basic satisfaction that Americans have felt toward the fundamentals of the political system—which is a sign of political health—has led to less voting. People are often motivated to vote where the differences among the parties are great and where the choice involves radically different visions of the ends of society, including whether the existing form of government should be maintained. These kinds of fundamental choices were common in many European nations, at least through the 1970s, when communist and socialist parties called for fundamental changes in the entire social structures of their countries. Paradoxically, then, it may be that in a comparative setting lower turnout can be a sign not of more, but of less, alienation. It is noteworthy that the two countries at the bottom of the list in Table 8.1 (the United States and Switzerland) have been two of the most stable and long-lived of the democratic states.

Historical Trends in Voting

A decline of turnout in relation to rates in the past is perhaps a more troubling question. Actually, the evidence here raises issues about two different trends. First, there has been a sharp decline reported in turnout rates among eligible voters from the nineteenth to the twentieth century; and second, there has been a gradual decline in turnout since 1960.

Turnout in the Nineteenth Century It came as a great surprise when analysts of voting behavior discovered that voters participated at a much higher rate in the nineteenth century than in this century. In the electorate today, increased participation is associated with greater wealth and higher levels of formal education. On the basis of these relationships, it was normal to expect that citizens of nineteenth century America, who were far poorer and had much lower levels of formal education than citizens today, would be much less likely to vote. Yet just the opposite is true.

To be sure, the figures for voter turnout in the last century are not entirely reliable. Statistics in many areas of the country were doctored to cover the corrupt practices of the time, as proven by the fact that in numerous instances counties reported turnout rates that exceeded the number of eligible voters! Sometimes figures were merely fixed, while at other times some citizens would be transported from one district to

Chapter 8: Voting Behavior and Political Participation ❖ **241**

8.1

Federal Definition and Protection of Voting Rights

Determining qualifications for voting was originally a state function, the sole exception being the Constitutional provision in Article 1, Section 2 giving the right to vote in federal elections for the House to the same people eligible to vote for the most numerous branch of the state legislature. Over the course of American history, Constitutional amendments, court cases, and federal laws have established what amounts to a national right to vote. Some of the major developments have been:

The Fifteenth Amendment (1870), providing that race shall not be a condition for denying suffrage.

The Nineteenth Amendment (1920), providing that sex shall not be a condition for denying suffrage.

The Twenty-Fourth Amendment (1964), prohibiting the use of the poll tax or any other tax as a means of denying anyone the right to vote.

The Voting Rights Act of 1965, outlawing the use of tests for denying anyone the right to vote in certain areas of the country.

The Voting Rights Act of 1970, banning literacy tests nationally.

The Twenty-Sixth Amendment (1971), guaranteeing 18-year-olds the right to vote.

Dunn v. Blumstein (1972), a Supreme Court ruling declaring long residency requirements unconstitutional.

The Voting Rights Act of 1975, requiring states to provide bilingual voting information.

another to vote two or three times—from which practice comes the ironic slogan for responsible citizenship: "Vote early and vote often." Yet even allowing for a considerable degree of corruption, most scholars still agree that turnout among those eligible to vote was much higher than today. In the late 19th century, turnout outside the South routinely reached 75–80 percent.

The reasons for this decline can be sought in looking at the three general factors identified earlier. First, legal reforms designed to help end corruption, such as the secret ("Australian") ballot and voter registration, made voting less "profitable" to some citizens and more "costly" to others.[5] Once the state began printing ballots, parties had more difficulty buying votes, and citizens now had to go to the additional trouble of registering to vote before elections.

Jim Crow laws and intimidation of African Americans further reduced turnout, which remains lower in the South. And the adoption of the 19th Amendment guaranteeing women's suffrage in 1920 initially led to lower turnout because women were slow to exercise their right to vote.

Second, the strength of political party organizations in the nineteenth century certainly helps account for the higher levels of participation.

Aside from some of their overly enthusiastic activities such as buying votes, the parties were busy organizing citizens and making sure that they made it to the polls on election day. Party organizations are weaker today and do not do nearly as much to bring citizens to the polls. Nor has any modern substitute—including the MTV-sponsored "rock the vote" campaign—come close to making up for the kind of direct personal contact that the parties once routinely provided. Thus, the individual citizen today is left more on his or her own in deciding whether to vote, and in the end fewer do.

Some who study this history, however, have raised the issue not just of the rate of voting, but of its quality as a political act. Given the extent to which the parties in the nineteenth century mobilized voters, sometimes without voters knowing exactly what positions they were supporting, can the act of voting in the 19th century really be compared to voting today? In this view, the decline in voting turnout is not the unhealthy development many have maintained, for the electorate today includes a higher percentage of citizens who truly want to vote and who see their vote as an instrument for policymaking.

Finally, in regard to citizens' attitudes toward the vote, politics may have occupied a more important place in people's consciousness in the nineteenth century. There were fewer alternative forms of entertainment, such as professional sports, movies or television, and politics was often the only "game" in town. Moreover, the substance of political controversy then revolved around highly emotional social issues, such as slavery and religious questions, that citizens could easily grasp. Some campaigns today, by contrast, focus on economic matters that may seem more distant and confusing, and some of the more emotional issues, such as civil rights and abortion, were—at least for a time— removed from direct political controversy and taken up as legal questions to be resolved by the courts or bureaucracies. The removal of these issues may have led many citizens to question the significance of electoral politics altogether.[6]

Turnout Since the 1960s Concern over low voter turnout has focused not only on the differences between participation in the nineteenth and twentieth centuries but also on the decline in turnout since 1960. Although turnout today is no less than it was in 1928 and 1932, the easing of registration requirements and other legal changes in the last thirty years would lead one to expect that participation should be increasing, not diminishing. Part of the explanation for the decline, of course, comes from the mandatory lowering of the voting age in 1971 from 21 to 18 years, which brought into the electorate more young people, who vote at a much lower rate.

Yet the decline has also resulted from the increasing belief that one's vote does not matter and a loss of interest in politics, particularly among younger generations. Citizens who have reached the voting age since the 1960s are less likely to vote and to participate in politics in general than older Americans. Younger generations may have become more cynical about politics because of Watergate and other scandals portrayed, or they may feel that their vote matters less, in part because of a decline in competition in many congressional races. In many districts, the incumbent candidate of one party has such a great advantage that voters may not see a reason to come to the polls. Younger generations are also less partisan and more independent, a worldwide trend that is correlated with declining turnout.

The 2000 election was another step in the era of declining turnout. About 51 percent of the adult population voted in the election, an increase of 2 percent over turnout in 1996, but still 4 points below 1992. The fact that only roughly half of the voting age population cast a ballot in 2000 was all the more surprising because other trends suggested that there would be an increase in turnout.[7] Registration requirements were eased in many states, people perceived that the contest between Bush and Gore would be close and thus their vote would matter, parties had their best get-out-the-vote effort in years, and education levels were up. Many people blamed weak candidates for the disappointing turnout, while others noted that peace and prosperity had dulled the edge of public discontent.

Nonvoters: Who Are They?

The fact that nearly half of the electorate does not vote in presidential elections could lead one to conclude that one half of the American people are disaffected citizens. Yet this is clearly false. Nearly half of the citizens do not vote in any particular election, but they are not the same people from one election to the next. In examining the reasons for nonvoting, it turns out that most nonvoters in a specific election have not removed themselves permanently as participating citizens. Some nonvoters are those who recently moved and did not manage to register; others are those who had something come up— they were ill, could not find transportation, or could not get a babysitter; and still others are those who deliberately sit out the election because of dissatisfaction with the particular candidates running. Thus most nonvoters will come back into the electorate in a subsequent election, just as many voters will for one reason or another not vote in some future election. In short, the nonvoter frequently turns out to be not an individual who is deeply alienated from the political system, but the average citizen— one's neighbor, one's teacher, one's parent, or perhaps one's own self.

Much of nonvoting is related to the life cycle. Voting declines among older voters, probably because of health or loss of interest. At the other end, citizens from age 18 to 24 also turnout at a very low rate. Many have not settled in communities and are not habituated to the duties of citizenship. Being young, however, is not a permanent affliction. Young people eventually grow older and then, surprisingly, begin to think and behave like older people.

The number of people who are truly alienated from the political system is more likely close to 10 or 15 percent than the nearly half who do not turnout to vote in presidential elections. It would be a serious problem if nonvoters were dramatically different from the voting population and were not represented. Surveys tell us, however, that the political views of non-voters are much the same as those of voters. Many politicians think that because nonvoters are more likely to be poor, less well educated, and nonwhite, they would be more likely to vote for Democratic candidates. This conclusion is far from clear. The largest groups of nonvoters are young people and the residentially mobile, both of which do not usually have settled partisan identifications.

The Problem of Voter Turnout

Voting is the citizens' chief instrument of democratic control. How power is allotted in our system and who governs are shaped in important ways by who votes. Voting provides a means by which various groups have been able to protect their interests and promote certain goals. On a larger scale, it is the basic mechanism by which the citizenry as a whole expresses its sense, not always with perfect clarity, of what the people (the majority) wants or does not want. Finally, the act of voting creates a feeling of connection between the individual and the political system and confirms for the individual that the government is not some alien mechanism, but an expression of the will of the citizens. Voting thus helps promote the overall level of support and legitimacy of the system.

For all these reasons, low levels of voting participation cannot be lightly dismissed. The decline in voter turnout may not represent quite the crisis that some have claimed, but it is surely

TABLE 8.3

Percentage of Different Groups Voting in the 1992 Presidential Election

VOTERS	PERCENT VOTING
Education:	
Grade School	35%
High School	57.5%
College	81%
Age:	
Under 21	38.5%
21–24	46%
25–44	53%
45–64	70%
65 and over	70%
Region:	
South	59%
West	58.5%
Northeast	61%
Midwest	67%
Employment:	
Employed	64%
Unemployed	46%
Not in labor force	59%
Race	
White	64%
Black	54%
Hispanic origin	29%
Sex	
Male	60%
Female	64%

Source: U.S. Bureau of the Census.

an important problem that merits close attention.

Voting Behavior

Few questions of political science have received more attention in the last thirty years than the attempt to explain why citizens vote as they do. Although more is known today about voting behavior than ever before, the complexities of human behavior are too great and the array of political stimuli too various to construct any foolproof predictive model of voting. What a generation of scholarship has taught is the difficulty, indeed the impossibility, of elaborating a purely scientific explanation of the "simple" act of voting.

It is possible nevertheless to list the general factors that influence voting behavior and to indicate their relative importance under different circumstances. The purpose of this kind of discussion is less to attempt to predict elections far in advance than to help one understand long-term trends in the electorate and to assess elections as they unfold. Knowledge of voting behavior is also important for a constitution maker's decisions about electoral institutions and reform.

The factors that voters assess in reaching their decision can be grouped under five general headings:

1. Partisan identification

2. The performance of the incumbent or incumbent party

3. The character and qualifications of the candidates

4. Issues and ideological stances

5. The moods, themes, and character of the times

Imagine, for example, a typical voter during the 2000 election campaign. This voter—let's call her Jennifer—thinks of herself basically as a Democrat, although she does not vote Democratic all the time. Her partisan identification predisposes her to vote for Al Gore, but she keeps an open mind. Jennifer will certainly think about Bill Clinton's performance as president, since he was a Democrat and is probably the best guide to what Gore's presidency would be like. She approves of Clinton's record as president, and this too makes her more likely to vote for Gore. But Jennifer also has to consider what she thinks about the character of the candidates. She likes Gore well enough, although she has some doubts about his sincerity. She also respects George W. Bush, whom she finds to be straightforward and honorable. But on some of the main issues that are discussed during the campaign, such as the environment, Jennifer feels closer to Gore, who is also the more "liberal" candidate. (Jennifer

thinks of herself as more liberal than conservative.) Finally, although she has some concerns about crime, Jennifer feels good about where America stands and is relatively confident about the future. All things considered, Jennifer's decision is a fairly easy one, as the basic factors for her weigh in Gore's favor. Fairly early on in the campaign, Jennifer makes up her mind to vote for Gore and will reassess only if some new major piece of information should come to light.

Imagine any different set of reactions of voters in regard to these five factors and this will help illustrate how they can weigh in a voter's decision. These factors not only can be used to determine what voters take into consideration, but they also can serve to identify the the different sorts of appeals made by candidates during the campaign. This connection is not surprising, as the candidates obviously attempt to fit their appeals to the way voters think. It is also the case, however, that voters respond in part to what is "offered" them by the candidates. Thus, if the candidates emphasize the issues, it is more likely that the issues will count more heavily for the voters. But this kind of effect is only partial, as much of the important information that the voters consider is determined before the campaign or comes from sources other than the candidates. A campaign is a momentary event, whereas some of the factors that influence voting behavior are rooted in long-standing attitudes. Incumbency, for example, is a key factor in congressional elections and, like many other factors, is determined before the campaign begins.

The five categories noted above overlap and influence each other. One's view of the character of the candidates, for example, inevitably affects one's assessments of their positions on issues and vice versa. And one's party identification, which generally exists before the campaign, importantly influences one's assessment of the other factors. Because of the overlap and interaction among these categories, it is difficult to build a model that can specify precisely which factor is most important. In any event, their relative weight varies according to different circumstances.

It depends in the first place on the type of election. Voters behave differently depending on whether the election is a primary or a general election or an election for president or for Congress. The choice is structured differently in these elections. Thus, to take the most obvious case, in primary elections the factor of partisan identification plays no role, because all candidates are from the same party. People may also weigh the various factors differently according to the office for which they are voting. Character—or certain traits of character—may count somewhat more in the case of evaluating candidates for the presidency than for Congress.

Second, the weight given to each of these five factors may vary over time, with changes in institutional arrangements and norms. For example, the importance voters ascribe today to partisan identification, though it is still considerable, is less than it was a century ago. Finally, the weight of the five factors varies in the short-term with the immediate conditions of the particular election. Sometimes the issues presented during the campaign seem to dominate, at other times it seems to be the character of the candidates that is decisive, and at other times still it seems to be the conditions in the country that virtually decide the outcome. Each campaign is a story unto itself.

Presidential Primaries

Turnout Who votes in primaries is often as important as how people vote. Turnout is generally low, on the average of about one-quarter of the electorate in states holding primaries. Yet these averages mask significant state-by-state variations, which ranged (in 2000) from 4.6 percent in Rhode Island to 42.9 percent in New Hampshire. Turnout is affected by a number of different factors, including the level of competitiveness (a close race that is still undecided will stimulate high turnout), the amount of attention the candidates and media give to a primary, the history and political culture of the state (states with a longer history of running primaries tend to attract a greater turnout), and the question whether the primary is only for presidential candidates or includes also primaries for other offices as well as statewide referendums.

Low turnout in primary elections has raised questions about how representative the primary electorate is of the party's following. In general,

the primary electorate contains a somewhat higher percentage of well educated and wealthy voters than is found in the electorate as a whole (or the electorate of each of the parties). These sociological differences do not necessarily mean, however, that the primary electorates are unrepresentative of the political views of the general electorate. On this point the prevailing view is that the electorate in primaries contains a higher percentage of ideologically minded voters than the electorate at large, as these kinds of voters tend to be among the more active and attentive part of the citizenry.

Voters in primary states must decide not only whether to turn out, but sometimes also in which party's primary they wish to participate. Primary laws vary considerably in the degree to which they permit citizens to vote in the party with which they are not normally associated—that is, a Republican or independent voting in a Democratic primary, or a Democrat or an independent voting in a Republican primary. In the states that make no real effort to restrict voting to party identifiers, cross-over voting is not unusual, and the candidates compete openly for the votes of independents and supporters from the other party.

In 2000, John McCain was competitive with George W. Bush for the Republican nomination because he was able to win the votes of many Democrats and independents in open primaries. McCain declared that the non-Republican votes showed that his campaign had broad appeal and would be successful in the general election. Candidates such as George W. Bush who were disadvantaged in open primaries sometimes seek to minimize their losses by claiming that open primaries do not indicate what party members want.

The Voting Decision Anyone who has followed the fate of candidates in the primaries is aware of the tremendous swings in popular sentiment that can take place during the primary season. A candidate leading by a wide margin in the polls at one moment can plummet and be trailing in the next. For example, in early January 1980, national polls of Republicans and independents showed Ronald Reagan leading George H. Bush by a margin of 29 points (32 percent to 6 percent); after losing the Iowa caucus, Reagan fell three points behind Bush (29 percent to 32 percent), only to pull comfortably ahead again by early March, to a 39 percent to 23 percent lead. The same thing occurred in 1988. Bush held a sizeable lead over Dole in all the polls until Dole upset him in the Iowa caucus. Dole then temporarily gained the lead, only to lose it after Bush defeated him in the New Hampshire primary.

Rapid shifts in voters' sentiments are sometimes taken as an indication of voter irrationality. But this conclusion hardly seems warranted. Although the voters' knowledge about the candidates' positions in the primary races is often vague or incorrect, it must be recalled that there is sometimes a large number of candidates who are relatively new to the voters. Volatility and shifts in public opinion may reflect the reality that people's preferences at this point are not very firm and are open to new information. Moreover, a change of preference may be an understandable and even logical consequence of the situation in primary contests in which voters are deciding among candidates from the same party. A primary election is in effect a nonpartisan race among candidates, many of whose ideological positions are often very similar. From the voters' viewpoint, therefore, the candidates may be seen as essentially interchangeable. Unable to choose on ideological grounds, voters may make up their minds on the basis of their assessment of the candidates' personal qualities or their perception of which candidate seems a likely winner. Opinions on both of these scores are subject to rapid changes, as voters get to see the candidates for the first time and as they evaluate (with the help of the media) how the candidate fared in the previous round of primaries.

General Elections for the Presidency

Each presidential election is a story unto itself, with its own issues, themes, and cast of characters. In the insert below there is a short survey of the presidential elections from 1952 to 2000 (see Box 8.2 at end of chapter). This overview should be consulted along with the general analytic points discussed below.

Turnout   The failure to vote should not always be viewed as a lapse or a sign of political disaffection. Sometimes it is a calculated act of political behavior, fully as political and rational as the choice of which candidate to support. For some voters who are firm opponents of one of the parties, the practical choice in a given election is not really between the two candidates, but between voting for one of the candidates and staying home (or, as they used to say, "going fishing").

In the latter half of the nineteenth century, when the electorate was strongly attached to political parties, elections were often decided less by people switching to vote for a candidate from the opposite party than by voters, unenthusiastic about their own party's candidate, taking the opportunity to "go fishing." The same kind of consideration takes place in modern elections. Thus in 2000 only a small percentage of black citizens considered voting for the Republican, George W. Bush. Their real decision was whether to vote for Al Gore or to express their disapproval or lack of enthusiasm for his vice-presidency by not voting at all. This kind of politically-motivated nonvoting is a frequent weapon of some groups who are committed partisans.

Assessing Incumbency   When an incumbent runs, most voters assess how that candidate has already performed and base their vote heavily on this assessment. What the candidates promise to do in the campaign may be less important than what the incumbent has already done. The voter here makes what voting analysts sometimes call a retrospective judgment, calculating like a "rational god of vengeance and of reward," whether to reelect the president or "throw the rascal out."[8] In this kind of voting, the voter is concerned in a general way with policy (how the president performed), but does not weigh the specific point by point comparison of proposed future actions. Despite the use of the term "retrospective," the voter is not merely looking backwards; the idea is that someone who has proven competent in the past is likely to perform well in the future and that someone who has proven to be a weak president should be retired, provided the alternative candidate appears at least generally qualified.

Retrospective judgments are strongly influenced by one's partisan identification. Thus Republicans are far more likely than Democrats to think that a Republican president has done a good job. Still, the assessment of how well a president has performed is made in some measure independently of party identification. For example, in the 1980 election, a large number of Democrats defected from their party because they judged that President Carter had not been an effective leader. This number far exceeded the number of Republicans in 1984 who defected to the Democratic party. The Republicans were overwhelmingly satisfied with President Reagan's performance.

Retrospective voting may operate in some sense even in campaigns in which an incumbent is not running. When vice presidents run as successors to presidents, they inevitably assume in the voters' minds much of the responsibility for the incumbent administration. A vice president cannot break completely with a president, although some vice presidents, like Al Gore in 2000, have tried to put a good deal of distance between themselves and the president. Either an incumbent president or vice president has run in 21 of the last 25 elections. Even where an incumbent president or vice president is not running, however, a partial retrospective element is present through the vehicle of the party. The nominee of the incumbent party is almost compelled to accept some responsibility for the performance of the past administration.

Retrospective voting on an incumbent is clearly quite compatible with the general idea of representative democracy. It is a form of voting that provides leeway for the president in making policy decisions rather than tying the president in advance to following specific policies. America's founders seemed to have this idea of voting in mind as the preferred standard for voting behavior. (*Federalist* 72)

Issues and Ideology   The voter's decision may also be based on the candidates' stand on major issues discussed in the campaign and on the candidates' general ideological position. For issue voting to occur, voters must be concerned about certain issues and must see differences between the candidates. Not all voters, however, think about politics explicitly in these terms, at least not all of the time. The extent of issue voting depends greatly on the situation. It increases in elections in which candidates take opposing stands on important issues, as in the elections of 1964, 1972 and 1980, and it diminishes in elections in which either the issues do not appear very important (1960 and 1976) or in which there is not much difference between the positions of the candidates on a key issue (1968).[9]

Voters may also decide how to vote on the basis of the candidates' basic ideological position and select the candidate whom they consider to be more liberal or conservative. Generally speaking, however, ideology is important not in and of itself, but in how it shapes voters' responses to specific issues: voters tend to think more in terms of specific and concrete matters than in terms of abstract categories. By knowing the ideological disposition of voters on various areas, one has a better idea of their likely responses to the issues that emerge in campaigns. For example, those who were conservative on questions of social order could be expected to respond favorably to George W. Bush's stand in the 2000 against abortion.

Character   Voters place a great deal of weight in their decisions on the candidates' qualifications and character. The presidency is a highly personalized office in which the individual attributes of the president count importantly in how well the nation is governed. Voters realize this, and they also realize that many of the critical decisions a president will face are not known in advance of an election, but emerge in response to events. For example, no one in 2000 could have known that the major decision an American president would face in the next term was how to respond to terrorist attacks. For all these reasons, voters want someone in the presidency whom they feel they can trust to do the job. This judgment, though influenced by the candidate's party and stands on the issues, is partly beyond partisanship and ideology. It rests on an assessment of the skill, experience, and maturity of the candidates.

The full set of qualities people esteem or dislike is not easy to determine. Clearly, most citizens—including those who voted against him—

had an immense amount of respect and admiration for Eisenhower, who had been a World War II hero. People admired his integrity and his strength. By contrast, many voters viewed McGovern in 1972 and Mondale in 1984 as weak and ineffective leaders. Beyond competence, therefore, people seem to be highly concerned with selecting "strong" leaders for the presidency, in realization of the kinds of decisions a president must make.

Judgments about character are highly compatible with the idea of representative government, again because they appear to leave somewhat more discretion to the elected official. The voter votes for the "person," not the position. At the same time, the importance of character, yet the difficulty in assessing it, can lead to judgments based on dangerous or trivial grounds, such as the good looks or good speaking voice of a candidate. In particular, many have worried about attempts by public relations experts to manufacture "images" of the candidates. It is a credit to the voters that these concerns play less of a role than many fear.

Partisan Identification

Partisan identification refers to the voter's own perception of the party to which he or she feels attached. It is not a legal concept, but a political reality of which politicians have long been aware and which pollsters now attempt to measure. They do so by asking which partisan position—Democratic, Republican, or independent—best describes a citizen's outlook. (The precise questions differ according to who is conducting the poll, and some polls attempt to probe the degree of partisan strength by asking whether people consider themselves to be strong or weak Democrats or Republicans, or independents that lean toward the Democratic or Republican party.)

Partisan identification is important because for many people it represents a fundamental attachment that structures or influences their view of candidates and politics. For a voter to think of himself or herself as a Democrat or Republican means that that voter, in some degree, feels connected to an ongoing "team" or organization that best represents the voter's views and interests. This identification in turn

means that each election is not viewed as an entirely new event conducted on a clean slate. Rather, the partisan approaches the campaign with a certain disposition or tendency to support a party. Thus, for the partisan, the presidential campaign is a race not simply between two individuals, but between two parties. In 2000 George W. Bush was not just an individual candidate by the name of "George W. Bush." He was the Republican party's nominee, and that fact weighed heavily with many voters.

In some cases, partisanship is almost enough by itself to determine the vote. Such "blind partisanship" was apparently quite common in the nineteenth century, as many were prepared to support one party or another virtually without concern for who were the candidates. This is still sometimes the case today, but the mechanism by which partisan identification functions is different. Partisan identification works as a kind of filter that influences how other factors, such as issues and the candidates, are judged. Thus in the case of presidential elections, most partisans do not make up their minds exclusively on the basis of party, but on how they judge the candidates, their position on the issues, and their themes. But their judgment on these matters is very much influenced by their partisan identification.

Evidence of the importance of partisanship is easily provided by comparing partisan identification and voting decisions (see Table 8.4). No one will be surprised to learn that in election after election, most Democrats vote for the Democratic candidate and most Republicans for the Republican candidate. Yet this simple fact is of great importance. The underlying ratio of partisan strength affects the probability of the outcome (the larger party has the advantage); and it influences the strategies adopted during the campaign (the majority-party candidate may often seek to emphasize the party label itself while the "minority" party candidate will emphasize other factors). Basic shifts in the electorate—realignments—are best described by looking at the underlying partisan balance.

How Partisanship Operates   It is important to consider how partisan attachments actually work to influence a voter's decision. Only by better

TABLE 8.4

Voting Patterns of Partisan Identifiers, 1960–2000

GROUP	1964 Dem.	1964 Rep.	30 Dem.	30 Rep.	Wallace	1972 Dem.	1972 Rep.	1976 Dem.	1976 Rep.	1980 Dem.	1980 Rep.	Anderson
Republicans	20	80	9	86	5	5	95	9	91	11	84	4
Democrats	87	13	74	12	14	67	33	82	18	66	26	6
Independents	56	44	31	44	25	31	69	38	57	30	54	12

	1984 Dem.	1984 Rep.	1988 Dem.	1988 Rep.	1992 Dem.	1992 Rep.	1992 Perot	1996 Dem.	1996 Rep.	1996 Perot	2000 Dem.	2000 Rep.	Nader
Republicans	3	97	5	95	10	73	17	13	80	6	8	90	1
Democrats	84	16	89	10	77	10	13	84	10	5	87	11	2
Independents	33	67	42	55	38	32	30	43	35	17	45	46	7

Sources: Gallup polls, 1960–1976; CBS/New York Times Poll, 1980–1988; New York Times/Voter Research Surveys, 1992–1996; Voter News Service, 2000.

understanding this connection can one get some idea of why and when voters may defect from their party. There are a number of ways in which voters form partisan attachments and in which these attachments in turn influence voting behavior. For some partisans, the attachment is chiefly a matter of habit and emotion, formed over a long period or inherited from their parents. Barring a major change in the fundamental issues of the political environment, they will vote for the party with which they identify. For these voters partisan identification is not entirely different from the loyalties they hold for other social groups or for their favorite team. An interview with a voter in the 1950s is typical of this kind of partisan attachment: "My father is a Democrat and I'm one by inheritance sort of. I know nothing about politics but I like the Democratic Party. . . ."[10]

For most partisans, however, the attachment is based on their commitment to certain positions or basic political orientations represented over the long run by their chosen party. Partisan attachment here is less emotional and more rational. It can be thought of as a tally of past

experience and an expression of political memory. This tally is applied to the specific election and used, consciously or unconsciously, to evaluate the other factors and to save time gathering information. In the words of another voter, "Democrats helped the farmers . . . and are more for the working class people. . . . I think the Republicans favor the richer folks."[11]

In a "typical" situation—that is, one without an especially important new issue or without especially compelling or repulsive candidates—partisan attachment in one of the two ways described above weighs very heavily on the voting decision. Democrats tend to vote Democratic and Republicans tend to vote Republican. Yet partisanship is not determinative. In every election millions of partisans deviate and vote for the candidate of the other party. For example, in 1980 Ronald Reagan won the votes of more than a quarter of all Democrats. And those who do vote for the candidate of their own party must still be won over in each campaign. Most partisans weigh the short-term factors of the campaign, and only a relatively small number of them are so committed to their party that they vote "automatically" for its nominee. Even for the most committed partisans, a radical deviation by the party from its own traditional positions will lead to defections. To take a hypothetical example, if George Wallace, a former proponent of segregation, had been nominated by the Democratic party in 1972, black voters would have voted against him, despite their partisan identification. This kind of hypothetical example—which has in fact occurred in some state and local races—shows that at the outer limit, very few voters are actually "automatic" or "habitual" partisans; they only appear so because the parties themselves remain inside an expected range. Habitual voting (and the voter practice of frequently ignoring the immediate issues of the campaign) rests on the background assumption that the parties maintain a degree of continuity and support some of the same basic positions.

Changes in Partisan Identification Partisanship is key in determining vote choice, but it should not take on supernatural status. There is some evidence that partisan identification is affected by politics. In the late 1940s, slightly more than half of those who identified with a major party were Democrats, but by the mid-1970s, the number was 70 percent. By 1984, the number had returned to slightly more than half. Scholars found that partisan identification varied in response to great swings in presidential popularity and large-scale changes state of the economy. Partisanship is relatively stable compared to other attitudinal measures, but it does seem to change in a limited and gradual fashion.

Long-Term Changes in the Nature of Partisanship Partisan attachment as a factor influencing electoral behavior has itself changed in character. Compared to forty years ago (and presumably compared to one hundred years ago) there is a smaller percentage of partisans (and of strong partisans), although this trend has been slowed or reversed in the 1980s. Some research has suggested that many independents tend to vote fairly regularly for one party or another and thus to behave like partisans. But even so these independents cannot be counted on to follow their "party" in the same way as committed partisan voters.

In addition, partisan attachment itself does not weigh as heavily as it once did in influencing the votes. Voters who identify with a party are less hesitant than they once were to vote for a candidate from the other party, no doubt because of the individualistic character of the nominating process, the decline in strength of local party organizations, and the increasing reliance on the mass media as a source of campaign information. Politics is structured far more than it once was around the candidates rather than the parties.

During the 1980s and 1990s, voting based on partisanship underwent a resurgence in presidential elections after a decline in the 1960s and 1970s.[12] Recent congressional elections tell a similar story: voters (especially in the South) have realigned their partisan congressional voting pattern to resemble their partisan presidential voting pattern. The 1990 elections had the lowest level of ticket splitting since the 1950s.

It remains nevertheless that the electorate as a whole is far less structured by partisanship than it was a half-century ago. More voters are potentially open to being won by either party (or by a third party) in any election, which has meant more volatility and greater swings from one party to another in succeeding elections. Formerly, because of the greater hold of partisanship on the electorate, each party's candidate could anticipate a solid base of support. Campaigns were directed at the relatively small portion of potential swing voters who could determine the outcome. Today, more voters are willing to switch from one party's candidate to the other from one election to the next or to move outside the parties and vote for an independent such as Ross Perot in 1992.

The fact that voters are potentially more responsive than they once were to the variable factors of each election—to the incumbent's record, the immediate issues, the character of the candidates, and moods and themes—does not necessarily mean that most voters are open to persuasion during the two-month period of what used to be considered the presidential campaign itself, that is, from labor day until election day. Voters' assessments of some of the variable

TABLE 8.5
Party Identification, 1954–2001 (Percent)

YEAR	DEMOCRAT	REPUBLICAN	INDEPENDENT
1954	46	34	20
1960	47	30	23
1964	53	25	22
1968	46	27	27
1972	43	28	29
1976	47	23	30
1980	46	24	30
1984	40	31	29
1988	43	29	28
1989	38	34	28
1992	38	35	27
1996	34	32	34
2000	39	35	27
2001	37	35	28

Source: Gallup, VNS Survey (2000), Greenberg (2001).

factors, such as the incumbent's record or the basic national mood, may be made before the traditional campaign ever begins. Still, the base of automatic support that each party can expect has diminished in comparison to the past, which makes campaigns potentially far more important, especially if one broadens the idea of the campaign to include the events that take place during the entire election year, beginning with the primaries.

The Group Basis of Partisanship and Voting

Partisan identification is the most important long-term factor that influences voting behavior. In tracing voters' partisan identifications to their origins—even if they have been inherited—we find in most cases that the partisan link has been forged in response to the voters' assessment of the party's basic stand and performance at a critical moment.

Citizens make these assessments in part as individuals according to their own personal views. But as we saw earlier, these assessments can often be traced in some way to social or group characteristics. This link "works" in two ways. First, people who share certain characteristics tend to view the world in similar terms and may be similarly affected by government policies. As a result, they may end up voting the same. Secondly, many people explicitly identify with a certain reference group and think that the group should act collectively in politics to promote and protect its interests. Politicians respond by actively seeking the endorsements of group leaders and making appeals to the voters in terms of group interests.

The group foundation of opinion and voting behavior is what enables one to pose the question "Who are Democrats and Republicans?" without responding with the unhelpful answer: Those who are Democrats or Republicans. One can say, for example, that Republicans are more likely to be businesspeople and farmers, and that Democrats are more likely to be union members and blacks (see Table 8.6). What is noteworthy today, however, is the extent to which the group basis of voting has grown weaker. In the past, it was possible to characterize a large part of party followings in terms of identifiable groups that supported or that were strongly weighted in

Table 8.6
Group Foundation of Vote for President in 2000

Percent of Total Vote			Democrat Gore	Republican Bush	Green Nader
48	Gender	Men	43	52	3
52		Women	54	42	2
81	Race	White	43	53	3
10		Black	90	8	1
7		Hispanic/Latino	63	33	3
2		Asian	55	41	3
2		Other	57	37	4
17	Age	18-29	48	45	5
33		30-44	48	48	2
28		45-59	48	48	2
22		60+	51	46	2
5	Education	No high school	59	38	1
21		High school graduate	48	48	1
32		Some college	46	50	3
24		College graduate	46	50	3
18		Postgraduate studies	53	42	4
23	Region	East	57	39	3
26		Midwest	48	49	2
30		South	43	54	1
21		West	50	43	5
65	Marital status	Married	44	52	2
35		Single	57	37	4
7	Income in $	Under 15,000	57	36	5
16		15.000-30,000	54	40	3
25		30,000-50,000	50	46	3
25		50,000-75,000	47	50	2
13		75,000-100,000	46	51	2
15		Over 100,000	43	53	3

Table 8.6 (cont.)

54	Religion	Protestant	43	55	2
27		Catholic	50	46	2
4		Jewish	79	18	1
6		Other	63	27	7
10		None	61	28	9
14	Frequency of attendance at religious services	More than once a week	36	62	1
28		Once a week	41	56	2
14		A few times a month	51	45	2
28		A few times a year	55	41	3
14		Never	62	29	6

Source: Voter News Service Exit Poll

favor of each party. Of course, it was never the case that everyone in any group voted exactly the same way. Still, one could characterize the Democratic coalition of the 1940s as consisting of labor union workers, southerners (whites), Catholics, and Jews. Today, by contrast, few identifiable groups can be considered safe members of a party, and more importantly the bulk of each party's support cannot be characterized in terms of distinct groups. Both parties end up getting most of their votes from middle-class voters.

Having said all this, however, the group basis of voting remains important and figures prominently in the formation of political strategies. Not only do strategists think in terms of the traditional grouping, but they are always sensitive to the emergence of "new" groups that show signs of distinct political behavior. Thus in the last two decades, religious fundamentalists became an important group, and also men and women began to display somewhat different voting patterns. In the following section we shall look briefly at the effects of ethnicity, race, religion, region, and gender on voting behavior.

Ethnicity

In the last century, voting behavior was strongly influenced by ethnic group ties based on European national origins, especially Irish, Italian, and German. Today, these groups are much less pronounced and acquire significance in national politics only when an ethnic-group member is a candidate (as was the case, for example, with Michael Dukakis as an individual of Greek origins).

One of the few ethnic groups of major political significance today are Hispanics. The Hispanic population in the United States has been growing rapidly for the past 30 years. Latinos now make up 12.5 percent of the population and are the nation's fastest growing racial or ethnic group.[13] The significance of Hispanic voting is all the greater because of its location: Hispanic voters today are concentrated in the largest states (such as California, Texas, Florida, and New York) and in some of the fastest growing states (Colorado and Arizona). Because the largest states weigh so heavily in the electoral college, and because Hispanic voters can be decisive in the outcome in these states, the Hispanic vote is crucial to the fate of the two parties, especially in presidential elections.

Hispanics constitute not one, but several different communities which do not necessarily vote the same. They may come from Mexico (mostly in the Southwest and Illinois), Puerto Rico (primarily in New York and New Jersey), and Cuba (largely in Florida). Salvadorans, Colombians, and Dominicans are among the other significant Hispanic groups.

The 2000 election was a turning point in Hispanic electoral history as both presidential candidates actively courted Hispanic voters, and Hispanic turnout was greater than in past elections. In 2000, Al Gore won 62 percent of the Hispanic vote, while Bush won 35 percent, which was less than his advisors had hoped but more than the previous Republican candidate, Bob Dole, had won. Further, Bush's one point advantage among Hispanics in Florida, largely thanks to traditionally Republican Cuban-Americans, was decisive in the outcome of the election. Both parties have made courting Hispanics a top priority because a large gain for one party among Hispanic voters would have momentous consequences for election outcomes. But as with other immigrant groups, the degree of group voting among Hispanics may begin to recede the longer they live in the United States.

Race

Race has been one of the key reference groups in American politics. It has been important for large numbers of white voters (who have seen their interest in terms of race) and for Indians, Asian groups, and blacks. Obviously, the racial division that has been most significant and evident in American history is that between whites and blacks. The distinct historical experience of black voters has led to a very distinct pattern of voting behavior that has its roots in issues of civil rights, but that extends beyond to identifiable views in a number of different areas.

Up until the New Deal, blacks were overwhelmingly Republican because of the historic commitment of the Republican party to racial equality. The Democratic party in the South was almost exclusively a white and a segregationist party. After the New Deal, blacks outside the South began to move into the Democratic party because of the party's position on economic and social welfare issues. A major turning point came in the 1960s, after President Johnson and the majority of Democrats led the way in promoting major civil rights legislation, which many Republicans opposed. Thus in 1960, 44 percent of the black population identified themselves as Democratic, whereas by 1968 the number jumped to 85 percent. Since the 1960s, most of the black leadership in the nation has identified with the Democratic party, and blacks today are the most solid supporters of the Democratic party of any identifiable group in the population. Democratic candidates for the presidency since 1980 have received between a quarter to a sixth of all their votes from black citizens.

Republicans in recent years have made attempts to gain inroads among black voters. Their idea has been that the views of many citizens in the black community are more compatible with the Republican than the Democratic party, but that few vote Republican because of the party's poor image among black citizens. Certain Republican political leaders such as Jack Kemp have taken to spreading the GOP's message. Thus far this effort has yielded only modest results, but in the 1990s Republicans elected two black members to the House of Representatives, Gary Franks of Connecticut and J. C. Watts of Oklahoma, although Franks was defeated in 1996. This compares to Democratic representation which in 2002 included 36 black members of the House.

Another rapidly growing demographic group is Americans of Asian Pacific origin. In 2000, this group comprised 4.8 percent of the population; but in California, the nation's most populous state, the figure was 12 percent. Asians, like Hispanics, do not form a unified voting block. Japanese Americans have been strongly identified with the Democratic Party, while those of Korean and South Vietnamese origin have tended to vote Republican. Chinese Americans have split roughly along the lines of the rest of electorate.

Religion

Religious affiliation has long been an important reference group for American society, but the religious cleavages have varied over time with changing economic and political conditions. In the nineteenth century, for example, there were severe strains between native Protestants and Catholics over such issues as parochial education, immigration policy, and Prohibition. Because of the hostility directed against them, Catholics came to think of themselves as a distinct and unified political group. In addition, the Catholic population in the nineteenth century tended to be concentrated in the great urban centers of the East and Midwest, where they were recruited in large numbers into the Democratic Party. Throughout the nineteenth century and, in fact, well into this century, religion was a strong "predictor" of party affiliation. The great majority of Catholics were Democrats, while the larger part of northern Protestants were Republicans.

With the decline of religious conflict between Catholics and Protestants in this century and with the changing economic status of Catholics (from predominantly bluecollar to whitecollar) differences between the groups on ideology and on most specific issues have greatly diminished. So too has the traditional division in party voting; in both 1972 and 1980, a majority of Catholics voted for the Republican candidate for the presidency, a result that would have been inconceivable a half century earlier. It remains true that Catholics overall vote somewhat less Republican than Protestants, especially Catholics who are working class and in labor unions. Indeed, 53 percent of American Catholics supported Bill Clinton in 1996, considerably exceeding the support given to him by white Protestants. This occurred despite the Catholic hierarchy's criticism of Clinton's support for legal abortion. But in general, the differences in voting behavior between Protestants and Catholics are not very great and have little to do with disputes over religious dogma.

Today the chief division within the Christian community relevant to voting behavior is found less between Catholics and Protestants in general than between religious traditionalists on the one hand and the secular on the other. The 1990s saw the rise of the Christian Coalition and other "religious right" groups. Such organizations receive most of their support from white fundamentalist Protestants, although they have

sought to reach out to blacks, Catholics, and Jews. Religious conservatives now form one of the Republican Party's most loyal constituencies: about two-thirds of "born-again" voters voted for Bob Dole in 1996 and an even higher percentage supported GOP congressional candidates. In 2000, exit polls showed Bush won 63 percent of the vote from white Protestants but only 47 percent of the Catholic vote. Bush's total is even higher among more religiously committed white Protestants.

The Republican emphasis on traditional values may have a special appeal to religious voters. George W. Bush courted religious groups in the primary contest, but tempered religious language during the general election campaign. Even so, Bush did substantially better than Gore among white, traditionally religious Protestants.

American Jews, mindful of the persecution and genocide of Jews in Europe as well as many experiences of discrimination in America, have had a long tradition of identification with liberalism and First Amendment freedoms. Like Catholics and blacks, Jews strongly supported the Democratic Party after the New Deal. This liberalism stretched across economic lines. Even as Jews became wealthier, their support for the Democratic Party remained substantially intact. In the 2000 presidential campaign, Al Gore named Joseph Lieberman, an Orthodox Jew, as his running mate and won more than three-quarters of the Jewish vote.

Regionalism

Just as a nation as a whole may have a particular political culture formed by its history, institutions, economy, and environment, so, also, to a much lesser extent can its regions develop subcultures more or less in harmony with the major beliefs of the national political culture. As a large continental nation, the United States has had a long history of sectional differences, based in part on the different economic activities of each section and in part on their different traditions, lifestyles, and attitudes.

Foremost, of course, has been the regional conflict between the North and South. Following the Civil War, southern whites, rejecting the hated Republican Party, made common cause with the Democratic Party, and the region became virtually a one-party area until the 1950s. For most of this period, the Democratic Party was more supportive of southern whites on the key issue of retaining segregation and white supremacy in the South. As the northern wing of the Democratic Party became more liberal on the race question, southern whites in the 1950s began to question their Democratic allegiance. By the 1970s, the whole context of southern politics had changed. The race issue had lost much of its significance in the South, which meant that the traditional reason that had kept southern whites within the Democratic Party had faded and if anything began to work in favor of the Republican Party. Many southern whites, who in general tend to be more conservative on cultural issues and "individualistic" on economic issues, began to change their voting behavior.

The move of many white southerners from the Democratic Party to the Republican Party is one of the most dramatic changes in 20th century voting behavior. Beginning in the 1960s, white southerners have given a majority of their votes in every presidential election to the Republican candidate—usually at a higher rate than white voters in the rest of the country. (Black voters in the South, by contrast, have voted overwhelmingly for the Democrats.)

This realignment in southern politics began in presidential voting, but gradually reached other levels of government. Since the mid-1960s, Republicans have made important inroads in congressional elections. In 1960, there were no Republican Senators from the eleven former Confederate states, and only 7 percent of the House members from that region were Republicans. By the mid-1990s, the Republican trend had permeated every level of southern politics. More than two-thirds of senators and about 60 percent of House members were Republicans. Most southern states had Republican governors, and the party began to gain power in the statehouses: after the 1996 election, Republicans had control of both houses of the Florida legislature, the first time this had happened in any southern state since Reconstruction.

Another regional divide is between the western states—dubbed the "sunbelt"—and the midwestern and northeastern states—dubbed the "frost belt." The western states have grown at a faster rate and many have added seats in Congress as their population grows, while the midwest and northeast have lost seats. Many of the western states tend to be more economically individualistic in their political values.

Gender

At the turn of the century, when it seemed likely that women would win the right to vote, politicians and analysts began to wonder how women would vote. One school of thought foresaw no major differences between male and female voters; another predicted very significant differences. According to the latter view, women would change the character of the political system. For some, this tendency was construed as dangerous to the nation's capacity to defend itself. For others, there was the optimistic belief that women's voting would improve protection for the family, bring a greater political concern for poverty, and diminish political pressures to go to war.

Initially, women voted at a much lower rate than men, almost certainly because cultural norms in many areas frowned on female participation in politics. As attitudes changed and a new generation of women attained voting age, the difference began to diminish and today men and women vote at about the same rate. As for voting behavior, we cannot say with any confidence whether women in the period after achieving suffrage voted differently than men. When scientific polls began to be conducted in the 1950s, it was discovered that there was little if any difference in the voting patterns of men and women. This held true throughout the 1960s, but in the 1970s analysts began to note a growing divergence between men and women in voting and in their opinions on key issues. This difference became known as the "gender gap." A higher percentage of women than men have cast their votes for the Democratic candidate in every presidential race since 1980.

Still, the character of the gender gap has often been misunderstood. Women are more likely to vote for a Democratic presidential candidate than men, but women have not always given the Democratic candidates a plurality. The majority of women and men have favored the same candidates, only in different degrees. For example, in 1988, both women and men favored George Bush over Michael Dukakis. Men voted for Bush by 57% to 41%; while women backed him by only 50% to 49%. But in 1996 for the first time men and women had pluralities on different sides. Bill Clinton won among women by 54%–38%, while Bob Dole carried men by 44%–43%. According to the 2000 VNS polls, Gore won 54 percent of the female vote and 42 percent of the male vote, a record 12 point "gender gap."

Since 1980 men and women seem to differ in their voting patterns, but there appears to be a gap within the gender gap. Married women tend to vote Republican, while single women tend to vote Democratic.

Many reasons were cited for this disparity. Specific issues related to women, such as the candidates' stand on abortion, explain part of the difference. But a greater part derives from marginal differences in general policy orientations. Women evidenced a distinctly more "protective" view, favoring a stronger welfare state and—going back to foreign policy issues of the last decade—a less confrontational posture by the government in world affairs.[14] Men are more prone to a view that endorses risk, both in domestic and international affairs. In surveys, men and women disagreed on what were the most important issues facing the nation: men were more likely to cite foreign policy, taxes and the deficit, while women focused more on Medicare and education. Gender, then, does have a marginal influence on political behavior. Whether this influence is the result of nature or nurture (environment), is a matter on which analysts of voting behavior can only speculate.

Political Participation

Voting is the most common form of participation. Other forms of participation are rarer, but activities such as organizing a political party or participating in a boycott are important ways to attain political goods. Taking the average of surveys carried out between 1973 and 1990, one in three citizens say they had attempted to persuade someone during the most recent presiden-

President Bill Clinton's 1996 re-election depended heavily on women voters, who gave him a large plurality; polls showed that if only men had voted, Bob Dole would have won. (Courtesy of the University Journal, University of Virginia. Used with permission)

tial campaign; one in ten say they have given money to a party or candidate; 8 percent say they attended a rally or political meeting, and 4 percent report that they worked on a political campaign. Outside of voting, the majority of Americans avoid political participation.

Providing accurate evidence of participation is difficult. Citizens may overstate their level of participation; and analysts may define it differently. Is participation defined as formal membership in an organization? Does simply writing a check or being on a mailing list count? What about non-political organizations such as soccer leagues?

Political participation must be considered not only in terms of its immediate impact on the conduct of national politics, but also in terms of its long-term effect on what we have called political virtue or citizenship. Political participation is a human activity that influences and changes human beings, providing them with certain qualities necessary for the well-being of a free society. People who participate in politics learn the art of working with others, of forming groups, and of considering and acting on the public good. Viewed in these terms, the act of voting is less important than other forms of participation that involve citizens in a more sustained way. When citizens serve on juries, take part in a local party caucus, or organize to change local school policies, they are engaging in activities that may give them a new perspective on politics and new skills as citizens. Voting, by contrast, is a solitary act that takes place quickly (if the voting machines are operating) behind a closed curtain.

Constitutional Perspectives on Participation

The authors of the Constitution knew they were creating a system that involved greater citizen participation for history's largest democratic nation. At the same time, they spoke infrequently during the Convention of political participation beyond the realm of voting. This inattention was the result of the task at hand, which was to create the institutions of a national government. Given the communications system of the time and the distance of government from the citizens, regular citizen participation, apart from voting, was not considered practical, nor, for those worried about majority tyranny, desirable.

Yet many of the founders emphasized the importance of citizen participation at the local level. This theme was of particular concern to some of the Anti-Federalists, who argued that republics could survive only if the citizens were public-spirited. Republics required direct political participation by the citizens, which is what led some Anti-Federalists to oppose any form of national government. Although the Anti-Federalists' opposition to a national government was rejected, their ideas were partly incorporated in the Constitution through their insistence on a strong role for state and local governments. Furthermore, encouraging political participation as an element of good citizenship became a matter of concern for many American thinkers.

Tocqueville It was the French political theorist Alexis de Tocqueville, however, who offered the most comprehensive theoretical treatment of the importance of political participation in a modern representative democracy. In his book *Democracy in America*, Tocqueville reflected on his observations of political participation in the United States, especially in New England. While Tocqueville emphasized the importance of representation for national institutions, he also stressed the need for extensive citizen participation at the local level. Most of this participation, he held, would involve issues of local concern. But the habits and talents citizens developed in local politics would also be used to form national associations, such as parties and interest groups. Tocqueville therefore clearly envisioned the formation of new kinds of participatory links between citizens and the national government.

At the center of Tocqueville's analysis was a very simple insight: participation in politics requires certain skills, habits, and attitudes that are not automatically forthcoming and that are therefore easily lost. Citizens must "practice" participation in order to be capable of participating effectively. Tocqueville discussed a number of different ideas and institutional mechanisms to encourage participation—decentralization of decision making (even at the expense of administrative efficiency), freedom of association, and an emphasis on the performance of citizens' duties, such as serving on juries. Citizens would learn to participate mostly in civic associations and local governments: "Local institutions are to liberty what primary schools are to science; they put it within the people's reach; they teach people to appreciate its peaceful enjoyment and accustom them to make use of it."[15]

Participation, Tocqueville believed, would be helpful to citizens, first, because it would integrate them into the community, overcoming what today is sometimes called "alienation"; and, second, because it would provide them the know-how to join together to promote their interests and ultimately to defend their liberties. Tocqueville never denied the importance of voting as a way of maintaining a free regime. To sustain the subtle mechanisms needed for liberty, he placed an equal emphasis on the development of citizens' capacity to organize and create associations. It was thus not just the quantity of participation that counted, but its character and quality.

Contemporary Views While American political thought in the 20th century stressed the need for basic political rights such as the right to vote, it tended until recently to ignore some of the deeper issues and themes connected with political participation. Part of the reason for this neglect was that some of the most vocal defenders in the 1950s and 1960s of states rights and federalism were abusing local power to deny civil and political rights to minorities. Frequently, moreover, participation in local communities has in reality been limited to certain groups. In some cases, local leaders resembling the fictitious Boss Hogg immortalized in the television show "The Dukes of Hazzard" could rule local fiefdoms and bar women, racial, religious, and other minorities from full participation.

As a result, many people in the 1960s turned to the federal government (and often to the judicial branch) to reform the localities. As the Supreme Court in this period produced decisions that protected substantial rights that were denied or threatened, the idea of strong popular participation in local decision making was often discounted, and many incentives for participation by citizens at the local level diminished.

Two movements in this century—progressivism and the reform movement of the 1970s—have made participation a major theme. Yet scholars are divided over whether these movements actually served to increase important kinds of participation. Progressivism took the power to nominate most elected officials from party organizations and vested it in the primary elections. In so doing, it allowed more citizens to take part in the nominating decision by the act of voting, but it severely reduced the power of political parties as intermediary organizations in which meaningful and ongoing participation takes place. In the case of the party reforms in the 1980s, the avowed goal again was to increase participation. While some of the changes have had this effect, others served again to diminish the role of party organizations and to substitute the minimal function of expressing a preference for a national candidate for the much more meaningful function of interacting in local party organizations. According to one analyst, "When these reforms are reexamined for their impact on intermediary organizations, the logical out-

Table 8.7
Trends in Political and Community Participation

	Relative change 1973-74 to 1993-94
Served as an officer of some club or organization	-42%
Worked for a political party	-42%
Served on a committee for a local organization	-39%
Attended a public meeting on town or school affairs	-35%
Attended a political rally or speech	-34%
Participated in at least one of these twelve activities	-25%
Made a speech	-24%
Wrote a congressman or senator	-23%
Signed a petition	-22%
Was a member of a "better government" group	-19%
Held or ran for political office	-16%
Wrote a letter to the paper	-14%
Wrote an article for a magazine or newspaper	-10%

Source: Robert D. Putnam, *Bowling Alone* (New York: Simon & Schuster, 2000), 45 and Roper Social and Political Trends surveys, 1973-1994

come of each appears to be not a strengthening of the bonds between citizens and their government, but a weakening of those bonds."[16]

Assessing the impact of institutional changes on political participation is difficult, especially as people are often unclear about what they mean when they speak of participation. Participation can refer to the broadest and most common activity (the act of voting), or it can refer to more sustained kinds of involvement in intermediary organizations. In the late 20th century, political reformers discovered that sometimes the arrangements that support greater mass participation by voting such as the rise of the candidate-centered campaign can weaken viable intermediary organizations. Mass democracy is no substitute for the richer and more complex forms of participatory politics that represent the views of citizens, if not equally, then certainly with depth and vigor.

Participation Resources

As with voter turnout, the rate of participation varies among groups. One neighborhood may be able to block a power plant's move into their community while another may not even be organized enough to contemplate collective action. Why such differences in participation? One answer is that it has costs. It requires skills and takes time and money. Factors such as family income, education, skill at organizing and communicating, and the belief that political action can make a difference explain why some groups participate more than others.[17] Local civic groups and churches that Tocqueville observed can act as "schools" to train people how to organize effectively.

Social Capital

In the 1990s, Robert Putnam expanded the notion of resources to include social capital, which refers to social connections, habits, norms, and interpersonal trust.[18] Sending a check to the Sierra Club, an environmental protection interest group in Washington D.C., is an act of political participation but it does not create social capital. Political participation through an urban political machine or a grassroots movement does, however. Joining a bowling league or the Lions club also creates social capital, even though these are not explicitly political acts. Following Tocqueville, Putnam believes that social capital developed through participation in associations is an important resource in political action because it binds people together and takes individuals beyond their private concerns.

Putnam found that civic engagement, which leads to the development of social capital, has declined over the past three decades. Membership in the PTA, the League of Women Voters, social clubs, bowling leagues, and all manner of civic groups have declined, despite rising education levels. Why are more people "bowling alone"? Putnam tells us that the "culprit is television."[19] Declining civic engagement began in the 1950s with the advent of television. In 1950 only 10 percent of American homes had a television, but by the end of the decade 90 percent did. Today, the average American watches three to four hours of television a day, and the more individuals watch television, the less they participate in civic groups or feel a sense of social trust.

Putnam's thesis presents starling data about the decline in civic participation, but it has not gone without criticism. There are other factors, some of which Putnam presents, that could lead to a decline in civic participation. Increased pressures of time and money, mobility and suburbanization, the changing role of women, and the rise of the welfare state could all contribute to a decline in individual's ability or desire to participate in community groups. Another question is whether there has been a decline in participation or just a change in the types of organizations people participate in. All male clubs where men wear funny hats and engage in secret handshakes may have fallen out of favor, but youth soccer leagues and book groups have exploded in popularity, and the level of participation in these new types of associations is not easily measured. Furthermore, some civic associations are harmful to democracy—the Ku Klux Klan and street gangs have high levels of social capital, but not the kind Putnam wants. Finally, even if Putnam is right that television is the main culprit in the decline of civic engagement, it is not clear what the proper remedy would be.

If Putnam's thesis is not the last word on social capital and political participation, then at least he has sparked a new round of debate about important democratic questions that have occupied American thinkers for generations.

Conclusion

The more one participates in politics, first by voting and then by more extensive activities, the more influence one is likely to have on the political system. Generally speaking, the voter has more influence than the nonvoter; and the campaign volunteer, whose assistance candidates need in all sorts of ways, will count more than the "average" voter. Political participation thus has the effect of skewing the policy process from what it would be under the hypothetical situation in which everyone participated equally. The paradoxical result is that participation is not "democratic," if by democratic one means the perfectly equal influence of all citizens on the politics of the nation. Those who participate are more equal than others.

The effects introduced by participation are difficult to determine. Educated people from the upper middle class may work for the interests of people from other classes. Probably, however, we can say that the effect of the greater influence by activists is to provide somewhat greater protection for upper-middle-class values and programs and to make our politics somewhat more ideological than it otherwise would be. Although there are institutional changes that might alter the effects of participation by regulating the character of permissible participation (as in the case of limitations on campaign contributions), many of the "biases" of participation are a product of a free society. To do away with such biases would require either forcing all people to participate in certain ways or preventing people from participating as much as they like. Enacting such measures in any extreme form seems unlikely.

In the final analysis, there is an inevitable tension between the freedom to participate and the goal of equality understood as each person's preferences counting exactly as much as another's. It is undeniable that some begin with more resources to participate, whether of time, money, or civic skills; in addition, some people simply want to participate more than others. Without imposing severe restraints, participation in a free society may lead to certain biases that favor some groups and tendencies within the population over others. Although rates of voting and participation do skew the system somewhat, it is not enough to negate the powerful majoritarian influence of presidential elections. A more serious question may involve sources of campaign funding for other elections in the United States.

Yet to dwell on the "problems" of participation at a certain point becomes perverse. An excessive concern with the tension between equality of influence and the freedom to participate obscures the common benefit of civic engagement. One of the most interesting debates in political science today is over the causes of an apparent simultaneous decline in voter turnout and participation in political and civic associations in the last half for the twentieth century. The debate is important because participation, even when all do not participate equally, serves to protect the liberty of the nation's citizenry.

Chapter 8 Notes

1. Russell J. Dalton, *Citizen Politics: Public Opinion and Political Parties in Advanced Industrial Democracies*, 2nd ed. (Chatham, NJ.: Chatham House, 1996).
2. Ronald Inglehart, *Culture Shift in Advanced Industrial Society* (Princeton: Princeton University Press, 1990).
3. Benjamin Highton and Raymond E. Wolfinger, "Estimating the Effects of the National Voter Registration Act of 1993," *Political Behavior* 20: 79-104. Glenn E. Mitchell and Christopher Wlezien, "The Impact of Legal Constraints on Voter Registration, Turnout, and the Composition of the American Electorate," *Political Behavior* 17:179-202.
4. Patricia L. Southwell and Justin I. Burchett, "The Effect of All-Mail Elections on Voter Turnout," *American Politics Quarterly*, vol 28, 2000, pp. 72-79.
5. For an analysis of the impact of the Australian ballot on turnout see Jac C. Heckelman, "Revisiting the Relationship between Secret Ballots and Turnout: A New Test of Two Legal-Institutional Theories," *American Politics Quarterly*, vol. 28, pp. 194-215.
6. Richard Jensen, *The Winning of the Midwest: Social and Political Conflict, 1888–1896*, University of Chicago Press, Chicago, 1971.
7. Richard G. Niemi and Herbert F. Weisberg, "Why Is Voter Turnout Low (And Why Is It Declining)?" Controversies in Voting Behavior, 4th ed (Washington DC: CQ Press, 2001) p. 33. Also see Steven Finkel and Paul Freedman, "The Half-Hearted Rise: Voter Turnout in the 2000 Election," Paper for the Conference on Assessing the Vitality of Electoral Democracy in the United States: The 2000 Presidential Election, Columbus, Ohio, March 9, 2002.
8. V. O. Key, Jr., *Politics, Parties, and Pressure Groups*, 5th ed. (New York: Thomas Y. Crowell, 1964), p. 568.

9. Morris P. Fiorina, *Retrospective Voting in American National Elections* (New Haven, Conn.: Yale University Press), 1981.

10. Angus Campbell et al., *The American Voter* (New York: Wiley, 1960), p. 238.

11. Angus Campbell et al., *The American Voter*, p. 136.

12. Larry M. Bartels, "Partisanship and Voting Behavior, 1952-1996," *American Journal of Political Science* vol. 44, pp. 35-50.

13. U.S. Census Bureau, "The Hispanic Population: 2000 Census Brief," May 2001.

14. See Gerald M. Pomper, "The Presidential Election" in Gerald M. Pomper et al., *The Election of 1996.* (Chatham, NJ: Chatham House Publishers, 1997) pp. 184–85. Kathleen Frankovic, "Sex and Politics: New Alignments, Old Issues," PS, vol. 15, no. 3, 1982. Karen Kaufmann and J.R. Petrocik, "The Changing Politics of American Men: Understanding the Sources of the Gender Gap," *American Journal of Political Science*, vol. 43, 1999.

15. Alexis de Tocqueville, *Democracy in America*, J. P. Mayer, ed. (Garden City, N.Y.: Doubleday, 1968), p. 63.

16. Byron E. Shafer, "Reform and Alienation: The Decline of Intermediation in the Politics of Presidential Selection," *Journal of Law and Politics*, vol. 1, no. 1, 1983.

17. Steven J. Rosenstone and John Mark Hansen, *Mobilization, Participation, and Democracy in America* (New York: Macmillan), 1993. Donald Kinder, "Opinion and Action in the Realm of Politics," in The Handbook of Social Psychology II, 4th ed, editors Daniel T. Gilbert, Susan T. Fiske, and Gardner Lindzey, (London: Oxford University Press), pp. 826-827.

18. Robert D. Putnam, "Tuning In, Tuning Out: The Strange Disappearance of Social Capital in America," *Controversies in Voting Behavior* 4th ed. (Washington D.C.: CQ Press, 2001), p. 39. Robert D. Putnam, Bowling Alone (New York: Simon & Schuster, 2000).

19. Putnam, "Tuning In, Tuning Out: The Strange Disappearance of Social Capital in America," p. 61.

BOX 8.2

A Survey of Presidential Elections, 1952–2000

1952 In their effort to recapture the presidency after twenty years of Democratic rule, the Republicans nominated former General Dwight Eisenhower, whose personal popularity was such that many Democrats had earlier sought Eisenhower out to be the candidate of their party. Eisenhower and the Republicans ran against the record of the incumbent party, blasting it alternately for mistakes made in the Korean war, the infiltration of communists into the government, and the corruption of certain high officials. These issues, and the general theme of an incompetent administration which they evoke, were summed up by the slogan "Korea, Communism, and Corruption." These attacks on the Truman administration were as important as Eisenhower's great personal popularity, which exceeded that of any politician of his day. Adlai Stevenson, the well-spoken governor of Illinois, became the Democratic nominee and sought to rally Democrats to their traditional party loyalty on the themes of the New Deal and Fair Deal. Partisan considerations were important, but a sufficient number of Democrats and independents went for Eisenhower to give him a comfortable measure of victory. The Republican campaign buttons in effect summed up what was most important: I LIKE IKE.

1956 The 1956 election was a repeat of the 1952 election, with Stevenson challenging Eisenhower as the incumbent. This campaign was one of the most uninspiring of recent times. Stevenson attempted to find fault with Eisenhower's record, with little success, and sought again to rally the traditional Democratic majority, and nearly all his votes came from Democrats. Although the president's record was not viewed as great or inspiring, it was nevertheless sufficiently creditable to allow independents and some Democrats to vote their personal preference for Eisenhower as a candidate.

1960 The Democrats chose Senator John F. Kennedy, the first Catholic to be nominated since Al Smith in 1928. The Republicans went with their vice president, Richard Nixon. Few major issues divided the candidates during the election, though the basic principles of the two men reflected the positions of their parties, with Kennedy more sympathetic to federal solutions to problems like health and education, and Nixon more reluctant to endorse federal programs. Kennedy, while not attacking Eisenhower directly nonetheless ran against the record of the Republican administration and appealed very strongly to the theme of "getting the country moving again." His rhetoric emphasized the vague idea of a "new frontier," which was a general appeal to a more active and progressive federal government. Nixon emphasized his personal experience (and Kennedy's inexperience), in addition to defending the Republican record. Nixon benefited from this appeal, but Kennedy, with the help of his running mate, Lyndon Johnson of Texas, was able to hold the support of enough traditional Democrats to win the election. The religious issue, though not debated by the candidates, played a significant role in voters' decisions. Kennedy did better than might otherwise have been expected among Catholic voters, and Nixon received somewhat more support from Protestants. The election was extremely close, with Kennedy winning by the narrowest of margins.

1964 The Democrats nominated the incumbent, Lyndon Johnson, who assumed the presidency after the assassination of President Kennedy in 1963. The Republican nominee was Senator Barry Goldwater, who was one of the most outspoken conservatives in the party. The ideological choice presented to the American people was more sharply focused than at any time since 1936, and it is not surprising that issues were important to voters. Goldwater argued that the American people had become disillusioned with the policies of Democratic liberalism and that the electorate was prepared to realign in support of the principles of conservatism.

The election, however, proved differently. Not only did Goldwater fail to attract the support of Democrats and independents, but he actually lost the backing of many Republicans. Indeed, there is evidence to suggest that a substantial number of Republicans began to reconsider their allegiance to the party, and certainly Goldwater hastened the exit of the small but still significant percentage of blacks who had been Republican adherents. Goldwater did, however, manage to convert some Democrats to the Republican side in the deep south, which was the only area of the country where he did better than Nixon had done in 1960. Johnson ran on his record and on the Kennedy legacy,

Box 8.2 (cont.)

Barry Goldwater/Lyndon Johnson (Goldwater photo provided by the Library of Congress.)

which he claimed to be carrying through. With the nation enjoying unprecedented prosperity, and with the passage of much new legislation, Johnson defeated Goldwater in a landslide.

1968 The 1968 election came in the midst of the Vietnamese war and after a series of racial riots that rocked the country. Divisions in the nation were much greater than usual, and political tensions ran high. In addition to the major party nominees, Nixon for the Republicans and Vice President Humphrey for the Democrats, there was a strong third-party challenge headed by George Wallace from Alabama. Wallace attacked the intrusion of the federal government into state and local affairs and decried the growing lawlessness of American society. His campaign fed on a reaction to the new social programs of the "Great Society"—Lyndon Johnson's extension of Democratic liberal policies—and on the frustrations of the Vietnamese war. Voters for Wallace were obviously not motivated by party attachment, as his party was a new one, but were activated by their response to the issues and themes of his campaign.

Humphrey led a divided Democratic party, trying in vain to defend Johnson's policies while putting enough distance between himself and Johnson to offer some kind of alternative. Nixon ran as the experienced statesman against the "failures" of the Johnson years and on the premise that new approaches to our foreign and domestic challenges were required. Nixon benefited in the race from the public's disenchantment with the Johnson record on the Vietnamese war, and from a growing reaction among Americans to aspects of the new phase of liberalism of the Democratic years.

The election raised a set of issues different from the standard economic issues of the New Deal era. These issues cut against the Democratic nominee, causing defections to Wallace and Nixon, but they did not provoke a permanent realignment in favor of the Republicans. Indeed, this election was nearly as close as the 1960 contest between Kennedy and Nixon.

1972 Repeating the Republicans' mistake of 1964, the Democrats nominated a candidate from the extreme of their party, the very liberal Senator George McGovern. McGovern based his campaign on opposition to the Vietnamese war, which he promised to conclude by a unilateral American withdrawal, and on a new plan for income redistribution. McGovern quickly became associated with elements who had supported his candidacy from the beginning of the primary season and who were viewed by many voters as radical. For those who have an interest in slogans, opponents of McGovern invented the "three A's"—"Acid, Amnesty, and Abortion"—which were depicted to be his campaign stand. An obvious exaggeration, this slogan nonetheless captured the picture many carried of McGovern as an extremist. His political positions were only part of the problem, however. Coupled with this were the doubts people had about McGovern's capacity as a leader. These were reinforced by his ill-fated choice of Senator Thomas Eagleton as his vice presidential nominee, which had to be

Box 8.2 (cont.)

reversed after Eagleton's medical record became known. McGovern's personal credibility suffered immensely, and voters generally came to doubt his competence to be president.

President Nixon ran on his record, on his attempt to project statesmanlike qualities (especially in foreign affairs), and on his pledge to end quickly American involvement in the war on "honorable" terms. The race ended in a landslide victory for President Nixon, and talk again surfaced about a new realignment in American politics. Such talk proved premature, however. Masses of Democratic voters turned against their own nominee and were no doubt also expressing concern against the "big government" programs bequeathed by the Democratic party. They were not, however, willing to switch parties, and any sentiments they may have had along these lines quickly changed with the revelations of Watergate, which discredited Nixon as a leader and shortly forced his resignation.

1976 The Democratic nominee, Jimmy Carter, faced the Republican incumbent, Gerald Ford, who had assumed the presidency after Nixon's resignation in 1974. Carter ran a campaign quite different from that of any of his Democratic predecessors. While professing to be a liberal, he nonetheless ran against the "big government" that liberalism had created. He promised to create a more efficient national government and directed much of his rhetoric against the waste and mismanagement of federal programs. Carter also ran against the economic record of the Ford years, blasting the administration for creating high unemployment and inflation. Perhaps the central element of the Carter appeal, however, was thematic. Carter promised truthfulness in government and proclaimed constantly his own honesty and integrity. This combined thematic and character appeal fell upon very sympathetic ears after the many revelations of corruption and wrongdoing in the Nixon administration. President Ford himself was not implicated in any of these activities, but inevitably had to take some of the responsibility for his party. Moreover, by pardoning former President Nixon, Ford opened himself to charges of having engaged in a deal for the presidency and of protecting someone who deserved criminal punishment.

Carter did manage to attract enough support among Democratic identifiers to gain a narrow victory, but by no means was the edifice of the old Democratic coalition solidly reconstructed. Indeed, Carter's appeal, which, as noted, was based on the theme of honesty more than on a support for liberalism, indicated part of the problem that existed for the Democratic party. Democrats remained nominally the majority party, but a good many of their adherents were no longer attracted by traditional Democratic programs or by the traditional Democratic concept of using the power of the federal government to solve major social ills. Republicans, starting in 1968, had been able to capitalize in part on this disenchantment with liberalism, but they were unable as of 1976 to convert voters permanently to their side. Indeed, many analysts questioned whether any kind of "permanent" realignment was still possible, given the decline of parties and the increased tendency of voters to be independents.

1980 The 1980 election was a great victory for the Republicans and showed definite signs of a realigning shift toward the Republican party on the presidential level. The Democratic nominee, President Jimmy Carter, survived a strong challenge for the nomination from Senator Edward Kennedy. The party managed to unite behind the president, but the enthusiasm for his candidacy was at best lukewarm. Lacking a clear belief in the liberal philosophy of government and tentative about his own record, Carter adopted a twofold campaign strategy of attempting to rekindle partisan sentiments among Democrats and attacking his opponent as extreme and unreliable. At one point, Carter implied that Reagan was a racist and at several other points suggested that he was a warmonger. This negative campaign did succeed for a time in raising doubts about Reagan, but in the end it backfired.

For his part, Reagan won his party's nomination more easily than most expected, surviving the challenges of a number of credible opponents, including his eventual vice presidential choice, George H. Bush. Reagan, who came from the conservative wing of the Republican party, articulated a "new" conservative program of progress and economic growth. He promised to cut the size of the

Box 8.2 (cont.)

federal government, while pledging also to increase defense expenditures and to take a much tougher stance toward the Soviet Union. While Reagan emphasized the positive aspects of his brand of conservatism, he also hammered away at Jimmy Carter's record, especially on the economy and on foreign affairs. His overall strategy, which proved successful, was to make people doubt Jimmy Carter's ability to govern while presenting a positive and credible alternative, both in regard to his personal qualifications and his governing philosophy.

John Anderson ran as an independent appealing largely to voters who thought Carter incompetent and Reagan too extreme. Drawing mostly from independents, and about equally from Democrats and Republicans, Anderson managed 7 percent of the vote, which qualified him retroactively for a share of public funds in 1980 and assured him of funding for 1984.

1984 Ronald Reagan was reelected in a landslide against Democrat Walter Mondale, who had been Jimmy Carter's Vice-President. Mondale was nominated in a tough race against six competitors, with strong backing from organized labor. At the Democratic National Convention Mondale chose New York Representative Geraldine Ferraro as his running mate, in an attempt to exploit a perceived "gender gap" in the elections. This was the first time a major political party had placed a woman on the national ticket. Mondale emphasized what he called the "fairness" issue: the domestic spending cuts and tax cuts of the first Reagan Administration, which Mondale claimed unfairly hurt the poor and advantaged the rich. He also attacked the growing federal budget deficit, and promised to raise taxes to deal with it.

Reagan was nominated without serious opposition, and emphasized both his own administration's accomplishments and Mondale's association with Carter. Inflation had been brought under control, and after a serious recession in 1981–82, the economy had rebounded strongly. Reagan was able to argue that his tax cuts and a reduction in the rate of increase of federal spending and regulation had led to prosperity for the nation as a whole. He also argued that his defense and foreign policies had reestablished America as a credible actor in the world, and that the Soviets had a new respect for the United States. Overall, the Reagan campaign had a theme of renaissance—it was, in the words of one commercial, "morning in America" again.

In contrast, Reagan pointed to the Carter years as years of economic stagnation at home and weakness abroad, and claimed that Mondale would reinstate the failed liberal policies of "tax and spend"—a charge Mondale inadvertently reinforced with his promise to raise taxes and his appearance as beholden to the AFL-CIO and other special interest groups. In the end, Reagan won all but one state and the District of Columbia.

1988 After eight years of the popular Ronald Reagan, Democrats believed they had an opportunity to regain the White House in 1988. Massachusetts Governor Michael Dukakis won the Democratic nomination and ran a campaign stressing his stewardship of the economic "Massachusetts Miracle," technocratic competence, and his Greek ethnic background. He deliberately avoided polarizing issues, and promoted a Democratic platform which was the shortest (and vaguest) such document in years. Dukakis and his supporters simultaneously attacked Republican nominee George H. Bush as aloof and insensitive to the needs of working Americans.

Bush, Reagan's vice-president, started the campaign far behind. Despite a reputation for caution, Bush quickly gained an overwhelming lead by taking the offensive and emphasizing the ideological contrast between himself and Dukakis. Bush and his campaign sought to portray the Massachusetts governor as a typical Northeastern liberal who was eager to raise taxes, and was soft on crime, weak on defense, and generally out of touch with the values of mainstream America. To this end, Bush made a "no new taxes" pledge the centerpiece of his campaign, and pointed out that Dukakis was a member of the ACLU and had once vetoed a bill in Massachusetts that would have required school classes to begin the day with the pledge of allegiance. Bush succeeded in convincing voters that Dukakis was too liberal, and that a Bush administration would continue the policies that by 1988 had produced six years of uninterrupted economic growth.

Box 8.2 (cont.)

1992 After twelve years of Republican control of the White House, Arkansas Governor Bill Clinton defeated incumbent President George Bush by an electoral vote total of 370 to 168. Clinton won the Democratic race over an exceptionally weak field; most of the major Democratic possibilities, believing that President Bush would be a certain winner, declined to run. Clinton, however, took the risk; after some damaging personal revelations in the early primary season that nearly knocked him from the race, he captured the nomination with little difficulty.

Meanwhile, President Bush's approval rating began a steady slide from its highpoint of over 90 percent following the Gulf War in 1991. An economy that failed to show noticeable improvement and a series of equivocations and missteps left Bush vulnerable, even as he faced a challenge to the nomination inside his own party from Patrick Buchanan.

In the presidential race, Clinton ran on the need for change. He called for a more active role for the federal government in stimulating economic development and job growth and blamed the weakness in the economy on the failures of Reagan-Bush "trickle-down" economic policies. Bush sought to focus on weaknesses in Clinton's character but to little avail.

A notable element of the 1992 campaign was the candidacy of Ross Perot, the Texas billionaire who ran as an independent. Perot emphasized his status as an "outsider" who could end the gridlock in Washington and begin to reduce the national debt. In the early summer, Perot actually led both major party candidates in the polls, and many began to think that the nation might have its first "independent" president. Perot began to falter however, and withdrew in July. He then re-entered in October, finishing with 19 percent of the popular vote, but no electoral votes. It was the best showing of any third party candidate since 1912, when Teddy Roosevelt received 27 percent.

1996 After a campaign that stretched the limits of tedium, Bill Clinton became the first Democratic president to win re-election since Franklin Roosevelt, by defeating former Senate Majority Leader Bob Dole. Two years before, many observers had written Clinton's political obituary after the Republicans captured both houses of Congress for the first time since the 1950s. But Clinton adapted to the new political environment with great skill, moving to the center on many issues, while portraying congressional Republicans as dangerous extremists. A surging economy further boosted Clinton's popularity, as unemployment fell to the lowest level since the 1980s.

A political veteran who had sought the presidency twice before, Dole won the GOP nomination after a brief but intense battle. Dole tried many ways to stir public interest, but to no avail. Sometimes he stressed cutting taxes, sometimes he emphasized his humble Kansas roots, and sometimes he criticized Clinton's character. Only at the very end of the campaign, in response to revelations of major campaign finance irregularities in the President's campaign, did Dole begin to make some gains. This last-moment Republican surge may have been especially important in the congressional elections, where the Republicans held on to their majorities in the House and the Senate. Clinton may have been helped by a reaction against the Republican Congress and its visible leader, Newt Gingrich. Clinton ran a campaign that stressed his centrist credentials and portrayed him as a man "building a bridge to the 21st century"—a subtle reminder that Dole, 73, was the oldest first-time presidential nominee in American history. Ross Perot sought the presidency again, but received only 8.5 percent of the vote—less than half of what he got in 1992.

Voter turnout in the election was under 50 percent of the voting-age population, suggesting perhaps voters' satisfaction with the nation's affairs and their lack of interest in a presidential campaign whose outcome was widely predicted.

2000 After a controversial decision by the U.S. Supreme Court that overruled a controversial decision by the Florida Supreme Court and five weeks after Election Day, George W. Bush was assured the presidency. Bush was also the first president since Benjamin Harrison in 1888 to win the electoral vote while losing the popular vote.

Box 8.2 (cont.)

How did 2000 become one of the closest races in history, and how did George W. Bush defy pundits and scholars who predicted an easy victory for Gore? First, partisanship is considerably weaker than it was earlier in the 20th century, and voters seem to be more willing to vote based on factors other than party. Social forces, too, are weaker than in the past. Few voters feel bound to a political party because of their class, religion, or ethnicity. Without a strong feeling of group affiliation, voters are more likely to switch their votes to another party.

A final part of the answer may lie with Gore's campaign. Mathematical models of presidential elections attempt to predict the winner by measuring long-term factors established before the election such as economic conditions and partisanship, and often these models are correct. But these models are premised on the idea that candidates run campaigns of equal strength, and many observers thought that Gore's campaign was unusually poor. Gore highlighted his environmental record and his opponent's inexperience, while avoiding mentioning the name of Bill Clinton—the popular president for whom Gore served as vice-president for eight years. While Clinton was popular with Democrats and won reelection by a large margin in 1996, he was unpopular with many centrist voters who questioned his character. Gore wanted to win many of these voters. But later in the campaign, Gore presented himself as an economic populist who demanded change—an odd pose for a man who served in the incumbent administration during an economic boom.

In the campaign, Bush countered the label that he was not qualified to be president through solid debate performances, though he also became known for his frequent verbal gaffes. In the end, Bush was able to win 90 percent of Republican party identifiers as well as some Democrats and independents. But it was Gore who won the majority of the popular vote, with especially strong support from African-Americans and single women.

The election result was in dispute for five weeks because of legal battles over the result of the election in Florida, where the difference in the vote totals between the two main candidates was smaller than the margin of error that electoral mechanisms could handle. After a Supreme Court decision overturning a controversial Florida court decision, Bush was assured victory, though subsequent vote tallies showed that had the Florida Court prevailed Bush would have likely been the eventual winner. Florida's problems caused the nation to rethink standards for voting equipment and procedures, and in 2002 both houses of Congress had passed versions of an electoral reform bill, which would impose national standards on elections.

Bush became president after an electoral dispute, but questions about his legitimacy and competency disappeared after his forceful but measured rhetoric and response to the terrorist attacks of September 11, 20001. Political leaders would questions Bush's policies but not his legitimacy or the result of the 2000 election.

9

Interest Groups

CHAPTER CONTENTS

To any foreign political observer visiting the United States, surely one of the most striking aspects of American government is the prominent and quite open role played by organized interest groups. While political theorists since Aristotle have noted the tendency of people to form groups, the open and ubiquitous state of American interest groups is exceptional. Interest groups, professional organizations designed to influence policy and policy-makers, have a presence all over town in Washington, D. C. There are offices for the major labor unions, for business groups, for religious organizations, for "public interest" groups, and even for organizations of other levels of government (states, counties, and cities). These groups spend much of their time and energy contacting ("lobbying") officials of the federal government, especially legislators; and many of the organizations, through their political action committees (PACs), openly contribute funds to candidates for political office, including of course to incumbent members of Congress. The contact between government officials and interest groups has become so commonplace that members of Congress routinely hire firms whose sole purpose is to facilitate fundraising events for the interaction between the two. This contact is frequent, ongoing, and highly important to both sides.

Americans themselves hold rather ambivalent attitudes toward all this interest group activity, cherishing the right and necessity of collective action and yet concerned about the influence moneyed interests hold over the governmental process. As just suggested, Americans probably regard most interest group activity as normal and legitimate. The reason goes back to the founding and to the case made from the outset in favor of developing a "large commercial republic." *The Federalist* is among the first works of political theory to develop the idea that a "multiplicity of interests" can be a positive feature of society and can lead to a safer and more moderate form of democratic government. The solution to the problem of factions, according to *The Federalist,* consists in part not in the attempt to suppress the formation of different interests, but to accept them and multiply their number.

Moreover, Americans could scarcely imagine or tolerate a situation in which their right to

form or join an interest group was denied. Groups, whether they be labor unions, veterans' groups, farm organizations or civil rights organizations, are a natural outgrowth of a system that protects freedom. Contrast this with the situation in totalitarian regimes, which have always disallowed the formation of free associations. Even more than limiting individual liberty, preventing free associations has been a characteristic of totalitarian systems, for associations independent of government represent a formidable source of power that can challenge political authorities. (Indeed, it was the assertion of an independent labor movement in Poland in the 1980s—called *Solidarity*—that led eventually to the fall of the communist government in that country and that helped precipitate the collapse of communism throughout eastern Europe.) By contrast, in liberal democratic regimes groups are an integral element in governing. In the United States, the First Amendment to the Constitution expressly guarantees the "right of the people peaceably to assemble, and to petition the government for a redress of grievances." Direct contact between interest-group representatives and government officials—lobbying—therefore has Constitutional protection.

From this starting point, Americans have come to develop a rather special outlook on policymaking. Whereas the politics of other nations often begins with the idea that the solution to any problem involves discovering a "general will" or right answer, Americans often begin with the very pragmatic notion that the starting point to making policy is to get together the various interests that are involved and let them negotiate or bargain among themselves. This bargain may not be exactly in the public interest, but it is often a good approximation of it or at any rate a reasonable place to begin. Participation by interest groups in governing is probably more visible and openly accepted in American politics than in the politics of any other democratic nation.

On the other hand, Americans have more and more expressed concern that this politics of interests—or "special interests"—is a threat to democratic government. In his farewell address in 1981, President Carter said: "We are increasingly drawn to single-issue groups and special interest organizations to ensure that, whatever else happens, our personal views and our private interests are protected. This is a disturbing factor in American political life. It tends to distort our purposes because the national interest is not always the sum of all our single or special interests." Three days later in his first inaugural address, President Reagan echoed the same theme: "We hear much of special interest groups, but our concern must be for a special interest group that has been too long neglected . . . 'we the people,' this breed called Americans."

In recent years, Americans have worried in particular that Congress has come too much under the influence of special interest lobbies and political action committees. The role that some interest groups played in financing the 1996 presidential election contributed to this concern and reinvigorated a movement toward campaign finance reform. For many, there is a feeling that there are so many groups and that they are so active in trying to influence the government that "the interests" are dominating the policymaking process; and that the large amounts of money that interest groups contribute to political campaigns and the numerous lobbyists that they employ mean that these groups are obtaining special favors for themselves. In 2002, due to this growing pressure, President George W. Bush signed a bill curbing the amount of money and the way interests can spend money in the political process.

The Problem of Interest Groups

The ambivalent feelings Americans have about interest groups are not new. They reflect a fundamental concern of constitution makers that has been present since the founding. That concern was to allow for the formation of interest groups (and even to profit from their existence), but not to become subject either to the rule of a certain privileged number of groups or even to the rule of all groups in such a way that a broad dialogue with the public as a whole is prevented. The public interest, in other words, must be protected against an imbalance in the organized power of groups and against a conception of the national interest as existing of simply a summation of all its particular interests.

Thus despite the openness of the American political system to interest groups and despite their protection under the Constitution, past constitution makers have seen certain dangers in excessive interest group influence. Interests, as James Madison made clear in *Federalist* 10, must be regulated by the same government in which they exercise a considerable degree of influence. Speaking of the variety of interests that grow up in modern commercial societies, Madison commented that the "regulation of these various and interfering interests forms the principal task of modern legislation and involves the spirit of party and faction in the necessary and ordinary operations of government." (*Federalist* 10) While interests must be represented in government, they also must be channeled and controlled, for each interest, left to itself, might impose its own view and, in the extreme cases of factions, enact measures "adverse to the rights of their citizens." Government, therefore, must stand above the interests in order to moderate the conflict among groups with opposing interests. In this manner government promotes the public interest. Madison also hoped that the competition between self-interested factions over a fixed supply of power might aid in this moderating effect.

Constitution makers and political scientists have long argued over whether the clash of interest groups can alone represent the national interest. At one extreme, a well-known political scientist of an earlier generation, Arthur Bentley, argued that all politics could be understood as the struggle among interest groups and that any notion of the public interest above this struggle (or any institutional attempt to discover it) is meaningless.[1] This view, however, has been widely criticized, as most have realized, for example, that if the government simply accedes to the demands of various interests for more and more benefits, the total of these demands can far outstrip the resources of government to provide them and will result in huge deficits. At the other extreme, some progressives came very close to identifying the public interest as something that almost always was in tension with the demands of particular interests. According to this view, government should be reformed to reduce the power of those institutions that are open to interest group influence (such as the Congress) and to expand the power of those institutions that supposedly have a national perspective (such as the presidency and a "professional" bureaucracy).

The original framework of the government stood somewhere between these two poles. The founders clearly recognized a public interest independent of the sum of particular interests. Their challenge, however, was not to theorize about such matters but to construct the institutional arrangements that would best promote the public interest in practice. The outline of those arrangements reveals that the public interest was most likely to be known by a process that both summed up interest and sought to ascertain the public interest independently of them. No institution in the government could be entirely representative of one approach; but it was clear that the founders expected that the House, with short terms and small districts, would be the most open to the pressures of groups, while the presidency, with a longer term and a larger constituency, would be much more likely to consider the general interest. The separation of powers was originally understood not simply as a partial division among the functions of the government, but also as a system for combining different methods of determining the public interest.

As long as we maintain the basic structure of our government, the issue we must confront is not whether interest groups should exist and influence public policy (they will), but how much influence they should exercise, under what conditions, and through what means. If their power has become excessive, why has this happened and what can be done about it? It is not an exaggeration to say that of all the links between the citizenry and the formal institutions of government, interest groups have caused the most profound controversies for democratic theory and practice.

The Interest Group System

Whatever attitude one adopts about interest groups, their substantial impact on government is undeniable. Interest groups are major intermediary instruments of American politics, connecting citizens to their government and the government to its citizens. They can be thought of

collectively as making up a patterned system, almost an "institution," that is involved in a major way in performing the following key functions of political intermediation:

❖   *Interest groups influence public policy.* They have a significant impact on how government operates, including what laws are passed, who wins elections, how agencies are administered, and who is appointed to important positions.

❖   *Interest groups represent the views of citizens.* They provide additional political representation, beyond that offered by elected officials, for the philosophies and policies of group members. This representation can be purer and more undiluted than that offered by elected officials, who ordinarily must appeal to a broad audience.

❖   *Interest groups provide information to government officials.* Since most interest groups specialize in certain types of issues, they often are able to provide information that is helpful to making policy decisions.

❖   *Interest groups provide information to the public.* Since interest groups usually seek public support, they often try to supply information to the general population to increase its knowledge about various public issues.

❖   *Interest groups help set the governmental agenda.* Many problems and ideas come to the attention of government officials in the first place as a result of the efforts of interest groups.

❖   *Interest groups monitor government.* Once laws are passed, interest groups often keep a close watch on their implementation and call attention to changes that they believe should be made.

❖   *Interest groups are a vehicle for citizen participation.* Many Americans desire more involvement with government than voting, and in an era of party decline participating in interest groups is one of the most common forms of citizen participation. This activity often epitomizes the ideal of good citizenship, where those who are genuinely concerned about what government is doing take the time to express their concerns and their ideas. At the same time, this activity trains individuals to be effective democratic citizens by affording them the opportunity to learn how to organize, discuss, and build effective political bases of power.

The system of interest groups clearly affects how all of these major political functions are performed in the United States. Yet how interest groups operate, indeed how they are organized, reflects certain basic elements of the American political system. For anyone who looks at interest groups in other countries, it becomes clear just how much the American interest group system is a product of the basic political structure.

Thinkers since Aristotle have theorized that it is natural for people to form groups. However, the large number of groups in the United States suggests there is more at play than this natural predilection. There are in fact two reasons for the large number of interest groups in the United States (apart from the great size of the country and the number of interests it includes). One reason is that it "pays" for groups to form interest groups. The dispersion of power in the American system, and in particular the dominant idea of representation, means that many government officials in the United Sates are potentially open either to the arguments or pressures of interest groups. In Great Britain, for example, the interest groups tend to speak to the top members of the government and party, because few others can really help them. Lower level administrators are following government policies, and members of parliament are almost always bound by party discipline to vote for what the party decides. It makes no sense to "lobby" members of parliament because they are not really free agents able to decide on their own. Compare this to the situation in Congress, where each member is in fact free to make up his or her own mind. Groups naturally organize and expend their energy to meet this situation. For the same reason, British interest groups tend to be national, whereas American interest groups may still find it helpful to work in a few regions where they are strong.

The second reason that helps explain the great number and activity of interest groups in the United States is the separation of the government from the economy. In certain, so-called "neocorporatist" democratic states, such as Japan and Sweden, the major interests are virtually brought right into the decision-making process and have a "seat at the table." Major governmental economic decisions are hammered out between business leaders and labor leaders and governmental officials. In the United States, no group has this kind of official power. Each group, including business, must scramble for influence. It is in part because they lack firm power that interest groups must organize and lobby to achieve what influence they can.

The Growth and Development of Interest Groups

An "interest group," as we use the term here, is an association of individuals that is formally organized and that promotes certain goals or objectives inside the policy process. An "interest," by contrast, is an actual or potential set of goals held by certain citizens. Not all interests have interest groups. For example, a consumer interest existed long before there were organized consumer interest groups. Nor are all interests accurately represented by interest groups, despite the claims of those groups. Many besides labor unions make some claim to represent the interests of labor.

American history has witnessed a continuous, though not steady, growth in the number of interest groups (though recently some have claimed that television, among other things, has diminished group forming). The formation of interest groups has tended to occur in waves.[2] For national interest groups that participate in national politics, the formation of these groups have had a good deal to do with changing demands on the federal government and the expansion of its role and activities.

In the initial years of the republic the number of interest groups was small, and there were virtually no national associations. The impact of interest groups was limited at the national level, in part because government itself had a limited role. Most formal interest-group activity that existed was found at the state and local level. Nevertheless there were certainly perceptible interests in the nation—urban, commercial, manufacturing, agrarian, slaveholding and the like—and because these were often grouped in specific geographical zones, many senators and representatives quite openly assumed the roles of "representing" these interests.

By the 1830s Tocqueville was celebrating the great number of associations in America: "In no country in the world has the principle of association been more successfully used or applied to a greater multitude of objects than in America."[3] The associations Tocqueville described were not always groups that exercised pressure on government, but often groups that sought to influence opinions in society or to perform certain functions, like distributing books, building hospitals, or caring for the poor. These groups often substituted for or supplemented government activity, for they performed important social functions.

The performance of important social functions by groups is known today by the term of "voluntarism." For Tocqueville, it was seen as a means of preventing the excessive growth of government. "At the head of any new undertaking, where in France you find government or in England some territorial magnate, in the United States you are sure to find an association."[4] There is still much truth to this observation, although different circumstances have clearly brought a greatly expanded role for government. Voluntarism nevertheless remains a major theme of American politics, and it continues in the rhetoric of recent presidents, as in President George W. Bush's call to raise the "armies of compassion."

The Civil War accelerated the nationalization and industrialization of American life. Following the Civil War government expanded and the articulation of interests by formal groups began to occur on a truly national scale for the first time. Farm organizations, social and fraternal groups, and business associations all formed by the turn of the century. Also, labor interests organized in response to the growth of large corporations.

The progressive era brought the next great wave of organization and as power tends to be a zero-sum game, group organization tends to bring with it counterorganization, both of eco-

nomic and noneconomic interests. The National Association of Manufacturers, the American Medical Association, chambers of commerce, the American Farm Bureau, and other economic interests organized in part because of the economic insecurity of this period and the development of new national economic legislation. Public interest counterorganizations such as the Consumers League, the Child Labor Committee, the National Civic Federation, and the Pure Food Association formed partly in opposition to the growing strength of economic interests. Groups such as the National Civil Service Reform and the Non-Partisan League grew in direct opposition to political party machines. The National Association for the Advancement of Colored People, the Urban League, and various religious groups originated during this period as well.

There is an instructive lesson in the growth of interest groups during the progressive era. The progressive movement itself was a reaction against the ill effects of commercial industrialism, the growth of private power, and the corruption of political machines. It was a majoritarian movement against interest groups, made in the name of "the people" or public opinion in opposition to special interests. Yet, quite apart from the fact that it stimulated the emergence of formal economic interest groups, which inevitably arose to protect their groups, the progressive movement itself relied on the formation of groups such as the Non-Partisan League. Of course, there is a difference between economic interest groups (whose goal is the promotion of group financial interests) and "public" interest groups (whose goal is the promotion of a common good that will not selectively benefit the group), but it remains that a reliance on organized groups is one of the fundamental characteristics of American politics.

The New Deal represented a major shift from limited to positive government and to the establishment of the welfare state. The growth in regulation of major parts of the economy led to a much more active role by economic interest groups, not just in the legislative process, but during the phase of implementation by administrative agencies, which were often given broad formal discretion to make important decisions.

Groups therefore sought to get close—indeed too close—to these agencies. Examples included the cozy relationship between the National Labor Relations Board and labor, and between the National Rural Electrification Administration and the National Rural Electrification Cooperation Association.

It was in response to this situation of strong interest group influence that one political scientist, Theodore Lowi, coined the term "interest-group liberalism."[5] By this term, Lowi meant to describe a situation in which increased government intervention for purposes of economic stability, national security, and social welfare had led Congress to delegate greater authority to executive agencies, which in turn resulted in much greater participation in the regulatory process by the affected interest groups. The consequence, he and others argued, was the virtual domination of certain areas of policy by "subgovernments" or "iron triangles." Iron triangles refer to the stable and often impenetrable codependency between bureaucratic agencies, congressional committees and subcommittees, and organized, moneyed interest groups. These iron triangles operate to form public policy and can block even the president from entering the policy process (aside from his explicit Constitutional powers). Whether this situation was as new or as pathological as Lowi suggested has been debated, but it is clear that the dimensions of this problem were clearly growing with the much greater role of the federal government.

The next great wave of interest group formation began during the 1960s and continued at least until the early 1980s. During this period, Lyndon Johnson's Great Society program dramatically increased the degree of direct federal governmental involvement in large areas of social welfare. Partly as a result (and partly in reaction), there was a large growth in the formation and the development of public interest and single-issue citizen groups, in such areas as gun control, civil liberties, women's rights, the environment, consumerism, and "good government." (Seventy-six per cent of all citizens groups and seventy-nine per cent of the welfare organizations in existence in 1981 were formed after 1960.) A growth of economic groups followed in the middle and late 1970s, adding sub-

stantially to their presence in Washington. (The number of business corporations operating offices in Washington increased from 50 in 1961 to 545 in 1982.) Close students of interest groups, such as Robert Salisbury, have spoken of a veritable "explosion" in the number of organized interests in Washington since the 1960s. Virtually every conceivable interest now has an active, organized interest group.[6]

Yet it is not clear whether this last wave in the growth of interest groups has led to an increase or—paradoxically—a decrease in their influence over policymaking. Robert Salisbury, after studying the 1986 Tax Reform Act, has concluded that the number of interests represented is now so large that the "major interests" (which once alone were organized) have lost relative influence and that government officials have gained greater leverage in relationship to groups.

Number and Types of Interest Groups

The number of interest groups in America is enormous. The *Encyclopedia of Associations* lists more than 1,900 national public affairs organizations. In addition, there are many thousands more interest groups that operate at the state or local level.

Many citizens today, as noted earlier, have expressed concern about an excessive influence of interest groups. Yet people are apt to forget that *someone* is supporting these groups or they would not exist. And that someone, it turns out, is us, the United States holding some 23,000 national organizations itself. No doubt, of course, the groups that *we* support are healthy for government, while the groups that *others* support are problematic "special interests." The problem is that others think just as we do.

Most Americans are involved in some fashion with at least one interest group, even if politics was not the main reason for becoming involved. A grocery store owner who joins the local chamber of commerce may see herself as mostly trying to support a healthy business climate for her town, but she also is the newest member of one of the most powerful lobbies in Washington, the U.S. Chamber of Commerce. Similarly, a carpenter may join a union because he believes it will lead to higher wages or even because only union carpenters can find work in his town, but his local union probably is affiliated with the AFL-CIO, the country's largest labor organization and another important political force.

We often become involved with interest groups even without realizing it. Many organizations try to influence government policy—and thus qualify as interest groups—even though their main reason for existing is nonpolitical activity. For example, most churches belong to associations of churches that have offices and employ lobbyists in Washington, D.C., such as the Southern Baptist Convention. The policies that such associations are concerned with need not be directly related to religious beliefs: for instance, groups that represent churches are likely to be quite concerned about whether donations made to them are tax-deductible and would push for expansive charitable choice legislation.

The large number of organizational affiliations that are maintained by Americans clearly suggests the enormous variety of purposes and objectives pursued by the groups in which they participate. For the sake of simplicity we can classify interest groups as consisting of three basic types: economic, ideological, and social.

Economic Groups

In *Federalist* 10 James Madison said, "The most common and durable source of factions has been the various and unequal distribution of property. . . . A landed interest, a manufacturing interest, a mercantile interest, a moneyed interest, with many lesser interests, grow up of necessity in civilized nations, and divide them into different classes, actuated by different sentiments and views." Few would deny the validity of Madison's observations for contemporary politics. Organizations that promote discrete economic (or property) interests are among the most powerful and enduring forces in the political arena. These fall into four general categories: business, labor, agriculture, and professional associations.

Business   In their relations with government, businesspeople are primarily concerned with regulations, subsidies, contracts, tax rates, inter-

est rates and international trade policy (quotas and tariffs). Any idea, however, that business constitutes a monolith that supports one viewpoint is false. Due to the overwhelming force of a competitive market, business can be unified or fragmented, depending on the issue. For example, businesses are frequently united on issues like corporate taxes, consumer policies, and labor legislation, yet they are often divided on matters of international trade. Textile manufacturers have supported quotas on the import of foreign textiles, whereas the merchandisers of clothing have opposed these quotas. In *The Logic of Collective Action*, Mancur Olson shows how even when a unified interest can be identified, such as maintaining high prices, the competitive market will often lead companies to act in ways that will hurt the group's interest.

Businesses are organized into a few umbrella organizations, the most prominent being the Chamber of Commerce, the National Association of Manufacturers (NAM), the Business Roundtable, and the National Federation of Independent Businesses (NFIB). The Chamber of Commerce, with 215,000 firms and individuals as members, is the largest and best known of these. Although most Americans know it as a local organization, an annual budget of approximately $70 million and a Washington staff of 350 give the Chamber of Commerce an impressive influence on Capitol Hill and at the White House. In order to avoid alienating any part of its wide and heterogeneous membership, the Chamber of Commerce maintains a high level of generality in its appeals. It is a vigilant defender of the private enterprise system and an opponent of high taxes. But it almost always avoids addressing matters that affect a particular constituent industry.

More so than the Chamber of Commerce, the NAM represents "big business" interests. Although it comprises only 6 to 8 percent of all manufacturers in America, among these are many of the largest in the country. Even more representative of big business, and potentially more influential, is the newest umbrella organization, the Business Roundtable, founded in 1972. The Roundtable is made up of about 200 chief executive officers of some of the nation's largest corporations, including General Motors

(GM), AT&T, and IBM. The Roundtable does not rely merely on lobbyists, but chooses instead to take advantage of its members' direct access to representatives, senators, and presidents. Finally, the National Federation of Independent Businesses (NFIB), also with a Washington staff of about 55 persons, is one of many organizations representing small businesses.

Although most business owners usually vote Republican, not all business groups engage in partisan activity. "Big business" groups such as the NAM and the Business Roundtable often either stay out of electoral politics, or split their support between the parties, usually backing incumbents. "Small business" organizations such as the NFIB and the Chamber of Commerce are more open in their embrace of Republican politicians and policies. During the 1980s, the Chamber of Commerce actively campaigned for approval of Ronald Reagan's economic programs, while more recently the NFIB has worked to elect Republican congressional candidates.

Along with these umbrella organizations, business is represented in Washington by scores of trade associations. These organizations predate the formation of the umbrella groups and include everything from the National Cricket Growers Association and the Paper Bag Institute to the American Petroleum Institute. Trade associations are especially active when it comes to legislation involving taxes and tariffs, as each trade usually will have the same interest and position. At the same time, these groups frequently oppose one another. When the Beet Sugar Association seeks higher sugar prices, it is vehemently opposed by the Chocolate Manufacturers Association of America.

The number of business organizations has led some to conclude that business runs the government. Nothing really could be further from the truth. The variety of groups testifies to the variety of interests inside the business community, which means that business groups are very often in conflict with one another. Moreover, as noted, the existence of business interest groups indicates the weakness of business in relationship to government, or at any rate its separation from government. In a number of countries, businesses are partners with government and are actively and almost officially brought into the decision-making process. In contrast, American businesses remain on the outside, acting as external pressure groups: because they lack clear power, they are obliged to seek influence.

Labor   Labor is the largest group in terms of membership and, though hardly monolithic, is considerably more centralized than business. Unlike most other interest groups, unions are not, strictly speaking, voluntary organizations. This is because of "union shop" or "closed shop" agreements by which nonunion members can be prohibited from employment in a given factory, office, or other location.

Also unlike most interest groups, labor unions take positions and lobby intensively on an assortment of issues that often only remotely concern their memberships. Although unions focus first on concerns such as higher wages, better working conditions, and a boost in the minimum wage, they also work to promote interests that are not simply their own, as they have done in social issues, civil rights, and foreign defense policy. Traditionally, labor has been affiliated with liberal causes and with the Democratic party. Organized labor was also one of the largest contributors to the campaign of Democrats such as Al Gore in 2000, spending almost 59 million dollars on Democratic candidates. In addition to money, labor unions are also one of the largest sources of less tangible campaign support such as holding signs at rallies and volunteering to distribute campaign literature.

In general, Republicans have followed the strategy of appealing to union members despite the official endorsements of the unions. All this being said, however, the union organizations remain a very important element in the Democratic party and continue to exert considerable influence both in national party circles and in the organizations of some of the states, like Michigan, where labor unions are very strong. Labor unions have long used members' dues to fund political campaigns. But the Supreme Court ruled in *Communications Workers of America v. Beck* (1988) that workers who refuse to join a union cannot be forced to pay for political activities that they oppose. Since unions can collect dues from nonmembers who work in otherwise unionized settings, *Beck* could hinder organized labor's activities by forcing unions to segregate money paid by nonmembers from that paid by members.

The largest union organization is the American Federation of Labor-Congress of Industrial Organizations (AFL-CIO). The AFL-CIO has 13.4 million members, including laborers, teachers, and white-collar workers. The AFL-CIO, a product of the merger of two formerly distinct organizations, clearly sets the tone for American labor. Its president for 25 years (1955–1980) was the cigar-smoking George Meany, who ruled the AFL-CIO with a firm hand and who consequently wielded considerable personal political influence. The union's political department, the Committee on Political Education (COPE), conducts fund-raising and voter registration drives, provides political party support, and, with its large pool of volunteer campaign workers, does much direct electioneering.

The proportion of American workers belonging to labor unions has been declining for decades. In 1945, 35.5 percent of American workers were union members; this figure remained steady through the 1950s. But union power has declined dramatically over the past 30 years. In 1980, 22 percent of American workers were unionized, but by 1999 that figure had fallen to 13.9 percent. This decline has been particularly dramatic in the private sector, the traditional base of American unionism. The largest private-sector unions are the International Brotherhood of Teamsters, which has 1.4 million members, mostly truck drivers; the United Food and Commercial Workers, which also has 1.4 million members; the United Automobile Workers (UAW), with 1.3 million members, mostly in the automobile and aerospace industries; and the Service Employees International Union (SEIU), with 1.1 million members. Other prominent private-sector unions include the International Brotherhood of Electrical Workers (IBEW), the Communications Workers of America (CWA), and the United Steel Workers (USW).

With the growth in government employment, especially on the state and local levels, public-sector unionism has become increasingly important. The most prominent public-sector unions are the nation's two leading teachers'

associations: the National Education Association (NEA), with two million members; and the American Federation of Teachers (AFT), with 900,000 members. The NEA is a formidable political presence, with an annual budget of about $200 million and a Washington staff of 525. The American Federation of State, County, and Municipal Employees (AFSCME) has 1.3 million members and wields great power in many cities. Other prominent public-sector unions include groups representing federal employees, postal workers and police officers.

Agriculture Although the farmers of the American Revolution, working small plots of land to provide themselves with the basic necessities of life, have given way to large-scale "agribusiness" enterprises specializing in one or a few crops, the farming life still retains a nostalgic appeal for Americans, and thus its public image as an interest group remains largely positive. Yet farm groups, like business and labor, have never presented a united front.

The largest farming organization, representing 4 million farmers, is the American Farm Bureau Federation, founded in 1920. The Farm Bureau originated with the U.S. Department of Agriculture's (USDA) Agriculture Extension Service, established to provide technical aid on a local level. It represents larger, more successful farm businesses, rather than the traditional family farm, and thus supports free market policies and opposes government regulation and price supports.

Agriculture, too, has its equivalent of trade associations, called "commodity associations," which represent dairy, tobacco, and other distinct commodity interests. These associations exercise considerable influence within both the U.S. Department of Agriculture and the congressional agriculture committees, thereby benefiting from price supports and subsidy policies. In 2002, President George W. Bush signed into law a farm bill that offered large subsidies for wheat farmers and an additional 73 billion dollars for farm programs.

Professional Associations There are hundreds of professional associations in the United States, ranging from the American Medical Association

(AMA) and American Bar Association (ABA) to the American Society of Golf Course Architects. Most professional associations exist not so much to influence public policy as to provide services to members. The American Political Science Association, for example, sponsors conferences, an employment service, and numerous publications of interest to political scientists.

Among those associations that are involved in politics, the AMA and ABA are perhaps the most active and powerful, exerting considerable influence in local, state, and national politics. Like some other professional associations, the AMA and ABA maintain licensing and training standards in their respective professions and, not surprisingly, can usually count on the generous support of their members. On the national level, the AMA lobbies against policies such as compulsory national health insurance (as it did against Medicare); and the ABA rates all candidates for the federal judiciary and has become a powerful factor in the selection process.

Ideological or Policy-Oriented Groups

Madison may have believed that the most durable source of interests derived from economic concerns, but he also realized that interests could form around "opinions"—that is, deeply held beliefs or convictions about public policy. Political scientist James Q. Wilson defines such policy-oriented groups as those that work "explicitly for the benefit of some larger public or society as a whole and not one that works chiefly for the benefit of members."[7]

Ideological groups can have a broad or a narrow focus, taking positions on a variety of different public policy disputes or concentrating their attention on one or a few issues. Examples of the former type of group, which are sometimes called "public interest" groups, are Common Cause, the League of Women Voters, Americans for Democratic Action, Americans for Constitutional Action, and the American Conservative Union, and the Christian Coalition. The so-called "single-issue" group, on the other hand, includes the Sierra Club (environment), the National Right to Life Committee (anti-abortion), the National Rifle Association (anti-gun control).

Ideological groups are based on commitments strong enough to induce active participation by members. For this reason they are often less flexible than economic groups. Members frequently bring zeal and militancy to their work. Rather than promoting a politics of bargaining or compromising interests, they give rise to a politics of principle or ideology. Many of these groups would rather lose with their principles intact than win at the cost of compromising firmly held beliefs.

Ideological groups are both old and new, large and small, little known and widely recognized. The Sierra Club was founded in 1892; the League of Women Voters, with its suffragist origins, in 1920; the Fund of Animals in 1967; and the Consumer Federation of America in 1968. Some ideological groups must make do with shoestring budgets and a few dedicated volunteers, while others, like the National Wildlife Federation, enjoy ample resources, professional staff, and a vast membership.

Many of the more recent groups can trace their roots to specific events or controversies and to the activities of particular individuals, sometimes known as policy entrepreneurs. Some environmental groups point to Earth Day, 1970, as their birthday. The Vietnam War and Watergate helped give rise to the "good government" organization known as Common Cause, whose founder John Gardner was former secretary of the Department of Health, Education, and Welfare (HEW) under Lyndon Johnson. But the most famous of the political entrepreneurs of the past two decades is the charismatic Ralph Nader. Nader used his talents for writing, speaking, organizing, and attracting publicity to turn a one-man show into a public interest conglomerate, Public Citizen Inc. with over 100,000 members.

The members of ideological groups noted above tend to be better educated, wealthier, younger, and more politically aware than the average citizen. This is also true of the staffs of these organizations (sometimes the only members are the staff), which have considerable freedom of action. Although most public interest activists are ostensibly nonpartisan, they tended initially in the 1960s and 1970s to support Demo-

On particularly controversial issues like abortion, groups often organize on both sides. That is not always the case on low-profile economic issues like farm price supports. (Courtesy of the University Journal, University of Virginia. Used with permission.)

cratic programs and initiatives and to embrace a liberal political ideology.

More recently, as public attitudes have become more conservative, and largely in response to the growth of these liberal groups, an increasing number of conservative groups have sprung up, also claiming to speak for the public interest. Many have focused their attention on "social issues" such as abortion, pornography, and school prayer. The most prominent of these groups in the 1980s was the Moral Majority, founded by Jerry Falwell; in the 1990s, the Christian Coalition, led by Pat Robertson, has become the leading organization of this type.

Social Groups

Social groups, which exist primarily to promote friendship or campaign among their members, are of many different types: ethnic (such as the National Association of Polish-Americans and the Loyal Order of Hibernians), religious (the B'nai B'rith and the Knights of Columbus), veterans' groups (the VFW and the American Legion), as well as lodges and fraternal orders (the Elks, Rotary, and Kiwanis). The most common impetus for creating groups of this kind is the feeling of shared identity and the sense of kinship or belonging. Members join primarily out of loyalty or pride, a desire for sociability and prestige, or a need for reinforcing some self-identification.

Many of these organizations have a special interest in noncontroversial community service activities such as sponsoring cultural and social events, fund-raising for charitable causes, promoting youth activities like Little League or summer camps, and providing college scholarships. Through these and similar activities, these groups seek to promote a sense of civic duty or responsibility at the local level. This is one way in which such avowedly nonpolitical groups contribute to the political health of the community. Another way in which social groups can be important politically is by serving as a conduit for political leaders or aspiring politicians to communicate, substantively or symbolically, with influential segments of a broader constituency. This is why politicians frequently speak before such group, eat pizza, blintzes, and sausage on the campaign trail; and march in St. Patrick's Day parades.

Civil Rights Groups

Some groups have purposes or functions that do not fit neatly into one specific category. The most important of these, and surely those that have left the most indelible imprint on American politics, have been the civil rights organizations formed to promote the well-being of black Americans. The best known are the National Association for the Advancement of Colored People (NAACP), the Southern Christian Leadership Conference (SCLC), and the Urban League. In one respect these are economic groups, for they seek to promote the material well-being of a segment of the population that has traditionally lagged far behind white Americans in income and wealth. In another respect they are ideological groups because their cause is part of a larger effort to fulfill the promise of America and bring about a more just society. Finally, they serve as social groups by enhancing group identity and feelings of solidarity among their members.

The civil rights groups played an important role in organizing black Americans during the civil rights struggles of the 1960s and 1970s. In addition, the NAACP in particular pioneered a strategy of litigation that relied on expert lawyers filing suits on behalf of blacks in a variety of different areas of social and economic life, such as *Brown v. Board of Education* (1954). Rather than seeing courts as merely an instrument for remedying specific cases, the NAACP in effect began to see the courts as an institution that could be used to effect major changes of public policy.

Organizations have arisen to assist members of groups other than black Americans. These associations include the National Organization for Women, the National Council of La Raza (Hispanics), the Gray Panthers (senior citizens), and the Human Rights Campaign (gays and lesbians). While most such groups tend to be on the left, some civil rights organizations such as the American Center for Law and Justice and the Rutherford Institute consider themselves conservative and focus on issues of religious freedom.

Governments as Interest Groups

A final type of interest group that does not fit neatly into any traditional category consists of the associations of state and local governments. In the extraordinarily complex web of intergovernmental relations that has developed since the time of the Great Society in the 1960s, state and local governments have become more dependent on the federal government for resources and have been touched more and more by federal programs and regulations.

As a consequence, the various associations of state and local governments, such as the National Governors' Association, the National Conference of State Legislatures, and the National Association of Counties, now lobby the federal government to protect their benefits and promote their interests. It is a testimony to the complexity of the system that governments now behave, as it were, as organized interest groups in relationship to other levels of government. Other governmental agencies, such as major public universities, also have lobbies in Washington.

How Organizations Form

Given the number and variety of groups in America, one might get the impression that maintaining substantial membership is the least of the problems facing groups' leaders. Yet this is far from the truth. Many groups are in fact quite small, even though they may claim to speak for millions. It is remarkable how many organizations in Washington, especially ideological groups, use the word "national" in their title but have a membership of only a few thousand. Often the organization consists of little more than the paid staff. Many such groups derive the funding necessary to support a Washington staff not from membership dues but from donations by foundations or corporations.

Of course, some groups, such as labor and farm organizations, do have millions of members. But it is important to consider carefully the question of why people join a group and invest their time or money on its behalf. Modern social scientists have given this question considerable attention, beginning with posing the hypothetical question of how a strictly "rational" or calculating individual might act. In doing so, they have arrived at a difficulty or situation known as "the free-rider problem."

The "Free-Rider" Problem

Consider, for example, a woman who works in a automobile factory. While she may believe that she and her fellow workers benefit from the efforts of the United Auto Workers, it does not follow that she would voluntarily join the union, as she might think that in a factory employing thousands of workers her membership is not crucial. Thus, she might hope to reap the benefits of a strong union (higher wages) without paying the costs, such as union dues and the attendance at union meetings.

This difficulty is an example of the so-called "free-rider" problem—the problem that someone can gain the benefits from the actions of the group at large, but does not find it rational (in a calculating sense) to become a member. If the benefits of the group can be collected without paying any of the costs associated with joining the group, why join? Of course if everyone tried to be a free rider, then organizations would find it impossible to recruit members. But this logic still may not prove convincing to any particular individual who after all cannot control how everyone else thinks. The free rider problem (in theory) would be especially acute for those groups which cannot restrict their benefits only to their members. There is no way, for example, for environmental groups to limit the enjoyment of cleaner air to those who actively work to promote clean air.

Organizations attempt to solve this problem by giving people good reasons for joining. In the case of a labor union like the United Auto Workers the reason is one of the strongest of all: membership in the union is a necessary condition of employment in a "closed shop." (Some states with "right-to-work" laws—mostly in the South and Southwest—prohibit closed shops.) Other groups provide reasons such as attractive monthly magazines, access to special services, and the personal satisfaction of working toward worthwhile goals. Although it may sound self-evident, it is worth noting that the largest interest groups are those that offer the most compelling reasons for joining to the largest number of individuals. This fact explains why the largest groups in the United States, that of the nation state, the individual states, and the localities, force the costs of membership through taxation.

Historical Events

One should remember, however, that the free-rider problem is sometimes more of a problem for the theorist than for the actual citizen. While it does point to a real difficulty that groups face, it should not be assumed that citizens always calculate in just this way. As we have already seen, individuals join groups because they believe in a cause and because they wish to participate in promoting it. Part of the logic of the citizen is to think and act in terms of justice

for society as a whole. In studying the "free-rider problem," we should not forget the other motives besides individual interest that characterize citizen behavior.

A study of the formation of interest groups shows in fact that other motives are decisive in explaining the formation of interest groups. Groups related to "moral purpose" or "public interest" arise when issues of public morality and national interest are prominent or salient as in the period before the Civil War, the progressive era, and the period of the 1960s. Economic interest groups have tended to form in response to new situations in government in which they have a stake in protecting or promoting their interests, as at the beginning of this century, during the New Deal, and in the 1970s.

Beyond these broader events, there are technological changes that affect the rate of formation of interest groups. Citizens today can communicate more easily with each other than ever before. These mechanisms of communication—telephones, fax machines and computers—considerably facilitate the technical obstacles to group formation and probably assist in the ease with which organizations form.

How Interest Groups Influence Politics

A well-known political scientist, V. O. Key, once observed that "where power rests, there influence will be brought to bear."[8] Political interest groups employ a variety of different means for gaining access to and influencing the policymaking process. The choice of tactics used in any particular case will depend on the nature of the political process, the character of the organization and its resources, and the issue at hand. Five basic tactics are available to groups: direct lobbying, grass-roots lobbying, electioneering, public protest, and litigation.

Direct Lobbying

Interest group representatives can simply tell government officials what they prefer, a practice known as direct lobbying. The growth in both the number and size of federal programs and the increasing numbers of groups in Washington have combined to greatly increase the prevalence of lobbying. A conservative estimate is that there are now about 11,000 professionals who are employed in lobbying one part or another of the federal government.

Of course, not all lobbyists spend all their time putting pressure on government officials. A large part of the average lobbyist's job is to obtain information about what the government is doing and to make assessments about trends in government policy. Businesses or health organizations need this kind of information to make their own decisions, and they rely in part on their lobbyists to supply it.

Unfortunately, there also are less benign examples of direct lobbying. Mark Twain once observed that Americans have the best Congress that money can buy. The point of Twain's comment was, of course, the supposed illicit connections that exist between interest groups and Congress. The notorious image of lobbyists wining, dining, and bribing public officials was in part deserved. The motto of Sam Ward, the king of the lobbyists in the 1870s, was "The way to a man's 'aye' is through his stomach." Nor was that the only appetite to which appeal has been made. Writing in 1873 about women "lobbyesses," Edmund W. Martin in *Behind the Scenes in Washington* observed that the "lever of lust is used to pry up more legislators to the sticking point than money itself avails to seduce."9 The question is whether in the contemporary Congress such behavior is the exception or the rule. The scandals of recent years have amply demonstrated that Congress is not free of instances of outright corruption. Yet Congress is a large body, and the misbehavior of a few should not be taken as measure of the standard of behavior of the many. It is only natural, of course, for the news media to focus publicity on the handful of representatives and senators involved in scandal, and there is little newsworthy in the absence of scandal. But in reality there is no evidence today of widespread, outright corruption involving the members of Congress and the lobbyists who seek to influence them. Whether there are troubling patterns of influence deriving from campaign contributions is a different—although related—question.

The traditional bad reputation of the lobbying profession is in part self-induced. In opposing each other, some lobbyists tend to exaggerate their own effectiveness, while disparaging their opponents as rich, unscrupulous, and conniving. If this is so, then why lobby? And if lobbying is not primarily wining, dining, or bribing, then what is it? Consider the conclusion of the political journalist Bernard Asbell, who spent nearly a full year following the daily activities of former Senator Edmund Muskie:

To the outsider who sees Capitol Hill only as a movie set, it may come as a surprise that more than ninety-nine percent of lobbying effort is spent not on parties, weekend hosting, and passing plain white envelopes, but trying to persuade minds through facts and reason.10

The fact is that the majority of lobbyists spend most of their time providing friendly, or at least persuadable, representatives and senators with facts and arguments to back up their legislative positions. Lobbyists help their friends in Congress to persuade other members of the soundness of their positions. Lobbyists also indirectly supply important "political" information to legislators. The reaction of lobbyists to various legislative proposals, the intensity of their views, and their willingness to work to promote or defeat a measure all give legislators cues about how constituents feel about certain issues. Interest-group representatives also help by communicating politicians' views to group members, in certain cases helping to explain why a member of Congress voted in opposition to the group's position. The lobbying relationship is, in short, a two-way street.

There is a kind of built-in quality control on the information lobbyists provide. It is in the lobbyist's long-term self-interest to be honest and straightforward in order to maintain the trust of the official and ensure future access. As one member of Congress put it:

It doesn't take very long to figure out which lobbyists are straightforward, and which ones are trying to snow you. The good ones will give you the weak points as well as the strong points of their case. If anyone ever gives the false or misleading information, that's it—I'll never see him again.11

Rarely do lobbyists directly pressure politicians. If there is pressure, it is from the politician making a calculation of the political damage that might come from going against a certain group. The image of interest groups directly co-opting members of Congress, committees, and executive agencies is largely overdrawn.

Grass-Roots Lobbying

Common Cause routinely includes an "alert" in its bimonthly membership magazine urging members to contact their representatives on a given issue. The National Rifle Association is famous for its ability to rouse its members to notify their elected officials of their opposition to pending gun-control legislation. And companies such as Mobil Oil regularly conduct national media campaigns to influence the course of public debate in order to have an effect on public policy decisions.

Grass-roots lobbying includes both specific efforts directed at a legislator's home district and general efforts to influence public opinion. The sharp rise in recent years of this form of lobbying is in part due to the growing importance of mass communication and the perfecting of Madison Avenue-style public relations techniques. It is also a response to the success with which it has been used. When interest groups provoke a storm from below, elected officials begin to think that they must vote a certain way or else face a possible loss of support back home.

This method is in a sense the very picture of democratic politics. It consists not in a lobbyist putting direct pressure on a politician, but in a group mobilizing popular support, which in turn puts pressure on politicians. Still, it is the interest group organizations that orchestrate these campaigns. And they often do so by forming coalitions with each other and attacking head on. One of the best examples of such a campaign was the successful effort in 1987 to block the Senate confirmation of Judge Robert Bork, whom Ronald Reagan had nominated to fill a seat on the Supreme Court. A coalition of interest groups, including feminist organizations and civil right organizations, led a grass-roots lobbying campaign that made a strong impression on many senators, who ended up voting against the nomination.

A common grass-roots lobbying technique is the letter-writing campaign. Legislators, however, are quick to identify and discount prepackaged, manufactured campaigns, in which they receive thousands of identical postcards. After all, how much effort or commitment does it take to sign a postcard? For this reason, some organizations refrain from providing members with specific wording or form letters. When representatives receive hundreds or thousands of independently drafted letters voicing similar views on pending legislative issue, they are quick to take notice.

Electioneering

Interest groups are not political parties. They neither nominate candidates for office nor seek to win elections under their own label. Indeed, it is unlikely that an AT&T candidate, or a Bow Tie Manufacturers Association nominee, or even a Chamber of Commerce candidate, could win an election. Groups often claim credit for determining the outcome of elections, but it would be an interesting test of their true strength if they tried to nominate and run their own candidate against either of the two major political parties.

Interest groups do, however, form alliances with political parties, usually of an informal nature. These alliances enable interest groups to influence platforms and nominations, and thereby affect the nation's political agenda. In recent years, groups such as the AFL-CIO, the National Education Association, women's groups, and groups on all sides of the abortion issue have actively sought to get their members elected as delegates to the major-party conventions and to write their own planks into party platforms. But such groups are not so much seeking working alliances with the parties as trying to obtain the party's support for their cause.

As elections have become more expensive and parties weaker, interest groups have come to play a greater role in the election process. Organizations such as the AFL-CIO's COPE provide money, workers, and expertise to candidates. Few groups can match the ability of unions to field workers for registration and "get out the vote" drives. In presidential nomination campaign, support by major interest groups, such as the National Education Association or the National Organization of Women, has played an important role in helping certain candidates launch viable campaigns. Interest groups also play a key role in financing political campaigns, especially in congressional races. Groups like EMILY's List (Early Money Is Like Yeast) raise and distribute funds to female candidates of both political parties. Many interest groups have their own political action committee which they use to solicit funds from group members to contribute to candidates or parties.

Some of the larger organizations such as the AFL-CIO and the Christian Coalition also engage in so-called "independent expenditure" campaigns, in which they spend money on an election independent of the candidates' efforts. These organizations will sometimes air "issue advocacy" advertisements, which present the group's view of a particular topic such as Medicare or education. The advertisement may also note the candidates' positions on that issue, but it will not directly advocate support for any candidate. These efforts are not considered to be contributions to candidates and so are not regulated by federal law.

Since (and largely as a result of) the strict campaign finance legislation that was enacted in the 1970s, there has been an enormous growth both in the number of PACs and in the sum total of their contributions to political campaigns (see Table 9.1 and Chapter 7). Virtually any organization can form a PAC, and not all PACs are interest groups. About 40 percent of the PACs are corporate (meaning essentially businesses), 10 percent labor, and the rest other kinds of organizations, including public interest and ideological groups.

Although each individual PAC is strictly limited in how much it can give in any race to any single candidate, the candidates for Congress are relying more and more on the PACs to finance their campaigns, as it is often easier to raise large amounts of money from PACs than from individual donors. Certain predictable biases appear in the PACs' pattern of contributions. Corporate PACs tend to favor Republicans; labor PACs favor Democrats. As reflected in their contributions, PACs overwhelmingly favor incumbents, reminding us that everyone loves a winner. And in congressional races, PACs disproportionately favor legislators on committees of interest to the organization.

Public Protest

Most interest groups do not engage in direct public protest when they are dissatisfied with the direction of public policy. Occasionally, however, an organization will stage a protest demonstration, boycott, march, or strike to call attention to its grievance in a particularly dramatic way. With the exception of violence, these tactics are extensively protected by laws and court decisions.

The Boston Tea Party constitutes one of the earliest uses of protest tactics in American politics. In recent decades, civil rights, antiwar groups and environmental groups have resorted to active protest. Today, the protest is a strategy of the right and the left, and it has been used extensively, for example, by right-to-life groups. Direct-action tactics usually reflect intense emotional commitment to an issue. The protest builds solidarity and commitment among the members. It is also frequently a measure to awaken public opinion. The strategy depends for its success on drama and media attention. It can backfire if the attentive public perceives neither the cause nor the chosen tactics as legitimate. On the other side, however, large public demonstrations against the Vietnam War were instrumental in ending American involvement. As a general rule, politicians respond more readily to their traditional publics than to protest groups.

Litigating

Most of the tactics of interest groups discussed thus far are as old as interest groups themselves. There is one strategy, however, that is relatively new, yet in a short time has become one of the most effective ways for groups to influence public policy: the practice of resorting to the judiciary, especially the federal courts, to achieve results.

TABLE 9.1
The Increasing Number of Political Action Committees

PAC Type	1974	1976	1980	1990	1994	2001
Corporate	89	433	1,2024	1,795	1,660	1,575
Labor	201	224	297	346	333	317
Trade/Members hip Health	318	489	574	771	792	860
Nonconnected	—	—	378	1,065	980	1,026
Cooperative	—	—	42	59	53	41
Corporation without stock	—	—	56	136	136	118
TOTAL	608	1,146	2,551	4,172	3,954	3,907

Source: Federal Election Commission press releases, Jan. 17, 1982, Aug. 19, 1981 and Jan. 20, 1986. 1992: Harold Stanley and Richard Niemi, *Vital Statistics on American Politics, 1992.* (Washington: LQ Press).

This practice was actually pioneered near to the turn of the century by the National Consumers League (NCL) and by its general counsel Louis Brandeis (who later became a Supreme Court Justice). Brandeis promoted worker protection by winning a test of the Constitutionality of an Oregon law that limited women's workday to ten hours (*Muller v. Oregon*, 1908). In the Muller case, Brandeis introduced what became known as a *Brandeis brief*, arguing the case based upon social science evidence as opposed to established law, which became a popular technique of interest group litigation. But the great landmark case that really inaugurated the use of litigation by an interest group to achieve substantive policy changes was the now famous 1954 school desegregation case *Brown v. Board of Education*. The Brown case was the climax of a carefully planned legal strategy devised by the NAACP. The judicial route was pursued because the NAACP had virtually no chance of success in the political arena. The white-dominated southern state legislatures would not dismantle the dual school system voluntarily; and civil rights advocates in Congress could not muster sufficient strength to overcome a southern filibuster

in the Senate (at least not until the 1960s), thus foreclosing a remedy through national legislation.

In recent decades the Supreme Court has made it easier to influence policy through litigation by liberalizing the rules on who has "standing," or the right, to sue in court and by allowing more class-action suits on behalf of a class of individuals in similar circumstances. The result has been a large increase in the use of the courts by interest groups, especially by ideological groups. The acquisition with the help of feminist groups of a right to an abortion was achieved through a litigation strategy in the case of *Roe v. Wade* (1973). (Recent decisions have returned control over certain aspects of this question to state legislatures, and the same feminist groups that pursued the litigation strategy have had to employ—quite successfully—electoral and lobbying techniques.) Few groups have made more use of the courts or done so more successfully than environmental organizations, which have relied on the broad language of environmental legislation to delay or stop actions they believe are harmful.

All the tactics discussed above represent means by which interest groups seek to influence the political process for objectives they deem important. The capacity of groups to employ these tactics effectively depends on the resources of the particular group in question. Resources, however, must be understood in a sense much broader than cash in the bank. While economic assets are very important, other resources that can be equally, if not more, important include the ability to mobilize members as well as the appeal of the group's cause and the skill of the group's leadership. For example, the success of the civil rights movement in the 1960s owed a great deal to the willingness of hundreds of courageous individuals to risk their own safety and freedom in marches and to the extraordinary political and rhetorical skills of Martin Luther King.

Regulating Interest Groups

Interest groups are an intrinsic and vital element of the American political system and enjoy extensive First Amendment protection, as a result of the guarantee of both free speech and the right to assemble and petition the government. Yet extensive as these protections are, it has not meant that interest groups must go entirely unregulated. Groups and lobbying activities have been affected by direct attempts at regulation, by campaign finance legislation, and by various conflict-of-interest laws and ethics codes that regulate public officials' relationships to interest groups.

Direct Regulation

There have been two main statutes that have involved more or less direct regulation. One is the Lobbying Act of 1946, which requires individuals or organizations who solicit funds "to be used principally to . . . influence, directly or indirectly, the passage or defeat of any legislation" to register with the clerk of the House and the secretary of the Senate indicating their general legislative goals and who it is that they represent. They must also submit quarterly financial reports detailing how much they spent to influence the passage of legislation. This law was challenged by organizations arguing that it unconstitutionally abridged the right of free speech and petition. In *United States v. Harriss* (1954) the Supreme Court upheld the law, but construed it rather narrowly to apply only to direct contacts between lobbyists and members of Congress, thereby excluding both contact with a legislator's staff and grass-roots lobbying. A further weakness of the legislation is its failure to provide coverage for organizations that do a significant amount of lobbying but are able to argue that their "principal" purpose is not influencing legislation. Many politically powerful groups have refused to register for just this reason. In 1995, legislation was passed that expanded the definition of lobbying and increased the amount of information that lobbyists must provide. They now have to disclose who they lobbied, about which issues, and which clients they served. The House and Senate also passed strict limits on the gifts that members may accept from persons other than friends or family. Senators may not receive any gift worth more than $50; representatives may not accept any gifts at all.

The other statute that affects certain groups is the Revenue Act of 1939, which stipulates that nonprofit organizations—which include many, though not all, interest groups—whose activities are substantially directed toward "attempting to influence legislation" must pay income tax. As tax-exempt status is important to many organizations, both for saving on taxes and receiving donations, this law might discourage some organizations from devoting a substantial effort to direct lobbying. Occasionally a group may lose its tax exempt status for excessive overt lobbying, as the Sierra Club did in 1968. Most groups that wish to lobby, however, sidestep the law by setting up one organization to lobby (which pays taxes) and the other which does not (which enjoys tax-exempt status). The Sierra Club, for example, revived its affiliated Sierra Club Foundation after 1968, which served as the nonprofit tax-exempt arm of the organization.

Campaign Finance Legislation

The 1976 and 2002 campaign financing laws, discussed earlier in Chapter 7, place restrictions and regulations on the financing of election campaigns for federal office. One of the major restrictions limits the role of special interest money in the electoral process. Before this law passed, individuals or organizations could give hundreds of thousands, or even millions, of dollars to a single candidate. The law now limits each PAC both in how much it can give to a single campaign ($5,000 per campaign) and in how much it can contribute annually to all federal election campaigns ($25,000). Moreover, all contributions are now publicly recorded.

The limitations do in fact work to free candidates of too much pressure from any single group. No group really can give enough money to "buy" a candidate, although coordinated action by a number of groups giving at once ("bundling") does change this equation somewhat. Moreover, the growing number of such groups in a sense also assures greater independence for the candidates (especially the incumbents), as they can pick up from one group what they may lose from another. Yet, because of the severe limitations on campaign contributions from individuals and because parties are now limited in what they can give to their own candidates, candidates must rely more and more for their total funding on PACs. Campaign finance reforms have therefore stimulated a greater reliance on groups (though a greater freedom in relationship to any particular group).

Miscellaneous Actions

A variety of actions with the purpose of somehow stopping illicit influence-peddling have been directed not at the groups themselves, but at the members of Congress and employees of the executive branch. These include provisions requiring financial disclosure by high governmental officials, prohibitions on any outside work that might create a conflict of interest, strict limitations on how much representatives and senators may earn in outside income, and "revolving-door" legislation forbidding executive agency personnel who leave government service from representing any private interest dealings with their former agency for at least one year. These kinds of measures are aimed at making it less likely that improper relationships will develop between those who make policy and those who are most directly affected by government.

Alternatives to Legal Regulation

There is an inherent difficulty in attempts to regulate interest groups by legislation. Interest groups are protected by fundamental rights; moreover, it is perfectly proper and desirable that interest groups should be able to press their views vigorously and without undue interference. Although certain kinds of clear influence-buying should and can be limited by legislation, it is impossible to imagine how legitimate efforts at influence could be controlled by legislation without violating fundamental rights. In the words of one expert: "to regulate pressure politics by suppressing these great liberties is to cure the disease by killing the patient."[12]

At the same time, however, virtually everyone is aware that excessive group pressure applied within the law can still pose risks for the quality and fairness of public policy. This conclusion has led analysts to look to "regulate" interest groups by institutional techniques that tend either to reduce the influence that groups can bring to bear on officials or increase the ability of official to resist their pressures.

The idea of relying on such institutional solutions was pioneered by the founders. Thus Madison argued that in a commercial republic legislators would be elected from fairly large and heterogenous districts, which would allow legislators to play off various interests inside their districts to gain a greater degree of freedom. Moreover, the great number of interests at play in the nation as a whole would limit the net power of any one group in relationship to the others. This old theory forms precisely one modern solution that many analysts have seen emerging in recent years and have sought to encourage. The idea is simply to limit the power of interests by having more and more groups organize and participate. This solution has been working, many argue, in the legislative and administrative arena, where, in Robert Salisbury's words, "more groups" mean "less clout." It has also been working, many argue, in the area of campaign financing, where more PACs mean less influence.

Yet there are almost certain to be limits to the success of this kind of mechanical solution. It is not enough merely to have groups check each other. Institutional means must also be studied to foster and strengthen the ability of national institutions to withstand interest group pressures and to be able to reach independent judgments about the public interest. This kind of institutional solution points to studying ways of strengthening political parties, which buffer candidates and politicians somewhat from pressure groups, and to making organizational changes in Congress which may limit some of the points of access by groups and promote greater deliberation.

Conclusion

Of all the links between the citizenry and the formal institutions of government, interest groups have caused the most profound difficulties for democratic theory and practice. While interest groups play a vital role in communicating public attitudes to government, they can also make the achievement of the public interest more difficult by distorting governmental policy in favor of politically powerful organizations or by fostering a view that policymaking consists of nothing more than bargaining among different groups. A political system designed to promote personal liberty will necessarily foster dynamic interest-group politics. Nonetheless, this same political system will be required to moderate and regulate the clash of interests.

The openness of the American political system to interest groups reflects a clear recognition of the legitimacy of pluralist elements in the decision-making process and the need to take into account, however imperfectly, the *intensity* of the views of certain groups and not just their numerical strength. Yet the desire to control and regulate group interests reflects an attempt to ensure that majoritarian concerns are not overwhelmed by the power of entrenched groups and that representative institutions are not incapacitated from acting on behalf of their perception of the public interest.

It is incorrect of course, to depict group interests as always being in tension with majoritarian concerns or the public interest. Interest groups are a vital component of majoritarian politics and an essential mechanism for discovering the public interest. Yet the potential conflict between the sum of organized interest groups and the wishes of the majority is of sufficient importance to merit laws and especially institutional arrangements that seek to limit and structure the access of groups to the political process.

Chapter 9 Notes

1. Arthur Bentley, *The Process of Government* (Chicago: The University of Chicago Press, 1908).
2. David Truman, *The Governmental Process,* 2nd ed. (New York: Knopf, 1971), p. 59.
3. Alexis de Tocqueville, *Democracy in America* (New York: Doubleday, 1969), p. 189.
4. Alexis de Tocqueville, *Democracy in America,* p. 513.
5. Theodore Lowi, *The End of Liberalism,* (New York: Norton, 1969).
6. Robert Salisbury, "The Paradox of Interest Groups in Washington—More Groups, Less Clout," in Anthony King, ed., *The New American Political System,* 2nd ed. (Washington, D.C.: American Enterprise Institute, 1990), pp. 203–229.
7. James Q. Wilson, *Political Organizations,* (New York: Basic Books, 1973), p. 46.
8. V. O. Key, *Politics Parties and Pressure Groups,* (New York: Thomas Crowell, 1958), p. 154.
9. Norman Ornstein and Shirley Elder, *Interests, Lobbying and Policymaking* (Washington, D. C.: Congressional Quarterly Press, 1978), p. 97.
10. Bernard Asbell, *The Senate Nobody Knows,* (Garden City, New York: Doubleday, 1978), pp. 370–71.
11. Norman Ornstein and Shirley Edler, *Interest Groups, Lobbying and Policymaking,* p. 77.
12. E. E. Schattschneider, *The Semi-sovereign People,* (New York: Holt, 1960), p. 42.

Part Three

The Institutions of Government

10

The Congress

CHAPTER CONTENTS

Congress today is perhaps both the most criticized and least understood of our national governing institutions. Sometimes, in dealing with an issue like the federal budget, Congress's procedures and institutional structures seem to make it incapable of formulating coherent policy. Occasionally, however, Congress acts with great speed and determination in translating a new idea into legislation. Congress has been attacked as a body of entrenched incumbents who win reelection by exploiting the advantages of holding office; yet all accounts show that members devote an enormous amount of time and energy to remaining on good terms with their constituents. On some issues Congress appears to favor special interests over the broader national interest, while on others it passes legislation that imposes substantial economic burdens on powerful corporations. In the recent past many have urged Congress to reassert its authority against an overly powerful executive branch, especially in the areas of budgeting and foreign policy; but after trying to do so, Congress has often been attacked for meddling in areas where it is not competent to act, or for interfering with the president's executive functions.

What are we to make of these divergent characteristics and views of Congress? Is it unrepresentative of the American people, or is it per-

haps too representative? Is Congress the captive of special interests, or does it too frequently seek idealistic ends without regard for the actual costs that must be borne by particular segments of American society? Does Congress intrude too greatly on the president's power, or has it failed to live up to its own proper role in the American separation-of-powers system?

Controversy about the Congress, while perhaps greater than usual today, is certainly not new. People have questioned the effectiveness of Congress from the outset. There has rarely been anything like a consensus about the proper role of Congress in the American political system. No matter how much the institution and its political environment change over time each generation seems vaguely dissatisfied with the national legislature yet equally uncertain about what could be done. One reason for this perennial dissatisfaction is that we expect so many different things from Congress and from those who serve in it.

The Functions of Congress: Original Intention and Historical Developments

When the founding fathers created Congress, they had in mind for it two key tasks: the passage of sound legislation and the faithful representation of what they called the "deliberate sense of the community." Over the years, Congress has taken on three other important functions: oversight of the bureaucracy, investigations to inform the public, and constituency service. A brief examination of these five functions illustrates the many different burdens placed on Congress.

Legislation

Article I of the Constitution of the United States begins with the words "All legislative Powers herein granted shall be vested in a Congress of the United State." It goes on to enumerate seventeen separate powers, some of which are among the most important exercised by any government—taxation, regulation of commerce, and declaration of war—and others of which seem less significant, such as the power to establish post offices and to exercise jurisdiction over the seat of government (Washington, D.C.). The list of specific powers is followed by a clause giving Congress the authority to "make all Laws which shall be necessary and proper for carrying into Execution the foregoing Powers." This clause makes it clear that the enumeration was not intended as a strict limitation on Congress. Although the president possesses a qualified veto over statutes passed by Congress, and the Supreme Court has successfully asserted the power to rule acts of Congress unconstitutional, Congress was designed to be the primary lawmaking institution of the national government.

For most of the nineteenth century Congress was, in fact, the government's chief policymaking instrument. This was especially true in the decades after the Civil War, a time when relatively weak presidents were no match for a determined House and Senate. During the twentieth century, however, the position of Congress as the nation's chief policymaking institution has been undermined by three broad developments. First, the president became increasingly important as an agenda setter for the nation and Congress. Second, with the growth of a large federal bureaucracy to regulate various sectors of the economy, more policy decisions are made by career civil servants or presidential appointees. Many of these decisions have the full force of law even though they are not directly passed by Congress. Finally, the importance of foreign policy

concerns after World War II enhanced the president's power at the expense of Congress, especially since much foreign policy is made by day-to-day decisions of the executive branch rather than by formal legislation.

In response to these developments, Congress, over the past quarter century, has made an effort to reassert its position. It has often been reluctant to take its direction from the president, especially when the president is of a different party than majorities in Congress; and it has built up its own institutional capabilities by adding large numbers of staff and new organizational units, such as the Congressional Budget Office, and by restructuring its procedures for exercising its authority to decide matters of taxing and spending. It has also become more skeptical of policymaking within the bureaucracy, overturning administrative decisions through statutes and placing new restrictions on the power it delegates to the bureaucracy. In the area of foreign policy, Congress enacted new legislative restrictions on the president, including the War Powers Act of 1973, which was designed to make Congress a full partner in decisions to undertake long-term military actions.

Congress has also attempted to retain its legislative prerogative over administrative agencies. In a practice known as the "legislative veto," Congress beginning in the 1930s gave itself the power to overturn the administrative decisions of executive branch agencies by a simple majority vote. In the early 1980s, the Supreme Court in *INS v. Chadha* decision (1983) found this practice to be a violation of the principle of separation of powers and declared all legislative veto provisions unconstitutional. In 1996, Congress instituted a new process known as "congressional review." It allows Congress to overturn administrative regulations, with the approval of the president, within sixty days of their announcement. This practice was first used in 2001 to reverse ergonomics regulations enacted at the end of the Clinton administration.

Representation

Before the modern era, the task of lawmaking was carried out by individuals (monarchs, tyrants), by small bodies of powerful leaders (hereditary nobles, the wealthy), or by the people directly (the Athenian democracy). In contrast to these schemes, modern liberal democracies place the official lawmaking responsibility in a representative body. Whether called a "congress," "parliament," "national assembly," or "diet," the lawmaking body is an assembly of individuals elected by the people who are expected to give voice to—to re-present—the attitudes and interests of the people themselves. The joining of the two tasks of lawmaking and representation into one body creates a strong likelihood that the laws passed by the government will broadly conform to popular desires, while not being subject to the convulsions of direct democracy. James Madison believed a representative assembly would "refine and enlarge the public views" over the often regionalized, narrow, and volatile views of a direct democracy (*Federalist* 10).

The representative principle takes two different forms in modern democracies. In most western European nations, the individual elected to the legislature represents primarily the views of a political party. The personal characteristics and background of the candidates are less important than their party affiliation. On election day, the voters in effect choose one of the contesting parties and its particular program to govern the nation. But in the United States the political party is less important. Individuals elected to Congress represent primarily those who reside in their legislative district (for House members) or state (for senators). Members of Congress act on their own, as spokesmen for the interests of the district or state or as independent deliberative agents.

This principle of *geographic representation* has several important effects. It virtually guarantees that interests and groups powerful at the local or state level will make themselves felt within Congress, while diffuse interests or values, such as a desire for a clean environment, may not be as well represented, especially if they conflict with powerful local interests. Generally, members of Congress analyze legislative proposals in terms of the impact on their districts or states and favor legislation that will benefit their constituents, sometimes at the expense of broader national considerations. Geographic representation also weakens party leadership within Congress by making the congressional district or state, and not the party, the first object of loyalty of representatives and senators.

Oversight

The federal government, especially in this century, has dramatically expanded its role in attempting to promote social and economic well-being by direct government action. As it has done so, a huge bureaucracy, numbering almost 3 million people, has grown up to administer hundreds of federal programs. The bureaucracy nominally serves under the direction of the president and is part of the executive branch of government. On paper at least, the executive branch has a pyramid-like, hierarchical arrangement with clear chains of command that bind even the lowest-level employee to the ultimate direction of the chief officers who serve the president.

Congress, however, has adhered to a very different notion of bureaucratic accountability under which officers of the government are principally responsible to the law, and therefore to Congress. Congress formulated this concept in 1946 when, in the Legislative Reorganization Act, it required that "each standing committee of the Senate and the House of Representatives exercise continuous watchfulness of the execution [of laws] by the administrative agencies."

Congressional oversight is carried out (1) through the review by committees of Congress of requests by executive branch officials for new legislative authority to continue ongoing programs, (2) through the annual budget process when the appropriations committees set specific funding levels for these programs, and (3) by the two government operations committees (one in each house of Congress), which have special responsibility for investigating and promoting the "overall economy and efficiency of government." More recently many committees in Congress have created special oversight subcommittees to consolidate their oversight responsibilities. The bureaucracy in the American system in effect serves two masters.

Investigations

If the members of Congress are uncertain about how faithfully or effectively the executive branch is carrying out its mandate, they may initiate a formal investigation by a congressional committee. Some congressional investigations, however, have a much broader purpose of publicizing a major problem, either to prepare the way for governmental action or to hold accountable (and check) executive officials, including the president. In the past decades, congressional investigations of organized crime, of hunger in America, of the assassinations of John F. Kennedy and Martin Luther King, Jr., and of the Watergate scandal all uncovered and publicized important information. In 2002, both houses of Congress conducted oversight hearings to determine the circumstances of the Enron Corporation's financial downfall. As a result of their findings, Congress has proposed various reforms to the rules governing accounting procedures to prevent another financial collapse like Enron. Another important investigation is the joint House and Senate Intelligence Committee probe into the handling of intelligence information prior to the September 11th attack on the World Trade Center. Many of these hearings took place in private, but they are almost certain to promote changes in the organization of the FBI and CIA.

Constituency Service

The growth in the programs and size of the national government over two centuries has put greater demands on the members of Congress to assist their constituents in their dealings with federal agencies. Consider what a Virginia congressman wrote to his constituents in a campaign newsletter:

> Thousands of your neighbors have asked Herb Harris for help in cutting through red tape to get information or action. Some need replacement of a lost Social Security check. Others need help in getting veterans benefits they deserve. Others are trying to get a straight answer from the SBA [Small Business Administration]. What they all have in common is that they want the system to work the way it's supposed to work: fairly.

When Congress first began operating, there was much less contact between individual citizens and the federal government and therefore less need for members of Congress to play this kind of service role. Now, however, constituency service consumes a large part of the resources of every congressional office, especially the time of personal staff. Senators and representatives assign this function a very high priority, for it can generate votes within the state or district. Unlike taking stands on controversial issues, constituency service tends to garner more support from voters. So important has this function become that many analysts of Congress worry that we are witnessing a transformation of some members from national legislators to errand-boys who devote the bulk of their time and effort to constituency service.

The variety and importance of these five functions give some idea of the vitality of Congress in the American political system. Congress is, without doubt, the most powerful and dynamic national legislature among the world's major liberal democracies. In the parliamentary systems of countries like Britain, Germany, and Japan, the executive branch—prime minister, cabinet, and bureaucracy—is the dominant governing institution. Although the parliament retains complete formal authority over public policy, in practice the majority party in the legislature nearly always supports the proposals of the party leaders, who head the executive branch. In the United States, the national legislature is, as it was designed to be, vigorously independent of the executive branch. It has a far greater independent impact on public policy than do the legislative bodies in other liberal democracies.

A Bicameral Legislature

Although we commonly refer to Congress as if it were a single institution, it is more accurate to think of it as two distinct legislative bodies: the House and the Senate. Each body is a world of its own, and there is surprisingly little formal interaction between the two houses, other than occasional joint sessions, a few joint committees, and conference committees to resolve differences in legislative proposals. The two bodies have separate office buildings and separate chambers for debate. Each body selects its own leaders, creates its own committee system, and determines its own rules and procedures.

This formal institutional division extends even to the architecture of the Capitol and surrounding buildings. If a line were drawn east-west through the rotunda in the center of the Capitol, it would divide the offices, chambers, and support buildings of the Senate (north of the line) from those of the House (south of the line). The fact is that a member of the House or Senate can work a full day "on the Hill" without even seeing a member of the other body.

But why have a bicameral legislature? What purposes are served by requiring two distinct institutions to agree on legislation? Why did the founders create both a House and Senate, and is their design still relevant today?

The Original Plan for the House and Senate

Bicameralism   The form of America's bicameral legislature, as discussed in Chapter 2, was related to the conflict between the small and large states within the Constitutional Convention. Many delegates from the larger states wanted a legislative branch in which membership was based on a state's population, while delegates from the smaller states feared that this system would result in a union dominated by the larger states. A compromise was finally reached whereby representation in the House was based on population and representation in the Senate on the equality of the states.

The attention paid to this "great compromise" has tended to obscure the fact that well before the conflict over representation even arose at the Convention, the delegates had decided in favor of a bicameral legislature. Bicameralism, they argued, would improve the quality of legislation by requiring the concurrence of two distinct bodies, each possessing attributes beneficial to the legislative process.

In constructing the new legislature, the founders thought that one branch had to be especially close to the people. The House of Representatives, according to George Mason, "ought to know and sympathize with every part of the community."[1] To ensure the democratic

character of the House, the founders instituted election directly by the people and short terms of office. Election by the people made it likely that representatives would share the basic values and political dispositions of their constituents. Short terms of office (with no restrictions on reeligibility) encouraged incumbents to act in ways broadly consistent with the desires of those they represented.

Although firmly committed to a democratic assembly in the legislative branch, the founders feared that it would be subject to some of the defects characteristic of the state legislatures during the revolutionary period. In particular, they were concerned that (1) a relatively large, popularly elected assembly would be a tumultuous and disorderly body easily manipulated by "factious leaders"; (2) the House would lack sufficient knowledge about national issues because members would serve only a few months out of each year, after which they would return to their primary occupations; (3) a rapid turnover of membership every two years would translate into frequent changes in the laws; and (4) the members of the House would too often judge legislative proposals on the basis of their immediate popularity rather than their long-term impact on the nation.

For these reasons the founders created a Senate that was considerably smaller than the House and whose members served six years instead of two. Senators were elected by the state legislatures, not directly by the people, and had to be at least 30 years old (five years older than the minimum for the House). To ensure a basic continuity of membership, only one-third of the Senate would come up for reelection every two years. The founders hoped that this new institution would be more knowledgeable about national affairs, more stable and consistent in formulating national policy, and more capable of resisting short-term popular pressures for unwise legislation. The Senate, Madison hoped, would function "with more coolness, with more system, and with more wisdom, than the popular branch."[2]

It was not the founders' intent, however, that the Senate should be immune from the pressures of public opinion. After all, senators interested in reelection would have to be sensitive to the political views predominant in the state legislatures, which were very democratic bodies and usually accurate barometers of public opinion within the states. In giving senators some insulation from direct popular control, the founders sought to create an institution that had the capacity temporarily to resist unsound popular desires at those "critical moments" when the people might be "stimulated by some irregular passion, or some illicit advantage, or misled by the artful misrepresentations of interested men." (*Federalist* 63) Such temporary resistance would give the people time to reconsider their actions and reach a more considered and thoughtful opinion.

Constitutional Powers   For the most part the House and Senate were intended to be equal partners in the legislative process. No bill can become a law unless both branches agree to precisely the same language. There is, however, some differentiation in function between the two bodies. The House, for example, is given exclusive authority to originate revenue bills, reflecting the founders' belief that the particularly sensitive power of taxation should be tied to the branch of government closest to the people. The Senate, nonetheless, retains full authority to amend House-passed tax measures as it sees fit.

On the other hand, the founders gave the Senate a special role in two important areas: the ratification of treaties and the confirmation of appointments to high executive offices and to the federal judiciary. The conduct of foreign policy in particular demanded qualities peculiar to the Senate: stability of membership, substantial expertise about national affairs, and a long-range view of the public good. Foreign policy according to the founders, was both too sensitive and too risky to be entrusted to a "popular assembly composed of members constantly coming and going in quick succession." (*Federalist* 64)

The House and Senate Today

The House and Senate are now very different institutions from those created nearly 200 years ago. The Senate has increased in size from 26 to 100, the House from 65 to 435. Where once only a handful of aides assisted the functioning of each body, there are now many thousands of such persons. The average size of a congressional district has increased from about 40,000 to more than sixteen times that amount (about 650,000); and senators from many states now represent more people than lived in the entire country in 1789. Moreover, since the passage of the Seventeenth Amendment in 1913 senators are elected directly by the people, rather than by the state legislatures.

Many things, of course, have not changed. The terms of office are the same; the Senate is still considerably smaller than the House; the House remains more important on revenue matters; and the Senate continues to play a larger role in foreign policy and appointments.

Membership Turnover   The founders expected —though they did not mandate—a rapid turnover of membership in the House. Since the early Congresses met for only a few months out of each year, there was concern that a body of short-term, part-time legislators might lack sufficient expertise about national issues. For a century the founders' expectation regarding turnover proved accurate. It was not uncommon in the nineteenth century for half the membership of the House to change at each election, and turnover was nearly always at least one-third.

Although part of this turnover resulted from incumbents being defeated for reelection, much of it was also due to voluntary decisions not to run again. Service in Congress was not nearly as attractive in the past century as it later became. Washington at the time was a relatively small and unexciting city and could not compete with the social and cultural attractions of Boston, New York, or Philadelphia. Moreover, those who sought to exercise great political power were not necessarily drawn to service in Congress; during a time when the national government played a rather limited role in domestic affairs, the decisions of state legislatures were often more important. Finally, since service in Congress was only a part-time job (three to four months each year), it took time and attention away from a member's principal occupation and source of livelihood.

The Rise of the Career Legislator The high turnover in congressional membership started to decrease around the turn of the twentieth century. As the national government began to exercise greater influence in both domestic and foreign policy, more members sought to remain in the House and establish careers there. After 1912, institutional changes were adopted which ensured that members who served a long time (that is, accumulated seniority) would gain substantial influence within the House. This, in turn, gave voters more reason to reelect incumbents, who could now be more helpful to the district. As a result, by the middle of the twentieth century, the House had been transformed into a body of full-time, professional legislators. Few incumbents voluntarily retired, and the vast majority who sought reelection were successful (see Table 10.1).

From 1950 through 1990, an average of only 32 representatives (7 percent of the body) voluntarily retired each two-year period, many to seek higher office. Members of the House served on average almost twelve years, and it was not uncommon for many to spend most of their adult lives in Congress. In 1992, however, there was a larger than usual turnover, as many members retired rather than risk being defeated by the tide of an anti-incumbency sentiment that swept the nation. Again in 1994 more House members than usual announced their retirement, and in the 1994 elections there was a much greater than average turnover of membership, as Republicans swept many Democrats from office. The elections of 2000, in which Republicans barely managed to retain their new majority status, continued the usual pattern of low turnover. Compared to the last century, members manage to stay for a much longer period of time in Washington.

The contemporary House thus does not suffer from one defect that the founders feared. Because members tend to serve for long periods, they build up substantial knowledge about national issues, and the low turnover has meant that the contemporary House is not given to dramatic shifts in policy every few years. Rather than a loose, informal, factious assembly of legislative amateurs, the House has become a highly structured institution where business is conducted by experienced legislators according to regularized rules and procedures. A similar tendency toward careerism has characterized the Senate. Senators from 1950 to 1990 were reelected at a slightly lower rate than House members (see Table 7.5). Since the Senate term is three times longer than the House term, senators generally end up spending more years in Washington than House members. The high rate of victory for incumbents, along with the staggered elections, means that membership in the Senate in any given year changes only at the margins.

Term Limits? The development of the career legislators, many have contended, creates a new problem for the Congress. In this view, members who seek to make a career in Congress lose touch, if not with the interests of their constituency, then at any rate with the way of thinking of the average citizen. The idea of the "citizen legislator," who serves in Congress and then returns to private life has been lost. More ominously, legislators may begin to conduct the business of governing with a view to keeping themselves in office, which corrupts the entire deliberative process.

One former congressman summed up the problem in the following way: "You give me a staff of fifteen people, a budget of over $600,000 a year, the ability to solve your personal problems with the government, the right to send you unlimited amounts of mail telling you what a good job I'm doing, combine almost unrestricted access to the local media, and I'll beat my opponent almost every time."[3]

The belief that there is a crisis both in representation and in the effective performance of Congress has spawned what has become known as "the term limits movement." This movement calls for a Constitutional amendment that would limit congressional careers, according to the most popular proposal, to 12 years: two terms for senators, six terms for members of the House. Proponents of this plan, however, have not waited for the passage of an amendment, which Congress has not been willing to endorse. Using the processes of initiative and referendum in the states, citizens in fifteen states between 1990 and 1993 passed some form of term limitation for

TABLE 10.1
Membership Turnover in the House, 1950–2000

Year	Retired	Defeated for Reelection	Percent New Members
1950	29	38	16.8
1952	42	35	18.6
1954	24	28	12.9
1956	21	22	10.6
1958	33	40	18.2
1960	26	30	13.8
1962	24	36	15.4
1964	33	53	20.9
1966	22	49	16.8
1968	23	13	9.0
1970	29	22	12.9
1972	40	25	15.1
1974	43	48	21.1
1976	47	16	15.4
1978	49	24	17.7
1980	34	37	17.0
1982	40	39	18.6
1984	22	19	9.9
1986	38	8	11.5
1988	23	7	7.6
1990	27	16	9.9
1992	52	43	25.2
1994	49	37	19.8
1996	50	23	16.8
1998	33	7	9.2
2000	33	6	9.4

Source: Norman J. Ornstein, Thomas E. Mann, and Michael J. Malbin, *Vital Statistics on Congress, 1989–1990* (Washington: American Enterprise Institute, 1990), p. 56; 1992 results from *New York Times* Election Returns.

congressional members. By 1997, however, the movement to limit congressional terms had lost much of its momentum. Several factors contributed to this development. First, in a landmark case in 1995, *U.S. Term Limits Inc. v. Thornton*, the Supreme Court struck down state term-limit laws as unconstitutional. According to the Court, states have no authority to enact such limits for a federal office whose qualifications are spelled out in the Constitution. (Term limits have also been adopted in many states for state legislators, but these laws pose no problems of

constitutionality and remain in effect.) Second, efforts in Congress to propose a term-limit amendment to the Constitution have consistently failed to muster the necessary two-thirds majorities. Interest in term limits has faded considerably since the mid-1990s. Even at the state level, one state, Idaho, voted in 2002 to overturn the term limits voters enacted through ballot initiative in 1994.

Continuing Differences Between the House and Senate If these changes mean that the dissimi-

Many senators have aspired to higher political office, but only two in this century—Warren G. Harding and John F. Kennedy—came to the presidency directly from the Senate. (Harding photo provided by National Portrait Gallery, Smithsonian Institution; Gift of Oswald D. Reich. Used with permission.)

larity between the House and Senate is not as great as the founders expected, they do not mean that important differences no longer exist. The difference in size alone has important consequences for the structure and functioning of the two institutions. Because the Senate is less than one-fourth the size of the House it is able to function much more informally. Rules are less rigid and can be more easily dispensed with. Procedural decisions like scheduling legislation, which are made by a Rules Committee in the House, are usually made in the Senate through informal discussion among the interested parties. Floor debate in the two chambers also reflects the effects of the difference in size. The House is so large that severe restraints must be placed on a member's opportunity to speak on the floor. In the Senate, on the other hand, any member may insist on debating a bill for a prolonged period (subject only to a vote of "cloture" to end debate).

Another difference between the House and Senate, at least partly the result of the contrast in size, is that the Senate is the more prestigious institution. Membership in the Senate is more highly prized than membership in the House, a point easily demonstrated by the fact that no senator has in recent times voluntarily resigned to run for the House, whereas many members of the House regularly resign to run for the Senate. Inside the two bodies, senators "count" more in the Senate than do representatives in the House; each senator is accorded privileges and prerogatives as an individual that are unknown to House members.

All these differences produce a contrasting political cast to the two institutions. The House today is a more democratic body in which the majority ultimately has its way. The Senate is far less majoritarian. Minorities or even individual senators can more easily hold up Senate action or extract concessions before allowing the body to proceed.

The Senate and Presidential Ambitions Because the Senate is smaller and more prestigious than the House, a larger number of its members are able to develop visibility and reputations in the broader national community. Though a number of House members (including Jack Kemp and Richard Gephardt) have become serious presidential candidates in recent years, it is easier for senators to develop national visibility. Lyndon Johnson, John Kennedy, Barry Goldwater, Ted Kennedy, Robert Dole and Al Gore all established national reputations and national constituencies while serving in the Senate.

Often senators consciously promote national visibility in order to foster presidential ambitions. Senators, in particular, have benefited in the last half century from the increased importance of foreign policy, over which the Senate has special responsibilities (ratifying treaties and confirming ambassadorial appointments), and from the growing dominance of television as the chief communicator of national news. (Senators are frequently asked to appear on major national news programs.) Before these developments, the governor's office, especially in the larger states, was the likeliest route to a serious attempt at the presidency. Today, senators are frequently involved in presidential campaigns, although since 1920 only one (John Kennedy) has actually been elected coming directly from the Senate. The lack of executive experience here may prove to be a disadvantage to senators.

The Senate and the Legislative Process   One way senators seek to develop reputations outside the institution itself is by investigating and publicizing national problems and actively promoting new policy initiatives. As a result, the Senate has become an "incubator" for national policy development, serving, in the words of political scientist Nelson Polsby, as

> a great forum, an echo chamber, a theater, where dramas—comedies and tragedies, soap operas and horse operas—are staged to enhance the careers of its members and to influence public policy by means of debate and public investigation. . . . [The Senate] articulates, formulates, shapes, and publicizes demands and can serve as a hothouse for significant policy innovation, especially in opposition to the President.[4]

The danger is that if senators are mainly interested in fostering higher political ambitions, they may give more attention to their public image than to the substance of the legislation they promote. This may lead to "statutes that are long on goals but short on means to achieve them" and laws with "ambitious 'public interest' aims" that cannot be realized.[5] Indeed, it is not uncommon for members of the House to regard the Senate as an irresponsible, publicity-seeking body rather than a serious lawmaking institution. As a member of the House Ways and Means Committee once commented on the way the Senate writes tax legislation:

> With all due respect to the Senate, they don't know what the hell they're doing over there. They're so damn irresponsible you can get unanimous consent to an amendment that cost a billion dollars! And the Senate is supposed to be a safety check on the House. We really act as the stabilizing influence, the balance.[6]

In the mind of at least this one member of Congress, the founders' original plan for a bicameral legislature has been turned on its head.

The lesson to draw from this brief comparison is that the House and Senate remain quite different institutions. Each makes a distinct contribution to the legislative and representative functions of Congress. This fact must be kept in mind as we examine in more detail the members of Congress, the organizational structure of the two chambers, the procedures used to pass legislation, and how Congress represents public opinion.

Members of Congress: Who They Are, What They Want, and What They Do

Personal Characteristics

The members of the House and Senate are not a cross-section of the American populace. If they were, then half of them would be women, over 12 percent would be African Americans, the average age would be around 35, a majority would not have college degrees, a sizable fraction would come from blue-collar occupations, and less than 1 percent would be lawyers. (In fact, almost all are college graduates and over forty percent hold law degrees.)

In terms of race and sex, Congress has become more reflective of the population during the past few decades. Once nearly an all-white and male club, Congress from 1947 to 2000 has seen the number of African Americans increase from two to thirty-eight, and the number of women from eight to seventy-four. There are also twenty-one Hispanics, eight Asians, and two American Indians.

The vast majority of members claim an affiliation with an organized religion. The figures for both Roman Catholics (28 percent) and Jews (7 percent) have increased significantly during the past several decades, and many of the newer Catholic and Jewish members represent districts or states that are overwhelmingly Protestant. The specific religious affiliation of candidates for Congress does not seem to matter nearly as much as it once did.

Constituency Senators' constituencies are automatically set by the boundaries of the states. In the case of House members, however, the constituencies must be determined after a reallocation of seats among the states and then a process of constituency drawing within them. The Constitution requires an adjustment every ten years in the apportionment of seats in the House of Representatives to reflect population changes among the states. Throughout this century the Northeast and Midwest have steadily lost representatives while the South and West have gained. These changes have been especially significant in the last twenty years, and the balance of political power in the nation has been increasingly moving south and west.

Within the states, the constituencies, as noted, reflect the principle of geographic representation. The determination of district lines, discussed in Chapter 7, is one of the most intensely political processes in larger states, where there are many districts to draw. All sorts of criteria come into play, including traditionally the number of persons from different ethnic and racial groups. In many areas before the 1960s, lines had been drawn to exclude the possibility of districts having a majority of black citizens. These kinds of racial gerrymanders were declared unconstitutional by the Supreme Court in 1960 in the decision of *Gomillion v. Lightfoot.*

By 1991, however, the situation had changed dramatically. The Voting Rights Bill of 1982 was understood by most states to require, wherever possible, the drawing of geographic districts in 1991 that included a majority of certain minorities (blacks, Hispanics, and Asians). Many of the new black and Hispanic members of Congress in 1993 came from these new districts. In some instances, the geographic basis of these districts was highly tenuous—in one case in North Carolina consisting for a good part of nothing but a corridor that ran up interstate 85 in order to join together different areas having a high black concentration.

The *requirement* of race-based constituencies, at least where the geographic boundaries are so oddly shaped, was challenged in the courts and led to a 1993 Supreme Court decision (*Shaw v. Reno*) in which Justice Sandra Day O'Connor, speaking for the Court, worried that "racial gerrymandering, even for remedial purposes, may balkanize us into competing racial factions." In subsequent cases brought in North Carolina, Texas, and Georgia, the Court has struck down a number of these districts where the district lines had been drawn with the clear intent of creating race-based districts. The issue here has not been completely resolved, but the system of districting used in the 1990s, in which race was taken to be a necessary criterion, has now been declared unconstitutional.

Party Perhaps no characteristic of those who serve in Congress is more politically significant than party identification. Nearly all members identify with either the Democratic or the Republican party. The majority party in each chamber has the responsibility of organizing that body. Each chooses its own leader, determines the committee chairs, and has considerable influence in deciding whether a pattern of cooperation or conflict is established with the executive branch.

From Franklin Roosevelt's election in 1932 until 1994, the Democratic Party dominated in Congress. From 1933 to 1981 they were the majority party in both houses in all but four years (1947–1948 and 1953–1954); from 1955 until

1981, a period of twenty-six years, Democrats controlled both chambers. From 1981 to 1994, the Democrats maintained control of the House and held the Senate for half the period (1987–1994). The Democrats had majorities in both houses under the Bush and first two years of the Clinton administrations (1987–1995). In a major and quite unexpected turn of events, however, Republicans took control of both houses in the 1994 elections, which ended a forty-year period in which Democrats held at least one chamber (the House) of the Congress. After the 2000 election, Republicans temporarily held control of all branches—the presidency, Senate, and House—but the Senate "majority" was based on a 50-50 split in the chamber. Five months into George W. Bush's administration, Vermont Senator James Jeffords switched parties and control of the Senate went to the Democrats.

Our national political parties are not, however, cohesive units of like-minded individuals. Voting within Congress is ample testimony of this fact. Majorities differ according to the specific issue being considered; and while a tendency to vote on party lines is usually noticeable, party-line voting does not describe the whole of congressional behavior.

For much of the period of Democratic party dominance in Congress, there has been a pattern of coalition building outside of the party. Beginning in the late 1930s, conservative southern Democrats commonly joined Republicans to vote against liberal northern Democrats. Proposals supported by a majority of the Democrats have often been defeated by this cross-party group known as the "conservative coalition." Southern Democrats provided the margin of victory for some of the major initiatives of the Reagan administration in the early 1980s.

Fewer conservative Democrats are being elected from the South, as most of the conservative voters are now selecting Republican representatives. Indeed, the center of power inside the Republican party in the House has been moving more and more to the South, as witnessed, for example, by the Republicans' selection in 1995 of Newt Gingrich, from Georgia, as the Speaker of the House, Dick Armey, from Texas, as the Majority Leader, and Trent Lott, from Missis-

sippi, as the Senate Majority Leader. In all likelihood, this development has also made the Republican membership as a whole ideologically more cohesive. The Republican majority that took control of Congress in 1995 showed remarkable unity early on, although there remain important differences of viewpoint between moderate and conservative elements within the party.

Goals

The members of the House and Senate have different backgrounds, interests, and ambitions. Four basic goals influence their behavior within Congress: reelection, power and prestige within the House or Senate, good public policy, and election to higher office.[7]

Reelection Although some members retire voluntarily as their terms expire, the vast majority work hard to get reelected. Members of the House in particular seem to be running for reelection all the time, as indicated by the dozens of trips they take home each year and the close attention they pay to constituency service. While some members seem content merely to maintain a seat in Congress, for most reelection is not an end in itself but rather a means—albeit an essential one—to other ends.

Power and Prestige within Congress Some members wish not only to be reelected, but also to hold important positions in Congress. Both the House and the Senate have been described as "little worlds all their own," in which members' reputations and standing have no necessary relation to how well they are known outside the body. J. Dennis Hastert, a relative unknown outside of Congress, was elected Speaker of the House after Gingrich's retirement in 1998. Though he had rarely been in the national spotlight, Hastert had built good relations with his fellow Congressional Republicans over many years. Members who wish to gain prestige and influence within the House and Senate seek to do so by treating colleagues courteously, carrying out legislative duties responsibly, and avoiding any actions that might bring the body into disrepute.

Good Public Policy Some members of Congress, however, are more interested in influencing public policy than they are in achieving a prominent position inside the body. They have strong opinions about what government should be doing and they work hard to bring about new policies by introducing legislation, informing the public through committee hearings and floor speeches, and taking their case directly to outside audiences. Sometimes, these members will forgo a measure of prestige and influence inside the Congress to pursue their goals. Often, these are the representatives and senators who become well known outside Congress.

Election to Higher Office Building a reputation outside of Washington can also serve a fourth distinct goal sought by many in the House and Senate: election to higher office. Members of the House often have their eyes on a Senate seat or on the governor's mansion, while some senators, as we have seen, focus their ambitions on the presidency. Those who aspire to higher office are especially inclined to find ways to use their legislative position to become better known in the home state or in the nation at large.

Personal Resources

Newly elected members of the House and Senate quickly discover that Congress provides them with ample resources to pursue their goals. In addition to a personal salary (in 2000) of $141,300, each member is given a suite of offices in one of the buildings across from the Capitol as well as a substantial sum for office expenses, for the rental of space for district or state offices, and for travel to and from the home state or district. In addition, members of the House receive over $550,000 each year to hire up to twenty-two assistants; senators get between $1.1 and $2.2 million dollars each year (depending on the size of the state) to hire as many assistants as they wish. (Some Senate staffs are as large as seventy members.)[8]

Not all these resources are applied to the legislator's service in Washington. Approximately one-third of all personal staff members work in district or state offices engaged in constituency service. Many members of Congress maintain two or even three such offices throughout the district or state in order to maximize their visibility back home. Members' personal visibility is also enhanced by the availability of the "frank": the privilege of mailing newsletters and other communications to constituents free of charge.

The Job of Serving as a Member of Congress

No single word better describes the task of serving as a representative or senator than "demanding." Consider the following comments made by an exasperated member of the House to a group of his colleagues one evening while waiting for a vote in the House chamber:

> I came here to make laws, and what do I do? I send baby books to young mothers, listen to every maladjusted kid who wants out of the service, write sweet replies to pompous idiots who think a public servant is a public footstool, and give tours of the Capitol to visitors who are just as worn out as I am. . . . Take today, I wanted to hear this debate, because I'm not real sure on this bill. Since noon I've had five long-distance phone calls, and seven different groups of tourists have called me off the House floor to show them the Capitol. Two of them insisted on seeing the President. Today! They couldn't understand why I didn't just pick up the phone and tell him they were coming over. I'm just about fed up![9]

The problem this legislator describes confronts nearly everyone who serves in the House and Senate. Sent to Washington to make laws, they soon find out that they must devote a sizable amount of their time (as well as that of their staff) to answering an enormous volume of mail, resolving constituents' problems with the bureaucracy, personally meeting with tourists or representatives of interest groups, and returning home to mend fences or otherwise maintain good relations with the district or state. Demands of these sorts obviously make it difficult to focus attention on lawmaking.

The problem is compounded by the many conflicting demands that the legislative process itself places on representatives and senators. Although the rules of the two bodies seek to impose order by reserving the mornings for committee and subcommittee meetings and the afternoons for floor debate, exceptions to this rule are quite common. Not only must legislators often choose between a committee meeting and floor debate, they must also decide among simultaneous meetings of the committees or subcommittees on which they serve. This is particularly a problem in the Senate where in recent years members have served on an average of eleven committees or subcommittees. House members, who on the average serve on about seven committees or subcommittees, are only slightly less affected by this problem.

Most members of Congress spend much of their time hustling back and forth from one meeting to another. With so many conflicting demands, they often arrive late, leave early, or miss meetings altogether. Committee and subcommittee meetings, as well as floor debates in both chambers, are often poorly attended. Sometimes, especially in the Senate, there is not the minimum number of members necessary to do business.

The Structure of Congress

The Importance of Committees

"There is one principle," Woodrow Wilson once wrote about Congress, "which runs through every stage of procedure, and which is never disallowed or abrogated—the principle that the Committees shall rule without let or hindrance."[10] Much about the congressional committee system has changed since Wilson's time. The number of committees has been reduced from over eighty to under forty (a result of the legislative Reform Act of 1946), and large professional staffs have developed to assist committees in their work. But one thing has not changed: the central importance of committees to the legislative process.

There are three basic types of committees: joint committees, select committees, and standing committees. Joint committees, whose membership comprises an equal number of senators and representatives, are one of the few devices that build bridges between the two chambers. Some are created to examine housekeeping matters of concern to Congress as a whole, such as

the joint committees that review the operation of the Library of Congress and the Government Printing Office. Perhaps the most important of the joint committees, however, is the Joint Committee on Taxation, which studies proposals for changes in the nation's tax laws and makes recommendations to Congress.

Select committees are created within each body for a specific purpose, often an investigation of some type. They usually go out of existence when their work is complete (although a handful of select committees have become more or less permanent). One of the most famous select committees was the Senate Watergate Committee, which uncovered many of the misdeeds of the Nixon administration, thereby leading to formal impeachment proceedings in the House of Representatives. In 1987, select committees of the House and Senate together conducted a highly publicized investigation into the "Iran-Contra affair"—the sales of arms by the Reagan administration to Iran and the diversion of part of the proceeds to the Nicaraguan opposition. More recently, in President Clinton's second year in office, a series of alleged financial misadventures involving the first couple led to investigations by regular standing committees, not a select committee.

By far the most important of the three types of committees are the standing committees of which there are now eighteen in the House and sixteen in the Senate. Each has jurisdiction over a specific subject area as set forth in the rules of the House and Senate. These committees are responsible for considering and reporting legislation to the full bodies. In the vast majority of cases, approval by the standing committee is necessary for a bill to pass in the House or Senate. The parent body may accept, amend, or reject legislation recommended for passage by the standing committee. Though the tradition, especially in the House, has been to defer to the recommendations of the standing committees, since the 1970s members have been more willing to propose amendments to legislation that has been recommended by committees or to reject committee recommendations altogether.

A committee, it might be thought, should be a microcosm of the full body, for then the results of its deliberations would approximate what the full body would have decided. This result, however, is seldom achieved. Some committees are more liberal or conservative than the full House or Senate, while others draw a disproportionate number of members from certain regions of the country. Members naturally seek to be appointed to committees on which they can secure benefits for their state or district. For example, committees that handle water projects generally have large numbers of Westerners, while those that review farm legislation are packed with members from farming states. Committees, then, are not neutral or impartial actors in the legislative process.

Most committees accurately reflect the parent bodies in regard to party membership. Thus, if 60 percent of the members of the Home are Democrats, then approximately 60 percent of the members of most House committees will be Democrats. But there are important exceptions to this rule. The ethics committees in both chambers, which are supposed to operate in a nonpartisan way, are equally divided in their membership between the two parties. Conversely, House Republicans reserve extra seats for themselves on the most important standing committees (including Appropriations, Budget, Rules, and Ways and Means) to strengthen the influence of the majority party over key committee decisions.

The number of standing committees in the House and Senate remained fairly constant from 1946 until 1994 (about 22 in the House and 16 in the Senate). When the Republicans took charge of the House in 1994, however, they made important changes in the committee structure, eliminating three standing committees entirely and reorganizing the jurisdiction of others. This reform was part of an effort by Republicans to reduce the number of congressional staff employees and cut back on Congress' own expenditures.

The Growth of Subcommittees

Subcommittees are agents of the full committees, made necessary because the full committees simply do not have sufficient time to consider carefully all the proposals referred to them. As a result, most bills are first analyzed in a subcommittee. If the subcommittee favors the legis-

lation, it is then taken up by the full committee. Although the full committees are not obligated to accept the recommendations of the subcommittees, they often do.

One of the most important developments in Congress during the past generation has been an increase in both the number and the power of subcommittees. The number of subcommittees grew enormously during the period from 1970 to 1994, when it totaled 227 subcommittees, 143 in the House and 84 in the Senate. (The number in the House has been scaled back to 87, in the Senate to 68.) Subcommittees also became more powerful, especially in the House. Until new rules were adopted in the 1970s, committee chairs exercised extensive control over subcommittees, appointing members and chairs, determining jurisdictions, and controlling staff and monetary resources. These powers now rest with the majority-party members on the full committee, which in practice has meant that the subcommittees have become far more independent and important policymaking units within committees.

Where once the term "committee government" was used to describe the working of Congress, now many prefer to speak of "subcommittee government." There are so many chairmanships now spread around that, at any rate for the majority, the old dream of "every member a chairman" has practically become a reality.

The Reduced Influence of Committee Chairs

The basic way of life in Congress in the 1960s was summed up in the following observation of a House member: "The best way to get things done in Congress is to live long enough to get to be a committee chairman, and be resilient enough to be a good one. If things can be done, they can do them."[11] Now, however, committee chairs have less control over how subcommittees deal with bills and less influence over the decisions of the committee as a whole. To be sure, committee chairs in the House remain important people who exercise authority over large committee staffs and make critical decisions on the timing of committee actions. But they no longer

BOX 10.1

Committees of the One Hundred Seventh Congress 2001–2002

HOUSE

Standing Committees

Agriculture

Appropriations

Budget

Education and the Workforce

Energy and Commerce

Financial Services

Government Reform

House Administration

International Relations

Judiciary

Resources

Rules

Science

Small Business

Standards of Official Conduct

Transportation and Infrastructure

Veterans' Affairs

Ways and Means

Select, Special, Other

Permanent Select Committee on Intelligence

SENATE

Standing Committees

Agriculture, Nutrition, and Forestry

Appropriations

Armed Services

Banking, Housing, and Urban Affairs

Budget

Commerce, Science, and Transportation

Energy and Natural Resources

Environment and Public Works

Finance

Foreign Relations

Governmental Affairs

Judiciary

Health, Education, Labor and Pensions

Rules and Administration

Small Business

Veterans' Affairs

Select, Special, Other

Select Committee on Intelligence

Select Committee on Ethics

Senate Committee on Indian Affairs

Special Committee on Aging

JOINT COMMITTEES

Joint Economic Committee

Joint Committee on Taxation

Joint Committee on Printing

Joint Committee on the Library of Congress

enjoy the power and autonomy of those who served before the 1970s reform era.

Other reforms of the 1970s further curbed the power of committee chairs by placing them more under the control of the majority party organization in the House. This change came as a result of a landmark decision by the House Democratic caucus (the group of all Democrats serving in the House) in 1975 to refuse to reappoint as chairs of their committees three senior members who most House Democrats felt had lost touch with mainstream Democratic opinion or had run their committees unfairly. For the half century preceding this decision, appointments to committee chairs had been made in almost every case on the basis of seniority: the chair was given to the majority-party member who had the longest continuous service on the committee.

Because the seniority principle made the selection of committee chairs automatic, it reduced any incentive the chair might have to follow the policy objectives of the party leadership or of the majority of party members. Liberals, in particular, criticized the seniority system for favoring conservative southern Democrats, who had little trouble getting reelected because of the absence of a strong opposition party in much of the South.

By the early 1970s, discontent with the seniority system became so widespread that Democrats in the House changed the rules to require that chairs must be elected by a secret vote of the Democratic caucus. The decision to depose three committee chairs in 1975 was a signal to all future chairpersons that they were not beyond the control of their party. The new system, according to David Obey of Wisconsin, "sends a message to all chairmen that they have to be more responsive . . . . [P]eople don't want to have to work around chairmen, they want to be able to work through them."[12] Although seniority is still one of the most important factors to be taken into account when choosing a committee chair, it is no longer an absolute rule, and committee chairs who wish to remain in power are now obliged to consider the views of other members of their party. The weakening of the rule of seniority in the House became even more apparent following the Republicans' capture of the House in 1994. In three important standing com-

mittees, the old tradition of seniority was bypassed to select chairmen more in accord with the views of the party majority and the leadership. In the Senate the rule of seniority, while not inviolable, is much more closely adhered to than in the House. Additionally, Republicans changed House rules to limit committee chairs to six years. In 2000, many chairmen were forced to step down for the first time under these self-imposed House chair term limits. Two very prominent chairmen, Bill Archer and Tom Bliley, took this opportunity to retire from the House.

Committee Assignments

Because committees are so important to the legislative process, members have a keen interest in serving on those committees that will best promote their legislative or electoral goals. In the Senate, the environmental and Public Works and Agriculture committees, for example, are especially valuable for reelection-oriented legislators, since service on them is likely to result in projects or legislation directly beneficial to constituents, be it a harbor improvement, a dam, or a higher price support for corn. The Rules, Ways and Means, and Appropriations committees in the House, on the other hand, are sought by representatives interested in power or prestige within Congress; they sometimes can be used for constituency purposes, but they are frequently relied on to make some of the tough decisions for the body as a whole. And some committees, like Education and the Workforce in the House, or Foreign Relations in the Senate, are especially sought after by those who wish to play an important role influencing public policy.

The decisions on committee assignments are made at the beginning of each new Congress by each party's "committee on committees" in the House and Senate. These decisions affect both new members seeking their initial favored committee choices and veteran legislators seeking to upgrade their committee assignments. The selection process is governed by a set of formal procedures, but it is heavily influenced by political considerations and personal relations among congressional members. The party leadership today is especially active in this process, and it has become one of the instruments at its disposal to reward helpful and loyal party members.

Strengths and Weaknesses of the Committee System

The greatest contribution which the committee system makes is the development of expertise on the issues that come before Congress. Most members of the House serve on one or two standing committees, most senators on three. Members obviously cannot become experts on all the issues. Instead, they are expected to focus their energy on a few areas of policy. By staying on the same committee for many years, a member may eventually develop expertise in a specific area that will rival that of anyone else in the government. This expertise frees Congress from dependence on those in the executive branch and enables it to reach independent judgments. Without some kind of committee system the Congress could hardly aspire to be the president's equal in guiding national policy.

The committee system, however, has several weaknesses. One is that there is no guarantee that the committees of the House and Senate will reflect the political views of the full membership. Regional or ideological variation is quite common from committee to committee, which results in decisions that are biased in one direction or another. A related problem is that some committees and subcommittees become advocates of the programs under their jurisdiction. The terms "subgovernment" and "iron triangle" are often used to describe the cozy relationship that sometimes exists among committees (or subcommittees), a bureaucratic unit, and the affected interest groups. Each participant has a stake in the preservation or expansion of current programs, even if these are difficult to justify in terms of the broader national interest.

Of course, the full House or Senate is always free to reject the recommendations of biased or unrepresentative committees. Yet the simple fact that only the committee members have thoroughly digested an issue usually gives committee proposals substantial weight in the decision process. After all, the very existence of the committee system presumes that nonmembers will tend to defer to committee requests.

Another problem of the committee system is that it decentralizes the decision-making process, making collective action difficult and contributing to a lack of coherence in national policy. When the decision-making authority in an institution is centralized in the hands of a single person or a small number of individuals, the institution can react more quickly and decisively to changing events and pursue a consistent series of measures designed to achieve its ends. When, however, the decision-making power is dispersed among relatively autonomous units within the institution, conflicting views and jurisdictional jealousies will often make it more difficult to pursue a consistent policy.

This problem has been amply illustrated in recent years in Congress' difficulty in dealing with the federal budget. When large budget deficits began to appear in the 1970s, Congress was faced with the need to set clear priorities among spending programs and to decide the proper mix of spending cuts and/or tax increases to bring the budget closer into balance. Yet authority over tax and spending decisions was spread among virtually all of the standing committees in the House and Senate, making the tasks of setting and enforcing budgetary priorities extraordinarily difficult. In response to this problem, Congress enacted organizational and procedural reforms intended to remedy some of the defects of a decentralized system of standing committees. Congress established budget committees in each chamber, set up a Congressional Budget Office, and mandated procedures for adopting an annual congressional budget.

Although structural alterations of these types can improve Congress's legislative capacity, they cannot wholly eliminate the basic effects of decentralized decision making. The problems of decentralization are unavoidable under a system that relies so heavily on standing committees. These problems can only be mitigated by other structures having a centralizing influence, one of which is the political party.

Political Parties in Congress

Political parties are the most important centralizing instruments in Congress and the most significant mechanisms for coordinating broad pol-

TABLE 10.2
Congressional Leadership in the One Hundred Seventh Congress (2001–2002)

HOUSE

Republicans

Speaker of the House
    J. Dennis Hastert (Illinois)

Majority Leader
    Richard Armey (Texas)

Majority Whip
    Tom Delay (Texas)

Conference Chair
    J.C. Watts, Jr. (Oklahoma)

Democrats

Minority Leader
    Richard Gephardt (Missouri)

Minority Whip
    Nancy Pelosi (California)

Caucus Chair
    Martin Frost (Texas)

SENATE

Democrats

Majority Leader
    Tom Daschle (South Dakota)

Assistant Majority Leader
    Harry Reid (Nevada)

President Pro Tempore
    Robert Byrd (West Virginia)

Republicans

Minority Leader
    Trent Lott (Mississippi)

Assistant Minority Leader
    Don Nickles (Oklahoma)

icy between the two chambers and with the president. Institutionally, the Democratic and Republican parties operate in Congress through three principal mechanisms: party caucuses, party committees, and an elective party leadership structure.

Party Caucuses   A party caucus (also called a "conference") is the collection of all the members of one party in one of the branches. Thus, there are four caucuses altogether. Earlier in our history the caucuses played an important role in the legislative process, meeting frequently to debate policy issues and often instructing party members how to vote. After 1920, however, party caucuses restricted themselves mainly to selecting party leaders and to confirming committee appointments. Since the 1970s party caucuses in both chambers have become slightly more active as forums for debating organizational reforms and policy issues and, in the case

of the Democratic party in the House, in challenging committee chairs.

Party Committees   Because the party caucuses are so large and unwieldy (after the 2000 elections the House Democratic caucus included 211 members, while the Republican conference had 221), certain tasks are assigned to smaller party committees. Serving only as agents of the party, these committees analyze policy issues, nominate committee members and committee leaders, and provide assistance for congressional campaigns. In most cases, the party committees do not act independently, but make recommendations to the full caucus to accept or reject.

Party Leadership   Atop the caucuses and the party committees is the party leadership system, a hierarchical structure designed to connect each party member to the broad interests of the party. Above all else this system is a communications network that sends information both up and down the party ladder, giving members a chance to express their views to the leaders and providing a channel for leaders to communicate their positions down to the full membership.

There are four distinct leadership systems, one for each party in each chamber (see Table 10.2). In the House the leader of the majority party is elected the Speaker of the House. Under the Speaker are the Majority Leader, who serves as a kind of Floor Leader for the majority party, and the majority whip, who is in charge of communications with party members. Under the majority whip are a number of deputy whips and a group of assistant whips who represent the different regions of the country. The minority party in the House has essentially the same structure with the exception that there is no equivalent to the Speaker; the highest-ranking minority member is the minority leader.

In the Senate, the highest-ranking officer is, according to the Constitution, the vice president, who serves as the president of the Senate. This gives the vice president the power to preside over the Senate and to break tie votes. As a rule, however, the vice president does not preside, reserving appearances for possible tie-breaking votes on important issues. When the vice president is absent, these powers devolve to the president pro tempore of the Senate, a position mentioned in the Constitution. In practice this has become an honorific post given to the most senior member of the majority party in the Senate.

The actual leader of the major party in the Senate and the most powerful senator is thus not an official Constitutional officer, but the majority leader. The majority leader with the assistant majority leader run the Senate, to the extent that the body can be run at all. The minority party has equivalent positions, known as the minority leader and the assistant minority leader. As in the House, the principal task of the majority and minority leaders is to oversee floor debate for their parties, and the job of the whip or assistant is to communicate with the other party members.

The greatest contribution that party leadership can make in Congress is to offset some of the defects of the decentralized decision making of the committee system. To the extent that party leaders can guide or influence the actions of individual members, they add a degree of unity or coherence to the legislative process. Their success depends both on the resources they have available and on the political skill they possess to get others to follow their lead. Their capacity for influence is limited, however, because they exercise almost no control over the electoral fate of their party colleagues. This situation stands in marked contrast to the power of party leaders in some parliamentary systems, who can deny a party endorsement to uncooperative members and virtually ensure their defeat at the polls. Congressional party leaders exercise no such influence.

Without the power to deny members their seats in Congress, party leaders possess only limited means of disciplining dissidents. And if the party should, for example, start denying choice committee assignments to those who deviate from majority opinion, it might force the dissidents into the hands of the opposing party. In January of 1983, House Democrats actually did discipline one of their colleagues, Phil Gramm of Texas, by removing him from the House Budget Committee. Gramm was singled out not because he had endorsed President Reagan's economic policies (other conservative Democrats had done likewise), but because he participated directly with administration forces in moving the President's bills through Congress. Rather than accept his rebuke, Gramm switched allegiance to the Republican party and was subsequently reelected as a Republican.

What happened to Gramm is quite rare. No party wants to reduce its share of congressional seats (and therefore committee seats) by forcing its dissidents into the hands of the opposition, especially if such a coalition would constitute a majority of the House or Senate.

Congressional leaders, however, possess a variety of other means by which they can exercise power over their respective parties or chambers. Some, like Speaker of the House Sam Rayburn and Senate Majority Leader Lyndon Johnson, had a great impact on their institutions. Part of what makes a leader effective is the skillful exercise of formal authority: the Speaker's power to preside over floor debate; the Senate Majority Leader's right to be recognized first in proceedings on the floor; and the power to make

Henry Clay, one of the most famous legislators in the nineteenth century was elected Speaker of the House for three separate terms and later served as a senator from Kentucky. (National Portrait Gallery, Smithsonian Institution; Transfer from the National Gallery of Art; gift of Andrew W. Mellon, 1942. Used with permission.)

appointments to special committees or commissions and to select members of Congress to serve on official delegations visiting foreign countries. More important, however, is a leader's skill in taking advantage of his strategic position in the legislative process. Lyndon Johnson, who served as leader of the Senate Democrats from 1953–1960, "made himself the leader by putting himself at the center of an enormous number of bargains in the Senate. . . . In this way, he could create coalitions of senators who would never have thought to get together on their own."[13] Finally, Newt Gingrich of Georgia, who began as Speaker of the House in 1995, achieved remarkable success early due in part to a new approach. He helped devise a national campaign strategy and platform (The Contract with America) on which Republican candidates for the House agreed to run in 1994 and which then became the basis for a legislative program.

Leadership struggles are certainly not unknown in Congress, though considerable efforts are made to present changes in a benign way. Recently, for example, James C. Wright of Texas, who served briefly as Speaker of the House from 1987 to 1990, was forced to resign after the House Ethics Committee concluded that his financial dealings might have violated House rules. Wright, who proved to be one of the most active House leaders in decades, may also in part have been a victim of his own aggressive leadership. He was succeeded as Speaker by Thomas Foley, a less combative leader who demonstrated a more collegial approach to leadership. The opposite occurred in the Senate in 1988, when Democrat Robert Byrd of West Virginia stepped down under pressure as Majority Leader and was succeeded by the far more active and outspoken George Mitchell. In the summer of 1997 House Speaker Gingrich survived a coup attempt by disgruntled Republicans, and in 1998 he resigned under pressure following the Republicans' poor showing in that year's midterm election.

Other Groups within Congress

In addition to the party organizations, there are several other sorts of groups in Congress that serve to link members together and that influence the legislative process. One of the most important of these are state or regional delegations. In the House, many state delegations seek to increase their influence by meeting together to discuss local or national issues. Democrats and Republicans in the delegation will often join forces to take a united stand on a pending issue that has a direct impact on the state.

There are also economic groups that form to protect different interests. Given the American concept of geographical representation, few forces in Congress are stronger than the desire of legislators to promote the economic well-being of their constituents. Thus, representatives from the Detroit area have led congressional efforts to soften the economic impact of pollution restrictions on the automobile industry, those from Texas and Louisiana have fought to protect the producers of natural gas and crude oil, and others from districts with military bases have used their influence to try to prevent closing of those bases. When specific economic interests cut across states or congressional districts, legislators often work together to develop legislative strategy, establishing numerous semi-official coalitions, or caucuses, among themselves to promote common economic interests in such matters as tourism, steel, textiles, beef, coal, and wine. There has even been a mushroom caucus in the House. Broader ideological dispositions rarely outweigh the desire to protect jobs or promote economic growth within the districts.

Ethnic and minority groups that have traditionally had little direct representation in Congress and that have certain distinct interests also have caucuses. Today, there is the Congressional Caucus for Women's Issues, the Hispanic Caucus, and, by far the most active, the Congressional Black Caucus. Comprising the black members of Congress, the Black Caucus takes stands on a variety of issues of concern to black citizens.

The various caucuses—regional, economic, ideological and ethnic—form yet other centers of power in Congress that sometimes compete with the more established centers in the committees and the parties. Because these groups cut across the traditional committee, subcommittee, and party organizations in Congress, they can contribute to the fragmentation of decision making, but proponents maintain that they make for more effective representation of important interests.

Conflicting Forces

The structure of Congress reflects the tension between decentralizing and centralizing forces within the institution. The committee system results in many important decisions by hundreds of small groups of legislators acting more or less independently of one another. This arrangement is good for promoting expertise and competence, but bad for fostering a coherent approach to complex public issues. On the other hand, the party system and the budget process seek to coordinate the activities of these smaller work groups and fashion common approaches to policy issues among majorities of like-minded legislators.

Changes in Congress in the past two decades have simultaneously centralized and decentralized power within the institution. In the House in particular, the majority party has become more influential as a result of reforms that have made committee chairs more responsible to majority party members. The Speaker has also acquired expanded powers over committee assignments and referral of bills to standing committees. The congressional budget process has developed into a potentially powerful mechanism for exerting more centralized control over money decisions. Yet power in both chambers has also been decentralized. This development has resulted from the increased authority and autonomy of subcommittees, which distributes power widely throughout Congress, and from the increased staffing for individual members, which provides them with the capability to act independent of committee and party leaders.

These two recent trends are in conflict. Rule by a strong and cohesive majority party is usually possible only when committees, subcommittees and individual members are willing to defer to the views of the majority of the party or its leaders, even if they disagree. A more democratized distribution of power, on the other hand, encourages individual members to act according to their own beliefs. In 1995, with Newt Gingrich assuming the position of Speaker for the Republicans, there was a much greater centralization of power in the House than had been seen in a very long time, although part of this concentration may prove to be temporary.

The way in which power is distributed within Congress affects its position within the broader political system. If Congress is ruled by a strong and cohesive party, as it was in the late nineteenth and early twentieth centuries, then it can assert itself as a forceful independent actor in relation to the president. But if power is widely distributed within Congress, if congressional leaders exercise little real control over their colleagues, then it becomes quite difficult for Congress to act with a consistent purpose. Congress can exercise a "negative power" of blocking presidential initiatives, but it cannot itself devise a coherent alternative program ("positive power").

There is then an interesting paradox in regard to the power of Congress. While most members of Congress gain greater influence from a wider distribution of power inside the body, the institution as a whole becomes less powerful in relationship to the presidency. Most observers today see power in Congress as being slightly more centralized than in the late 1970s and early 1980s, but still far from the centralized hierarchical leadership system that was present in the early twentieth century.

How (and Why) a Bill Becomes a Law

Congress passes only a small fraction of the bills and resolutions that are introduced during each two-year session. In the 106th Congress (1999–2000), for example, only about 19 percent of the bills introduced in the House survived to final passage, and only three percent were also passed by the Senate and enacted into law. In order to examine the legislative process it is useful to look at the passage of one particular bill—the Tax Reform Act of 1986—which seemed to have everything against it when it was first introduced, but which eventually overcame the many obstacles of the legislative process and became the law of the land.

The Tax Reform Act of 1986

The comprehensive tax reform proposal submitted to Congress in May 1985 was one of the most important economic policy changes in years and also the most important domestic policy initiative of President Reagan's second term in office. The administration's proposal asked Congress to eliminate hundreds of billions of dollars worth of "loopholes" and special preferences in the tax system, and to use the new tax revenues to lower basic tax rates for all individuals and businesses and remove millions of low income families from the tax rolls. Tax experts agreed that the tax system was in need of a major overhaul. Yet because of limited public interest in tax reform and opposition from the many well organized economic interests who benefited from the special tax provisions, few in Washington expected tax reform to succeed. According to two *Wall Street Journal* reporters, Jeffrey Birnbaum and Alan Murray, "The conventional wisdom in Washington held that tax reform was destined to lose, and the conventional wisdom had plenty of history to back it up."[14]

A comprehensive tax reform bill nevertheless passed Congress, and President Reagan signed it into law in October 1986. Why, then, did Congress pass tax reform in 1985–86, and what does this case tell us about the forces that affect the legislative process more generally? Four factors played key roles: policy, personality, procedures, and politics.

Policy The structure and procedures of Congress are designed to help members determine which public policy initiatives will be good for the nation and which will not. Serious efforts are made to accumulate and assess relevant information, to consider opposing arguments, and to reach intelligent judgments about the merits of legislative proposals. Congress is, at least in part, a deliberative institution. Of course, not every good idea is guaranteed of success, nor is every bad one destined to fail. But despite a good deal of fashionable cynicism in journalistic reporting on Congress, ideas about what constitutes good public policy do play a significant role in congressional politics.

Part of the explanation for the success of the tax reform bill lay in a broad consensus among tax experts and economists, both liberal and conservative, that tax reform would be good for the nation. Policy experts argued that the existing tax system was too complex and that it hindered economic growth by encouraging investment decisions based on tax breaks rather than on what would generate economic productivity and produce the best returns. Liberal Democrats had long sought to eliminate tax preferences in order to make wealthy individuals and corporations pay their "fair share" of the nation's tax burden. Conservatives in the Republican party saw tax reform as the means to achieve lower tax rates, which would in turn stimulate new savings, investment, and economic growth. Once the Reagan administration proposed a tax reform measure, the broad array of arguments in favor of reform placed those who opposed it on the defensive, and made them appear to be defending "special interests" against broader interests (fairness, simplicity, economic growth

Personality Like the citizens they represent, members of Congress are influenced by a variety of personal characteristics and by personal relations with their colleagues. Within Congress, the progress of the tax reform bill was shaped decisively by two individuals: Dan Rostenkowski, Democrat of Illinois and chairman of the House Ways and Means Committee, and Robert Packwood, Republican of Oregon and chairman of the Senate Finance Committee. Though neither had been a proponent of tax reform prior to 1985, as chairmen of the standing committees responsible for reviewing tax legislation in each chamber each became responsible for steering the bill through his chamber. As Birnbaum and Murray describe the two chairmen:

> The two had little in common: Packwood was a maverick legislator from a largely rural state; Rostenkowski was a machine politician from a big city. Packwood was cerebral, analytical, a collector of rare books and special editions; Rostenkowski was physical, a man of gut instinct, a devotee of red meat and golf. Packwood was new to his chairmanship and still uncertain of how to wield the power that accompanied it; Rostenkowski was accustomed to his high-ranking post and well-trained in the mechanisms of power.[15]

Yet despite these differences, both chairmen became strongly committed to tax reform and each worked hard to win support for the bill, first in committee and then on the floor.

Procedures The procedures of Congress are not neutral to the passage of legislative proposals. They can create obstacles in the path of new policy initiatives or smooth the way to final passage into law. Critical to the passage of tax reform were procedures that limited access to the legislative process at key points. Interestingly, the procedures used to pass tax reform represented a reversal of some of the "democratizing" reforms enacted in Congress during the 1970s.

Committees in both the House and Senate wrote the actual tax reform legislation in sessions that were closed to the public and press. Both chambers also used procedures that limited opportunities for amending the legislation while it was being considered for final passage. In each case, the restrictive procedures shielded the legislation from powerful interests that sought to "water it down." According to one political scientist, "Open meetings, open rules, and unlimited recorded votes seemed like good ideas when they were proposed, and they were backed by Common Cause and others who sought to reduce the power of special interests. . . . We now know that open meetings filled with lobbyists, and recorded votes on scores of particularistic amendments, serve to increase the powers of special interests, not to diminish them."[16]

Politics The tax reform bill was also subject to a complex interplay of political forces, including the political motives and ambitions of the major actors, members seeking to protect important local and regional interests, and competition between the two political parties for credit and support from the voters. Rostenkowski, for example, worked hard for the tax reform bill not only because he thought it was good public policy, but also because it would be a legislative achievement to enhance the prestige of the Ways and Means Committee and his own reputation as an effective chairman. Packwood was up for reelection in 1986, and he was sensitive to being labelled a captive of special interests by his opponent if a credible reform bill failed to emerge from the committee he chaired.

Local and regional interests came into play in the politics of tax reform because some of the tax preferences slated for elimination would have had a disproportionate impact in certain areas of the country. An important case in point was the proposed elimination of the federal income tax deduction for income taxes paid to state and local governments. For members of Congress from states and localities with low income taxes or no income taxes at all, the provision was of little importance. But to members from states in the northeast with high state and local income taxes, this was a major provision that would have substantially increased income taxes on many of their constituents.

In order to maintain support for reform among these members, Chairman Rostenkowski negotiated a deal with those from the northeast who served on the Ways and Means Committee: he would remove the objectionable state and local tax provision, and they would promise to support the bill.

Finally, a distinctive aspect of the politics of this bill involved the competition between the two political parties to take credit for tax reform. Though public reaction to the issue ultimately was fairly limited, at the time leaders in both parties thought that a bill removing special tax provisions and lowering tax rates might have a powerful appeal for the voters. Some congressional Democrats, including Dan Rostenkowski, viewed Reagan's initial tax reform proposal as an attempt to lure away traditional Democratic voters by portraying the Republican party as allied with average taxpayers against special interests. Under these conditions, the divided party control of Congress in 1985–86 may actually have helped propel tax reform through to passage. The House Democratic leadership had a strong desire to pass a tax reform bill so that their party would share in the credit to be gained from the voters. Once the Democratic House approved the bill, the Republican-controlled Senate also had to act, or face having the party be blamed for having "killed" tax reform.

As the history of the Tax Reform Act illustrates, Congress is a dynamic and complex collection of 535 distinct individuals in which personal ambition, interest, bargaining, political party allegiance and the exercise of power all make a contribution to the final product. With this in mind, we can turn to the procedures according to which a bill becomes a law.

Introduction of Bills

Only the members of each chamber have the authority to introduce formal legislative proposals into Congress. Even presidents, with all their stature and power, cannot personally introduce bills. When presidents present their legislative programs to Congress, they seek influential members of the House and Senate to sponsor their bills. Many of the bills introduced in Congress are thus not written by the legislators who sponsor then, but by executive branch officials, interest groups, or even private citizens.

Although we commonly assume that representatives and senators introduce bills because they want them to become law, in fact they often introduce measures for their symbolic significance, to mollify powerful interest groups, or to

stimulate new thinking about a problem. This partly explains why so many bills are introduced during each legislative session. Not all of the bills that are introduced, however, are actually different proposals, but often merely the same proposal with a different number. This technique allows many members to claim credit for introducing a popular measure.

In the House, a bill is introduced by placing it in the "hopper," a box at the front of the chamber. In the Senate, a bill is given to one of the clerks and is usually accompanied by a statement on the floor by the sponsoring senator. In each chamber, bills are numbered consecutively, following the initials "H.R." for the House and "S." for the Senate. Usually these numbers have no particular significance except for the designation "H.R. 1" or "S. 1," which is reserved by the leadership for a high priority item.

Committee Stage

The most important stage in the movement of a bill through Congress is its consideration by the standing committee to which it is referred. Committees have traditionally had rather clear spheres of authority, but with the increasing complexity of modern legislation, bills often fall into the jurisdiction of several committees. Disputes among committees have therefore become more frequent, and the leadership has had to play a more active role in awarding control to contending committee chairmen. Most bills, once they reach the committee, will then be sent to the subcommittee of the full committee with jurisdiction over its subject matter. Subcommittee consideration takes two forms: hearings and mark-up.

Hearings The most important decision to be made within the subcommittee is whether to hold hearings on a bill at all. Time limitations allow only a fraction of bills to reach the hearing stage; consequently, most bills die in subcommittee. The decision to hold hearings on a bill is no guarantee of eventual subcommittee approval, but it is a necessary first step.

The hearings are designed to elicit the relevant information on the matter at hand and the major arguments on both sides of the issue. Most hearings are open to the media and the public. The format is quite simple. Witnesses for and against the bill appear before the subcommittee, present brief oral statements, submit longer formal statements for the record, and respond to questions from subcommittee members. On important bills, witnesses will include the sponsors of the legislation from the House and Senate; high-ranking members of the administration (often department heads or their deputies); representatives of interest groups (including leaders of public interest groups); and experts from academia, think tanks, or private foundations.

Mark-Up When the hearings are completed, the subcommittee meets to determine whether there is sufficient support to "mark up" the bill. The mark-up is a line-by-line reading and often redrafting of the original proposal. Although occasionally the subcommittee may bring in an outside expert to help, especially one from the executive branch, most of the work at this stage is done by the members themselves and the subcommittee staff. After the mark-up is completed, there is a vote on the final proposal. If a majority support the bill, then it is referred back to the full committee with a recommendation that the committee report the bill to the full House or Senate.

Full Committee Consideration At this point the committee has three options: (1) to do as the subcommittee requested, (2) to refuse to report any bill at all, or (3) to amend the subcommittee proposal and then report it to the full body. Although the full committee is not bound to accept the subcommittee's recommendation, it is definitely influenced by it, since in most cases the subcommittee members can reasonably argue that they know more about the issues involved than others on the committee. If the committee decides in favor of the original or an amended bill, a written report is prepared (usually by the staff) explaining and defending the main features of the bill. Committee members who oppose the bill have the option of preparing a dissenting opinion which is included with the report. The presence of a written dissent is often a good measure of the intensity of feeling of those against the bill.

Scheduling Floor Debate

The Senate Once a bill has been reported back favorably to the full body, it must be scheduled for floor debate. This is one area where the procedures for the House and Senate are quite different. In the Senate, decisions are made through informal consultation among the leaders of both parties, the sponsors of the bill, and other interested senators. When agreement has been reached as to when the debate should take place, how long it should last and who should control the apportionment of time during debate, then a unanimous-consent agreement is presented to the full Senate. It is usually accepted, since the arrangements have been cleared ahead of time with all the interested parties. If agreement on the rules for debate cannot be reached, this is usually a sign that opponents of the measure are planning to use obstructionist tactics, including the filibuster, to prevent passage of the bill.

The House: Importance of the Rules Committee In the House, the procedure for scheduling debate is much more formalized. With few exceptions, bills can get to the floor only through the Rules Committee, a standing committee with a relatively small membership of thirteen. The Rules Committee's main job is to determine the rules under which bills will be debated on the floor of the House. The Committee is the "traffic cop" for House business. Its decisions serve the same function as the unanimous-consent agreement in the Senate, setting the time for debate and determining which members shall control the apportionment of time.

A rule will also stipulate whether and what kinds of amendments may be offered on the floor. On some complex matters, like tax legislation, amendments may be prohibited if they are not supported by the reporting committee (a closed rule). If there are no restrictions at all on amendments, the rule is called an open rule. A rule which allows only specified amendments or which limits amendments to specific parts of a bill is called a modified closed rule. The argument for debating bills under a closed or modified closed rule is that the complexity and political sensitivity of some issues (like the tax reform bill discussed above) make it impossible for the full body to do a responsible job of writing legislation on the floor.

An important development over the past decade has been the increased use of closed or modified closed rules which restrict amendments on the House floor. During the 94th Congress (1975–76) only 16 percent of the rules recommended by the Rules Committee and adopted by the House were closed or modified closed rules; by the 99th Congress (1985–86) close to half (45 percent) of all rules adopted by the House prohibited or restricted amendments.[17] The increased use of restrictive rules drew sharp criticism from House Republicans, who argued that these rules prohibited amendments or alternatives from being proposed by members of the minority party. The Democratic leadership, which worked closely with the Rules Committee, responded by defending restrictive rules as necessary to manage the more individualistic politics of the contemporary House and as a legitimate prerogative of the majority party. Although Republicans promised more open rules when they gained control of the House in 1994, their leadership has sometimes employed restrictive rules in order to facilitate the flow of business and speed the passage of priority legislation.

The recommendations of the Rules Committee, however, are not absolute and technically must be passed upon by the full House. In fact, they are rarely overturned today, which is evidence that the Rules Committee now does a fairly good job of reflecting the majority sentiment of the larger body it serves. Earlier in the century, the Rules Committee under "Judge" Howard Smith of Virginia had been more assertive in acting upon its own independent judgment of the merits of a bill, occasionally against the wishes of the membership and the leadership of the majority party. A revolt in 1961 against Smith led to a Rules Committee that has increasingly served as an arm of the majority leadership; this connection was further strengthened in the 1970s by the adoption of a new procedure giving the Speaker of the House the prerogative of nominating Democratic members to the committee.

Floor Debate

One of the great disappointments of tourists to the nation's capital is to sit in the gallery of the House or Senate chamber and observe a handful of representatives or senators reading speeches in a nearly empty room. In the Senate it is not uncommon for important bills to be "debated" with as few as three or four senators present. In the House, attendance is usually higher, but most of those present often seem more interested in private conversations, reading the paper, or even napping than in the discussion on the floor.

There are two basic reasons for the low level of interest displayed by members of Congress in floor debate. One is that the demands on their time are so great that they find it difficult to justify spending several hours on the floor to hear a bill discussed which they may know little about or have little interest in. The other is that by the time a bill reaches the floor, most of the serious deliberation on the measure has already been completed. Dozens of committee members may have spent months working out the details of a complex measure before it goes to the floor to be debated for a few short hours. In most cases, it is simply more efficient for a representative or senator to take guidance from the committee as a whole or some member of it whose views and judgment he or she respects than to try to learn enough in the debate to make an informed decision.

This is not to say that debate never affects votes. Debate may be especially important on controversial and closely divided issues of great national significance. The House and Senate debates in January 1991 on authorizing the use of military force in the Persian Gulf, for example, took place before heavily attended sessions and with a number of members still undecided about which way they would vote. In this case, large parts of the floor debates were followed by the American people on television and had a dramatic effect on forming people's opinions about various members of Congress.

Procedurally, formal debate begins in chambers with a statement by the bill's leading proponents (usually subcommittee or committee chairs and other senior committee members) explaining and justifying their proposal. In the course of making their case for the bill, the proponents may be interrupted with questions from the floor. Some of these will come from the opposition, probing for weaknesses in the argument. Other questions, arranged in advance, will lead to a "colloquy," an exchange between two supporters of the bill which seeks to clarify an ambiguous point or to get a particular interpretation of the bill "in the record" (for possible later use by the court or administrative agencies in seeking to ascertain congressional intent). The opponents of the bill are given equal time to deliver their speeches against the measure, subject again to interruption from the floor. Although any member of the House or Senate may seek recognition to speak on a bill, debate usually tends to be dominated by the members of the reporting committee.

The Filibuster　In the Senate, opponents of a bill have available to them a parliamentary strategy that cannot be used in the House. They may refuse to agree to any limit on debate and then proceed to engage in extensive speechmaking to prevent a bill from coming to a vote. This practice is known as a filibuster. Until 1917 there was no rule at all in the Senate limiting the amount of time that an individual senator could speak on the floor—a position reflecting the traditional respect which the Senate accorded the views of each of its members. Until the twentieth century, however, this privilege was not often used as a parliamentary device to prevent the full body from voting on a bill. But in 1917 a group of isolationist senators (labeled by President Woodrow Wilson a "small group of willful men") filibustered to prevent the passage of legislation authorizing the arming of American merchant ships.

In response to this action, the Senate enacted its first cloture rule, providing those present and voting with the authority to cut off debate and force a vote if two-thirds of them so desired. With only minor changes this rule remained in effect until 1975, when the Senate reduced the number needed for cloture to three-fifths of the membership of the Senate (sixty members). The Senate again revised the cloture rule in 1986, reducing the time allowed before debate is cut off after the cloture vote from 100 to 30 hours.

Although the Senate has placed restrictions on filibusters, it has been unwilling to allow a simple majority to cut off debate and bring an issue to a vote. This remains true even as filibusters (and threatened filibusters) have become more and more frequent. As Senator David Pryor of Arkansas observed in 1988, "During the 25 years from 1940 to 1965, there were only 18 filibusters in the Senate. During the 22 years since then, the number of filibusters skyrocketed to 88."[18]

Though some have voiced the concern that such frequent filibustering is an abuse of Senate procedures, the tradition remains that majority rule must be tempered in the Senate by the minority's right to have its say. In reality, many so-called filibusters begin as serious efforts by the opposition to explore the relevant issues at length, hoping that, given enough time, other senators will change their minds. Some senators might be influenced by the arguments themselves, others by increasing opposition in the broader political community. The filibuster must be judged not merely as a parliamentary device but also for the opportunity it gives for extended deliberation on complex contemporary issues.

Voting　Each chamber has its own rules governing the voting procedures on amendments and final passage. In the House, there are actually five different ways of voting. The voice vote requires members to call out "aye" or "nay" at the appropriate time. In the division vote, the legislators stand to demonstrate approval or disapproval. During a teller vote, the members walk down the aisle in one of two lines and are counted as voting aye or nay. The recorded teller vote, instituted in 1970, is similar to the teller vote with the addition that members turn in cards with their names so that individual votes can be recorded and subsequently listed in the Congressional Record. The roll-call vote has been carried out electronically since 1973: members insert a special personalized electronic card into one of several devices on the floor and press a button for aye, nay, or present. In the electronic roll call individual votes as well as a running total are displayed on the wall at the front of the chamber. This makes it particularly easy for those voting near the end of the fifteen-minute period set aside for the roll call to seek voting "cues" from committee members or other representatives to whom they look for guidance.

Resolving House-Senate Differences: The Conference Committee

In order for a bill to become law it must be passed in identical language by both the House and the Senate. Each chamber is free to accept the language of the bill as passed by the other body. Often, however, the two branches disagree on a variety of points, ranging from the trivial to the fundamental. When differences exist between the House and Senate versions of a bill, a conference committee is appointed to resolve disagreements. A conference committee works on only one bill; and when its work is completed, it disbands. The members of the committee are chosen by the leadership in each chamber and usually include the senior members of the reporting committee, including some who may be opposed to the bill. Settlement is reached within the committee whenever a majority of both delegations agrees to a final version of the bill.

The committee then reports the new version back to the House and Senate, and each branch votes on the compromise proposal. Although both bodies are free to reject a bill entirely or send it back to conference for a try at a more acceptable version, they nearly always accept the conference committee's recommendation. The result is that conference committees are very important and powerful, even more so now than in the past. Much significant legislation today is done in omnibus bills of great length and complexity that may require extensive revisions in conference committees to resolve House and Senate differences. Some observers have dubbed these conference committees "third houses" of the legislative branch.

Presidential Action

The Constitution requires that any bill passed by Congress must be presented to the president before it becomes law. At this stage, there are three options. (1) The president may sign the bill, thereby making it the law of the land. (2) The president may formally veto the bill and return it to the chamber in which it originated, usually with a statement listing various objections to the bill. A two-thirds majority in each branch is then necessary to override the president's veto. (3) Finally, if the president does nothing for ten days and Congress is in session, the bill becomes a law. If Congress has adjourned, the bill does not become law. This is known as a "pocket veto." The vast majority of vetoes are not overridden, even when the White House and Congress are controlled by different parties. Since the presidency of Harry Truman, fewer than 15 percent of the nonpocket vetoes of public bills have been overridden by Congress.

The existence of the veto power obviously gives the president a substantial influence in the legislative process. Not only can presidents reject laws they disapprove of, but they can seek to modify the content of laws earlier in the process by threatening to veto them if changes are not made.

Assessing the Legislative Process: A Bias against New Laws?

Lawmaking in Congress is a complex process. Not only are two separate institutions involved, but within each one there are numerous distinct points in the decision-making process: the subcommittee, committee, and the full chamber. Proponents of a new law must achieve success at each stage; opponents need only block a measure at a single point. This fact has led many to conclude that the procedures of Congress are biased against passing new laws, that it is much easier to stop a law than to pass one. To some extent this is true, and it was one of the explicit objectives of the founders in creating a bicameral legislature. Their experience with state legislatures during the "critical period" (1776–1787) demonstrated the dangers of numerous and constantly changing laws. The Senate in particular was intended to make the legislative process more orderly and responsible. Although some good laws would not be passed as quickly as under a unicameral legislature, in the founders' view the price was worth paying to guard against passage of hastily drafted, ill-considered, and unwise measures.

Yet, it is important not to exaggerate the degree to which the structure and procedures of Congress inhibit the passage of new proposals. In fact, the modern Congress regularly passes 500 or more laws during each two-year session. Some of these, of course, are trivial or symbolic, but others deal with the most important matters facing the nation: in the mid-1960s, the passage of Medicare and Medicaid, civil rights laws, and federal support of elementary education; in the late 1960s and 1970s, new laws controlling environmental pollution, regulating safety in the workplace, altering mandatory retirement policy, and prohibitions of various kinds of discrimination based on sex or physical disability, and deregulation of the airline and trucking industries; in the 1980s, cuts in many earlier programs found to be unsatisfactory and a far-reaching reform of the nation's tax system; and in the 1990s, the free trade agreement with Mexico and Canada (NAFTA).

Some of these laws were enacted with surprising speed, while others required many years to move from idea to national policy. In either case they demonstrate that the procedures of Congress are not an insurmountable barrier to the enactment of novel proposals. In certain cases, moreover, the complexity of the legislation involved has made the long wait helpful in improving the laws and in winning broad support for their enactment.

Congress and the Public: The Task of Representation

Having examined the structure and procedures that govern lawmaking within Congress, we must now consider whether the product of congressional legislation is broadly consistent with the wishes of the American people. In other words, is Congress a truly representative institution?

How Important Are Personal Characteristics?

The membership of Congress is not a mirror image of the American people. Proportionally, there are considerably fewer women, blacks, and other minorities than in the general population, and the social class make-up is even more different. Yet it is clear that if every group were to be represented according to its ratio, it would be necessary to establish in advance all the relevant groups and accord them official status. Such a process would obviously be in conflict with the principle of geographical representation and its consequences.

Although the helpfulness of direct group representation cannot be denied, legislators need not always be members of a specific demographic group to represent that group's interests in Congress. Because members of Congress are subject to reelection, they have an incentive to be responsive to the strongly held views of their constituents, whether or not they share the same class, race, religion, or sex. Thus, in the 1960s and 1970s, Congress—despite the small number of minority and women members—passed landmark civil rights statutes and enacted a variety of laws to prohibit unfair discrimination against women in pay, employment, and credit. The number of women and minorities in Congress began to increase significantly beginning in the 1970s, as these groups increased their participation in the political process.

When the founders drafted the Constitution, they had in mind a concept of representation different from merely mirroring the population. If Congress was to be an effective and responsible lawmaking body, the founders thought it should be filled with citizens who are knowledgeable and experienced in public affairs. The effort of many today is to ensure that this general idea can be maintained and implemented in a way that provides for an adequate variety in the composition of Congress.

Representation and Elections

The founders thought that frequent elections would ensure the democratic character of the House of Representatives. Citizens would elect representatives who shared their basic views, and the prospect of reelection would encourage representatives to remain faithful to their constituents' interests. Some political scientists challenged this view on the basis of a 1958 election survey that showed that more than half of the electorate knew virtually nothing about their candidates for Congress and that a large fraction of those who could identify the candidates had no knowledge of their positions on policy.[19] The authors of the study concluded that, once elected, members of Congress were largely free to do as they wished: "The Congressman . . . knows the constituency isn't looking." Frequent elections, they concluded, did not have the democratic effect that the founders had intended.

This conclusion has since been disputed for three reasons. First, the recruitment mechanisms within congressional districts generally ensure that those who become major-party candidates tend to share the basic beliefs of their constituents. Second, local elites such as newspaper editors, labor and business leaders, interest groups, and local public officials communicate information about congressional candidates and their voting records to the voters, and major differences between a member of Congress and the basic views of his or her constituents become known. For example, if a Democrat from a blue-collar district began to vote against prolabor legislation, union leaders in the district would waste little time in voicing their displeasure to a wider audience. Finally, prospective challengers keep a sharp eye on the actions of incumbents in order to exploit any divergence between their records and the interests or views of their constituents.

Members of Congress are well aware of these mechanisms for enforcing constituent views, and they usually try to anticipate how constituents would react to new issues. According to political scientist R. Douglas Arnold, "legislators use a form of political intuition that comes with experience. They talk with and listen to their constituents, they read their mail, they watch how past issues develop over time, they look for clues about salience and intensity, they consider who might have an incentive to arouse public opinion, they learn from one another and from others' mistakes."[20] Most members believe that what they do in Congress will make a difference in their reelection, and that they must work very hard, both personally and through their staff, to promote good relations with the voters back home.

Delegates and Trustees

While most members of Congress seek to fashion a voting record that will contribute to their reelection, they do not all understand the representative function in the same way. Some see themselves as essentially the agents of those who elected them to Congress, sent to do their bidding. As one member commented, "I'm not here to vote my own convictions. I'm here to represent my people."[21] This understanding of the representative's function is known as the "delegate theory" of representation.

Many members of Congress look on this view with open contempt. In the words of one representative:

> All some House members are interested in is "the folks." They think "the folks" are the second coming. They would no sooner do anything to displease "the folks" than they would fly. They spend all their time trying to find out what "the folks" want. I imagine if they get five letters on one side and five on the other side, they die.[22]

These members insist that it is an intrinsic part of their job to exercise their own best judgment on the issues that come before them. When asked what he would do if a majority of his constituents signed a petition requesting that he vote in a particular way, one member of the House responded:

> If that did happen, then no, I would not vote for it. I would still have to use my own judgment . . . . You can express opinions. I have to make the decision. If you disagree with my decision, you have the power every two years to vote me out of office. I listen to you, believe me. But, in the end, I have to use my judgment as to what is in your best interests.[23]

This view is known as the "trustee theory" of representation.

Although the delegate and trustee roles of representation are easily differentiated in theory, the distinction in practice is much fuzzier. Members of Congress who think of themselves as trustees realize that if they want to be reelected, they must vote in ways broadly consistent with the strongly held views of their constituents. On the other hand, those who subscribe to the delegate theory face hundreds of decisions each year on matters on which a clear constituency opinion does not exist or cannot be easily ascertained. Delegates are forced to exercise their own judgment, while trustees are invariably led to take account of their constituents' opinions.

This overlap of the delegate and trustee aspects of representation corresponds well with what most Americans probably expect from their legislators: effective representation of their basic interests and desires, but not blind obedience on every single point.

Representation, Reelection, and Nonlegislative Activities

The desire to be reelected, in addition to encouraging members of Congress to represent the dominant interests and views of their constituents, also leads to a variety of nonlegislative activities useful for fostering electoral support. These include (1) "advertising" the legislator's name back home by sending newsletters or questionnaires to constituents; (2) claiming credit for federal grants or projects that benefit the district (even if the legislator was not primarily responsible); (3) taking popular public positions on issues of concern to constituents; and (4) assisting the citizens of the district or state in their dealings with the federal bureaucracy—the "constituency service" function described earlier.[24]

Many argue that members of Congress have become increasingly skilled at getting reelected by focusing their energies on these kinds of activities at the expense of traditional legislative duties of drafting proposals, contributing to committee sessions, reading committee reports, and attending floor debate. Greater political benefits can be had from maintaining a sophisticated public relations operation than from devoting hours to the process of formulating legislation. As the members of Congress become better at getting reelected, Congress becomes less and less a deliberative institution, or so it seems.

While there is no doubt that some of the nonlegislative activities of members of Congress do serve to help them win reelection, it is too cynical to regard this as their only purpose. Many of these activities are appropriate elements of the representative function. As Richard Fenno has argued, the legislator "cannot represent any people unless he knows, or makes an effort to know, who they are, what they think, and what they want; and it is by campaigning for electoral support among them that he finds out such things."[25]

To be a representative means to engage in a real communications process with constituents, including explaining to them why one has voted in a certain way. Members of Congress are not simply receptors of opinions or demands from the citizens back home; they are also a source of information and instruction about national problems and Congress's attempts to deal with them. Members who explain their particular contributions to the policy process may generate considerable respect and trust from their constituents, who may in turn grant them a greater degree of freedom or flexibility in legislative actions. Representation and legislation are two sides of the same coin.

Representation and the Growth of Congressional Staff

Another development in the contemporary Congress that has raised questions about its representative function is the enormous growth in congressional staff. In 1947 the committees of the House and Senate had a total support staff of 399. By 1999 this number had grown to over 2,200. During the same time period, the personal staffs of representatives and senators increased more than five-fold from 2,030 to nearly 11,500. As of 1999, the 535 members of the House and Senate were far outnumbered by a staff that totaled over 16,000.

What do all these staff people do? While some perform clerical and secretarial functions, others take a direct and active role in the legislative process: drafting legislation, scheduling witnesses for committee hearings, negotiating with other staff personnel and representatives of interest groups over the details of pending legislation, and briefing their bosses. The total amount of staff time devoted to drafting a bill and navigating it through Congress often far exceeds the time devoted by the members of Congress themselves. The large staff clearly helps Congress in two respects. First, individual members are able to make more informed judgments when advised by personal aides who research and analyze legislative issues. Second, Congress as a whole has increased its independence of the executive branch by having its own experts to advise it on policy issues.

Yet there are also grounds for concern about the role of large staffs. If the thousands of nonelected staff members who work for Congress have a real impact on lawmaking, then how can we be sure that national policy represents the people's desires? And who is to be held responsible if important classified information is leaked, consciously or inadvertently, by staff members? In fact, a large staff can have distorting effects in Congress, even if it does not always run directly counter to the public's wishes. The tremendous increase in the workload in Congress in recent decades is the result in part of the increase in staffing. Staff members, anxious to impress their bosses and to have an effect on shaping the nation's public policy, have a strong interest in developing and pushing legislative proposals. Large staffs also mean that members spend more of their time speaking to their own staff and managing their offices and less time interacting with other members of Congress.

One fact that makes the growth of congressional staffs less of a threat to the representative character of Congress is that most high-level staff persons do a rather good job of reflecting the interests and desires of the members. Representatives and senators tend to recruit as aides people who share their basic policy dispositions, and most staff professionals are intelligent enough to realize that they could quickly lose their jobs if their actions deviate from the views of the legislators. Still, while the staffs add to the congressional process, their growth beyond a certain point threatens to undermine the effectiveness of Congress as a deliberative body.

Conclusion

Who Rules?

The United States Congress is hardly a passive medium through which the American people shape and direct public policy. It is a unique institution with its own traditions, norms of behavior, and organizational structures and rules. How it is organized and operates influences both the role it plays in the political system and the kinds of policies it enacts.

As we saw in Chapter 1, it is necessary in the United States to speak not only of *who* governs but also of *what* governs. Congress is not merely a collection of elected officials, but an independent deliberative institution that puts its own stamp on governing the nation. This does not mean, of course, that Congress is isolated from the broader political community. Public opinion works through Congress, but in so doing it has other consequences than if it acted directly to fashion national policy.

There are two distinct ways in which public opinion influences Congress, following the pluralist and majoritarian models described in Chapter 1. Insofar as organized interest groups influence Congress, the pluralist model holds. Millions of Americans belong to organizations that seek to influence public policy. Interest groups contribute to political candidates, testify before congressional committees, and orchestrate letter-writing campaigns to members of Congress. People debate how much influence interest groups have in Congress, but no one doubts that it is substantial; and while interest group influence is easy to attack as corrupt and wicked, it is important to recall that it fulfills the legitimate need to represent the wishes and ideas of large parts of the public and that it serves to make known the intensity with which certain views are held by some citizens.

Yet the sum of the views of interest groups does not necessarily represent the will of the public at large, and policy dictated by the demands of interest groups (and the best organized among them) could deviate substantially from what the majority desires. There is a mechanism through which the majority influences Congress. The process of periodic elections tends both to bring into Congress individuals who share the electorate's basic policy goals and to ensure the fidelity of incumbents to the essential interests and desires of the voters. The electoral connection keeps Congress in line with the majoritarian model of policymaking.

Congress in Its Third Century

Although it is not possible to predict with any certainty how well Congress will meet its twin constitutional responsibilities of representation and legislation in its third century, several conclusions seem warranted from what we have learned about the operation of Congress.

Representation Despite many problems, Congress remains a vital and dynamic representative institution. The increasing diversity of its membership, the many opportunities to influence decision making in its decentralized power structures, the proliferation of informal groups devoted to specific economic or ideological ends, and the increased sophistication of members of Congress in serving their constituents ensure that interested individuals and groups will be able to be heard within the institution.

One danger in these trends is that as Congress becomes more open and accessible to so many interests and points of view, it may be less able to work in an effective and coordinated way to serve the national interest. Another is that, despite its openness to listening to different views, Congress may remain unable to respond to deeper currents of opinion because of high reelection rates and the methods employed to win reelection. Members of Congress have developed an interest of their own in securing reelection.

Legislation As a lawmaking institution Congress will preserve the strengths of its committee and subcommittee systems that promote specialized expertise and technical competence. And since this expertise is coupled with an independent membership supported by a substantial staff, there will be no lack of novel ideas or policy initiatives to deal with whatever issues may appear on the horizon.

Yet these resources do not mean that Congress possesses all the qualities necessary for passing sound and effective legislation. The dispersal of power to many different points may produce too many legislative ideas that are insufficiently coordinated; or it may miss aspects of the overall picture which go beyond the confines of each particular subcommittee. Like the issues of the federal budget deficit and health care, many future issues will be highly complex, cutting across traditional subject areas and requiring coordinated action in a variety of fields. Through its budget process and more active party leadership, Congress has attempted to overcome the decentralizing forces present in the committee and subcommittee system and a highly independent membership. The tensions between decentralizing and centralizing forces will grow more acute in an era in which resources available to government are limited and issues are highly interdependent.

Congress has proven to be a remarkably resilient legislative body, retaining influence well beyond that of any other national legislative body in the world. Yet it remains to be seen how well Congress can meet the challenges of this third century under the constitutional system.

Chapter 10 Notes

1. Max Farrand, ed., *The Records of the Federal Convention,* vol. 1 (New Haven: Yale University Press, 1937), p. 48.
2. Max Farrand, ed., *The Records of the Federal Convention,* vol. 1, p. 151.
3. Cited in Tom Coles "Congressional Elections in the 1990s: Can the Times Be Changing?" *Extensions,* Spring, 1994, p. 11.
4. Nelson W. Polsby, *Congress and the Presidency,* 3rd ed. (Englewood Cliffs, N.J.: Prentice-Hall, 1976), pp. 98–99
5. David R. Mayhew, *Congress: The Electoral Connection* (New Haven: Yale University Press, 1974), pp. 134–135.
6. John F. Manley, *The Politics of Finance* (Boston: Little, Brown, 1970), p. 251.
7. Richard F. Fenno, Jr., *Congressmen in Committees* (Boston: Little, Brown, 1973), p. 1.
8. Norman Ornstein and Thomas Mann, *Vital Statistics on Congress 1999–2000* (Washington, D.C.: American Enterprise Institute Press, 2000). Staff expenditures allowances are given for 1999.
9. Donald G. Tacheron and Morris K. Udall, *The Job of the Congressman,* 2d ed., (Indianapolis: Bobbs-Merril, 1970), pp. 1–2.
10. Woodrow Wilson, *Congressional Government*, p. 66.

11. Clem Miller, *Member of the House: Letters of a Congressman* (New York: Scribner, 1962), p. 39.

12. Janet Hook, "Younger Members Flex Muscle in Revolt against Chairmen," *Congressional Quarterly Weekly Report* 48, December 8, 1990, p. 4059.

13. Nelson Polsby, *Congress and the Presidency,* p. 97.

14. Jeffrey H. Birnbaum and Alan S. Murray, *Showdown at Gucci Gulch: Lawmakers, Lobbyists, and the Unlikely Triumph of Tax Reform* (New York: Random House, 1987), p. 13.

15. Birnbaum and Murray, *Showdown at Gucci Gulch,* p. 255.

16. R. Douglas Arnold, *The Logic of Congressional Action* (New Haven: Yale University Press, 1990), p. 275.

17. Steven S. Smith, *Call to Order: Floor Politics in the House and Senate*, (Washington: Brookings Institution, 1989), pp. 74–83.

18. Roger H. Davidson and Walter J. Oleszek, *Congress and Its Members,* 3d ed. (Washington: Congressional Quarterly Press, 1990), p. 330.

19. Donald E. Stokes and Warren E. Miller, "Party Government and the Saliency of Congress," *Public Opinion Quarterly,* Winter 1962, pp. 531–546.

20. R. Douglas Arnold, *The Logic of Congressional Action,* pp. 11–12.

21. Richard F. Fenno, Jr., *Home Style* (Boston: Little, Brown, 1978), p. 160.

22. Richard F. Fenno, Jr., *Home Style,* p. 160.

23. Richard F. Fenno, Jr., *Home Style,* p. 161.

24. See David Mayhew, *Congress: The Electoral Connection;* and Morris P. Fiorina, *Congress: Keystone of the Washington Establishment,* 2d ed. (New Haven: Yale University Press, 1989).

25. Richard Fenno, *Home Style,* p. 233.

11

The Presidency

CHAPTER CONTENTS

The American president is often referred to as the "chief executive." The dictionary definition of an executive implies carrying out someone else's decisions. Early at the Constitutional Convention, one delegate conceived the presidency in just this way, as "nothing more than an institution for carrying the will of the Legislature into effect."[1] But the founders emphatically rejected so narrow a conception of the presidency. Instead, they created an office having an independent sphere of action that was endowed with major responsibilities of its own.

Under Article II of the Constitution, the President is charged to "take care that the laws be faithfully executed." This responsibility is clearly greater than just carrying out a law passed by Congress, because the Constitution itself is part of the law. Presidents have cited the "take care" clause when they have acted to defend the Constitution as a whole. But even when the president is carrying out an ordinary law, he may need to exercise a considerable degree of discretion about how to handle a difficult situation.

To take one example, Congress passed a law in the 1940s making it illegal for federal government employees to strike. In 1981, the Air Traffic Controllers Union called for a strike, thinking that the Secretary of Transportation would negotiate and accept the union's demands. President Reagan decided to take matters into his own hands. He announced that the strike was illegal and that any air traffic controller who did not show up for work would be fired after two days. Then, to the surprise of many, he did just that, letting go more than 11,000 workers. Congress forty years earlier had never thought about how to meet such a situation.

The task of executing the law is thus not always simple or automatic. Far from it. Decisions must be made about how, how much, and by what means a law will be executed. In fact, where executing a law is simple, routine, or relatively unimportant, it probably will not come to the president's attention, but will be handled by someone at a much lower level. The president is left with the tough choices that require discretion.

Seeing that laws are executed, important as this task is, is not all that presidents do. Consider another example. In the summer of 1990, Iraq invaded Kuwait and then threatened Saudi Arabia, placing in jeopardy the supply of oil to the industrial world. The United States had to decide how to respond. For weeks, a series of immensely important diplomatic and military decisions had to be made, including whether to send military forces to the area, whether to blockade Iraq, what position to take in votes in the United Nations, and when or whether to commence hostilities. All of these decisions were made by President Bush. Of course, he consulted members of Congress and kept his eye on whether they supported his actions. Congress was in a position to pass measures that could have constrained the president, and in this respect Congress was present as a potential check. But the initiative for action and decision lay entirely with the president up until the moment when Congress had to decide whether to support the president in beginning a war.

To be the chief executive, therefore, means more than to "carry the will of the Legislature into effect." The president has an independent sphere of authority. He can act with discretion in situations of crisis where a series of specific and perhaps swift and secret decisions may be required.

Consider a final example. After waging a campaign for the presidency in 1980 that promised fundamental changes in the policies of the federal government, President Reagan on assuming office in 1981 proposed to Congress a series of highly controversial measures to substantially cut planned growth in domestic spending and to reduce federal taxes. This program required legislation to be put into effect. Still, it was President Reagan who took the initiative and led the political offensive, defining the issues and urging the American people and members of Congress to back his program. Once again the president was doing more than "carrying the will of the legislature into effect." He was attempting to shape that will and to set and control a national agenda for action. Such efforts are something Americans now expect of a president.

These, then, are the three major tasks that presidents perform. They execute the law (which itself often involves substantial choice and discretion); they essentially decide for the nation (within limits) in the conduct of important areas of foreign affairs, especially in crises; and finally, they attempt to set a political agenda and chart a course for the nation.

"Leadership" refers to a president who does not limit himself to administering the government, but who sets a course in foreign affairs and seeks to lay out a domestic political agenda. The presidency, in Woodrow Wilson's words, should be the "vital place of action in the system."[2]

The extent to which the founders intended the presidency to be the seat of leadership remains in dispute. The very first president, George Washington, certainly exercised this role. Yet during long periods in the nineteenth century, presidents did not take the lead, in part no doubt because crises in foreign affairs were so infrequent. For the past half century, however, Americans have come to regard leadership as central to the presidential office, and many of the distinguishing characteristics of the modern presidency, as well as many of its problems, derive from its role as the "vital place of action in the system."

The Tasks of Presidential Leadership

One way to gain insight into the varied tasks of the president is to examine the daily activities of a chief executive (Box 11-1). On June 23, 1981, the White House allowed reporters from the weekly magazine *U.S. News & World Report* to attend President Reagan's meetings and functions, public as well as private. The President and advisors no doubt selected an especially full day, but it was not exceptional in regard to the kinds of activities a president performs.

The Activities of a President

Reagan attended a total of seventeen meetings on June 23. Some of these, like the picture-taking session with new ambassadors, the lunch with Jacques Cousteau, and the reception for the teenage Republicans, illustrate the symbolic role of the presidency. The president is the head of state in this country; there are few higher public honors than to meet with him personally. The rest of President Reagan's meetings, however, had less to do with symbolism and formality than with the business of governing.

To govern effectively, presidents need information and advice, much of which they now receive from their personal staff. Meetings with the president's staff are integral parts of his daily schedule. On June 23, President Reagan met with his three most senior advisors in the morning, his chief congressional liaison and press spokesman in the afternoon, and received his daily briefing on international events from his National Security Advisor. While all presidents are to some degree dependent upon their staff, they have great latitude in how they structure and interact with the staff organization.

Presidents get their advice not only from personal aides but also from those they appoint to head the various departments and agencies of the executive branch. On this day President Reagan sought the advice of department heads in three different forums: individual meetings (with the Treasury Secretary and Director of the CIA), a session with a specific group of department heads (the Cabinet council on commerce and trade), and a meeting with the entire Cabinet (all the department heads and selected other high-level officials who are given Cabinet ranking). Usually, meetings with executive branch staff and officials are supplemented by briefing books on the issues that the president faces. On this day alone President Reagan received a staff summary on the day's news, an inch-thick briefing book on the events for the day, a written report on national security matters, and a staff memo on the issue under consideration by the Cabinet council on commerce and trade.

Those outside the executive branch who are most important to the success or failure of a president's program are members of Congress. This is illustrated by the fact that on June 23 Reagan met with 239 members of Congress. As a general rule, the larger the number of representatives and senators who meet with the president, the less likely it is that the meeting will involve a serious discussion of political business. Still, sessions like the reception for the House Republicans can serve to build personal relations, which can translate over the long run into a greater willingness on the part of members of Congress to see things the president's way. Beneath the institutional forms of government, it is well to remember that there is a community

---

BOX 11.1

Ronald Reagan's Schedule, June 23, 1981

4:30 A.M. The President, having trouble sleeping, gets up and does some paper work. Goes back to bed about 6.

8:00 A.M. Reagan receives wake-up call from White House switchboard.

8:41 A.M. Senior aides James Baker, Edwin Meese and Michael Deaver join the President in the family quarters to discuss the day's schedule.

9:08 A.M. Reagan walks from second-floor residence down to the State Dining Room for breakfast with 38 Democratic lawmakers who backed his budget cuts.

10:15 A.M. The President goes to the Oval Office for daily national security briefing. Among those attending are Vice President Bush and National Security Adviser Richard Allen. Meeting concludes at 10:34.

10:37 A.M. At his desk, Reagan is briefed on the days developments by aides Baker, Meese, Deaver, Max Friedersdorf, David Gergen and Larry Speakes. At 10:46, the meeting ends.

10:50 A.M. U.S. News & World Report editors interview the President.

11:09 A.M. White House advisers Melvin Bradley and Thaddeus Garrett enter Oval Office to prepare Reagan for meeting with NAACP officials Benjamin Hooks and Margaret Bush Wilson.

11:13 A.M. Hooks and Wilson begin discussions with the President. Also present are Vice President Bush and White House aide Elizabeth Dole. Meeting ends at 11:59.

12:01 P.M. Reagan poses for photographs in Oval Office with new U.S. Ambassadors Arthur Burns, Maxwell Rabb and Ernest Preeg and their families.

12:15 P.M. Ocean explorer Jacques Cousteau enters for lunch with Reagan, Deaver and White House aide Richard Darman on patio outside the Oval Office.

1:31 P.M. Treasury Secretary Donald Regan briefs the President in the Oval Office on tax developments in Congress.

1:39 P.M. Reagan walks across the hall to the Roosevelt Room to meet with 11 Republican members of the Senate Finance Committee. Meeting ends at 2:01.

2:08 P.M. The President enters the Cabinet Room for meeting with the Cabinet Council on Commerce and Trade. Session ends at 2:27.

2:34 P.M. The Chief Executive convenes a meeting of the entire Cabinet. It concludes at 3:38.

3:46 P.M. The President goes to the State Dining Room for meeting with the Presidential Advisory Committee on Federalism. Session ends at 4:24 and Reagan returns to the Oval Office.

4:33 P.M. Personnel Adviser E. Pendleton James enters Oval Office to discuss presidential appointments.

4:48 P.M. CIA Director William Casey enters for meeting with the President.

5:09 P.M. Reagan goes to Rose Garden reception for 175 teen-age Republicans.

5:16 P.M. The President returns to the Oval Office to do some paper work.

5:51 P.M. Reagan enters the East Room for a reception in honor of 190 House Republicans.

6:12 P.M. The President goes back to the family quarters, has dinner alone, telephones Mrs. Reagan in California, catches up on some reading and retires at 11:15 P.M.

Source: *U.S. News & World Report*, July 6, 1981, pp. 16–17.

of officials in Washington for whom personal relations have an important bearing on how they act.

Although Reagan's activities on June 23 provide a good glimpse into the day-to-day business of governing, there are at least three things the president did not do that day that are important elements of presidential leadership. First, he did not give a televised address to the nation, which is something Reagan did quite effectively during his tenure. Nor did he hold a press conference. The nationally televised freewheeling session with the White House press corps has become a virtual institution in American politics. How well presidents relate to the press can be very important to how well they get their message across to the American public. Second, the president did not meet any foreign heads of state. Although the Constitution created three separate branches of government, it designated the president as the one official representative of the United States in meeting with foreign ambassadors and, by implication, with foreign leaders generally.

Finally, less common than delivering a presidential address or meeting heads of state, but still of crucial importance, is crisis management. As commander in chief of the armed forces and director of foreign relations, the president is responsible for the initial reaction to any military or international crisis that threatens the nation's interest or well-being. The normal daily schedule may be abruptly canceled in favor of hurried meetings with military and foreign policy advisers, briefings on rapidly changing events, and confidential communications with world leaders. Congress may eventually contribute to the final resolution of a dispute with a foreign nation, but in the first few hours or days the crucial decisions are up to the president. As Robert Kennedy related in his account of the Cuban Missile Crisis, when President Kennedy had to decide how to respond to the introduction of Soviet missiles into Cuba: "Saturday morning at 10:00 I called the President at the Blackstone Hotel in Chicago. . . . It was now up to one single man. No committee was going to make this decision. He canceled his trip and returned to Washington."[3]

Governing Style and Personality

The kinds of activities which President Reagan engaged in on June 23 are not much different from those of other recent presidents. If one looked at typical presidential schedules of any modern administration, it would be difficult to determine which president went with which schedule. This surface similarity, however, obscures fundamental personal differences in how the occupants of the Oval Office actually go about the business of governing, for each president has an individual style of governing (see Box 11.2).

The presidency cannot be understood apart from studying particular presidents. The presidency is the most personalized of the national governing institutions. As Woodrow Wilson once noted, "it is easier to write of the President than of the presidency."[4] By its very nature as a "unitary" institution headed by—indeed, embodied in—one person, the presidency is and was intended to be an office that provides wide discretion to its occupant. Statesmanship, the founders realized, was not an attribute of collective bodies.

Some presidents are intensely energetic and delve into the fine details of administration and governing (Johnson, Carter, and Clinton); others delegate matters of detail to the White House staff and reserve their own time and energy for broader issues (Eisenhower and Reagan). Some prefer a highly structured and smoothly functioning staff organization (Eisenhower and Nixon); others see advantage in a looser and less settled division of staff functions and chain of command (Kennedy, Johnson, and Carter). Some treat their personal aides with consideration and respect (George H. Bush, Reagan and Carter); others harass, intimidate, and embarrass them (Johnson). Some are guided by deep-seated beliefs in a few fundamental principles about society and government (Reagan); others have a more problem-solving type of approach to the task of formulating public policy (Bush).

The list could go on and on. Some like meetings; others don't. Some are effective one-on-one persuaders; others do better communicating to millions through television. Some pre-

BOX 11.2

The Governing Styles of Three Modern Presidents

Ronald Reagan (1981–1989)

Reagan keeps a tight schedule, but spurns long hours in the office. He spends most of his day with people, not papers. He insists on hearing an issue debated before making a decision. He sets broad policy and allows aides to work out the details.

As an administrator, Reagan is detached and sometimes formal. He never removes his suit coat in the Oval Office, even when he's working there alone with his feet propped up. Although he spends most of the day in meetings, he seldom joins in the debate and rarely asks questions.

At the same time, the Chief Executive makes strangers feel comfortable in his presence. . . . A good storyteller, he often rewards visitors to the Oval Office with a joke. . . .

Reagan occasionally yawns during long meetings. He doodles with paper and pencil, chews on his right index finger or plays with his glasses. . . .

Unlike most Presidents, Reagan is not usually an early riser. His day began at 8:00 A.M. and ended at 11:15 P.M.

Jimmy Carter (1977–1981)

He grasps issues quickly. . . . He would resolve technical questions lucidly, without distortions imposed by cant or imperfect comprehension.

He is a stable, personally confident man, whose quirks are few. . . .

Carter is usually patient, less vindictive than the political norm, blessed with a sense of perspective about the chanciness of life and the transience of its glories and pursuits. . . . He would leave for a weekend at Camp David laden with thick briefing books, would pore over budget tables to check the arithmetic, and during his first six months in office, would personally review all requests to use the White House tennis court. . . .

Carter thinks in lists, not arguments; as long as the items are there, their order does not matter, nor does the hierarchy among them. Whenever he gave us an outline for a speech, it would consist of six or seven subjects ("inflation," "need to fight waste") rather than a theme or tone. . . .

For certain aspects of his job—the analyst and manager parts—Carter's methods serve him well. He makes decisions about solar power installations and the B-1 on the basis of output, payload, facts, not abstract considerations. But for the part of his job that involves leadership, Carter's style of thought cripples him. He thinks he "leads" by choosing the correct policy; but he fails to project a vision larger than the problem he is tackling at the moment.

. . . While Carter accepts challenges to his ideas and is pleased to improve his mind, he stubbornly, complacently resists attempts to challenge his natural style.

Lyndon B. Johnson (1963–1969)

With his own men, Johnson commanded, forbade, insisted, swaggered and swore. Verbal tirades and fits of temper became an integral part of his image. On occasion, it seemed as if Johnson needed to make his staff look ridiculous, that he was strengthened by his exposure of inadequacies in others. . . .

His energy [when he succeeded to the presidency] seemed redoubled. He talked with chiefs of state; sent messages to the Congress; issued orders to the executive branch; met with businessmen, labor leaders, and civil servants. The hours between 2 and 6 A.M. were all that Johnson grudgingly gave to sleep. Endowed with an encyclopedic memory, he had a command of the details of matters significant to his power and its exercise that was prodigious. In one sitting, he would deal in turn with issues of education, finance, poverty, and housing. His mind remained resilient even when his body was fatigued. He tended to rest from one kind of activity by engaging in another. . . .

BOX 11.2 (cont.)

His hierarchy was an orderly structure with many fixed relationships, but he alone was at the top with direct lines of communication and authority to the several men who occupied the level below. . . . The President was his own chief of staff: he made the staff assignments; he received the product of his staff's work and reconciled or decided between the competing reports; he set the pace of action and the tone of discussion. . . . And he extended that control down to the least significant levels of activity, handling such details as approving the guest list for social functions, checking the equipment for the White House cars, determining the correct temperature for the rooms in the Mansion. . . .

Sources: *U.S. News & World Report,* July 6, 1981, pp. 13–15; James Fallows, "The Passionless Presidency," in Peter Woll, ed., *Behind the Scenes in American Government,* third ed. (Boston: Little, Brown, 1981), pp. 141–157; and Doris Kearns, *Lyndon Johnson and the American Dream* (New York: Harper and Row, 1976), pp. 176, 178, 239–240.

fer the challenges of foreign policy; others focus on domestic affairs. The governing styles of presidents reflect their personal attributes and qualities—their views of executive leadership derived from long experience, their strengths and weaknesses, their goals and public philosophy, and, finally, their character and personality.

Descriptions of individual presidents are found in biographies, memoirs, and historical treatments of different administrations. What strikes one in reading these accounts is the diversity in backgrounds, characteristics, and talents of those who have served. Some were brought up in families of great prestige or wealth (John Quincy Adams, Franklin Roosevelt, John Kennedy), while others faced boyhoods of unusual difficulty (Richard Nixon and Ronald Reagan). There are some whose dignity and sobriety are striking (like Washington), and others who seem vain and undistinguished (like Harding). Some were clearly "in control" of themselves—here one thinks of the well-integrated personalities of Gerald Ford or George H. Bush—while others seem to have been "driven" by unconscious needs and desires which they may never have fully understood or mastered, like Woodrow Wilson, Lyndon Johnson, Richard Nixon, and Bill Clinton. The sketches below (see Box 11.3) of three presidents—Lincoln, Wilson, and Nixon—give an indication of some of the different qualities of those who have occupied the office.

But as important as personality is to the study of the presidency, each individual still acts within constraints and inducements set by the presidential office. That office possesses certain powers, has certain expectations placed on it, and—increasingly—has a fixed organizational structure that surrounds it. To some extent, therefore, we can speak of properties of the institution itself without reference to individual personalities or style. These institutional properties are the product of a long history of evolution and of deliberate attempts by certain constitution makers to create and adapt the office.

The Development of the Office: The Original Design

Today, the presidency is generally regarded as the seat of political leadership in the nation. Yet neither the Constitution nor our early history provides conclusive support for ascribing to the presidency a premier position among the triad of national institutions. The Constitution vests the office with powers that, while they may suggest, by no means require a leadership role in the national government. Moreover, for much of our history, Congress—not the presidency—has been the more influential branch.

It is only, in fact, since the New Deal administration of Franklin Roosevelt that the presidency has achieved a permanent leadership role in the political system. Before Franklin Roosevelt there were strong presidents, but the norm for much of our first century and a half was congressional dominance of national policymaking. The roots of the modern presidency can, however, be

BOX 11.3

Personality Sketches of Lincoln, Wilson, and Nixon

Abraham Lincoln

Lincoln must have been taxed near to the limit of what men have endured without loss of judgment, or loss of courage or loss of ordinary human feeling. There is no sign that any of these things happened to him; the study of his record rather shows a steady ripening of mind and character to the end. . . . He had within his own mind two resources. . . . In his most intimate circle he would draw upon his stores of poetry, particularly of tragedy; often, for instance, he would recite such speeches as Richard II's: "For God's sake let us sit upon the ground and tell sad stories of the death of kings. All murdered." Another element in his thoughts . . . [was the] play of humour in which he found relief . . . to the end.

Woodrow Wilson

Men require ways of expressing their aggressions and of protecting their self-esteem. Wilson's ways of doing both, unhappily, involved demanding his way to the letter and hurling himself against his opponents no matter what the odds, no matter what the cost. . . . He must fight to have his way. But in doing so he must prove his devotion to the Treaty [of Versailles]. He must demonstrate that he had no personal motive for taking the position he took, that matters of great principle were involved. He must demonstrate his moral superiority and his opponents' "selfishness." He must be ready to die for his cause.

Richard Nixon

Most men mature around a central core; Nixon had several. This is why he was never at peace with himself. Any attempt to sum up his complex character in one attribute is bound to be misleading. The detractors' view that Nixon was the incarnation of evil is as wrong as the adulation of his more fervent admirers. On closer acquaintance one realized that what gave Nixon his driven quality was the titanic struggle that never ended; there was never a permanent victor between the dark and the sensitive sides of his nature. Now one, now another personality predominated, creating an overall impression of menace, of torment, of unpredictability, and, in the final analysis, of enormous vulnerability.

Sources: Lord Chamwood, *Abraham Lincoln,* 3rd ed. (New York: Henry Holt, 1917); Alexander and Juliette George, *Woodrow Wilson and Colonel House* (New York: Dover, 1964); and Henry Kissinger, *Years of Upheaval* (Boston: Little, Brown, 1982).

traced to the Constitution and to the broad potential grants of power that the founders gave the executive. According to one scholar, the friends of a strong presidency at the Convention "gained a version [in the Constitution] that provided the opportunity for the exercise of a resideuum of unenumerated power. . . . Much of the subsequent history of the presidency would involve the incumbent's claim that he had the power to act, and his critics' counterclaim that his exercise of authority was unconstitutional."[5]

The Experience of the Articles

The Constitution was written after eleven years of political experience following the country's declaration of independence in 1776. The form the founders gave to the presidency owed much to what they had learned about the need for effective executive power during those years. At the beginning of the revolutionary period, Americans shared a deep distrust of executive power resulting from the abuses ascribed to King George III, whom the Declaration of Independence attacked for being guilty of "every act which may define a tyrant." These actions of the king had followed a long history of conflict in the colonies between popularly elected assemblies, which represented the colonists views, and the royal governors appointed by the monarch.

The mistrust of a strong executive as a threat to liberty was reflected both in the Articles of Confederation and in the new state constitutions written in the early years after the Revolution. The Articles established no independent executive authority. All the power vested in the national government resided with Congress. Important executive tasks nevertheless had to be performed, such as directing the war effort and negotiating with foreign nations. Congress at first assigned executive functions to committees of the legislature, later to semi-independent boards with both members of Congress and private citizens, and finally to distinct departments that were separate from the legislature but answerable to it.

These experiments in developing an effective administrative apparatus were failures. Fearful of the growth of a powerful independent bureaucracy, Congress refused to divest itself of the details of administration. Both legislation and administration suffered. Jefferson complained that the "smallest trifle of [administration] occupies as long as the most important act of legislation and takes place of every thing else." Hamilton echoed the same sentiment, contending that "Congress is properly a deliberative corps and it forgets itself when it attempts to play the executive."[6] By 1787, many concluded that effective conduct of the national business required a separate administrative branch energized and supervised by a single head with a clear chain of command and protection from irregular legislative intrusions into the details of administration.

During the same eleven-year period (1776–1787), events in the states taught a similar lesson, but for somewhat different reasons. In the eleven states that drew up new constitutions after independence, provisions were made for a separate executive branch headed by a governor. But in almost every instance, the executive branch was made decidedly subordinate to the legislature. Terms of office for governors were short (usually one year), and many states prohibited reeligibility. The most common mode of election was by a vote of the legislature. The gubernatorial office was further weakened by the existence of executive councils that could overrule the governor on many important matters. Finally, most governors received their powers not from the state constitution but directly from the legislature

Although these provisions did prevent executive tyranny, they had the unwelcome effect of fostering a form of legislative tyranny in the new state governments. In the absence of effective political checks, the state legislatures regularly overstepped their proper constitutional authority and encroached upon the executive and judicial spheres. As Jefferson noted, "173 despots would surely be as oppressive as one. . . . An elective despotism was not the government we fought for."[7] In addition, unchecked legislative power resulted in excessive and constantly changing legislation that made the policies of these governments highly unstable.

The conspicuous exception to this pattern of legislative usurpations and irresponsible lawmaking was the state of New York. There the constitution established a relatively powerful and independent executive branch that was more than a match for the legislature. The governor was elected directly by the people for a three-year term with no limits on reeligibility; and gubernatorial powers were granted by the state constitution, not by the legislature. With the exceptions of appointments and vetoes, the governor was unchecked by an executive council. As a result, Governor George Clinton, who held office for eighteen years, became the dominant force in the state, employing the executive powers to maintain public order and to guide measures in the legislature. Under Clinton's firm leadership, New York probably enjoyed a more stable and competent administration than that of any other state. The New York governorship taught the founders that a powerful executive could be consistent with republican government, and it served as a partial model for the founders when they designed the presidency.

The Constitution of 1787

By the time the Constitutional Convention met in 1787, most delegates already agreed that the executive office should be sufficiently strong and independent not only to provide for an effective administration of national law, but also to counteract legislative tyranny and instability. This latter function implies a political executive who plays a role in the policy process and who may occasionally thwart the legislature's will. In addition, the delegates saw the need for a stronger hand in the conduct of the nation's diplomacy, if not in formulating the essential policies then at any rate in carrying them into effect. In four different ways the Constitution of 1787 went beyond the practices in the states to establish an executive that would have a will of its own and the Constitutional means to resist legislative encroachments on the executive sphere.

Constitutional Grant of Power Most states allowed the legislature to define the powers of executive branch. In contrast, Article II of the Constitution begins, "The executive Power shall be vested in a President of the United States of America." This cryptic declaration has served as a focal point of debate between those who think the president has certain inherent powers that are part of the "executive power" and those who insist that the phrase adds nothing to the president's authority beyond what the Constitution otherwise expressly grants. The Constitution then goes on to spell out a variety of specific powers, including the power to command the armed forces, to issue pardons, to recommend measures to Congress, to veto legislative enactments, and to receive ambassadors. These powers are the president's alone. Two others are shared with the Senate: to appoint ambassadors, justices of the Supreme Court, and other high-level federal officers; and to make treaties with foreign nations. Formally, then, the source of much of the president's power lies not in statutes passed by Congress, but in the Constitution.

Structural Independence from Congress The founders sought to ensure an institutionally independent executive by limiting Congress's control over a president's salary and by providing the president with an independent electoral base. Both of these provisions differed from the prevailing practices in most states. In regard to salaries, Congress may raise or lower the presidential salary for future terms, but it cannot alter the salary of a sitting president during the current term.

The question of salaries, incidentally, was discussed at some length at the Convention. The delegates rejected a proposal by Benjamin Franklin to have the president serve without pay on the grounds that such a plan would exclude all but the wealthiest (or else subject poorer incumbents to the temptation of corruption). To avoid an elitist or oligarchic spirit to the government, the founders argued for reasonable salaries for elected officials.

As for the method of election, the founders removed the choice of the president from the legislature.[8] They did so to protect the president's independence, realizing that the body that selects can also usually control. In place of legislative selection, they created the new institutional mechanism of the electoral college, which gave the decision to temporary bodies of special representatives who would be directly or indirectly responsive to the people. (State legislatures decided in each case how the electors would be chosen.) Members of Congress were prohibited from serving as electors.

Substantial Term of Office and Indefinite Reeligibility The Constitution established a four-year term for the president and placed no restrictions on reeligibility. These provisions were designed to promote continuity and stability in the administration of the government and to give the president an interest in protecting the executive domain from legislative encroachments. The founders were keenly sensitive to the force of personal ambition in the political arena and knew full well that highly spirited persons would be attracted to the presidency. Consequently, they tried to construct the office in such a way that as presidents pursued their own interest, they would also promote the interest of the nation. Because good performance in office might be rewarded with reelection, presidents would come to see that personal goals—whether in the form of perquisites of the office, the prestige of the position, the power to affect national life, or the glory resulting from great accomplishments—could be best achieved by a responsible exercise of the powers of the presidency.

Opponents of indefinite reeligibility worried that popular presidents might serve for life and thereby become dangerously powerful. This concern was partly laid to rest when George Washington and later Thomas Jefferson retired after two terms, setting a (loose) two-term precedent. (Both Ulysses Grant and Woodrow Wilson seemed interested in third terms.) It was not until Franklin Roosevelt, who was chosen four times, that a president served more than eight years. In 1951, six years after Roosevelt's death, the states ratified the Twenty-second Amendment, limiting presidents to two terms. This amendment was passed largely from fears, especially among Republicans at the time, that the presidency under Roosevelt had become too powerful.

Since then, two quite different proposals on reeligibility have been seriously entertained. One idea, advocated by Presidents Ford and Carter, is to do away with reeligibility entirely and to extend the presidential term to six years. Proponents of this single, six-year term maintain that it would free presidents from concern with the narrow political consequences of their actions so that they could concentrate on the broad national interest. Opponents answer that presidential leadership depends on the "political" nature of the office; that a prohibition on reelection would undermine the president's influence with Congress; that the nation is well served when presidents are forced to defend their policies in a reelection campaign; and that an inflexible six years is too long for an ineffective president and probably not long enough for an especially able chief executive. The other proposal, favored by President Reagan, is to abolish the Twenty-second amendment and return to the original plan of indefinite reeligibility.

Unity Perhaps the most important characteristic of the presidency, in the founders' view, was the unity of the office: "That unity is conducive to energy will not be disputed. Decision, activity, secrecy, and dispatch will generally characterize the proceedings of one man in a much more eminent degree than the proceedings of any greater number; and in proportion as the number is increased, these qualities will be diminished." (*Federalist* 70) An effective executive must be able to make decisions quickly, to carry them out forcefully, and at times to do so secretly. A single individual is more likely to function in this way than a group.

The founders thus rejected one proposal that would have created a committee of three or more, perhaps selected from different parts of the country, to function as chief executive; and another that would have established an executive council, like those in the states, to share the

authority vested in the presidency. A plural executive, moreover, would make the office less accountable to the public and therefore more dangerous, for "plurality in the executive . . . tends to conceal faults and destroy responsibility." (*Federalist* 70) With one person in charge, the people know whom to reward for distinguished service and whom to punish (that is, refuse to reelect). Voting studies have shown that the main criterion citizens employ when voting on an incumbent is precisely this: whether to reward a president for what the people believe has been a successful administration, or else to reject the president and change to someone else.

Although the founders sought to construct an independent and energetic executive, not all of them had in mind the idea of the president as the focal point of governmental leadership. On this issue, there were differences of opinion and much uncertainty about how governmental initiatives would normally be formulated. Certainly, the bare grants of power in the Constitution do not—and probably could not—mandate a role for the president as the principal national leader. But there is enough in these powers and in the position of the president in the system to enable a strong leader to assert the role of national leader.

The Presidency in the First Century

Anyone who has tried to memorize the list of presidents knows that some were rather minor figures. Along with such famous persons as George Washington, Thomas Jefferson, Andrew Jackson, and Abraham Lincoln are some rather obscure names: William Harrison, Zachary Taylor, Franklin Pierce, and Chester Arthur.

For the most part, the presidency during the nation's first century was not an office of political leadership. This limited role for the president can be explained by the nation's minor responsibilities (after 1815) in foreign affairs, the modest use of federal power generally, and the development of opposition to a strong presidency, first by the Democratic-Republican party and later by the Whig party. Nevertheless, the presidents who did offer strong leadership illustrate some of the capacities of the office. These presidents not only ensured that the presidency did not

GENERAL WASHINGTON.

As the first President of the United States, George Washington (1732–1799) established many of the informal conventions, norms, and precedents that govern presidential behavior to this day. (Photo provided by the National Portrait Gallery, Smithsonian Institution. Used with permission.)

wither into a merely ceremonial office, but they also established some of the precedents on which certain twentieth century presidents built the more permanent, institutional foundation of the strong presidency. Four administrations were especially significant in setting the stage for later development: those of Washington, Jefferson, Jackson, and Lincoln.

George Washington (1789–1797)

As the first president, George Washington was keenly aware of the precedent his actions would hold for the future. The Constitution charted the bare outlines of the office; it was up to Washington to bring the office to life. For Washington that meant making clear from the beginning that the presidency was Constitutionally and politically independent from Congress, especially in the area of foreign affairs.

An early episode served to emphasize this independence. In 1793, while France and England were at war, Washington issued a Proclama-

tion of Neutrality, asserting that the existing treaty between France and the United States—the same treaty that had brought France to the aid of the Americans during the Revolutionary War—did not require American intervention on the side of France. Such a policy declaration, which today seems fully within the president's power, was strongly criticized by many in Congress as an unconstitutional usurpation of Congress's authority to declare war (and thus decide matters of war and peace). None of the specific grants of power in Article II, they contended, allowed the president to make foreign policy in this sense. Indeed, the Constitution does not contain a "power to conduct foreign relations."[9] For Hamilton, however, who defended Washington's view, the "executive power" encompassed the power to conduct diplomacy; and authority over foreign policy therefore belonged to the president, "subject only to the exceptions and qualifications which, are expressed" in the Constitution.[10]

In the domestic sphere, where the presidency has less formal authority, Washington could have limited himself mainly to the faithful execution of congressional policy. Instead, through the vigorous leadership of Secretary of Treasury Alexander Hamilton, in voicing to the Constitutional injunction to "recommend to [Congress] . . . such measures as he shall judge necessary and expedient," Washington's administration took an active part in determining the nation's early economic and commercial policies. Important bills were prepared in substance and sometimes detail in the Department of the Treasury and then submitted through members of Congress. The success of the new government in establishing sound national credit and in fostering the nation's economic well-being demonstrated some of the virtues of presidential policy formulation.

What is remarkable in looking back on the Washington presidency is its strikingly "modern" character. Although the presidential office lacked most of today's institutional trappings, such as the large White House Staff, the executive performed the same key functions as today, conducting the nation's foreign affairs and proposing a major legislative agenda. To be sure, Washington could not take to the airwaves, hold press conferences, or travel in Air Force One, and he probably would have found such constant and direct contact with the public beyond the proper boundaries of presidential leadership. But even in the realm of managing public opinion, Washington's administration—often acting through Treasury Secretary Hamilton—prepared major state papers intended for public as well as congressional purview and defended administration programs, as well as presidential powers, in the newly established newspapers.

Thomas Jefferson (1801–1809)

The growing strength and assertiveness of the executive office during Washington's two terms caused some to fear that the national government was moving toward a kind of monarchy. Washington's successor, John Adams, faced an increasingly assertive Congress, and in 1800 Adams lost his bid for reelection to the man who led the "antimonarchist" forces: Thomas Jefferson.

To the surprise of friends and foes alike, Jefferson did not subordinate the presidency to Congress. On the contrary, he exercised considerable leadership over Congress on most of the important issues of the time. Indeed, he used presidential power to its fullest by purchasing the Louisiana Territory from Napoleon without prior congressional approval—a step over which even Jefferson agonized.

For the most part, however, Jefferson's use of presidential power was exercised more through his leadership of the Democratic-Republican party, which controlled both houses of Congress, than by the boldness which characterized his purchase of the Louisiana territory from the French. During his two administrations, trusted allies of Jefferson served in key positions in the House and Senate, and they were usually willing to follow his lead. Where Washington had given shape to the Constitutional dimensions of the office, Jefferson was the first to use the political party, an extra-Constitutional institution, to enhance the influence of the presidency.

Indeed, Jefferson's presidential legacy is an ambiguous one. His party came to power very much in opposition to a strong presidency, and Jefferson gave expression to many of these views. He did not think it appropriate to employ

As third President of the United States, Thomas Jefferson (1743–1826) sometimes held a cautious view of executive power even as he often acted with great boldness. His acquisition of the Louisiana Territory from France more than doubled the size of the country. (Jointly owned by Monticello, the Thomas Jefferson Memorial Foundation, Inc., and the National Portrait Gallery, Smithsonian Institution. Purchase funds provided by the Regents of the Smithsonian Institution, the Trustees of the Thomas Jefferson Memorial.)

some of the capacities implicit in the Constitution, such as delivering the State of the Union address in person to the Congress. By acting as a party leader, he exercised strong leadership not just outside of formal channels, but in a sense at their expense. He exercised his strong leadership not just outside of formal channels, but in a sense at the expense of them. Jefferson is remembered as a strong president, but certainly not as one who strengthened the presidency. John Marshall, never one of Jefferson's admirers, predicted this result in 1800: "By weakening the office of President, he will increase his personal power."[11]

Andrew Jackson (1829–1837)

Jefferson's close friend James Madison followed him into the presidency in 1809. Neither Madison nor his immediate successors, James Monroe and John Quincy Adams, were able to give the presidency the influence it had under Jefferson. None possessed the stature of Jefferson within his party, and in any case the party had by 1816 more or less collapsed from its own success. Moreover, from 1800 until the early 1820s, the Republican method of nominating presidential candidates by a caucus of congressional party members strengthened Congress and threatened to invalidate the founders' guarantee of presidential independence by allowing the president to be selected by the legislature. Those who sought their party's nomination had to curry favor with members of Congress. In 1818, Supreme Court Justice Joseph Story wrote in a letter to a friend, "The Executive has no longer a commanding influence. The House of Representatives has absorbed all the popular feeling and all the effective power of the country."[12]

The election of Andrew Jackson to the presidency in 1828 reversed this decline of presidential power. A military hero of the War of 1812, Jackson was at the time the most popular political figure in the country, especially in the fast-developing regions west of the Appalachians. By 1828 the extension of white manhood suffrage and the introduction of the popular election of presidential electors had effectively vested the selection of presidents in the hands of the people. And Jackson was the people's choice, as he often reminded his opponents.

Extending Jefferson's example, Jackson asserted a new basis of authority for the president as the special representative of the American people. Under the original design, the mode of presidential election was not by direct popular vote, and the principal foundation of presidential authority was not generally conceived in popular terms, but somewhat more on the powers of the office as granted or implied by the Constitution. Jackson emphasized a much more immediate connection between the people and the presidency than any of his predecessors. The president was elected by all the people and had a claim to being their representative equal to that of Congress. (Indeed, Jackson proposed eliminating the electoral college mechanism and instituting a direct popular election.) Jackson began as a nonpartisan leader, but by his reelec-

tion campaign of 1832 he joined with Martin Van Buren, who was committed to rebuilding the party system, and connected the idea of the popularly elected president to the idea of the president as head of the majority party. By adding to the presidency the claim of being the public's truest representative, Jackson expanded on Jefferson's extra-Constitutional basis of presidential authority, freeing the presidency from some of the shackles of his predecessors and altering the character of the institution.

No power exercised by Jackson had greater consequences, or generated greater controversy, than the veto. The six presidents who preceded Jackson vetoed a total of nine bills. The understanding of Republican-democratic presidents was that the veto was intended for extraordinary circumstances, especially to guard against legislative encroachments on the executive, not to give the president a regular check on the policymaking process. Jackson rejected this view—in effect embracing the view of *The Federalist*—and legitimized the use of the veto on policy grounds, maintaining that he had a responsibility as the direct representative of the people to oppose legislative measures that were not in the public's interest. During his eight-year administration he vetoed eleven bills.

Under Jackson, more than under any president until Lincoln, the presidency became the focus of public attitudes and desires. Jackson, however, did not use his power to expand the scope of the national authority, but on the contrary to limit it. As an heir of the Jeffersonian tradition, Jackson was fearful of an energetic national government and frequently used his power in a "negative" way, as with the vetoes, to protect the powers of the states against the federal government. But Jackson was not prepared to see the union itself endangered. In the nullification crisis in 1832, when South Carolina threatened to withdraw from the union if a tariff law was enforced, Jackson declared his willingness to use force to protect the union, thus demonstrating the power of the presidency to act on behalf of the nation against internal rebellion.

The strong Jacksonian presidency, even if used largely for denying power to the federal government, provoked great opposition. The Whig party that emerged to challenge Jackson and the Democrats had sought to limit presidential powers, especially as exercised by a popularly elected figure. Various Whigs sought legislation or amendments to limit the president's veto power, to establish a single term for the presidency, and to eliminate the president's discretion in dismissing executive officials. Above all, the Whigs subscribed to the view that the president was not the leader or initiator, but merely an executor carrying out duties explicitly assigned by the Constitution or the laws. The existence of such "anti-executive" views by a major party throughout the period, even if its proposals were not put into effect, probably served as a check on presidential power. The origins of both of the nineteenth century parties thus reflected a mistrust of the executive.

Abraham Lincoln (1861–1865)

On assuming office, Abraham Lincoln faced precisely the political crisis foreshadowed by the nullification controversy: the formal secession of southern states from the union. Between Lincoln's election in November of 1860 and his inauguration in March of 1861, seven southern states formally seceded from the union and established the Confederate States of America. When Lincoln took office, armed hostilities had not yet begun between the North and South, and he sought in his inaugural address to persuade the southern states that secession was both Constitutionally illegal and politically unwise. In contrast to his predecessor James Buchanan, who stated that "it is beyond the power of any President, no matter what may be his own political proclivities, to restore peace and harmony among the States," Lincoln declared his determination to defend the authority of the federal government.[13] He firmly stated, "I shall take care, as the Constitution itself expressly enjoins upon me, that the laws of the Union be faithfully executed in all the States." One month later Fort Sumter fell to Confederate forces, four more states seceded, and full-scale hostilities began.

Congress during this time was not in session and was not due back until December. Lincoln issued a call for Congress to reconvene for a special session. But before Congress met, he initiated a variety of military measures. He called out

Faced with the nation's gravest crisis, Abraham Lincoln (1809–1865) assumed vast powers in the exercise of the presidency. Lincoln is generally regarded as the greatest of all presidents. (Photo provided by the National Portrait Gallery, Smithsonian Institution. Used with permission.)

75,000 members of the militia, asked for volunteers to increase the size of the regular Army and Navy, instituted a blockade of southern ports, and authorized the selective suspension of the writ of habeas corpus, thereby allowing the arrest and detention of suspicious persons without having to show cause. Constitutional historians have long debated whether Lincoln possessed the authority to undertake these and other actions he took during the Civil War, including the issuance of the famous Emancipation Proclamation, "freeing" all the slaves living in areas still under Confederate control. Some scholars have gone so far as to label Lincoln's actions the equivalent of a military or "Constitutional dictatorship."[14]

Lincoln, who began as a Whig, saw in this emergency situation a clear justification for unusual powers. He defended his vigorous exercise of the "war powers" on several grounds. First, he maintained that some of the powers were logical implications of the explicit language of the Constitution. Second, he argued that it was often necessary for the president to act for the national government as a whole until Congress could examine the matter and prescribe future actions. Third, he referred to both the "take care" clause ("he shall take Care that the Laws be faithfully executed") and the presidential oath ("I do solemnly swear . . . that I . . . will to the best of my Ability, preserve, protect and defend the Constitution of the United States") as evidence that the president bears a special responsibility for the preservation of the nation. Finally, he suggested that violations of specific laws or Constitutional provisions might be justified and legal if necessary to preserve the Constitutional order as whole: "Are all the laws but one to go unexecuted, and the Government itself go to pieces lest than one be violated?"[15] Or, as he put it in a letter to a newspaper editor,

> "Often a limb must be amputated to save a life; but a life is never wisely given to save a limb. I felt that measures, otherwise unconstitutional, might become lawful by becoming indispensable to the preservation of the Constitution, through the preservation of the nation."[16]

Lincoln's argument in defense of certain otherwise illegal actions under extraordinary circumstances is known as the doctrine of executive prerogative. It was spelled out nearly two centuries earlier by the political philosopher John Locke. Because the legislature is not always in session and because law, being general in nature, cannot foresee all situations, "the good of the Society requires that several things should be left to the discretion of him that has the Executive Power." Prerogative consists in the discretion to act "for the public good, without the prescription of law, and sometimes even against it."[17] In such cases the people—or, in the American system, the legislature through its power to impeach—must judge whether the assumption of such powers is justifiable and "for the public good."

President Lincoln, without ever explicitly claiming a prerogative power, contended that the Constitution granted the president extraordinary authority during a national crisis. Even if the existence of such power has remained in a gray area from the point of view of the Supreme Court and strict legal interpretation, the fact stands that President Lincoln did exercise such powers. And despite grumbling in many quarters, the people and Congress made the judgment that his actions were justifiable "for the public good." (It was quite a different story when President Nixon, quoting Lincoln, sought to justify on the same grounds certain illegal activities undertaken by a special unit established by the White House; the public and Congress in this case were entirely unimpressed.)

Lincoln's assumption of extraordinary powers may have established certain precedents for presidential power in time of war or emergency, but it did not add to the powers of the office in "normal" times, and it may even have helped provoke a reaction against the presidency. For some thirty years after the assassination of Lincoln, the presidency dropped to its historical nadir in power and prestige. For most of the rest of the century Congress was the supreme branch of the national government, often reducing the presidency to little more than a mere administrative office.

The Rise of the Modern Presidency

Signs of revival of the presidential office could be glimpsed in the first administration of Grover Cleveland (1885–1889) and in the administration of William McKinley (1897–1901). McKinley came to power after the realigning election of 1896 with solid majorities for the Republicans in both the Senate and the House. Through close cooperation with powerful members of Congress, McKinley, as leader of the governing party, was able to restore some of the effectiveness and influence of the executive office. Ironically, however, it was the assassination of McKinley in 1901 that marked the beginning of the modern presidency, for it brought into the office a man of exceptional vigor and personality, Theodore Roosevelt.

Theodore Roosevelt (1901–1909)

By character and disposition, Teddy Roosevelt was incapable of being a "mere" administrator. He was one who loved—or needed—to take the initiative, whether it was in charging up hills in

A dynamic chief executive, Theodore Roosevelt (1858–1919) articulated the "stewardship" theory of the presidency, according to which a president should act with broad discretion for the public good except where explicitly limited by the Constitution. (Photo provided by the National Portrait Gallery; Smithsonian Institution, Gift of Joanna Sturm. Used with permission.)

Cuba as a Rough Rider in the Spanish-American War or in sending the Navy around the world while president. Roosevelt was able to project an image of dynamism at a time when the U. S was emerging as a regional international power and Americans were looking to the national government for the solutions to domestic problems, and when the press was beginning systematic news coverage of Washington politics. Roosevelt touched the imagination of the public and brought the presidency into the headlines of the daily news. He did so quite consciously, realizing that a strong public image and the capacity to reach the people directly could be powerful resources on behalf of the presidency. It was Teddy Roosevelt, characteristically, who first spoke of using the presidency as a "bully pulpit" to influence public opinion.

The personal factor was one element in Roosevelt's strengthening of the presidency. He also acted, however, with a conscious view of the possibilities of the presidency as an institution. The president, he argued, should assume the role of a prime mover in the political system, not waiting to be told what to do, but initiating action. Rejecting Whig notions of a modest presidency, Roosevelt embraced the concept of a president who was at liberty to act in the public interest, limited only by what the Constitution prevented or the laws forbade:

> My view was that every executive officer . . . was a steward of the people bound actively and affirmatively to do all he could for the people, and not to content himself with the negative merit of keeping his talents undamaged in a napkin. . . . My belief was that it was not only [the president's] right but his duty to do anything that the needs of the nation demanded, unless such action was forbidden by the Constitution or by the laws. . . . I did not usurp power, but I did greatly broaden the use of executive power.[18]

Roosevelt's "stewardship theory" is a succinct theoretical defense of unilateral presidential action. But it was Roosevelt's deeds rather than his words that contributed to the development of the modern presidency.

Woodrow Wilson (1913–1921)

The most elaborate theoretical case for the modern, activist presidency was made by Woodrow Wilson well before he became president. Wilson was not only a political actor but also an accomplished scholar of the American political system. His views about the presidency are important not only because they influenced his subsequent behavior, but also because they set out a theory of how the office should function that greatly influenced later generations of Americans.

Wilson developed his theory on the simple proposition that in the American political system only the president is capable of providing leadership. Because the individual member of Congress is elected by only a small portion of the nation, no single representative or senator can truly claim to speak for the American people as a whole. But this is not true for the president:

> The nation as a whole has chosen him, and is conscious that it has no other political spokesman. His is the only national voice in affairs. Let him once win the admiration and confidence of the country, and no other single

Possessing a prodigious intellect as well as a keen political sense, Woodrow Wilson (1856–1924) furnished the most sophisticated and lasting argument for an activist presidency. (National Portrait Gallery, Smithsonian Institution; Gift of Aileen Conkey. Used with permission.)

force can withstand him, no combination of forces will easily overpower him. His position takes the imagination of the country. He is the representative of no constituency, but of the whole people. When he speaks in his true character, he speaks for no special interest. If he rightly interpret the national thought and boldly insist upon it, he is irresistible; and the country never feels the zest of action so much as when its President is of such insight and calibre. Its instinct is for unified action, and it craves a single leader.[19]

This positive view of the presidency and the presidential office was one Wilson reached late in his career. How he reached it shows both his ambivalence about the Constitution and the ways in which he was attempting to transform it. First, Wilson argued that although a few of the founders (above all Hamilton) saw the need for making the president the central national leader, the theory that finally triumphed at the Convention of 1787 was opposed to a strong presidency. The problem with the Constitution was that the policymaking power in the government remained divided between the president and Congress. The founders preferred to balance power rather than concentrate it. Developing a strong executive, according to Wilson, was an extra-Constitutional—perhaps even an anti-Constitutional—project.

Second, for many years it was unclear to Wilson that a strong executive force could ever develop inside the Constitutional system. For a time he favored scrapping the Constitution and adopting a parliamentary system in order to foster greater energy and concentration of power. Later—and it is from this stage that the above passage is taken—Wilson argued that a strong presidency could be developed inside Constitution, if there was a change in people's attitude toward the presidency. The Constitution did not actually intend presidential leadership, but it had on occasion allowed it. This possibility could become the norm: "The President is at liberty, both in law and conscience, to be as big a man as he can." In the end it is not so much the document written in 1787 that determines the president's power and authority as it is the special relationship that the president develops with the American people. If the people are on the president's side, then Congress will allow the president to set the direction of national politics. In line with this idea, Wilson called for a change in the nature of the party system in which members of the president's party in Congress would (somehow) be obliged to follow the president's lead.

Finally, Wilson insisted not only that the basic policymaking agenda of the nation was a presidential responsibility, but also that presidents should be judged by how successful they have been in achieving the enactment of their program. Wilson thus sought to increase expectations people had for the presidency, which he believed would help strengthen the office. Wilson thus sought to increase people's expectations of the presidency, which he believed would strengthen the office. In effect, creating the expectation that the office could do more would in practice allow it to do more.

During his eight years in office Wilson worked to make his theory of presidential leadership a reality. Breaking a 100-year-old precedent, he became the first president since John Adams to deliver his state of the union message in person before a joint session of Congress. Moreover, he took the lead in promoting important new legislation, using the Democratic party to help secure its passage. Wilson met with Congressional members of the party in policy caucuses, and for a time the party behaved almost like a parliamentary party. At the beginning of American involvement in World War I, Wilson received vast delegations of authority from Congress to mobilize the nation's economy for the war effort and proved himself to be a forceful wartime leader.

It was after the war that Wilson met with his greatest failure. As part of the peace treaty he negotiated, Wilson proposed The League of Nations, an international body that would provide a forum for the peaceful resolution of international disputes. The Senate refused to ratify the treaty without certain amendments and reservations that Wilson judged unacceptable. In conformity with his theory of presidential leadership, Wilson took his case directly to the people to stimulate public pressure on the Senate. In a three-week period, he delivered thirty-seven speeches in twenty-nine cities. The ardors of this tour led to a physical collapse that incapacitated him for the balance of his term. Wilson had written that the president "has no means of compelling Congress except through public opinion."[20] His failure to turn the country around on the League of Nations demonstrated the practical limits to popular leadership.

Franklin D. Roosevelt (1933–1945)

Theodore Roosevelt and Woodrow Wilson had laid the foundations for the modern presidency; but the three presidents who followed Wilson—Warren G. Harding, Calvin Coolidge, and Herbert Hoover—declined to make it the focal point of leadership in quite the way that Roosevelt and Wilson had envisaged. Just as there had been a reaction to the concentration of "emergency" power in the presidency after the Lincoln administration, so too was there a swing away from the presidency following Wilson's wartime administration.

It was Theodore Roosevelt's fifth cousin, Franklin D. Roosevelt, who finally established

Franklin Delano Roosevelt (1882–1945) realized the vision of his predecessors Theodore Roosevelt and Woodrow Wilson as the model of the activist president. Roosevelt was first elected president in 1932 and was the only president to serve more than two terms, winning four presidential contests. (Photo provided by the National Portrait Gallery; Smithsonian Institution; Transfer from the National Museum of American Art; gift of Willard Hubbell, 1964. Used with permission.)

the modern presidency as a permanent feature of American politics. He did so less by theorizing about it than by acting—creating a permanent change in public expectations. Elected to the office four times, by large majorities, Roosevelt maintained the confidence and support of the people, guiding the nation through two of its greatest crises: the depression and the Second World War. During Roosevelt's tenure, several major changes were also made in the institutional arrangements of the office, with the creation of the White House staff and the expansion of some of the support agencies in the executive office (these are discussed later). When Roosevelt died in office in 1945, he left a presidency very different from the one he entered in his first inauguration in 1933. After Roosevelt, people expected "leadership" from the office, and changes began to be made so that the office would be institutionally equipped to supply it.

Like Theodore Roosevelt and Woodrow Wilson, Franklin Roosevelt brought into office an activist view of presidential responsibilities, especially in the crisis situation of the depression. "I assume unhesitatingly," he announced in his inaugural address of March 4, 1933, "the leadership of this great army of the people, dedicated to a disciplined attack upon our common problems." He expressed the hope that the "normal balance of executive and legislative authority" could be preserved, but went on to note that an "unprecedented demand and need for undelayed action may call for temporary departure from that normal balance." It was the presidency that the people looked to for leadership, and it was only the presidency that could provide it: "In their need [the people] have registered a mandate that they want direct, vigorous action. They have asked for discipline and direction under leadership. They have made me the present instrument of their wishes. In the spirit of the gift I take it."[21]

Roosevelt wasted no time in making good on his promise. He called a special session of Congress, which in the famous "hundred days" deferred to Roosevelt's leadership on virtually every important point. It passed laws delegating to the president broad discretionary authority over commercial transactions and creating the Civilian Conservation Corps, the Agricultural Adjustment Administration, the Employment Service, and the National Recovery Administration. Some of these laws were passed within a few short days after their introduction. Others took only a few weeks or months to move from presidential recommendation to law of the land. Through these and other enactments the national government assumed direct responsibility for alleviating the human suffering caused by the depression and for fostering economic recovery. At no other time in our history has Congress passed so much novel legislation so quickly. (Many key elements of the program were, however, soon declared unconstitutional by the Supreme Court.)

With war approaching in Europe during his second term, Roosevelt's attention shifted to international relations. Isolationist sentiment was so strong during the 1930s that Congress passed several laws prohibiting the sale of arms to belligerent nations. Roosevelt attempted to persuade the public, initially with only some success, that the security of the United States was bound up with that of France and Great Britain. After war broke out in Europe in 1939, Roosevelt continued with his efforts to help the Allies, though Congress rebuffed some of his proposals for direct assistance. In September of 1940, Roosevelt acted without legislative authorization to transfer to Great Britain, which was by then standing alone against the Axis powers, fifty old American destroyers in exchange for long-term leases of British naval bases in the Atlantic. The action seemed to violate both statute and Constitutional law, demonstrating again the willingness of "strong" presidents in extraordinary circumstances to "act for the . . . public good, without the prescription of law, and sometimes even against it." After the United States entered the war in 1941, Roosevelt exercised tremendous powers; but in nearly all instances he did so with powers delegated to him by Congress.

Truman to Clinton: The Activist Presidency Accepted

Throughout American history, activist presidents have usually provoked congressional efforts to reassert their authority. Congress has often been supported in these efforts by a public uncomfortable with prolonged presidential dominance. Many historians have likened this movement to that of a pendulum: the center of gravity within the governmental system swings from periods of presidential preeminence to those of weak presidents and a dominant Congress.

After Roosevelt's death in 1945, the same historical pattern reemerged. Congress acted in several ways to reduce the power of the presidency. It created two new advisory groups in the executive branch, the Council of Economic Advisers (1946) and the National Security Council (1947), with the hope that these groups would reduce presidential discretion in national security and economic affairs by formalizing the decision-making process, thereby creating elements of a plural executive the founders had rejected. No law, however, can force the president to take advice, and in practice presidents have either ignored these councils or used them as they have wished as resources for the presidency. In the 1950s, Congress also made several unsuccessful attempts to initiate Constitutional amendments restricting the president's power to enter into executive agreements with foreign nations. Finally, in a direct attack on the Roosevelt legacy, Congress initiated action on the Twenty-second Amendment, which limited the president to two terms.

In retrospect, however, Congress's reaction to Roosevelt's presidency appears relatively mild by historical standards, and did not even come close to matching the blatant encroachments of the post-Civil War Congress on the president's Constitutional powers. Moreover, the broader public demonstrated little desire to shackle the presidency. On the contrary, Roosevelt's twelve years as the "vital center of action" created enduring public expectation for the presidency and fostered the belief that presidential leadership was necessary. In many respects, Roosevelt fulfilled Wilson's model.

Under Roosevelt's immediate successors, Harry Truman and Dwight Eisenhower, the presidency retained its central importance. Eisenhower's presidency was especially important, since under Franklin Roosevelt the expanding power of the presidency had become a partisan issue. Liberal Democrats tended to defend a powerful presidency for its contribution to a welfare state, while conservative Republicans saw it as the engine of a growing governmental machine that threatened personal liberty. Eisenhower exercised a strong presidency, though for different ends than Roosevelt, thereby solidifying the power of the office across partisan lines. If there was any doubt whether Republicans supported a strong executive, it was ended by Richard Nixon. Following the two self-proclaimed activist presidencies of the Democrats John Kennedy and Lyndon Johnson, President Nixon left no doubt that he as a Republican embraced a modern view of the presidency: "The days of a passive Presidency belong to a simpler past. . . . The next President must take an activist view of his office. He must articulate the nation's values, define its goals, and marshal its will."[22]

In the aftermath of the Vietnam War and the unfolding of the Watergate crisis, the pendulum again swung against the presidency. Congress began to attack what was called the "imperial presidency"—an office that had swallowed up nearly all of the warmaking power and many domestic powers as well. Congress passed fundamental structural legislation in the 1970s that sought to define and delimit the president's role in the conduct of war and in the impoundment of public monies. In addition, Congress became far more assertive in the formulation of the budget and in foreign policymaking. For a moment, some in Congress even spoke of a return to "congressional government" in which the seat of national agenda setting and leadership would be the Congress. The partisan dimension to the conflict also began to change. With the Republican party in the White House at the close of the Vietnam War and during the Watergate crisis (as well as most of the time since), liberal Democrats now led the attack on the presidency while Republicans came to its defense.

The changes made in the 1970s were far more significant in curbing the president's power than the measures enacted after World War II. The principal institutional debate about the presidency today is a legacy of this reaction. On one side are those who argue that the presidency remains an imperial institution which needs to be further checked and restricted. On the other side are those who argue that many of the restrictions on the president adopted after Watergate went too far and now prevent the presidency from effectively performing its necessary role. In this view, what we have is a "fettered presidency."

The reaction against a strong presidency in the 1970s, however, did not remove the presidency from its position of political leadership. Congress has proven simply too fragmented to assume this role, and Americans have learned to look to the presidency to provide—or at any rate propose—an overall direction. By the time of President Reagan's inauguration in 1981, the presidency again was at the "vital center of action." Some likened Reagan's activism in his first year in charting a new direction of government policy to that of President Roosevelt in 1933, a comparison that shows that the presidency remains the center of action, whether in the hands of an avowed liberal (Franklin Roosevelt) or avowed conservative (Ronald Reagan).

Explaining the Rise of the Modern Presidency

The reactions to the modern presidency in the 1970s demonstrate that the pendulum continues to swing back and forth between our two national political institutions. But while the oscillations continue, the point from which the most recent swing of the pendulum began is far closer to the presidency than it was in the nineteenth century. What explains this historical dynamic? Why is presidential leadership now the rule rather than the exception? Along with the changing doctrines about the presidency, three historical developments have been particularly significant in accounting for the growth of presidential power: the increasing importance of international relations to the nation's well-being, the growth of the social welfare state, and the development of mass communications technologies.

The Importance of International Relations   For most of the nineteenth century, American foreign policy embraced the principles of neutrality. Americans looked upon the 3,000 miles that separated the new world from the old as a natural buffer against attacks or interference from powerful foreign nations. Events in the twentieth century, especially the Second World War, completely changed America's relationship to the rest of the world and left the United States as a major world power actively involved in world affairs.

As foreign policy has become more important to the overall task of governing the nation, the presidency has inevitably become more influential. The executive branch is the driving force in foreign affairs arguably by Constitutional design and now by tradition and the nature of the duties performed. Although the president's power in foreign affairs has also ebbed and flowed, the presidency began with—and has always maintained—a much greater share of power in foreign than domestic affairs.

The Growth of the Social Welfare State   A distinguishing feature of national policy in the twentieth century is the federal government's assumption of responsibility for guaranteeing a minimum level of social welfare, as in laws that set a minimum wage, that provide various kinds of assistance to the unemployed, the poor, the disabled, and the elderly, and that regulate safety in the workplace. Although laws of this sort are a sign of the expanded reach of congressionally-passed legislation, they also have added to presidential power in two ways.

First, they enhance the importance of presidential policy formulation. The growing reach of national policy has led to much greater complexity and has immensely increased the planning burden of the government. Because of its hierarchical structure, ready access to a mass of information, and a broader view of the well-being of the whole nation, the executive branch has become the chief policy planner in the national government. In a number of cases, Congress has positively encouraged the president—sometimes through legislative mandate—to set the agenda for congressional deliberations, as in assigning to the president the responsibility of preparing and sending to Congress each year a comprehensive national budget proposal or of regularly formulating proposals designed to foster a healthy economy. These delegations of the (initial) planning function to the president reflected Congress' recognition that on many matters the presidency is better-suited for analyzing complex issues and fashioning appropriate responses. Since the 1970s, however, Congress has added to its own ability to assess information, and congressional mandates for planning have become a burden that Congress imposes on the executive.

The other way in which the growth of the welfare state has increased presidential power relates to the execution of laws after they are passed. The complexity of many programs often leads Congress to vest in the executive branch substantial flexibility and discretion in determining how to carry out the laws. Congress delegates discretionary decisions to the administration because it cannot foresee all the subtle issues that will arise in carrying out a program and because it may wish to avoid the political difficulties that come from making final decisions on some controversial issues. Broad discretion allows a departmental secretary or agency head to issue rules or regulations specifying grant levels, contract requirements, and eligibility criteria. These executive branch decisions have the full force of law, and they constitute the policy of the federal government as much as the original congressional statutes. Thus, as the power of the executive branch has grown so too in some degree has the president's.

Yet here again some important qualifications are in order. Despite what organizational charts may suggest, not all power shifted from Congress to the bureaucracy is automatically given to the president. The reality of American politics is that many matters within the executive branch are not fully (or easily) controlled of the president, who only has the time and energy to focus on certain matters. Not only do large bureaucratic agencies develop a will of their own, but also Congress writes certain laws to seal off agencies from presidential direction and to make these agencies pliable to informal pressure from congressional committees.

The Development of Mass Communication The growth in the importance of foreign affairs and the rise of the welfare state have increased the president's power, but it is the development of radio, television, and internet communications that has brought the presidency to the center of the nation's attention. Franklin Roosevelt first made extensive use of the radio in his famous "fireside chats" to communicate directly with the American people. Television has given subsequent presidents even greater opportunities to reach the people, either through formal addresses on subjects of immediate national concern or through live, televised press conferences, begun by President Kennedy. In addition, network news programs cover the day-to-day activities of presidents, from his score in a round of golf to his occasional informal responses to journalists' questions. The modern presidency is above all a visible presidency.

Radio, television and the Internet give the presidency a public relations advantage over the Congress. Because Congress is a large institution with a highly decentralized power structure, it is difficult for the broadcast media to cover its actions and more difficult still for Congress to communicate with the American people. The president inevitably will speak in a clearer voice. Yet Congress has not been closed out of the media battleground altogether. The emergence

of C-SPAN's coverage of Congress played a pivotal role in making Newt Gingrich the Speaker of the House in 1994. Moreover, televised congressional hearings have allowed Congress to engage or compete with the president.

Even though television provides the president with an extraordinary new instrument of communication, it has not always helped the president. Most of what Americans daily see and learn of the president comes not from his speeches or press conferences, but from news reports. Thus the president appears to the public not exactly in the way he wants to be portrayed, but in the way journalists wish to portray him. Journalists will observe the president through their own lens, stressing what they find to be newsworthy. They will scrutinize the president's every move, often emphasizing information that presidents would rather see ignored, such as the presence of conflicts within the administration, or interpreting presidential actions in ways that presidents often disapprove of.

The relationship between presidents and the press tends therefore to be characterized by frequent tension on both sides, mitigated usually by the common understanding that each in some sense needs the other. Presidents have varied greatly in their ability to get along with the press. Their caution was evident from early on. Jefferson, who celebrated the press in his theoretical writings before becoming president, complained while president that "newspapers present only the caricature of disaffected minds." In modern times, journalists were very friendly to President Kennedy, to the point where many later conceded that they had been taken in by the grace and charm of "Camelot." But the press changed and grew far more mistrustful of the presidency with the Vietnam War. Journalists were often openly adversarial in their relationship to President Nixon, who in turn did little to hide his contempt for the press. Nixon's press conferences on occasion degenerated into thinly veiled verbal wars. Presidents Reagan and Bush had slightly better relations with the press, and President Clinton was both praised and assailed, making any easy generalization impossible. It is no longer a simple matter to manipulate the press, as it has become too powerful and independent a force to be co-opted by the presidency.

The Powers and Power of the Presidency

The president's formal powers derive from the Constitution and from statutory law. In the case of the Constitution, the president's powers depend not only on the plain meaning of the words of the Constitution but also on precedents of former presidents and on how the Constitution has been interpreted by the Supreme Court. In the case of statutory law, Congress grants discretion to the president to make certain decisions, such as the power to impose wage and price controls. Where the power in these statutes does not overlap with or clarify a Constitutional power, it may be revoked by law or, if granted temporarily, simply allowed to expire.

The president's Constitutional powers, contained mostly in Article II, read initially like an odd mixture of three different types: powers that are (seemingly) minor (such as requiring the opinion of executive officers, receiving ambassadors, and providing Congress information on the state of the union); powers or responsibilities that are highly important (such as the veto, nomination and appointments, the pardon, negotiating treaties, and the role as commander-in-chief); and grants of power or responsibilities that are general (the "executive power clause" and the "take care" clause). Let us look at each of these.

The Lesser Powers

The (seemingly) insignificant powers turn out, on further reflection, to be far more important than they appear. The Constitution in these instances sometimes seems to be sketching in law an idea of the *position* of the president in the political system. The powers to make recommendations to Congress and to give information on the state of the union, for example, suggest a president who has every right (and even a duty) to be an active participant and initiator in the legislative process. The power to require opinions of executive officers leaves no doubt that the president is the head of the executive branch, free of any possible constraints from a council or Cabinet. Finally, the power to receive ambassadors, while not without significance in its own

right, has established the president as the "head of state" in international affairs and, together with the treaty power and the "executive power" clause, makes the president the chief diplomat of the United States. With the backing today of federal law, the president is the only one able to carry out or authorize diplomatic negotiations.

The Major Specific Grants of Power

Two of the president's most significant specific grants of power are in the areas of national security and foreign affairs: the role of commander in chief and the power to negotiate treaties. The power of commander in chief, in combination with the executive power, also gives the president his most controversial implied power, which is to commence hostilities and thus virtually to commit the nation to war.

Another major power is partly legislative: the veto. Although many initially considered the veto to be a tool restricted to the president's view of what the Constitution required or what was needed to protect his own office, the veto since Andrew Jackson has been used more freely as a policy instrument. It gives the president a formidable weapon to stop a legislative initiative, unless the veto is overridden by two-thirds of the members of both houses, which occurs only infrequently (less than 4 percent of the time). The veto is an even more formidable weapon than it may appear from the instances in which it is actually used. Anticipation that it might be employed often forces Congress to abandon a legislative proposal or to modify it to suit the president's wishes.

Some presidents clearly have not been shy about using the veto. In his first term (1885–1889) Grover Cleveland vetoed 414 bills, the record for any single term. (This figure includes "pocket vetoes," which refers to instances in which the president does not sign a bill after Congress has gone out of session, thus letting the bill simply expire.) Only two were overridden. Franklin Roosevelt collected 635 vetoes during his tenure to lead the list of most vetoes by any one president.

The veto has been an especially important weapon in recent times, when control in the national government has been divided. Presidents Ford, Reagan, and George H. Bush relied on the veto to thwart opposing majorities and to influence national policy. President Clinton did not use the veto during his first two years in office (1993–94) when there were Democratic majorities in both houses, but after the Republicans captured the Congress in 1994 he began to use it with great effect, blocking Republican policies and forcing changes in their program.

The appointment power gives the president the authority to name, subject to the approval of the Senate, all Supreme Court justices, ambassadors, federal judges, Cabinet members, and, by law, non-civil service officials. In the last group now are some 2,700 persons who serve in sub-Cabinet-level positions and on various agencies and boards. These people, along with the Cabinet members, help supervise the nearly 3 million federal civil servants. Presidents use their power to appoint executive branch officials not only to help manage the government by placing their own people at high levels in the bureaucracy, but also to fulfill the demands of patronage and to reward those who have given faithful party service.

Curiously, the Constitution does not say whether presidents may remove those whom they have appointed to positions in the executive branch. (Congress, of course, may impeach any executive official.) By extension of the appointment power presidents very early on asserted the power to dismiss officials, although there were always questions about whether Congress by statute could share or restrict this power. The Constitutional basis of the president's power to dismiss appointees was finally recognized by the Supreme Court in 1927 in the case of *Meyers v. United States*. This power may be limited, however, in the instance of appointments to independent regulatory commissions.[23]

The power to pardon comes closest to being a prerogative-type power explicitly endorsed in the Constitution. It gives the president the authority to set aside, at discretion, the normal process of the criminal law. Mercy may be one reason for granting pardons, but The Federalist makes clear that its primary justification is to enable presidents to promote national security or the general welfare. The most famous recent use of this power occurred in 1974, when Presi-

President George H. Bush used his powers as Commander-in-Chief to commit half a million troops to the Persian Gulf before the war with Iraq. (Courtesy of the University Journal, University of Virginia. Used with permission.)

dent Ford pardoned former President Nixon from any possible prosecution relating to his conduct while president. Ford justified this highly controversial decision on the grounds that it was needed to end the trauma of the Watergate affair and to allow the nation to get back to the business of governing. A long criminal trial of a former president, Ford believed, "would be disastrous for the nation. America needed recovery, not revenge."[24]

The General Grants of Power

The Constitution vests the "executive power" in the president and gives the president the power (or imposes on him the obligation) to "take care that the Laws be faithfully executed." In addition, the president must take an oath, included in the text of the Constitution, to "preserve, protect and defend the Constitution of the United States." Read in broad terms, as presidents like Lincoln and Franklin Roosevelt chose to read them, these general grants or responsibilities give the president truly formidable power. The "executive power" clause may give the president the powers to carry out any inherently executive task, including conducting the nation's foreign policy in specific situations and assuming a broad emergency power not otherwise provided by law. The "take care" clause enables the president to employ the means necessary, including the use of armed force, to ensure compliance, as presidents have done on numerous occasions.

These general grants of power, often in combination with more specific ones, form the foundation of certain of the president's implied powers. One of these, just noted, is the power to dismiss, which flows in part from the president's obligation to "take care" that laws be faithfully executed. (If the president cannot fire an official, the reasoning goes, how can he ensure the faithful execution of law?) Another implied power is known as "executive privilege," meaning the right to refuse to divulge information about the executive requested by other branches. (If the president cannot be certain of a degree of confidentiality in internal deliberations within the executive branch, how can he carry out his essential executive duties?) This last power, while recognized by the Supreme Court, is not unlimited, as the Court required President Nixon in 1974 to divulge information to a lower court to scrutinize for possible use in a criminal trial *(United States v. Nixon)*.

Certain presidents, including Lincoln and Roosevelt, have either claimed the power they felt they needed to meet a particular situation or else threatened Congress that they were prepared to claim such power if Congress did not delegate it to them by statute. Although the Court on several occasions has given very broad interpretations of the president's power, it has never gone so far as to recognize any inherent power of prerogative. By contrast, the Court has on occasion issued presidents certain legal rebukes. For example, with respect to actions taken by President Lincoln, the Court ruled against the president well after he had taken action and achieved his purpose *(Ex Parte Milligan,* 1866). In another important case, *Youngstown Sheet and Tube v. Sawyer* (1951), the Court directly rebuffed President Truman's attempt to seize and operate the nation's steel mills to avert a strike during the Korean War. Truman had cited as the basis of his power the "authority vested in me by the Constitution and laws of the United States." Truman backed down.

While all these legal precedents are important, in the final analysis the limits of presidential authority in unusual situations or emergencies may be determined less by legal reasoning than by the character of the circumstances the nation faces. The president's broad assertion of prerogative power is not exactly a legal one, but one that points to the very limits of law. Jefferson, himself often suspicious of executive power, perhaps expressed this point best: "An officer is bound to obey orders; yet he would be a bad one who should do it in cases for which they were not intended, and which involved the most important consequences."[25]

The Power of the President

The specific powers of the presidency, while significant, do not seem to add up to the formidable role of the president in our political system. The power of the president, it seems, is more than the sum of the office's specific powers. This fact has led some to assert that the president's authority is in large measure extra-Constitutional. But this conclusion is not warranted. The president's power derives in large part from his *position* in the political system; this position—as a single individual able to command all the separate powers and as an individual who enjoys a separate and independent electoral base—in turn derives substantially from the Constitution. Many of the capacities of the presidency are thus rooted in or owe much to the Constitution, even where a specific power to cover a particular function cannot be named.

For many of their actions, presidents do not rely on automatic powers of command. Instead they use their unique position in the American system (backed of course by their formal powers) in an effort to induce others to go along with them.[26] They must induce or persuade rather than command because they need the assistance of others who are partly independent of them and who are capable of thwarting them. Because a president's success often rests in some part on inducing others, his effective power is not constant; it changes from year to year and even from month to month. The capacity of presidents to persuade varies with many political or nonlegal factors, such as their standing with the public or with Congress. As perceptions of presidents' future political strength vary, so does their effective power to accomplish what they want. At one moment a president may seem invincible; at the next, quite vulnerable.

While the president's power is greater than the sum of his formal powers, it falls short of what is needed to meet the expectations many now have for the office. The gap between expectation and power is a central fact about the modern presidency. It is the result of the Wilsonian legacy that raised hopes for the office well beyond its capacities. Today, presidents are often blamed (or credited) for more than they can control. Certain commentators who view the president from the inside find the president's powers inadequate because the president lacks the authority to do all that is expected of him. Viewed from the outside, however, the issue is not what is best for presidents but what is best for the Constitutional system as a whole.

The Institution of the Presidency

The modern presidency is more than just the president. It includes thousands of individuals who serve under the presidents and act in their name. These individuals in the executive branch can be placed into four categories according to their proximity to the president and to their function: the White House staff, the Executive Office of the President, the Cabinet, and the departments and agencies of the government.

The White House Staff

The White House staff grew substantially in number from the mid-1950s to the mid-1970s, before leveling off and then, during the Reagan years, declining. The growth and changing role of the staff have raised some serious questions about the operation of the presidency: Are presidents truly capable of overseeing and controlling the actions of those who act on their behalf? Is too much political power being wielded by presidential appointees who are unaccountable to Congress and the American people? Are the authority and morale of the departments and agencies of the executive branch being undermined by the centralization of decision making

in the White House? Does the presidential staff apparatus do a good job of communicating different ideas to the presidents, or does it insulate them from discordant views? Let us turn to some of these issues.

At the beginning of this century only a handful of people served as personal aides to the president. The executive branch consisted mainly of the president, the Cabinet members and the employees who served under the Cabinet officers in the agencies of the government. During Franklin Roosevelt's administration, it became clear—in the words of the Brownlow Committee, which studied the organization of the presidency—that the "President needs help." The Brownlow study led to the formation of the modern White House staff, which numbers today (depending on whom one counts) over 500 people. As originally conceived, the major staff members would provide the president with advice from a presidential perspective—that is, advice not bound by the particular interests of the departments—and help to see that the president's decisions were carried out. The staff would serve as the president's "eyes and ears," being directly responsible to the president and appointed without the need of Senate confirmation. Above all—in words that seem almost curious today—the aides "would have no power to make decisions or issue instructions in their own name. They would not be interposed between the president and the heads of the departments. . . . They would remain in the background, issue no orders, make no decisions, emit no public statements."[27]

Today, a few high-level advisers, known usually as the "senior staff," meet with the president regularly to help in planning strategy and making decisions. In his first year, President George W. Bush, for example, has worked closely with Karl Rove, Karen Hughes, and Condoleezza Rice. The personal staff are generally longtime associates of the president, often aides during the presidential campaign, in whose loyalty he has total confidence. This trust of the president, along with their direct access to the Oval Office, makes these officials among the most powerful figures in government.

Below this small group are another 150 or so professional aides, usually anonymous to the public, who assist the top advisers and otherwise serve the president, handling such tasks as liaison to the press, drafting speeches, and maintaining contacts with Congress and other outside groups. With the growth in the importance of news coverage by the national media, the job of Press Secretary is among the most important in the administration. The rest of the White House staff are clerical and lower-level administrators who perform such additional functions as answering the enormous volume of mail that the White House receives.

A major criticism of the White House staff in recent administrations is that it has grown too powerful and makes decisions that should properly be made by the regular departments and agencies. Not only does this concentration of power in the White House undermine morale in the departments, but it also blurs political accountability, since members of the president's personal staff, unlike department heads, are not answerable to Congress and usually do not testify.[28] These criticisms were especially pronounced during the Johnson and the Nixon administrations, when many charged that the president was trying to run the government from the White House, ignoring or avoiding the permanent executive establishment. During President Nixon's first term, for example, the President's chief aide in formulating and implementing policy was his National Security Adviser, Henry Kissinger, not the Secretary of State, William Rogers.

Another criticism of the White House staff is that it creates a "palace guard" around presidents that limits access and denies them the benefit of diverse opinions. Although the inability of certain leaders to solicit diverse opinions or recognize flatterers is not a new problem, the staff system arguably makes matters worse. Because high-level staff members usually share the president's basic policy views and have no independent base of political power, they may behave toward the president as "courtiers" and build a powerful barrier to "presidential access to reality," creating what some have called a bunker mentality.[29]

More than a half century after its inception, the White House staff has become a permanent institutional appendage of the modern presi-

dency. The staff clearly helps the president, but it has also produced certain harmful consequences. Paradoxically, a staff that came into being to help coordinate the bureaucracy has sometimes itself become bureaucratic and unmanageable; and it has created tensions of its own by interfering with Cabinet officials. Moreover, while the White House staff may provide the president with personal advice that may unify the administration, it can provide an additional source of competing tensions. Like so many institutions, the White House staff has become a mixed blessing; it may be absolutely necessary, but it is not always helpful.

The Executive Office of the President

President Roosevelt formally created the Executive Office of the President (EOP) in 1939 under authority that Congress granted him. Not including the White House staff, it now consists of approximately 1,700 people divided among several offices or councils, the two most important of which are discussed below.

Office of Management and Budget The Office of Management and Budget (OMB) began as the Bureau of the Budget in 1921. Congress created the agency to assist presidents in carrying out their new responsibility to formulate and present Congress a coherent national budget proposal each year. Originally located in the Department of the Treasury, it was moved to the new Executive Office of the President in 1939 and in 1970 was renamed by President Nixon to reflect its broadened responsibilities for the general management of the executive branch. With over 500 employees it is now the largest single agency in the Executive Office.

OMB has both a political or policymaking function and an administrative function. Its policymaking function follows on the emergence of the budget as the major domestic political issue. With the growth of the budget deficits, budget politics have moved to center stage, and the budget has become a major point of decision making for almost all activities of government.

OMB also has a major management role. In preparing the administration's budget proposal, OMB serves as the voice of the president in deal-

BOX 11.4

The White House Staff

Henry Kissinger, national security adviser to President Richard Nixon from 1969 to 1973, describes the mentality of the Nixon White House staff:

I had a better sense than almost anyone of the environment out of which—nearly imperceptibly—had grown the cancer of Watergate. The White House is both a goldfish bowl and an isolation ward; the fish swim in a vessel whose walls are opaque one way. They can be observed if not necessarily understood; they themselves see nothing. Cut off from the outside world, the inhabitants of the White House live by the rules of their internal coexistence or by imagining what the outside world is like. This in the Nixon White House became increasingly at variance with reality until suddenly the incommensurability between the two worlds grew intolerable; the bowl burst and its inhabitants found themselves gasping in a hostile atmosphere.

SOURCE: Henry Kissinger, *Years of Upheaval* (Boston: Little, Brown, 1982),

ing with the departments and agencies of the executive branch. It attempts to translate the priorities of the president into the hundreds of detailed requests that constitute the national budget. Its power derives from its ability to say no to the departments, to refuse to approve new spending plans when they are inconsistent with broader budget realities. This power extends not only to the preparation of the budget but also to the submission of legislative proposals to Congress. Through the process of central legislative clearance, the OMB examines legislative proposals requested by an executive department or agency before they are submitted to Congress. Only if a proposal receives endorsement from the OMB may it be officially sent up to Capitol Hill (although some bureaucrats may risk going around the OMB through informal contacts with members of Congress).

National Security Council The National Security Council (NSC) was created by Congress in the aftermath of the Second World War (1947). Its membership, defined partly by statute, includes some of the highest-level executive branch officials with responsibility for defense and national security issues, among whom are the president, the secretaries of state and defense, the director of the CIA, and the chairman of the Joint Chiefs of Staff. The NSC's functions include giving presidents advice on national security matters and enhancing coordination among the many actors who play a role in this area. The Council has attached to it the National Security Advisor and their staff who serve the president.

The Council's origins, as noted above, reflected an attempt by some in Congress, dubious of President Truman's abilities, to reduce the president's discretion by establishing a formalized institutional structure. In fact, the NSC has had no such effect. President Truman, who opposed the NSC's creation, virtually ignored it and conducted foreign and security policy working directly with Cabinet secretaries in arrangements he devised. The Constitution's clear implication that the president is the head of the executive branch, able to dismiss as well as "to require the opinion, in writing, of the principal Officer in each of the executive Departments," made it impossible for Congress to saddle the president with a decision-making system he disapproved of.

President Eisenhower met with the Council regularly to seek advice, yet never let it constrain him, often using the NSC to legitimize his own decisions. Eisenhower's use of the Council showed that it could be helpful insofar as it served as an advisory and coordinating body subject entirely to the control of the president. Since the Kennedy administration, presidents have relied only intermittently on the NSC. Certain presidents, like Kennedy and Johnson, preferred to establish senior advisory groups of their own choosing, while others have made extensive use of the NSC, especially in crisis situations.

In another display of how the National Security Council law has aided more than constrained the president, most presidents have used the National Security Advisor as a close personal counselor on foreign and security affairs. Presidents have turned to the National Security Advisor and staff as a source of information independent of the agencies and departments in order to develop a uniquely presidential perspective on these matters.

Far more problematic and controversial has been the reliance on the security advisor and staff to formulate and implement foreign policy. This practice was most fully exhibited under President Nixon, with NSC advisor Henry Kissinger operating what was often referred to as the "little state department" inside the White House. In a lesser degree, but still significantly, President Carter also relied heavily on NSC advisor Zbigniew Brzezinski. President Reagan sought to lower the profile of the NSC and to return the general operation of diplomacy and security to the departments and agencies. Reagan largely succeeded in this aim, but with one exception that was so glaring and significant that it produced the most important crisis of his presidency: the Iran-Contra Affair.

In this matter, President Reagan uncharacteristically went around his major departmental secretaries and gave his National Security advisor operating responsibility for a plan to sell arms to Iran as a way of securing the release of American hostages in Lebanon. The NSC advisor and staff handled the whole operation, no doubt in an effort to maintain secrecy (which they did in part by misleading or lying to members of Congress and destroying certain documents). Moreover, a (then) obscure national security staff member, Oliver North, who was involved in managing the Iran arms sale, came up with what he later called the "neat idea" of transferring part of the proceeds from the arms sale to the Contras in Nicaragua. This transfer was unknown (apparently) to the President, the Secretaries of State and Defense, and certainly

to anyone in Congress, which at the time had voted a ban on further aid to the Contras.

The scandal exploded with the revelation of this activity, and congressional hearings revealed a runaway operation under no one's clear—or, at any rate, admitted—control. The Tower Commission that studied the affair not only found fault with the whole lax system of administration that prevailed in implementing this policy, but made a special point of calling on the National Security advisor and especially members of the NSC staff to stop performing any operational role. In light of this experience, it will no doubt be some time before the NSC staff ever ventures again into carrying out governmental missions.

The Cabinet

The history of the president's Cabinet is largely one of neglect. The Constitution does not provide specifically for a Cabinet, and while the term was probably used as early as 1793, it was never mentioned in an official statute until 1907.[30] As a formal institution, the Cabinet includes the head of each of the executive departments and a few other officers of the government who may be given Cabinet rank by the president. Since the Cabinet as an organization has no Constitutional status—the founders expressly rejected an executive council—its role within the executive branch depends on the president. Some recent presidents have begun their terms by expressing high hopes for regenerating its influence in executive branch decision making; but they have generally concluded that Cabinet meetings are not very useful forums for conducting the business of government. Among presidents in the past half century, only Eisenhower made much use of the Cabinet.

The reasons for the limited use are fairly obvious. First, the departments deal with such a variety of issues and policies that it is a waste of time for experts in one field (say transportation) to sit through a long discussion on a completely unrelated subject (foreign policy, for example). As President Kennedy once remarked, "Cabinet meetings are simply useless: why should the Postmaster [formerly a member of the Cabinet] sit there and listen to the problem of Laos?" Second, because each department secretary is highly jealous of his or her jurisdiction, an implicit understanding is usually reached between them to refrain from trying to influence administrative policy in each other's areas. As a result, useful proposals or ideas often remain unexpressed. Finally, presidents have discovered that the advice they receive in Cabinet meetings is very much colored by each secretary's desire to promote the programs and interests served by his or her department. Cabinet members often "go native," making them, in the cynical words of one presidential adviser, "the natural enemies of the President."[31]

It might be wondered, then, why presidents call full Cabinet meetings at all. The answer probably has something to do with maintaining a general team spirit within the administration and even more with effective public relations. Americans like to think of the Cabinet as a group of experienced and dedicated public servants whose collective wisdom will be an invaluable asset to the presidency. Regular Cabinet meetings foster the notion that the president is running a truly "open" administration, seeking the best possible advice from a variety of sources before acting.

The Executive Branch

Beyond the White House staff and the Executive Office of the President lies the executive branch, which consists of fourteen departments and some sixty other agencies. It is tied to the president by the Cabinet heads and the limited number of upper-echelon department and agency officials whom the president appoints.

A difficult distinction for those outside Washington to appreciate is between the president (along with his staff) and the executive branch. In public administration textbooks, the president is the "head" of the executive branch. But in the day-to-day politics of Washington, this title is often more nominal than real. Executive agencies, though "beneath" the president, must also consider the wishes of Congress, which writes the laws that create the bureaus and appropriates the budget; moreover, government workers deep in the agencies are civil servants with permanent tenure, not the personal appointees of the president. Presidents, in fact, appoint well

under one percent of the civilian members of the executive branch.

When presidents choose to, they can usually exert their authority in the executive branch. But in many cases the obstacles to their succeeding are so great that they may not be worth the effort. Most recent presidents have expressed a frustration similar to that voiced by Harry Truman: "I thought I was the President, but when it comes to the bureaucracies, I can't make them do a damn thing."[32] Moreover, the resources of time, energy, and political will are limited. A president cannot personally manage the thousands of decisions of government, and it is not his job to do so. Until or unless a matter becomes one of importance as the president sees it, he will leave it to the departments. Similarly, within the departments, a secretary cannot manage each and every question in his or her domain. Many decisions, inevitably, are taken at lower levels in the agency.

The Vice President

Besides the president, the vice president is the only other nationally elected official. Until recently, this fact has been about all vice presidents could boast of. Woodrow Wilson's vice president, Thomas Riley Marshall, remarked that his "only business as vice president was to ring the White House bell every morning and ask what is the state of the health of the president." Nelson Rockefeller, Gerald Ford's vice president, was more active: "I go to funerals; I go to earthquakes." The list of former vice presidents includes many names that only a Jeopardy! champion might recognize: Richard Johnson, William King, Thomas Hendricks, and Charles Curtis. Generally, only vice presidents who have succeeded presidents, or managed later to become president on their own, have achieved much renown.

The Constitution is sparing in its description of the office. By awarding the office (originally) to the person who finished second in the presidential election, the founders sought to ensure that the vice president would be a person of national stature and experience. Yet the Constitution gives vice presidents little to do. Their principal power is legislative, not executive. The vice president is officially the president of the Senate. Vice presidents may preside over Senate proceedings (which they do now only occasionally), and they may vote to break a tie in the Senate. Vice President John Adams still holds the record for breaking twenty Senate ties during Washington's administration.

The rise of political parties, with their slating of candidates for the presidency and the vice presidency, and the Twelfth Amendment's single-vote system for the two offices, overturned the founders' original mode of selection. Vice presidents became party allies of the president, selected chiefly for considerations of political "balance." With the growth in the number of assassination attempts, commentators put more emphasis on the need to consider the vice president's qualifications as a potential president. Furthermore, campaigns with televised vice-presidential debates have made the vice presidential candidates far more visible than in the past.

Until recently, the safest generalization that could be made about vice presidents is that they have been about as important (or unimportant) as the presidents wanted them to be. There have been instances in which presidents have almost entirely ignored their vice presidents. Thus, President Franklin Roosevelt did little to involve Vice President Truman in the administration, even though Roosevelt by 1945 knew of his own impending death. Truman was forced to assume office with little direct knowledge of such highly sensitive security issues as the administration's negotiating positions for ending the war in Europe and the plans for using the atomic bomb. President Kennedy promised a much greater role to the already well-known Lyndon Johnson, and he relied on Johnson to relieve some of the ceremonial burdens of the office. But he thought little of Johnson, and there were bitter feelings between Johnson and many of Kennedy's personal staff.

An important change in the vice president's role appears to have begun under President Carter, who integrated Vice President Mondale into his staff hierarchy and relied on him extensively for advice and assistance. Vice Presidents Bush (1981–1989) and Quayle (1989–1993) retained some authority under Presidents Reagan and Bush, while President Clinton made Vice President Gore one of his most important advisors. More recently, President George W. Bush has made Vice President Richard Cheney an important part of his administration. As a matter of precedent and expectation, vice presidents have now become much more important figures in the institutional presidency. This larger role seems to fit with their enhanced political standing under the current nominating system as likely future front-runners.

The central importance of the office, however, lies in the possibility of vice president's succession to the presidency. Since the ratification of the Twenty-fifth Amendment (1967), the Constitution designates two kinds of succession for the vice president: one in which the vice president serves as "Acting President," when the president is temporarily disabled and "unable to discharge the powers and duties of his office," and the other in the case of the president's removal, death or resignation, in which case the vice president becomes president.

Vice President John Tyler was the first to succeed to the presidency, when he assumed the office as well as the duties of the president in 1841 after the death of William Henry Harrison, who served just one month in office. (The original Constitution was not clear about whether the vice president should become president or merely act as president.) Since Tyler, seven vice presidents have become president after an incumbent's death (Millard Fillmore, Andrew Johnson, Chester Arthur, Theodore Roosevelt, Calvin Coolidge, Harry Truman, and Lyndon Johnson) and one, Gerald Ford, assumed the presidency after the resignation of President Nixon in 1974. Five others (John Adams, Thomas Jefferson, Martin Van Buren, Richard Nixon, and George Bush) were elected as presidents on their own.

The Importance of Popular Leadership

When Ronald Reagan became president in January of 1981, he brought with him into office one indispensable skill: the ability to communicate effectively with the public, which earned him the epithet of "The Great Communicator." Communicating with the public is clearly an important part of being president. But how exactly does it translate into political effectiveness? What makes this skill so important for the contemporary American presidency?

Under the system of separation of powers, the president's institutional means for influencing Congress are limited. Presidents can try to persuade legislators of the merits of their recommendations; they can bargain with legislators, using the resources the office makes available (for example, the allocation of federal projects); or they can generate a public sentiment so strong that members of Congress interested in reelection would be foolish to ignore it. Recent presidents have frequently employed this last technique, confirming Woodrow Wilson's slightly exaggerated dictum that the president "has no means of compelling Congress except through public opinion."[33]

Influencing Public Opinion

Perhaps the most direct way a president has of trying to influence opinion is the nationally televised address. Yet since a single speech by itself may not, especially in the case of a proposal for a domestic legislative program, have a major and immediate impact on the people, presidents will often follow up an address with a carefully orchestrated rhetorical campaign. For example, President Bush mobilized public opinion with his speech to Congress and the American people after the terrorist attacks on the World Trade Center and the Pentagon. Such campaigns may include news conferences, informal meetings with prominent reporters, presidential addresses in various parts of the country, and, in President Clinton's case, the use of televised "town meetings" with questions from ordinary citizens. At worst, such efforts take on the look of public relation campaigns designed to manipulate public attitudes; at best, they contribute to public awareness and understanding of pressing political problems.

Although the president, more than anyone else, has both access to the public and opportunity for influencing it, these advantages are no guarantee of success. President Carter discovered this early on when he failed to mobilize

public opinion on the energy issue after a full-blown campaign of persuasion that began with a televised fireside chat and continued with many other speeches and appearances. Later in his term, he was more successful in selling an administration proposal when he managed to get the Senate to ratify his Panama Canal treaties turning the American-built canal gradually over to the authority of the Panamanian government.

The importance of public support for a presidential program was demonstrated even more dramatically when Ronald Reagan, after only a few weeks in office, presented to Congress a plan to reduce expected growth in federal expenditures and taxes. Because many groups derived specific benefits from these expenditures, Reagan believed that his only chance of success in turning around "business as usual" in Washington was to generate broad-based public support for his package of reductions. He prepared the way by several nationally televised addresses over the course of the next few months. By the end of the summer of 1981 Reagan had succeeded in getting nearly all of his tax and spending package through Congress, and his effective appeal to public opinion was decisive in generating congressional support for his policies.

The success of presidential appeals to the public through televised addresses has thus been mixed. Studies comparing public opinion before and after presidents have spoken on an issue indicate some increase of support for the president's position. This increase has ranged from the negligible (a 4 percent gain for a tax cut following an address by President Kennedy on April 18, 1963) to the dramatic (a 43 percent increase in support for sending troops into Cambodia following President Nixon's address of April 30, 1970). In cases involving presidential action in foreign and security crises, the tendency of the nation to support the president—at least temporarily—is much greater. This so-called "rally-around-the flag" effect is well-known to Washington politicians, who realize that presidents have the first opportunity to influence public opinion. But here too subsequent challenges from other leaders and the collision of predictions with reality can quickly erode any temporary gains. In the case of the invasion of Cambodia, support for Nixon's policy quickly dissipated and he was forced to end the mission sooner than was planned.[34]

Besides seeking to persuade the public about the wisdom of particular policies, presidents seek to persuade the people that overall they are doing a good job. That is, they seek in a general way to defend themselves and their record so that the American people will think highly of them. A positive evaluation by the American people is important to presidents for two practical reasons: first, if a president is planning to run for a second term, he will need the people's support and confidence by the election; and second, when a president is popular he finds it easier to persuade people on specific issues. An unpopular president is more likely to be discounted and ignored, a popular one to be listened to. Thus, popularity is a political resource and a fairly important one.

Yet the qualifications to note here are as important as the main points. Popular support in the short term cannot be an end in itself. Even if a president is thinking in terms of reelection, his goal must be to have a reasonable level of popular confidence at election time. Policies that may bolster popularity in the short-term may fail over the longer term. By contrast, policies that may succeed over the longer term may cost a president support in the short-term. The general point is that efforts at persuasion and good speeches cannot cover for what are seen as palpable policy failures, while policies that succeed will help to persuade in the end far more than a good speech. Hence, a president who wishes to succeed must be willing to risk losing, in the short term, popularity and approval.

These points are illustrated in the case of Reagan's approval ratings during his first term. When his plan for economic improvement appeared to be failing in 1982, his approval rating dropped sharply to 37 percent; but when these policies in 1983 appeared to work, Reagan's approval ratings steadily grew. By the end of 1983, 53 percent of the American people approved of his performance, setting the stage for his landslide victory the following year.

"Moral Leadership"

In addition to attempting to persuade in behalf of their own program or record, presidents sometimes assume the burden of influencing the public in a sphere often referred to as "moral leadership."

First, presidents lead by moral example. As the occupant of the most prestigious position in American society and the object of unremitting attention, a president's own personal conduct—not only what he says but also what he does—can influence public morality. If a president sets a high standard of personal behavior, this can help foster norms of good conduct throughout society. As President Eisenhower once observed, "the President of the United States should stand, visible and uncompromising, for what is right and decent—in government, in the business community, in the private lives of the citizens."[35] Eisenhower began regular church attendance only after he was elected president, on the grounds that his conduct as president had consequences it did not have when he was a private citizen.

The failure of presidents to serve as good examples can have negative results. One of the worst consequences of the Watergate scandal was how President Nixon's actions undermined respect for the office and reduced the public's trust in the institutions of government in a similar vein. Respect for the office deteriorated with the events leading up to the Clinton impeachment debacle, reaching its nadir with the release of Independent Council Kenneth W. Starr's 1998 report to the House Judiciary Committee. The Starr Report gave new meaning to the phrase "presidential exposure," as Clinton's trysts with the White House intern Monica Lewinsky were outlined in graphic detail.

Many now complain that the inclusion of the whole personal life of the president for public scrutiny has gone too far. Clearly, elements of the personal lives of presidential candidates and presidents today receive public scrutiny and comment in a way that they did not only twenty years ago. Whether the emphasis on these aspects of character is helpful has been widely debated; but the fact remains that the public image of the president has important consequences, and today nearly everything is public.

Second, presidents on occasion are expected to "lead" in the sense of buoying the confidence of the nation and helping it, psychologically, to endure its travails. The capacity of President Lincoln, by word and deed, to provide solace and hope to millions during the Civil War was one of his great qualities as a leader. Similarly, Franklin Roosevelt saw his responsibility in 1933, during the depths and despair of the Great Depression, not just to promote specific pieces of legislation that would improve economic conditions, but also to reinvigorate confidence in the nation and its institutions. In his first inaugural address, Roosevelt declared that the "only thing we have to fear is fear itself—nameless, unreasoning, unjustified terror which paralyzes needed efforts to convert retreat into advance." More recently, after the terrorist attacks of September 11, 2001, President George W. Bush has effectively exhorted and consoled the American people.

In a related activity, presidents may attempt to summon the American people and inspire them to perform something higher or more noble. Recent presidents have not faced crises as severe as the Great Depression or World War II, but some of them have acted as if the model of inspirational leadership is at the core of the modern presidency. When running for the presidency, John Kennedy maintained that the country "will need a president . . . who is willing and able to summon his national constituency to its finest hour—to alert the people to our dangers and our opportunities—to demand of them the sacrifices that will be necessary."[36] Perhaps the most unusual example of a presidential effort to inspire the American people was an address given by President Carter in 1979 in which he warned, in a speech about the energy problem, that the nation was suffering from a national "crisis of confidence" that threatened to "destroy the social and political fabric of America." A united effort to solve the nation's energy problem could become the first step on the path of a revival of common purpose.[37] President Clinton has referred to his universal health care plan in very similar terms. Some presidents have clearly met with more success than others in attempts at inspirational leadership, although it

Monica Lewinsky is shown here embracing President Clinton at a White House reception. President Clinton's denial of a sexual affair with Ms. Lewinsky, both in public and in sworn testimony, formed the background to his impeachment by the House of Representatives on December 19, 1998. The Senate declined to remove the President from office in a trial that ended on February 12, 1999. (Photo courtesy of AP/Wide World Photos.)

is now clear that many Americans look to the presidency in some degree as the primary source of this kind of leadership.

Finally, presidents attempt to articulate principles and educate the American people (and perhaps the world as well) about the nation's convictions and commitments. Presidents are uniquely situated to educate in this sense. They can give expression to the major ends of American society and make those principles come alive for the American people, perhaps refining and adapting them in the process. For example, in response to the terrorist attacks on the World Trade Center and the Pentagon, President George W. Bush's speech to Congress and the American people articulated the ends of American society as freedom and equality. It is no accident that a major legacy of certain presidents has been their words, which often continue to be cited as fundamental constitutional texts.

Assessing Popular Leadership

Popular leadership is clearly among the most important responsibilities of the modern presidency. As President Truman once observed, "one of the great responsibilities and opportunities of the president is to lead and inspire public opinion." But it is possible for presidents to overestimate the effectiveness of popular leadership.

When it comes to promoting their agenda or program, presidents face significant limitations in efforts to pressure Congress by generating public support. Raising the public against Congress can succeed, but it is a weapon that can only be used sparingly and that can sour presidents' relations with Congress. It requires in immense effort on the president's part, and the public can only be called upon to focus attention in a few instances. As for attempting to win general support for the performance of the administration, the president faces even greater limits. Fine speeches and skillful press conferences or town meetings can no doubt help a president to explain what he is trying to do. But words in the end are no substitute for performance, and the American people will by and large judge a president's performance by consulting sources besides the president's own words.

Popular leadership is also fraught with broader dangers. In attempting to persuade the public, presidents can fall prey to rhetorical techniques and arguments that may have harmful long-term consequences. For example, to win support they may exaggerate the benefits of prospective programs or promise much more than they can possibly deliver. The result can be to raise unrealistic expectations, which if repeated can lead to public disenchantment with political leaders and institutions. Or presidents may make "inspirational" pleas that unnecessarily transform ordinary political situations into tests of national moral character. By overestimating the willingness of the American people to make sacrifices, they can promote dissatisfaction with the whole political order.

Finally, popular leadership can undermine the representative or republican role of the president. Popular leadership emerges, at least in the Wilsonian view, on the basis of the claim that the president, as the only leader elected by all the people, speaks for the nation. Sound leadership, however, requires office holders who have confidence in their own judgments, even if these vary from the immediate opinions of the majority and even if persuasion in the short run is not possible. By the same token, sound leadership

requires a citizenry that is prepared to accord a degree of discretion to its representative institutions. The more the public comes to think of the president as essentially the voice, or "tribune," of the people, the more the task of effective political leadership is placed in jeopardy.

Conclusion

Those who created the presidency wanted it to be strong and independent enough not just to provide for effective administration of the law, but to serve as a force to act decisively for the nation in diplomacy and crisis as well as play a creative role in the policymaking process. For much of the first century, it was Congress that was the dominant direction-setting institution in national policymaking. A few presidents, however, demonstrated that the office had capacities that could place it at the forefront of national affairs. These capacities include the ability to formulate coherent domestic and foreign policies, to guide the legislative process (often through the leadership of the dominant political party), to act forcefully to meet military threats, to serve as a focus for popular expectations, and to guide and instruct the citizenry.

In this century, changes in our relations with the rest of the world, the rise of a more activist national government, and the development of new communications technologies have made leadership in the executive office essential to the effective functioning of the political system. With the growth of the president's new responsibilities has come the emergence of a presidential bureaucracy to assist presidents in carrying out their job. The office, however, remains highly personalized and presidential discretion has not been restricted in a significant way.

The unity of the office, along with selection by the public as a whole, have made the presidency the focus of popular leadership. In a way that neither Congress nor the Supreme Court can match, the presidency is the foremost communicator with the American people. While this capacity makes for a formidable majoritarian office, it poses the dangers of raising unrealistic expectations and pandering to popular sentiments. An emphasis on the president's role as the people's "voice" can also obscure the distinction between guiding public opinion and merely following it.

The solution to these problems of popular leadership is not to return to a nineteenth-century idea of the president as mere administrator. Historical events and the capacities of the office have thrust the presidency into the "vital place of action in the system." Contemporary presidents are not free to ignore the responsibilities that the times have placed on the office. Their task rather is to carry out those responsibilities in a way which both recognizes the opportunities and dangers that come with the exercise of great power and respects the Constitutional role of the other branches.

Chapter 11 Notes

1. Comment of Roger Sherman on June 1, 1787 as recorded in James Madison's *Notes,* Adrienne Koch, ed. (New York: Norton, 1969).
2. Woodrow Wilson, *Constitutional Government in the United States* (New York: Columbia paper back edition, 1961 [originally published in 1908]), p. 73.
3. Robert F. Kennedy, *Thirteen Days* (New York: New American Library, 1969), p. 47.
4. Woodrow Wilson, *Constitutional Government in the United States,* chapter 3.
5. Richard M. Pious, *The American Presidency* (New York: Basic Books, 1979), p. 38.
6. Louis Fisher, *President and Congress: Power and Policy* (New York: Free Press, 1972), pp. 254–264.
7. Merrill D. Peterson, ed., *The Portable Thomas Jefferson* (New York: Viking, 1975), p. 164.
8. The House of Representatives does, however, choose the president when no candidate receives the requisite number of electoral votes.
9. Louis Henkin, *Foreign Affairs and the Constitution* (Mineola, N.Y.: Foundation Press, 1972), p. 16.
10. Richard M. Pious, *The American Presidency,* pp. 51–52.
11. Cited in Wilfred Binkley, President and Congress, 3rd ed. (New York: Vintage, 1962), p. 63.
12. William W. Story, ed., *Life and Letters of Joseph Story,* vol. 1 (Boston: Little, Brown, 1851), p. 311.
13. Robert S. Hirschfield, ed., *The Power of the Presidency,* 2nd ed. (Chicago: Aldine, 1973), pp. 66–67.
14. Richard M. Pious, *The American Presidency,* p. 57.
15. James D. Richadson, ed., *The Messages and Papers of the Presidents, 1789–1897* vol. 6, (Washington, D.C.: U.S. Government Printing Office, 1896), p. 25.
16. Robert S. Hirschfield, ed., *The Power of the Presidency,* p. 80.
17. John Locke, *Two Treatises on Civil Government,* Peter Laslett, ed. (New York: Mentor, 1965), pp. 421–422.
18. Theodore Roosevelt, *The Autobiography of Theodore Roosevelt,* Wayne Andrews, ed. (New York: Scribner, 1958), pp. 198–199.
19. Woodrow Wilson, *Constitutional Government in the United States,* p. 68.
20. Woodrow Wilson, *Constitutional Government in the United States,* p. 71.
21. Robert S. Hirschfield, ed., *The Power of the Presidency,* p. 165.
22. Robert S. Hirschfield, ed., *The Power of the Presidency,* p. 165.
23. This restriction was accepted by the Court in the case of *Humphrey's Executor v. United States* (1935).
24. Gerald Ford, *A Time to Heal* (New York: Harper and Row, 1979), p. 161.
25. Christopher Pyle and Richard Pious, *The President, Congress and the Constitution* (New York: The Free Press, 1984), p. 64.
26. Richard Neustadt, *Presidential Power: The Politics of Leadership from FDR to Carter (New* York: Wiley, 1980).
27. Joseph E. Kallenbach, *The American Chief Executive* (New York: Harper and Row, 1966), p. 441.
28. The purely personal staff almost never testifies officially before Congress. The heads of the two most important offices in the Executive Office of the President—the National Security Advisor and the Budget Director—will testify.
29. George Reedy, *The Twilight of the Presidency* (New York: New American Library, Mentor Books, 1970), p. 99.
30. Thomas E. Cronin, *The State of the Presidency* (Boston: Little, Brown, 1980), p. 254.
31. Elmer Cornwell, Jr., *Presidential Leadership of Public Opinion* (Bloomington, Indiana: University of Indiana Press, 1965), pp. 180–181.
32. Calvin MacKenzie, "Personal Appointment Strategies in Post-War Presidential Administrations," a paper delivered at the Midwest Political Science Association, Chicago, April 24, 1980.
33. Woodrow Wilson, *Constitutional Government in the United States,* p. 71.
34. George Edwards, III, *The Public Presidency* (New York: Saint Martin's, 1983), pp. 43–45.
35. Robert S. Hirschfield, ed., *The Power of the Presidency,* p. 123.
36. Robert S. Hirschfield, *The Power of the Presidency,* pp. 117, 133.
37. *Congressional Quarterly Weekly Report,* 1979, pp. 1470–1472.

12

Congress and the Presidency: Conflict and Cooperation

CHAPTER CONTENTS

In 1980, Lloyd Cutler, who served as White House Counsel to Presidents Carter and Clinton, wrote a controversial article for the highly respected journal *Foreign Affairs*. "The separation of powers between the legislative and executive branches," Cutler maintained, "whatever its merits in 1793, has become a structure that almost guarantees stalemate today." The American system of government has a "structural inability . . . to propose, legislate and administer a balanced program for governing." Voicing frustration with the unwillingness of Congress to pass many of President Carter's proposals, Cutler criticized a system in which a president can be elected to carry out certain expressly articulated goals but then denied the authority to translate them into public policy. Our system requires three separate bodies—the House of Representatives, the Senate, and the presidency—to agree before most general policies can be formulated, approved, and executed. The difficulty of meeting this requirement, according to Cutler, inevitably leads to "stalemate."[1]

Cutler's critique of the separation-of-powers system is hardly new. As long ago as the late nineteenth century, Woodrow Wilson lamented that "the federal government lacks strength because its powers are divided, lacks promptness because its authorities are multiplied, lacks wieldiness because its processes are roundabout, lacks efficiency because its responsibility is indistinct and its action without competent direction."[2] In the 1980s, critics of the separation of powers added another element to their argument: "divided government," or the situation in which the presidency is in the hands of a different party than either one or both houses of Congress. Divided government, these critics charged, is characterized "by conflict, delay and indecision, leading frequently to deadlock, inadequate and ineffective policies or no policies at all. . . . The President and Congress are motivated to try to discredit and defeat each other."[3]

Many of these critics propose altering our structure of government and moving toward a parliamentary form as it exists in Great Britain or Canada. In a parliamentary system the leaders of the executive branch—the prime minister, cabinet, and subcabinet (simply called the "gov-

ernment")—are chosen by the majority party in the legislature (or by a coalition of parties that constitute a majority of the legislative body). These leaders retain their seats in the legislature while also serving as high executive officials. An equivalent arrangement in the United States would consist of having only congressional elections and then allowing the winning party to install its leaders as president, vice president, and department heads. These officials would still be members of Congress, debating and voting on the very bills they were introducing in their capacity as officials in the executive branch.

The selection of the leaders of the executive branch by the legislature makes for much more cohesion between the branches of government than exists in the American system, where the Constitution expressly prohibits anyone from serving in both branches simultaneously (with the exception of the vice president, who is also the president of the Senate). The cohesion of the parliamentary system is reinforced by the practice that dictates that if the parliament rejects a key part of the government's program or votes a resolution of "no confidence," then the government must resign and a new one must be formed out of the parliament, or new legislative elections must take place. Political leaders in parliamentary governments, at least where there is a single majority party, very rarely lose votes in the parliament. Almost no one in the majority party wants the government to fall, as this might mean facing an election and giving up office.

While this system seems on first analysis to give all the power to the legislative branch, in reality the exact opposite is true. It is the prime minister and cabinet that are the real powers, at least in a situation in which a single party has a clear majority. The "government" proposes policies and, unlike an American president, can be almost certain that they will be enacted by the parliament. Thus the government possesses virtually the whole of the executive and legislative powers and retains almost all of the initiative in policymaking. Parliamentary governments, according to critics of the separation-of-powers system, display the merits of coherent policy formulation and implementation, prompt and consistent responses to external events, and clear accountability to the voting public.

BOX 12.1

On the Separation of Powers—Against and For

Against:

Any part of the president's legislative program may be defeated, or amended into an entirely different measure, so that the legislative record of any presidency may bear little resemblance to the overall program the president wanted to carry out. . . . This difficulty is of course compounded when the president's party does not even hold the majority of the seats in both Houses. . . . The former ability of the president to sit down with ten or fifteen leaders in each House, and to agree on a program which those leaders could carry through Congress, has virtually disappeared. The Committee chairmen and the leaders no longer have the instruments of power that once enabled them to lead. . . .

In this century the system has succeeded only on the rare occasions when there is an unusual event that brings us together, and creates substantial consensus throughout the country on the need for a whole new program. . . . Except on the rare issues where there is . . . a consensus, the structural problems usually prove too difficult to overcome. In each administration, it becomes progressively more difficult to make the present system work effectively on the range of issues, both domestic and foreign, that the United States must now manage even though there is no large consensus. . . .

We are not about to revise our own Constitution so as to incorporate a true parliamentary system. But we do need to find a way of coming closer to the parliamentary concept of "forming a Government," under which the elected majority is able to carry out an overall program, and is held accountable for its success or failure. . . . The most one can hope for is a set of modest changes . . . with somewhat less separation between the executive and the legislature than now exists.—Lloyd N. Cutler

For:

Mr. Cutler has a philosophy of governance that is at odds with what the framers of the Constitution embodied in that document. To Mr. Cutler good policy or good government is the product or the act of a single will. It is an act of management, of allocation, of balance. The framers, by contrast, thought that good policy could be recognized when it appeared, but to achieve it in the real world required a process of ambition counteracting ambition, leading thereby to the formation of coalitions—coalitions of partial, self-interested groups. They hoped the Constitution would lead these coalitions to emerge only on the principle of the common good. . . .

[Separation of powers] facilitates scrutiny, sometimes at the expense of action; it protects the particular and the individual, sometimes at the expense of the general. But it has brought about the capacity to engage in great national commitments when important national emergencies arise, and above all it has permitted a union to be created out of great diversity by providing separate constitutional places on which individuals could focus their loyalties. . . .

If we compare American policy with that of most parliamentary democracies, its leading characteristic is its moderation. There are many policies I do not approve of and regularly call immoderate. Taken as a whole, however we tend to temper the enthusiasm of temporary majorities by the need constantly to reformulate that majority. . . .

If reforms are to be sought, we should seek them from within the American experience on the basis of those institutional arrangements to which the American people have become accustomed. We should not reach overseas for an approximation of the parliamentary system; we should look at state and city governments in this country and ask what modifications in federal arrangements already tested at the city and state levels might commend themselves.—James Q. Wilson

Sources: Lloyd N. Cutler, "To Form a Government," *Foreign Affairs,* Fall 1980, pp. 126–143; and James Q. Wilson, "in Defense of Separation of Powers," in Thomas E. Cronin, ed., *Rethinking the Presidency* (Boston: Little, Brown, 1982), pp. 179–182.

In this chapter we will examine the ways in which Congress and the presidency interact and how this interaction affects the ability of our governing institutions to achieve the purposes for which they were created. Specifically, we will (1) analyze the ways in which one especially effective president tried to influence Congress, (2) study the underlying sources of conflict between Congress and the presidency, (3) consider the resources available to each branch when it does battle with the other, and (4) examine the forces that make for cooperation between the two branches. In the conclusion we will return to the questions of the effectiveness of the separation-of-powers system and the desirability of reforms modeled on the parliamentary form of government.

Both the presidency and Congress have an independent sphere in which they can act on their own. The president as the chief executive can, for example, decide when to extend diplomatic recognition to new governments and can even commit troops in certain kinds of military actions. The president may consult with members of Congress in these cases, but it is not clear that he is obliged to do so. Thus President Nixon on his own decided in 1972 to move toward recognition of the Chinese communist government in Beijing (which had been in existence since 1949), and President Reagan in 1983 decided to send armed forces to the island of Grenada. In one of the most dramatic assertions of presidential power in recent history, President Bush decided in 1990 to deploy hundreds of thousands of American troops in Saudi Arabia in response to Iraq's invasion of Kuwait.

For its part, Congress can also take certain actions on its own. It can hold major hearings of which the president might disapprove, it can pass legislation that the president opposes (even over his veto), and it can impeach a judge or an executive branch official against the president's will. Thus as much as he might have wished otherwise, President Reagan could not halt the politically damaging Iran-Contra select committee hearings in 1987. Nor could President Clinton stop congressional impeachment proceedings against him in 1998.

Yet as important as these separate actions may be, they constitute only a part of the activities of the government. In conducting most of the major business of government, common action of some kind will need to be taken by *both* the president and the Congress. This is the case on the one hand because a president can only do so much without congressional support and on the other hand because the president holds a major share of the legislative power. While a president may be able to send in troops in a quick strike action, he cannot sustain that action for long without a congressional vote of funds. Or while a president may be able to recognize and establish formal diplomatic relations with a nation at his own discretion, he will only be able to carry out a larger diplomatic aim, such as providing economic assistance or offering favorable terms for trade with this country, with the help of Congress.

Accordingly, for conducting any kind of sustained policy, domestic or foreign, both the president and Congress must be involved, and there is a need for cooperation and coordination. Yet each of these two institutions is proud, independent, and endowed with a will of its own. Cooperation is a goal that is widely preached, but not always practiced. The president and Congress often do not see matters in the same light, or they may have very different priorities. This brings us to the complex and intriguing politics of executive-legislative relations in Washington, D.C.

The President as Chief Legislator: The Case of Lyndon Johnson

An American president clearly has a much harder time getting initiatives through the legislature than a British prime minister does. Yet some presidents have been far more successful than others, and in a few instances certain presidents have enjoyed, at least for a brief period, enough support in Congress to push through large parts of a program that has altered the nation's basic direction of public policy. The most notable of these presidents have been Woodrow Wilson (from 1912–14), Franklin Roosevelt (from 1933–35), Lyndon Johnson (from 1965–66), and (to a lesser extent) Ronald Reagan in 1981.

There is no single key to presidential success that holds true in all of these cases. Much depends on the political style of each president and on the instruments of power in Washington, some of which change from one period to the next. A good deal can be learned, however, from focusing on one of the most effective modern presidents in dealing with Congress, Lyndon Johnson, and in examining just how much energy and effort are needed, in Johnson's words, to "crack the wall of separation" that divides the executive and legislative branches. We will also make some comparisons with other presidents, especially Ronald Reagan.

Lyndon Johnson served as president from November of 1963 (when John Kennedy was assassinated) to January of 1969. Like the other successful presidents in this group, Johnson had a major legislative program or agenda that he wanted to implement. The name Johnson gave to his program was "The Great Society," which covered a range of new social welfare legislation in areas like education, health care, and civil rights. In fact, all of the four presidents noted above have had labels that they or others have attached to their basic program: Wilson's was The New Freedom, Roosevelt's The New Deal, and Reagan's The Reagan Revolution. In each case, too, the presidents were able to win support for the idea that their programs were essential to a nation that was in crisis and facing a special need for leadership.

Johnson's period of greatest legislative success came in 1965–1966. It followed his landslide election victory over Barry Goldwater in November of 1964 in which Johnson won 61 percent of the popular vote and in which Democrats won 295 of the 435 House seats (61 percent) and maintained a lopsided majority in the Senate of 68 of the 100 seats. Given the dominance of the Democrats in the Eighty-Ninth Congress, Johnson clearly had much going for him in pursuing his legislative program, although other presidents with large party majorities have failed to achieve their objectives. The backing of a strong party majority in Congress, following on an impressive electoral victory, were also factors favoring Wilson in 1913 and Roosevelt in 1933. Reagan lacked a Republican majority in the House in 1980, but his party's gain of thirty-three

seats in that body was impressive, and Republicans had posted a net gain of twelve seats in the Senate, enough to capture a majority.

President Johnson exhibited a skill and intensity in his dealings with Congress that was unmatched by any president since at least Franklin Roosevelt. He relied on a direct personal relation with Congress, which he described as follows:

> There is but one way for a President to deal with Congress . . . and that is continuously, incessantly, and without interruption. If it's really going to work, the relationship between the President and Congress has got to be almost incestuous. He's got to know them even better than they know themselves. And then, on the basis of this knowledge, he's got to build a system that stretches from the cradle to the grave, from the moment a bill is introduced to the moment it is officially enrolled as the law of the land.[4]

The first ingredient in Johnson's approach to Congress was thus an intimate knowledge of the structure, procedures, and personalities that constituted the House and Senate. For this task Johnson came into the presidency well equipped, having served in Congress for a total of twenty-two years, ten in the House and twelve in the Senate, of which his last six were as the majority leader. But Johnson did not rely simply on past knowledge:

> In the Eighty-Ninth Congress (1965–66), his favorite reading was the Congressional Record. A White House messenger picked up the newest issue at the Government Printing Office every morning, and an aide then read it before dawn, clipping each page on which a member of Congress praised or criticized Johnson [and gave it to Johnson to read at breakfast]. . . . Before retiring at night, Johnson read detailed memos from his staff on their legislative contacts of the day, specific problems that arose, and noteworthy conversations, all of which he absorbed rapidly and thoroughly. When Congress was in session, he received continuous status reports. . . . Congress was for Johnson "a twenty-four-hour-a-day obsession."[5]

The second ingredient of Johnson's system—his "cradle to grave" contact with Congress—included special White House briefings with congressional leaders before a legislative message was sent to Capitol Hill, regular Tuesday morning breakfast meetings with the congressional leadership to review the legislative schedule, and frequent contact, on the telephone or in person, with undecided legislators. The special briefings were generally at dinner meetings in the White House to which Johnson invited the chairmen of the appropriate committee and subcommittee, the party leadership, and other legislators who were likely to be influential on a particular issue. The legislators would go over the President's legislative messages with key Cabinet officials and members of the White House staff, who would provide background information and answer questions. Johnson likened these briefings to the "question period" in the British system—"an opportunity for the members of Congress to get an advance look at my documents and then to confront my Cabinet members with all sorts of questions. . . . It gave the chosen ones a knowledgeable understanding of what often turned out to be complex legislation."[6]

At his Tuesday breakfast meetings, Johnson would stand beside an immense chart which showed the course of each of his bills: which were still in subcommittee, which were ready for the mark-up, and which were ready for consideration on the floor. The chart, which seemed to accompany Johnson everywhere, was also used to prod the members of his Cabinet, allowing him to request or demand explanations from the Secretaries whose departmental legislation was shown to be lagging.[7]

Ronald Reagan's technique was different, as he lacked Johnson's interest in and personal knowledge of the workings of Congress. He was also far less of a "detail" man than Johnson. But Reagan was very much the skilled politician, and he was solicitous of members of Congress. His political rival at the time, the Democratic House Speaker Thomas ("Tip") O'Neill, gives the following description of the President's technique: "Reagan had tremendous powers of persuasion. . . . The President was continually calling members of the House. He didn't always get his way, but his calls were never wasted." What Reagan lacked in his personal knowledge of Congress, he made up for with a very experienced and effective legislative liaison staff at the White House.

According, again, to O'Neill, "all in all, the Reagan operating team in 1981 was probably the best run political operating unit I've seen."[8]

There was a final element in Johnson's strategy, which he used effectively: the appeal to the public by a speech, sometimes delivered in a special session before Congress. Johnson preferred to negotiate directly with members of Congress and was not an especially good public speaker. But at certain times he could rise to the occasion; and with his huge majorities in Congress, his speeches were used more to inform and educate the public than to pressure or convert members of Congress. With Reagan the case was different. Lacking a majority in the House, he needed to mobilize public opinion in an effort to put pressure on members of Congress to vote for his program. Speeches were thus far more important for him than for Johnson, and it was very much to his advantage that he was so masterful an orator.

Johnson's success in getting his way with Congress in 1964 and 1965 was unmatched in the period since World War II. By 1966, however, Johnson's effectiveness with Congress began to ebb. In the midterm election of 1966, the Democrats lost forty-eight seats in the House and four in the Senate. Throughout Johnson's term the Vietnam war continued to escalate, robbing the president of the goodwill of important elements in his own party. Moreover, fiscal conservatives increasingly attacked his attempts to provide both "guns and butter," that is, to fight a war while adding more domestic programs. Federal deficits soared, taxes were increased, and Johnson's public popularity quickly eroded. By the end of his term, Johnson was regularly being thwarted by Congress.

Johnson himself well understood the cyclical nature of presidential influence with Congress and the importance of striking just after a presidential election. He assessed the possibilities of presidential leadership of Congress as follows:

You've got to give it all you can that first year. Doesn't matter what kind of majority you come in with. You've got just one year when they treat you right, and before they start worrying about themselves. The third year, you lose votes. . . . The fourth year's all politics. You can't put anything through when half of the Congress is thinking how to beat you. So you've got one year. That's why I tried. Well, we gave it a hell of a lick, didn't we?[9]

What lessons, then, about the system of separation of powers can we draw from Lyndon Johnson's administration? One point is clear: the gap between Congress and the presidency is not unbridgeable, and under certain circumstances the president can truly become the force that pushes a broad program or agenda through Congress. But these circumstances are not present in the normal course of presidential-congressional relations. Most new presidents do not, like Johnson, come to office with an electoral landslide or with the advantage of overwhelming majorities of the same party in control of the House and Senate. Nor are most as experienced as Johnson was in the ways of Congress. Finally, even when a president gains effective control over the legislative process—as Lyndon Johnson did in 1965–1966 and Ronald Reagan did in 1981—that control will not persist throughout the president's entire term in office; Congress will always in time reassert its independence from the president.

Sources of Conflict

Legislative successes of the degree that Lyndon Johnson enjoyed in 1965 and 1966 and Ronald Reagan enjoyed in early 1981 are rare in American politics. In more normal circumstances the forces that generate conflict between the branches seem to predominate. This fact is hardly surprising, as the founders designed the system to foster a certain amount of competition between the branches of government. They hoped that each institution would oppose the excesses of the other, thereby preventing a dangerous consolidation of all power in a single set of hands. In itself, then, conflict (at least in some degree) is not altogether a bad thing.

There are three main sources of this conflict: institutional jealousy, structural differences between the branches, and differences in the way each branch represents the public.

Institutional Jealousy

A considerable amount of conflict between the president and Congress results from the desire of officials to protect and enhance the power and prerogatives of their institutions. Differences over polices are also often at stake, but it is remarkable—especially for foreign observers—how often these conflicts involve institutional loyalties rather than policy positions.

An episode in 1978 illustrates the importance of institutional loyalty. President Carter negotiated an agreement on the limitation of strategic (nuclear) arms with the leaders of the Soviet Union, which most expected he would submit to the Senate for ratification as a treaty. Increasingly fearful, however, that he could not obtain the necessary two-thirds of the Senate to support this agreement, Carter indicated that he was considering submitting the proposal in the form of a joint resolution, which would need only a simple majority vote in both branches.

Reaction in the Senate was swift and negative. A respected Republican senator, Charles Mathias from Maryland, warned that such a step "would be viewed as an effort to circumvent" the Constitutional role of the Senate. Even the President's natural allies in the Senate, the Democratic leaders, opposed the move. Majority Leader Robert Byrd of West Virginia chided the administration for trying to "end-run . . . the Senate." "A pact as important as this," Byrd argued on the Senate floor, "must be sound in every respect and be able to withstand the constitutional test of advice and consent." Given the strength of Senate criticism, Carter dropped the idea of a joint resolution and submitted the agreement in the form of a treaty.[10] Even those senators who were inclined to support this agreement did not want to see it passed in a way that violated the Senate's proper role in the ratification process.

Similar efforts by members of other institutions to resist actions that seem to encroach on their institution's Constitutional prerogatives are not at all uncommon. Many members of Congress were incensed at actions taken by the Reagan administration during the Iran-Contra affair, which a congressional inquiry charged directly "bypasse[d] the checks and balances of the system."[11]

For their part, presidents throughout history have resisted congressional actions designed to weaken the executive branch. Some have gone to extreme lengths. For example, President Andrew Johnson refused in 1867 to comply with a law, passed over his veto, that stripped from the president the power to dismiss his own cabinet members. For this, Johnson was impeached by the House and nearly convicted by the Senate.

Historical experience has demonstrated, then, that those who serve in the legislative and executive branches develop a personal attachment to the institution in which they serve, exactly as was envisaged by the founders:

> The great security against a gradual concentration of the several powers in the same department consists in giving to those who administer each department the necessary constitutional means and personal motives to resist encroachments of the others. The provision for defense must in this, as in all other cases, be made commensurate to the danger of attack. Ambition must be made to counteract ambition. The interest of the man must be connected with the constitutional rights of the place. (*Federalist* 51)

In a properly constructed government, individual officeholders will have a personal interest in preserving the "constitutional rights" of their office. Their ambition to play an important role in national policymaking will incline them to protect the institution which is the source of their influence. Members of each institution develop "opposite and rival interests" that prevent any one branch from consolidating all power: the "private interest of every individual [officeholder becomes] a sentinel over the public rights." (*Federalist* 51)

Structural Differences

Another source of conflict between the presidency and Congress lies in the fundamental structural differences between the two institutions. The presidency is more unified and hierarchical, the Congress more pluralistic and collegial. The institutions were designed in this way to give them the qualities most suited to their particular function in the governmental system: a large legislative branch consisting of members of roughly equal power, the founders believed,

would promote "deliberation and wisdom," while unity in the executive would contribute to "decision, activity, secrecy, and dispatch" as well as a more unified view of the common interest.

These points of emphasis did not, of course, mean that the founders wanted a chief executive who would act without taking account of varied viewpoints, or a legislature that could not on occasion act quickly. On balance, however, the structure of the legislative branch should foster deliberation that results from the interaction of a multiplicity of interests and opinions, while the structure of the executive branch should promote the kind of energy and forcefulness and unity of vision that comes from vesting power in a single person.

Each institution may occasionally exhibit the defect of its virtue. There is a danger of hasty or precipitous action by a president that is taken on the basis of incomplete information, without sufficient attention to a variety of viewpoints, or perhaps without broad-based public support; by contrast, there is the risk that the slow and more deliberative legislative process may result in unwarranted delays or failure to make decisions on pressing national problems. What we sometimes find, therefore, are conflicts that arise because presidents tend to grow impatient with a legislative body that often seems incapable of acting decisively, while Congress becomes resentful of an executive branch that may want to act too quickly or claim too much of the credit.

Representational Differences

The final source of conflict between Congress and the presidency derives from the different ways in which these two institutions relate to the American people. Members of Congress usually think of themselves in the first instance as representatives of their own districts or states. Congress represents the entire nation, but in the form, as it were, of a summation of its different pieces. The president, as the sole elected official chosen in a national election, represents the nation as a whole. Besides their different electoral constituencies, the two branches also have different terms of office. Presidents serve a four-year term, renewable only once. House members serve a two-year term, senators a six-year one, both indefinitely renewable.

These differences in constituency and term promote quite different perspectives. Consider, first, the time-frames under which the two institutions tend to operate. The presidency works on a four-year cycle, while Congress works on a two-year cycle. Every two years the entire House and one-third of the Senate are re-elected. The result is that Congress—in particular the House—tends to be more closely attuned to short-term changes in public opinion, while a president can discount somewhat these same changes during the first two years of a presidential term.

Events during the first two years of the Reagan presidency illustrate this point. Reagan, as noted, was elected with a large electoral majority in the 1980 presidential election, and there was much sentiment in Congress, even among his foes, to go along with parts of his legislative program. Yet as the economy began to deteriorate late in 1981 and as Reagan's personal popularity waned, many Democratic members shifted and demanded a reversal of the President's policies, especially after the Democrats gained 26 seats in the House in the 1982 midterm election. The President stood firm, resisting pressure to slow increases in defense spending and to raise income tax rates that had been cut in 1981. His responsibility, he claimed, was to "stay the course" and give a full chance to the program for which he had been elected in 1980.

The American system is unusual among the liberal democracies not only because it selects members of Congress in separate and distinct elections from the president, but also because half of the congressional elections (so-called midterm elections) occur in a year when there is no election for the presidency. Both branches can—and do—claim to be reading the sentiments of the people. But they read public sentiment in different ways and also at different times. This, too, is an invitation to conflict.

A second difference in representational perspective reflects the fact that presidents, while they are better able to resist immediate pressures of public opinion than Congress (and in this sense can take a longer view), are often more in a hurry to get a program enacted. They

enter the White House with four, or at most eight years, to make their mark on history. Especially if they are "activists," they will seek quickly to demonstrate their ability to lead, to shape events, and in general to "get things done." They will try to push their legislative program through Congress quickly and thus often express impatience and frustration with the snail-like pace and less-than-efficient procedures of the House and Senate. For their part, members of Congress, while they must be responsive to short-term public opinion, may well be less in a hurry. Many members of Congress today are looking to make a career of being in Congress and thus plan to be in office much longer than the president. They may have far less incentive to see things done quickly.

A third difference in representational perspective derives from the plurality of Congress in contrast to the (relative) unity of the presidency. The fact that Congress is an institution of many relatively equal members, especially in a system in which party members do not always vote the same way, means that different majority coalitions form from one issue to the next. This flexibility enables Congress to be responsive to different sentiments of Americans on different issues. Some issues may pit the northern "frost belt" states against the southern "sun belt" states, while others divide urban areas from rural areas. In a sense, it is difficult to ask the Congress always to be logically consistent among its policies, for it is not the same individuals who are responsible for each majority. The case is different for the executive branch, because the ultimate decision maker is a single individual. That individual is likely to possess a rather stable set of political beliefs or attitudes, and in any case the president will at least attempt to explain how and why all the particular decisions taken by him or in his name fit into some kind of consistent program.

A fourth difference reflects the differing susceptibility of the two branches to special interests. Members of Congress are often more susceptible than the president to the force of special or narrow interests. The smaller the constituency, the more leverage any particular special interest can exercise. In the nation as a whole, however, the influence of any one group

Even though Congress was dominated by his own party, Jimmy Carter had difficulty achieving enactment of his legislative agenda. (Courtesy of the University Journal, University of Virginia. Used with permission.)

is diluted by the sheer size of the electorate, and there are so many different groups, often with conflicting aims, that they have a tendency to balance each other out. Having a nationwide constituency therefore puts presidents somewhat "above the battle," whereas the members of Congress often look first to the short-range interests of their districts or states.

An excellent illustration of this difference of approach is the controversy that broke out early in the Carter administration over federal water projects (dams, irrigation projects, and river and harbor improvements). Traditionally, Congress had insisted on playing the preeminent role in determining national water policy. President Carter believed, however, that policy was being made not on genuine assessments of national needs, but instead on the desire of individual members to get all they could for their constituents. This situation led, in Carter's view, to wasteful overspending on a system lacking any coherent national purpose. When Carter tried to change prevailing practices, he met with intense opposition and had only minimal success.

When Congress and the presidency do battle over these kinds of issues, it is always fair to ask which institution is accurately reflecting public opinion. The answer is probably both, but in two quite different ways. Congress effectively gave voice to the millions of individual citizens or groups who wanted better flood control, cheap hydroelectric power, improved irrigation of farmlands, more water transportation, and expanded outdoor recreational facilities. Congress expressed the concrete interests of these citizens, and people often want their member of Congress to be primarily concerned with the needs and interests of their own district or state.

The presidency, by contrast, articulated the general public sentiment for economy in government and for rational and coherent national policies, a sentiment shared even by those who favored the water projects. Here, too, the President may have been doing the job that Americans expect: reflecting the more generalized or diffuse values of the American people and goals like a balanced budget, reduced inflation, and a clean environment. Individual members of Congress often share these same goals; but if achievement of these ends imposes substantial short-term costs on their constituents—for example, closing a military base, terminating or reducing federal programs, or shutting down a polluting factory—they often vote to forestall the costs. Members of the House in particular can hardly be faulted for behaving in this way, since the system was designed precisely to foster their close attachment to the strongly held views of the people.

Many also ask which institution does a better job representing the people's long-term interests. To pose these questions is to realize how difficult it is to provide definitive answers. Keep in mind that we have only been speaking of general tendencies of the institutions, not iron-clad rules. There are many cases when it is clear that presidents are beholden to certain important special interests in their own party and when Congress is taking a broader view. More important, the presidential view, which often asserts the "high ground" of seeking the national interest by standing above special interests, can by its very general and abstract perspective miss the true national interest. In complex issues of public policy, it may be said that the best way to arrive at the national interest is to respond to, if not exactly echo, specific concerns and interests as they are articulated at the local or regional level.

In the final analysis, the national interest may best be approximated neither by an institution that claims to grasp it as a whole, nor by an institution that tends to sum up its particular parts. Perhaps the best arrangement is one that allows for an ongoing dialogue and system of negotiation between two institutions that represent the nation in different ways.

Instruments of Institutional Conflict: The Presidency

Given that conflict between the executive and legislative branches is a deep-seated characteristic of American national government, we should turn now to an examination of some of the legal, constitutional, and political instruments available to each branch. For presidents, the most important of these weapons are taking the initiative, influencing public opinion, using persuasion, cutting deals, and exercising the veto.

Taking the Initiative

No single factor benefits presidents more in trying to get their own way than their ability to take the initiative, especially in cases where they can act at their own discretion on existing Constitutional or statutory authority. Presidential actions can create facts or realities to which members of Congress must then respond, sometimes in ways they might not have originally chosen if they had control of events.

There were several important examples of this during the first century of American government. President Washington seized the initiative in 1793 by proclaiming that the United States would remain neutral in the war between Great Britain and France. Many in Congress believed that the United States was obligated to come to the aid of France under the terms of the treaty of 1778, which had brought France in on the side of the Americans during the Revolutionary War. Constitutionally, Congress retained the authority to declare war against Great Britain; but in practice this would have meant opposing the settled judgment and decision of the highly respected chief executive, and thus they backed down. An even more striking instance occurred in 1845, under the administration of President

President Polk's decision to provoke a confrontation with Mexico in 1845, an action which was followed by a reluctant congressional declaration of war, illustrates the efficacy of presidential initiative. (National Portrait Gallery; Smithsonian Institution; Gift of the James Knox Polk Memorial Association of Nashville and the James K. Polk Memorial Auxiliary of Columbia, Tennessee. Used with permission.)

James Polk. Opposition to fighting a war with Mexico was very strong in Congress. Polk, who wanted the war, moved American troops into a piece of disputed territory in Texas, whereupon there was a clash between the Mexican and American forces. As one historian aptly concluded, "The President's initiative left Congress no choice but to accept a *fait accompli* by declaring that a state of war existed."[12]

More recently, President Bush initiated the deployment of American troops in the Persian Gulf region in August 1990. Then, in the face of criticism from influential members of Congress including Senate Armed Services Committee Chairman Sam Nunn of Georgia, in November 1990 the president further increased troop strength to a level adequate to initiate offensive action to expel Iraq from Kuwait. Only after American forces were at full strength and an endorsement of the use of force had been secured from the United Nations did President

Bush request formal approval of his actions from Congress.

The capacity of the president, especially in military matters, to present Congress with a *fait accompli* has often been criticized. Some have complained that the president's capacity to act in this fashion allows the nation to be taken to war too easily. Once the president has actually sent troops into a combat zone, it is particularly difficult for Congress, if it is opposed to the president's actions, to undo what the president has done (especially given the public's tendency to "rally around the flag" in the midst of a crisis).

But Congress has ways to respond. Congress can pass resolutions to make known its sentiments, or it can threaten to cut off funding for a specific military deployment. One attempt to resolve this matter in a more general fashion was the War Powers Act of 1973. It states that the president "in every possible instance shall consult with the Congress before introducing United States Armed Forces into hostilities or into situations where imminent involvement in hostilities is clearly indicated." The act also provides: 1) that the president must seek formal approval by Congress within sixty days of introducing American forces into hostilities, and 2) that American forces must be withdrawn within 90 days if Congress directs or if it does not formally approve the president's action.

The constitutionality of these last two restrictions on the executive's war powers is very much a matter of dispute. Presidents who have served since the passage of the Act have generally declared them to be unconstitutional. According to one observer, today "a substantial number of members [of Congress] . . . have doubts about the constitutionality of the law and hold opinions of inherent power very close to those of recent presidents."[13] A clear resolution of these issues has yet to occur, in part because the Supreme Court has refused to become involved in what it has viewed as a political dispute over the proper boundaries of the two branches, and because Congress has voted approval of troop commitments in the most important cases to which the act might have been applied (the deployment of American forces in Lebanon by Reagan in 1982-83, U.S. participation in the multinational force that expelled Iraq from Kuwait in 1991, the peacekeeping force sent to the Balkans in the 1990s, and the troops sent to Afghanistan to remove the ruling Taliban and the Al Qaeda terrorist organization following the attacks on the World Trade Center and Pentagon in 2001.)

While presidents since Washington have found it relatively easy to take the initiative in foreign policy, the same cannot be said of domestic policy. In this realm, the president's latitude to proceed on his own is generally more hemmed in by specific provisions of statutory law. What presidents can do, however, is to take the initiative in another sense: to recommend action to the Congress and to the nation and thereby focus attention and attempt to set the agenda for congressional deliberations.

The prerogative to set the agenda is by no means fully recognized, either by law or tradition, as belonging to the president. Indeed, through much of the nineteenth century it was Congress that usually decided what domestic problems needed to be solved and what legislative solutions were required. Congress generally set the domestic policy agenda and jealously guarded this prerogative.

But there is also a basis in the Constitution for the idea of the president as the agenda-setter. It is contained in Article II section 3, which assigns the president the right or duty of giving to Congress "information of the state of the union" and of recommending to Congress "measures as he shall judge necessary and expedient." At the turn of the twentieth century, Woodrow Wilson sought to give this power a far more active force than it had throughout most of the nineteenth century, arguing (in an indirect criticism of some of the more diffident nineteenth century presidents) that it is not necessary "that recommendations should be merely perfunctory. . . . The Constitution bids [the president] to speak and times of stress must more and more thrust upon him the attitude of originator of policies."[14] As President, Wilson himself freely made use of this power. He returned to the old practice (abandoned by Jefferson) of giving the state of the union address in person, and he delivered several special messages to Congress—some in writing, others in person—to recommend elements of his New Freedom program.

Modern presidents employ the same two mechanisms (state of the union addresses and special messages) to present their legislative programs. In addition they are also now required by statute to submit each year a budget report that outlines the administration's spending priorities. Combined, these messages give presidents an important tool for defining and highlighting policies of importance to them. Congress may reject a president's recommendations, but—given the intense media coverage the president receives—it is usually difficult for it to ignore them.

Since the 1920s, accordingly, presidents have increasingly fought for and been generally accorded the "right" to attempt to set the congressional agenda themselves. In modern American politics, it is expected that a president will have a legislative program every year and that he will actively use his influence to fight for that program. (In fact, when Dwight Eisenhower declined to submit a program to Congress in 1954, he was widely criticized, even by members of Congress.) The expectation that presidents have a legislative program gives them some leverage in determining what problems and issues will be debated in Congress as well as in the media and by the attentive public. Yet while presidents have gained this advantage in dealing with Congress, they now suffer the disadvantage of often being judged by the public according to how well they can control Congress and get their program enacted into law.

Even in the modern era, however, Congress under certain circumstances can seize the initiative in defining the public agenda. When the Republicans took control of both Houses of Congress in 1995, they were highly energized by their victory. The Speaker of the House, Newt Gingrich, laid out a program that for a time dominated public discussion. The agenda-setting power of Congress was revealed when, for a time, even Clinton seemed to acquiesce to the Republicans' leadership. Nevertheless, the bicameral organization of the Congress, coupled with the demands of parochialism, soon led to the decline of Gingrich and his national program. The president's position (with the vice president) as the nation's only elected official almost insures that the president will maintain the role in most circumstances as the chief agenda setter.

Influencing Public Opinion

Presidents, especially modern presidents, attempt to generate public opinion supportive of their policies. They do so because strong public backing of a measure will make members of Congress more likely to support it. As Woodrow Wilson observed, a president has "no means of compelling Congress except through public opinion."[15] This Wilsonian idea overstates the case, but the reliance of certain presidents on extensive public "campaigns" for their programs certainly testifies to their confidence in this technique. No president employed such campaigns with more regularity than President Clinton, who made scores of trips and gave hundreds of speeches to promote his legislative agenda.

Congress has, of course, means of its own in influencing public opinion. Some congressional debates are widely publicized; individual members of Congress spend long hours in their districts explaining their activities in Washington and seeking to build public support; and congressional investigations can, under certain circumstances, capture the nation's attention.

The president, however, has tremendous advantages over Congress in access to the media and in his ability to communicate directly to the public. In the end, the hundreds of individual efforts by members of Congress cannot match the impact of a single, well-executed presidential address on national television. Coupled with the suggestion, which presidents sometimes explicitly make, for citizens to contact their representatives and senators on a specific question up for consideration before Congress, a speech can sometimes play an important role in pressuring members of Congress to follow the president's lead. Yet it also appears that this technique can begin to wear itself out by over use. Presidents may speak, but the public may cease to listen.

Using Persuasion

One instrument often overlooked in popular accounts of Washington politics is the executive branch's ability to marshal a case on the merits for its proposals. Persuasion takes place in several ways. Sometimes, it is exercised directly by the president or his closest aides in contacts with members of Congress, as in frequent briefings given at the White House or by meetings or telephone calls to members of Congress. Members of Congress are not easily swayed, however, they are likely to be impressed by the very fact of being contacted by the president, and they are certain to give his arguments due consideration. When the president calls, you listen.

To assist in the task of persuading members of Congress, each president since Dwight Eisenhower has employed a congressional liaison staff with specific responsibility for presenting the president's case on Capitol Hill. Though its principal function is to communicate the president's objectives to legislators and persuade members to vote in support of those objectives, an effective congressional liaison staff also serves as a channel of communication in the other direction as well. Staying abreast of the climate of opinion in Congress, anticipating congressional reaction to presidential initiatives, and communicating special concerns of key members back to the White House are important functions a skilled congressional liaison staff can perform for a president who seeks to persuade members of Congress to follow his lead.

The White House congressional liaison staff is well known for getting information that supports the administrations's position into the hands of members of Congress. Executive agencies also have (smaller) congressional liaison staffs, and to a more limited extent, the bureaucracy itself follows the "line" of the administration—although members on various committees usually have their own sources of information in the agencies. Still, the bureaucracy does generally attempt to generate information more favorable to the administration's line. If, as is often said, "information is power," then these efforts are important. Consider the following comment made by Walter F. Mondale when he was serving as a senator from Minnesota:

I have been in many debates . . . that dealt with complicated formulas and distributions. And I have found that whenever I am on the side of the administration, I am surfeited with computer print-outs and data that comes within sec-

onds, whenever I need it to prove how right I am. But if I am opposed to the administration, computer print-outs always come late, prove the opposite point, or always are on some other topic. So I think one of the rules is that he who controls the computers controls the Congress. . . .[16]

Most efforts at persuasion by the executive branch occur through formal congressional hearings when officials make the administration's case for or against a legislative proposal. Through the congressional hearings process the expertise and the vast information resources of the executive branch—from the White House staff down to the most obscure bureaucrat—can be marshaled to support the president's programs. Of special importance are the appearances of cabinet officers, as these are occasions when members of Congress have the opportunity to hear directly the arguments of the administration.

Cutting Deals

Administration officials do not, of course, limit their dealings with members of Congress to reasoned persuasion through facts and arguments. Often a representative or senator may hold out for a more tangible or immediate benefit that can be of help to the political career of the representative, which is usually an item meant to benefit constituents, such as a new federal project, a tax break for a local industry, higher price supports or subsidies for agricultural products grown in the area, or the postponement of a planned closing of a military base. Sometimes presidents are in a position to act directly; at other times they may be asked simply to support or oppose other measures that will come before Congress.

Yet as much as journalistic accounts like to emphasize the importance of such deals (after all, it makes for good reading), their use is surprisingly infrequent. Some presidents find this kind of bargaining quite distasteful. As Jimmy Carter noted: "Horse-trading and compromising and so forth have always been very difficult for me to do. I just don't feel at ease with it, and it is a very rare occasion when any member of Congress or anyone else even brings up a subject that could be interpreted by the most severe cynic as a horse-trade."[17] Even presidents who are less squeamish about bargaining for votes, however, must be quite cautious. An aide to President Lyndon Johnson explained why: "If it ever got around the Hill that a President was trading patronage for votes, then everyone would want to trade and all other efforts at persuasion would automatically fail. Each member would tell his neighbor what he got for his votes and soon everyone would be holding out, refusing to decide until the President called."[18] Thus, presidential favor is usually bestowed in reward for a broad pattern of support, rather than for a single supportive vote, and most bargains are based on implicit, not explicit, understandings.

A far more frequent source of deals involves presidents' granting or withholding political favors, rather than governmental benefits. A popular president, for example, can be of immense help to a member of Congress from his own party running for re-election. The president can campaign for a representative and speak at a fundraiser, helping to fill the campaign's coffers. A president may even have something to offer to members of the opposition party, who may make their support for the president's policies contingent on a promise that the president will not actively campaign against them. In the spring of 1981, President Reagan took the initiative in suggesting this kind of arrangement when he let it be known that he would find it very difficult to campaign against any Democrat in 1982 who supported him on his key budget proposals. This appeal was directed specifically to conservative Democrats in the South, where Reagan was highly popular. Obviously, in all these kinds of political bargains, the more popular and successful a president is, the more political capital he has to work with.

Exercising the Veto

When all else fails, the president retains his power to block congressional action by the veto, perhaps the most powerful instrument the president possesses next to the position of commander-in-chief. The veto, of course, may be overridden by two-thirds of the House and Senate, but, as noted earlier, in the vast majority of cases presidential vetoes are upheld, and the threat of a veto alone can sometimes prevent Congress from acting.

The major limitation of the veto is not that it can be overridden, but that it operates negatively. The veto can be used to prevent Congress from acting, but not to make it act where the president would like to see initiatives taken. President Reagan, for example, could prevent Congress from taking action to raise income taxes by threatening a veto (in fact he challenged congressional Democrats to "make his day" by giving him the opportunity to veto a tax increase); but the veto power was of little use in winning support for the budget cuts he sought from Congress to reduce federal deficits.

Nevertheless, the importance of the veto cannot be underestimated. It became a far more frequently used weapon in the recent periods of "divided government," when Congress has been under the control of a different party than the president. Republican presidents used the veto to check the Democratic-controlled Congress, to thwart Democratic policy initiatives, and in some cases even to get their own way. Where Congress under the Democrats wanted action of some sort, such as in the areas of clean air legislation and civil rights laws, Presidents Reagan and George H. Bush were able to tell Congress that it had to meet some of the presidents' own terms or have no bill at all. President Clinton masterfully employed the same tactic against the Republicans in 1995, vetoing the budget bill and forcing the Republicans to agree to some of his legislative priorities.

The president's power was momentarily enhanced when Congress enacted what was called the "line item veto" in 1996. This measure enabled the president to cut out certain tax and spending portions of a bill and veto them, while allowing the rest of the bill to become law. Presidents since Ulysses S. Grant had supported the idea, arguing that it would permit them to trim unnecessary items from an otherwise acceptable bill. Many hoped that it would be used to remove pork or other wasteful appropriations proposed by Congress. President Clinton made use of this provision in 1997, but the Supreme Court found it to be unconstitutional the following year on the grounds that the Constitution only permits the president to sign a bill or veto it in its entirety.

Instruments of Institutional Conflict: The Congress

As formidable as the president's resources are, they have not created a permanent imbalance in the system of separation of powers. Far from it. Congress, after all, has its own resources to draw upon in a conflict with the executive. The most important of these are formal lawmaking authority, congressional staff, the midterm mandate, investigations of the executive branch, the Senate's authority over confirmations of presidential appointments, the congressional budget process, the legislative veto, and the impeachment power.

Formal Lawmaking Authority

Congress possesses the formal authority to pass legislation for the national government. Yet as obvious as this simple fact is, its full implications are sometimes overlooked. The American people often seem to hold the president to account for the successes and failures of the governmental system, even though the president can do little, especially in the domestic arena, without positive legislation. A Congress reluctant to amend or revoke old laws and to pass new ones can thwart the best efforts of an activist president. To create (or abolish) social programs, to set agricultural price supports, to promote (or retard) the civil rights of American citizens, to increase (or diminish) the number of people in the armed forces, to build (or cancel) a weapons system, and to raise (or lower) taxes are all powers that require legislation and thus pass under the purview of the Congress. A president may recommend policies in these areas and may influence how congressional statutes are interpreted and carried out, but Congress retains the decisive authority.

Nor has Congress hesitated to wield that authority in an active way, even in periods of supposed presidential dominance. Congress itself is very often the source or originator of policy. A close study of ninety major laws enacted from 1880 to 1945 found that presidents could take most of the credit for influencing final passage of 20 percent of the laws, Congress 40 percent, joint presidential-congressional efforts 30 percent, and external pressure groups 10 percent. In many cases bills were originally introduced without presidential backing, where they sometimes languished for years, only to be adopted later by presidents who revived them and pushed them through Congress.[19] Similar studies since that time have shown that, while the presidency has clearly gained in importance as the agenda-setter, Congress continues to take important policy initiatives, with or without presidential backing, in science, consumer and environmental protection, antipoverty programs, transportation, civil rights, labor policy, taxation, and even foreign affairs.[20]

There are several ways in which Congress can take the initiative. In some cases, Congress may see a need for legislation, draft a bill, hold hearings and mark-up sessions, and enact a law, even over presidential opposition. The Taft-Hartley Act of 1947, passed by a Republican-controlled Congress over President Truman's veto, is an important example of such start-to-finish legislation. A more recent case of start-to-finish congressional initiative is the Water Quality Act of 1987, which provided $20 billion in grants to state and local governments for water treatment plants. Though President Reagan had opposed the bill from the outset as a "budget buster" and had killed the legislation through a pocket veto in 1986, Congress repassed the bill and overrode a second presidential veto in 1987.

In other cases, Congress may lay the groundwork for legislation, after which the president may adopt the initiative. The basic outlines of the comprehensive tax reform legislation proposed by President Reagan in 1985 were based upon proposals developed earlier by Senator Bill Bradley, Representative Jack Kemp, and others. Finally, Congress sometimes takes the policy initiative indirectly, by spurring the executive into action. After the successful launching of the Soviet satellite Sputnik in 1957, for instance, Congress examined American space and defense policy and threatened to develop its own program for space exploration. The Eisenhower administration took the hint and came up with an alternative program. Congress may also formally require the president to initiate new legislation, as it did in 1988 when it asked President George H. Bush to develop and submit to Congress a national drug control strategy.

No one today questions the importance of the executive branch in initiating policy, but Congress plays a considerable and often innovative part in the process. Its decentralized structure undoubtedly enhances its ability to develop the most diverse and complex legislation. Subcommittee assignments permit members of Congress to specialize and to acquire expertise rivaling that of executive branch officials. Those who suggest that the "president proposes and Congress disposes" have underrated Congress as the country's supreme lawmaking power.

One final way in which Congress may use its formal lawmaking power to control the executive is by enacting provisions into law which require the president to submit reports to Congress or which place very narrow restrictions on how appropriated funds may be used. By law, Congress now requires the president to submit detailed reports in a variety of areas, including both foreign and domestic policy activities. In recent years Congress has also enacted an increased number of specific, detailed restrictions on actions of the president or other executive branch officials in legislation providing for the expenditure of federal funds. Among the most controversial restrictions of this type was the 1984 Boland Amendment, named for its sponsor, Massachusetts Democratic Representative Edward Boland. This legislation restricted the actions of the president by prohibiting the use of any funds provided to the Defense Department, Central Intelligence Agency, or other intelligence agencies for providing either direct or indirect support to the *contra* rebels in Nicaragua, who the Reagan Administration wanted to support. The desire of the Reagan administration to keep the *contra* forces in the field in the face of this prohibition led to some of the actions involved in the Iran-Contra affair. Other restrictions on the executive inserted by Congress in spending legislation have dealt with relatively minor administrative details such as the specific staffing levels and locations of executive agencies.

For proponents of congressional power, these restrictions and reporting requirements have been defended as legitimate extensions of Congress's formal lawmaking power; others have decried these provisions as "micromanagment" that denies the president and other executive officials the discretion that is necessary to perform executive functions effectively.

The Congressional Budget Process

Along with the formal lawmaking power, a key source of congressional influence over the governing process is the power of the purse. The Constitution provides that "Congress shall have power to lay and collect taxes, duties, and excises, [and] to pay the debts" of the United States, and it further stipulates that "No money shall be drawn from the Treasury, but in consequence of appropriations made by law." (Article I, sections 8 and 9) Unlike most other nations in which legislatures have formal control over money decisions, but real control resides in the executive, Congress has jealously guarded its power over taxing and spending. Although the modern presidency inevitably plays an important role in budget matters, Congress has actively sought in recent years to strengthen its capabilities in this area. These efforts have included major organizational changes as well as new procedures for making budgetary decisions. Among the procedural changes adopted during this period is a controversial budgeting mechanism that has become known as "Gramm-Rudman-Hollings."

Though the president has submitted an annual comprehensive budget proposal to Congress since the 1920s, as recently as the 1970s Congress had no mechanism for considering the budget as a whole. Instead, the president's budget proposal would be broken down into its component parts (proposals for new programs, proposals for funding for existing programs, and proposals for changes in tax policy) and referred to the relevant standing committees in each chamber. Each standing committee worked more or less independently of the others, and there existed no formal procedure for relating the parts to the whole. During the 1970s, growing budget deficits and conflicts between Congress and the Nixon administration over budget priorities led to the enactment of a major piece of reform legislation, the Budget and Impoundment Control Act of 1974.

This act established formal restrictions on the authority of the executive to defer or rescind expenditures approved by Congress, created the Congressional Budget Office (CBO) to provide Congress with its own budget agency, and reorganized the way in which money decisions are made. A standing Committee on the Budget was created in each house with responsibility for developing an annual budget resolution through which Congress would set budget policies for the upcoming year. The budget resolution establishes explicit levels for overall government spending, tax revenues, budget deficit or surplus, and overall federal debt. Also included in the 1974 Budget Act was a procedure called reconciliation, by which majorities in each house can order the standing committees to report out any legislation (such as spending cuts or tax increases) needed to stay within the figures adopted in the budget resolution. Thus, in theory at least, the new budget process created a centralizing mechanism (consisting of the Budget committees and the budget resolution/reconciliation procedure) to offset the difficulties of making coherent budgetary decisions within a highly decentralized committee system. The passage of this act was seen by many as an important step in reasserting the congressional power of the purse.

In practice, budgeting remains a task that strains the decision-making capabilities of Congress and that produces continual conflict between Congress and the president. With the emergence of large federal budget deficits during the 1980s, the congressional budget process became the focus of protracted and sometimes highly partisan debates over national priorities. The underlying pattern in budget politics from 1982 to 1997 remained one of political deadlock.

Attempts were made to find institutional mechanisms to break this budgetary deadlock. In 1985 three senators—Phil Gramm, Warren G. Rudman and Ernest Hollings—proposed a new budgetary law in which federal deficits would either be reduced annually to levels that would produce a balanced budget within five years, or else automatic spending cuts would be triggered through a process known as sequestration. The law passed over objections that it would create a "doomsday machine" which would slash federal domestic and defense spending, creating massive hardships. It did not, but neither did it realize its objective of a balanced budget.

At best, the law had mixed success. By the early 1990s it seemed that a balance budget was still well out of reach. It was for this reason that many supported a Balanced Budget Amendment to the Constitution, believing that an amendment might succeed where ordinary legislation has failed. At this point, however, it seems that a balanced budget may be possible without any such measures. The Republican Congress won President Clinton's acceptance of a balanced budget, and economic growth led to rapidly shrinking deficits in the late 1990s. But the recession that began shortly after 2000 and the September 11 attacks reversed this trend. Nevertheless, the preoccupation with the budget question as *the* issue of domestic politics has faded.

Whether the different budget procedures enacted since the 1970s have enhanced congressional influence in relationship to the executive on budget matters is unclear. At times the threat of automatic spending cuts seemed to strengthen the president's hand, at other times it has given leverage to the congressional leadership. What is clear, however, is that Congress remains determined to maintain its power of the purse. With the expertise of its own budget agency (CBO) and the potential centralizing capabilities of the new budget process, it remains well-equipped to engage the president in battles over issues of taxing and spending.

Congressional Staff

The 535 members of Congress could hardly hope to master their modern responsibilities and maintain a position of strength without some assistance. Consequently Congress now employs some 25,000 people in supportive staff roles. This number marks a tremendous increase since the 1960s and reflects a desire by many in Congress to be more assertive in dealing with the executive branch.

Control of information in Washington is a major source of power. The executive was able to dominate Congress in certain areas in earlier decades because of a lack of congressional expertise and thus the necessity by Congress of relying on information coming from the executive branch. Today, by contrast, congressional staffs supply a potential counterweight to executive branch information in almost every area. Usually the executive agencies still enjoy an advantage, but it is hardly as great as it once was. As noted, in the area of budgeting Congress now has the Congressional Budget Office (CBO) to prepare alternative budgets and economic forecasts to match those prepared by the Office of Management and Budget (OMB) in the executive branch. Similarly, in foreign affairs, the increase in the last decade in the number of foreign affairs and intelligence experts as staff assistants has allowed Congress to involve itself in details of foreign policy that formerly were beyond its reach.

In some cases a greater staff capacity allows members of Congress to assume more effectively their legislative role in a system of separation of powers. But another possibility is that staffs have grown too large and have created an artificial incentive for legislators to challenge the executive. Although the original impetus for increasing the size of the staffs came from members of Congress, once in place staff assistants seeking to establish their own reputations generate more work and encourage members to become more active in different policy areas. Some critics have complained that the size of staffs has led to a situation in which members of Congress are merely overseeing a decision-making process that they no longer fully control. Responding in part to this view, the Republicans upon assuming the majority in Congress in 1994 cut back considerably on the size of committee staffs in the House without any noticeable loss of effectiveness.

Midterm Mandate

Another important source of congressional power is the fact that Congress, as a result of the midterm election, possesses a partial mandate of its own which congressional leaders can use to justify opposition to the presidency. This power is enhanced by the fact that the president's party almost always loses seats in Congress in the midterm election (an occurrence in every midterm House election since 1934). Thus, for half of the time in American politics, it is Congress, not the president, that can claim to have taken the latest "sounding" of the American people.

The most striking recent example of the mid-term mandate came in 1994, when the Republicans captured majorities in both chambers. Having campaigned to an unusual degree on a national platform, the Republicans claimed a strong mandate and proceeded to try to set the national agenda from the Congress, asking the President to follow. President Clinton did in fact step to the background for much of 1995, although he returned with great visibility in 1996 to block Republican measures that he sensed had gone well beyond their earlier mandate.

Investigations

One of the most important powers of Congress is the power to conduct formal investigations into the operation of the executive branch. This power, while not specifically mentioned in the Constitution, has been accepted as a logical extension of the prerogatives of the legislative body. Congress holds investigations for many different purposes: to acquire information, to seek evidence of illegality or wrongdoing in executive departments or agencies, to discover whether government officials have undermined the original intention of congressional statutes, to determine whether problems exist within the functioning of the executive branch which should be made public, and sometimes (though this reason is never officially avowed) to harass or embarrass the administration for partisan reasons.

Congressional investigations are often more than internal affairs for the edification of members of Congress. They can be a way for members to highlight an issue or a concern before the American people. Highly publicized investigations represent efforts to influence public opinion, very often to check the executive branch and sometimes to weaken the administration's political standing. One of the most controversial congressional investigations in the past half-century was the series of hearings conducted by Senator Joseph McCarthy in the early 1950s into allegations that many Communist sympathizers had infiltrated important positions within the State Department. McCarthy used the hearings to appeal to widespread public fears of a communist menace in America. His highhanded tactics—misuse of evidence, guilt by association, innuendo—constituted an abuse of the congressional investigatory power, although few initially were willing to challenge him.

Probably the most famous congressional investigation in American history was conducted in 1973 by a Senate select committee chaired by Sam Ervin, which considered allegations of wrongdoing by the Nixon administration arising out of the Watergate affair. The revelations that came to light before Ervin's committee, followed daily by the American public on television, led to impeachment proceedings against President Nixon in the House of Representatives and ultimately, before a trial was held in the Senate, to Nixon's resignation from the presidency.

In more recent times, a joint House-Senate select committee inquired into the Reagan administration's secret sale of arms to Iran and diversion of funds to the anti-communist *contras* in Nicaragua (the so-called Iran-Contra affair). The investigation captured the attention of the nation for months in 1987, during which time President Reagan lost not only a great deal of personal popularity, but also for a time the capacity to shape events. In 1997, the hearings of the Senate Government Affairs Committee chaired by Senator Fred Thompson produced some startling revelations of campaign finance abuses by the Democratic party during the 1996 presidential campaign. Congressional investigations can have more than just symbolic effects. When effectively used, they provide a formidable weapon for promoting the power of Congress at the expense of the executive.

Confirmations

One of the most important checks and balances set forth explicitly in the Constitution is the Senate's veto power over high-level presidential appointments. Nominations to the cabinet and other important executive positions, and appointments of ambassadors must be approved by a majority of the Senate. So too must all members of the federal judiciary.

Traditionally, the Senate has granted chief executives substantial leeway in making appointments to the executive branch on the theory that administrative officials are most directly serving the president. Still, the Senate is willing on occasion to reject presidential nominees, and in doing so it sets certain standards it may have in mind for future appointments as well. In the recent period of divided government, the Senate has also appeared slightly more willing to delay or even reject presidential nominations, as occurred during the presidencies of George H. Bush, Bill Clinton, and George W. Bush. These rejected nominations involved political differences between the two parties, although in all instances the Senate majority has raised substantial questions about the candidate's personal qualifications or fitness for the job.

The Senate has long accorded somewhat less deference to the president in the case of Supreme Court nominations, and these appointments have grown even more contentious during recent periods when the presidency and Senate have been in the hands of different parties. Richard Nixon charged that the Democratic Senate's refusal to confirm his nomination of Clement Haynesworth to the Supreme Court was the result of the anti-southern and liberal biases of his political opponents, even though the ostensible reason given by most who opposed him was a breach of judicial ethics. A more striking case occurred in 1987, with the Senate's rejection of President Reagan's nomination of Robert Bork. As a distinguished legal scholar and former solicitor general and appeals court judge, Bork could not be opposed on the grounds of a lack of qualification. The Senate rejected him because of the majority's opposition to his legal philosophy. This rejection opened the nomination process to a much more overtly political atmosphere, which was repeated in the confirmation hearings of Judge Clarence Thomas in 1991, and, more recently, some of George W. Bush's nominees to federal courts of appeals and district courts.

For appointments to the federal district courts and local United States attorneys, the usual order of nomination by the president and confirmation by the Senate is often modified in practice. The reason is the norm known as "senatorial courtesy," according to which members of the Senate will not confirm the nomination of anyone opposed by a senator of the president's party in the state in which the nominee would serve. Presidents thus often will informally request from senators the names of acceptable candidates at the very beginning of the appointment process. By selecting one of these, the president in effect "confirms" the person "nominated" by the senator.

Legislative Veto

One device Congress has employed to maintain its influence over decisions made by the executive branch is the "legislative veto." In the typical case, a statute authorizes the president (or an executive agency) to undertake certain kinds of actions, but reserves for Congress (by vote of a majority in one or both houses or occasionally by a standing committee) the right to overturn the president's (or the agency's) actions within a specified period of time. Presidential actions that were subject to this kind of control included reorganization of the executive branch, actions to defer the spending of appropriated funds, and the sale of weapons to foreign nations.

The increased use of the legislative veto during the 1970s and early 1980s was strongly opposed by Presidents Ford, Carter, and Reagan on both policy and Constitutional grounds. President Carter, for example, complained that "the legislative veto injects the Congress into the details of administrating substantive programs and laws [and] infringes on the Executive's constitutional duty to faithfully execute the laws."[21] Congress maintained that the veto was the only effective way to control the vast delegations of authority it made to the executive branch. After repeated efforts by opponents of the legislative veto to have the courts adjudicate its Constitutionality, the Supreme Court in 1983 finally decided that many legislative veto provisions violate the explicit requirement in the Constitution that legislative powers be exercised through action by both houses of Congress and presentation to the president for signature or veto (*Immi-*

gration and Naturalization Service v. Chadha, 1983).

Many legislative veto provisions were voided by this decision, but something like the legislative veto is still alive and well with which Congress exercises control over the executive. A number of statutes enacted since the *Chadha* decision, for example, simply require that executive branch officials notify congressional committees before taking certain types of actions. Because administrators will usually be hesitant to incur the wrath of the standing committees that oversee their budgets and programs, committee disapproval has much the same inhibiting effect as a formal legislative veto. Other statutes have required that certain presidential actions must be approved within a specified period of time by passage of a joint resolution. Such a statute satisfies the Constitutional requirement that congressional power be exercised through the normal legislative process (joint resolutions must be passed by both houses and submitted to the president for his signature), yet because majorities in both houses must approve the resolution, the practical effect is again to allow either house a veto over the president's action.

Impeachment

As important as all these resources are to Congress for upholding its place in the American system of separation of powers, they pale in comparison with the power of impeachment. Impeachment and removal of a president from office is the ultimate check available to the legislative branch on an aggrandizing chief executive. Once viewed by most Americans as a weapon too severe to be frequently employed, impeachment in recent years has moved from the unthinkable to the thinkable.

Under the Constitution, a president, a vice president, a high-level executive branch official, or a federal judge may be removed from office if accused, or "impeached," by a simple majority of the House and then convicted by two thirds of the Senate of "treason, bribery, or other high crimes and misdemeanors." In the case of a president's impeachment, the Chief Justice of the Supreme Court presides over the trial of the president in the Senate. This provision brings the judicial branch into the proceedings and adds to the weight of any verdict.

Prior to 1974, Andrew Johnson was the only president seriously involved in an impeachment proceeding. Johnson, who acceded to the presidency after Abraham Lincoln's death in 1865, was bitterly opposed by large majorities in both branches of Congress for his moderate Reconstruction policies. Radical Republicans in Congress finally pushed for removing the president on the grounds that Johnson violated the Tenure of Office Act (which he did, in part, in an attempt to have the Supreme Court test the act's constitutionality). Johnson was impeached by the House, but survived conviction in the Senate by only one vote. The failure of this effort, combined with the judgment of later generations that Congress had dangerously abused its authority in 1866, made subsequent impeachment efforts less likely. By the middle of the twentieth century, many Constitutional scholars considered the impeachment provisions a dead letter: too drastic a penalty to contribute to the subtle dynamics of the separation of powers.

The presidency of Richard Nixon changed this assessment. Revelations that President Nixon's subordinates had helped to plan a break-in at the Democratic party's national headquarters in the Watergate office building in June 1972, and that others obstructed the FBI investigation into the case, led in 1974 to the initiation of formal impeachment hearings before the Judiciary Committee of the House of Representatives. After several months of deliberation, the committee voted out three articles of impeachment. Before the matter was taken up by the full House, however, the Supreme Court ruled unanimously in *United States v. Nixon* that the President had to turn over to the special prosecutor tape recordings of certain conversations between Nixon and his top aides. Nixon, who had repeatedly denied any involvement in the break-in or its cover-up, had been withholding these tapes on grounds of executive privilege. These tapes contained the clearest evidence that Nixon had been involved in the cover-up, and the little support he still had in Congress rapidly dissolved. Bowing to the inevitable, Nixon resigned from office in August 1974 before the impeachment process could be completed.

Watergate transformed Americans' perception of impeachment and the office of the presidency. In 1974, Congress and the public still regarded both institutions with a good deal of reverence. Legislators were clearly uncomfortable assuming the power to impeach—even when confronted with direct evidence of Nixon's transgressions—and many responsible legislators agonized publicly over whether to impeach a sitting president for criminal wrongdoing. At the same time, however, Watergate planted the seeds for future assaults on the presidency. Public distrust of the president in 1974 heightened just as journalists were rethinking how they went about reporting on the White House. The investigative reporting of *Washington Post* reporters Carl Bernstein and Bob Woodward on the Watergate crisis was a watershed, forever altering the relationship between the presidency, the public, and the press. After Watergate, the press and the presidency assumed a much more adversarial relationship, with the press seeking information to confirm the public's distrust and disillusionment with their elected leader. Subsequent administrations frequently became mired in scandal. Jimmy Carter suffered politically from the investigations of aides Bert Lance and Hamilton Jordan, and Ronald Reagan spent much of his second term defending his administration against charges of illegalities stemming from the congressional investigation of the Iran-Contra affair.

The scandal for which Bill Clinton was ultimately impeached was not the first to arise in his administration. Clinton's first term was marked by a number of Watergate facsimiles: Travelgate, involving the questionable firings of White House travel office personnel; Filegate, alleging White House mishandling of classified FBI files; and especially Whitewater, concerning a shady land deal from the Clintons' Arkansas days. The most serious allegations against Clinton surfaced on January 21, 1998, and centered on his potentially criminal conduct just a few days earlier in a legal case then proceeding against him. On January 17, Clinton had been deposed in the civil suit of Paula Corbin Jones, an Arkansas woman who claimed that the President had sexually assaulted her years earlier in an Arkansas hotel room. In that deposition, Clinton denied having had sexual relations with yet another woman, Monica Lewinsky, when she had served as a White House intern in 1995 and 1996. When it was revealed on January 21 that a White House employee, Linda Tripp, had recorded telephone conversations with Lewinsky contradicting the President's account, it invited speculation that the President had lied in the Jones deposition and may have encouraged others, including Lewinsky and presidential secretary Betty Currie, to lie as well.

Clinton forcefully denied the allegations, and encouraged his Cabinet and staff to support him. When physical evidence corroborating Tripp's tapes emerged the following summer, Clinton relented somewhat, admitting on August 17 to an "inappropriate relationship" with Lewinsky. He still insisted on his technical innocence, however, testifying before a grand jury on August 17 that his responses in the January 17 Jones deposition had been based on a novel interpretation of the phrase "sexual relations." This legal parsing prompted Independent Counsel Kenneth W. Starr to deliver to the House on September 9 a report outlining in embarrassing detail the exact nature of Clinton and Lewinsky's relationship. The report persuaded the Republican majority in the House that Clinton had lied in his grand jury testimony of August 17, prompting them on December 19 to approve two articles of impeachment, the first charging him with giving "perjurious, false and misleading testimony to a federal grand jury," and the second charging him with obstruction of justice.

Clinton was acquitted by the Senate, in a vote cast, once again, largely along party lines. His success was due to the strong support of fellow Democrats, together with the high levels of public approval he enjoyed throughout the scandal. In frequent polls, the public expressed their distaste for removing a president from office for possible crimes committed while trying to conceal an extramarital affair. Although the public ultimately believed Clinton should not be removed from office for his personal indiscretions, it remains that the press today is far more prone to pry into and report on such matters, and many in the public are eager to hear about them. Previous presidential indiscretions, most notably the affairs of Franklin D. Roosevelt and

John F. Kennedy, had been deemed material inappropriate for the press. Watergate changed matters. Presidential gaffes and indiscretions are now the public's business, serving as legitimate grounds for criticism and making impeachment on these grounds a viable possibility.

It is interesting that impeachment was employed only a few years after many scholars had argued that the presidency had achieved "imperial" dimensions under Nixon. In the short span of twenty-five years, Congress twice demonstrated its willingness to force a president from office for violating his Constitutional obligations to "take care that the laws are faithfully executed" and to "preserve, protect, and defend the Constitution." What will this reassertion of the impeachment power mean for the future? It is difficult to say. The partisan nature of Clinton's impeachment, culminating in his acquittal by the Senate, will likely discourage future legislators from resorting to impeachment too quickly, much as Andrew Johnson's trial discouraged future impeachment efforts for well over a century. But Americans will probably not have to wait another century for the next presidential impeachment. Although impeaching a president may prove very difficult in the near future, the standard has most likely been lowered. Opposing parties in Congress may now be more inclined to impeach sitting presidents when plausible justifications can be found, even when they lack the two-thirds majority in the Senate necessary to remove a president from office. If used too readily, however, impeachment's symbolic importance as a blight on a president's record may decline.

Bases for Cooperation

It is common in accounts of the American separation-of-powers system to emphasize the ongoing conflict between the legislative and executive branches of government. This emphasis is hardly surprising, since the very idea of allowing for a degree of disharmony between these two fundamental governing institutions is one of the most unusual—and even incomprehensible—features of American government when viewed by those accustomed to a parliamentary system. Yet it would be a mistake to conclude that just because the system allows for conflict it was intended to promote stalemate. The founders, while they were willing to pay some price in terms of efficient policymaking to secure liberty, did not want to prevent government from addressing problems within its purview or block needed governmental action. In the period before the adoption of the Constitution, they had seen enough of a government characterized by "tedious delays, continual negotiation and intrigue [and] contemptible compromises of the public good." (*Federalist* 22)

For government to be able to act effectively and to pursue any long-term general policy, some degree of cooperation between the president and Congress is necessary. Let us turn now to some of the forces that encourage harmony, some of which are inherent in the Constitutional system and others which have developed as institutional arrangements within the Constitutional framework to help secure cooperation.

Crisis

Perhaps the most powerful, if shortest-lived, stimulus for interbranch cooperation is the existence of a national crisis. Whenever there is the perception that there is a genuine emergency situation, Congress and the presidency usually seem to set aside their differences and work together, perhaps out of mutual fear of the dire consequences of inaction. Thus, the economic collapse of the 1930s did more than any other single factor to foster a close cooperation between the presidency and Congress in Franklin Roosevelt's first term. The bombing of Pearl Harbor in 1941 had the same effect in the military and foreign policy areas in Roosevelt's third term.

Some more recent examples demonstrate this same tendency. In 1981, President Reagan told the American people, "We're in the worst economic mess since the Great Depression." Opinion surveys indicated clearly that Americans felt they were in the midst of such a crisis and that a genuine emergency situation was at hand. This sense was clearly felt by Congress. According to Democratic Speaker Thomas "Tip" O'Neill, it became impossible under these circumstances not to act: "I was afraid the voters would repudi-

ate the Democrats if we didn't give the President a chance to pass his program. After all, the nation was still in an economic crisis and the people wanted immediate action."[22]

A final example of the effects of a crisis situation on executive-legislative cooperation is the overwhelming consensus that immediately developed following the September 11 attacks in New York and Washington in 2001. Congress immediately rallied behind George W. Bush and, within days of the attacks, passed the Patriot Act, which provided the President with increased law enforcement capabilities to carry out the War Against Terrorism. In addition, Congress quickly appropriated money for the war effort and offered its support for the use of U.S. troops in Afghanistan. Times of crisis, however, do not always help presidents in every area, as this case displays. Though Congress was fully supportive of the War Against Terrorism, President Bush still faced stiff opposition in the areas of domestic policy and judicial confirmations. Democrat Tom Daschle, the Senate Majority Leader, captured this distinction when he said:

> [In] the battle against terrorism, President Bush and his national security team are doing a superb job. They've united our nation, and virtually the entire world, in defense of freedom and civilization. They deserve our support, and our praise....[But] when it comes to our second battle, our economic battle, I think most Americans would probably agree that the news hasn't been so good lately....Unfortunately, last spring, Republicans chose exactly the wrong solution. They made a huge tax cut their number one priority—ahead of everything else—and discarded the framework of fiscal responsibility.... There are those who say the reason the surplus deteriorated so quickly is the attacks on America and the war against terrorism. Clearly, September 11th was a major blow to our economy....But September 11th and the war aren't the only reasons the surplus is nearly gone. They're not even the biggest reasons. The biggest reason is the tax cut.

Common Purpose

Amidst all the political squabbles, institutional jealousies, and the clashes of interest and perspective, those who serve in the two political branches often share a genuine desire to work together to achieve common goals, such as a sound national defense, a healthy economy, and the protection of the rights and liberties of the American citizenry. Agreement on certain basic ends may cut across partisan as well as institutional barriers and thereby foster cooperative efforts among members of both parties and both branches. This is not to say that conflict will be absent from the political arena (is it ever?), but only to point out that conflict need not necessarily divide the institutions. Very often, the president and a majority of Congress (even when it may be in the hands of the opposite party) find grounds for common action because they agree on what should be done and what is best for the nation. In his first year of office, for example, President George H. Bush and members of Congress agreed on the need for major new legislation to deal with the problems of the environment and drug abuse.

In this respect, the sense of common purpose is like the reaction to a national crisis: the members of the two branches work together to meet a recognized national need. It is different, however, in that it is usually less forceful, less urgent, and of a longer duration than the reaction to a crisis. Although this force for cooperation is often ignored in accounts of presidential-congressional interaction, which often emphasize more self-interested motives, its consequences are quite real.

Political Party

One political institution that can make a significant contribution to bridging the gap between the presidency and Congress is the political party, which has had a very real, although—in comparison to the nineteenth century—a declining, influence on securing cooperation between the two political branches. The president, after all, is the effective leader of one of the two major parties, and the parties play an important role in organizing the House and the Senate. The leaders of the president's party in Congress tend to be his allies and to work closely with the president to promote his programs. Thus the party gives the president a base of support in Congress (although the opposition party likewise provides a base of opposition). The formula some have

used to express the role of parties captures at least a measure of the truth: what the Constitution separates, parties join.

It is important to keep in mind the limitations as well as the usefulness of parties in "joining" these two branches. Members of Congress consider their party affiliation to be only one of the legitimate constraints acting on them, to be weighed against the interests of their constituencies and their own personal judgments of what is in the national interest. Thus it is almost always the case that some party members will break with the president, even on key issues, and there are more than a few paradoxical cases in which presidents have actually enjoyed more support from the opposition party than their own. Another difficulty the party has in bridging the gap between the presidency and Congress occurs when a different party controls the White House and one or both houses of Congress. This situation of divided government was once the exception in American politics. From the time of President McKinley through President Truman (1896–1952), the same party controlled the presidency and both houses of Congress 86 percent of the time (in 48 out of the 56 years) and the presidency and at least one house 93 percent of the time (52 out of 56 years). From 1952 through 2002 the president's party controlled both houses of Congress only 34 percent of the time (17 out of 50 years) and at least one house just 48 percent of the time (24 out of 50 years).

Divided government does not mean that parties are of no help in promoting cooperation between the two branches. Obviously a president is helped by a strong and loyal following from his own party. A frequent pattern is for the president to rely on his party to form the core of a potential majority and then to go shopping among members of the other party for the requisite votes needed. Nevertheless, the existence of divided government in our system shows the importance not only of parties being fairly strong, but also of their not being too strong. If party members voted with their party consistently and acted as a strictly organized phalanx, the opposition party could always defeat the president and his party. The situation of divided government would then make American government entirely unworkable. The president, especially in an era of divided government, must be able to forge majorities across party lines and learn to work with the leaders of the opposition party. So too must the leaders of Congress learn to work with the president. The incentives here are complicated, but neither the president nor the majority party in Congress gains from trying all the time to block and frustrate the initiatives of the other. When nothing gets accomplished, both the president and the majority party in Congress can risk the electorate's disapproval. The pattern under divided government is thus a mix of confrontation and cooperation.

Mandates and the Coattail Effect

Almost every president who is elected is apt to *claim* a mandate for his policy program. This claim, which is often politely ignored by Congress, carries greater weight when the presidential candidate has run as a party leader on a clear national party program, which many members of his own party have also made an important part of their own campaigns. If the president's party receives a majority, or makes a significant gain in the number of seats it holds, the president will use the argument of a mandate in attempting to secure passage of elements of his program. Such was the case for Lyndon Johnson after the 1964 election and Ronald Reagan after the 1980 election.

A mandate, then, is not a legal concept but a rough political calculation. Its existence is judged in part by the electoral phenomenon known by the colorful name of "the coattail effect." This term refers to the circumstance in which a popular presidential candidate has helped to pull members of his own party into office on his "coattails." The effect works as follows: if a presidential candidate generates enthusiasm, some voters are more likely to vote for congressional candidates running under the president's party, and other voters—who probably would have otherwise stayed home—also come out to vote for the president and for candidates for Congress from the same party as the president. Thus a number of candidates have presumably been elected in no small part because of the presidential candidate and his program. In addition to any debts of gratitude

they may feel, these members of Congress are likely to think that their chances for re-election are tied to the president's record of accomplishment, and they may therefore be especially disposed to cooperate with him.

In the past few decades, the diminished tendency of voters to vote a "straight ticket" has weakened the coattail effect. Still it is far from being negligible, and in some elections—such as 1980—many members of Congress clearly perceived the effect to be substantial. Reagan's victory in 1980 was accompanied by dramatic Republican advances in Congress: twenty-seven Republican challengers ousted Democratic incumbents from the House, and nine Republican challengers did the same in the Senate. The existence and strength of the coattail effect (like mandates) are always, of course, going to be subject to interpretation, for the reasons why people vote as they do are never fully known. But whatever the true explanation, what matters most is whether many members of Congress *think* that they owe their election at least in part to the president. Perception in this case may be more important than reality.

Conclusion

The sources of conflict between Congress and the presidency are powerful and deep. These differences were intentionally built into the system by the founders, and their design has effectively achieved its principal purpose: to keep either branch from concentrating all powers within its hands and thereby to protect the liberty of the American people. It has been rare in American history that one branch of government has been truly dominant. The only cases might be Congress just after the Civil War and the presidency during Franklin Roosevelt's first term.

Even when one branch has gained some degree of ascendancy for a certain period of time, it has been unable to sustain it for very long. On the contrary, a temporary concentration of power in the hands of one institution has often been followed by a reaction from the other branch. Historically, there has been a pendulum-like pattern, where power swings back and forth between the branches. Whenever one seems to overstep its proper Constitutional bounds, the other employs a variety of weapons to resist these excesses. This self-correcting process promotes both adherence to the Constitutional framework and stability in the governmental system.

Critics of the system of separation of powers complain that the conflict between the two branches does more harm than good: that it makes coherent policymaking almost impossible, that it drastically slows down the response of government to pressing national problems, that it hinders public accountability, and that it results finally in a "stalemate" between the branches of government. Though few serious critics today argue that a full-blown parliamentary system is feasible or desirable in the United States, some have proposed less drastic reforms inspired by parliamentary regimes that would encourage greater legislative-executive cooperation. These proposals include: a team ticket in which the presidential candidate and candidates for Congress from the same party would be formally linked on the ballot; changing the terms of office for representatives and senators to eliminate the midterm election (representatives could, for example, serve four years and senators eight); allowing special elections to be called at the request of either the president or Congress in cases where government has become deadlocked or lost effectiveness; and allowing members of Congress to serve in the executive branch.[23]

Whether such structural reforms, designed to introduce a more efficient majoritarian system, would really improve the character of the government is doubtful. Often conflicts and deadlock reflect divisions and uncertainty in society. In that case, perhaps prolonged discussion and debate are better than rushing forward to "do something." The system of separation of powers encourages the building of consensus, the gradual working out of the "cool and deliberate sense of the community." The reformer must ask whether the increased efficiency and unity that might be obtained in a parliamentary-style system would be worth the loss of the tendency toward moderation and the capabilities for deliberation and representation of a wider variety of interests.

There are undoubtedly inconveniences connected with a separation-of-powers system, and even its strongest supporters would not deny that it carries significant costs. It is messy and disorganized. It often responds slowly to controversial problems and on occasion leads to a blurring of responsibility. Yet *every* system has certain inconveniences attached to its virtues. The question that Americans must ask is whether some amount of inefficiency in policymaking is not a worthwhile price to pay for maintaining the benefits of a separation-of-powers system.

Chapter 12 Notes

1. Lloyd N. Cutler, "To Form a Government," *Foreign Affairs*, Fall 1980, pp. 126–143.
2. Woodrow Wilson, *Congressional Government*. Reprinted in Ann G. Serow, W. Wayne Shannon and Everett Carl Ladd, eds., *The American Polity Reader* (New York: Norton, 1990), p. 137.
3. James Sundquist, "Needed: A Political Theory for the New Era of Coalition Government in the United States," *Political Science Quarterly* 103, Winter 1988, p. 629.
4. Doris Kearns, *Lyndon Johnson and the American Dream* (New York: Harper and Row, 1976), p. 226.
5. George C. Edwards III, *Presidential Influence in Congress* (San Francisco: Freeman, 1980), pp. 117–118.
6. Doris Kearns, *Lyndon Johnson*, pp. 223–224.
7. Doris Kearns, *Lyndon Johnson*, p. 223.
8. Thomas P. O'Neill, Jr., *Man of the House: The Life and Political Memoirs of Speaker Tip O'Neill* (New York: Random House, 1987), p. 345.
9. Harry McPherson, *A Political Education* (Boston: Little, Brown, 1972), p. 268.
10. Gary Schmitt, *Executive Agreements and Separation of Powers* (Ph.D. Dissertation, University of Chicago, 1980).
11. *Report of the Congressional Committees Investigating the Iran-Contra Affair with Supplemental, Minority and Additional Views.* House Report 100-433, Senate Report 100-216 (Washington: Government Printing Office, 1987).
12. Wilfred E. Binkley, *President and Congress* (New York: Vintage Books, 1962), p. 123.
13. Christopher J. Deering, "Congress, the President, and War Powers: The Perennial Debate," in James A. Thurber, ed., *Divided Democracy: Cooperation and Conflict Between the President and Congress* (Washington: Congressional Quarterly Press, 1991), p. 189.
14. Woodrow Wilson, *Constitutional Government in the United States* (New York: Columbia University Press, 1908), pp. 72, 73.
15. Woodrow Wilson, *Constitutional Government*, p. 69.
16. William J. Keefe, *Congress and the American People* (Englewood Cliffs, N.J.: Prentice-Hall, 1980), p. 111.

17. George Edwards, *Presidential Influence in Congress*, p. 175.
18. Doris Kearns, *Lyndon Johnson*, p. 236.
19. Lawrence H. Chamberlain, "The President, Congress, and Legislation," in Aaron Wildavsky, ed., *The Presidency* (Boston: Little, Brown, 1969), pp. 440–453.
20. Ronald C. Moe and Steven C. Teel, "Congress as Policy-Maker: A Necessary Reappraisal," *Political Science Quarterly*, September 1970, pp. 443–470; John R. Johannes, "Congress and the Initiation of Legislation," *Public Policy*, Spring 1972, pp. 281–309.
21. "Legislative Vetoes: Message to Congress, June 21, 1978." Administration of Jimmy Carter, *Public Papers of the Presidents of the United States: Jimmy Carter, 1978* (Washington, D.C.: Government Printing Office, 1979), Book 1, p. 1147.
22. Tip O'Neill, *Man of the House*, p. 344.
23. See James L. Sundquist, *Constitutional Reform and Effective Government* (Washington, D.C.: Brookings Institution, 1986), chapters 4–9.

13

The Judiciary

CHAPTER CONTENTS

The power of the Supreme Court is indeed great, but it does not extend to everything; it is not great enough to change the Constitution. . . ."[1] These words have a contemporary ring, for in recent years the federal judiciary has often been accused of reading its own policy preferences into the law. Yet the voice is that of Spencer Roane, chief justice of the Virginia Supreme Court, registering his indignation at the decision of *McCulloch v. Maryland* (1819), one of the early landmark cases of the United States Supreme Court.

As Roane's words suggest, controversy about the role of the courts in American politics is nothing new. Thomas Jefferson railed against the Supreme Court, warning that the nation was in danger of falling under a "judicial despotism." The Supreme Court hastened the Civil War with its decision in *Dred Scott v. Sanford* (1857), which struck down the Missouri Compromise and ruled, in effect, that black people could not be legal citizens of the United States. In the 1930s, the Supreme Court declared much of President Franklin Roosevelt's New Deal program unconstitutional, leading to his plan to "pack" the Court with new justices more favorable to his views. During the 1950s, the Supreme Court's decision in *Brown v. Board of Education* (1954) outlawing school segregation provoked widespread resistance in the South and served as a catalyst for the entire civil rights movement of the next decade. In the 1960s and 1970s, decisions outlawing prayer in the public schools, extending the rights of criminal defendants, requiring the reapportionment of state legislatures, granting women a right to abortion, and limiting the states' ability to combat obscenity placed the Supreme Court at the center of political controversy. In the past decade, congressional legislation or constitutional amendments have been introduced to overturn the Court's decisions on abortion, school prayer, busing, and burning of the American flag.

For better or worse, the courts have been deeply involved in political issues for most of American history. As Alexis de Tocqueville remarked in the 1830s, when the role of the courts was much more modest than today, "There is hardly a political question in the United States which does not sooner or later turn into a judicial question."[2] This was seen in the dramatic events surrounding the 2000 election when the Court had an opportunity to determine who would be the next president of the United States. When compared with the politics of other western democracies, the extraordinary power of the courts is surely the most distinctive feature of American politics. In some sixty nations, the law proclaims the power of judicial review, and in a few cases—India, Australia, Germany, and France—the judiciary will occasionally exercise it. The increasingly federalized European Union has sought to emulate some of the features of the United States federal court system, including the broad scope of its judicial review. But these institutions are not yet developed enough to wield such power with widespread public acceptance. But in no nation does the level of judicial involvement in key decisions approach that played by courts in the United States. Decisions in other democratic nations that would be considered entirely "political" and made by elected officials are routinely made or influenced in the United States by appointed judges.

Yet, while conflict over judicial decisions is nothing new, the courts' involvement in ordinary policymaking over the past quarter century has increased dramatically in both its scope and its character. According to the critics of this development, the courts have become virtually another legislature, intervening in a variety of policy areas that are primarily political in nature, such as welfare administration and environmental policy; and rather than merely deciding conflicts between litigants, the courts have used individual cases to announce broad policy decisions that require political authorities not just to desist from conduct deemed illegal or unconstitutional (which was the nature of most judicial remedies in the past), but to establish positive programs, like the busing of schoolchildren, to change existing circumstances. The courts have even devised some of these programs on their own, engaging in what looks very much like legislating and administering. This role for the courts, critics maintain, far exceeds anything the founders ever had in mind and has created a guardian institution that is remaking American society according to its own standards, undermining popular government in the process.[3]

This criticism of the judiciary, which has been a major theme of the Republican party over the past twenty years, is now beginning to influence the judicial system, as judges appointed by Republican Presidents Reagan and Bush have begun to alter court majorities. But not all commentators have shared these Presidents' objections to the expanded role of the judiciary. Some deny that the courts' decisions mark a radical departure from the past, contending instead that the courts are merely enforcing legal and Constitutional norms in new fields of governmental activity. As Congress and federal administrative agencies venture into new policy fields, creating additional legal requirements, they necessarily prompt litigation and thereby requiring more judicial involvement. Others acknowledge that the courts have taken on unprecedented responsibilities, but defend this development on the grounds that it increases government's responsiveness to certain public needs, especially those of underprivileged groups inadequately represented in the ordinary political process.[4]

This debate raises a fundamental controversy over the role of the courts in contemporary American politics and whether the courts' more involved or active posture in recent decades has been a positive or a negative development. These modern questions, however, cannot be intelligently discussed until we have first analyzed the nature of the judicial power, the organization and operation of the federal court system, and the special place of judicial review.

The Role of the Courts

"It is emphatically the province and duty of the judicial department," Chief Justice John Marshall proclaimed in *Marbury v. Madison,* "to say what the law is." The courts do this in the course of deciding disputes (cases) that require the interpretation and application of law. Federal law comes primarily from three sources: the United States Constitution, Congress (which passes federal statutes), and federal administrative agencies (which promulgate regulations giving further specificity to federal statutes and spelling out certain procedural rules that agencies must follow). In addition, our system of law also includes the state constitutions, state and local laws, and state and local administrative rulings; these too can be subjects for litigation in federal courts when they touch upon issues of federal law.

In deciding cases, the courts are involved in interpreting all types of law. But an important distinction must be drawn between judicial interpretation of statutes and regulations on the one hand and the Constitution on the other. In the case of statutes and regulations, court decisions—important as they may be—represent an attempt to define the intent of Congress or an administrative agency and to fill in the gaps in their laws or rules. If Congress or the administrative agency disagrees with a court interpretation, it can attempt to overturn it by passing another law or writing another regulation. By contrast, when the courts interpret the Constitution, they speak for the Constitution, which is the fundamental law of the land and which is therefore higher than any legislative enactment or administrative ruling. Since the other political agencies are bound to respect the Constitution, they are left with no ordinary recourse. This is the essence of the doctrine of judicial review.

The Meaning of Judicial Review

"Judicial review" is the power of courts to rule on whether government actions conflict with the Constitution and are therefore null and void.* Such actions include laws passed by Congress, regulations written by agencies, laws and regulations enacted by state or local authorities, or actions taken by any government official, from the president down to the local police officer. All courts theoretically possess the power of judicial review. In practice, however, when state courts

---

* Technically speaking, judicial review also refers to a court decision that sets aside any law that conflicts with another law that is of a higher authority, as when a state law or a state constitutional provision conflicts with a federal statute or treaty. Our focus on judicial review in this chapter will be exclusively on the interpretation of the United States Constitution.

BOX 13.1

A Glossary of Legal Terms

Affirm To uphold the decision of a lower court.

Amicus curiae brief "Friend of the court" brief. A brief submitted with Supreme Court permission by an interested group which is not a party in a case.

Appeal A petition to a higher court for review of a lower court decision.

Appellate jurisdiction The power of a court to hear appeals.

Brief A document prepared by legal counsel which presents legal arguments, facts, and other considerations which support his or her client's position in a case.

Certiorari "To make certain." A petition for Supreme Court review of a lower court decision, which the Court has complete discretion to grant or refuse.

Civil law The division of law dealing with the definition and enforcement of legal rights. These rights may result from either private action (for example, contracts between parties) or governmental action.

Conference The closed meeting of Supreme Court justices, in which they vote on whether to hear cases and both discuss and vote on cases in which they have heard oral argument.

Constitutional law The division of law dealing with the interpretation of the Constitution and with determining the validity of laws and official actions taken under its authority.

Criminal law The division of law dealing with crimes and punishments.

General-jurisdiction courts Courts authorized to hear cases involving all subjects within federal jurisdiction.

Jurisdiction The power of a court to hear a case. This power may be limited to specific geographical areas, subject matters, or persons.

Limited-jurisdiction courts Courts limited to hearing only cases involving certain specific subjects.

Magistrate A judicial officer authorized to hear minor cases and act for district court judges in certain court functions, such as setting bail.

Original jurisdiction The power of a court to hear and decide cases before their consideration by any other court.

Per curiam "By the court." An unsigned opinion issued by the court collectively.

Precedent A decision on a point of law which provides guidance for the decision of subsequent cases.

Reverse To overrule the decision of a lower court.

Stare decisis "Let the decision stand." The doctrine that principles of law enunciated in judicial decisions should not be overruled in subsequent decisions.

---

or lower federal courts pronounce an important statute unconstitutional, their rulings are invariably appealed and ultimately reach the Supreme Court. During the time an important case is under appeal, the ruling of a lower court generally holds only for the immediate case on which that court has decided. Everyone awaits a more definitive decision from the Supreme Court to resolve the issue for the whole nation.

The power of judicial review extends well beyond cases in which the courts actually hold certain actions unconstitutional. As in the case of the president's veto power, the power of judicial review "works" in part by anticipation. It is the "restraining power of its presence," as much as the frequency of its application, that makes judicial review so important, because legislators are aware that their decision making must take Constitutional considerations into account.[5]

The most dramatic instances of judicial review occur when courts review a federal statute passed by Congress or an action taken by the president, because in these cases the power of the judicial branch is posed against the will of institutions chosen by the entire nation. Consider two such examples. In 1989, the Supreme Court in *Texas v. Johnson* nullified a federal statute (as well as laws in 48 states) that forbade burning of the American flag on the grounds that flag burning was a form of speech protected under the First Amendment to the Constitution. Congress quickly passed another anti-flag burning act designed to meet the Court's objections, but it too was struck down. In 1973, President Nixon, citing the doctrine of "executive privilege," refused to divulge either to Congress or to the courts the contents of a series of tape recordings that included private discussions on the subject of the break-in at the Democratic National Committee Headquarters at the Watergate Hotel. Rejecting part of Nixon's argument, the Supreme Court in *United States v. Nixon* (1974) ruled that Nixon must surrender the tapes to a lower court for use in a criminal prosecution. This decision forced the disclosure of an incriminating discussion that ultimately led to Nixon's resignation.

The Supreme Court since 1790 has declared slightly more than 100 provisions of federal statutes unconstitutional (see Table 13.1)[6] (Reference is made to provisions of federal statutes, because in some cases only that part of the law said to violate the Constitution is voided, while the rest of the law is left to stand.) Table 13.1 must be considered with care, for the number of provisions declared unconstitutional in each historical period is not always a good indication of the importance of the Court's influence. The Court in the early nineteenth century was clearly reluctant to strike down federal statutes, but its ruling in *Dred Scott v. Sanford* (1857) has probably been the most consequential decision in American history. After the Civil War, the Court voided important civil rights legislation and declared the income tax to be unconstitutional. Most of the activity in striking down federal laws, statistically speaking, has come in this century. In the 1930s, the Court struck down much of Franklin Roosevelt's New Deal economic legislation. Since the 1950s, the Court has been active in a number of different areas, although many of the provisions it has declared unconstitutional have been relatively minor.

The Court's power of Constitutional interpretation involves not only deciding on the substance of governmental actions, but also helping to define the respective powers of the institutions of the national government. Although the Court has generally been reluctant to involve itself in the ordinary struggles between the president and Congress, it occasionally has stepped in to define the nature and boundaries of the executive, legislative, and judicial powers. In the aforementioned *United States v. Nixon,* the Court began to define the scope of the president's "executive privilege," while in *Immigration and Naturalization Service (INS) v. Chadha* (1983), the Court voided the legislative veto, a device that had been used since the 1930s to allocate authority between Congress and the executive branch.

Less dramatic, but equally important for understanding the power of the courts, is judicial review of state and local laws and of the activities of state and local officials (see Box 13.2). Under this application of judicial review, for example, the courts have acted to desegregate public schools, to provide a right of abortion, and to adjust the powers and behavior of police officers and prosecutors in conducting interrogations and searches for evidence. The Supreme Court and federal courts have been less hesitant to strike down state laws as unconstitutional, with the Supreme Court alone invalidating over 1,000 state laws and constitutional provisions and other federal courts voiding many times that number.

The most obvious explanation for the federal judiciary's more frequent invalidation of state and local laws is that there are more of them. Other factors, however, also play a role. First, the Constitutional basis for judicial review of state legislation is considerably clearer than for federal legislation, as the Constitution explicitly stipulates the supremacy of the Constitution, federal laws, and treaties over state constitutions and laws (Article VI). Second, the Court has accorded less deference to the Constitutional judgment of a local political majority than to that of a national political majority as expressed by a coequal branch of government. (Frequently,

TABLE 13.1
The Exercise of Judicial Review by the Supreme Court, 1789–1998

Year	Acts of Congress Overturned*	State Laws and Local Ordinances Overturned
1789–1800, Pre-Marshall	0	0
1801–1835, Marshall Court	1	18
1836–1864, Taney Court	1	21
1865–1873, Chase Court	10	33
1874–1888, Waite Court	9	7
1889–1910, Fuller Court	14	88
1910–1921, White Court	12	125
1921–1930, Taft Court	12	143
1930–1940, Hughes Court	14	83
1941–1946, Stone Court	2	32
1947–1952, Vinson Court	1	45
1953–1969, Warren Court	25	166
1969–1986, Burger Court	34	201
1986–(1998), Rehnquist Court	17	87

* In *Immigration and Naturalization Service v. Chada* (1983), the Supreme Court effectively ruled unconstitutional all legislative vetoes, which were contained in 212 statutes. *Chada* here is counted only as one act of Congress overturned.

Source: David O'Brien, *Storm Center* 4th ed. (New York: Norton, 2000), p.30.

however, the state laws struck down do have the support of national majorities, as evidenced by the fact that many or all states may have similar kinds of laws.) Finally, state legislatures are more likely than Congress to adopt unconstitutional legislation because of the far greater probability of factional majorities occurring at the state or local level.

Today the federal courts play a major role in policing state and local authorities. Since the 1920s the federal courts have dramatically widened their jurisdiction into areas of state action by "incorporating" most of the requirements of the Bill of Rights into the due process clause of the Fourteenth Amendment. Now, the Bill of Rights applies to all individuals in their relationship to all levels of government. (Before "incorporation," the Bill of Rights related to citizens only in their relationship to the federal government.) After the 1960s, court review of state activity expanded still further under a much

broader interpretation of the Fourteenth Amendment's requirement that states assure "equal protection of the laws." The consequence today is that federal courts regularly review in some form a large part of the legislation passed by the states.

Statutory Interpretation

Although judicial review may represent the most dramatic instance of judicial participation in governing, it is by no means the only way in which the courts exercise power. Typically, about two-thirds of Supreme Court cases—and less than 5 percent of lower federal court cases—involve Constitutional questions. The remaining cases generally involve the interpretation of federal statutes and federal administrative regulations. In expounding the meaning of the statutes, the courts often must resolve major policy disputes.

The need for judicial interpretation of statutes is inescapable in any legal system, for statutes are rarely "self-interpreting." In part, the necessity of interpretation stems from the difficulty inherent in attempting to control future events. As Justice Felix Frankfurter once noted: "The intrinsic difficulties of language and the emergence after enactment of situations not anticipated by the most gifted legislative imagination reveal doubts and ambiguities in statues that compel judicial construction."[7] Frequently the need for interpretation results from intentional ambiguity by the drafters of statutes. Since it is easier to agree on broad goals (for example, equality of educational opportunity) than on specific means of achieving those goals, members of Congress who are eager to secure passage of legislation may often word statutes vaguely in order to secure maximum support. In doing so, legislators open the door not only to broad discretion on the part of the bureaucrats who administer the law but also to the courts, since broad and vague statutes are almost certain to be challenged by citizens who are unhappy with administrative decisions.

The Court may also take some liberty in interpreting the "spirit" behind a statute, as in the controversial case of *United Steelworkers of America v. Weber* (1979). Title VII of the 1964 Civil Rights Act prohibited job discrimination on the basis of "race, color, religion, sex, or national origin." The Kaiser Aluminum and Chemical Corporation and the United Steelworkers union devised a plan for a Louisiana factory which reserved one half of the positions in an on-the-job training program for blacks. Brian Weber, a white worker excluded on account of his race, filed suit contending that the company policy violated Title VII. The Congressional history behind this provision seemed to support Weber's claim, and two lower federal courts, based on the congressional debates and the language of Title VII, had upheld Weber's contention that the Act had indeed been violated. But the Supreme Court held otherwise, contending that the lower courts had followed the letter of the Civil Rights Act of 1964, but not its spirit. Justice Brennan asserted that Congress had intended the Act to help the economic plight of blacks and that it would be ironic if Title VII

would be used to prohibit, "all voluntary private, race-conscious efforts to abolish traditional patterns" of discrimination.[8]

When the courts interpret statutes, Congress retains the authority to overturn such interpretations by passing another law specifying its intentions. Congress occasionally will do so. But statutory interpretation gives the courts a great deal of authority, because it generally takes far less political muscle to stop a law from being passed than to pass one in the first place. Hence Court action in statutory interpretation can change the entire political equation. Moreover, when the courts interpret federal statutes, they often deal with statutes that were passed many years ago, and the members of Congress who enacted those statutes have long since departed. Unless the current Congress is highly dissatisfied with a decision, the court opinion will usually stand.

Review of Administrative Activity

The actions and regulations of federal administrative agencies also come under judicial scrutiny when it is charged that they violate or do not properly fulfill the purpose of federal law. Major societal interests are often affected by decisions that involve what seem to be technical areas of administrative law. But the importance of this power of the courts today cannot be overemphasized. Much modern legislation in such fields as environment, safety, and health is very broad and leaves tremendous discretion to administrative agencies to devise rules to fulfill the law's vague or sometimes contradictory goals. The courts have carved out a huge role in reviewing both the substance of these rules and the procedures by which these rules have been made. The courts, moreover, usually have the last word, as they determine the definitive meaning of a statute against any administrative rule.

The Federal Court System

Of the first three articles of the Constitution which define the powers, scope and structure of the three branches of the federal government, Article III is decidedly the shortest. It sets out the broad outlines of the judicial power and marks its outer boundaries, but it leaves many of

BOX 13.2

The Supreme Court Rules A State Action Unconstitutional:
Board of Education of Kiryas Joel Village School District v. Grumet (1994)

The parties

The Board of Education of Kiryas Joel Village, New York; Louis Grumet, the director of the New York State School Boards

The issue

The state legislature of New York created a special school district for the handicapped children of the Kiryas Joel, in Orange County, New York. Because the community was entirely populated by Satmar Hasidic Jews, Louis Grumet challenged the creation of the school district on the grounds that it was a violation of the First Amendment's establishment clause.

The background of the case

The school district was created in 1989 because the leaders of Kiryas Joel did not want to send 200 handicapped children to the surrounding school districts because the Hasidic Jew's distinctive dress and use of Yiddish might expose already vulnerable children to more stress and ridicule. All of the other children in the school district attended private religious schools. These other schools did not have the resources to adequately educate children with special needs.

The legal confrontation

The lower state courts of New York and the New York Court of Appeals ruled that the school district violated the establishment clause because it had the effect of aiding a religion. After losing in state court Kiryas Joel appealed to the Supreme Court.

The Court's decision

In a six to three decision, the Supreme Court ruled that the school district was unconstitutional because it aided religion. Writing for the majority Justice Souter said that the school district was unconstitutional because "the benefit flows only to a single sect." In dissent Justice Scalia contended that the Constitution only prohibits a state from officially establishing one church for the state. Creating a special school district for handicapped children, he argued, was not the "establishment of Satmar Hasidism" as the official state religion.

the essential choices about the structure and character of the courts to the Congress. Thus the creation of the judicial branch, more than either of the other two branches, has been left to subsequent legislation.

The Scope of the Federal Judicial Power

Article III defines the federal judiciary's jurisdiction by reference either to subject matter (cases under the Constitution, federal law or treaties) or in terms of the parties involved in the case (such as the United States government, a foreign government, or citizens of different states). The founders devised this broad language first to ensure that all cases having important national implications could ultimately be handled by federal, not state, courts; they did not intend to grant powers to the federal government that could not be adjudicated in federal courts, nor did they intend to allow state courts final say over matters involving fundamental sovereignty or cases affecting the nation's foreign relations.

Second, the founders extended the federal judicial power to the kinds of cases in which the neutrality of the state courts might be suspect. This forms the basis for what is known as the federal judiciary's "diversity jurisdiction." Because state courts might conceivably favor their own citizens or state governments, a practice that could easily have led early on to the disintegration of the Union, the Constitution permits out-of-state parties to bring suit in federal court.

The Judiciary Act of 1789

Article III left Congress the task of creating the institutional structure of the federal judiciary and of assigning to these courts their respective jurisdictions. This task was one of the first great questions Congress took up in its first session, and it served to open up many of the controversies over the Constitution itself.

Despite the broad grant of potential jurisdiction to the federal courts, some opponents of the Constitution—or at any rate of a strong national government—hoped to use Congress' authority to set up a court system to achieve objectives they had apparently lost during the Constitutional Convention in 1787. Their aim was to limit the power of the federal courts by not employing the authority of Article III to its fullest and by structuring the court system in a way that would give more control to the state courts. What some had in mind was to have the state court systems to double as the lower court system of the national government and to limit the kinds of cases that could be appealed to the Supreme Court.

In the end, the first Congress, in the Judiciary Act of 1789, remained basically true to the founders' national aims, although the system it created was more restrictive than it could have been under the broad terms of Article III. Most important, Congress created a distinct system of federal courts. The structure of the federal judiciary was not to be extensive, consisting of two lower levels and a Supreme Court. To limit the number of non-criminal cases heard in federal court, Congress limited jurisdiction to cases involving only relatively large amounts of money. The Judiciary Act explicitly gave the Supreme Court the authority to overturn state constitutions and laws found in conflict with the federal Constitution and to review state supreme court decisions that denied (but not affirmed) federal claims.[9]

Through the Judiciary Act of 1789 Congress emphatically declared that the legislative branch could regulate the jurisdiction of all federal courts. Congress has subsequently altered the jurisdiction of the federal courts, in some instances increasing it while in other instances—involving diversity jurisdiction—limiting it to cases involving more than $50,000. In general, however, the federal court system has gained more authority than it has lost not just through explicit grants of jurisdiction by Congress, but more importantly through the judiciary's own interpretation of the Constitution and its requirements for the exercise of the judicial power.

The Lower Federal Courts

Remarkably, the fundamental structure of the federal courts remains basically unchanged to the present day. Beneath the Supreme Court, there continue to be two levels of general-jurisdiction courts: the district courts and the circuit courts of appeals. Congress has added various limited-jurisdiction courts, such as the United States Court of Claims and the United States Tax Court, which have significant powers within their designated domain (see Box 13.3).

The District Courts The district courts serve as the major original-jurisdiction (trial) courts of the federal court system, handling both criminal and civil cases. A single district judge—sitting with a jury unless all parties and the judge agree to waive it—hears a tremendous variety of major and minor cases that arise under federal law. These cases range from matters involving personal bankruptcies, to kidnappings (an automatic federal offense), to suits over fundamental civil rights. Since less than 15 percent of the decisions of district courts are ever appealed, district courts make the final rulings in the vast majority of federal cases.

Altogether, there are 94 district courts staffed (in 2002) by 672 judges. These courts have experienced a large increase in the number of cases filed over the last few decades. The expanded case loads have resulted in long delays in the processing of cases. In 2001, for example, the median time for a civil trial to be heard after filing was 21.6 months, with a further 8.7 months to dispose of the case. The median time for disposing of a criminal case in 2001 was 6.6 months, more than double the time it took in 1980. To relieve case-load pressures, Congress enacted legislation in 1978 and on four subsequent occasions to increase the number of district court judgeships from 399 in 1978 to the present number of 672. Congress also expanded the duties of the federal magistrates, who are officials assigned to assist the district court judges. Magistrates today are authorized not only to relieve the judges of routine tasks, such as setting bail, but also to try some civil cases and all federal misdemeanor cases. Yet these measures have provided only temporary relief from the pressure of ever-increasing case loads. Other methods of relieving court congestion remain under consideration, such as narrowing the jurisdiction of federal courts and eliminating jury trials in complex civil suits.

Not only has the number of cases handled by district courts been increasing, but district court judges have become more heavily involved in the ongoing supervision of governmental activity. Some of the responsibilities that district court judges have assumed in the last few decades have been unprecedented. For example, Judge Arthur Garrity, who ordered the desegregation of Boston public schools in the mid-1970s, responded to noncompliance with his orders by placing a Boston high school in "receivership" and taking over the administration of the schools.

Courts of Appeals   Litigants dissatisfied with district court decisions have a right of appeal to the federal court of appeals serving their region. These courts are frequently referred to as "circuit courts," because Supreme Court justices were required by the Judiciary Act of 1789 to travel around to various towns in a given area or "circuit" to hear cases with other local district judges. Early justices complained about this burdensome duty, especially in an era when travel was primarily by horse, but the practice was not totally eliminated until 1891. Today, each circuit is technically supervised by a Supreme Court justice who hears certain pleas arising from court actions within his or her circuit including pleas from inmates on death row.

Congress created permanent appeals judges in the Judiciary Act of 1891. These judges today conduct virtually all the work at the appellate level. Currently, there are thirteen courts of appeals, eleven of them based on geographical districts in the states and territories, plus one for the District of Columbia and one that supervises some of the specialized courts. In 2002 there were 179 authorized appeals judgeships. But years of disagreement and delay by the Senate in confirming appointments means that a large number of these positions are vacant—29 in May 2002, roughly one in six positions. There are also judges with senior status who, although retired, can still hear cases as and when required to help alleviate work pressure on the active judges. There were 87 senior appeals judges in 2002. The actual number of judges assigned to each circuit varies from 6 to 28 depending upon population and work load.

The courts of appeals exercise an exclusively appellate jurisdiction—that is, they do not hear cases in the first instance but only cases that are appealed from other courts. They receive appeals not only from the district courts but also from federal independent regulatory commissions (such as the Federal Communications Commission) and certain administrative agencies (such as the Environmental Protection Agency). Thousands of Appeals are filed each year, but many of them are dropped, having been settled by the parties before a hearing or summarily disposed of after screening by the judges. Only in about half the cases filed do the courts of appeals actually consider arguments. To decide most cases, the courts divide into three-judge panels, with the judges rotating the panels on which they serve. Only in cases of national importance or in controversies that have resulted in conflicting decisions within the same circuit do all the judges of any appeals court sit as a unit (*en banc*).

Like the district courts, the appeals courts have been plagued by increasing case load pressures. From 1970 to 1980, the number of appeals that were filed more than doubled, and while the rate of the increase now is no longer as dramatic as that, the number is still increasing by a significant number every year. In 2001 the number of appeals filed was nearly 6,000 more than in 1996, though no extra judgeships were created in that period. The flow of cases through the federal courts is sluggish and the median time from filing in a district court to a decision in the courts of appeals is around two years.

BOX 13.3

The Federal Court System (2002)

The Regular Courts

The Supreme Court of the United States
- .9 justices

United States courts of appeals
- 12 circuit courts (plus 1 special court of appeals)
- 179 judges

United States district courts
- 94 courts
- 672 judges

United States magistrates
- Created by the Federal Magistrates Act (1968)
- 471 full-time, 59 part-time, 3 combination clerk/magistrate
- Assist in processing of cases

Specialized Courts

United States Court of Federal Claims*
- Created in 1855
- Primarily concerned with claims arising out of public contracts
- 16 judges

United States Court of International Trade
- Created in 1956
- Primarily concerned with disputes about customs duties and the value of imported goods
- 9 judges

United States Court for the Federal Circuit
- Created in 1909
- Reviews the decisions of the U. S. Court of International Trade, the U. S. Court of Federal Claims, the U. S. Court of Veterans Appeals, and U. S. Patent Office
- 12 judges

United States Tax Court*
- Created in 1924
- Considers citizen challenges to Internal Revenue Service tax decisions
- 19 judges

United States Court for the Armed Forces*
- Created in 1950
- Reviews appeals from courts-martial
- 3 judges with fifteen-year terms

United States Court of Appeals for Veterans Claims
- Created in 1988
- Reviews decisions of Board of Veterans Appeals
- 3 to 7 judges with fifteen-year terms

*A court created under Article I of the Constitution. The decisions of these courts are not directly reviewable by other federal courts.

The district courts and courts of appeals are subordinate to the Supreme Court, which stands at the apex of the judicial system and has the power to review decisions of lower courts. These lower courts, however, have very considerable authority. For cases on their way up, the Constitutional and statutory interpretations of the lower courts often influence the Supreme Court's ultimate resolution of the issues. In the implementation of Supreme Court decisions, the lower courts—especially the district courts—play a crucial role. Supreme Court decisions often restrict themselves to the general principles of law, with the cases being remanded (turned back) to lower courts to implement the actual decision in the particular cases and to decide other cases of the same type. This task usually involves a great deal of discretion. Finally, the lower courts make the final decision in the vast majority of cases that enter the federal courts. In 2001 the district courts heard over 295,000 cases. The courts of appeals heard over 57,000 appeals, less than 20 percent of the cases dealt with by the district courts handled that year. The Supreme Court was petitioned to take almost 8,000 cases, but it heard only 86 of them, a tiny fraction of the cases in federal courts.

The relationship between the courts of appeals and the Supreme Court resembles more a division of labor than a sifting process in which all important cases make their way to the top. Since the Supreme Court is primarily concerned with Constitutional issues, nonconstitutional issues of great practical importance are routinely decided by the courts of appeals.

The Supreme Court

The Supreme Court serves as the final arbiter in cases coming from the federal and state court systems. Its decisions are final for the litigants, for there is no court to which they can appeal a Supreme Court's decisions. Supreme Court decisions are final as well for the lower courts, establishing precedents which guide their decisions in subsequent cases. Most important they are final in most instances for the entire political system.

In practice, however, the finality of Supreme Court interpretations is less definitive than this purely legal account might suggest. The other branches may challenge or thwart the Court in some measure, based in part on claims that the Constitution never gave the Supreme Court the final say on Constitutional questions. Even within the judicial system itself, compliance is not absolute. The lower federal courts and the state courts, while "under" the Supreme Court, have latitude in interpreting its general orders and may sometimes resist—by omission or subversion—its policies. The Court, unlike an executive, is not in a simple "command" relationship with its subordinates, but must instead proceed by hearing cases or issuing legal orders. The state courts on occasion have been particularly slow in interpreting cases in the exact spirit intended by the Supreme Court, as in many school desegregation cases during the 1950s and 1960s.

Beyond the court system itself, administrators and other officials may not always comply with Court rulings. The Court system is not a national police system, and in some areas—where suits have not been brought in every jurisdiction—compliance with interpretations of the Court is limited. In a large number of public school classrooms, for example, prayers are routinely recited each day. And there are still many, many instances in the nation where police officers do not follow each and every item required by Court rulings.

The Business of the Supreme Court The Supreme Court is a court of both original and appellate jurisdiction—that is, there are some cases it hears in the first instance and others that it hears on appeal. Original jurisdiction is defined in Article III and usually involves cases involving foreign diplomats or two or more states (such as border or land and water disputes). While the Court's original jurisdiction can only be changed by Constitutional amendment, appellate jurisdiction can be changed by Congress. In practice, the Court's original jurisdiction is infrequently used, amounting to only about ten cases per term.

Under the statutes regulating the Court's appellate jurisdiction, there are two primary modes of access to the Court: "appeal" (in certain kinds of cases in which litigants theoretically have a right to have their case heard) and "cer-

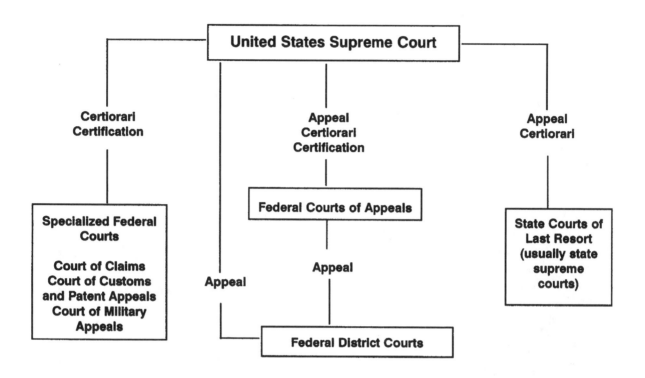

Figure 13.1 How cases reach the Supreme Court.

tiorari" (in which litigants ask for the privilege of having their case reviewed, with the Court agreeing to do so as a matter of discretion). Today, almost 99 percent of petitions for review are on writ of certiorari. As for appeals, a 1988 law provides that the Court is hardly ever obliged to hear a case under appeal, as it can dismiss any appeal that in its judgment fails to raise a "substantial federal question."[10] For all intents and purposes, therefore, the Supreme Court exercises almost unlimited discretion in determining what cases it will decide. This control makes the Court no ordinary tribunal doing justice on the demand of litigants. Rather, it is a kind of legal policy tribunal that sifts through a mass of potential cases and decides for itself which ones it will hear based on the significance of the issues that are raised.

The number of cases that the Court is petitioned to review has increased in recent years, though the number heard by the full Supreme Court remains quite small in comparison. In 1999 more than 7,300 petitions arrived, but only

83 were argued. In 2000 the number of petitions increased by nearly 500, but only 86 cases were argued before the Court. Since the justices receive far more petitions for review than they can possibly grant, they have established a process in which the individual justices and their law clerks screen all incoming petitions. These petitions range from the polished products of prestigious law firms to the handwritten pleas of prisoners and indigents. Unless at least one justice favors hearing a case, it is "dead-listed" and review is automatically denied. Roughly 75 percent of all cases are eliminated in this fashion. Surviving petitions are then acted upon collectively by the justices during conference. A case is accepted if four justices vote to hear it (the so-called "rule of four"). The vast majority of the petitions considered by the Court are rejected. In 2000 the Court heard barely 1 percent of the cases in which review was sought.

In deciding which cases to hear, the Court is not primarily concerned with righting individual wrongs. "Everyone who comes here," a former chief justice once noted, "has had one trial and one appeal already."[11] Rather, the Court hears cases that raise issues of major legal or practical importance. Often these include the most pressing political issues in the nation.

The Decision-Making Process   In making its decisions, the Court relies heavily on four sources of information: decisions of lower courts, the legal briefs of the parties in a case, legal briefs of interested parties (*amicus curiae* briefs), and oral argument before the Court. Once the Court decides to hear a case, counsel for both parties submit briefs. These briefs are essentially "partisan" documents designed to persuade the Court. By providing interpretation of relevant legal materials (precedents, statutes, and the Constitution) as well as factual information favorable to their case, lawyers attempt to convince the Court to rule in favor of their clients or position.

The Court, at its discretion, may permit *amicus curiae* briefs by parties declaring their desire to help and perhaps having a tangible interest in the outcome of the case. Organizations that frequently file amicus briefs include the American Civil Liberties Union (ACLU), the National Association for the Advancement of Colored People (NAACP), the AFL-CIO, various veterans' groups, and numerous activist or consumer groups such as Common Cause. In recent decades, the U.S. Government has filed amicus briefs, especially in reapportionment-redistricting, sexual discrimination, and segregation-integration cases. Amicus briefs provide additional perspectives on the issues confronting the Court and alert the justices to the broader implications of their decisions.

Briefs in cases today rely not only on pure legal reasoning, but also on attempts to show the policy implications of a decision. The discussion of policy concerns, though certainly not a twentieth-century innovation, is clearly done today with much greater openness and less attempt to integrate the arguments with pure law. Parts of judicial briefs today hardly differ at all from the types of information supplied to legislators or administrators.

The final opportunity to influence the justices comes during the stage of oral argument, when the lawyers appear before all the justices in a formed session. In the early nineteenth century, oral arguments were often great occasions, when the Court would be packed with spectators anxious to hear the long and often eloquent discourses of famous lawyers such as Daniel Webster. In the early days of the Court oral arguments often lasted for several days, or even weeks and could be used to go over every detail of the case and the implications of the Court ruling in different ways. Today the Court generally limits oral presentations to a half hour for each party, during which time the justices often interrupt counsel with questions and requests for clarification, seeking to gauge the strengths and weaknesses of their arguments. For the unprepared or inexperienced lawyer, oral argument can be a harrowing experience. In one recent case, an unprepared lawyer was forced to scan his briefs frantically when he could not answer the probing questions of Justice Antonin Scalia. Impatient with the delays, an exasperated and impish Scalia told the unlucky lawyer to yell "Bingo!" when he found the answer. Effective response to the justices' questions can influence the outcome of a case, especially if some justices are undecided. As Justice John Marshall Harlan once acknowledged, oral argument "may in many cases make the difference between winning and losing, no matter how good the briefs are."[12]

On Wednesdays and Fridays during the Court's term, the justices meet in closed conference to discuss the cases heard during that week. Disagreement is common—clear-cut cases are seldom accepted for review—and debate can be heated. At the conclusion of their deliberations, the justices take a non-binding vote on each case. A decision is then made about which justice will have the responsibility to draft the opinion of the Court (majority opinion). This is a matter of great significance, as the justices are not just deciding the outcome of a specific case but also stating the reasoning behind the decision, which will dramatically affect the disposition of other cases. If the chief justice has voted with the majority, he assigns who writes the majority opinion. Otherwise, the most senior justice in the majority makes the assignment. Chief justices voting in the minority have been known to switch their votes so that they can control who writes the opinion and thus attempt to moderate the resulting opinion.

A vote in conference is not binding and marks only the beginning of a sometimes lengthy process of deliberation. This deliberation is conducted under the strictest secrecy. During the period between the vote and announcement of the Court's decision, the opinion of the Court and dissenting opinions are prepared and circulated among the justices. These draft opinions are carefully reviewed. A persuasive opinion may convince justices to switch votes, and a draft dissent might in this way even become the opinion of the Court. But even if no votes change, this phase of the process is vitally important. Justices may request changes in the language or argument of an opinion as a condition for endorsing it. Argument over the content of opinions at times reflects a concern with the soundness of the legal justification for the Court's decision. Even more, it may reflect the individual justices' concern about the implications of the Court's arguments, since Court decisions serve as precedents that will influence the course of future cases.

Once the justices have reached their final position the Court announces its decision in open court. In addition to the opinion of the Court, the other justices remain free to express their views in concurring or dissenting opinions. The justices writing separate opinions explain their reasons for disagreeing with the majority opinion, whether over the result of the case, or the reasoning used to get that result. Copies of all of the opinions are published in the *United States Reports*. By the conclusion of the Court's term in late June, the process will have repeated itself more than 150 times, and the justices will have written opinions filling four or five volumes of *United States Reports,* totaling over 4,000 pages.

The State Court Systems

Under our federal system, judicial power is divided between the federal courts and the state court systems. While the federal courts, especially the Supreme Court, receive much of the attention from the media, the state courts are the unsung workhorses of the judicial system. Of all legal cases in the United States, over ninety-nine percent take place in state courts. The average individual is more likely to encounter state courts because of common matters such as traffic violations, domestic relations (such as divorce or child custody), probate concerns (e.g., wills, estates, and deeds), or small claims (damages of a certain dollar amount). The Constitution lists the type of cases which federal courts may hear (in Article III and the Eleventh Amendment), and state courts by implication have jurisdiction over all other questions. They handle initially all matters that arise exclusively under state law as well as some matters involving federal law.

Some cases may be heard in either state or federal courts, or both. For example, if a citizen of one state sues a citizen of another and the case involves more than $50,000, the plaintiff can sue in either court. Moreover, when a federally insured bank is robbed, the burglar has violated both state and federal law and could be prosecuted in either system. Prosecutors in such cases will often file suit in the system where the penalty will be higher; similarly, plaintiffs in civil suits will examine which system may give the client better treatment.

The constitutions of each state define the structure of their particular judicial systems. Thus, there are fifty separate systems in addition to the federal system. The individual structures may differ from state-to-state, but in general there are three levels: the trial court, the appellate court, and the state supreme court. Litigants may appeal cases within the state systems up to the supreme court of each state, which gives the most authoritative interpretation of the law in that state and binds all the lower state courts. The rulings of the state supreme courts are final unless the case involves a "substantial federal question," as determined by the United States Supreme Court. If the Supreme Court concludes this, the case may be transferred to the federal courts.

The Supreme Court can use its power of review over state court decisions to ensure the uniform interpretation of federal law and to move into new areas of litigation. Without this power, the state courts would be able to interpret or ignore federal law as they pleased. State cases enter the federal court system when at least four justices determine that an issue is ripe for consideration and agree that there has been a substantial violation of federal law. This has increasingly occurred in the last half century with the incorporation of the Bill of Rights to apply to the states and with the extensive litigation that has taken place under the Fourteenth Amendment's "equal protection" clause.

One example will illustrate how matters can move from state to federal courts. In 1968, William Furman was convicted under a Georgia state law and sentenced to the death penalty. This matter, which until then had always been an issue for the states, became a federal question when the Supreme Court agreed to hear Furman's appeal that the death penalty constituted a violation of the Eighth Amendment ban on cruel and unusual punishment. In *Furman v. Georgia,* 1972, the Court overturned Furman's sentence and held that all existing laws were too arbitrary. This decision touched off a decade-long struggle on the limits of capital punishment. Ultimately, thirty-five states rewrote their laws in attempts to conform with the Court's objections to the death penalty. Since 1976, the Supreme Court in a series of opinions has ruled that the death penalty is not inherently "cruel and unusual punishment," but has set stringent criteria under which the states can apply it.

The Judges

When Justice William Brennan retired in 1990, he had served on the Supreme Court for almost 34 years. His judicial career spanned the administrations of eight presidents. Yet remarkable as Brennan's tenure is, it is so only in degree. In order to safeguard judicial independence, the Constitution specifies that judges "shall hold their offices during good behavior" and receive a salary "which shall not be diminished" while in office. Although judges are liable to impeachment, it has not been used as an instrument

against the opinions of the judges. Only a few federal judges, and no Supreme Court judge, have been removed by this process.*

Long tenure typifies the federal judiciary, and prolonged life expectancy may have increased the average tenure. Long tenure enables individual judges to exercise a considerable influence over the development of American law by participation in thousands of cases. On his retirement, Justice Brennan was often referred to, by both his supporters and opponents, as the single most influential person in American political life since President Franklin Roosevelt.

The Politics of Judicial Selection

The Constitution provides that the president shall appoint federal judges with the advice and consent of the Senate to hold their office "during good behavior." During the ratification debates, many anti-federalists charged that the lifetime tenure of judges would lead to a dangerous expansion of the federal judicial power. Alexander Hamilton responded in *The Federalist* that life tenure would provide judges with the needed independence from political pressures and give them the time to develop a firmer and deeper knowledge of the law and its principles.

There have been occasional attempts to alter the judicial selection process. During the 1840s and 1850s, abolitionists asserted that selection and tenure provisions insulated the judiciary from public demands to abolish slavery; and in 1867 some Republicans in Congress led an effort to pass a Constitutional amendment requiring the election of federal judges, clearly with the aim to get rid of Democratic judges appointed before the Civil War. In the early twentieth century many progressives called for judicial elections in the belief that the courts were "too indifferent to the rights of the people and not sufficiently responsive to present day needs."[13] Teddy Roosevelt, during his campaign for president in 1912, also proposed the idea of a recall of judicial decisions: "When a judge decides a con-

---

*   1969 Justice Abe Fortas resigned from the Supreme Court, almost certainly because of the fear that impeachment proceedings would be brought against him. The reason had to do with a possible economic conflict of interest, and not directly with his judicial opinions.

stitutional question, when he decides what the people as a whole can or cannot do, the people should have the right to recall the decision if they think it is wrong."[14] A few decades later, a group of Alabama legislators, motivated by their opposition to *Brown v. Board of Education* (1954), revived the judicial election proposal, and asked other states to join in a "crusade to reform the federal courts" by "putting them back in touch with the people."[15] In all, Congress has rejected proposals for ten amendments and thirteen bills calling for the election of Supreme Court justices.

Lower Court Judges   Although the appointment process is formally the same for all levels of the federal judiciary, the simplicity of the Constitutional language masks a more complex reality. Different actors play decisive roles in the selection of lower court judges than Supreme Court justices. An assistant attorney general in President Kennedy's administration aptly characterized the process for selecting district court judges when he remarked, "The Constitution is backwards. Article II, Section 2 should read: 'The senators shall nominate, and by and with the consent of the president, shall appoint.'"

While the Constitutional responsibility for nominating judges is lodged with the president, the primary power in selecting district court judges often resides in fact in the Senate—and more particularly with the senators from the state in which the judge is to serve. Under the unwritten policy of senatorial courtesy, the Senate rejects any nominee who is opposed by a Senator from the president's party who represents the state in which the vacancy occurred. This policy allows the Senate to largely control the selection of district court judges. Presidential advisors must negotiate with a state's senators from their own party to ensure confirmation. District court judgeships represent major patronage positions. If a state's senators favor a particular candidate, that candidate ordinarily will receive the nomination.

Traditionally, the nomination of judges for the courts of appeals has followed a similar pattern. Because of the importance of these positions, the attorney general and other high officials of the Justice Department typically play a much more active role in determining prospective nominees for the appeals courts. Nevertheless, a modified form of senatorial courtesy has operated here as well. Although the appeals court encompasses more than a single state, senatorial courtesy has been extended to specific seats informally allocated to each state in the circuit. Thus, agreement between the executive branch and the appropriate senators has remained a necessity for confirmation.

President Jimmy Carter attempted to depoliticize the process by establishing the U.S. Circuit Judge Nomination Commission to help him fill vacant judgeships. Carter hoped that panels in the individual circuits would identify and suggest members of "underrepresented" portions of society such as women and various minorities; however, this commission did not work well because several senators refused to give up the practice of senatorial courtesy. Senator James Eastland reportedly told Carter's Attorney General, Griffin Bell, "I'll hand you a slip of paper with one name on it, and that'll be the judge."[16] The Reagan administration formally abolished the commission in 1981. Carter was more successful in his effort to encourage senators to establish merit advisory groups within their individual states to search for nominees for district judgeships. This effort did not really strip senators of their appointment perks, and by 1981 40 senators representing 30 states had created such panels.[17]

The selection process for lower court judges has a definite impact on the kind of person selected. Judges have usually been politically active members of the president's party. Judge Joseph Perry, recounting how he was appointed to the federal bench, recalled his realization that "if I wanted that appointment, I had better get back into politics—which I did."[18] Since state party contacts are particularly important in securing support, the judges have typically been active in state or local, rather than national, politics. They therefore almost always are inhabitants of their own state and tend to share its political perspective. Thus district judges are not, as in some countries, a corps of national officials sent to different regions. This can be a problem, as was illustrated by the reluctance of some southern district court judges to enforce the Supreme Court's school desegregation decisions. Finally, members of multijudge courts are selected in part to provide representation for ethnic and religious groups served by their court, and this practice was especially pronounced during the presidency of Jimmy Carter.

Supreme Court Justices The appointment process consists of two or (in a few instances) arguably three stages. The first stage is the optional one. It occurs in cases in which the direction of the Court becomes an important theme in a presidential election campaign, as in 1860, 1936, and—more recently—in 1968 and 1980. In the last two instances, candidates Nixon and Reagan made clear their intention to appoint justices having a different judicial philosophy from that of the majority on the Court. In these cases, the parties and the public in a sense take part in the selection process. The victorious candidate may attempt to claim a kind of popular mandate for a certain kind of nominee. Of course, no one can ever say which particular question decides an election, and in any event the Senate still has its own constitutional duty to perform.

The next—and more regularly the first—stage in the process is the nomination by the president. The appointment of Supreme Court justices is among the president's most important responsibilities. Historically, four qualities have characterized presidential nominees for the high court: (1) they have been high in national stature and distinguished service; (2) most (85 percent) have shared the same party affiliation as the president; (3) many have been members of groups whose presence on the Court has been sought to "balance" its composition (geography, race, religion, and now gender have been considerations); and (4) they have generally shown compatibility with the president's views on major Constitutional issues.

The final stage is confirmation by the Senate. The Senate has not been reluctant to reject proposed candidates. As of 2002, the Senate failed to confirm 28 out of a total of 146 Supreme Court nominees; however, only 5 rejections have occurred during this century. The Senate rejected several nominees during the nineteenth century because of political opposition to the president. President John Tyler, for example, who had alienated his party's senators, named six nominees before the Senate finally accepted his choice.

Earlier in this century, there were two highly disputed nominations—Louis Brandeis in 1916 and John Parker in 1930—whose suitability for the Court was openly debated in the Senate in part in terms of their judicial philosophies, which in fact sometimes meant their political positions. Brandeis was narrowly confirmed after strong opposition from various business groups, who considered him a political radical. Parker was eventually turned down, having been opposed by many labor unions and several black organizations.

After 1930 and until very recently, the Senate has ostensibly used "objective," nonpartisan standards—character and qualifications—in debating appointments, although political considerations have always been present beneath the surface. Thus, breaches of judicial ethics doomed President Johnson's attempt to promote Justice Abe Fortas to chief justice; yet it was also clear that many in the Senate were beginning to grow dismayed with the Court's liberal direction. The Senate's rejection of President Nixon's nomination of Clement Haynesworth in 1969, again on questions of ethics, clearly involved liberal opposition to a conservative jurist. The undeniably undistinguished judicial service of Harold Carswell, nominated by President Nixon, prevented his confirmation. In all these cases, even where considerations of judicial or political philosophy may have played a role, the major public debate turned chiefly on questions of qualifications.

An important change occurred in 1987, when the Senate rejected President Reagan's nomination of Court of Appeals Judge Robert H. Bork. By objective standards, Judge Bork was among the best-qualified Supreme Court nominees in recent decades. He had served as solicitor general during the Nixon Administration and was a former law professor at Yale and Chicago Universities. But his outspoken judicial philosophy was highly criticized by the National Organization for Women and the American Civil Liberties Union. This negative campaign against his judicial philosophy derailed his nomination.

TABLE 13.2
Occupations of Supreme Court Designees at Time of Appointment

Federal officeholder in executive branch	22
Judge of inferior federal court	30
Judge of state court	22
Private practice of law	18
U.S. senator	8
U.S. representative	4
State govern	3
Professor of law	3
Associate justice of U.S. Supreme Court*	3
Justice of Court of International Justice	1

* Justices White, Stone, and Rehnquist, who were promoted to the chief justiceship in 1910, 1930, and 1966.

Source: Henry Abraham, *The Judicial Process*, third and fourth eds. (New York: Oxford University Press, 1980), p. 65, table III, updated to 1994.

Reagan's previous nominees could depend on a friendly Republican majority in the Senate; however, the Democrats had regained control of the chamber in the 1986 elections. In the end, the Senate rejected Bork, 42–58, on a largely partisan vote.

Bork's judicial philosophy was clearly a large part of the reason for his rejection. Yet opening the process to this consideration also opened it to the more direct use of politics. Many senators were clearly counting votes back home, and the interest groups were hardly shy in threatening senators with political retribution if they did not oppose Bork's nomination. The process accordingly became highly politicized, and many now feared that this example could set a precedent that detracts from a careful process of deliberation.

The Senate eventually confirmed U.S. Circuit Court Judge Anthony M. Kennedy as Powell's replacement.[19] Despite his conservative record, Judge Kennedy's hearings attracted little controversy and a weary Senate confirmed him without difficulty. Unlike Judge Bork, Judge Kennedy had spent most of his career as a legal technician

on the bench, giving the Senate little to discuss besides his judicial decisions. Some observers have expressed concern that a legacy of Bork's rejection will lead presidents to pass over impressive candidates who have left extensive "paper trails" that express their views on many of the legal issues of the day. Bork himself has worried about a possible tendency "to nominate and confirm persons whose performance once on the bench cannot be accurately, or perhaps even roughly, predicted either by the President or the Senate."[20] In 1990, President Bush in his first Supreme Court appointment seemed to have the Bork case very much on his mind, nominating Judge David Souter, an individual who had not publicly expressed himself on most controversial questions. The 1991 nomination of Judge Clarence Thomas, while giving rise to great controversy over questions of both qualifications and judicial philosophy, in the end passed by a narrow margin.

Despite the rejection of Robert Bork, Presidents Reagan and Bush managed to alter somewhat the direction of the Court. Although the Senate may be able to block a few appointments, the American people would probably not tolerate a permanent opposition posture. The president retains the initiative and will generally prevail. President Clinton's two nominees, Ruth Bader Ginsberg and Stephen Breyer, were confirmed by the Senate in harmonious proceedings and with support of Senators from both parties.

There is nothing wrong with presidents seeking a large degree of "real" compatibility between their nominees and their own judicial philosophy. This mechanism is precisely one of the ways in which a degree of popular control is exercised over the judiciary and in which current views of judicial philosophy are brought on the bench. Moreover, there are limits to how far a president can go in fully achieving his aims. One limit is the number of appointments to the Court that any single president is likely to make. Since a vacancy on the Court occurs about every two years on average, a single-term president can usually not count on having a decisive influence on the direction of the Court. (Fate occasionally deals an unlucky hand, as in the case of President Carter who made no appointments to the Court.) Second, any effort to achieve real compatibility depends on a president being truly serious in considering the effects of Constitutional interpretation. In this respect, some presidents seem to have been unaccountably remiss. When asked if he had made any major mistakes during his administration, President Eisenhower replied: "Yes, two, and they are both sitting on the Supreme Court." (He was referring to Chief Justice Earl Warren and Justice William Brennan.) In both of these cases, Eisenhower almost certainly could (and should) have been able to foresee their development.

Finally, there are limits to presidential control that are, so to speak, unavoidable—and rightly so. In selecting a highly qualified and independent-minded nominee, a president can never know how that individual will view future issues or how he or she will develop on the bench. The whole idea, indeed, of selection for life is to encourage and protect the justice's independence. The prospective justice, while wholly dependent on the president up to the moment of nomination, becomes entirely free of any presidential pressure thereafter. Nor can a president know what the great legal and constitutional questions of the next era will be. As one judicial scholar noted about the appointment process: "You shoot an arrow into a far-distant future when you appoint a Justice, and not even the man himself can tell you what he will think about some of the problems he will face." President Harry Truman put the same point more bluntly, "Packing the Supreme Court simply can't be done. . . . I've tried it and it won't work."[21]

State Court Judges   The states are not obliged to follow the federal government's method of selecting judges, and in fact many of the states have very different selection procedures. A few of the various systems include selection by partisan election (as in Arkansas and Alabama); nonpartisan elections (as in Ohio and Michigan); legislative selection (as in Virginia and South Carolina); and gubernatorial selection (as in Massachusetts and New Jersey). Several states have experimented with a new method developed during the progressive era of the early twentieth century that combines elements of popular election with merit selection. Some states employ more than one method, depending

on the level of the particular court, but despite these variations, almost fifty percent of all state judges are elected by the voters.

The experience of the states in judicial appointments has differed from that of the federal government.[22] Most state constitutions have been periodically revised or rewritten through conventions, giving advocates of popular election of judges numerous opportunities to change the system. Initially, most states followed the federal method, with either governors or legislatures appointing judges. In 1832, Mississippi set a precedent by establishing popular elections for all of its judges. New York followed in 1846 and set off a chain reaction; by 1900, more than 70 percent of the states elected their judges through the popular ballot. This movement was largely led by lawyers who sought to instill democratic accountability within the state judiciaries while simultaneously providing judges with a source of popular support to check legislative excesses. Critics, however, began to complain that partisan infighting and corruption in the judicial selection process was compromising the independence and impartiality of state judiciaries.

During the 1930s, reformers successfully implemented a new variation on judicial appointments aimed at minimizing partisan influence, providing a degree of security of tenure, and maintaining an element of popular control. This method, which combines both the appointment and election methods, was first approved in California in 1934 and Missouri in 1940 and is now employed in whole or in part by sixteen states. Under this system governors make judicial appointments, with a nonpartisan commission playing a role either in approving the appointment (California) or screening the initial list (Missouri). Approved nominees serve for a minimum of one year and then must face the voters at the next general election in order to be elected to a full term. Judges run unopposed with the ballot question asking voters, "Shall Judge X be elected to the office for the term prescribed by law?" If the voters reject a judge seeking retention, the entire process repeats itself. This method is designed to combine democratic accountability with merit selection. The election allows for popular electoral control, while the absence of an opponent allows the judge to run on his or her record and avoid the partisan politics of running against another candidate.[23] In practice, voters rarely reject judges seeking retention. In 1986, California voters, however, created a notable exception when they defeated Chief Justice Rose Bird and two other state Supreme Court justices who had refused to invoke the death penalty or weaken measures protecting criminal defendants.

The Personal Factor in Judging

Justice Owen Roberts once suggested that, in ruling on Constitutional questions, the judicial branch has only one duty: "to lay the article of the Constitution which is invoked beside the statute which is challenged and to decide whether the latter squares with the former."[24] But this description of judicial decision making is far too simple. Broad Constitutional mandates, such as "due process of law" and "equal protection of the laws" provide general directions but not precise instructions. Judicial interpretation is not an automatic process, but one that is influenced by judicial philosophies, political opinions, and the personalities and experiences of the justices.

Judges are affected by their own concerns and viewpoints and, like all human beings, are occasionally "driven" by petty concerns in their relations with others, including, of course, their colleagues on the Court. The personal experiences of judges also affect their opinions, and justices are susceptible to the impact of historical events, which can change their views. As Justice Benjamin Cardozo remarked, "The great tides and currents which engulf the rest of men do not turn aside in their course, and pass the judges idly by."[25]

It would be a mistake to conclude, however, that because judges interpret the law, they simply read their own policy preferences into it, voting as legislators and then justifying their views in legal language. Undoubtedly, this can and does occur. But there are constraints that limit the justices' inclination and ability to turn their personal opinions on issues into the basis of their legal interpretations. For the most part, justices tend to be guided by their conceptions of their

role as judges and by their idea of judicial interpretation.

First, judges are obliged to seek direction from the law in deciding cases, and they cannot simply disregard either the text of the law or past decisions. In interpreting the law, all judges accept that they are at least partly constrained by the doctrine known as *stare decisis,* according to which precedents normally bind current decisions. The justices, in other words, feel some responsibility to adhere to the Court's previous rulings; if they did not, every decision would be challenged and the entire notion of interpreting the law would become a mockery. This does not mean, however, that the Court worships blindly at the alter of precedent. It sometimes will ignore precedents where the rulings are ambiguous; and it will occasionally overturn a decision, admitting that an earlier argument was false or is now somehow inapplicable. One famous instance of such a reversal occurred in the case of *Brown v. Board of Education* (1954), which overturned the infamous *Plessy v. Ferguson* (1896) decision that had endorsed racial segregation. Both sides in the abortion controversy take differing views on *stare decisis.* Individuals who wish to ban abortion believe that *Roe v. Wade* was wrongly decided and should thus be overturned while advocates of abortion rights believe that *Roe* formally and correctly recognized abortion as a Constitutional right and that *stare decisis* should apply in future cases.

Second, judges must write legal opinions that publicly justify their decisions. Judges wishing to influence their colleagues must employ persuasive legal arguments. Studies of the inner workings of the Supreme Court have consistently shown that justices are deeply concerned with the quality of the legal arguments. The possibility of dissenting opinions reinforces this concern, as dissents can expose the weaknesses of decisions not rooted in the law. Sometimes a well written dissent will convince a future court to overturn a decision. Although district court judges need not convince colleagues, the possibility of appeal and reversal serves as a constraint on their decisions.

Finally, judges are constrained by their own conception of their role and duties as a judge. As Justice Frankfurter once observed:

There is a good deal of shallow talk that the judicial robe does not change the man within it. It does. The fact is that on the whole judges do lay aside private views in discharging their judicial functions. This is achieved through training, professional habits, self-discipline, and that fortunate alchemy by which men are loyal to the obligation with which they are entrusted (*Public Utilities Commission v. Pollack*, 1959).

In sum, while judges cannot escape exercising personal judgment in deciding cases, numerous constraints channel that judgment and generally transform it into something other than the mere personal opinions that judges might express as citizens. Yet while limiting the role of personal opinions may assuage, it certainly cannot relieve all concern about the latitude of judicial policymaking. Even conscientious judges who strive to limit all elements of personal decision making can—and do—disagree among themselves and operate under controversial conceptions of their role as judges.

The Expanding Role of the Courts

Federal courts in the past two decades have been deciding more cases than ever before, an increase that far exceeds what would be expected from population growth. Not only are the courts deeply involved in contentious policy issues, but they have also been active in supervising the details of administration of various governmental programs.

Why the Judicial Role in Governing Has Grown

What accounts for the increased level of judicial activity? Four interrelated factors are primarily responsible for the judiciary's broader role in governing: (1) changes in the overall scope of governmental activity, (2) an increased disposition of groups to make use of the courts to pursue political objectives, (3) a lowering of barriers limiting access to the courts, and finally (4) a growth (during the 1960s and 1970s) of an activist judicial philosophy among judges and an increased confidence by the courts in their institutional power.

The Growth of Government Government at all levels has grown over the past few decades. Expanding the scope of governmental responsibility inevitably increases the level of legal regulation; and when government increases the body of law, it creates new legal obligations and thereby promotes litigation designed to enforce those requirements. Yet it is not so much the number of congressional statutes that has accounted for the expanded scope of law as the number of administrative regulations. The volume of public bills passed annually by Congress has not increased since 1946–1948, but the number of administrative regulations has shot up dramatically. The size of the *Federal Register,* in which administrative regulations are published, has grown from 2,619 pages in 1936 to more than 65,000 pages at present.

The expansion of administrative regulation is particularly important in promoting litigation, for litigants often challenge administrative regulations as being inconsistent with congressional legislation. Congress has also passed legislation that grants a right to review many regulatory actions which in some cases facilitates legal challenges; any individual who is "adversely affected or aggrieved" may challenge administrative decisions. Environmental groups, for example, frequently petition the courts to provide stricter enforcement of environmental regulations.

Litigation as a Political Strategy Beginning in the latter years of the Warren Court during the 1960s, a growing number of political organizations—civil rights groups, consumer groups, and environmental groups, to name a few—began pursuing their objectives through litigation. These groups perceived that the courts had become more receptive to their claims; and they recognized that even without winning favorable rulings, a litigation strategy can bring considerable benefits.

The National Association for the Advancement of Colored People's (NAACP) Legal Defense Fund was the pioneer in employing this strategy during the 1930s and 1940s. Their victories in a series of cases in which litigants sued to require the states to provide the "separate but equal" facilities mandated by *Plessy v. Ferguson* (1896) ultimately prepared the way for *Brown v.*

Board of Education in 1954. After *Brown,* the Legal Defense Fund continued filing lawsuits to ensure that the school systems in numerous cities across the country were complying with the desegregation orders.

Groups that are unable to achieve their objectives with the legislative or executive branches often fare better in the courts. One reason is that the criteria for success in the courts differ from those in other forums. Whereas success in the political arena may depend upon the number and influence of those supporting a position, in the courts the primary criterion is legality. Thus even politically powerless groups—aliens, for example—can win major victories by convincing the judges the federal law or the Constitution supports their claims. Certain groups also found the Warren Court, and to a lesser extent, its successor, the Burger Court, to be unusually receptive to attempts to overturn government policies. The willingness of the courts to overturn government policy has in turn encouraged other groups to file lawsuits, thereby expanding the range of policies subject to judicial review.

Access to the Courts   During the 1960s and 1970s, the judiciary increased its role in governing by lowering procedural barriers that previously had prevented some politically charged issues from coming to the courts. Under Article III of the Constitution, the federal courts' jurisdiction extends to "cases" and "controversies." Courts in the past had interpreted this as a limitation on judicial power by refusing, for example, to decide cases in which the party instituting the suit lacked "standing," that is, a personal stake in the outcome of the case. Since the 1960s, however, the courts have greatly reduced this limitation and have expanded the parties who can challenge governmental actions in court.

A particularly important development in this area has been the Supreme Court's decision to open the judicial system to more class-action suits. In a class-action suit, one or more persons bring suit for themselves and for "all others similarly situated" who claim a common legal right. These suits can relieve the courts of the burden of deciding a succession of cases involving the same legal right. Even more important, they increase the use of the courts by greatly reducing

Earl Warren, who served as Chief Justice from 1953 to 1969, led a Supreme Court known for its willingness to overturn federal and state laws to promote a national vision of civil rights. (Photo provided by the Library of Congress.)

the costs of litigation for litigants and by increasing the potential rewards. A great many consumer groups have sued businesses on this basis, and the class-action suit has been widely used in the area of employment discrimination.

In response to the barrage of litigation caused by the easing of the rules of standing, the Supreme Court began during the mid-1970s to make it more difficult to bring class-action suits. In a 1982 opinion, Justice Rehnquist lectured that the Court would not condone the use of the federal courts by citizens who sought to use them as if they "constituted as ombudsmen of the general welfare" or as speaking platforms for those who "would roam the country in search of government doing wrong."[26] The Court in recent years has emphatically stated that standing to sue is not a citizen's right, but instead is a set of prudential rules.[27]

Judicial Activism   In 1972, patients involuntarily confined in Bryce Hospital, Alabama's largest state mental health facility, filed a class-action suit, arguing that the state had not provided minimum standards of care as mandated by the Constitution. In *Wyatt v. Stickney,* 1971, a federal district court judge agreed and ordered the Alabama Department of Mental Health to remedy the situation. When state officials did not make acceptable progress, the judge intervened once more and established detailed standards for care, treatment, and rehabilitative programs at the hospital. In prescribing a remedy, the judge assumed the tasks normally performed by the legislators and state administrative officials. Largely as a result, Alabama's expenditures for mental health institutions jumped from $14 million in 1971 to $58 million in 1973.

Although *Wyatt* represents an unusual example of judicial intervention, it is hardly unique. This "positive" type of intervention, in which the courts prescribe broad remedies, dates from the Supreme Court's 1955 implementation decision which provided a remedy for *Brown v. Board of Education* that authorized district court judges, if necessary, to impose their own plans. The success of the federal courts in supervising this particular effort, along with a growing belief on the part of some judges that the courts can effectively undertake these responsibilities, led to further such "positive" judicial interventions. Moreover, courts have been asked to provide more of these kinds of remedies because of the nature of the modern state, in which cases involve complaints of governmental failure to meet its affirmative responsibilities to achieve certain results. In such circumstances, where judges also conclude that they cannot rely on administrative officials to remedy the situation, they have actively chosen to participate in the formulation and implementation of remedial programs. As Judge Frank Johnson, who decided *Wyatt v. Stickney,* observed:

> Desegregation is not the only area of state responsibility in which Alabama officials have forfeited their decision-making powers by such a dereliction of duty as to require judicial intervention. . . . State officers by their inaction have also handed over to the courts property tax assessment plans; standards for the care and treatment of mentally ill and mentally retarded persons committed to the State's custody; and the procedures by which such persons are committed.[28]

With increasing frequency, courts make decisive determinations on important public issues. When they require specific remedial measures, they establish public policy; and in supervising the implementation of their directives, they administer it. Moreover, in directing governmental attention and funds to the solution of a particular problem, the courts inevitably influence the entire public policy process, for by requiring that government address one problem, they necessarily divert funds and personnel, which are limited, from other programs.

Should the courts play such an important role? Can they do so successfully? Such questions might, of course, seem inappropriate. If the courts are simply "saying what the law is," then the obvious answers are that the courts should be involved exactly as they are. But proponents scarcely less than opponents of an active role for the courts seem to agree that the courts have gone further than what a strict or modest interpretation of the law requires. (Opponents deplore this, while proponents applaud it.) The courts in some measure have voluntarily expanded their policymaking role, and it is therefore important to question their effectiveness as policymaking bodies.

Commentators have identified a variety of factors that affect the success of governmental policies. Among those mentioned are, first, the adequacy of information used by those who make decisions. Courts here suffer from the problem that the information they obtain may apply to the special case in front of them, but may not be typical of most situations that a general decision may affect. As Donald Horowitz his observed, "Because courts respond only to the cases that come their way, they make general law from what may be very special situations."[29] Judges may also lack the capacity to digest all the relevant information. Judges tend to be very busy and lack the staff resources of many legislators or executives. They may be deciding cases in areas in which they have little or no expertise. How much, for example, may a particular judge know about education or housing, when that judge may be making decisions that have a tremendous impact on local schools or housing?

Second, policymakers are more likely to be able to deal with certain problems where they can be flexible in their responses and change tactics to meet new circumstances. Yet courts have considerably less flexibility than the other branches. Because courts must decide on the basis of law, judicial policymaking focuses on solutions cast in terms of the rights and duties of the parties in a dispute. This permits little consideration of compromise solutions. If the policy does not succeed, courts cannot easily admit the failure of a previous directive and backtrack from it. Judicial policymaking also limits the balancing of costs and benefits: if persons possess a right, they possess it regardless of cost. Thus in *Wyatt v. Stickney,* for example, the effect on Alabama's entire budget could not be a consideration in the court's decision. These attributes of the legal process are precisely those that ought to be involved in matters where Constitutional rights or duties are at stake; but when (or if) the legal process is extended into the policymaking area, these same attributes can become inflexible impediments to the resolution of problems.

Finally, policymaking bodies often rely on a degree of consensus in the community to successfully implement certain policies. Court decisions can sometimes create this consensus, but in other cases the necessary community support is lacking. Many of the court-ordered busing programs in the end failed to achieve their objective of racially-balanced schools, as affected groups either moved out of the jurisdictions or opted out of the public schools. For such programs to have worked, a broader popular base of support would have been required.

The Impact of Judicial Intervention

The greater activity of courts has led some in society to alter their method of pursuing political objectives, abandoning their struggle in the political arena and turning instead to a strategy of litigation. Groups rely more on specialized lawyers to plead their cases in a judicial setting than on mobilizing constituencies in a legislative setting. By the same token, the political branches, aware that the courts are involved in more areas, have sidestepped difficult political issues, allowing the courts to "take the heat." Both by encouraging reliance on the courts and

by underwriting political irresponsibility, the expansion in court activity, according to certain critics, has undermined the vigor of popular government. Of course, if valid Constitutional rights have been abridged, it is clearly the role of the courts to intervene; but a result-oriented activism, while it might achieve certain policies, could weaken the ability of democratic institutions to operate effectively in the long run.

Judicial Review and the Limits of Judicial Authority

Judicial review is the power of the courts to pronounce the laws or actions of any government in the United States, or any officials of those governments, contrary to any higher law and therefore null and void. When the courts interpret the Constitution, they seem to possess an awesome power from which there is little recourse except the difficult process of amendment. What is the basis of this power? What problems does it pose in a representative democracy? And what kinds of checks exist against it?

The Historical Foundation

Marbury v. Madison (1803) ranks as the Supreme Court's most important decision, because it *authoritatively* established the power of federal courts to review the Constitutionality of federal laws.[30] Chief Justice John Marshall's classic argument began by asking what happens if Congress exceeds its Constitutional bounds and enacts laws "repugnant to the Constitution." His answer was disarmingly simple. Since the Constitution is the fundamental law and superior to ordinary legislative enactments, laws that conflict with the Constitution are necessarily void. When deciding cases that involve a conflict between the Constitution and a legislative enactment, the courts must apply the Constitution and refuse to apply the law. The duty to say what the law is entails the power to say what it is not—and therefore includes the power to strike down laws as unconstitutional (see Box 13.4).

Marshall's argument has been criticized by those who contend that the founders never intended for the courts to exercise so formidable a power. Nowhere in the Constitution, they note, is the power of judicial review explicitly granted. Nor do the records of the Constitutional Convention show that the delegates ever explicitly debated granting this power to the judiciary. Marshall's opinion in *Marbury,* in this view, represents one of history's great thefts—the stealing of a power that rightfully belonged to or was shared by Congress and the president.[31]

Yet a close examination of the historical record suggests that the delegates at the Convention regarded judicial review in some form as implied by the nature of the government being adopted. Certainly the leading treatise on the Constitution, *The Federalist,* explicitly argued that the courts would exercise this power: "whenever a particular statute contravenes the Constitution, it will be the duty of the judicial tribunals to adhere to the latter and disregard the former." *(Federalist 78)* To grant that the courts have a power of judicial review is not, however, to resolve all issues. For there still remain the questions of how often and in what circumstances the courts will actually choose to exercise it, and whether the other branches and the people must automatically accept that the Court's interpretation of the Constitution is final and definitive.

Judicial Review: The Fundamental Problem

The doctrine of judicial review poses a fundamental problem in a political system based on the principle of self-government. In the words of legal scholar John Hart Ely: "A body that is not elected or otherwise politically responsible in any significant way [is] telling the people's elected representatives that they cannot govern as they'd like."[32] This counter-majoritarian aspect of judicial review is most evident when the Supreme Court strikes down the actions of a coequal branch of government, Congress or the president, for these branches are responsible through elections to national majorities. But it applies no less forcefully to certain state laws that have the backing not only of local majorities but of a majority of the American people as a whole.

The conflict between majority rule and judicial review is not, however, absolute. There is a very plausible democratic argument that goes

some way to reducing this conflict. It runs as follows. Because the Constitution creates a system of limited powers, not a system that allowed an unbridled majority to work its will, the Court in striking down unconstitutional acts protects the Constitution, which represents the expression of the public's most solemn will. Judicial review does not set the judges over the legislature, but, in the words of *Federalist* 78, "only" supposes that "where the will of the legislature, declared in its statutes, stands in opposition to that of the people, declared in the Constitution, the judges ought to be governed by the latter rather than the former."

This argument has served as one justification for judicial review. Yet it slides over two thorny problems: one is that a majority of the people, expressing their will through their legislators, may actually hold views in conflict with the Constitution; the other is that the judges may interpret the Constitution in a way that is contrary to the views of the public and that is perhaps at odds with a plausible interpretation of the Constitution. In the first case, most Americans have been prepared to accept, at least in theory, the general premise that current majorities ought to yield to what is truly in the Constitution. The Constitution is not—and was never intended to be—a purely majoritarian document. The second case raises far greater difficulties. It leads to the question of how much discretion and authority should be given to unelected judges in making decisions.

The controversy over judicial review is made more difficult by the fact that the exercise of judicial review has not been limited to issues of marginal concern to the public, but often has involved key issues of the day, from slavery, to the management of industrial relations, to civil rights, to matters of privacy and life and death. Moreover, when the Supreme Court exercises judicial review, it now claims that its rulings are the final, and thus the decisive, determination of the meaning of the Constitution. Unless the Court reverses itself in a later case, its ruling that a law or official action is unconstitutional can be reversed only by Constitutional amendment, which happens only rarely.

The task of Constitutional interpretation, even when undertaken in good faith, is not a

BOX 13.4

Marbury V. Madison: Establishing the Power of Judicial Review

The parties

William Marbury and other persons appointed as justices of the peace in Washington, D.C.; James Madison, secretary of state under President Thomas Jefferson.

The issue

Marbury and the plaintiffs were asking the Supreme Court to issue a *writ of mandamus* ordering Madison to deliver the commissions entitling them to take office as justices of the peace.

The political context

The case arose during the waning days of President John Adams's administration. Adams and his Federalist party had been soundly defeated in the election of 1800 by Thomas Jefferson and his forces. Adams sought to safeguard his party's interests by appointing as many Federalist judges as possible before leaving office; the lame-duck Congress, which the Federalists dominated, cooperated by creating fifty-eight new judgeships. William Marbury was appointed to one of those positions, but John Marshall—who was still serving as secretary of state despite his recent appointment as chief justice of the Supreme Court—failed to deliver Marbury's commission before Jefferson's inauguration. President Jefferson was furious at Adams's attempt to pack the judiciary and, although Marbury and others had been appointed and confirmed by the Senate, ordered Madison not to deliver their commissions.

Chief Justice Marshall had little love for Jefferson, his cousin and longtime political adversary. However, he recognized the political peril posed by Marbury's petition. Congress, which was now dominated by Jefferson partisans, had already postponed the Supreme Court's term and abolished some courts created during Adams's administration. If Marshall ruled in favor of Marbury, Jefferson would certainly still refuse to deliver the commissions and thus demonstrate the political impotence of the Court. Indeed, a ruling in favor of Marbury might well trigger impeachment proceedings against the justices. On the other hand, Marshall did not wish to endorse Jefferson's refusal to deliver the commissions.

The Court's opinion

Marshall initially made clear that Marbury had a right to the commission and that Madison was duty-bound to deliver it. He also noted that mandamus was the proper remedy in the case. He held, however, that the Supreme Court could not issue the writ. The Constitution specified the Court's original jurisdiction, and Congress could not add to it by ordinary legislation. In sum, the Court could not issue the writ because the legislation granting it that power was unconstitutional.

The effects of the decision

The immediate effect of the decision was that Marbury and the other petitioners did not receive their commissions. Marbury never did receive his and eventually became a bank president. In a sense, therefore, Jefferson had won, although he complained about "twistifications" in Marshall's opinion, particularly his gratuitous criticisms of the failure to deliver the commissions. But in denying that it had the power to issue the writ, the Court secured a much more important power, the power to declare acts of Congress unconstitutional.

Chief Justice John Marshall's opinion in *Marbury v. Madison* in 1803 established the Supreme Court's power of judicial review. Marshall had the longest tenure of any Chief Justice, serving from 1801 until 1835. (Photo provided by National Portrait Gallery; Smithsonian Institution; Transfer from the National Gallery of Art; gift of Andrew W. Mellon, 1942. Used with permission.)

technical or mechanical one. In most cases that reach the Supreme court, the questions to be decided are complex and ambiguous. The Constitution, while a law in some sense, is not an ordinary law with hundreds of qualifications and definitions. Often, its words are very general, and it is therefore impossible to place a statute beside the Constitutional provision in question and easily determine the validity or invalidity of the statute. Consider, for example, the First Amendment which prevents Congress from passing any law that abridges the freedom of speech. Does this ban any attempt by Congress to limit what a candidate for federal office can spend on his or her own behalf, as the Court ruled in *Buckley v. Valeo* (1976)? Or can Congress limit what an individual can spend to promote their issue or candidate of choice in an election, as it proclaimed in the McCain-Feingold Campaign Finance Reform Act of 2002? Obviously, the text of the Constitution, taken by itself, does not supply automatic answers.

Although the breadth and generality of the language of certain parts of the Constitution does not necessarily mean that its language is without content, it does mean that the Constitution must be interpreted and that any act of interpretation is not an automatic or simple process. Judges, as fallible human beings, can make mistakes or exceed what might reasonably be considered a valid effort at interpretation. In any case, in instances where there is considerable room for interpretation, should the view of judges hold sway over the view of legislatures and the people? Many have been unwilling to accept the Court as the final interpreter without any checks or balances.

Stated in its most unqualified form, the problem of judicial review seems threatening: The Supreme Court says what the Constitution means, and the Constitution is the final and highest law of the land; therefore, the Court rules as it wants. Yet this formulation overlooks a number of important limitations on the judiciary. It cannot be supposed that most judges want to "govern" beyond the mandate of the Constitution; and the method of selecting judges by the president and Senate usually ensures some degree of conformity between public officials and the judiciary. Moreover, the other institutions do not simply accept what the Court says and offer no resistance. In fact, there is often a struggle between the institutions when they are in conflict, with each calling on certain resources. Let us look first at the potential checks that can be called on by others against the Court and then at the ways in which the Court itself has behaved in the system of separation of powers.

External Checks on the Power of the Courts

Are the other branches obliged to recognize the Supreme Court's Constitutional rulings as authoritative? If they disagree with those rulings, what steps may they legitimately undertake to change them? The answers given to these questions throughout our history demonstrate that the authority of the Supreme Court is not unlimited. Yet, far more than the checks and balances between the president and the Congress, the limitations on the Court are often rather ambiguous doctrines; their use has been called into question, and today they seem to offer less of a check on the courts than they did in the past.

The Doctrine of Concurrent Responsibility Judges may "say what the law is" in cases coming before them, but this does not necessarily determine the binding force of those pronouncements. The doctrine of concurrent responsibility, espoused in its fullest form by some presidents in the nineteenth century, held that each branch had a responsibility to determine the Constitutionality of matters within its own sphere. In short, the Court might say what the law is, but so could the president and Congress.

President Jefferson first put forth this view, arguing that "the opinion which gives to the Judges the right to decide what Laws are constitutional, and what not, not only for themselves in their own sphere of action, but for the Legislative and Executive also in their own spheres, would make the Judiciary a despotic branch."[33] For Jefferson, the "branch which is to act ultimately, and without appeal, on any law, is the rightful expositor to the validity of the law, uncontrolled by the opinions of the other co-ordinate branches." President Jackson fol-

BOX 13.5

SOME WHO HAVE QUESTIONED JUDICIAL REVIEW

To consider the judges as the ultimate arbiters of all constitutional questions is a very dangerous doctrine, and one which would place us under the despotism of an oligarchy.

—Thomas Jefferson, Letter to William Charles Jarvis

The candid citizen must confess that if the policy of the government, upon vital questions affecting the whole people, is to be irrevocably fixed by decisions of the Supreme Court, the instant they are made, in ordinary litigation between parties, in personal actions, the people will have ceased to be their own rulers, having, to that extent, practically resigned their government into the hands of an eminent tribunal.

—Abraham Lincoln, First Inaugural Address

There appears to be only one means by which the federal courts, including the Supreme Court, can be brought back to constitutional legitimacy. That would be a constitutional amendment making any federal or state court decision subject to being overruled by a majority vote of each House of Congress.

—Robert Bork, *Slouching Towards Gomorrah*

lowed Jefferson's reasoning, arguing that the president must "be guided by [his] own opinion of the Constitution—and support it as he understands it, and not as it is understood by others."[34]

Where there is no direct conflict of institutional power, this doctrine poses no serious problem. For example, there is no difficulty when a president vetoes a bill in the belief that it is unconstitutional, even if the Court had considered similar legislation to be Constitutional. But in those instances in which the Court seeks to prevent the president or Congress from doing what either believes to be Constitutional, or in those instances in which the Court requires executive assistance to enforce a ruling of unconstitutionality with which the president disagrees, there is a direct conflict. Here the doctrine that each branch should be "guided by its own opinion of the Constitution" can result in profound uncertainty. (In one instance, involving a Supreme Court decision on a state law that conflicted with a federal recognition of an Indian nation, President Jackson allegedly responded, "John Marshall has made his decision, now let him enforce it."[35]) Jefferson was aware of the difficulties posed by the doctrine of concurrent responsibility, but he thought that the resulting ambiguities were less dangerous to the nation

than giving the Court alone ultimate authority over all Constitutional questions.

In this open and unabashed form, the doctrine of concurrent responsibility seems to have lost support as a respectable Constitutional doctrine. Prior to the steel seizure case in 1952 and the Watergate tapes case in 1974, both Presidents Truman and Nixon declined to say whether they would comply with an unfavorable judicial ruling. After the decisions, however, both gave in and submitted to the Court, although it is certainly possible in the future that another president under different circumstances might act differently. By and large, however, members of Congress and presidents in this century have come closer and closer to recognizing that the Court has the definitive last word in Constitutional interpretation.

Limited Applicability of Court Decisions The *Dred Scott* decision in 1857 interpreted the Constitution in a way that was directly at odds with a central plank in the Republican party platform. In dealing with this problem Abraham Lincoln, then a U.S. Senate candidate in Illinois, sought to clarify the possible limits on the authority of Supreme Court rulings. Court rulings, he argued, do two things simultaneously: they decide the specific case before the Court, and they create precedents that may serve as the basis of further decisions. According to Lincoln, a Court decision is always authoritative with regard to a particular case, but its value for determining future cases is subject to question. Some decisions, by virtue of their consistency with established legal principles, fully settle Constitutional questions. But decisions that many find to be without Constitutional foundation, like *Dred Scott,* can be a legitimate subject of debate in the political arena by political parties and candidates for public office. Victory by a party opposing a Supreme Court decision can be taken as a sign that the Court's decision should be reversed. (Following his election Lincoln appointed to the Supreme Court men who shared his opposition to the *Dred Scott* decision.)

In Lincoln's view, then, the pronouncement of a Constitutional interpretation need not end the debate and leave people with the sole—and difficult—remedy of a Constitutional amendment. Rather, widespread public opposition can reopen the discussion of Constitutional questions in the political arena. This position involves a subtle distinction between respect for the Court's rulings in particular cases and opposition to a general policy enunciated by the Court. Lincoln was not arguing that a majority of the people should always decide Constitutional questions; but he was arguing that the political process and the President—and not just the courts—had a definite role to play in resolving great Constitutional issues. Others have recently adopted the same view. The Republican party in its platforms of 1980, 1984, and 1988 opposed the Court rulings in *Roe v. Wade,* and in 1986, Attorney General Edwin Meese directly challenged the view that Supreme Court cases automatically create blanket Constitutional rules that should be accepted by the people or the other branches of the government.

This view contends, then, that political parties and other institutions may actively confront the Court in controversial issues with their own understanding of what the Constitution means. Since the 1970s, some members of Congress have employed certain techniques to express their "dissatisfaction" with the Court by introducing laws that assume different interpretations from those that have been employed by the Court. Since the 1970s, numerous bills have been introduced to limit the use of busing as a remedy for school segregation, while others were introduced to modify or overturn *Roe v. Wade.* These proposed laws, which run directly counter to the thrust of the Court's Constitutional interpretations, were intended to register public sentiment and thereby perhaps to "encourage" the Court to shift ground, though attempting to change the position of the Court in this way can often entrench the undesirable holding. After Congress passed a law that sought to change the requirements for voluntary confessions to the police as set out in *Miranda v. Arizona*, the Court ruled in *Dickerson v. U.S* (2000) that Constitutional decisions of the Court cannot be overturned by an Act of Congress. This strong statement in support of keeping the rule as set out in *Miranda* makes it less likely that the Court will change its position in the near future.

"Disciplining" the Court   There are a few potential weapons that Congress and the president potentially have at their disposal to curb the power of the Court. One is impeachment, which President Jefferson once seriously considered using as a way to win control of the judiciary from the Federalists. However, very early on, in 1805, the Senate's acquittal of Justice Samuel Chase in an impeachment trial established the precedent that judicial impeachment was not a tool to discipline the opinions of the judges, but an instrument for dealing with instances of corruption or dubious ethical behavior.

A second device is to change the size of the Court, since the number of judges is set not by the Constitution but by law. Congress therefore could increase or diminish the number of judges in order to influence its rulings. In fact, it did so three times during the 1860s, the last time to deny President Andrew Johnson the ability to replace retiring justices. In response to the Court's rejection of many of his New Deal programs, President Franklin Roosevelt after his landslide 1936 reelection proposed a plan to add one additional justice—up to a maximum of fifteen—for each justice over age seventy who refused to retire. Ostensibly, Roosevelt justified the proposal as a means to ease the judicial workload; however, Congress saw it as an illegitimate attack on judicial independence. The effort nonetheless apparently convinced one justice of the seriousness of the threat to the Court, leading him to change his mind on several key decisions that came before the Court in the next term; historians and judicial scholars have labelled this reversal as the "switch in time that saved nine." Since President Roosevelt's partial failure with the Court-packing plan, the present size of the Supreme Court (nine justices) has become virtually an accepted part of the unwritten constitution.

A final possible means of checking the Court would be for Congress to remove its jurisdiction over certain kinds of cases. The Constitution gives the Supreme Court original (or automatic) jurisdiction over cases in only a few areas; most of the cases that reach the Court come to it under its appellate authority, which is based on federal statute and which could possibly, therefore, be revoked, either in its entirety or in part. In one instance, following the Civil War, Congress used this power to curtail the Court's jurisdiction, and the Court accepted Congress's authority to do so in *Ex parte McCardle*, 1869.

In the 1970s and 1980s, many attempts were made in Congress to remove the jurisdictional authority of the federal courts in large areas of policy such as school desegregation, school prayer, and abortion. But no such law ever passed. Many legislators who opposed Court decisions nevertheless voted against limiting its jurisdiction, on the grounds that this kind of action would compromise the independence of the judicial system. Moreover, some argued that—despite the *McCardle* precedent—any such curtailment would be an unconstitutional infringement of the "judicial power" vested in the judiciary under Article III. The Supreme Court until now has purposely avoided answering this question. As with the technique of changing the size of the Court, changing its appellate jurisdiction to check its power would be extremely difficult.

The Amending Process Congress can initiate and the states can ratify Constitutional amendments to overturn Court decisions. Amendments have overturned Court decisions on at least four occasions: the Eleventh Amendment, broadening state immunity from lawsuits, which over-

turned *Chisholm v. Georgia* (1793); the Fourteenth Amendment, guaranteeing citizenship for blacks, which overruled *Dred Scott v. Sanford* (1857); the Sixteenth Amendment, permitting a federal income tax, which overruled *Pollock v. Farmer's Loan and Trust* (1895); and the Twenty-Sixth Amendment, establishing 18 years as the legal voting age, which overturned part of the decision of *Oregon v. Mitchell* (1970). During the last decade, a number of different amendments were pushed, unsuccessfully, to overturn Court decisions in the areas of school prayer, abortion, and flag burning.

All twenty-seven amendments to the Constitution have been proposed by Congress; however, Article V also mandates that Congress shall call a constitutional convention when one is requested by two-thirds of the states. This provision has never been utilized since the original Constitutional convention in 1787 and many scholars fear what might be proposed by another one; nevertheless, by the late 1980s, over thirty states had passed resolutions calling for a constitutional convention to draft an amendment requiring a balanced federal budget. As this number approaches two-thirds Congress may be prodded into proposing an amendment of its own. In this instance, a convention is intended as a check on Congress; however, it could also be employed to check the judiciary.

Reliance on the amending process is a difficult hurdle to clear, and making frequent use of it might greatly add to the length of the Constitution. Moreover, it can only with much hesitation be spoken of as a check on the Court. When those disagreeing with the Court's Constitutional interpretations resort to the amendment process to make changes, they in effect concede that the Court is the ultimate arbiter of the meaning of the Constitution.

Internal Restraints on the Power of the Court

Internal restraints refer to the doctrines that judges and courts employ to limit their own involvement in major policies, either as a matter of prudence or as a matter of judicial philosophy. The willingness to adopt internal restraints depends partly on the strength of external checks, which will clearly affect the behavior of judges.

Prudential Restraint Considerations of prudence derive from the justices' analysis of the Court's power position in the political system. The Court's authority rests in large part on the public perception that it is a nonpolitical body exercising a judicial function. If this perception is endangered, so too is the position and power of the Court. From what happened to the Court after the Civil War and what nearly occurred after the New Deal, justices must be aware of the possibility that they can become too actively engaged in political affairs and provoke the other institutions into efforts to restrict the Court's authority. Part of the Court's restraint, in other words, may come from the justices' calculation of what will maintain the Court's power over the long term, and avoiding certain controversial questions may well be the best tactic.

Yet the judges' willingness to show restraint based such calculations of prudence will obviously depend on their estimation of the likelihood that the other branches may use some of the checks that they have at their disposal. To the degree that judges can be confident that the other branches will not employ these weapons, the restraints imposed by prudence will correspondingly diminish. By the 1970s, many judges had clearly come to doubt that any kind of check would be used against them.

The Nature of the Judicial Power One way the judicial branch has been able to avoid controversy, at least traditionally, derives from the nature of the judicial power. The courts themselves do not initiate judgment, but rather make judgments in response to specific cases or controversies brought to them in the course of trying criminal cases or hearing civil suits. The courts, in other words, are "passive" instruments; it is not for them to step in where they please and devise general rulings.

This limit on judicial involvement, however, is not entirely automatic. Partly it is a matter of the courts' own choice. Our entire society has become more given to suits and litigation, which is a change that the courts themselves facilitated by easing the definition of what constitutes a "case" and "controversy." The sample of policy questions that arrives before the courts, therefore, is much larger than ever before. This has enabled the courts to become involved in more areas. Many judges and lawyers also have sought to increase the scope of court involvement in policy matters and to end the idea that courts should be "passive" bodies.

Specific Techniques of Restraint Supreme Court justices have devised certain judicial doctrines to sidestep certain issues that are too touchy or that might not admit easily of any judicial remedy. The most important of these is the political-question doctrine, under which the Court refuses to rule when the challenged government action involves matters that the Constitution leaves directly to the discretion of one of the two political branches.

What constitutes a "political question" is of course something that the Court itself decides. Issues that have been judged political questions in one era—for example, the problem of malapportionment of legislatures—have subsequently been declared proper subjects of judicial remedy and intervention in another era. In general, however, the political-question doctrine provides the Court with a reason for not taking action in certain difficult areas, frequently those involving the discretion of the president in the conduct of foreign affairs. For example, during the Vietnam War, the Supreme Court, using arguments based on prudence, avoided the political thicket and repeatedly refused to rule on the Constitutionality of the American military presence in Indochina.

The usefulness of this doctrine in avoiding interbranch conflict is illustrated by *Goldwater v. Carter* (1980), in which the Court refused to decide whether President Carter could terminate a treaty with Taiwan without congressional authorization. Stressing the president's authority over foreign relations, Justice Rehnquist argued that the Court should stay out of this "political" feud between the president and Congress; this case was "a dispute between coequal branches of our government, each of which has resources available to protect and assert its interests, resources not available to private litigants outside the judicial forum."[36]

A second doctrine the Court has employed in the past to limit its role is that of according the actions of Congress or the president a "presumption of Constitutionality." As noted, no more than 105 federal laws have been struck down, most of them of minor importance. This deference reflects an acknowledgment that the Constitutional judgment of coequal branches is entitled to great weight. In the words of Justice Harlan Fiske Stone, "courts are not the only agency of government that must be assumed to have the capacity to govern" *(United States v. Butler,* 1936). As in the case of the political-question doctrine, however, the success of the "presumption of constitutionality" in avoiding excessive judicial intervention depends on the Court's willingness to adhere to it. At times the Court has been extremely deferential, while at other moments it has seemingly tried to settle by itself the most "political" questions facing the nation. Finally, it should be observed that both the doctrines noted here apply only to the Court's relationship to the other branches of the federal government and not to its relations to the states.

Judicial Philosophies: Activism and Restraint
The frequently employed labels of "activism" and "restraint" are easily misapplied. In using these terms, many people confuse the involvement of the Court (the number of laws, for example, that it finds to be unconstitutional) with the Court's intentions (the extent to which the Court does or does not want to make policy). In fact, the degree to which the Court becomes involved may be much less dependent on its intentions than on the activities of Congress and the states. If Congress or the states happen to pass a great deal of clearly unconstitutional legislation, then the Court, in saying "what the law is," would necessarily appear active in striking down these laws. To do less in such circumstances would be not so much to show restraint as to abdicate. By the same token, if the other branches or the states are careful and pass no clearly unconstitutional legislation, but the Court nonetheless imposes its own will on a few occasions, its level of activity would be limited, but its intentions would be activist. It is obvious that what one sees as activism or restraint will depend greatly on how one interprets the Constitution in particular instances.

Recognizing the difficulty of using these terms with precision, we can nevertheless apply them to refer to a certain mood or disposition on the part of the judges. As such, the terms reflect judicial intentions about their role. Restraint refers to a judicial disposition that accords a "presumption of constitutionality" to the actions of the other branches and the states. Where a tenuous interpretation is involved, advocates of restraint say that it should be the views of the political branches, and not those of the courts, that should prevail. This restraint is all the more important, some judges argue, because the formal checks on the Court as the final interpreter are so tenuous. According to Justice Stone, "While unconstitutional exercise of power by the executive and legislative branches of government is subject to judicial restraint, the only check upon our own exercise of power is our own sense of self-restraint" *(United States v. Butler,* 1936). Judges who believe in restraint may have doubts as well about the ability of judicial solutions to in fact resolve many problems. Activism, by contrast, refers to a judicial disposition that holds that the courts can and should involve themselves in broadly interpreting the law and finding in it new doctrines of growth and development. A particularly strong form of activism holds that the courts should "use" the law with some license to make "good" policy (see Box 13.6).

Few judges readily admit to strong forms of activism, as this philosophy claims more authority for courts than the public at large is prepared to give them. Yet certain scholars have been willing to discuss these matters more bluntly; and for those who entertain an activist position, the key question becomes not simply whether the Court is activist, but for what and for whom. The largest number of defenders of activism today deplore the type of activism of the Court during the late nineteenth and early twentieth centuries, when the decisions were made on behalf of property rights and a laissez faire philosophy; instead, they favor an activism that protects rights of free expression or helps to secure the interests of those said to be inadequately represented in the political process. Law professor Arthur S. Miller has stated what is probably the

---

BOX 13.6

Judicial Activism and Restraint

One advocate of judicial activism is Abram Chayes, professor of law at Harvard University:

> . . . The growth of judicial power has been, in large part, a function of the failure of other agencies to respond to groups that have been able to mobilize considerable resources and energy. . . . In my view, judicial action only achieves . . . legitimacy by responding to, indeed by stirring, the deep and durable command for justice in our society. . . . In practice, if not in words, the American legal tradition has always acknowledged the importance of substantive results for the legitimacy and accountability of judicial action.

In his dissenting opinion in *West Virginia State Board of Education v. Barnette* (1943), Supreme Court Justice Felix Frankfurter argues for judicial restraint in assessing the Constitutionality of a West Virginia statute compelling students to salute the flag in classrooms:

> It can never be emphasized too much that one's own opinion about the wisdom or evil of a law should be excluded altogether when one is doing one's duty on the bench. The only opinion of our own even looking in that direction that is material is our opinion whether legislators could in reason have enacted such a law. In the light of all the circumstances, including the history of this question in this Court, it would require more daring than I possess to deny that reasonable legislators could have taken the action which is before us for review.

Source: Walter F. Murphy and C. Herman Pritchett, *Courts, Judges, and Politics,* second ed. (New York: Random House, 1974), pp. 60–61; 729.

---

most extreme version of activism, arguing that the Supreme Court should function as a "Council of Elders" whose work would be "result-oriented" in upholding human dignity through more judicial intervention in the political process.[37]

A theory of judicial interpretation that many find to parallel restraint—but that is not necessarily the same thing—is known as "originalism." The essence of this position is that judges should decide cases on the basis of meanings that are stated or clearly implicit in the words of the Constitution. Where there is doubt about what those words mean, the justices should look to the intent of those who drafted or ratified the text. They should strictly avoid reading their own views or contemporary theories of justice into the Constitution. The opposing view is known as "non-originalism." The essence of this position is that meanings change and justices have as their duty to interpret the text in light of evolving standards of right or justice. According to Justice Brennan, "What the constitutional fundamentals meant to the wisdom of other times cannot be their measure to the vision of our times."

The Institutional Resources of the Courts

The emphasis in this section has been on the problem of judicial review and hence on the potential for conflict between the courts and the other institutions. Much of the time, however, there is little or no conflict. Judges, appointed by the president and confirmed by the Senate, are not usually "out of step" with the majority. Nor do they—usually—have a desire to involve the Court in conflict. For their part, the other branches and the public both respect and support an independent judiciary having a legitimate claim to judicial review (though perhaps not to an uncontested role in interpreting the Constitution).

Still, serious conflicts do occur, and there are periods when the relationship between the Court and the political branches is the major institutional question facing the country, as at the time of the *Dred Scott* decision, during the stormy decade of the Great Depression, and, most recently, in the later years of Chief Justice Warren's term. In the test of will that ensues between the courts and the other bodies, the courts have important resources to call on. They have the political support of the groups that benefit from their decisions; the general support of the legal profession, which constitutes a powerful element in society that tends to respect the principle of judicial determination of policies; and finally, to a remarkable degree, a general level of support from the American public, which accepts the basic idea of the role of the courts as interpreters of the Constitution.

Yet the courts clearly have certain disadvantages in a contest with the other branches. They lack the direct popular backing of the public that the executive or legislature possesses. The president and Congress (if not the state governments) also possess certain legal weapons that they can conceivably bring to bear against the courts, although in recent times these have perhaps appeared more as distant threats than immediate possibilities. While the courts may well have backed off from certain areas to avoid too much public dissatisfaction (an outright ban on capital punishment being perhaps a case in point), the courts today seem to be in a stronger position than at any point in our history. The other branches have seemingly accepted judicial supremacy in Constitutional interpretation and have avoided any direct assaults on judicial authority. Therefore, the extent to which judges will continue to involve themselves in policy will depend less on external restraints and more on the judicial philosophies of those who are appointed as judges.

Conclusion

In a democratic political system, the judiciary stands out as a striking exception. By the method of choice (appointment), the length of tenure (life), and the mode of deliberation (secrecy), the federal judicial system embodies attributes that are in tension with the normal practices of democratic institutions. The founders intended the judiciary to have such characteristics precisely because the protection of the rule of law would be enhanced by an independent and non-democractic institution. Although the founders clearly wanted this institution to be powerful, they did not seek to establish judicial supremacy over the other branches. The power balance among the institutions, rooted in their compet-

ing claims of authority as established by the Constitution and by tradition, was not fully resolved by the founders and remains a question that faces each generation.

Cases Cited

Baker v. Carr, 369 U.S. 186 (1962).

Branzburg v. Hayes, 408 U.S. 665 (1972).

Brown v. Board of Education of Topeka, 347 U.S. 483 (1954); and 349 U.S. 294 (1955).

Buckley v. Valeo, 421 U.S. 1 (1976).

Chisholm v. Georgia, 2 Dallas 419 (1793).

Colegrove v. Green, 328 U.S. 549 (1946).

Dickerson v. United States, 530 U. S. 428, 2002.

Dred Scott v. Sanford, 19 Howard 393 (1857).

Furman v. Georgia, 408 U.S. 238 (1972).

Goldwater v. Carter, 444 U.S. (1979).

Griggs v. Duke Power Company, 401 U.S. 424 (1971).

Hunt v. Washington Apple Advertising Commission, 432 U.S. 333 (1977).

Marbury v. Madison, 1 Cranch 137 (1803).

McCardle, ex parte, 7 Wallace 506 (1869).

McCulloch v. Maryland, 4 Wheaton 316 (1819).

Miranda v. Arizona, 384 U.S. 436, 1996.

Oregon v. Mitchell, 400 U.S. 112 (1970).

Plessy v. Ferguson, 163 U.S. 537 (1896).

Pollack v. Farmer's Loan and Trust, 157 U.S. 429 (1895).

Public Utilities Commission v. Pollack, 343 U.S. 451 (1951).

Rummel v. Estelle, 445 U.S. 263 (1980).

United States v. Butler, 297 U.S. 1 (1936).

United States v. Curtiss Wright, 299 U.S. 304 (1936).

United States v. Nixon, 417 U.S. 683 (1974).

West Virginia State Board of Education v. Barnette, 319 U.S. 624 (1943).

Wyatt v. Stickney, 344 F. Supp. 373 (1971).

Youngstown Sheet and Tube Co. v. Sawyer, 343 U.S. 579 (1952).

Chapter 13 Notes

1. Gerald Gunther ed., *John Marshall's Defense of McCulloch v. Maryland* (Stanford: Stanford University Press, 1969), p. 11.
2. Alexis de Tocqueville, *Democracy in America,* J.P. Mayer ed. (Garden City: Doubleday, 1968), p. 270.

3. Ward Elliott, *The Rise of the Guardian Democracy* (Cambridge: Harvard University Press, 1974); Robert Nisbet, *Prejudices: A Philosophical Dictionary* (Cambridge: Harvard University Press, 1982).

4. John Hart Ely, *Democracy and Distrust* (Cambridge: Harvard University Press, 1980); Richard Neely, *How Courts Govern America* (New Haven: Yale University Press, 1981).

5. Henry Abraham, *The Judicial Process* (New York: Oxford University Press, 1975), p. 319.

6. This figure does not count each separate instance of the approximately 200 legislative veto provisions that were struck down by the Court in 1983.

7. Walter F. Murphy and C. Herman Pritchett, *Courts, Judges, and Politics* 2nd ed. (New York: Random House, 1974), p. 414.

8. Quoted in Abraham, p. 522.

9. The Supreme Court upheld this review power in *Martin v. Hunter's Lessee,* 1 *Wheaton* 304 (1816). Congress did not give the Court the power to review cases which affirmed Supreme Court decisions until 1914.

10. This had resulted from congressional legislation—most notably the Judiciary Act of 1925—narrowing the categories of cases in which parties have a right of appeal to the Court. In 1988, Congress eliminated almost all of the Supreme Court's remaining mandatory appellate jurisdiction, except for appeals in reapportionment cases, suits under the Civil Rights and Voting Rights Acts, antitrust laws, and the Presidential Election Campaign Fund Act. See Gerald Gunther, *Constitutional Law* supplement (Westbury, N.Y.: Foundation Press, 1989), pp. 4–5, and David O'Brien, *Storm Center* 2nd ed. (New York: Norton, 1990), pp. 187, 196–7.

11. Fred Vinson, "Work of the U.S. Supreme Court," *Texas Bar Journal,* December 1949, p. 551.

12. Anthony Lewis, *Gideon's Trumpet* (New York: Vintage, 1964), p. 162.

13. Senator Coe Crawford, (R-S.D.) quoted in Hall, "Why We Don't Elect Federal Judges," *This Constitution,* Spring 1986, no. 10, p. 24.

14. Henry F. Pringle, *The Life and Times of William Howard Taft,* vol. 2 (Hamden, Conn.: Archon, 1939), p. 768.

15. Quoted in *This Constitution,* no. 10, Spring 1986, p. 20.

16. Quoted in O'Brien, 1990, p. 70.

17. Keefe et al., 1990, p. 538.

18. Murphy and Pritchett, p. 169.

19. President Reagan next nominated circuit court judge Douglas Ginsburg, but was forced to withdraw this nomination within 10 days because of allegations that Ginsburg had smoked marijuana as a Harvard Law School professor and because of growing concerns about his lack of judicial experience.

20. Robert H. Bork, *The Tempting of America* (New York: Free Press, 1990), p. 347.

21. Abraham, p. 75.

22. "Why Do We Elect State Judges," *This Constitution,* Spring 1986, no. 10, p. 25.

23. Henry Abraham, *The Judicial Process* 5th. ed. (New York: Oxford University Press, 1986), p. 39.

24. *United States v. Butler* (1936).

25. Benjamin N. Cardozo, *The Nature of the Judicial Process* (New Haven: Yale University Press, 1921), p. 168.

26. *Valley Forge Christian College v. Americans United for the Separation of Church and State* 454 U.S. 464, at 473, 487; quoted in Abraham, 1985, p. 372.

27. O'Brien, 1990, pp. 204–5.

28. Frank M. Johnson, "The Constitution and the Federal District Judge," *Texas Law Review,* June 1976, p. 906.

29. Donald L. Horowitz, *The Courts and Social Policy* (Washington: Brookings Institution, 1977), p. 44.

30. Justices had challenged a federal law in three cases prior to *Marbury v. Madison—Hayburn's case* (1792), *Van Horne's Lessee v. Dorrance,* (1795), and in *Cooper v. Telfair* (1800). But in none of these cases was the doctrine of judicial review fully presented and argued for in depth.

31. James B. Thayer, "The Origin and Scope of the American Doctrine of Constitutional Law," reprinted in Gary L. McDowell ed., *Taking the Constitution Seriously* (Dubuque: Kendall Hunt, 1981). Originally published in 1873.

32. Ely, pp. 4–5.

33. Quoted in David O'Brien, *Constitutional Law and Politics* (New York: Norton, 1991), p. 7.

34. President's Veto Message (July 10, 1832), reprinted in James D. Richardson ed., *Messages and Papers on the Presidents,* vols. 1–10 (Washington: U.S. Government Printing Office, 1917), p. 582.

35. Quoted by Edward Corwin, *The Doctrine of Judicial Review* (Princeton: Princeton University Press, 1914), p. 14.

36. *Goldwater v. Carter* 444 U.S. 996 (1980).

37. Arthur Miller, *Toward Increased Judicial Activism: The Political Role of the Supreme Court* (Westport, Conn.: Greenwood Press, 1982).

14

The Bureaucracy

CHAPTER CONTENTS

To carry out policy, modern government requires a variety of organizations, which are referred to as the bureaucracy. This is the part of the government that most Americans are likely to have direct contact. This is the part of the government with which most Americans are likely to have direct contact. Often this contact will be with officials of state and local governments—a city police officer, a state highway patrol man, or a public school teacher. In the case of the federal government, on which we will focus here, the contact might be in the form of a "friendly" chat with a tax collector from the Internal Revenue Service (IRS), an urgent visit to a doctor in the Veteran Affairs Department (VA), or a call to an agent of the Federal Bureau of Investigation (FBI). In addition, in our complicated system of federalism, citizens often deal with state and local officials who are being paid in part with federal funds and who are carrying out policies defined partly by the federal government, such as school teachers in many special education programs.

While citizens often have great confidence in the particular government worker they are dealing with, they generally have a different idea of the bureaucracy as a whole. For most people, bureaucracy conjures up the frightful image of legions of obscure people, employed in vast impersonal organizations, who take delight in frustrating citizens with thousands of incomprehensible rules. No wonder, then, that so many who run for political office find good sport in attacking "pointy-headed government bureaucrats" and in promising to clean up the "bureaucratic mess" in Washington—until, that is, a bureaucracy like the Defense Department, after years of being criticized, performs brilliantly in an operation like the Gulf War in 1991.

A public bureaucracy is composed of persons employed directly by government (other than the elected officials). It generally refers to the *structures and organizations* that have been established to carry out public policy—agencies like the aforementioned IRS, VA, or FBI. (Almost all large bureaucratic agencies seem to carry alphabetic labels!) Many important governmental policies are designed and implemented by a handful of high-level personnel—such as when the president decides with his secretaries of Defense and State on a foreign policy position and then instructs one of them to negotiate with a foreign government. Usually, however, the policies of modern government cannot be devised or implemented without the assistance of an organization, and often a large one. Defending the nation, for example, requires the whole of the armed services and the Defense Department (in all more than a million people), and conducting the nation's diplomacy relies on the expertise and the skills of those in Intelligence agencies and the State Department. The task of carrying out policies in the broadest sense is known as public administration. Today bureaucracy is one of the main instruments of public administration. When we speak of governing in the modern world, we speak of bureaucracy.

A bureaucracy, whether public or private, can be defined as a large organization with a hierarchy of superior-subordinate relations. Individuals in a bureaucracy have official positions with fixed limits of authority, and (except at the highest levels) they are generally appointed on the basis of "objective" tests of their ability to perform their jobs. An individual who begins his own business as a pizza maker and hires his brother-in-law to make deliveries is not part of a bureaucratic organization; as the owner, that person can decide how long to work, who to hire and fire, and when to call it quits. Not so for a bureaucrat. He or she is generally part of a large organization with a predefined mission (for example, inspecting coal mines for possible violations of safety regulations) and faces all kinds of rules about how to act on the job. After the bureaucrat has left, the organization will almost certainly continue to exist.

Bureaucracy is so important for modern government that political scientists have tried to describe what bureaucratic organizations do and why they do it, in hopes of explaining the character of the political system by reference to their behavior. Two overarching theories about modern government have emerged from the study of bureaucracy. The first is what we have called the "bureaucratic politics" model. In this view, beyond the functions that organizations are assigned, each develops an interest in protecting and sometimes increasing its own power within the government. Agencies act to defend their own turf. In many versions of this model, it is held that the policies of the government can often be explained by understanding the power relationships among the different bureaucratic units and the compromises that are struck among them.

A second general theory is that bureaucracy sums up the central reality of modern government and its relationship to society. In this view we live in what is sometimes called the "bureaucratic state," or the "administrative state," which refers to a system where government regulates or directs large spheres of human activities, using bureaucracies as its agent. Political decisions are made less and less by elected representative bodies that pass laws and more and more by administrative agencies that write rules and regulations. Businesses and universities, for example, find that many of the decisions they make about employment may face scrutiny from one federal agency or another, which may instruct them to alter their hiring practices based on federal anti-discrimination or affirmative action statutes. Bureaucracies under this theory may also abuse their discretion and act in a high-handed or arbitrary fashion. Congressional hearings in 1997 into alleged abuses by the Internal Revenue Service (IRS) demonstrated how the arbitrary actions of a powerful bureaucratic agency can have dramatic effects on the lives of American citizens. In one example, the IRS threatened to seize the bank account and car of a New York priest because of a mix-up over a charitable trust he managed for his dead mother. Another witness remarked that the IRS is "judge, jury and executioner—answerable to none."

These two general theories of bureaucracy raise major questions about who really rules in the American political system, regardless of what official constitutional policies may proclaim. After surveying the development of public administration in the United States, we shall ask how accurate or helpful these theories are in capturing the reality of how American bureaucracy actually operates.

The Bureaucracy: Constitutional Foundations

The founders were keenly aware of the importance of sound administration and regarded the inability of the government of the Articles to execute its policies as one of its main defects. This failure, most founders agreed, resulted from the absence of a strong and independent executive. A legislative body, while it might formulate general rules, was ill-suited to putting them into effect. Running the government—administration—was a distinct process that required an institution that was capable of command and energy. The decision taken in 1787 to establish an independent presidency was therefore a major step in changing the government's capacity for administration. But it clearly did not resolve all of the issues in this area. The Constitution, in fact, left open or only partly settled many fundamental questions of administration. In some instances this might have been by oversight. But the founders were also consciously aware of the limits of a written constitution in resolving many administrative matters, and they deliberately left much in this area to future generations to determine.

The Constitution accordingly does not specify the exact units of administration, referring only to the "executive departments" (Article II, section 2). Certain principal departments were already so much a part of the operation of government—War, Treasury, and State—that there was no need to list them. As for other departments, they would need to adapt to changing circumstances. There was, for example, no Department of Energy or of Labor in 1789. The Constitution thus gives the legislature the authority to establish and abolish administrative units. The task of creating an administrative structure fell initially to the First Congress, which created five departments—State, Treasury, War, Attorney General, and the Post Office—each headed by a single secretary.

The Constitution also does not fully resolve how these administrative units should be arranged. It indicates that departments should be headed by a single individual, but it does not say explicitly that departments are the only kinds of administrative units that can exist. During the first century, nearly all governmental administrative units were placed inside departments. But by the 1880s Congress began to create agencies, such as the Interstate Commerce Commission, outside the immediate control of any department—the purpose usually being to try to create some degree of independence from immediate presidential supervision. Some of these agencies have been headed not by single individuals, but by boards or committees. This practice of establishing important government agencies outside the normal departmental chain of command, which is now so common, has created a bewildering maze of rules and authority within the modern bureaucracy.

Finally, the Constitution does not definitively determine who in fact will exercise the decisive control over the administrative departments. The ambiguity here is an inevitable byproduct of the separation of powers, in which the president, the Congress, and even the courts have certain claims to supervising the bureaucracy. Of course, the president seems to have the strongest claim as head of the executive branch, and no doubt the president has usually had the upper hand, at least for the central core of government agencies. But the history of control of administration in the United States has been one of constant conflict among the branches. This conflict has never fully been resolved, and—however much some deplore this situation—probably never can or will be. At different times, the president and Congress have been more assertive in their claims to control the bureaucracy, but neither has fully yielded to the other. As one scholar has aptly noted, "The Constitution lays the basis for a contest between the executive and the legislature for the control of the administrative agent."[1]

Consider for a moment the different Constitutional foundations of authority for controlling the bureaucracy. The president in Article II is vested with the broad "executive power" and has the solemn responsibility to "take care that the laws be faithfully executed." A claim to direct the bureaucracy seems at the very least implicit in these powers. Moreover, the president "may require the opinion" of the chief officer of each executive department, again suggesting the idea that the president is in charge of the bureaucracy. But it is Congress that passes the laws that set up these units and that defines their tasks. In writing the laws, Congress may try to devolve power from the president to the department or agency head, creating expectations that they will act independently of presidential control. Thus the Attorney General (the head of the Justice Department) and the director of the FBI have their own responsibilities for protecting the law and would be expected in some areas to protect their independence of the White House. Independence can be greater as the law removes the agency from any kind of direct presidential supervision, as in the case of the Federal Election Commission.

The Constitution also leaves room for competing claims with regard to two other key instruments for controlling the bureaucracy—hiring and firing. The president is given the power to appoint top agency personnel. But they must be confirmed by the Senate, and in the course of their confirmation hearings they may make certain promises or assurances to the Senate. (Personnel beneath the top level may be appointed according to a system established by legislation, and today these appointments are handled by one form or another of the merit system, in which neither the president nor Congress plays a direct role.) When it comes to firing top-level appointees, the Constitution is not explicit. The First Congress, with Vice President John Adams casting the tie-breaking vote in the Senate, gave the president by statute the sole power to remove executive officers. (A contrary decision might well have made the agencies totally dependent on Congress*). Later, Congress tried to revoke this power, but presidents claimed that it rested on a Constitutional foun-

---

* The issue of presidential versus congressional removal of administrative officers arose again during the Reconstruction period following the Civil War. The House impeached President Andrew Johnson for violating the Tenure of Office Act of 1866 which mandated that the President must also have the consent of the Senate in order to fire a Cabinet Officer. Some historians and political scientists speculate that if Johnson had been convicted (he was saved by one vote), the United States government would have evolved into a quasi-parliamentary system.

dation—and the Supreme Court eventually largely agreed.[2] Even without direct control over personnel, however, Congress has been able to influence and at times almost run certain agencies. Usually, of course, it is not Congress as a whole that exercises this power, but one of its committees or subcommittees. Congress exercises its influence over the bureaucracy through its control of the purse (appropriations) and by its power to oversee administrative activities, if need be by highly publicized formal investigations.

The effect of the division of authority on the character and effectiveness of the bureaucracy has been one of the most frequently studied issues in American politics. Not surprisingly, no single pattern has been found to hold across the whole of the bureaucracy. In some instances, where bureaucratic agencies have learned to manoeuver adroitly among the president, the Congress and the courts, divided political supervision has meant a considerable degree of autonomy for the agency from higher political control. More often, however, divided supervision has led to agencies that are greatly influenced by political authorities, far more than is the case in most other democracies. Agencies are frequently under conflicting pressures from the three branches of government. (Where the executive has broad control, there is of course the possibility of close management from the top, but also a likelihood that agencies will have a substantial degree of independent discretion.)

American bureaucratic agencies frequently find themselves in a strange situation. By law administrative officials are often assigned a wide degree of discretion, but in practice they may find they cannot exercise that discretion according to their own better judgment. Under pressure or likely to be overruled by Congress or the courts, they often act in a way that tries in advance to take these constraints into account. Although some form of political control of the bureaucracy is clearly necessary and desirable, it does not follow that all forms promote responsible oversight or effective administration.

The Development of the Bureaucracy

The Constitution permits the bureaucracy to develop within rather broad limits. Within these limits, the character and structure of the bureaucracy have been shaped by different theories of administration, by the tasks government has had to perform, and by the impact of major events. Some of the most notable elements of each of these factors are discussed below.

The Case for Energetic Administration: Alexander Hamilton

Alexander Hamilton gave more attention to the question of administration than any other founder, and he is generally acclaimed as one of the first systematic theorists of public administration in the modern world. As the Secretary of the Treasury under President George Washington, Hamilton also had the opportunity to put some of his ideas into practice. Although he did not fully have his way in government—and in the end faced a substantial reaction against his plans—Hamilton's ideas and practices have influenced all subsequent thought about public administration.

The first element of Hamilton's administrative theory was that the bureaucracy should be under the supervision of the chief executive. Organizing administration in this fashion enables the president to exercise leadership: "Energy in the executive is . . . essential to the steady administration of the laws." (*Federalist* 70) Lines of responsibility must be clear, and all executive officials "ought to be considered as the assistants and deputies of the Chief Magistrate and . . . ought to be subject to his superintendence." (*Federalist* 72) Placing administration under the responsibility of the president is not, however, a plan for diminishing the importance of administrators. On the contrary, it is the way to give administrators the greatest possible responsibility consistent with republican government. No president can make every decision himself; he must rely on his top officials, who in turn must often rely on those underneath them. These administrators can then be trusted to run things and be held accountable when they fail.

Executive responsibility thus ordinarily provides for broad administrative discretion, at least where the president does not try to interfere and run everything himself.

Second, Hamilton stressed that administration is a distinct and important aspect of governance, not merely a mechanical or technical function. Administration involves making choices. Few tasks of government, especially important ones, are self-executing; they require someone to put them into effect who must make very important and often politically sensitive judgments. Accordingly, effective governance should allow administrators, acting under the supervision of the executive, to have a reasonable degree of discretion.

The third element in Hamilton's theory concerned the character of administrative personnel. Hamilton favored a stable and professional civil service. This objective would be achieved not by means of guaranteed job tenure but as a matter of practice. Government service should attract highly qualified personnel and then keep them in government service. The experience and knowledge of civil servants would be an invaluable aid to the functioning of the government, helping to provide for "the stability of administration."

Fourth, Hamilton stressed the interrelationship between administration and policy formulation. The officials who are largely responsible for directing or carrying out certain functions should not be reluctant to propose to the president new programs and legislation. High level administrators should be policy initiators. The president, acting in part at the behest of his department heads, should be an active force in the legislative process. Indeed, few individuals in American history have played as a large a role as Alexander Hamilton did in proposing, as Secretary of the Treasury, a program and direction for domestic legislation.

The final element of Hamilton's theory was connected directly to the immediate task after the founding: building unity in the new nation. Sound administration, Hamilton argued, was one of the best ways to attach people to a government, as people naturally turn to a system that is well-run and efficient. It was essential, therefore, that American citizens, especially persons in the commercial class, see their new government in action and appreciate its importance and efficiency. The task of nation building, in Hamilton's view, only began with the adoption of the Constitution, which provided the instrument by which effective leaders and administrators could bind the people to the new government and wean them away from their excessive attachment to the states. The real founding for Hamilton therefore included the governmental program that the Washington Administration sought to put into effect in the 1790s. Toward this end Hamilton favored a broad interpretation of the powers of the federal government, although he was by no means in favor of unlimited federal power and feared that a federal government that penetrated too deeply into local communities would undermine national administration itself.

The Reaction to Hamilton: Jeffersonian Republican Administrative Theory

Hamilton's economic plan for funding the national debt and for encouraging native industries, as well as his method of implimentation, provoked strenuous opposition. Among his chief critics were Thomas Jefferson and James Madison. Both feared that Hamilton was attempting to use administrative discretion to win the support of the urban commercial interests. These interests would then constitute the basis of a party in Congress that could be commanded and controlled by the president, effectively overcoming a real separation of powers and concentrating all authority in the presidency. Such a system is what they termed, perhaps a bit loosely, "monarchism."

In response Madison and Jefferson formed the Republican-Democratic party, which espoused very different ideas about administration. The Republicans would shortly establish congressional committees to oversee executive departments and make independent assessments of budgetary and legislative recommendations from the Treasury. The dominant view in the party was that Congress was the ultimate guardian of the public good and that executive branch officials should enforce the will of Congress and heed the wishes of its committees.

Republicans regarded the Secretary of the Treasury, who was the official most responsible for providing fiscal information to Congress, as being more or less independent of the president and responsible to Congress. Finally, to ensure obedience and reduce discretion of government employees, Republicans passed a law in 1820 imposing fixed time limits on tenure for all government posts, a measure that was designed to guarantee a continual turnover among government workers.

Andrew Jackson's Idea of Public Administration

Andrew Jackson and his followers claimed to be the heirs of the Republican-Democratic party, which they now called simply the Democratic party. But in the domain of administrative theory, Jackson developed his own ideas, some of which differed from the orthodox views of the old party members.

On the power and unity of the executive branch in relation to the departments, Jackson seemed to follow Hamilton's thinking. In 1832, Jackson wanted to close down the National Bank before its charter expired. To do so, he proposed simply removing all federal money from the Bank. The law establishing the Bank, however, gave immediate authority for removing funds—and apparently independent discretion—to the Secretary of the Treasury. Jackson ordered his Treasury Secretary, W. J. Duane, to remove the funds, but Duane refused to do so. Jackson then dismissed Duane and appointed a new Treasury Secretary, who then proceeded to remove the funds. Opponents of Jackson in the Senate condemned this action, contending that the Secretary of the Treasury was in this matter to be responsible to Congress. In their view, Jackson's firing of Duane and the removal of Bank funds marked the beginning of a presidential dictatorship. Jackson by contrast defended his power of dismissal as necessary to executing the laws, and he rejected any idea that Congress could bypass the president and work its own will with department heads. Jackson thus insisted on clear lines of authority within the administrative agency beginning with the chief executive.

Jackson also broke with his predecessors on the question of tenure in the federal administration. Although government workers at the time had no legal guarantee of job protection, the early presidents—Federalists and Republican-Democrats—did not engage in wholesale dismissals when they came into office, even in 1800 when the presidency changed hands from Federalists to Republicans. The early presidents sought to combine political responsiveness in the bureaucracy (by appointing officials sympathetic to their political views) with maintaining a substantial degree of merit and experience. For the upper levels of the civil service, this practice meant appointing individuals of a high level of education (and often "proper" social standing), who were then continued in office if they had served competently. Early administrators tended to have more education and more wealth than most Americans.

President Jackson gave expression to a new understanding of government service that would soon completely transform government personnel policies, even though Jackson's practice did not break sharply from that of his predecessors. Worried about the elitist cast of the bureaucracy, Jackson argued that advanced training and experience were not essentials for government service. The tasks of administration could be performed by common people of ordinary intelligence. The democratic idea required that government positions should change hands often and not remain the property of a distinguished few. This argument would later be used as part of the foundation for the spoils system:

> The duties of all public officers are, or at least admit of being made, so plain and simple that men of intelligence may readily qualify themselves for their performance; and I can not but believe that more is lost by the long continuance of men in office than is generally to be gained by their experience.[3]

Jackson proposed two new methods to control the bureaucracy. First, in place of the judgment of a more or less permanent group of civil servants, Jackson would rely on specific rules to encourage proper behavior by office holders; accurate bookkeeping, close inspections, and regularized procedures would accomplish what "good character" was previously supposed to guarantee. Second, government positions would be reserved for the political supporters of the party or presidential candidate as rewards for their support. These supporters could in turn be counted on to follow the program of the victorious party or candidate. The bureaucracy would be responsive to the people's wishes as expressed through the last election. This idea, together with the democratic notion of rotation in office, laid the foundation for the spoils system.

The Spoils System

The spoils system was the most notorious of all institutional practices of nineteenth-century politics. "To the victor belong the spoils of the enemy," said Senator William Marcy of New York in 1832. With each election, most government jobs would change hands and go to the supporters of the victorious party (or, as time went on, to supporters of the victorious faction within the party). Typical of this wholesale replacement on a partisan basis were the actions of Democratic President Grover Cleveland, who when he took over the presidency in 1885 from his Republican predecessor, Chester Arthur, fired about forty thousand Republican employees and hired Democrats in their place.

The spoils system had its strong points. It helped maintain the political parties, which were the foundation of democracy. It limited the development of too powerful or independent a bureaucratic establishment. It insured, at least in theory, the responsiveness of the bureaucracy to elected officials. And it was highly democratic: it kept government positions from becoming the exclusive preserve of an upper class and distributed them to average Americans. Where the bureaucracy in some European systems was becoming more powerful, elitist and imperious, in the United States it remained highly popular.

The defects of the spoils system, however, grew evident as time went on. It created two major problems. First, it led to a decline in the competence of the federal bureaucracy. People selected because of the party or candidate whom they supported often lacked qualifications for their jobs. The constant turnover of workers undermined the experience of government employees and detracted from any sense of professionalism. Horror stories circulated, many of them true, of illiterates, crooks, and various incompetents holding government positions. Customs agents and inspectors often demanded bribes and drank heavily on the job, while employees of the Office of Indian Affairs regularly defrauded Indians. Examples of this kind could be multiplied throughout the government.

Second, the spoils system had a debilitating effect not just on the civil service, but on the entire political system, especially the parties and the electoral process. With thousands of jobs changing hands after each presidential election, the control of jobs now became a main concern of politicians and parties. Presidents-elect were besieged by insistent job seekers. President James A. Garfield, for example, complained to his wife that he "had hardly arrived [in Washington] before the doorbell began to ring and the old stream of office-seekers began to pour in. They had scented my coming and were lying in wait for me like vultures for a wounded bison."[4] It was not presidents alone, however, who controlled all this patronage. Powerful state officials would condition their support of presidential candidates at nominating conventions on how much patronage a candidate promised to put at their disposal. The nomination and electoral systems were thus influenced by calculations about patronage, and the entire spirit of the government—or so reformers argued—was corrupted by the spoils system.

The bureaucracy in the latter part of the nineteenth century suffered from another problem unconnected to the spoils system: a decline in presidential authority. President Jackson had fought for presidential control over the bureaucracy, but he won the battle only in the short term. After the Civil War it was Congress, not the president, that came to exercise greater control over the bureaucracy. Presidents in this era experienced growing difficulties in managing the government's growing apparatus, and department heads often worked directly with members of Congress on major policy matters as well as day-to-day operations. Legislators participated in patronage deals, examined the details of agency spending plans, scrutinized bureaucratic

---

BOX 14.1

Spoils and Merit: Contrasting Perspectives

A century ago, at the time of civil service reform, the spoils system seemed to many to be one of the major problems with American government. The reformers argued that a merit system was necessary for true representative government. As one put it:

> The villages, the cities, the army posts, the special agencies, the custom-houses, the mayors, the governors, the consulates, the revenue officers, the president—in short, public affairs of every nature and officers of every class—are involved in distrust and are degraded in popular estimation, by reason of the opportunities afforded by a partisan-spoils system of office and the use that is made, or is believed to be made, of these opportunities. . . . Can anyone undertake to estimate how much it has done to impair confidence in institutions, to cast suspicion over all official life, to disgust the people with the very name of politics, to drive good men from the polls, to bring republicanism into disrepute both at home and abroad?

Yet in modern times a number of people criticize civil service because such systems, by protecting bureaucrats from political interference, also shield public employees from the people or their elected officials. One observer of the federal establishment has argued:

> Anyone who has had a reasonable amount of contact with the federal government has encountered people who should be fired. . . . Yet fewer than one per cent are fired each year. . . . I would urge cutting [the civil service] by 50 per cent, and filling the remaining half with political appointees who can be fired at any time. . . . If the government is to work, policy implementation is just as important as policy making. No matter how wise the chief, he has to have the right Indians to transform his ideas into action, to get the job done.

Sources: Dorman B. Eaton, *Civil Service in Great Britain* (New York: Harper, 1880), p. 444; Charles Peters, "A Kind Word for the Spoils System," in Charles Peters and Michael Nelson (eds.), *The Culture of Bureaucracy* (New York: Holt, 1979), pp. 263–267.

operations, and overturned certain agency decisions.

Civil Service Reform

Problems with the spoils system became so widespread after the Civil War that demands for its reform grew stronger. Reform was based on the idea of establishing a neutral and competent bureaucracy that would be free from the manipulation by politicians (see Box 14.1). Civil service reform associations formed in thirteen states during the late 1870s and on the national level in 1881. The assassination of President Garfield by a deranged office-seeker, also in 1881, provided the added impetus for congressional action. Two years later, in 1883, Congress passed the Pendleton Act that began to institute the merit system.

Today almost all full-time federal employees—except nearly three thousand upper level political appointees—are hired under the merit system. Hiring decisions are based in large part on competitive examinations that rate candidates on their ability to perform specialized tasks, such as skills in typing or accounting or managing the work of others. After a trial period, federal merit system employees receive considerable job security that makes it very difficult to dismiss them.

The merit system not only encourages individuals to make government service a full career, but it also limits political intrusion into administrative issues. Workers cannot be fired for resisting pressures to perform tasks to help one party or another. The guiding idea is that the civil servant, while bound to respect the legitimate policy decisions of political superiors, is not the servant of a party or administration, but of the laws and the government. "Responsiveness" in the sense of following election returns is no longer the goal. Rather the civil service is to be respon-

TABLE 14.1
Number of Civilian Employees in the Federal Government 1816–2000

YEAR	TOTAL
1816	4,837
1851	26,274
1881	100,020
1901	239,476
1921	561,142
1930	601,319
1940	1,042,420
1945	3,816,310
1950	1,960,708
1960	2,398,704
1970	2,921,909
1980	2,875,866
1990	3,128,267
1995	2,918,674
2000	2,425,898

Source: *Statistical Abstract of the United States*, 1996 (Washington, D.C.: U.S. Department of Commerce, Bureau of Statistics), p.345.

sive—if this is the right word—to the permanent interests of the nation. This understanding opens the way to a greater degree of autonomy for the bureaucracy, but at the same time it poses a danger that the bureaucracy might become too independent and resistant to direction from above.

Although civil service reform addressed the problems of the corruption and incompetence of government workers, it left unresolved the questions of who would control the bureaucracy and what role administration should play in governing. These issues were taken up by progressive theorists of public administration, the most well known of whom was Woodrow Wilson. Like with Hamilton's ideas, not all of the progressive theories were adopted. They have, however, influenced the way in which many people think about bureaucracy, all the more so because it was in this period that public administration became an academic discipline. Professors now began to teach courses about how to organize, administer, and control government agencies. Initially at least, progressive ideas had by far the greatest influence on shaping the content of this new academic enterprise.

Social Change and Governmental Response in the Late Nineteenth Century

Understanding progressive theory requires attention to some major social transitions that were taking place at the turn of the twentieth century. The economy was being transformed from a system in which the production of goods and services changed from markets made up of small entrepreneurs to markets dominated by large-scale economic enterprises employing hundreds of industrial workers. At the same time, the population as a whole was shifting rapidly from isolated rural areas to urban centers. The rise of the modern corporation and the development of a national economy led to increasing calls for the federal government to deal with new and more complicated tasks

As the economy became more complex, the government gave formal recognition to particular economic sectors. This recognition within the administrative branch could already be seen in the latter part of the nineteenth century in the creation of separate departments for agriculture, commerce, and labor. Previously, departments had been organized around general governmental functions, such as foreign affairs (State) and finance (Treasury). The new units were intended not only to handle the emerging problems associated with particular sectors of the economy, but also to promote these sectors' respective interests by conducting research, publishing statistics, and acting for the welfare of their clientele. The federal bureaucracy grew considerably in size during this period, expanding by more than two hundred thousand employees between 1861 and 1901 (see Table 14.1).

During the latter part of the nineteenth century, the national government also began to enact new kinds of policies. Regulatory legislation first was adopted in 1887, when the Interstate Commerce Commission was established to control rates charged for transporting people and goods between the states, chiefly on railroads. The Interstate Commerce Act was a landmark for public administration in more ways than one. It created a federal commission with discretionary powers to set rates and routes. Thus major governmental authority was delegated, at least formally, from Congress to an agency, and this authority was exercised without precise standards set by Congress. An administrative agency was left to reconcile conflicting goals and set policy in a political environment marked by rival interests and rapidly changing technology. The Interstate Commerce Commission was also set up outside of the usual structure of government and was not accountable to a department head. It was an "independent" agency, structured to allow it to make decisions free of immediate political control from either the president or Congress. The commission became a precedent for other federal regulatory programs.

Progressive Administrative Theory

According to progressive thinkers, the problems facing the United States at the turn of the Twentieth century could not be solved merely by reforming the personnel policies by the merit system. The nation needed a much broader idea of public administration, one that allowed for a new relationship of the federal government to society. For many progressives, this new relationship could only be created by replacing or modifying the Constitution itself.

Woodrow Wilson and other progressive reformers began with the premise that American government as organized in the late nineteenth century was incapable of providing the kind of administration and regulation needed for a modern and increasingly technological society. The political system was too decentralized and political power was too fragmented. What the nation needed, according to Wilson, was a much greater capacity for concentrated action at the center and for effective administration. Wilson criticized the entire political system as it then operated, which he sometimes took to reflect the Founders' thinking. At other times, however, Wilson suggested that the problem lay with Jeffersonian ideas, which he held to be responsible for weakening administration well beyond what many of the founders had wanted. Wilson often praised Hamilton's views and claimed to follow

his theory. But in the final analysis, Wilson's views appeared to be rooted in a different tradition that relied on European—mostly German—administrative theory and on European ideas of a large and highly active central government.

For Wilson the new age required a more active government that would engage in planning and executing complex new programs. These programs in turn demanded large bureaucracies administered by experts who understood the numbing details and puzzling technologies of a given field. To ensure that bureaucratic government would remain responsible to the public, authority should be centralized in relatively few hands, culminating in the president. The president could be held accountable to the voters through periodic elections, assuring a kind of democratic control. The bureaucracy would be transformed into a fine-tuned machine that would efficiently execute policy decisions made at the top. Administrators would be given in practice a wide range of discretion, although they would remain subject at all times to direct presidential control. Wilson for a time proposed changing the Constitution to a parliamentary system that he thought would provide both more effective political leadership and more efficient administration.

As a variation on this general theme, some progressives favored removing politics entirely from administration and making administrative units independent of any direct political control. In this view, the broad political decisions would be made by political bodies, but their execution would be the responsibility of administrative experts. This idea provided part of the underpinning for "independent" administrative agencies.

Second, on the question of the degree of discretion for bureaucratic agencies, Wilson argued that large amounts of authority could be given to the agencies because they would make decisions not on political, but technical, grounds. Policy and administrative decisions were quite separate, and a good corps of administrators could be entrusted with making most of the administrative decisions. Government acts in a two-step process: it makes decisions and it executes them. Policymaking is a political task; implementation of those policies is the job of public administration:

The field of administration is a field of business. It is removed from the hurry and strife of politics; it at most points stands apart even from the debatable grounds of constitutional study. It is a part of political life only as . . . machinery is part of the manufactured product.[5]

Government's administrative agencies can be compared with vending machines: policy is inserted at the top, winds its way through the bureaucratic mechanism, and emerges at the bottom—carried out by experts but essentially undamaged and unchanged. Administrative agencies thus strengthen democratic government by increasing its ability to implement the popular will. Civil service reform insulates politically neutral technocrats from partisan meddling, but they still carry out the goals of popular government.

Third, on personnel matters, Wilson stressed the importance of a stable and competent civil service. In contrast with Hamilton, however, he placed more emphasis on judging competence on the basis of technical skills. Wilson had much greater faith in the science of public administration, than in the kind of broad political judgments that Hamilton emphasized.

Finally, the progressives had great confidence in "the administrative state" and thought that fundamental societal problems could be solved by governmental programs based on techniques of administration. They were among the first to champion the utility of modern "scientific" social science as the key to resolving modern social problems, and they called for the establishment of schools and departments of public administration to train future civil servants in the social sciences. The key problems facing modern government, according to Wilson, were administrative in nature, not Constitutional.

Administrative Developments in the Twentieth Century

The two most important changes in public administration since the Progressive era have been an increase in instruments of presidential management of the bureaucracy and the delegation of large (formal) regulatory powers to administrative agencies. These two developments both owe something to progressive theory,

although matters often have not turned out in the way progressives envisaged.

Presidential Management

To counteract the predominance of Congress over the executive in the late nineteenth century in controlling administrative agencies, proponents of presidential authority reasserted the idea that the president was the general manager of the bureaucracy and sought to build new institutional mechanisms to support this claim. A starting point was with influence over spending. During Wilson's presidency (1912–1920) a proposal was put forth for the president to devise and submit an overall budget to Congress. More presidential influence over the budget, it was argued, would lead not only to greater economy and efficiency in government but also to greater presidential control over the agencies. The president would be in a position to review the budget of the agencies and offer them rewards or threaten them with cuts.

Many in Congress feared granting this authority to the president. But in 1921 Congress approved legislation establishing a Bureau of the Budget, the predecessor of today's Office of Management and Budget (OMB), which was charged with coordinating the requests from individual departments and consolidating them into a single recommendation for the president to send to Congress. Granting the president this authority gave him no more than the official opportunity to set budget priorities, as the power for voting the budget remained with Congress. Still, this was more power than the president had possessed in the past.

Further changes came during the New Deal years of President Franklin D. Roosevelt, with the establishment of the White House Staff and the Executive Office of the President. Hamilton's idea of presidential management, which the progressives shared, acquired greater acceptance. It was supported in 1937 by a blue-ribbon commission on public administration—the Brownlow Committee—which argued that the president should be responsible for running the bureaucracy. To do so, the president must have a staff immediately responsible to him, outside of any of the departments. Congress agreed and in

1939 created the Executive Office of the President (EOP). This act also transferred the Bureau of the Budget from the Treasury Department to the EOP, and it further strengthened the president's management role by recognizing in law the concept of legislative clearance. This provision requires executive agencies to submit their budget estimates and requests for new legislation first to the budget director and the president rather than Congress. Of course, agencies unofficially contact members of Congress, and Congress can always find out what it wants to know. Still, legislative clearance enables the president to balance the requests of competing agencies, at least in the planning stage. The concept behind legislative clearance has been expanded since World War II to include the practice of having the president submit to Congress an annual legislative program, which accords more recognition to the president as an initiator of legislative policy.

The impact of these institutional changes, along with the rediscovery of the general idea of presidential management, should neither be minimized nor exaggerated. The president's hand with the bureaucracy has clearly been strengthened. Since Roosevelt's time, presidents have used their personal staff and the staff of OMB to ensure that presidential objectives are not forgotten within the government. But the idea that the president is the "boss" or "manager" of the administrative branch, in anything like the same sense that the head of the General Electric corporation is the manager of that firm, has never been accepted in Washington. Furthermore, Congress has never given up its own instruments of control over the bureaucracy. While the president is often represented as the head of the bureaucracy on organizational charts, Congress continues to exercise a great deal of detailed control over many agencies. Bureaucratic units are thus often caught in a crossfire between two masters, the executive and the legislature.

Delegation and Broad (Formal) Administrative Discretion

The Great Depression led to demands for far more government involvement in the economy—for setting industrial prices, determining how much farmers could produce and sell, and regulating activities of the stock exchange. When government acts to regulate in such areas, the laws passed by Congress often do not make the actual determination of the price or the amount. Instead, the statutes set out an administrative process for making these decisions and establish guidelines, which in some cases may be very general. The actual decisions are turned over formally to those administering the program.

Delegating broad authority to administrative bodies already had some precedent, in the Interstate Commerce Commission (1887), the Federal Reserve Board (1913), and temporarily in the economic management program during World War I. These instances of delegation, however, were few and largely regarded as exceptional. The experience of the New Deal forced the nation to confront two new questions: whether Congress should delegate broad authority to administrative agencies on a regular basis and whether such delegation was Constitutionally permissible. These issues were resolved in favor of broad delegation, and administrative agencies have since been created to regulate such matters as the allocation of radio and television frequencies (Federal Communications Commission), the effectiveness and purity of food and drugs (Food and Drug Administration), the operations of the stock exchanges (Securities and Exchange Commission), nuclear power safety (Nuclear Regulatory Commission), basic working conditions (Office of Occupational and Health Safety Administration), and equal employment opportunity practices (Equal Employment and Opportunity Commission). The importance of these programs makes it necessary to examine the logic and status of this whole framework of delegation.

Congress may wish to delegate formal authority for at least three reasons. First, Congress simply cannot operate at a level that is too specific and debate all of the issues and make all of the decisions in areas it wishes to regulate. For example, federal law requires that dangerous foodstuffs be kept from American supermarkets. How can politicians determine which foods are harmful, and how much evidence is needed to make that determination? In this area, Food and

Drug Administration officials combine their skills with general administrative guidelines to draw conclusions and make decisions.

Second, Congress may realize that certain kinds of decisions require a high degree of technical knowledge and that bureaucrats are in a position to use their expertise to judge complex evidence. Thus Congress may decide that it wants air pollution to be reduced. But it may believe that, at least initially, it is beyond its competence to say in a law exactly how much such pollution should be reduced and by what means. As a result, these problems may be turned over to an administrative agency, which is directed to take certain broad factors into account, such as health and economic development, and make decisions in the public interest. (Of course, someone at some point, as we shall see, will have to make certain hard political choices.)

Third, sometimes when a controversial issue arises, Congress and the president may establish an administrative agency and ask it to search for a solution. This approach is very likely when political leaders know that the people want government action, but when these leaders do not know exactly what the policy should be or when taking a stand on a particular policy would be politically hazardous. Such has been the case, for example, in the area of ensuring equal opportunity in employment, where the exact means of accomplishing this objective were turned over to administrative units. Many agencies spend considerable amounts of time and resources developing policy precisely because they have been asked or are expected to do so. If agencies develop policies that go beyond what the statute may originally have allowed—and the new policy is challenged in the courts—legislators who favor the new policy may seek to put it into a law. In other words, the bureaucratic agency may be used to try out new policies, which may then develop a clientele.

But is this kind of broad delegation Constitutional? The issue was raised most directly in the 1930s, when these broad new programs for regulatory administration were first being considered. One objection dealt with the allegation that these regulatory programs, which involved extensive new governmental intervention into private markets, violated certain private rights of contract. Along with this claim of rights, there was also a question of procedure. The Constitution gives to Congress the power to regulate commerce among the states (Article I, sec. 8), and on this ground many argued that the legislature could not give up this power to an administrative agency; to do so was tantamount to giving nonelected bodies the power to make what were, in effect, laws. Up through the mid-1930s, in fact, the Supreme Court had held that an administrative agency in domestic affairs could only act when applying clear standards. In 1935, for example, the Court rejected a major price-setting program of the New Deal on the grounds that the Congress "left the matter to the president without standard or rule, to be dealt with as he pleased." (*Panama Refining Co. v. Ryan*) But this doctrine was dropped after 1937, and the Court began to uphold laws that assigned powers to agencies to make decisions that "serve the public interest." Almost any Court-enforced Constitutional limitation on broad delegation has therefore been removed. The courts are active in a different way: they now play a major role in judging the procedures followed by agencies and in ensuring that agency regulations respect all parts of the Constitution.

In many areas today, the law turns over very substantial formal power of decision making to administrative agencies. But who really exercises this power? Is it the nominal manager of the whole bureaucracy (the president), the heads of the departments (Cabinet officers), the heads of certain regulatory commissions, or the permanent civil servants? Or is it—despite the formal delegation contained in the laws—Congress or the courts? There is no single answer to this question, as the real flow of power varies considerably from one area to another. But this much is certain: those in the administrative branch charged with administering the programs do not exercise anywhere near all of the formal power that they are granted in statutes. The courts, the Congress, and of course the President are very much involved.

Today's Bureaucracy: Its Structure and Its People

The federal bureaucracy today contains nearly three million employees, excluding military personnel and part-time or seasonal federal workers. Surprisingly, the number of federal workers has increased only slightly in the last thirty years, and relative to the population it has declined quite dramatically. These figures are misleading, however, if they are taken to mean that the government does less than it did in 1970 or that the federal bureaucracy has less influence over our lives. Although the power of the federal government has slowed or stopped in many areas in the last decade, it has grown considerably since 1960. How is it, then, that the number of federal employees has not increased?

One reason is that not all the work of the federal government is done by federal employees. Much of it is farmed out to private individuals or companies which work on contracts for the government. Agencies often use consulting firms to handle nonroutine tasks or to circumvent limits on the number of federal employees. The Energy Department is a major example, with more than three quarters of its budget spent on private contracts, especially those to operate government-owned laboratories. Another reason is that the federal government does not administer all of its programs by itself but works through state and local governments. State and local bureaucracies have expanded greatly over the past thirty years, in large part to carry out programs that have been funded or mandated by the federal government. Federal administrators play an important role in directing and auditing certain activities of these state and local bureaucrats.

To measure the scope and influence of federal administration, it is therefore not enough to count federal employees. The federal budget may give a somewhat more accurate picture, although it too only begins to tell the story. Certain programs that spend a great deal of money can do so fairly easily without a bureaucracy having much discretion. For example, the social security program involves mailing out billions of dollars to people in certain fairly clear-cut categories. It is a technically demanding job, but not one in which the agency exercises very much discretion. (Indeed, it was only when the Social Security Administration took charge of administering certain disability programs, where the categories of beneficiaries had to be determined by the agency, that many began to criticize it for exercising power arbitrarily.) In the final analysis, therefore, the only way really to determine the influence of the bureaucracy is through an in-depth study of its agencies and programs.

The Shape of the Federal Bureaucracy

Organizational charts of the executive branch normally refer to all of the administrative units as agencies or bureaus. But these common names mask the very different kinds of bureaucracies that exist and the variety of tasks they perform. Figure 14.1 gives some idea of the complexity of the federal bureaucracy, but even this picture is greatly oversimplified. For instance, each of the fourteen Cabinet-level departments is itself composed of multiple bureaus. The Department of Agriculture, for example, consists of over twenty major subunits that handle such diverse tasks as education, regulation, subsidization, rural development, and foreign aid.

Federal agencies are the conscious creations of the nation's elected officials. Each is established to carry out some purpose that has been authorized by law. For example, in response to terrorist threats, legislators made airport security personnel federal employees, creating a new bureaucracy housed inside the Department of Transportation. Several types of public agencies compose the nation's executive branch, and a brief description of each type may help provide a road map of the bureaucracy.

The Executive Office of the President This important unit, discussed in the chapter on the presidency, has as its aim to assist the president in performing his duties, to help him plan strategically for the whole government, and to help ensure that what the president has decided will actually be implemented by the regular agencies. Most of the important employees in the Executive Office of the President, other than an important group of career officials in the Office of

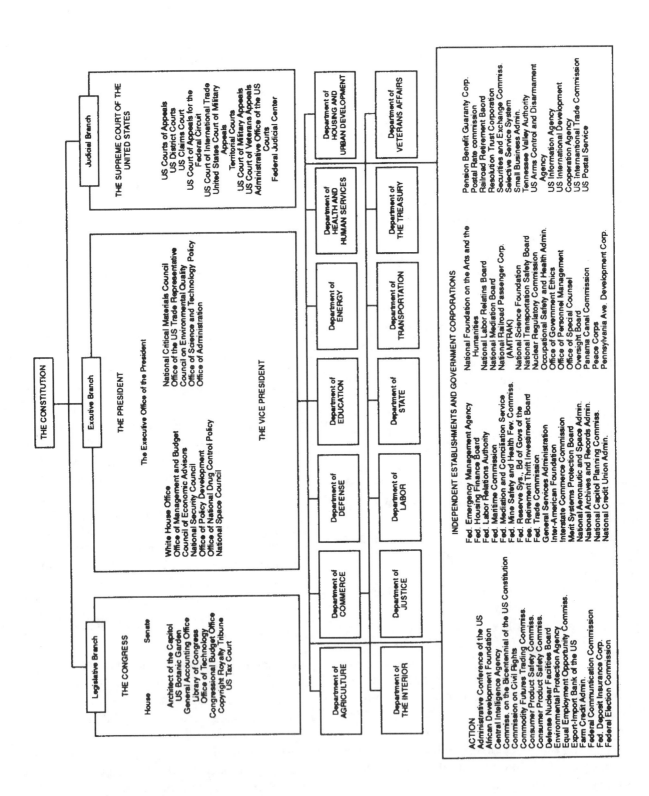

Figure 14.1 The Government of the United States.

TABLE 14.2
Size of Selected Federal Agencies

AGENCY	CIVILIAN EMPLOYMENT (1995)
Nuclear Regulatory Commission	3,212
Environmental Protection Agency	17,910
National Aeronautics and Space Administration	21,635
Social Security Administration	66,850
Department of Agriculture	113,321
Veterans Administration	263,904
Department of Defense	830,738
Postal Service	845,393

Source: *Statistical Abstract of the United States, 1996* (Washington, D.C.: U.S. Department of Commerce, Bureau of Statistics), p. 345

Management and Budget, are presidential appointees who will change with each president.

The Executive Departments While the Executive Office of the President is a twentieth-century creation, executive departments are referred to in Article II of the Constitution. Departments can be established or abolished by law, as the Congress and president see fit. The number of departments has changed in the course of history in response to different ideas of administration or perceived changes in the importance of different problems. Thus in 1970, the Post Office lost its departmental status, when its functions were assumed by a new government corporation, the U.S. Postal Service. The departments of Energy and Education were created in the past quarter century in recognition of the growing importance of these issues for the federal government. More recently, in 1988, the Veterans Administration was elevated from an independent agency to department status. Interest groups often lobby for the promotion of a favorite agency to department status, so that it will have more prestige and that its head will be a member of the president's Cabinet. It is therefore difficult to eliminate any department once it has been created, since that means demoting a certain interest and its clientele. Throughout the 1990s, the Republicans made efforts to eliminate the departments of Commerce, Education, and

Energy, but these efforts all failed. In response to terrorist threats, President George W. Bush has recently proposed a new Cabinet level Department of Homeland Security that would absorb large parts of the executive branch, including the Coast Guard, Secret Service, Federal Emergency Management Agency, Immigration and Naturalization Service, Customs, and the Transportation Security Agency. This proposal reflects the fact that the bureaucracy must change as the tasks facing the nation change. It remains to be seen whether this department will take shape as the president proposed. The president chooses all department heads, subject to Senate confirmation and may dismiss a Cabinet member without congressional approval.

Departments vary significantly in size and budget (see Table 14.2). Some of the larger departments are actually amalgamations of what operate as quite different agencies. The Department of Health and Human Services, perhaps the best example, supervises numerous duties, among them the provision of assistance to poor families, the funding of medical care for the elderly, the disbursement of social security, and the control of contagious disease. The size of the department, however, is not always a measure of its importance. The State Department, for instance, is one of the smaller departments, but it has responsibility for directing the nation's diplomacy. Moreover, Cabinet status itself is not always the best predictor of agency influence. Many presidents have ignored certain department heads while deferring to lower-ranking officials. For example, J. Edgar Hoover, director of the Federal Bureau of Investigation (FBI) from 1924 to his death in 1972, often could get to see the president more easily than could his nominal superior, the Attorney General.

Agencies Headed by Single Executives Besides the departments, there are other single-headed agencies that implement important national policy, such as the Environmental Protection Agency (EPA), the National Aeronautics and Space Administration (NASA), and the Central Intelligence Agency (CIA). Normally, the chief administrators of these bureaus are presidential choices, and, like the department heads, serve at the pleasure of the chief executive. These agencies generally exist outside the standard department structure for historical or symbolic reasons. By and large they function much the same way as departments.

Independent Regulatory Commissions Regulation refers to the general authority of government to set rules that limit the discretion of persons and corporations in what would otherwise be private economic activity. Regulative powers have in many cases been assigned to agencies inside the regular departments. But the powers in question here are so broad and politically sensitive that Congress often has not wanted to put them in an agency under the president's direct control. It has therefore created a new kind of administrative entity—the independent regulatory commission—outside of the direct line of command of the president or a Cabinet officer.

The most important of these independent bodies today is the Federal Reserve Board, which supervises banks and determines the nation's money supply and monetary policy. It is the most influential government body for setting interest rates and plays a major role in establishing overall economic policy, especially in regard to the rate of inflation. Another important regulatory commission is the Federal Communications Commission (FCC), which sets certain rules for television, radio, and the internet. Most television programs in the United States are pro-

duced privately by the networks or production companies, aired by privately owned stations, and financed by business through commercial advertising. But the FCC determines who receives the licenses required to operate a radio or television station, allocates broadcast frequencies, influences the spread of technological innovations such as cable or high resolution television, decides rules for obscenity and slander, and fixes general rules for the airing of political views (such as the right of all parties to purchase equal time).

In addition to the Federal Reserve and the FCC, the federal government has established independent commissions or agencies that regulate other aspects of the private economy, such as the stock market (Securities and Exchange Commission), the airlines (Federal Aviation Administration), and pharmaceutical drugs (Food and Drug Administration). These commissions exercise quasi-legislative and quasi-judicial responsibilities. They devise rules that have the impact of laws and can also penalize those who violate their rules.

Regulatory commissions are structured to insulate them from the usual kind of political controls. Of course the president appoints commissioners, subject to Senate confirmation; and Congress establishes general guidelines for commission rules. But these commissions are unlike regular departments. They are usually headed by multi-member boards, instead of single administrators. The commissioners serve for fixed terms (for example, six years), and cannot be removed by the president. Their terms are staggered so that all members cannot be appointed at the same time. Presidents can, of course, apply indirect pressure by speaking out about commission policy, but they cannot dictate it.

Congress is often in a better position to influence regulatory commission policies. Congress controls the budget of these agencies and may determine in law their exact grant of authority (subject, of course, to the president's veto). Still, commissions cannot usually be controlled by Congress either, as commissioners do not owe their immediate appointment to Congress. Furthermore, for members of Congress to put too much pressure on commissioners would seem to

BOX 14.2

Influences on Agency "Personality"

Just as with individuals, no two federal agencies are alike. Each has its own distinctive organizational personality. The character of a bureau today may be shaped by a number of factors, including past decisions and events, the nature of the unit's dominant professions and sense of mission, and the political executives appointed to head the unit.

The **Federal Bureau of Investigation** (FBI), for instance, cannot be understood without recognizing the importance of such factors. J. Edgar Hoover, who directed the agency for decades, left a permanent mark on the FBI, which only now is beginning to fade. Hoover established the Bureau's personnel system and built respect and support for the organization. Even the tight supervisory practices, the "clean-cut" image, and the distrust of political dissidence characteristic of the Bureau's operations were extensions of Hoover's own slightly paranoid personality. The dominant professions of law and accounting are the recruiting pool for agency positions, and these groups reinforce the agency's self-perception as an elite law enforcement outfit. In the 1980s, the FBI suffered from criticism of its illegal tactics employed in earlier years to gather intelligence and monitor protesters. Recent political appointments have sought to refurbish the FBI's professionalism and sense of mission.

The **Foreign Service** officer corps of the U.S. State Department constitutes the elite professional group in that agency. These are the nation's diplomats. For years the department recruited liberal arts graduates from the country's most prestigious universities. Selection criteria deemphasized technical specialists and favored the hiring of those who tended to dislike conflict. The promotion system established in the unit further discouraged open, frank communication within the bureaucracy; and political attacks from outside the department (for example, allegations in the 1950s that the State Department contained many communists) encouraged the organization to be very cautious in its operations. A series of reforms during the past decade has been aimed at stimulating more innovation, expertise, and productive debate within the Foreign Service. Yet the American diplomatic community remains a target of criticism for many.

The **U.S. Department of Agriculture (USDA)** is one of the best examples of a long-standing federal agency operating to benefit a particular clientele group. The department is composed of a number of bureaus, each handling a separate portion of the unit's task, such as inspecting grain or compiling agricultural statistics. Mostly, the bureaucrats performing these duties think of their job primarily as one of helping the agricultural community in this country. The USDA attracts professional staff disproportionately from rural areas. The personnel tend to feel protective and supportive of the farmer, and this pattern is reinforced by the political environment of the department. The Extension Service provides an intricately held network of contact with the agricultural interests on a county-by-county basis throughout the country and via the land-grant college system state by state. Secretaries of agriculture are recruited from the same fold.

The **Environmental Protection Agency (EPA)** was created during a time when the nation perceived itself in the midst of an environmental crisis in 1970. Federal activities on this front were consolidated in a new agency for a coordinated attack on the problem. The agency attracted a highly motivated young group of professional lawyers and environmental specialists who often saw their task as protecting the nation's resources for the long term against "special interests," especially economic ones. The first several EPA directors also had favorable reputations among conservatives. During the Reagan administration, however, the president sought a change in the direction of EPA. Staff and budgets were reduced, and greater consideration was given in some areas to economic development. Temporarily, these changes created turmoil in the agency and angered environmental groups. The agency in 1982 was embroiled in controversy and scandal, and a major shake-up occurred in 1983. In recent years, there has been a concerted effort to elevate EPA to the status of a cabinet-level department.

BOX 14.3

Bureaucratic Successes and Failures

Successes

Among the most obvious bureaucratic success stories are these:

The Fleet Ballistic Missile Program (FBM). This activity developed, procured, and deployed the Polaris missile on nuclear-powered submarines for the United States. The program was administered by the Special Projects office of the Department of the Navy, and its success played a major role in the nation's strategic defense system from the 1960s into the 1980s. The program produced a technically superior product several years ahead of schedule and within budget.

The Implementation of the Voting Rights Act of 1965. The execution of this policy stimulated major changes in electoral politics. As of 1965 racial prejudice kept blacks from voting in many locations in the South. In Alabama, for instance, several counties with tens of thousands of black citizens had no blacks who had been able to register to vote. The passage of this act enabled federal marshals from the Justice Department to enforce the right to vote in locations throughout the South. Black voting increased dramatically within a few years.

The Apollo Space Program. President John Kennedy announced in 1961 the goal of placing an American on the moon by 1970. The Apollo program in the National Aeronautics and Space Administration was established, the technological and administrative developments necessary to achieve this result were accomplished (albeit at a cost of tens of billions of dollars), and the goal was achieved in 1969.

Operation Desert Storm. After suffering years of criticism for cost over-runs and too sophisticated weapons systems, the Pentagon was called on to fight the Gulf War of 1991. Under the direction of Generals Colin Powell and Norman Schwarzkopf, the United States performed the extraordinary logistical defeat by quickly deploying a huge army thousands of miles from home. Many of the high-tech weapons proved indispensable to the war effort. The successful air campaign was followed by a one-hundred-hour ground war in which the American army encircled the Iraqi army and forced their surrender.

---

violate the quasi-judicial status these commissions are supposed to hold.

Independence does not, however, remove commissions from politics; it merely changes the kind of political environment in which they operate. Like many other federal agencies, commissions must generate support for themselves to ensure their survival and influence; they must demonstrate that they serve an important constituency. Because of their insulation from much of the government, commissions are often forced to seek support from the groups most interested in their decisions. As the constituency of many regulatory commissions is the regulated industry itself, there is a danger that commissions will become overly dependent on the businesses it regulates. Yet it is too simple to say that all commissions end up being the "captives" of their regulated industries. Commissions can also win important political backing by taking tough

stands against an industry and winning the favor of organized consumer or environmental groups, as the Federal Trade Commission did in the 1970s.[6]

The structure of regulatory commissions reflects one of the two conflicting strains of progressive administrative theory. While certain progressives wanted to give the chief executive more control, others sought to remove the administration from politics altogether. Commissions are an example of implementation of the latter idea at the expense of the former. Some observers and regulated businesses approve of this arrangement, as they feel that regulatory decisions that can affect significant segments of industry should be reached in an independent, insulated, and fairly impartial tribunal. Others, however, view this arrangement not only as Constitutionally suspect, but insufficiently accountable to any political authority.

BOX 14.3 (cont.)

Failures

These are some of the programs that few in the American bureaucracy ever mention:

The Mohole project. In the 1960s the National Science Foundation sought to manage the drilling of a hole in the ground, a hole deeper than any ever before. The goal was the development of scientific knowledge about the earth's crust and mantle. The project was characterized by cost-overruns, delayed schedules, and fights among scientists, engineers, and contractors for control of the program. The project was abandoned after millions were expended and very little learned.

The Tuskegee syphilis experiment. The project began as an effort of the Public Health Service (PHS) in the 1930s to beat this venereal disease in six rural black populations in the South. Funding problems, bureaucratic decisions, and the influence of the medical community contributed to a change in program from one of treatment to one in which medical assistance for syphilis was systematically denied to a group of 400 men—even after penicillin was shown to be an effective cure. The subjects of the experiment were monitored for forty years, until publicity forced an end in 1972. Many untreated victims had died from the disease or suffered permanent damage; but the program was fostered and protected by many PHS bureaucrats, including a number of physicians, to the end.

The swine flu fiasco. Federal officials were concerned as the winter of 1976–1977 approached that there might be an outbreak of a swine flu epidemic like the one that killed millions in 1918–1919. A $135 million crash program of mass inoculations was established. The expected flu never developed. The results of the program were large expenditures; confusing implementation; 120 deaths and numerous other injuries from side effects, especially Guillain-Barre syndrome; and liability claims against the government of approximately $1.2 billion. Although the bureaucratic agency involved, the Department of Health, Education and Welfare (HEW), was not entirely to blame for the program—it was endorsed by President Ford and passed by Congress—HEW did have responsibility for testing the vaccine, supervising inoculations, and developing warnings. The agency had also pushed hard for rapid mass inoculations, rather than a more limited program aimed at particularly vulnerable populations.

Government Corporations Some activities the federal government performs are akin to those of the private sector in that they involve the provision of the sorts of services provided by "normal" business enterprises. They are public agencies, however, because at one time or another they have been deemed to involve an especially public function that perhaps could not or should not be operated at a profit. Instead of running them through a department, however, Congress chooses to make them government corporations. The government corporation is a type of agency that looks and operates somewhat like any other sort of corporation, but with more public constraints and with a certain implicit public trust that effectively eliminates the possibility of bankruptcy. A government corporation is chartered by Congress, given a mandate and a set of powers, and exempted from many of the restrictions placed upon regular government agencies. They have a substantially freer rein regarding personnel hiring, task assignment, and salary determination, and they have had more flexibility in meeting deadlines and avoiding red tape. The government owns all or most of these corporations' stock.

Two well-known government corporations are the U.S. Postal Service (which was once a department) and Amtrak (which took over train travel from private companies). Whether either or both of these corporations should remain public, however, is a matter of some debate, and a number of economists have called for turning them both over to private control. Two other public corporations—The Federal Deposit Insurance Corporation (FDIC) and until 1989 the Federal Savings and Loan Insurance Corporation (FSLIC)—indicate how much government corporations may differ from regular private firms. These corporations, created in the aftermath of the collapse of the banking system during the Great Depression, insure the bank and savings deposits of virtually all Americans. It looks like they play the role of a private insurance company. Yet they are not, finally, like private corporations in the sense that they cannot go bankrupt—or rather, the government may not let them go bankrupt. As a result, when these corporations ran out of money in the late 1980s after the collapse of many savings and loan banks, the government continued to make good on the insurance claims of the depositors at a cost to the government of billions of dollars.

The Nation's Bureaucrats

Just as there is really no such thing as a typical federal agency, so is there no such thing as a typical bureaucrat. The bureaucracy contains experts in nearly every imaginable field—medicine, social work, law enforcement, geology, biology, and physics. Despite popular impressions that all bureaucrats work in Washington, D.C., the great majority of them (approximately 87 percent) work "in the field" away from agency headquarters in localities or in foreign countries.

In most respects—such as family background, regional origin, and age—federal employees resemble their private sector counterparts. It is also the case that the upper levels of the civil service in the United States are probably more representative socioeconomically of the public than are the top groups of civil servants in most other nations. Nevertheless at its upper levels, the bureaucracy is far from being a perfect picture of the populace. It is more white, more male, and more liberal.[7]

Responsiveness to the Public   The nation's bureaucrats will always require some discretion in making their decisions. Accordingly, there would be a problem for republican government if the federal bureaucracy consisted of persons too greatly divorced in their political views from the citizenry. Research on the political views of bureaucrats shows no great overall difference with the general population.[8] But the general similarity between the public and the federal bureaucracy masks an important point. Individual units of the bureaucracy often tend to be unrepresentative with respect to their own function, largely because bureaucrats choose their

agency in light of their own commitment. Thus liberals and Democrats tend to be over represented in social service agencies, while conservatives and Republicans tend to be overrepresented in defense agencies.[9] Of course, a bureaucracy that perfectly represents public opinion is not really the ideal. Up to a certain point, it is desirable that bureaucrats should be devoted to their missions. Moreover, almost no one wants the bureaucracy to use its discretion merely to follow public opinion. One reason for having permanent experts to help in decision making is so they can use their experience and expertise to solve problems. A public health official, for example, should be someone who knows something about public health and who uses that knowledge within the limits of the law to pursue an objective. It brings a degree of expertise and, through its long collective memory and love of procedure, it can exert a stabilizing influence on the actions of the government—on occasion, perhaps, too much.

Training and Career Patterns   It would certainly be a cause for great concern, however, if agencies systematically used their discretion in ways that were at odds with what most Americans wanted. On this point, many analysts have expressed concern that in the United States bureaucracies are run too much by those who seek to promote the particular mission of their agency and who seem unwilling to see that mission in the context of the needs of the entire government. This tendency is reinforced by the training and career patterns in the bureaucracy. Typically, when American bureaucrats join an agency, they spend their entire career inside it—unlike, for example, their British counterparts who are periodically rotated to other departments. As one civil servant observed, assignments and promotions tend to occur within one bureau:

> The ordinary civil servant comes into government being hired by a particular person in a bureau. Then he'll probably have a training program and a set of promotion possibilities laid out in the bureau and pretty soon he's walking down the hall almost as if he had a badge out in front of him saying, "I'm a Bureau X man," or "I'm a Bureau Y Man."[10]

This kind of career pattern typically elevates technical specialists to public managers, thereby reinforcing the bureaucrats' tendency to view their own unit as most important. For example, the Forest Service mainly hires recent graduates of forestry schools and then promotes primarily from within. The agency works with the schools to ensure that their curricula reflect the skills and, to some extent, the values of the Forest Service itself.[11] The result is a coherent sense of mission throughout the entire agency. In Great Britain, by contrast, upper-level management positions normally are filled by "generalists" who are well educated in a classical sense but not necessarily skilled in their agency's technical specialty. Because of this difference, British civil servants are less likely to develop a specific agency viewpoint.

To modify what many considered to have become an overspecialization among senior public administrators, Congress in 1978 passed legislation creating a Senior Executive Service (SES). This plan established a cadre of the government's top few thousand permanent bureaucrats who would be available for flexible assignments by the president. Outstanding service was to be rewarded with cash bonuses. But congressionally imposed pay ceilings, budget cuts, and traditional hostility to an "elite" civil service corps has limited the effectiveness of SES.

Between the Experts and the Politicians: The Political Executives

Atop the permanent bureaucracy is a layer of top-level officials, about 3,000 people, whom the president appoints and the Senate confirms. These political appointees serve as the link between the president and the civil service. (Three thousand positions is a significant number, although it is only about one-tenth of one percent of the entire bureaucracy.) If presidents had no political allies to help them manage the bureaucracy, their ability to exercise control over the bureaucracy would be impaired. Presidents select individuals to fill these slots without being bound by conventional civil service merit criteria, and in most cases the president can dismiss these individuals at his discretion.

At the peak of most federal agencies sits a rather small group of political executives that includes the secretary of the department, the undersecretaries and most assistant secretaries. Presidents usually fill these offices with individuals whom they believe are competent managers and who can be trusted to carry out the administration's program. Still, not everyone selected can be devoted fully to the president. Appointing the Cabinet involves a delicate political balancing act that is aimed at satisfying different elements and constituencies within the party and the nation. In the past, the Cabinet was in large part a political body designed to help the president acquire support, and often presidents had to select cabinet heads whom they could not entirely trust. Such political considerations still play a role. But today more emphasis is placed on making certain that the Cabinet includes representation from certain demographic groups based on race, sex, and ethnicity. Within this basic constraint, presidents can look more for officials whom they think will be loyal and effective. The appointees today need not be, and often are not, politicians, but business persons, technical experts or administrators of private institutions.

Only the top few hundred of the some three thousand presidential appointees usually receive close presidential attention. A president will worry about who will be his secretary of defense, but not about his appointees in the U.S. Patent Office. For these positions, presidents-elect have used panels of outside evaluators, plus a rather small staff hired during the transition period between election and inauguration to sort through and seek out promising applicants. Political support of the party and president can be an important factor. Very often strong Cabinet members win the right to select many of their subordinates (assistant and deputy secretaries), although recent presidents have maintained a fairly centralized system of control with their own personnel staffs in the White House. The White House is then in a position to watch its own Cabinet secretaries and try to assure their loyalty to the president's mission. Presidents also must "share" some appointments with members of Congress and interest groups.

Not all appointees, accordingly, begin as dedicated loyalists to the president. Moreover, even when appointees have close ties to the president, they may come under pressure to defend their agency from White House policies that may assign their agency a low priority. Ambitious political executives can only make a name for themselves by being successful at running their agency, and this may sometimes require deviating from the White House's line. Agency heads must also worry about winning the confidence of the permanent civil service, without which life can become very difficult. For this reason, Cabinet members and agency heads have a tendency, in the jargon of presidential staff members, to "go native" and join the agency against the president.

Political appointees usually do not stay very long in office. Occasionally they are fired or asked to resign by the White House. Sometimes they resign on their own accord, finding that they cannot accomplish what they wanted. In particular, those who have worked in the private sector often end up being frustrated by the limits and constraints on their discretionary authority. In recent administrations, the average appointee has remained in office only about two years.[12]

What Does Bureaucracy Do?: A Look at the Department of Veterans Affairs

For each major task government undertakes, there is a bureaucratic unit assigned to carry it out. Every day federal bureaucrats manage the nation's defenses, enforce drug laws, care for vast tracts of federal land, and direct airplane pilots to safe landings. Furthermore, a large number of units spend most of their time and resources administering other administrative units (usually state and local governments) that are actually carrying out the programs.

The Department of Veterans Affairs (VA) is a prime example of a federal bureaucracy that directly executes important policy. The agency's general task is to help former military personnel who have sacrificed for the nation's welfare. A series of specific laws has given the department a remarkably broad and complicated range of policies to administer.

For instance, the VA operates subsidized loan programs to help veterans purchase homes at favorable interest rates. Permanently disabled veterans are eligible for VA grants to purchase houses specially equipped to meet their needs. In carrying out this policy, VA bureaucrats must appraise properties, make sure that new homes are constructed properly, and supervise lending banks which cater to veterans. The agency also carries out policies designed to improve educational opportunities for veterans by distributing funds to allow them to complete high school, college, and vocational or professional education. Here VA employees work with the states to ensure that various schools meet certain quality standards. Furthermore, the VA distributes various compensation and pension benefits, for example, life insurance, vocational rehabilitation for disabled veterans, and disability compensation and pensions. The VA even operates the National Cemetery System, through which some veterans may be buried free of charge in national cemeteries.

The greatest portion of the agency's work load, however, consists of medical care for veterans. Almost everyone has seen huge VA hospitals, VA clinics for psychiatric or drug problems, and VA nursing homes serving thousands of old and disabled veterans. In these facilities, tens of thousands of federal bureaucrats quietly and often conscientiously tend to the nation's policy commitment to those who have served in the armed forces.

"Cutting the bureaucracy" is a favorite political slogan—in the abstract. But when one looks at the specific tasks of an agency like the VA, a different story can emerge. Government agencies are involved in carrying out activities that a large number of people want. Although a number of programs might well be dismantled and others turned over to the private sector, there are important services that Americans want their government to perform. This is why some anti-bureaucratic rhetoric proves more popular in political campaigns than it does in actual pieces of legislation.

The Political Character of Today's Bureaucracy

Administrative units are not just products of the political process. They are participants in it. Agencies seek support for their programs and vigorously defend their own turf. This behavior is a result not only of self-interest but of an agency's belief in its own mission. People in the Environmental Protection Agency naturally worry about protecting the environment, just as those in the Defense Department worry about assuring the nation's defense. And so with almost every other agency. Yet devotion to the mission can become worrisome when agencies become their own major advocates and seek to expand their influence beyond what is in the public interest. Bureaucratic power poses a challenge to democratic rule when agencies become primary actors in forming and influencing political decisions.

Studies of bureaucratic agencies demonstrate that they jealously seek to defend their programs from other agencies and from budget cutbacks. Competition is specially intense among units that perform similar functions. For instance, the Bureau of Reclamation (in the Interior Department), the Army Corps of Engineers, and the Soil Conservation Service (in Agriculture) battle each other for water projects and geographical jurisdiction. Competition may keep bureaucrats on their toes, but it can also lead to duplication and waste. When new policy initiatives are likely to generate significant political support or substantial new resources, various bureaus may squabble for a piece of the action. Take the case in the 1970s when Congress began consideration of a major solar energy plan. Several existing agencies argued that this responsibility properly belonged to them: the National Science Foundation, the Department of Housing and Urban Development, the Federal Power Commission, the National Aeronautics and Space Administration, the Energy Research and Development Administration, and the Atomic Energy Commission. The policy seemed lost for a time amidst the intensity of this bureaucratic turf war. Ultimately, the matter was assigned in 1977 to the newly created Department of Energy.

In protecting their jurisdictions, agencies seek the support of the public and especially of interest groups that are closely connected to the agency. When agencies, related interest groups, and the relevant congressional committee or subcommittee agree that maintaining some kind of policy is desirable, they form what has been referred to as a "triple alliance" or an "iron triangle." Each component of this triangle may have a somewhat different point of view, but all of them may share an interest in keeping disagreements about the policymaking process "in the family." There is a kind of pluralism at work here, but it can be very limited, involving the subunit of an agency, a few legislative committees, and a handful of interested groups.

Depending on such factors as the size and strength of a bureau's constituency and the nature of a unit's jurisdiction, some agencies enjoy much more success than others in winning support. The Department of Veterans Affairs, with its large, diversified, and well-organized constituencies (including the American Legion, the Veterans of Foreign Wars, and the Disabled American Veterans) can readily mobilize on behalf of VA programs. Other agencies face more difficulties. The Agency for International Development (AID), which provides loans and foreign aid programs mostly to poorer nations of the world, may perform worthy services, but no American politician worries much about the votes of AID beneficiaries. As a result, AID usually has a tough time in the annual budget process.

The efforts of bureaucratic agencies to play politics frustrates those who think that bureaucracies should work on behalf of the overall public interest rather than for particular interests. Yet thinking in terms of the general interest is not easy in a political system that is characterized by a dispersion of power in which no one, least of all bureaucrats, can impose one overall view of the public interest. Bureaucrats know that if they do not actively defend their agencies, few others will do so. As one political scientist has explained:

> It is clear that the American system of politics does not generate enough power at any focal point of leadership to provide the conditions for

an even partially successful divorce of politics from administration. Subordinates cannot depend upon the formal chain of command to deliver enough political power to permit them to do their jobs. Accordingly they must supplement the resources available through the hierarchy with those they can muster on their own, or accept the consequences in frustration.[13]

It is one thing, however, to say that agencies seek to promote their own interests and quite another to assert that bureaucracies are the principal actors in the government and the major influences in government decision making. The latter is the claim of the bureaucratic politics model. On this point, no single judgment can be rendered, and policy outcomes differ from case to case. It would appear, however, that the major directions of public policy are set by broader political factors and that bureaucratic influences operate more in the interstices and details. For example, the end of the Cold War brought a broad political judgment about the need for an extensive cut in military expenditures, after which bureaucratic factors and inter-service rivalries among the Army, Navy, Air Force and Marines played an important role in deciding where cuts would be made. While the extent of bureaucratic influence on government policy-making, especially on the politics of how a policy will actually be implemented, is much greater than most Americans probably think, bureaucratic influence is not regularly the determining factor on the most significant government decisions. The political actors—the president, the Congress, and of course the people—have not become the captives of their nominal servants, although their servants surely do not always play the role of obedient and submissive underlings.

Bureaucracy and Democracy: The Recurring Problems of Effectiveness and Control

A century ago reformers viewed the federal bureaucracy as being too closely controlled by political leaders through patronage. Today many worry that we live in an "administrative state" characterized by powerful bureaucracies that make important governmental decisions affect-

ing vast areas of American society without the people's consent. Although some would reply that the United States certainly attempts to do less than many other modern democratic states, less is still a great deal. The federal government over the past sixty years, and especially since the 1960s, has established many programs regulating large areas of American life—from setting safety rules for industries, to shaping sports programs for men and women in college athletics, to establishing plans for controlling air pollution, to deciding what new drugs will appear on the market. To be sure, some important areas of business have seen regulation considerably relaxed in the last two decades under the impetus of a vast deregulation movement—this includes the setting of airfares, trucking costs, and natural gas prices. The point nevertheless remains that modern government does indeed assign a great deal of decision-making authority to administrative agencies.

A striking example is found in the anti-tobacco campaign initiated by the Food and Drug Administration (FDA), led by Commissioner David Kessler, in 1995. Using an obscure clause of the Safe Medical Devices Act of 1990, Kessler charged that nicotine was an addictive drug and that cigarettes and smokeless tobacco were "drug delivery systems" and thus fell under the regulatory purview of the FDA. The new weapon that Kessler utilized was the restricted device clause of the Safe Medical Devices Act of 1990, which no one in Congress had ever intended would apply to nicotine or tobacco. Tough new regulations—that required children under 18 years of age to produce identification when purchasing cigarettes; banned cigarette vending machines from many areas; required tobacco companies to educate children on the dangers of smoking and chewing; and introduced many restrictions on the content and location of tobacco advertisements—were introduced by the FDA in 1995. President Clinton approved this policy and made it an important part of his political appeal in the 1996 presidential election. Thus a high level agency head—with the President's support—provided the impetus for new policy towards tobacco.

Yet in general, it is incorrect to argue, as the model of the administrative state suggests, that it is the experts in administrative agencies who exercise most of this power. American bureaucratic agencies, despite often having very large formal grants of power under the law, find in fact that their decisions constantly encounter outside interference—from political superiors, Congress, or the courts. Anticipating these checks from outside, bureaucratic agents often act on the basis of discovering a consensus among the relevant political actors rather than on the basis of their judgment of administrative efficiency or good public policy. Moreover, the difficulty of achieving consensus leads many department heads to avoid revisiting decisions, giving rise to a numbing conventional wisdom.

Congressional subcommittees and committees, in a sometimes bewildering process, adjust the legislation that is the original source of bureaucratic activity and exercise oversight authority over agencies, including the oft-used device of congressional hearings and investigations. These committees also write "reports," which are not statutes passed by Congress as a whole, in which they more or less specify to agencies how they want certain things done. All this activity is in addition to the informal contacts between agencies and key lawmakers. Federal courts are another important source of control over the bureaucracy, and they have not hesitated to review many agency decisions. Interest groups now frequently take matters into the courts when they are unhappy with the decision of a bureaucratic agency. Thus an agency's decision, far from being final, will often merely signal the first round of a long process involving extensive litigation and selective intervention by the courts.

These additional checks on administrative agencies may seem desirable, as few relish the idea of giving administrators too much power. Yet it does not follow that the kind of arrangement of checks in the United States is a healthy one. For one thing, the federal government does exercise a great deal of power under the programs noted, and thus someone or some process is exercising discretion. If this discretion is not in the hands of administrative agencies under general supervision from the executive, can the programs be run effectively? Clearly, the extensive political safeguards that exist make bureaucrats

act and decide with great care, but they also may deny to bureaucrats any capacity to be able to administer a program successfully. For another thing, it is far from clear that the kinds of political checks on the agencies result in responsible political control that operates in the general public interest. Recall here that the controls often come from the courts, which means that policy is set by one form of expert (the administrator) and then "checked" by other kinds of expert (lawyers and judges) in complex process of litigation. Thus the controls circumvent the public and broad processes of political representation. The same may hold true even of controls coming from Congress. The congressional oversight may come from a limited number of members on certain committees and subcommittees, who may be seeking benefits for their own constituencies or be spokespersons of particular interests.

There is, then, a disturbing pattern. Congress and the president establish an administrative agency and make grand claims that it will have the power to promote the public good. Once launched, however, the agency will often find that it lacks the discretionary authority to carry out its mission. It is placed into an environment in which, in addition to the usual controls deriving from higher executive authorities, it is pressured by members of Congress, lobbied by various interest groups, and taken into the courts to fight long and drawn-out legal battles. Bureaucrats are at the center of this process, but they are pressured from all sides and are often unable to act on the basis of their own judgment. A political process evolves in which an agency must learn to accept and live with a series of checks—political and legal—that may proceed without much regard for the original intent of the program. The operation of today's federal bureaucracy is thus often "pluralistic," in the sense that many different interests have a say. But it is not always arranged in ways that enhance either sound management or responsible political control.

Some have argued that problems in efficient administration are an inherent part of the American system of government and a price we pay for a separation of powers system. Instead, therefore, of putting all our efforts into reforming the administrative process to reach a perfect result, we ought to be looking to remove as much as possible from direct administrative controls and seeks strategies of privatization or market solutions to achieve our objectives. If any kind of administrative reform is needed, it would be to grant administrators in the fewer areas where public administration is required more real discretion in their administrative tasks. More real discretion might often mean not formal legal independence, but a concentration of power in a regular department of government that can rely on the entire executive branch to supply it with support.

Conclusion

The bureaucracy, a frequent target of attack by politicians in recent years, is a necessary part of modern government. Today's bureaucracy is huge, staggering in its expenditures, and widely dispersed geographically. It consists of many different kinds of bureaus organized in a variety of ways, ranging from executive departments tied closely to the president, to agencies highly dependent on certain congressional committees, to commissions that are granted (and that in a few cases actually exercise) a considerable degree of independence from both the president and Congress.

Bureaucratic agencies do not only implement policy but, through the use of their discretion, help to develop it as well. Moreover, in instances where there has been broad delegations of authority to bureaucratic agencies, administrators are formally asked to often make the first attempt at formulating government policies.

Bureaucratic agencies engage in struggles for resources in what is often a highly political process. The unusually high degree of politics is further encouraged by a separation of powers system, the effects of which permeate almost every aspect of public administration in the United States. In a few cases, when agencies succeed in playing political authorities off against each other for influence, this system can provide agencies with a considerable degree of independent discretion. For the most part, however, the separation of powers has meant that agencies are subject to checks from a number of different points in the political system. Not all of these checks foster effective administration or promote the general public interest, and efforts at administrative reform are sure to continue.

Chapter 14 Notes

1. Martha Derthick, *Agency under Stress* (The Brookings Institution: Washington, D.C.: 1990), p. 10.
2. See *Myers v. United States* (1926), which recognized the president's constitutional grounds for dismissing any presidential appointee. This power can be limited, however, in the case of appointments to regulatory commissions. See *Humphrey's Executor v. United States* (1935).
3. Paul Van Riper, *History of the United States Civil Service* (Evanston, Ill.: Row, Peterson, 1958), p. 36.
4. Leonard D. White, *The Republican Era* (New York: Macmillan, 1958), p. 6.
5. Woodrow Wilson, "The Study of Administration," *Political Science Quarterly*, vol. 2, no. 2, 1887, pp. 209–210.
6. The agency did, however, "suffer" by having some of its power taken away from it.
7. Stanley Rothman and Robert Lichter, "How Liberal are Bureaucrats?" *Regulation* (November–December 1983).
8. Kenneth J. Meier, "Representative Bureaucracy: An Empirical Analysis," *American Political Science Review*, vol. 69, no. 2, 1975, pp. 526–542; Stanley Rothman and S. Robert Lichter, "How Liberal Are Bureaucrats?" *Regulation* (November–December 1983)
9. Joel Auerbach and Bert Rockman, "Clashing Beliefs within the Executive Branch: The Nixon Administration Bureaucracy," *American Political Science Review*, vol. 70, no.2, 1976, pp. 456–468.
10. Hugh Heclo, *A Government of Strangers* (Washington, D.C.: Brookings Institution, 1977), p. 116.
11. Herbert Kaufman, *The Forest Ranger* (Baltimore: Johns Hopkins Press, 1960).
12. Hugh Heclo, *A Government of Strangers*. Norton Long, "Power and Administration," in Francis E. Rourke (ed.), *Bureaucratic Power in National Politics*, 3rd ed. (Boston: Little, Brown, 1978), p. 9.

Part Four

The Policy Process

15

The Public Policy Process

CHAPTER CONTENTS

People become engaged in politics not just because they want power or believe they have some duty to serve, but because they care about what the government does or does not do. It is the policies of government that give rise to much of the interest in politics.

Almost all Americans have a concern about some public policy. What can government do to alleviate poverty or to improve the quality of education? Should the nation require registration of handguns? Should human cloning be discouraged or considered an acceptable medical practice? What should be the nation's responsibility toward the children of the poorest families? Who should be admitted as immigrants?

The study of public policy should concern itself with more than the substance of the decisions. The careful study of public policy focuses on how policy is made through investigating how problems are identified or put on the agenda, how policies are implemented, and how results are evaluated. The study of public policy should also attempt to assess broader questions, for instance about who controls the policymaking process or about how democratic it really is or should be.

The Importance of the Policymaking Process

The problems modern American government faces are immense, ranging from environmental concerns and lingering poverty to the task of devising a foreign policy for a new international situation. Many commentators have expressed doubts about whether the government—particularly as currently arranged—will be able to meet these challenges. Yet it would be a mistake to think that concerns about the policymaking process are new. They were present from at least the time of the nation's founding, when political leaders had to deal with such problems as developing a national market, reestablishing economic stability, and designing a coherent foreign policy.

The Constitution represented in one sense the founders' response to the great challenges of the day. Yet it was a very distinct kind of response. A glance at the Constitution reveals very little of the founders' views on specific policy issues. It does not, for example, fix tax rates or outline a certain foreign policy. The document was designed not to decide in advance particular policies, but to establish a general structure for the policymaking process. The Constitution addresses mainly the questions of who and what governs and how governmental decisions are made.

Of course, fundamental policy choices are implicit in determining how much power government would have and in arranging the institutions in specific ways. Thus separation of powers and checks and balances are *processes* of decision making, but clearly part of their purpose is to protect liberty and property. While these goals are implicit, the Constitution is sparing in setting down specific policies to pursue them. This is why the United States Constitution is often referred to as a "short constitution," which distinguishes it from the "long constitutions" of some countries (and several of our states) which attempt to resolve in the written document itself a large body of policy questions.

In our discussions thus far of the formal institutions mentioned in the Constitution (the Congress, the presidency and the courts) and of other major intermediary institutions (political parties, interest groups, and the media), we have already dealt with important elements of the policymaking process. In studying the policymaking process itself, we look at these institutions not as separate entities, but in terms of how they interact to address policy problems.

What Is Public Policy?

If policies are decisions about what to do, what are *public* policies? There is probably a temptation to say that they are decisions that affect the people at large. Yet this is not exactly the case, as there are many decisions affecting large numbers of people that we normally do not consider to be *public* policy. If a major corporation decides to close a manufacturing plant in a small town, that choice has a dramatic effect on the citizens of the community. The decision, however, is in private hands.

The notion of public policy refers in a strict sense to decisions of the government. By this criterion, decisions made by private companies are excluded (but not public measures designed to encourage or discourage decisions by private corporations). The distinction between public and private realms is, of course, based on a prior fundamental decision that is profoundly political—a constitutional decision of how to protect freedom by limiting the scope of government involvement in people's lives.

More difficult is understanding the role of institutions of civil society like churches, community groups, unions and other private associations in the stages of the public policy process. Public policy, or the rules and institutions created by government, is increasingly concerned with how governmental decisions affect civil society. Advocacy groups, recreational associations, issue networks, religious groups, and a myriad of other associations can support the public realm in a democracy by encouraging the habits of citizenship, providing representation, and promoting public deliberation. Public policy must be mindful of its effects on private associations.

Intentions versus Practice

Sometimes the government enacts a policy, and everything proceeds smoothly: the bureaucracy carries out the decision, and the outcome is just about what was anticipated. The Voting Rights Act of 1965 is such a case. The federal government enacted a law, the intent of which was to make sure citizens could exercise their basic right to vote. The policy was aimed primarily at eliminating discrimination against black voters in the South, who had been prevented from voting by a variety of methods—including literacy tests, fraud, and gerrymandered election districts. In certain areas, federal marshals were to be used to enforce the provisions of the new law.

After passage of the statute, the Justice Department began to execute its provisions, and by virtually any measure the results met the expectations of those who framed the act. Black registration and voting dramatically increased by hundreds of thousands within months. In some states the change was truly revolutionary. Mississippi went from having 7 percent of its blacks registered before the act to 61 percent by 1967. Today, blacks register and vote at a rate only slightly lower than that of white citizens. The law worked.

Symbolic Policies Sometimes, however, formal policies like laws differ from the actual operations of government. Occasionally, even those responsible for formulating a formal policy do not intend it to be taken literally or to have a direct policy effect. The major reason for adopting the policy may be its political benefit.

The Humphrey-Hawkins Bill, passed by Congress and signed by President Carter in 1978, is a good example. The law proclaimed that it was the government's intention to reduce unemployment to a level at or below 4 percent of the work force by 1983 and to lower the inflation rate to zero by 1988. Yet the final version the law provided no real mechanism by which these goals could be accomplished, partially because there was no agreement on what would work. Furthermore, it is clear from the process by which the law was enacted that no one expected much to happen. Policies of this sort may be considered symbolic policies.[1]

In political life, many actions have at least some symbolic component to them. Sometimes, this component exists merely to serve the political benefit of a politician or party. But in other instances, symbols can be meant to send signals about future policy actions. In foreign affairs, for example, presidents have sometimes ordered military exercises with a friendly government that has been under threat. This symbolic action of support may send a signal to other countries of future intentions for real policy decisions.

Implementation and the Bureaucracy Even when policymakers intend to accomplish a policy objective, difficulties may arise. One set of problems relates to the implementation of policy. Sometimes a policy says one thing, but those charged with carrying it out do something else. The bureaucracy is usually given the responsibility for implementing policy, and usually bureaucracies are responsive to political direction. But in some cases, a bureaucracy might do nothing, delay, or do something different from the intentions of the original policymakers. An agency's organizational culture and history or professional orientation might lead some bureaucrats not to comply with their superiors.[2] For example, the Civil Rights Division of the Justice Department enforces civil rights laws, often through pursuing court cases. The natural inclination of the division's lawyers to argue increases the likelihood that career bureaucrats, who carry out much of the work, would question the commands of political appointees.

Unintended Consequences A second set of problems may occur even after a policy is established and implemented as directed. The policy may simply not work, or it may have side-effects that create more problems than the one that has been solved.

Earlier in this century the first freeways were built in and around the nation's cities. Many policymakers expected that these roadways would reduce traffic congestion. The expressways were completed (that is, the policy was implemented), but the result was an increase in traffic congestion and pollution. New roads meant that more people bought cars and more car owners drove more often. When a well-implemented policy does not have the expected result, there is a problem of *unintended consequences.*

Many attempts at social engineering run afoul of the "law of unintended consequences" as it is sometimes called. Welfare programs designed to alleviate poverty by transferring wealth to the poor might create a culture of poverty by providing more incentives to stay on welfare than to seek work.

The fact that policies may not meet with success because of problems of implementation and unintended consequences illustrates the complexities of the policy process. The creation of a public policy by no means guarantees the conversion of governmental intention into action. The process of policymaking does not stop with the passage of a law or the announcement of a decision. For government to serve the people, not only must appropriate policies be selected, but they must be implemented properly and achieve the desired results.

Inconsistent Policies

Policies are sometimes adopted and put into effect that work at cross purposes or contradict each other. One example is the conflicting federal policies that were in place for many years regarding tobacco use. One policy, a law dealing with agricultural subsidies, paid farmers to grow tobacco. Another—in the form of other federal law and regulations of the Federal Trade Commission and the Federal Communications Commission—sought to limit smoking by prohibiting cigarette commercials on radio and television and by requiring a cautionary message on cigarette packages and advertisements.

Laws and regulations, then, sometimes conflict with each other in their policy effects. Different actors in the government disagree, or they are simply operating with a different set of priorities or a different focus, such as helping farmers and protecting people's health. To some degree, this follows from the fragmentation of power in a system of separation of powers. Inconsistency is further promoted by writing legislation in scores of congressional subcommittees and the implementation of policies by administrative units subject to pressures from different congressional committees and different forces within the administration. While logic and consistency in policymaking clearly have their advantages, many of the inconsistencies we find in government policy are the result of a system trying to respond simultaneously to conflicting desires and interests.

Policies as Guidelines

Policies can be made incrementally or in a single comprehensive action and through any of several units of government: a law passed by a legislature, an executive order of the president, or an order or regulation issued by an agency are all considered policymaking. State and local governments also make policy in similar ways.

But, not every decision by a unit of government involves the making of policy. First, there are decisions to apply a policy that is already established to a specific case. An example would be when an agent of the Drug Enforcement Administration (DEA) decides to investigate and arrest a suspected narcotics dealer. Second, there are government decisions that establish goals, rules, standards or practices designed to be applied over time to a series of actions or cases. These decisions, intended to have a general effect and some stability, are what we normally call policies.[3]

The distinction between applying and making a policy, however, is not absolute. Many policies are made in the process of being applied, as many discrete decisions begin to add up to a more general policy. Thus a series of decisions made by a bureaucratic agency about how to apply a policy—for example, decisions by the DEA about what kinds of drug dealers to pursue—establishes a set of practices that in effect defines the policy. Courts also define policy in this way by applying rules in specific cases in such a way that, over time, a distinct policy finally emerges.

So far, we have raised a number of questions about what public policy is. By thinking about what constitutes policy, we are alerted to several important facts about government. First, public policymaking is important, but so are many private decisions. Second, there is often much more—or less—to policy than the formal documents and statements of government officials: the process begins long before the legislative debate and may continue past the signing of laws, judicial decrees and the publishing of regulations. American public policy is not a neat, consistent set of rules, but rather, a complex, shifting, partially contradictory amalgam of choices. Finally, there is not simply *one* process, but *many* policymaking processes. There are many ways to enter the system and to influence how matters are settled.

In addition to rules issued by legislatures, courts, the executive, or bureaucracies, policy can be made by restructuring an agency to set the tone for future policy decisions. After the terrorist attacks of Sept. 11, 2001, the Federal Bureau of Investigation went through several stages of reorganization at the request of Congress and the president to make counter-terrorism a larger part of its mission. Reorganizing the FBI involved proposals to restructure its hierarchy, add new technology, increase cooperation with the Central Intelligence Agency, and add new divisions to increase anti-terrorism intelligence gathering and a division for internal security to counter spying.[4]

Agency reorganization may be necessary, but it has often proved to be a Herculean task. The FBI was created to concentrate on large-scale crime not covered by state or local authorities, such as bank robberies across several states. But over time, agencies like the FBI acquire new tasks which are hard to relinquish. Since the 1970s, Congress has created more than 1,000 new federal criminal statutes, each of which entails a new responsibility for the FBI. As a consequence, sometimes FBI agents spend time tracking minor crimes such as drug violations rather than large scale terrorist operations. Simply passing one more law adding to the anti-terrorism duties of the FBI is not enough to produce real change. Agency reorganization is necessary because policy makers must work through institutions to carry out policy.

Different Views of Policymaking

How is policy made, and who governs? Policies are made within the institutions of the government, and officials act with a large degree of discretion in carrying them out. Thus judges judge, legislators legislate, and administrators apply the law. To understand how policies are made and put into effect, one must, in the first place, understand the operation of these institutions.

As noted in Chapter 1, these institutions rule in the name of, and are influenced by, certain forces. Four different views of who governs and which forces move the policy process are found in the models of policymaking: bureaucratic politics, elite domination, majoritarianism, and pluralism.

A Bureaucratic State?

The bureaucratic model of governance asserts that it is really the administrative apparatus that is in control of the modern state. The evidence we have discussed, especially in the chapter on the bureaucracy, shows that for certain kinds of decisions the bureaucracy does seem to direct policy. And it is undoubtedly true that large bureaucracies have a way of acting on their own that can defy the will of even the most determined political leaders. Yet the big decisions—those that set the basic directions of policies—are made by the political actors. Thus while the Pentagon may have various military options for almost every case, the decision of when to use a military option is made by elected officials.

Bureaucracy in the American system, far more than in the case of most other major democracies, is subject to a variety of direct political influences even in the conduct of administrative decisions. The American constitutional system of separated powers is less prone to administrative-led reform because it is more fragmented and has political oversight of administration. Seymour Martin Lipset summarizes the situation: "No other elected national government except the Swiss is as limited in its powers."[5]

Bureaucrats carry out many activities—from providing health care to protecting the environment—and inevitably possess some degree of discretion in doing so. Yet in reality, the bureaucrats are not formulating the broad contours of public policy. American bureaucracy exists because politicians decided that it should be there.

Elite Domination?

Anti-globalization activists assert that there is a power elite or establishment that governs the United States. Popular culture gives expression to concerns that a secret cabal or "cigarette-smoking man" is behind important national policies, as in the television series "The X-Files."[6]

A softer or milder version of the elitist model holds that there is a core of highly educated, well-positioned people who make the important decisions. If this means a closed group that gives little account to the views of the "average person," then it is clearly undemocratic, even if the places of the well-positioned are in theory open to all. But in a slightly different sense—in the sense of highly qualified individuals seeking to serve the people—it is not at all a concept that is opposed to representative government. Jefferson himself spoke of a government by a "natural aristoi" or meritocracy, meaning a government by the qualified and the talented serving on behalf of the public. The very idea of an executive senior service in the bureaucracy is based on finding and promoting such an "elite."

There are clearly elements of American policymaking that are strongly influenced by elites in one or both of the senses just mentioned. In many areas of policymaking in Washington, there are groups of experts who are important players, some of whom attempt to guard their influence. For years, for example, there was a fairly well-defined group that felt it had an informal prerogative to discuss and define the terms of foreign policy—the so-called "foreign policy establishment." For the most part in Washington today, however, we are speaking not of a single group, but of different groups—different elites—that possess more or less influence in a particular policy area.

The more significant question about elite domination relates to whether the elites operate cohesively and make decisions in the interest of a particular segment of society. The stricter version of the elitist model raises these concerns.

Karl Marx, the famous nineteenth century political theorist, argued that in advanced nations economic power more or less determines political power. Those who own the capital, the money and business necessary for the production of goods make sure that their interests are served, if need be at the expense of the majority. Marx was not alone in his belief. An American sociologist of the twentieth century, C. Wright Mills, studied the exercise of influence in this country's public life and concluded that a "power elite" controlled policy. Mills' claim was that a relatively small number of high-level military leaders, politicians, and business executives made all the key decisions. This group functioned as a single unit even if its members never actually sat down together to develop a "party line." Furthermore, this group made decisions in its own interest, not in the public's interest.[7]

Analysts concerned about elite domination, from Mills to contemporary anti-globalization activists, contend that many significant questions in American policy are not discussed because elites frame public discourse. If the public merely follows the set of opinions put forth by political, business, and media elites, then the deliberations leading to policies cannot be said to be fully democratic or representative. John

Zaller provides examples of public opinion following the positions advocated by elites, even on such contentious issues as the Vietnam War.[8]

Others worried about elite domination argue that there is a concentration of economic power in the hands of a fairly small group of people. This is significant because the economy and economic power have significant influence on the policymaking process. Wealthy industries lobby and stay abreast of decision-making in Washington and other world capitals with an effectiveness that most other interests, such as organized labor, envy. Given the importance of business to the well-being of the nation, leading business people, by claiming what is needed to keep business healthy, are in a position to exercise considerable political power.[9]

Business is not the only powerful interest in society, though, and it is not clear that there is even a single group of business leaders; instead there are distinct businesses and industries with sometimes competing interests. The problem with arguments about elite domination is that it is difficult to identify a single elite that shares the same policy objectives across several issues.

In modern society, as we have seen, information is an important influence on political power, and therefore the nation's major newspapers and journalists constitute another important interest with its own norms and reasons for acting. Moreover, ideas are a source of policy, so that those who are major forces in academia—let us say law professors—constitute a significant "establishment."

There is a big difference between saying that a power elite (such as a group of business executives, perhaps in concert with certain others) controls the policy process and saying that in this process certain interests (such as business) possess significant advantages. In fact, it would be very difficult to support a generalization that any single interest wins on every policy issue, or even on every policy issue about which it may care greatly. There are many policies that clearly benefit big business, from tax policy, to various subsidies, to tariff protection. But there are also other policies that work against businesses, and businesses are often in competition with each other. If the federal government's relaxation of mileage standards for American cars represents a victory for the industry, the 1970 policy requiring pollution control devices on those same vehicles was achieved over the determined opposition of the automobile makers. The oil business has repeatedly been rebuffed in recent years in its bid to drill in Arctic National Wildlife Refuge (ANWAR). And timber interests in the Northwest have had to yield in large measure to environmental groups.

Majoritarianism?

If by "pure democracy" one means a system in which the people directly determine the content of public policy with each person's preferences counting the same, the United States is a far cry from being a democratic system. The framers of the Constitution designed a republic in which the views of citizens would be filtered through political representatives and complex institutional arrangements. Some parts of the nation's policymaking apparatus, like the court system, are intentionally insulated from popular opinion. Moreover, the most democratic elements of the system are themselves not pure. Not all citizens' preferences "count" equally. Not all people vote, and fewer still ever make known their preferences on policy issues to their representatives. Those Americans who do participate in the political process are not fully representative of the entire populace.

Still, many initially adopt the model of strict majoritarianism—a system in which the majority of citizens get to control policy—as the unambiguous ideal against which the policymaking system should be judged. But consider a thought experiment: if we as constitution makers could start from scratch, ignoring the designs of the founders and creating a new system, would it be possible or desirable to seek a purely majoritarian arrangement?

First, we might decide that we would not want pure majoritarianism. Certain matters such as freedom of religion, speech, the press, and assembly are so deserving of protection that we would not allow a popular majority to ban one form of religion or shut down a newspaper by a simple majority vote. We might prefer to put these freedoms in a written constitution where they would have the added guarantee of protec-

---

BOX 15.1

One Problem with Pure Democracy

Even if citizens were well informed and had the time and inclination to make important public policy decisions directly, there would be no neat and simple way to translate their views into policy. The rules used for collecting their preferences and converting them into a decision can never be neutral. Any rules will influence the result.

To illustrate this point, we pose a hypothetical situation. Assume that current estimates are that next year's federal budget as presently projected will be in deficit by $200 billion, and citizens can vote directly what to do about the deficit. For simplicity's sake, assume that only three options are being seriously considered: (1) across-the-board spending cuts to balance the budget; 2) an income tax increase to cover the deficit; or 3) allowing the deficit as projected.

Suppose all Americans of voting age gave clear opinions on the matter in a survey. Their (hypothetical) views were as follows:

> 30% liked option (1) best, and option (2) second-best
>
> 30% liked option (2) best, and option (3) second-best
>
> 40% liked option (3) best, and option (1) second-best

Thus, no alternative would have a majority. To decide policy, suppose we arranged one vote between two of the options, with the winner placed against the third alternative.

Consider the results. If option (1) were first tested against option (2), the first would win 70% to 30%. In the runoff between (1) and (3), (3) would win 70% to 30%. Thus, it would seem that pure democracy requires continuing to allow a deficit.

But suppose we had started the contest with (1) versus (3). The latter would have entered the runoff against (2) and lost—60% to 40%! Increasing income taxes would seem to be the people's choice.

If the first race had been (2) against (3), with the winner to battle (1), the outcome would be spending cuts, by a 70-30 margin. Can you see why?

Notice that the outcome changed, despite the fact that people did not change their minds and despite the apparent fairness and neutrality of the rules. What the public prefers is often not so easy to identify.

Source: Kenneth Arrow, *Social Choice and Individual Values*, 2nd ed. (New York: Wiley, 1963).

---

tion by an independent judiciary, on occasion even against majority wishes.

Second, even if we wanted pure majoritarian decision-making on all other matters of public policy, there is no neutral or unbiased way of putting together, or aggregating, individuals' preferences on anything—including policy issues or candidates for office—to decide a collective outcome. Part of the attractiveness of a strict majoritarian system comes from the illusion that if we count everyone's view, we thereby remove bias since there are then no back-room deals between special interests or bargaining between elites in the policymaking process. But *all* ways of deciding policies—including voting, with

majority rule determining the winner—are biased, not in the sense of being dishonest but in the sense that they make some outcomes more likely than others. This concept may be a difficult one to grasp, but Box 15.1 provides a simple illustration of how a seemingly fair and unambiguous voting rule is not neutral toward the policies being decided.

Consider health care policy as an example of the problem of translating majority opinion into policy. In surveys, many people indicate that they want a national health care plan in the abstract, but when confronted with details they often express concern about "big government" and the complexity of a new federal program.[10]

Another classic example is when people favor a balanced budget, lower taxes, and increased government services all at the same time.

Third, there might be some deviations from pure majoritarianism that we might favor, at least up to a certain point. If one part of the democratic ideal is that a majority should be able to have its way, another is that those who care the most (or are the most directly affected) by a policy should have a greater say. Yet if we set policy by simply allowing people to indicate their preference—through polling, voting, or whatever—we shall have counted an intensely held opinion only as much as one expressed by the least interested citizen. An apathetic majority of 51 percent may outweigh a passionate minority of 49 percent—a result that many would consider unfair.

No democratic system can ever be so pure that it is free from all traces of bias. Furthermore, certain deviations or biases from a pure majoritarian standard may be justifiable. The whole purpose of constitutions is to structure choices and therefore to influence the general character of policy outcomes. The United States system does this in many ways. For example, the president and Congress are often in conflict, partly because the presidency was designed to be especially sensitive to crisis situations and problems affecting the whole nation, while the Congress was meant to pay closer attention to the concerns of particular regions and interests. Serious considerations other than pure majoritarianism were clearly evident at the founding, and thus it is not mere perversity or ill will that has kept the United States from adopting a purely majoritarian system.

Even though we do not have a purely majoritarian system, majoritarianism in a looser and more relaxed sense is one of the basic principles in the policy process. The rule of the majority helps to set or to limit the broad direction of public policy. Policies at the national and state levels are by no means always in line with public opinion—but majority opinion does exert leverage on policymakers and institutions, especially on the most important issues that capture the attention of the citizenry. Elections and representative institutions provide a mechanism whereby popular values are transformed into policy.

Pluralism

Along with majoritarianism, the other major principle in the policy process is pluralism. A pluralist system is one in which power is dispensed among a number of groups such that no single group can consistently control the outcomes. In a pluralist arrangement power is shared, and policymaking is the product of competition, bargaining, and accommodation among those who participate.

One version of a pluralist policymaking process was clearly favored by the founders as an important element of the constitutional system. As Madison explained, the idea was to construct the political system so that any "faction," even one to which a majority of the people belonged, would have difficulty enacting a policy that worked against the real interests of the public as a whole. The constitutional provisions for separation of powers (segmenting influence across Congress, the president, and the courts) and for a federal structure (separating national from state power) were conscious attempts to institute important pluralist elements into the policy process.

Today, along with the pluralist elements that act through the formal governmental institutions, there are other components of the political system that have added to the pluralist character of policymaking. These include the media, organized interest groups, and political parties.

One might also mention the bureaucracy, which though it is part of the official government and existed from the beginning, has added a new pluralistic dimension by the way it functions. Bureaucracies have become so large and important that they occupy a place in the pluralist power structure that the founders could probably not have foreseen. Departments such as agriculture developed their own issue networks and constituencies that rely on the Agriculture Department to represent their interests.

Policymaking in American government is complex enough and involves such a number of participants that it can often be described as a process of pluralism. How democratic are pluralist systems? How quickly, accurately, and frequently do they translate citizens' preferences into public policies? A pluralist system is certainly no guarantee of democratic government. Pluralism may prevent a single force from monopolizing power, but it can also be arranged to exclude significant segments of the public. If the major automobile manufacturers were to sit down with labor representatives from the United Auto Workers, an adviser to the president, and a few key members of Congress to work out a policy restricting the importation of foreign cars into the country, these actors would not all have the same interests at heart. There would probably be much bargaining and disagreement before any policy achieved consensus. But it would be quite possible for these participants to reach agreements that ignored certain interests or conflicted with the views of most citizens. Thus, the pluralist model may still mean that on some issues the bargaining among groups is restricted to a narrow range of options defined by a limited number of groups.

This kind of policymaking occurs in many instances, especially after a major initiative has been undertaken and the specific content of the policy remains to be "filled in." In filling in the details of policy—and often the details turn out to be far more important than anyone imagined—the specific groups affected are bound to pay much more attention to what occurs and to devote far more resources in attempting to achieve their objectives. Nevertheless, to say that a pluralist policymaking process can sometimes ignore the wishes of the public is not to say that it necessarily must do so. There are majoritarian influences at work ensuring that in many policy areas decisions are made that allow for a large number of players and for a consideration of the wishes of the general public. Moreover, with the growth in the last twenty-five years in the number of interest groups, including interest groups designed to watch and check some of the more powerful traditional interest groups, pluralist decision-making processes often include a broader range of players than before.

Pluralism can sometimes lead to "gridlock" in which the parties involved in bargaining cannot reach consensus, a phenomenon most often associated with redistributive policies that have well-organized stakeholders. The government shutdowns of the 1990s when Congress and the president failed to agree on a budget are examples of gridlock. Yet gridlock happens much less often than critics of pluralism might expect, even in a highly partisan environment.[11] During the past 15 years, Congress and presidential vote totals have been split about 50-50 between Democrats and Republicans. Despite the parties' disagreements, the past decade saw important policy innovations such as welfare reform, the North American Free Trade Agreement, deficit reduction, and deregulation of many industries

The Stages of Policymaking

As there is not just one American policy process but many, there is also no single way to describe all policymaking. But policymaking can be understood as a process that involves a series of distinguishable stages. We describe them here, in logical order, although in the real world things never proceed in so neat and orderly a fashion. As some policies are being executed, others are just being conceived. Certain public decisions are even being undone almost before they are put into place. In American government, policy is made not once and for all but in an unending series of steps.

Setting the Agenda

Policymakers must focus on a relatively limited number of questions. Those issues that actually do get considered and discussed constitute the *agenda* for decision making. Government sets policy in so many different areas today that it is hard sometimes to believe that it is not making policy about everything at once. On an average day a typical representative might find it necessary to devote attention to policies about handgun control, consumer product safety, postal rates, pesticide regulation, issues affecting regulated utilities and their consumers, and ideas about how to energize the Democratic Party as well as attend receptions for interest groups and meet with constituents. (This list is a partial enumeration of the items on the schedule of Representative David E. Price on February 23, 1999.[12])

Yet many matters a representative might devote attention to are never seriously considered for government action.

What constitutes a problem worthy of inclusion on the agenda of policymakers is not always clear-cut, so the process by which issues become of public concern and enter onto the political agenda in the first place is an important one. The boundary line identifying the issues that might be included on the policy agenda is not set in stone, but has shifted over time. The general tendency has been toward inclusion of more issues on the agenda of government. This tendency was especially in evidence from the 1930s through the mid-1970s, when the demands on government grew very rapidly and when expectations of what government could accomplish were very high. Since then there has been a partial reaction and an effort to take certain items off the agenda of government, as in the policies to deregulate some industries or to give responsibility for providing welfare and assistance to the poor to the states or to private charities.

Reducing the items on the political agenda is usually a difficult task, since existing programs tend to develop well-organized backers and people tend to think that a matter once public in principle will always remain so. But it is possible to remove items from the list of political concerns. Below we survey some of the factors that help explain the shifts in the items on the government's agenda.

The Impact of Ideas Policy studies often begin with the pluralist model in which interest groups such as the National Rifle Association, the National Organization for Women, and the Sierra Club play a large role in politics, and policy outcomes are the result of bargains struck by these groups. While not denying the role of interest groups, students of politics should also be sensitive to the impact of ideas on policy. Ideas shape policy in several ways. For instance, the ideas of a president, governor, or legislator may be important in how he or she votes. Politicians respond to voters and interest groups, but they are also purposive actors with their own values.

The public's general ideas about the role government should play in society also affect the policy agenda by changing the number and type of items considered appropriate for government intervention. In the nineteenth century, curing poverty was not a policy of the federal government, because most Americans thought of poverty as a private hardship or evidence of moral weakness, or at any rate a problem of state and local governments.

Since the New Deal of the 1930s, however, more and more citizens have come to view the government—and ultimately the federal government—as being responsible for ensuring certain basic needs of all citizens. This belief is the cornerstone of the social welfare state, and even President Reagan, a conservative Republican, endorsed the idea of maintaining a social "safety net" for all Americans.

Ideas about the role of government usually tend to change over a period of several years, as parties and influential presidents fight a battle of ideas about basic public philosophies or ideologies. Occasionally, however, a particular stimulus may trigger a shift in policy in a somewhat narrower area. In 1961, the newly elected president, John Kennedy, read a book entitled *The Other America* by Michael Harrington, which poignantly illustrated the great amount of relatively invisible poverty that still existed in the United States. Kennedy was so impressed with the book that he worked to place the poverty issue on the public's agenda. Harrington's argument, and Kennedy's sponsorship of the issue, quickly stimulated considerable public discussion and, ultimately, some new policies.

But over time, the dominant opinion shifted: people were less optimistic about the power of government to "cure" poverty and people began to worry about dependency and a self-perpetuating culture of poverty. By the 1990s, poverty was still on the agenda, but the dominant understanding of the problem had changed.[13] People were less concerned that no jobs were available, since millions of jobs requiring little or no skill were created in the 1980s and 1990s. Opinion leaders also became concerned about the problem of out-of-wedlock births and no longer believed that poor single mothers could raise children as well as a two-parent family. Even when controlling for income, children in one-parent families are much more likely to drop out of school, to be both out of work and out of school, and to become single parents themselves.

In 1996, welfare reform, formally titled The Personal Responsibility and Work Opportunity Reconciliation Act, replaced a social program known as Aid to Families with Dependent Children (AFDC) with a new program called Temporary Assistance to Needy Families (TANF). The reforms had three goals: 1) to increase employment, 2) to reduce child poverty, and 3) to reduce out-of-wedlock births. Welfare policy is complex, but the essence of TANF was the addition of time limits and compulsory work requirements to aid provisions.

Changing ideas among the public about what welfare should be influenced both a Republican Congress and a Democratic president (Clinton) to work for reform. Intellectuals who study and write about social life also had an influence on agenda setting. Many of the ideas behind complex policies such as welfare reform sometimes develop through a "policy stream" of participants outside the public view, consisting of government specialists, academics, and interest groups or private research units, known as "think tanks." Loosely knit groups of specialists exist in different policy areas in which ideas bubble around and spew forth in what has been called "the policy primeval soup" where there are "many ideas floating around, bumping into one another, encountering new ideas, and forming combinations and recombinations."[14] These specialists debate ideas and formulate possible solutions, but they need a problem to arise and a political proponent before their ideas are considered on the public agenda.

Ideas Outside the Policy Process: Nondecisions
The reigning ideas and principles of a society may also set the boundaries of policy options. For instance, the range of distribution of wealth and income for individuals in the United States is very wide. It would of course be possible for government to enact public policies to reduce the income disparity, which might be done by major alterations in inheritance law, nationalization of key industries, sweeping revisions in the income tax code, or major new income transfer programs. All of these plans for completely "remaking" the income distribution have been

enacted in at least one foreign country, but they are seldom seriously entertained in the American policymaking process. Public decision makers in the United States, and even many of the poorest citizens, believe strongly in property rights and in the principle of an individual's freedom to use income however he or she chooses.

Some of the most far-reaching options for dealing with certain questions or problems are not actively discussed. In many areas, the consideration of policies that might achieve certain goals (for example, reducing income disparity) is foreclosed by the acceptance of fundamental ideas or principles such as the sanctity of private property. These background choices, which apply basic constitutional principles, influence which issues are taken up for debate. The issues that are not actively considered—some political scientists call them "nondecisions"—are often far more important than the options government actually considers during policymaking debates.[15]

The principle of equality of opportunity frames the debate in many policy areas. In the 1960s, Great Society programs including Medicare, Medicaid, and anti-poverty programs were "wrapped up in a concept of opportunity for the disadvantaged that seemed fully in tune with the American political philosophy."[16] What did not happen in the 1960s was as important as what did happen—the political authorities did not consider a more far-reaching program of income redistribution and social change. Public policy was made according to the principles of individualism and opportunity. The debate over affirmative action, too, is often framed in the language of equality of opportunity by both its supporters and opponents.

Ideas Outside the Policy Process: Path Dependence
The options readily available to policy makers might also be limited by what is called path dependence. Theories of path dependence were first used to explain why certain technologies became the standard in their fields even though they were not the most efficient or advanced available. When typewriters were designed with a QWERTY keyboard, people made investments of time and money in that technology, and the QWERTY design continues on today's computers.[17] If a better keyboard

design were possible, as some maintain there is, it would be difficult to replace QWERTY because of the initial investment.

The central claim is that once a policy decision is made, it is difficult to radically change course. Initial actions, and even careless ones, put us on a path that cannot be left without a cost, which is often greater than simply living with the inefficiencies of the existing system.

Path dependence may characterize the political world even more than the economic world. The founders puts limits on government action (the separation of powers, bicameralism and federalism) that add veto points and increase the pluralist character of the American policy process.[18] Some Americans think that the institutions of the founders are key to the strength of American democracy, while others think these institutions are unwieldy. Either way, initial decisions to create certain institutions sent us down a path that is difficult, though not impossible, to reverse.

Path dependence is a fashionable term that can amount to the assertion that "history matters." In policy development, where we are today is a result of what has happened in the past. For instance, the reasons for the policy changes of the 1996 welfare reform act do not make sense without understanding the major welfare policy developments of the 1960s and 70s. But the fact that policies do change is a reminder that the decisions of political actors are important and that political action has the power to send us down the road we choose.

Science and Technology In less direct ways, the generation of new knowledge can help set the public agenda. As technology develops, it usually creates new problems for government to deal with, and it often provides government with new capabilities to act. In the 1940s, when physicists unlocked the secrets of the atom, the idea of nuclear weapons received the secret but immediate attention of the highest military and civilian government officials during World War II. This great scientific discovery has since added a huge number of items to the political agenda, both in the sphere of military and foreign policy (such as nuclear strategy and arms control) and in the sphere of domestic policy (problems related to nuclear power plants and nuclear waste disposal). By the same token, in 2001 and 2002 some scientists (prematurely) announced that they would soon be able to clone human beings. The problem of whether and how to control this potentially dangerous tool leapt onto the national policy agenda, and Congress and the president began to consider proposals for a ban on human cloning.

Increased knowledge and technological advances can also lead to certain issues being removed in part from the public agenda. As observed in our discussion of the media, the early history of television took place in an era in which only a limited number of stations could broadcast and in which the federal government believed it had to regulate aspects of television programming to protect the public interest. Cable and satellite technology now allow for hundreds of channels, and certain kinds of regulations are now less necessary and are in the process of being modified or abandoned. For example, under the "fairness doctrine," the Federal Communications Commission once required stations to seek out and give time to those who opposed any editorial view of the station. This measure has now been eliminated, in large part because current technology allows for many stations with multiple points of view.

Crises The occurrence of crises or prominent events can sometimes quickly add issues to the agenda. The Great Depression in the 1930s stimulated a new set of policy discussions about the role of government in the economy; the huge oil spills off the coast of Santa Barbara, California in 1969 and off the coast of Alaska in 1989 gave widespread public attention to the environmental movement; and the terrorist attacks on New York City and the Pentagon in 2001 prompted policy changes in national defense and the creation of the Office of Homeland Security.

Sometimes major events or tragedies are utilized as resources by interest groups that have long been struggling to attract the attention of policymakers. Federal gun-control policy provides a useful illustration. In 1968, the assassinations of Martin Luther King and Senator Robert Kennedy within two months of each other shocked and outraged millions of Americans.

Gun-control advocates made use of the tragedies to push for a new law, which was swiftly approved by Congress (the Gun Control Act of 1968). The new policy was not all the proponents had hoped for, but it did impose new restrictions on access to handguns.

Interest-Group Activity: Multiple Channels
Even when no major ideas or technological advances spur consideration of new policy issues, or no crises or prominent events take place, the activities of individuals or interest groups may succeed in attracting the attention of policymakers. Depending on the issue and the political makeup of the proponents, interests may use various routes—with varying degrees of success—to get an item on the agenda.

If somebody can interest a bureaucratic agency in a new policy, it stands a good chance of eventually receiving a serious hearing. Bureaucrats possess expertise and near-permanence, and they are in a position to propose an issue coherently and repeatedly. Even if the immediate political climate is not ripe for a particular policy, bureaucrats may eventually find ways to get attention directed to it. They are, after all, often the ones who help draft the speeches, provide information, write legislation, and frame the programs. Potential policy ideas may incubate in agencies for years before attracting a wider public.

Congress is another major channel for bringing an item onto the national agenda. The Senate has been particularly active in this respect in recent years, as senators have sought new issues to generate national attention—sometimes to gain personal exposure for a possible run for the presidency. Senator John McCain made his cosponsorship of campaign finance reform legislation a central issue in his 2000 campaign for the Republican nomination for president.

Because of the decentralized nature of Congress and the importance of committee work in the policy process, the legislature is an excellent point of entrance for a group seeking to add a new item to the agenda. A sympathetic committee or subcommittee leader may at least be able to initiate hearings on a subject. On the other hand, if an item gets access to the agenda through a congressional sponsor or committee,

there is no guarantee that Congress as a whole will resolve the issue in the group's favor. Some legislators may introduce an item onto the agenda to satisfy a constituency but have no intention of seeing it through the committees' winnowing process to completion.

The courts also offer access to the policy agenda for some interest groups. In general, one needs a strong case, but not necessarily strong political support, to get serious consideration of an issue. It is this feature that often makes the courts the starting point for groups that may lack an initial strong base of political support.

Not all issues receive attention by the courts, and judicial remedies can often be limited. Traditionally, the judiciary has been a reactive policymaking institution, validating, interpreting, and making consistent the policies established by the more political organs of government. Yet in recent periods, particularly since the 1960s, the courts have been far more willing to venture into new fields and undertake the kinds of remedies that formerly were supplied only by legislative or administrative bodies. Tobacco policy is one example of the move toward "adversarial legalism" in the policy process (see box 15.2).

The chief executive has become the nation's prime agenda setter, and much of congressional business consists of reaction to or investigation of the proposals put forward by the occupant of the White House. The president is responsible annually for some of the most obvious and formal agenda-setting activities of the government, such as delivering a state of the union address and producing a detailed budget proposal and legislative programs. When an interest group has attracted the president's attention to a policy issue and it becomes a priority of the president, it gets noticed and often becomes the nation's business.

The problem of civil rights appeared prominently on the policy agenda in the 1960s through the courts (school desegregation cases) and through the media (dramatic scenes such as police dogs attacking defenseless blacks on national television). But probably the most important channel was the presidency. Civil rights groups such as the National Association for the Advancement of Colored People (NAACP) and the Congress on Racial Equality

---

BOX 15.2

TOBACCO POLITICS

Tobacco lawyers and state attorneys general may have usurped powers traditionally reserved for lawmakers.

From the 1960s to the 1990s, tobacco policy was made through what some have called "ordinary politics." Legislation was the product of competing interests, and public health advocates and tobacco growers and manufactures hammered out compromises which were enacted into law. After three decades of moderately coercive laws, adult smoking was cut by half.

Tobacco policy underwent a fundamental shift in the 1990s, when policymaking was largely removed from the legislatures and was conducted through litigation in the courts. One attempt at bypassing legislative authority came from a federal agency. David A. Kessler, the commissioner of the federal Food and Drug Administration from 1990 to 1997, asserted his jurisdiction over tobacco regulation. Under Kessler, the FDA initiated aggressive regulations including an advertising program and sting operations to test retailers' compliance with rules banning cigarette sales to minors. The regulation advocates were up front about wanting to put tobacco companies out of business. In a newspaper interview, Kessler said "I don't want to live in peace with these guys. If they cared at all for the public health, they wouldn't be in this business in the first place. All this talk about it being a legal business is euphemism. They sell a deadly, addictive product. There's no reason to allow them to conduct business as usual." The FDA's power was challenged in federal court, and in March 2000, the Supreme Court ruled that the FDA did not have jurisdiction over tobacco policy. But the ruling did not stop tobacco regulation—it just meant that state governments and courts would be the center of action.

The other attempt to affect policy while bypassing the legislative process came through litigation in the courts. In the fall of 1998, the United States embarked down the path of "adversarial legalism" in tobacco politics when more than 40 state attorneys general filed lawsuits against the major cigarette manufacturers. The lawsuits were primarily though not exclusively based on claims for recovery of Medicaid costs allegedly attributable to smoking. There were four immediate individual settlements by state governments (Mississippi, Florida, Texas, and Minnesota) and then one large settlement, the Master Settlement Agreement of 1998 (MSA), covering the remaining 46 states.

Unlike some public health advocates, the state attorneys general were not in the business of trying to drive tobacco companies into bankruptcy. In fact, states had an interest in keeping tobacco companies healthy. The high taxes imposed on cigarette manufacturers provided a revenue windfall.

(CORE) were able to convince Lyndon Johnson to elevate this issue to prime importance. The President used his political skill to help produce several new policies, including the dramatic civil rights bills of 1964 and 1965. In a similar way, groups interested in more federal money for "faith-based" programs to help the poor have looked to win influence with President George W. Bush.

Presidents usually add only a few select issues to the agenda. They use their political influence cautiously by picking a few items to emphasize, usually items that have already become objects of considerable attention. Thus, many of those who seek access for their concerns must find another channel for placing an item on the agenda.

Less powerful groups that may initially have trouble being taken seriously by major institutions have limited options. One way for these groups to raise issues is through the media. Another way to seek attention for a problem or issue is to resort to protests or other "media events" as a way of attracting a broader audience. The civil rights march from Selma to Montgomery, Alabama in 1965 is an example of

Box 15.2 (cont.)

The tobacco settlements cause problems for the standards usually applied to policymaking in a democracy. The MSA was negotiated privately, without public comment. There is no record of the debate leading up to the settlement, and it is difficult to hold those responsible for the agreement accountable. The settlement benefits the parties who made it—states get richer, and attorneys general get publicity. Tobacco companies were able to win exemptions from antitrust laws and thus were able to raise prices even more than the settlement required. By contrast, a legislature might have debated the fairness of a tax that falls most heavily on the poorest and least educated segments of the population.

What is the best way to make policy in the case of tobacco politics and in others cases like it? The supporters of state litigation would say that theirs was the only effective method of reducing tobacco use, because Congress had failed to act. Supporters of FDA regulation might say that the agency was able to put anti-smoking campaigns on the national agenda while avoiding the excesses of state litigation. But supporters of ordinary politics, public policy enacted through compromises in legislatures, would find problems in the new adversarial legalism which is conducted outside the constitutional channels. Tobacco policy also raises larger moral issues such as how far should a government go in protecting its citizens against vice? Tobacco politics is emblematic of other contemporary policy issues in which there are several avenues for political actors to pursue policy change, but it also raises important questions about the separation of power, the roles of interest groups and courts, and government regulations versus individual rights.

Source: Case comes from: Martha A. Derthick, *Up in Smoke* (Washington DC: CQ Press, 2002). Kessler quote is from: Jeffrey Goldberg, "Big Tobacco Won't Quit," *New York Times Magazine*, June 21, 1998, 36ff.
For more on "adversarial legalism" see Robert F. Kagan, "Adversarial Legalism and American Government," in Marc K. Landy and Martin A. Levin, eds., *The New Politics of Public Policy* (Baltimore: Johns Hopkins University Press, 1995), pp. 88-118.

an effective protest. The activity was covered in detail by the national press and attracted even more attention when state police began to beat peaceful marchers. Civil rights activists used the demonstration as a political symbol of repression that was communicated by the media and ultimately had a direct impact on the passage of the Voting Rights Act.

Very often it is groups having a moral element to their cause that seek to make use of the media. Anti-war protesters in the early stages of the Vietnam War and later in the Gulf War held demonstrations in an attempt to raise awareness of their cause. Opponents of abortion have staged rallies and demonstrations in front of clinics that perform abortions in an attempt to gain media coverage and thereby a broader hearing for their views. Anti-globalization activists have also staged well publicized protests and demonstration around the world that have attracted media attention.

The multiplicity of channels for bringing items to public agenda makes the policy process con-

fusing. But it illustrates one of the primary characteristics of pluralistic decision making. The many points of access to the system increase the chances that government will give some attention to the needs, wants, and expectations of citizens. This conclusion does not necessarily mean that everybody can obtain a serious hearing on any issue. The agenda is limited, and all the institutions of government have at least some ability to influence which issues they will address.

Nor do all groups have the same difficulty in getting attention for their causes. The best-organized and most well-financed groups, and those with the most cohesive and sizable constituency, have an advantage. As one observer has remarked: "The flaw in the pluralist heaven is that the heavenly choir sings with a strong upper-class accent."[18]

Yet it is false to say that the upper classes alone set the agenda. The civil rights movement of the 1960s is one major example that proves the contrary, as is the antiwar movement of the 1960s and 1970s and the pro-life movement of the 1980s and 90s. Neither is the agenda always set by long-established and politically experienced interests.

The success achieved by the Christian Coalition in the late 1980s and 1990s shows how people can begin from outside major existing sources of political power and achieve influence. The group's leaders used print, radio, and television to organize thousands of supporters into a conservative group, the Christian Coalition, whose members had traditionally participated in politics at a much lower rate than other Americans. The Christian Coalition brought new voters into politics and trained nearly 16,000 potential political leaders, many of whom have since become legislators, mayors, and school-board members. "We took a system that was scary and complex and had an unseemly taint, and made it understandable and friendly, something people want to participate in," said D.J. Gribbin, one of the key architects of the coalition's grassroots networks.[19]

Defining the Problem

When the topic of energy appeared on the national agenda in the 1970s after the Arab oil embargo, almost everyone was prepared to admit that there was an energy crisis. But there was little agreement about exactly what the source of the crisis was. Was it a conspiracy of oil companies to create artificial shortages in order to reap exorbitant profits? Or was it an example of misguided government regulations draining capital from a critical sector of the economy that needed massive investment? Or the fault of American consumers for being so inefficient in their use of power that they squandered energy on gas-guzzling automobiles and buildings that were air conditioned in the winter? Or was it a foreign policy problem—a few oil-rich nations exploiting the rest of the world?

Defining the nature of a problem is of great importance in policymaking, because the way a problem is defined begins to determine the kinds of policies that will be considered and adopted. If the energy problem was one created by the oil companies, that would require more government regulation; if it was one of too many existing regulations, that would imply getting rid of regula-

tions. And so on. For almost every major problem, there are several ways of defining it, and from this definition various options will make more sense than others.

Developing Options and Building Support

The task of defining a policy problem, however, rarely takes place independently of certain other activities: developing policy options and building support for various alternatives. One can separate these features of the process for analytical purposes, but they often occur simultaneously. Presidents, for instance, make use of television to define problems, propose solutions, and stimulate popular enthusiasm, all within the time it takes to make a brief address. Lyndon Johnson did so on the issue of civil rights, Jimmy Carter on energy, Ronald Reagan on the economy, and more recently George W. Bush on terrorism.

Interest-group representatives draft legislative proposals, find friendly sponsors to introduce them, and seek to build coalitions in support of their alternatives. They often will bargain with other interest groups, with members of Congress, or with the president. Party ties at this point sometimes help coordinate support for alternative proposals among legislators and between the president and Congress. Coalition building on behalf of various alternatives often takes place in an atmosphere of compromise. Many of the participants know that they must deal with each other on many other decisions over a long period of time, so for the central actors there is considerable incentive to seem "reasonable." This bargaining stage is therefore often marked by a limitation on the intensity of conflict, a frequently observed characteristic of the American policymaking process.

Another way interest groups seek to build support for their position is to demonstrate that their views are backed by a large number of citizens. Officers and staff members of interest groups contact their membership to inform them of various policy proposals and to encourage them to contact legislators in support of or against particular measures. One reason why the National Rifle Association (NRA) has, over the years, been so effective in limiting gun control is that the organization has regularly been able to generate hundreds of thousands of letters to Congress within a couple of days. Legislators know that NRA members are extremely interested in gun-control issues whereas many citizens who support tighter regulation do not care nearly so much and may never base their vote on this one issue. Sometimes the policy process works to benefit intense minorities at the expense of a less intense majority.

The bureaucracy also often plays a role at this stage of the policy process. Many of the bills considered and approved by Congress are actually drafted in the agencies that will eventually implement them. These units furthermore are seldom neutral or idle among various policy options that are under consideration for dealing with a policy problem. Agency officials will work with friendly members of Congress and their staffs and with the leaders and staffs of important interest groups. In one case an agency was even instrumental in helping to create an interest group to support the agency's proposals. The Agriculture Department successfully did so years ago when it helped to organize the Farm Bureau.

The courts stand apart as an alternative path in the policymaking process. They are not active initially in formulating options, and they do not seek to generate popular interest in different proposals. The courts instead respond to parties in legal disputes, although it is certain that many judges take into account the support and opposition to the "policies" that result from their legal decisions. Courts may sometimes be used as policy paths by those who may have difficulty building strength for their issues in other arenas. The NAACP won on the school desegregation issue in 1954, despite the lack of support for its position with President Eisenhower and the Congress. In the 1970s, advocates of legalized abortion relied on the federal courts to strike down state laws that limited or banned a woman's access to the procedure. More recently, lawsuits by state attorneys general against tobacco companies have effectively set tobacco policy (see box 15.2).

The amount of conflict generated as policy problems are defined, options are developed, and support is built varies considerably from issue to issue and from one area to another. In one case, the difference in the way policy is made is a result of the design of the Constitution. Major foreign policy issues are handled in a process in which the president will always have a greater degree of power and influence than in other areas. In domestic policymaking the fundamental rules may be roughly similar from one area to another, but the process may differ in fact according to the kinds of policies—in particular to whether they are perceived to have a broad effect on most citizens or whether they may deal only with a few specific groups.

Making Decisions

Policy options can get sidetracked or vetoed, may be compromised or incorporated into newer options, or might adopted as public policy. A typical situation in the process is for some participants to be pushing anxiously for a decision, while others find their interests served by delay. The pluralist process is likely to have an effect on the sorts of decisions eventually reached.

Veto Points Multiple access points help get issues onto the agenda. Yet the same structure that supports easy access for consideration also makes it very difficult for any single group's policy option to make it all the way through unscathed. There are a remarkable number of veto points in the American policy process. Some are obvious, such as the president's power to veto bills. Others derive from the complicated twists and turns of the legislative process. Before any major proposal arrives on the president's desk, it must surmount a host of formal hurdles—votes in subcommittees and committees of both houses, approval by each house, (probably) a conference committee to resolve differences between the versions passed in both houses, and then another vote in each house. Given all these means to stop a policy proposal, accommodation to diverse points of view is especially likely if policy on a major issue is to be enacted. Even if an interest group is not able to generate support for its own proposals at every stage of the decision-making process, it may well be able to find enough support to block others' alternatives. Because of these realities, major policies which emerge from the process often either reflect only incremental changes from existing policy or are short on specifics.

Incrementalism   Incrementalism refers to the making of decisions that differ only slightly (by "increments") from the previous decisions on the same subject. Incrementalism may be characteristic of decision making in almost all governments, as it helps to simplify matters. With incrementalism, there is no need to reevaluate the worth of an entire program and risk offending its supporters. All that needs to be done is to add or subtract a little bit.

Yet if incrementalism is characteristic of much governmental decision making, there is good reason to think that it is even more characteristic of decision making in the United States. In the American system of separation of powers, federalism, and multiple veto points, individual actors realize how difficult it is to make a dramatic change. This process produces a great deal of stability. It also, of course, works against "comprehensive" and rationalistic approaches to problems that rely on the analyses of social scientists and policy analysts.

Imprecise Policies   The process of policymaking also may produce fairly vague decisions, especially on legislation. As participants bargain and jockey for support, options may have to become somewhat more general in order to attract a sufficiently large coalition to ensure passage. This outcome is especially likely when policymakers are in agreement about a problem but do not know exactly what to do about it. Often, participants in the process—such as bureaus or interest groups—who see their preferred options disappear in early legislative attempts may then favor a vague policy in the legislature instead. Their strategy is to push the real decision-making process to the implementation stage. When the laws are very general, the real tasks of policymaking are sometimes devolved to the bureaucracy, to the courts, or to state and local governments.

The "Triple Alliance"   Not all policies attract so many participants that decision makers have to consider many diverse points of view. If an issue is framed so that it does not attract a large audience, it may be decided without much of the skeptical scrutiny afforded more prominent items. In American policymaking, there are a number of issues like this—matters that may even affect everyone, but in such a way that only a very few find it worth their while to pay attention.

Subsidies for certain agricultural crops, such as soybeans or sugar beets, are examples of this situation. Everyone pays the cost in more expensive foods, but not many people write letters to Congress or decide their presidential choice on the basis of a few pennies in a household budget.

Some federal policies tend to be produced by a relatively few participants who have a direct interest in the policy at hand. In such cases, three policy actors—interest groups, bureaucratic agencies, and congressional oversight committees—constitute the most significant decision-making center, watched today very often by a fourth "group" of policy experts from a think tank. There are many such centers throughout the government dealing with all kinds of substantive policy topics. They are referred to by various labels, such as "subgovernments," or the "triple alliance," or the "iron triangle." Whatever the label, the result is the same: intense minorities or special interests exert weight greatly in excess of their numbers.

Policymaking in the United States varies greatly in the degree to which it is responsive to the public. Some decisions are especially sensitive to national majorities; others, as in the case of price supports for certain commodities, are most heavily influenced in settings favorable to minorities with intense preferences; and still others, for instance court decisions, may be quite insulated from popular opinions, whether of a majority or a minority.

Implementation and Impact

The policymaking process does not stop with the passage of laws or the giving of orders. These decisions must be executed, and in the process of implementation, policy is also created. Vague statutes obviously require the bureaucracy to make decisions during implementation. But these are not the only instances in which implementers create policy. Even carefully crafted laws or seemingly unambiguous directives require the continual exercise of judgment by agencies.

One day in August 1971, President Nixon announced a major policy by executive order pursuant to an earlier legislative statute. The policy appeared to be one of the clearest and most straightforward statements ever made by a public official. Nixon imposed an immediate freeze on all wages and prices for almost everyone in the country. A few items, such as raw agricultural products, were to be exempted, and the policy was to remain in effect for a strictly limited period. But when the Office of Emergency Preparedness and the Cost of Living Council began to implement President Nixon's order, they discovered that even in this case the policy left hundreds of questions unanswered. For example, were interest rates to be considered prices and therefore frozen? Was fish an agricultural product and thus able to be sold at a higher amount? Were labor union members who had already signed an agreement with their employers for wage hikes to be denied the increase in violation of their contract? The agencies found themselves swamped with such sticky policy decisions.

Every year, thousands of pages in the *Federal Register*, the newspaper printed by the government, are filled with important policy decisions made by administrative units during implementation. The bureaucracy often plays a decisive role in the implementation stage, although frequently it is closely watched by members of Congress and by interest groups prepared to take matters into the courts.

Policies sometimes have their intended impact, but very often they do not. As government has moved from handling relatively simple tasks to attempting to solve more complex problems, the likelihood of achieving clear success becomes more problematic. Today there is more and more of an effort made, both inside and outside of government, to evaluate systematically the impact of various policies and to consider whether the policies were worth the expenditures or could have been achieved better through other options. The "discipline" of making such systematic evaluations is known today as policy analysis. Of course, some people have

always been engaged in such analysis, which is why we hesitate to call it a discipline. There are many different standards for judging policies that involve many different kinds of expertise. Still, the very self-conscious and systematic efforts to evaluate policies and consider unintended consequences has become a new part of social science and a new force in the policymaking process.

Policy analysis is an effort to interject a rational consideration of policies and potential policies into the government's process of decision. The government itself employs thousands of such analysts in various agencies of the bureaucracy, as well as on the staffs of congressional committees and legislative units like the Congressional Budget Office. Many more work in and around Washington, for instance in think tanks such as the Brookings Institution and the Heritage Foundation.

Policy analysts typically begin from the perspective of economists. They seek a systematic, usually quantitative, evaluation of the costs and benefits of policies. The idea seems to be to temper the influence of purely political factors in the policy process, so that mere power does not solely determine what government does. Policy analysis can raise the level of thought given to policy problems by comparing alternatives and encouraging explicit consideration of the connection between intentions and actions.

Yet there is no way that policy analysis can replace the politics of policymaking. Evaluating policies is a tricky business. For instance, one can seldom be confident of what might have happened had a policy not been in effect. Many of the costs of policy alternatives are difficult to measure with precision. And many of the benefits cannot be effectively compared with each other. Is it worth spending an additional several billion dollars on nuclear power plant safety to slightly reduce the chances of a major accident with 10,000 lives lost? No analysis can answer this question without facing such deeply political questions as how much a human life is worth. Yet the strengths of policy analysis are such that many participants in the process employ it as a tool to inform themselves, convince others, and improve outcomes.

Conclusion

In this we have paid particular attention to the constitutional question of how closely the policy-making process adheres to standards that are consistent with democratic rule.

Interest in public policy is what attracts many to the activity of government. Yet, as the study of policymaking reveals, exactly what constitutes public policy is more complicated than one might initially think. Many decisions that have a broad public impact lie, by general constitutional design, beyond the control of a single government institution. Governmental policies frequently meet with failure, and sometimes inconsistent decisions make it difficult to decipher whether there is a governmental intention. There are nevertheless thousands of discernible public policies, meaning governmental decisions that establish goals, rules, standards, or practices that apply over time to a series of actions or cases. The study of the policymaking process looks at all of the institutions and forces—formal and informal—that play a role in fashioning these policies.

The attempt to explain who controls American policymaking by reference alone to models of who rules is impossible. Policy is made in large part by governmental officials performing their tasks: legislating, judging, executing and administering. But these officials clearly act on behalf of and are influenced by forces in society that seek to achieve favorable policy results. The two models that describe the greatest amount of policymaking are majoritarianism and pluralism. Majoritarianism applies in a loose but definite way to establishing many of the broad goals of public policy as well as many important and highly visible specific policies. Pluralism, the dispersion of power among a number of centers, provides an explanation of policymaking that is consistent, at least in broad outline, with a good deal of specific decision making. At times a pluralist process may consist of a wide range of participating groups that represent the viewpoints of many elements of society. At other times, the process may consist of a limited number of groups that represent those who have the most to win or lose by a particular policy.

There are normally numerous participants in the process of domestic policymaking—some designated by the Constitution, others less formal but no less important, as in the case of policies effectively made through litigation. Pluralism can be seen at work in the several stages of the policy process: when the public agenda is established; when various parties take part in defining policy problems, developing options, and building support; when decisions are reached; and even, to some extent, when the policy is implemented. The precise nature of the process in a particular case is affected by many factors, including the kind of problem, the institutional channels that are used at various stages, and the way the options are framed.

How consistent is American policymaking with the standards of popular government? There is no one answer to this question. Different stages and channels vary greatly in their accessibility to the people. Some parts are more in tune with the depth of public opinion than with its breadth, whereas in other segments the opposite is true. No single group or interest seems to control policymaking, yet some interests clearly have more weight than others. The policy agenda is finite, yet growing. Access to it, while not always easy, is also not limited to the wealthy and established. We have described the major influences on the system as being majoritarian and pluralist, though there are also clear instances of elite and bureaucratic control. Yet it is worth remembering that the system was designed primarily to protect against tyranny, not to implement a strict or pure form of democratic rule. The founders planned that the public should be an *important* determinant of policy, but certainly not the *sole* one. This intention still describes contemporary policymaking in the United States.

Chapter 15 Notes

1. Murray Edelman, *The Symbolic Uses of Politics* (Urbana, Ill.: University of Illinois, 1964).
2. Marissa Martino Golden, *What Motivates Bureaucrats? Politics and Administration during the Reagan Years* (New York: Columbia University Press, 2000).
3. Charles O. Jones, *An Introduction to the Study of Public Policy* (Boston: Duxbury, 1978).

4. Robert S. Mueller, III, "Statement for the Record on FBI Reorganization Before the Senate Committee on the Judiciary," Washington, D.C. Accessed 06/04/02 at http://www.fbi.gov/page2/reorg529temp.htm

5. Seymour Martin Lipset, *American Exceptionalism: A Double-Edged Sword* (New York: W.W. Norton, 1990), p. 21.

6. Paul Cantor, "Mainstreaming Paranoia: The X-Files and the Deligitimization of the Nation-State," *Gilligan Unbound*, Rowman & Littlefield Publishers, Inc., New York, 2001), pp. 111–198.

7. C. Wright Mills, *The Power Elite* (New York: Oxford University Press, 1956).

8. Zaller defines "elite domination" of mass opinion as "a situation in which elites induce citizens to hold opinions that they would not hold if aware of the best available information and analysis." John Zaller, *The Nature and Origins of Mass Opinion* (Cambridge, U.K.: Cambridge University Press, 1992), p. 313.

9. Charles E. Lindblom, *Politics and Markets* (New York: Basic Books, 1977).

10. John Kingdon, *America the Unusual* (Boston: Bedford, 1999), 40.

11. Aaron Wildavsky, "The Politics of the Entitlement Process," in *The New Politics of Public Policy*, ed. Marc K. Landy and Martin A. Levin (Baltimore: Johns Hopkins University Press, 1995), 143–179.

12. David E. Price, *The Congressional Experience*, 2nd ed. (Boulder, Co.: Westview Press, 2000), pp. 60–63.

13. For an account of the shifts in the dominant ideas about American poverty policy, see Joel Schwartz, *Fighting Poverty With Virtue: Moral Reform and America's Urban Poor*, 1825–2000, (Bloomington: Indiana University Press, 2000).

14. John W. Kingdon, *Agendas, Alternatives, and Public Policies* (New York: Harper-Collins, 1984), p. 109.

15. Peter Bachrach and Morton Baratz, "Decisions and Nondecisions: An Analytical Framework," *American Political Science Review*, vol. 57, no. 3, 1963, pp. 632–642.

16. Hugh Heclo, "The Political Foundations of Antipoverty Policy," in Sheldon Danziger and Daniel H. Weinberg, editors, *Fighting Poverty: What Works and What Doesn't* (Cambridge, Ma., Harvard University Press: 1986), p. 321.

17. Paul David, "Clio and the Economics of QWERTY," *American Economic Review*, vol. 75, pp. 332-337.

18. Kingdon, *America the Unusual*, pp. 79–84. E. E. Schattschneider, *The Semi-Sovereign People* (New York: Holt, 1960), p. 35.

19. Nina J. Easton, "The Power and the Glory," *The American Prospect*, May 20, 2002.

16

Civil Liberties and Civil Rights

CHAPTER CONTENTS

Imagine that you had been born in South Africa during the era of Apartheid. The schools you could attend, the job you could get, the place you could live, even your ability to move freely about the country would depend on your skin. Change in your imagination to China, and think of yourself as a person living today in Tibet wishing to practice your ancient religion. All of your activities will be monitored by the authorities, and you will have no freedom to read what you want or to speak or write certain views. A failure to comply can mean imprisonment or even death.

It is no wonder that when we Americans take pride in our country, it is most often because of our tradition of protecting civil rights and liberties. The core of what most citizens believe to be good about the United States is found in our freedom to think, believe, and say what we want without fear.

Yet when one looks at the record of the United States in protecting civil rights, there is cause for humility as well as pride. One whole race of people was held in slavery until the Civil War and then throughout many states in the South denied the elementary political rights of voting and serving on juries for nearly a century. Until the 1960s, the laws of many states prevented blacks from going to the same schools as whites, eating in the same restaurants, or riding in the same sections of trains and buses. Other groups and many individuals have also faced significant infringements of their rights. Japanese Americans on the west coast were forced into relocation camps during World War II, Hispanics have often been denied their lawful rights to vote and work free from harassment, and women have been barred from certain jobs by arbitrary physical standards. Although the United States, by the Declaration of Independence and the Constitution, is dedicated to protecting the rights of its citizens, the political problem has been to translate this dedication in principle into laws, customs, and attitudes that provide daily protection for these rights.

In this chapter we shall look at the American experiment in guaranteeing rights, considering what rights are, and how they can be protected.

What Are Rights and How Are They Protected?

There are four important questions citizens and political leaders must consider in trying to secure the equal rights of all citizens.

First: *What is a right?* While Americans are accustomed to thinking of their rights as *legal* protections that are embodied in the Constitution, in state constitutions, or in laws, the term "rights" goes beyond this purely legal idea. A right is ordinarily thought of as a standard to which the laws are supposed to conform—hence the connection of the term "rights" to what is "right" or just. A right is a just claim to the possession or use of something, be it a material object (like a piece of property), one of our faculties (like our ability to speak), or a key political privilege of participation (like voting or serving on a jury). The idea of a right as a standard is expressed in the Declaration of Independence, which tells us that people have certain rights and that legitimate government exists to protect these rights. People also use the term as when they make claims about certain things they think government should protect (whether or not it now does so), such as a "right to choose," "a right to life," or a "right to die."

Second: *Who has rights?* When people speak of "natural" or "human" rights, they are referring to rights that people have simply because they are human, not because they are citizens of a particular country. All people, according to the Declaration of Independence, are "endowed by their Creator" with the rights to "life, liberty, and the pursuit of happiness." On the basis of these natural or human rights, many condemn situations where these basic rights are not recognized or realized, whether because there is no effective government at all (and gangs prey on each other) or because a government itself takes away basic rights. Protecting rights, therefore, requires government and government of a certain kind. In the words of the Declaration, "to secure these rights, governments are instituted among men. . . ."

Securing and protecting of rights is thus in part the work of government for its citizens. Noncitizens who live in the United States are granted the protection of many rights that exist for Americans, but by no means all of them. They do not vote or serve on juries even if they pay taxes. And on occasion, certain basic rights may be curtailed for noncitizens. In 1979 during the period in which American hostages were being held by the Iranian government, the United States government restricted the freedom of Iranian visitors living in the United States to engage in demonstrations or to move freely about the country. These people could not claim the full protection of the Constitution.

Third: *How are rights reconciled with other rights and duties?* The protection of one person's rights may conflict with the protection of another's or with the security of the country or orderly civil life. The general and widely-accepted idea that government exists to secure rights thus does not provide automatic answers to what must be done in all cases and situations. Far from it.

Conflicts between rights provide the clearest case of the difficulties. Take the case of Dr. Sam Sheppard, a wealthy Cleveland doctor, who was tried in 1954 for murdering his wife. (The television show and the movie *The Fugitive* were based roughly on this case.) The newspapers and radio covered the story and Dr. Sheppard's love life in lurid detail. Journalists flooded the courtroom, frequently disrupting the proceedings. The Supreme Court ruled that such freedom for the news media had undermined Dr. Sheppard's right to a fair trial as recognized under the sixth amendment (*Sheppard v. Maxwell*, 1966).

The question of deciding when a right might need to yield to the nation's security or to orderly life in the community is more difficult. Obviously, government's power to restrict behavior in these areas could be used—and has been—to stifle opposition and dissent. Yet even in a system that tries to go as far as possible in protecting individual rights, these rights cannot be absolute. In time of war, for example, an unrestricted right to publish anything might conflict with the government's duty to secure the lives of its citizens and the victory of its armies. The government could not, for example, allow the publication of troop movements or a divulging of the names or positions of American undercover agents. When Charles Schenck mailed circulars to young men urging resistance

to the draft during World War I, the Supreme Court ruled that the threat of disruption of the war effort was such an evil that Schenck's freedom to publish could be restricted (*Schenck v. United States*, 1919).

Free speech is not the only freedom that poses a risk to national security, nor has it been the only one curtailed in the past. During the Civil War, President Lincoln imposed martial law to ensure conviction of disloyal persons in the North, denying them criminal trials and the protections associated with them, such as civilian juries. The Supreme Court did rule after the war that military tribunals could not be so used whilst the regular courts were operational in *Ex parte Milligan*. In the aftermath of the September 11th terrorist attacks there have been calls for similar measures to respond to the threat to national security, though the question, as always, is how much weight should be given to this claim. In a move reminiscent of Lincoln, a number of suspects have been arrested and held without charge as material witnesses. They could have been charged and deported, but they have been held for indefinite periods with no idea as to when they will be released, or in some cases, if they are linked to the terrorist attacks. Terrorist suspects apprehended in Afghanistan are to receive military trials for criminal offences despite the fact that the federal court system is obviously functioning.

These restrictions go deeper than suspects and alleged terrorists though, with charges of racial profiling being used at airports and calls for those entering the country to be fingerprinted as a guard against false documents. Outside of areas of international travel, the Federal Bureau of Investigation has been given more powers to conduct surveillance in public places and the exigencies of national security seem to demand even more sacrifices in terms of individual liberty, such as suspicionless searches and proof of one's identity through biometrics. These measures have created unease, both in traditionally liberal camps such as the American Civil Liberties Union, and in those of conservative commentators, making their future uncertain. The United States has usually accepted an abrogation or suspension of liberties during times of emergency and ceded power to the executive. However, the Constitutional system of checks and balances tends to draw these powers away from the president after the danger has passed. The question for the future is how grave the danger posed by terrorism will be perceived to be and when will it recede sufficiently to allow for a return to normalcy?

Fourth: *How are rights protected?* Which level of government and which institutions have the responsibility of protecting rights? There is a tendency today to think of rights as being protected mostly by the federal government and by federal courts. This way of thinking probably comes from the prominence given to Supreme Court cases in the news and to claims of many in the legal profession that rights are somehow the special province of courts. But in fact, while federal courts are indeed very important in the protection of rights, they by no means have the exclusive responsibility in this area.

In the complex system of government found in the United States, there are many institutions involved in rights protection and major disputes about who should have responsibilities. Should rights be protected by state and local governments or by the national government? Defenders of the states (and many conservatives) argue that local and state officials better understand the particular problems of an area in attempting to reconcile the conflicting claims characteristic of civil rights enforcement, while defenders of the national government (and many liberals) argued that national protection, especially by federal courts, is needed to guard against local prejudices. Within the national government, where should protection originate? All of the branches of government have assumed some responsibility in protecting rights. Over the past thirty years Congress has passed civil rights acts protecting minorities against private segregation, discrimination, and limitations on the right to vote as well as legislation to assure citizens access to information (the Freedom of Information Act of 1966) and certain protections of privacy (the Privacy Act of 1974). The president has supplemented these with executive orders and has used presidential powers to enforce laws and court orders. Finally, of the three major branches, the judiciary has been the most highly active institution in the area right protection.

The courts' visibility in this area is a result not only of how much they have done but also of how they do it. Court decisions often are based directly on interpreting the Constitution and the meaning of Constitutional rights, while actions by Congress and the president that deal with matters of rights are often seen as being merely policy decisions.

Although courts today receive most of the attention in the area of protecting rights, the question remains where the primary responsibility for this task really lies—with elected representatives who have their fingers on the pulse of the country, or with judges protected from popular prejudices. We shall focus mainly on courts and legal decisions in this chapter, but it should be kept in mind that the other institutions often play a more important role in this process. In fact, the protection of rights is a complex process in which all of the institutions play a part—and the state governments as well. Where there are conflicts among the branches, as there have been in many areas in recent times, there have been long and drawn out struggles for setting the nation's final policy for protecting rights.

Finally, we have yet to mention administrative agencies, which have enormous day to day power in deciding issues of rights protection. Much civil rights legislation is general in character, which often leaves to administrative agencies the task of deciding how broad commands of the law are to be interpreted in specific rules. For example, the use of specific goals for minority groups in hiring and contracting was not a direct result of orders from Congress, but of decisions made by such agencies as the Department of Labor and the Department of Transportation. Although Congress could step in to change administrative rulings, a majority may not exist in Congress to undo a certain policy, whatever Congress may have intended in the first place. By their desire to avoid difficult problems or by their unwillingness to discipline bureaucracies, elected representatives often end up allowing fundamental public policy to be made by unelected officials.

BOX 16.1

Extension of Civil Rights and Liberties by Constitutional Amendment

Amendment 13	Prohibits slavery.
Amendment 14	Prohibits states from abridging the "privileges and immunities" of citizens, or denying persons the "due process" or the "equal protection" of the laws.
Amendment 15	Prohibits denial of the right to vote on account of "race, color, or previous conditions of servitude."
Amendment 19	Prohibits denial of the right to vote on account of sex.
Amendment 24	Prohibits poll taxes
Amendment 26	Prohibits denial of the right to vote on account of age for those over 18 years old.

Constitutional Protection—The Bill of Rights

Protection of some of the most important rights in the United States rests upon explicit provisions of the Constitution. When Americans think of civil rights, the Bill of Rights immediately comes to mind. The first ten amendments to the Constitution, passed by the First Congress and ratified by the states in 1791, contain specific substantive and procedural protection of civil rights and liberties. The First Amendment protects the core to republican liberty: freedom of religion, speech, press, and assembly. Amendments 2 through 8 guard the individual against the threat of arbitrary force by the state. Amendments 2 and 3 protect against abuses by the military forces. Amendments 4 through 8 protect against abuses by legislatures, police, prosecutors, judges, jailers, and others who are in a legal position to take away people's property (through fines or confiscations) or liberty (through jailing) or lives (through execution).

But important as the Bill of Rights is, it does not exhaust the list of rights that are given Constitutional protection. The original Constitution contains provisions that define and protect civil rights, such as prohibiting titles of nobility and religious tests for public offices, and some of the subsequent amendments have added important protections (see Box 16.1).

The most significant extension of Constitutionally protected rights by means of court interpretation has occurred through the gradual "incorporation" of the Bill of Rights into the Fourteenth Amendment. Originally, as noted in Chapter 3, the Bill of Rights was confined to actions only of the *national* government in its relation to the citizens. Thus, the national government could not pass a law abridging the freedom of speech. People in the states were protected in various ways by their own traditions and bills of rights in their state constitutions, but not by the federal Bill of Rights. Through the process of "incorporation" the core of the Bill of Rights now applies to the laws and actions of all political authorities in the United States—national, state, or local.

The case of *Gitlow v. New York* (1925) began the process of interpreting the Fourteenth Amendment, which protects liberty against the actions of states, to include various provisions of the Bill of Rights. At first this process moved slowly. In a series of cases from *Gitlow* (freedom of speech) to *Everson v. Board of Education* (prohibition on establishing religion) in 1947, the Court incorporated the First Amendment freedoms into the Fourteenth Amendment. Most of the protections guarding criminal procedure contained in the Fourth through Eighth Amendments did not yet apply to the states. But under the leadership of Chief Justice Earl Warren (1953–1969), the Court moved rapidly to declare most of the remaining provisions of the Bill of Rights to be "fundamental" and thus protected by the Fourteenth Amendment. Of the various criminal procedures, only the Fifth Amendment requirement of grand jury indictments in criminal cases and the Seventh Amendment requirement of jury trials in civil cases remain as important provisions of the Bill of Rights not applied to the states. The Second Amendment, understood by many as protecting an individual's right to bear arms, has also never been incorporated to limit the states.

The list of rights contained in the Constitution is not meant to be exhaustive of all the rights that individuals possess. The Ninth Amendment of the Constitution notes that there are other fundamental rights that government should protect that are not specifically listed among the first eight amendments. One reason that certain rights cannot be listed is that it would be difficult to embody them in a meaningful Constitutional provision. Some rights require protection by lengthier statutes elaborated in the context of changing social and economic conditions. Thus, property rights and privacy rights are both clearly fundamental, but their definition is often complex. Congress has been intimately involved in the protection of these rights, even though often times its statutes protecting them may not be considered by some as dealing directly with a Constitutionally-guaranteed right.

Protection by Government or from Government?

Underlying the disputes over how to protect rights is the question whether rights are secured primarily by a strong government with the will to protect them, or primarily by placing restrictions upon government. The American system—indeed, any system that protects rights—must embody elements of *both* of these traditions. But the two traditions point in different directions. The first thinks in terms of empowering a government to work effectively for protecting rights using its discretion about how this should be done, the second in terms of explicit limitations upon government that can be enforced by a branch of government most removed from political pressures, the courts.

There is some tension between these two traditions. An emphasis on one more than the other may not only lead to different results, but also to the cultivation of different attitudes among citizens. Should people see themselves primarily as participants in or adversaries of government? Should people learn the art of forming political coalitions or that of arguing court cases? Although the easy answer is both, the attitudes required for the two courses are sufficiently diverse that in practice one is likely to be employed at the expense of the other.

The ultimate protection for civil rights in a republican system rests with the character of its people and the opinions they hold. The most important right involved in trials, the presumption that one is innocent until proven guilty, is not mentioned in the Bill of Rights, but it is just as securely protected as the rights that are mentioned because people would be outraged should judges begin to declare people guilty before the evidence is heard. Without a constitutional level of public opinion that supports equal rights for all, the protection afforded by the Constitution, the courts, Congress, and the president are likely to be short-lived. All the discussion of rights and liberties, therefore, takes place within the context of a system dedicated fundamentally to the realization of liberalism, although there have been different interpretations of the meaning of liberalism and powerful motives at times for ignoring its precepts.

Rights, then, are secured in the United States by a complex mixture of actions by state and national governments, by courts, legislatures, and administrative agencies. Enshrined in the Constitution, they are protected both by the arts and forms of self-government and by explicit prohibitions on government. Ultimately they are protected by public opinion. Yet all these means have never perfectly guaranteed people's rights. In part this is because of the strength of opposing interests and prejudices. It is also because of the difficulty of reconciling conflicts between the rights of some and those of others, and between the rights of individuals and the security of all.

Let us turn, now, to look at some specific liberties and rights.

Civil Liberties

The terms civil liberties and civil rights are often used synonymously. But scholars sometimes use the terms to make a distinction between two kinds of rights. Civil liberties here refer to the freedoms of individuals *from* governmental control. The emphasis is on things that the individual can do on his own and that government should not do. For example, an individual may speak or write, and government must not prevent or abridge this freedom. Civil rights here refer to things to which the individual has a just and equal claim; the emphasis here is often on what government must do to ensure this claim. A right to vote or to have free access to any place of business are examples of civil rights.

Civil liberties are protected by a complex array of opinions and doctrines deriving from the Constitution, laws, court decisions, and executive actions. The protecting of civil liberties is considered to be good not only for individuals, but also for the common good. In this section we shall discuss the two most important liberties protected by the First Amendment (freedom of speech and religion) and the rights of the accused protected by the Fourth through the Eighth Amendments.

Freedom of Speech

"Congress shall make no law . . . abridging the freedom of speech. . . ." This phrase from the first amendment is one of the most well-known of the entire Constitution. In different form it is found in the constitutions of almost all of the states.

Shortly after the end of World War II, in which some 6 million Jews died in Nazi concentration camps, an American Nazi and defrocked priest by the name of Terminiello held a rally in a Jewish neighborhood of Chicago. The advertisements for the gathering spoke disparagingly of Jews and were filled with invective and hatred. The night of the meeting, angry citizens gathered in protest outside the building in which the meeting was held. Inside, the Nazi leader gave a fiery speech inciting his audience to hatred of Jews. He referred to his adversaries as "slimy scum," "snakes," and "bedbugs." Outside the crowd grew more angry, yelling, "Fascists, Hitlers!" at those seeking to go inside. Rocks were thrown and windows broken. After asking Terminiello to desist, and not receiving cooperation, the police arrested him for "breach of the peace." Terminiello claimed that his Constitutional rights of free speech had been violated, and eventually a 5–4 Supreme Court decision agreed with him. The police maintained that the alternative to his arrest would have been riot, since they did not have the personnel to control the mob and since public safety was endangered (*Terminiello v. Chicago*, 1949).

Was the decision of the Court correct? What factors are relevant to determining the answer to this question? Does the issue turn on the likelihood of riot? Would it make a difference if the Nazi leader were instead a partisan of the Democratic party in a Republican stronghold? Should Terminiello have the right to say what he wanted regardless of the consequences, or should a large number of people be able to suppress speech they find offensive?

Such cases show that the protection of free speech often involves competing claims. It is good that a person can say what he or she wants; it is also good to maintain peace so that no one gets hurt. How the balance is to be drawn requires sensitivity to the character of particular circumstances; it also requires an understanding of the character and place of free speech in republican government and what ends or goods it is intended to promote. Speaking (or writing), unlike our unspoken thoughts, is not merely a private activity but also a means by which to communicate with others. The doctrine of free speech has been defended on the grounds of its benefits for the political order and of its contribution for the development of culture (art, literature, and philosophy). We shall first speak of the political benefits of speech, then consider some of the wider implications of this freedom.

Free speech has been understood to be necessary for a free government because where people can voice their complaints and communicate and concert their actions, they can defend themselves against a despotic government. For just this reason, totalitarian and authoritarian regimes have always tried to restrict speech. Free speech also enables people to discuss different possible policies, criticize existing ones, and examine the behavior of government officials. This free discussion is thought to increase citizens' participation in governing and, over the long run, to enhance government performance.

But reasonable people have also long recognized that free, democratic government also requires some restrictions on speech. Some speech can harm or destroy the rights of other persons. No one, as Justice Holmes said, can claim a right falsely to shout "Fire!" in a crowded theater and cause a panic (*Schenck v. United States*, 1919). Some speech can harm the country as a whole, jeopardizing the lives of its agents or undermining the nation's security. No one, for example, can publish the names of CIA agents working under cover.

Restrictions on Speech The general presumption in the United States is that speech is free; the burden of proof is upon those who wish to restrict it. What restrictions, under what circumstances, are justified? This question has been posed at the national level by Congress and then, following World War I and the beginning of "incorporation" of the first amendment, by the Supreme Court. It has also been discussed in all of the state legislatures and in thousands of cases in state courts.

There are four kinds of speech that governments have often tried to restrict: (1) speech which would tend to undermine officially supported religious opinions, (2) speech that tends to damage the reputation or property of other people, (3) speech that threatens to disrupt public order or undermine the government, and (4) speech considered obscene.

In the first area, because the principles of American government stand in opposition to state-supported religious opinions, freedom of religious speech under the First Amendment is virtually absolute. Americans have generally agreed with Thomas Jefferson that there is no public injury if their neighbors say there are twenty gods or no God. In the second area, libel laws that penalize speech endangering the reputation of other individuals have generally been accepted. To sue for libel, ordinary private individuals must show that statements made against them—let us say in a newspaper—are false and

injurious and that the author was negligent in making them. When it comes to public officials, however, the Supreme Court has made it much harder to win a libel suit. In *New York Times v. Sullivan* (1964), the Court decided that a public official must prove to a jury not only that statements made against him were false but that the person (or news agency) that made them either knew that they were false or acted with reckless disregard of the truth. This same standard now also apples to persons who have become prominent in the news, such as Donald Trump or Monica Lewinsky. This standard is extremely difficult to meet. It provides great latitude to news agencies in dealing with public affairs, but it sometimes can prove detrimental to individuals whose reputations may have been unfairly harmed.

But it has been in the third and fourth areas—restricting criticism of the government and its policies and controlling speech labeled obscene—that the disagreements have been greatest. We shall examine below the development of aspects of legal doctrine and rights protection in these two areas.

No "Prior Restraint" The records of the First Congress, which wrote the Bill of Rights, do not show extensive discussion of the meaning of free speech. The authors of the First Amendment appeared to have accepted the traditional view of English law regarding freedom of speech and press, according to which there could be no prior restraint upon publication—that is, the government could not require a license *before* works could be printed or prevent a work from being published. *After* publication, however, the author could be held responsible and fined or thrown into jail if the views expressed undermined the security or welfare of the government, or the safety, character, or property of individuals.

Although today we would regard such an interpretation of free speech as too narrow, freedom from prior restraint is still a bedrock of protection. When the *New York Times* in 1971 began a serial publication of the "Pentagon papers," a classified government document stolen by an anti-Vietnam War activist, the Justice Department sought to prevent the newspaper from publishing any more of it. The Supreme Court held that the *Times* was free to publish the papers even though they might have been stolen and protected by a legitimate government classification (*New York Times Co. v. United States*, 1971). The Court reasoned that the attempt to stop the *Times* constituted an effort at prior restraint of publication, which could be justified only by the most compelling reasons. The Court left open the possibility that the *Times* might later be prosecuted for what was actually published, although the government never pressed charges. The insistence that one can be punished for a writing only after publication is important, because it means that those who would restrict speech must prove to a court that a work is illegal before it can be suppressed; they cannot first suppress a work and then put the burden of proof upon the publisher to show that it should not be censored. All the safeguards of the judicial process—such as a public trial, a jury of one's peers, the right to present evidence—will be in effect *before* censorship can take place.

Truth as a Defense and Trial by Jury This traditional English common law of freedom of speech informed the thinking for the first national law that attempted to limit speech—the Sedition Act of 1798. In the charged atmosphere created by the French Revolution and a growing domestic partisan struggle, the Federalist majority in Congress made it a crime to write, utter, or publish "any false, scandalous, and malicious writing" against the president, the Congress, or the government "with the intent to defame" the government or to "excite against [the government] the hatred of the people." The Sedition Act, along with its companion the Alien Act, provoked strong opposition by the Republicans, led by Jefferson and Madison.

In defending this law (an example of a law of "seditious libel"), the Federalists argued that although the First Amendment prohibited prior censorship of the press, it did not prohibit punishing a newspaper for a false and malicious story. Just as an individual has a right to protect his reputation by suing someone for libel, so, they argued, does a government have a right to sue to protect its reputation. A government's reputation, after all, may be much more important for the common good than the reputation of any individual. (This argument slid over the

problem that political officials may easily confuse damage to their own reputation or position with damage to the country.) The issue raised here was not met head on, because most Republicans agreed in principle with the Federalists. Their objection was not that prosecutions for seditious libel should not to be made at all, but rather that they could not be made by the *national* government, which was forbidden to do so by the First Amendment. The matter was to be left to the states to handle. Republicans thus saw the issue as one of states' rights, rather than as one of freedom of speech.

The Alien and Sedition acts expired with the Republican victory of 1800, and Jefferson pardoned all who had been convicted under them. The courts never ruled on their Constitutionality. But the Federalists were so damaged politically by these acts that no attempt was made by the national government to prosecute its critics by means of a federal seditious libel statute until World War I. The election of 1800 had partly decided the question of how rights should be protected.

The controversy aroused by the Alien and Sedition acts led to reform in state laws. Two aspects of the traditional doctrines of English common law in particular were rejected as being incompatible with American democratic principles. First, under English law persons could not defend themselves against a charge of seditious speech simply by arguing that the words spoken were true. If the words harmed the government, that was enough to convict. Respect for the government and the monarch's reputation was more important than the public's right to know. Such reasoning, which may have had some logic in protecting a monarch who could not be deposed, was inapplicable in a democracy. If people are to control their government, they must be free to speak the truth about it, even if it brings it into disrepute. American laws were accordingly changed to allow truth as a defense in libel actions. Second, under the new laws passed in the states, the juries rather than judges were given responsibility for deciding whether the words spoken were actually libelous. The average person on a jury, it was thought, would be less likely than a government official (the judge) to see libel in criticism of the government. Thus, under the guidance of state legislatures and courts, the laws protecting free speech were extended and strengthened in accordance with the principles of democratic government.

The Development of National Protection Jefferson's Republicans had maintained that the states, rather than the national government, should have the responsibility for any laws restricting speech. The states, they argued, would be unlikely to abuse this power because of their closeness to the people. But experience did not always bear out this view. The Republican position was used by some southern states before the Civil War to restrict abolitionist publications. (At the same time that they upheld the states' authority in this area, many southerners also wanted to enlist the aid of the national government in restricting speech.) In any event, experience clearly showed that liberty could not be protected simply by relying on the discretion of the states, as the Republicans had maintained.

In the aftermath of World War I, the Supreme Court finally interpreted the free speech provision of the First Amendment. An antidraft agitator, Charles Schenck, published a pamphlet denouncing conscription and circulated it to young men about to be called to military service. He was charged under the Espionage Act of 1917 with obstructing the draft. Justice Oliver Wendell Holmes, Jr., speaking for a unanimous Court, laid down a test for determining what kind of speech could be Constitutionally punished. Holmes distinguished between language that merely criticized the government and language that incited people to illegal acts. "The question in every case," he said, "is whether the words used are used in such circumstances and are of such a nature as to create a clear and present danger that they will bring about the substantive evils that Congress has a right to prevent" *Schenck v. United States*, 1919). Although the Court ruled that Schenck's pamphlet met this test and hence that Schenck could be punished, in subsequent cases Justice Holmes, joined by Justice Brandeis, developed the "clear and present danger" test in a way that provided much greater protection for free speech and that made government prosecutions far more difficult. They stressed that to meet the test the danger

must be imminent and serious and that the speech must actually incite people to action, not merely advocate a dangerous course.

A second step in developing national protection of free speech occurred in the case of *Gitlow v. New York* in 1925. The Supreme Court ruled for the first time that the freedom of speech provided by the First Amendment was among the "fundamental personal rights" protected against state action by the due process clause of the Fourteenth Amendment, beginning the aforementioned incorporation of the Bill of Rights. Since the *Schenck* and *Gitlow* cases, the Supreme Court has dealt with cases ranging from someone shouting obscenities on a street corner, to religious groups refusing to salute the flag, to organized conspiracies trying to overthrow the government, and to speech in the form of spending and advertisements in political campaigns.

The great variety of contexts in which issues of free speech arise provides occasion for many disputes, as do the Constitutional standards that judges have applied in approaching these contexts. Various Constitutional tests have been devised, most of which are variants of either a "balancing" test or an "absolutist" interpretation of the First Amendment. The "clear and present danger" test is an example of a balancing test: freedom of speech is weighed against other goods, such as national security, to see if the statute is reasonable. Such tests seek to provide a means by which weight can be assigned to various goods to answer the question "What is the value of free speech in relation to the value of national security, of civil peace, of orderly administration?" People may, of course, disagree about whether the test assigns too great or too little weight to free speech. And beyond this, there is the fact the tests are applied by the judges, who determine the weight of each factor according to their own discretion. Some argue that this process in the end does not provide adequate protection of free speech.

To meet this objection, some have argued for an "absolutist" interpretation of the First Amendment. The leading exponent of this view on the Supreme Court was Justice Hugo Black, whose career on the bench spanned more than thirty years (1937–1971). Speech, Black argued, is fully protected by the Constitution, regardless

---

BOX 16.2

Dennis v. United States (1951)

The facts

Dennis and ten other leaders of the Communist party were charged and convicted under the Smith Act of conspiring to advocate and teach the violent overthrow of the United States government and to organize the Communist party for the same purpose.

The majority opinion of Chief Justice Vinson

Overthrow of the Government by force and violence is certainly a substantial enough interest for the Government to limit speech. Indeed, this is the ultimate value of any society, for if a society cannot protect its very structure from armed internal attack, it must follow that no subordinate value can be protected.

The dissenting opinion of Justice Douglas

The political censor has no place in our public debates. Unless and until extreme and necessitous circumstances are shown, our aim should be to keep speech unfettered and to allow the process of law to be invoked only when the provocateurs among us move from speech to action.

The decision

The Court upheld the convictions.

---

of the other goods that might come in competition with it. There is a legitimate question, in Black's view, about what is to be considered "speech"—whether, for example, burning one's draft card is a form of speech, or whether films or pieces of art are speech. But once something is deemed to be speech, it is protected completely, whether done in wartime or peacetime, whether it threatens to disrupt the draft or not. Many object to an absolutist interpretation, claiming that a total preference for free speech endangers other rights and goods.

Communist Prosecutions In 1940, Congress, worried by the threat of both Nazi and communist subversion, passed a sedition law known as the "Smith Act." Unlike the Sedition Act of the eighteenth century, it did not seek to punish those critical of the government, but sought to punish those who willfully advocated the overthrow of the government by force and violence. Not the content of the speech but its intended effect was the standard by which speech was to be judged. The Smith Act also made it illegal to organize, or be a member of, a group that advocated the forceful overthrow of the government. After World War II, the act was used to prose-

cute leading figures of the Communist party in the United States.

In bringing leading members of the Communist party to trial, the government alleged that these men and women were teaching and advocating the violent overthrow of the government, or that they were members of an organization they knew to be advocating its overthrow. In the case of *Dennis v. United States* (1951), the Supreme Court ruled 6–2 that the conviction of leading communists under the act was Constitutional. Interpreting the "clear and present danger" test to mean that the danger of an attempt to overthrow the government did not need to be imminent, or have any likelihood of success, the Court said the government did not have to wait "until the *putsch* is about to be executed, the plans have been laid and the signal is awaited." The evil of such an attempt to overthrow the government was so great, the Court argued, that the government had a right to prevent it, even though the attempt or its success was very unlikely (see Box 16.2).

Although many were prosecuted under the Smith Act, the act gradually became a dead letter. The climate of opinion in which the Court ruled changed. During the early 1950s there was a widespread fear of communist subversion of the government, which had some basis in fact but which was also fanned by unsubstantiated charges made by Senator Joseph McCarthy of Wisconsin. By 1954 this climate had changed, and McCarthy himself was censured by the Senate for his actions. Without declaring the Smith Act unconstitutional, the Court moved in the direction of interpreting the requirements needed to prosecute someone successfully under the act in such a way that convictions became increasingly difficult and finally impossible. The major step in this process was the *Yates* case in which the Court distinguished between the expression of a philosophical belief and the advocacy of an illegal act (*Yates v. United States*, 1957). Thereafter the government had to prove that a person actually intended to overthrow the government and that the words spoken were actually calculated to incite overthrow, not merely that the individual favored overthrowing the government. This test was virtually impossible to satisfy.

The provisions of the Smith Act and of varying state laws making it a crime to belong to organizations advocating the overthrow of the government were also gradually eroded. In 1967, the Court ruled that Communist party membership as such did not disqualify one from teaching in public schools, and in 1974 it held that the Communist party of Indiana could not be kept off the ballot because its officers refused to file an affidavit that the party did not advocate the violent overthrow of the government (*Kayishian v. Board of Regents*, 1967; *Communist Party of Indiana v. Whitcomb*, 1974). Today, a citizen can be punished for advocating political opinions only if his or her words are directed to inciting imminent lawless action *and* are likely to produce such action (*Brandenburg v. Ohio*, 1969).

Determining the limits of free speech has not just been a legal matter. It is a process that has been affected by the climate of opinion in the country at large. Sometimes changes in these limits have been the result of actions of the states, sometimes of those of Congress or the executive, and often of decisions by the federal courts.

Obscene Speech   While the founders clearly meant the First Amendment to protect religious and political speech, it is much less clear what

other kinds of speech, if any, they meant to protect. Courts have interpreted the amendment to cover many other kinds of speech, including speech in the realm of literature, philosophy, and art—and not just speech, but expression more generally, including pictures, photos, films, musical lyrics, and dramatic presentations.

But does the freedom to speak in this sense cover any kind of publication regardless of its character or quality? In fact, American law has never supported such a position. Speech that is deemed obscene has not been protected by the First Amendment, and governments (national, state, or local) may pass laws to ban it. But the definition of obscenity has been narrowed in recent years so that this exception is a shadow of what it used to be. The concern of the Court has been to protect artistic expression, which can easily be interfered with by broad conceptions of obscene material. The current standard for judging obscenity, established largely in the case of *Miller v. California* (1973), says that a work may be judged obscene if it appeals to "prurient interests" as judged by the "average person using contemporary community standards," if it portrays specifically defined sexual conduct in a patently offensive way, and if the work taken as a whole lacks "literary, artistic, political, or scientific value." Meeting this standard is not easy, and the industry that produces material at or near the line of the obscene is flourishing. The Court does not apply this standard, however, when child pornography is involved. Child pornography was held to be a "category of material outside the protection of the First Amendment" because of the state's great interest in protecting minors (*New York v. Ferber*, 1982). States may even ban the possession of child pornography in the home, though if they choose to do so, the states can protect child pornography under their state constitutional free speech protections. The Court in *Ashcroft v. Free Speech Coalition* (2002) clarified its rationale, saying that child pornography cannot be censored because the material is intrinsically repugnant, but because of the harm caused to children in its production. "Virtual" child pornography that appears to include children, but does not in fact do so, has the protection of the First Amendment. By ruling in this way the Court rejected the argument that even though the images in virtual child pornography were produced without harm to children, they could incite its viewers to abuse real children.

Although the Court has made it difficult to censor material considered to be obscene, the issue is likely to be revisited in view of changes in technology and in the culture. Concern over obscenity on the Internet prompted Congress to pass the Communications Decency Act of 1996, which would have imposed criminal penalties on those making indecent materials available on the net to those under eighteen. The law was declared unconstitutional by the Supreme Court on the grounds that it was too broad and vague—that its limitation of "indecent" materials unconstitutionally restricted free speech (*Reno v. American Civil Liberties Union* 1997). There is the question, too, of just what kind of medium is the Internet. Are materials on the Internet disseminated as on the electronic media of the radio and television, or is the Internet akin more to newspapers or even to "private" conversations among various individuals? In fact, the Court has placed the Internet in the category of a medium that has full First Amendment protection, unlike television and radio. Despite this Court ruling in this case, passage of the Communications Decency act and of many recent local statutes indicates a renewed political concern with trying to discover limitations on certain kinds of materials. Not only do some traditionalists argue for greater censorship, but some in the feminist movement contend that the degrading portrayals of women in pornography ought to be more strictly limited. Whether a republican government that depends on the character of its citizens can be indifferent to works that may corrupt that character is certain to remain an important issue.

Other Forms of Expression   Some activities other than speaking or writing seem to share the qualities that make speech protected under the First Amendment. When students in a Des Moines school wore armbands to school to protest the Vietnam War despite school regulations, the Court held that they were exercising a Constitutionally protected form of expression (*Tinker v. Des Moines School District*, 1969). But

expressive actions have generally received less protection from the Court than has speech itself. In *United States v. O'Brien* (1968) the Court held that burning one's draft card could be punished even though it might be a means of protesting governmental policies. The majority argued that the government's interest in an efficient system of selective service outweighed any infringement on the right of expression.

But more recently protection of expression has been broadened. In a highly controversial decision by the Supreme Court in 1989, *Texas v. Johnson* (see Box 16.3), the Court held that the burning of an American flag was beyond the reach of government to proscribe. The facts were these. At the Republican National Convention in Dallas in 1984, Johnson and a group of companions burned an American flag to protest the policies of the Reagan administration. Johnson was then convicted, fined, and sentenced to prison under a Texas statute prohibiting the desecration of a venerated object. (Forty eight states and the federal government had similar laws in effect at the time.) The Supreme Court overturned the conviction, holding that Johnson was clearly communicating an opinion and that the government could not restrict the use of the flag as a symbol to communicating an officially prescribed opinion. The action of burning the flag—not, literally, speech itself—was held to be protected speech. Responding to a great outcry, Congress passed the Flag Protection Act of 1989 which made it a crime to "knowingly mutilate, deface, physically defile, burn, maintain on the floor or ground, or trample upon" the United States flag. The Court, however, held this act to be unconstitutional as well (*United States v. Eichman*, 1990).

Freedom of Religion

"Congress shall make no law respecting an establishment of religion, or prohibiting the free exercise thereof. . . ." Freedom of religion both protects religious belief and worship from dictation by government and prevents religion from dictating to the government. It stems from the premise that government's purpose is to protect people's rights, not to tell them how they should save their souls.

BOX 16.3

Texas v. Johnson (1989)

The facts

As part of a protest against Reagan administration policies while the Republican National Convention was taking place in Dallas in 1984, Johnson unfurled the American flag in front of Dallas City Hall, doused it with kerosene and set it on fire. While the flag burned, the protesters chanted, "America, the red, white and blue, we spit on you." Johnson was charged with violating a Texas law which made it illegal to desecrate a venerated object. He was convicted, sentenced to one year in prison, and fined $2,000. He appealed, arguing that his conviction violated his freedom of speech under the First Amendment.

The majority opinion of Justice Brennan

If we were to hold that a State may forbid flag burning wherever it is likely to endanger the flag's symbolic role, but allow it wherever burning a flag promotes that role . . . we would be permitting a State to "prescribe what shall be orthodox." The way to preserve the flag's special role is not to punish those who feel differently about these matters. It is to persuade them that they are wrong.

The dissenting opinion of Justice Rehnquist

The American flag, then, throughout more than 200 years of our history, has come to be the visible symbol embodying our Nation. It does not represent the views of any particular political party, and it does not represent any particular political philosophy. . . . [The] public burning of the American flag by Johnson was no essential part of any exposition of ideas. . . . Johnson was free to make any verbal denunciation of the flag that he wished. . . .

The decision

The Court overturned Johnson's conviction.

Even with widespread agreement in the United States in favor of religious freedom, there are many areas of controversy. First, does the Constitution protect the right of a person to disobey an otherwise valid law because of religious conviction? The traditional answer to this question was no. In *Reynolds v. United States* (1878), the Supreme Court held that a Mormon who claimed polygamy as his religious duty was not exempt from the federal law making bigamy a crime. The Court said that people were free to *believe* whatever they wanted, but the *actions* of religious people could be subject to the same constraints as the actions of anyone else. The Court also expressed a fear that allowing people to claim religious exemptions from generally applicable laws might result in each individual becoming "a law unto himself."

But in later cases, the Court has changed its positions and said that people may be exempt from laws because of their religious convictions. In *Sherbert v. Verner* (1963), the Court held that a Seventh-Day Adventist who could not find employment because she would not work on Saturday was entitled to unemployment compensation in spite of a law barring benefits if a worker failed to accept "suitable work when offered." The Court held that the law was generally valid and could be used to compel others to work on Saturday, but interfered with the free exercise of Ms. Sherbert's religion. In another case, *Wisconsin v. Yoder* (1972), the Court ruled that the Amish need not obey a compulsory school attendance law of Wisconsin—a law valid for other citizens of the state.

But the Court has not been consistent, and more recently it has returned to the view that a valid law does not allow groups in the name of "free exercise of religion" to claim exemptions carved out by the Court. Presumably, the legislatures that wrote the law have already taken this claim into account and have done the balancing of all the rights and claims. Hence, the Courts would not perform their own balancing test a second time (*Oregon v. Smith*, 1990). In reaction to this line of reasoning, Congress in a highly unusual step passed a law, The Religious Freedom Restoration Act of 1993, rejecting the Court's interpretation and requiring that the First Amendment be read in a way that would allow a burdening of the free exercise of religion only if laws met a "compelling interest" and proceeded by the "least restrictive means." The Court declared this law to violate the Constitution on the grounds that the Congress has no authority to interpret and enforce the First Amendment in so broad a fashion (*City of Boerne v. Flores* 1997). In effect, the Court held that it alone has the authority to interpret the Constitution on issues relating to the Bill of Rights.

The second question in dispute concerns the establishment clause. Everyone agrees that the clause prevents Congress from establishing a state church (a particular church supported by state funds and given special privileges). But controversy has arisen about whether the government may accommodate religious belief in a general and non-sectarian fashion in places or times when this is natural; and whether government can give aid to religion or religious groups provided the aid is given to achieve nonreligious ends.

The most important cases raising this question have involved education and tax exemption for churches. May public schools have prayers or Bible reading as part of their program or release children from school time in order to receive religious instruction? May government give aid to church-related schools? The Supreme Court has developed a three-pronged test for dealing with these questions. First, the aid or religious practice must have a secular purpose to be Constitutional. Second, its "principle or primary effect [must] neither advance nor inhibit religion." Finally, it must not foster an "excessive government entanglement with religion" (*Lemon v. Kurtzman*, 1971).

The difficulty of defining rights in concrete circumstances is illustrated in the area of education. In *Everson v. Board of Education* (1947) the Court ruled that a New Jersey law authorizing school districts to reimburse bus fares paid by children traveling to and from schools, including church-related schools, had the secular purpose of getting children safely to school and was neutral between religious believers and nonbelievers. The law was therefore Constitutional. On the other hand, in *Abington School District v. Schempp* (1963) the Court held that a Pennsylvania law requiring Bible reading in the public schools was unconstitutional because the Bible reading was a religious exercise violating the required neutrality between religious believers and nonbelievers. The Court has firmly maintained a ban on anything resembling a religious exercise in the schools, including state laws mandating a moment of silence for meditation or voluntary prayer (*Wallace v. Jaffree*, 1985). This approach has been extended to official prayers at graduation ceremonies (*Lee v. Weisman,* 1992) and student led prayer at school sporting events (*Santa Fe Independent School District v. Doe*, 2000) with both being declared by the Court to violate the establishment clause.

Many forms of aid to religious schools, but not all, have been held unconstitutional because of the difficulty of distinguishing the secular purpose of such aid from the pervasive religious character of parochial schools. If the Court believes that the motivation of a law is religious in character, it is apt to strike down the law even if it is neutral in appearance. In *Edwards v. Aguillard* (1987) the Court declared unconstitutional a Louisiana law that required the teaching of both evolution and creation science.

It is sometimes difficult to see consistency in the Court's opinions. Why should tax exemption for churches, a very substantial and seemingly direct aid to religion, be Constitutional while state payments to church-sponsored schools to cover the costs of tests and reports mandated by the state, an indirect aid serving a required state purpose, be unconstitutional? (*Levitt v. Committee for Public Education*, 1973) History, fear of public reaction, desire to accommodate diversity, as well as Constitutional principles seem to play a role in this controversial area of adjudication.

Many Americans have disagreed with recent Court rulings in the area of religious freedom. There have been persistent attempts in Congress to pass a Constitutional amendment permitting prayer in the public schools. These disputes have frequently stemmed from deep cultural, as well as religious differences. The Court is sharply

---

BOX 16.4

Application of Criminal Procedural Rights to the States

Right	**Case and year**
Fourth Amendment	
Unreasonable search and seizure	*Wolf v. Colorado* (1949)
Exclusionary rule	*Mapp v. Ohio* (1961)
Fifth Amendment	
Grand jury clause	Not incorporated
Double jeopardy clause	*Benton v. Maryland* (1969)
Self-incrimination clause	*Molloy v. Hogan* (1964)
Sixth Amendment	
Speedy trial clause	*Klopfer v. North Carolina* (1967)
Public trial clause	*In re Oliver* (1948)
Jury trial clause	*Duncan v. Louisiana* (1968)
Notice clause	*Cole v. Arkansas* (1948)
Confrontation clause	*Pointer v. Texas* (1965)
Compulsory process clause	*Washington v. Texas* (1967)
Right-to-counsel clause	*Gideon v. Wainwright* (1963)
	Argersinger v. Hamlin (1972)
Eighth Amendment	
Excessive fines and bails clause	Not incorporated
"Cruel and unusual punishments" clause	*Robinson v. California* (1962)

Source: Ralph Rossum, The *Politics of the Criminal Justice System: An Organizational Analysis* (New York: Dekker, 1978), p. 125.

divided on the meaning of the three tests mentioned, and some members do not think the tests are the proper ones. Some think the Constitution permits more aid to religion than the tests seem to allow, others less. The Court simply ignored the *Lemon* tests in holding that prayers opening legislative sessions are Constitutional on the grounds that they are a long-accepted part of our historical practice (*Marsh v. Chambers*, 1983). Some members of the Court have given indications that they are open to reconsidering the *Lemon* standards, and it is likely that some modification will occur in the next few years.

Rights of Those Accused of Crimes

In our federal system the administration of criminal justice is principally a function of the states. But with the process of incorporation of the Bill of Rights, most of the protections in the Fourth through the Eight Amendments for those accused of crimes have been held to apply to the states. As a result, since the 1960s the Court has increased requirements related to the right to counsel (Sixth Amendment) and protections against unreasonable searches and seizures (Fourth Amendment) and against self-incrimination (Fifth Amendment). It has also used the Eighth Amendment's prohibition of cruel and unusual punishments to place restrictions upon capital punishment.

The increased protection of rights in criminal cases extended by the Warren Court during the 1960s created great controversy. Richard Nixon promised during the 1968 presidential campaign that he would appoint judges who favored crime prevention over procedural rights, and Congress acted to try to overturn or modify several of the

Court's decisions. This opposition had some effect upon the Court. Although the Burger and Rhenquist Courts have not retreated from the basic protections extended by the Warren Court, they have sometimes interpreted them more narrowly. Let us look at the four main areas in which the rights of the accused have been extended.

Searches and Seizures The Fourth Amendment prohibits "unreasonable searches and seizures." The central meaning of this prohibition is that the police may not search a person or premises without a warrant issued by a magistrate upon demonstration that there is a probable cause to believe that there is something illegal or incriminating to be found. But there are several circumstances in which police may make searches without a warrant. The most important of these is a search incident to a lawful arrest. An arresting officer may search the person being arrested and the immediate vicinity without a search warrant in order both to make certain that the arrested person does not have a concealed weapon which might endanger the officer and to keep evidence from being destroyed.

While there has been disagreement about how much discretion the police should be given to perform their job, the chief controversy surrounding searches and seizures has involved the "exclusionary rule." This rule states that evidence unconstitutionally or illegally obtained cannot be used in a trial. It is a means which courts have used to enforce due process protections. If the police gain evidence without a search warrant or extract a confession without the accused having been given the right to counsel, the evidence or confession cannot be used in a trial (*Weeks v. United States*, 1914). Although the Court held that the prohibition against "unreasonable searches and seizures" applied to the states in the case of *Wolf v. Colorado* in 1949, it was not until the case of *Mapp v. Ohio* in 1961 that the Court ruled that this prohibition must be enforced by means of the exclusionary rule. Those who favor the rule argue that it discourages illegal actions by police to obtain evidence. Those who oppose it argue that it merely encourages police officers to give false testimony about how they obtained evidence.

The alternative (as practiced in many other countries) would be to admit illegal evidence at a trial, but then make the offending officers subject to penalties. Proponents of the exclusionary rule argue that it is difficult to punish law enforcement officials when they have succeeded in catching criminals, even if they have acted illegally. Police may be reluctant to collect evidence against their fellow officers, prosecutors to bring cases, and juries to convict. Besides, they argue, it is demeaning to the law to enforce it by illegal means. Those on the other side argue that it does not make sense to let a known criminal go free, even if the evidence has been illegally obtained. The proper penalty should be applied to the offending officer, not to society as a whole. Although the exclusionary rule has not been abandoned, the Court in recent years has been moved by this latter argument to interpret it more narrowly. For example, the Court has held that if the evidence was likely to be discovered anyway, it is admissible even though it was actually obtained illegally (*Nix v. Williams*, 1984). The Court has also generally narrowed what constitutes a search or seizure, denying that it was a seizure when police boarded a bus to question passengers and inspect their luggage (*Florida v. Bostick*, 1991). But it did rule that police could not use thermal imaging devices to peer inside houses without either a warrant or probable cause (*Kyllo v. U.S.* 2001).

Self-Incrimination One of the most important of several provisions contained in the Fifth Amendment is that "no person . . . shall be compelled in any criminal case to be witness against himself." This privilege may be invoked before any official body with the power to compel testimony under oath. It thus applies to legislative committees and grand juries as well as to criminal trials.

As in the case of searches and seizures, the major controversy in the last two decades has centered on the question of the admissibility of confessions at trials. The Court had long held that coerced confessions were not admissible on the grounds that they might be unreliable, but that voluntary confessions could be. Torture was not a good way to the truth. However, the Court gradually came to see this exclusion as a means of regulating the police as well as preventing false confessions, blurring the distinction between voluntary and coerced confessions. Instead of looking for evidence of physical torture, the Court looked at evidence that psychological pressure had been applied. Because all police inquiries involve some psychological pressure, the issue became how much pressure there must be before the confession cannot be admitted in court.

In the case of *Malloy v. Hogan* in 1964, the Court held that the protection against self-incrimination is included within the due process protection of the Fourteenth Amendment. This led to decisions in the cases of *Escobedo v. Illinois* (1964) and *Miranda v. Arizona* (1966) establishing the rule that a confession would not be admissible in Court unless the accused had been advised both of the right to remain silent and of the right to counsel. (The privilege against self-incrimination and the right to counsel are intimately connected because lawyers will immediately advise clients not to incriminate themselves.)

While the Court has not reversed this basic position, it has narrowed the *Miranda* decision by making a number of exceptions. It has ruled that a confession obtained in violation of the *Miranda* rule might be introduced in court for the purpose of challenging a defendant's testimony although not for the purpose of proving he or she is guilty of the crime (*Harris v. New York*, 1971). And it has held that if a police officer gains a confession without reading the suspect his or her rights, the mistake may be corrected by reading the rights later and obtaining a second confession (*Oregon v. Elstad*, 1985). Finally in 1991 the Court held that the introduction of an illegally obtained confession as evidence in a trial need not automatically overturn a conviction, but might be treated as a "harmless error" if there was sufficient other evidence for a conviction (*Arizona v. Fulminante*, 1991).

Right to Counsel   It has long been recognized that a fair trial may require the assistance of legal counsel. Few persons are able to defend their own cases effectively, especially given the complexity of modern criminal law and procedures. Before 1963 the Court had held that a state was obliged to provide counsel for a defendant who could not afford one in a capital case but not in less serious crimes. In *Gideon v. Wainwright* (1963), the Court expanded this protection to include the provision of free legal counsel for indigent defendants in noncapital cases. In the cases of *Escobedo* and *Miranda* it held that counsel must be provided in the pretrial stage if confessions are to be admitted in court. The general rule is that counsel must be available at every "critical stage of the prosecution" where there is a possibility of a custodial sentence, even one that is suspended, because of the potential loss of liberty (*Alabama v. Shelton*, 2002).

Cruel and Unusual Punishment   In 1972 the Supreme Court ruled that the death penalty statute of Georgia violated the Eighth Amendment's prohibition against "cruel and unusual punishments." (*Furman v. Georgia*, 1972) But only two of the justices argued that all capital punishment was unconstitutional. The others in the 5–4 majority argued that the statute allowed too wide discretion to judges and juries, was too infrequently used, or was applied in a discriminatory manner. If the intention of some on the Court was to ban the death penalty altogether, this plan met widespread disapproval. Many states enacted new death penalty laws to meet these objections. In *Gregg v. Georgia* (1976) the Court upheld a new Georgia death penalty law which contained procedures directing the jury to the particular circumstances of the crime involved and provided general rules to guide the jury as to when the death penalty should be invoked. The Court has refined its criteria governing the procedures required in meeting Constitutional standards since *Gregg*. In *Coker v. George* (1977) the Court forbade the use of the death penalty to punish rape. The death penalty apparently passes Constitutional scruples only when it is used in murder cases, and then only if careful procedural requirements are met.

After *Gregg* there was a resurgence of public support for the death penalty and a seemingly ever higher number of executions. This trend has slowed somewhat in recent years, partially as a result of DNA testing that has shown a number of death penalty convictions to be unsupported by the evidence. While a majority of Americans still support capital punishment, Illinois imposed a moratorium in 2000 on its executions and a number of other states appear poised to follow. This could open another national debate over whether America wishes to continue as the only western industrialized nation to use the death penalty.

Civil Rights

In the issues we have examined thus far in this chapter, individual liberty has been uppermost. In the ones we will now turn to—those we are calling "civil rights"—the issue is primarily one of equality. The questions here include the protection of the rights of blacks, Hispanics, other minorities, and women who have been denied full participation in the country's political life or have been treated as second-class citizens under the law. There are two related aspects to fulfilling the promise of the equality of all persons in our Constitutional system. One is guaranteeing equal participation in voting and other aspects of the governing process. The other is protecting the individual's right to be treated equally under the laws. As we have discussed voting and other political rights in other chapters, we shall concentrate here on the issue of treating people equally under the law.

The Fourteenth Amendment guarantees all persons the equal protection of the laws, and the courts have held that the due process clause of the Fifth Amendment has a similar "equal protection" component. This does not mean that the laws cannot make distinctions between individuals or groups. Tax laws, for example, require people with high incomes to pay taxes at a higher rate than those with low incomes. This is not a violation of the equal protection of the laws, because the distinction made by the law is held to be a reasonable one that is not arbitrary and is related to a legitimate policy goal, such as raising revenues. But some distinctions between individuals or groups do violate civil rights, as in the case of policies that once excluded blacks from voting in many states in the South. How to decide whether or not a particular classification is reasonable forms a large part of the difficulties in this area of the law.

Racial Equality

Before 1954 the Court's understanding of what equality under the law meant with regard to race had been established in the case of *Plessy v. Ferguson* (1896). The majority in that case held that legally mandated segregation in Louisiana trains was Constitutional. No one was injured so long as the separate facilities were equal; required separation did not imply the inferiority of either race; and the purposes of ensuring public order and providing for the convenience and comfort of passengers were sufficient to justify the segregation.

Through the efforts of the National Association for the Advancement of Colored People (NAACP) and others, the courts were gradually induced to move away from the entrenched segregationist position established in the wake of *Plessy*. The great change came in 1954. In the years preceding 1954 various instances of educational discrimination had been ruled unconstitutional because the education offered to blacks was not equal to that offered to whites. In the early 1950s, Oliver Brown tried to enroll his daughter in an all-white public school in Topeka, Kansas. When the NAACP took the case to court, the lower federal court ruled that the black and white schools of Topeka were equal in quality and therefore Constitutional under the *Plessy* doctrine. Accepting the judgment that the schools were equal in most exterior ways, the Supreme Court faced the question: Were separate but equal schools Constitutional? In an atmosphere of great drama, the Supreme Court, on May 17, 1954, announced its unanimous decision: segregated schools are inherently unequal and therefore in violation of the equal protection clause of the Fourteenth Amendment (*Brown v. Board of Education of Topeka*, 1954). Although the decision involved only public education, it signaled the end of legalized segregation everywhere. In subsequent decisions, the Court began to strike down legally supported segregation wherever it was found.

The *Brown* decision marked a great advance for racial equality in the United States. Although resistance was initially massive and progress toward desegregation slow, by 1970 the dual school systems of the nation were destroyed. At the same time it helped to spur new *political* efforts to increase legal protection for civil rights. The civil rights movement of the 1950s and 1960s, begun with the nonviolent movement of Martin Luther King, continued through a variety of organizations and helped to dramatize the issue and form public opinion. The cause of segregation was discredited by brutal murders and beatings of civil rights workers, and moderate whites and blacks joined to form a broad coalition in favor of new protection for civil rights.

President Johnson seized the moment of the assassination of President Kennedy to galvanize opinion in favor of legislative action. The result was the Civil Rights Act of 1964. Although some civil rights legislation had been passed in 1957 and 1960 (covering aspects of voting rights), the 1964 law was more sweeping in its scope, adding protections for the right to vote and the right to access to public accommodations, and for desegregation of public facilities and education, and increasing the powers of the Commission on Civil Rights (charged with enforcing important aspects of civil rights legislation). It also contained provisions banning discrimination in federally assisted programs and guaranteeing equal employment opportunities. Racial distinctions were to be eradicated from American law and practice. The Civil Rights Act was followed by the Voting Rights Act of 1965, which was meant to assure blacks and others of the right to vote. Subsequent legislation in these areas has been passed, but the acts of 1964 and 1965 were the most sweeping and important.

The *Brown* decision and its aftermath, both legally and politically, brought a great advance for equality under the law. But the meaning of the Constitutional guarantee of equal protection of the laws has not been fully clarified and is a source of renewed controversy in contemporary politics. Justice Harlan, in the *Plessy* case, issued a ringing dissent in which he said, "In view of the Constitution, in the eye of the law, there is in this country no superior, dominant, ruling class of citizens. There is no caste here. Our Constitution is color-blind and neither knows nor tolerates classes among citizens." The Court in the *Brown* case did not make a blanket declaration that all racial discrimination in the law was ille-

gal, but rather that racial discrimination that stigmatized black children and caused them harm was illegal.

The Court subsequently developed a view of the equal protection clause which held that most classifications and distinctions made by law would be Constitutional provided they were reasonably related to some valid governmental objective. But in some cases the standards were higher, and the laws would have to pass *strict scrutiny*. In those cases the government would have to prove that it had a compelling governmental interest and that its classification imposed the fewest restrictions possible, while still achieving its objective. Under this type of scrutiny the presumption is that the government's actions are unconstitutional. This more difficult standard is required if burdens are put upon a class of persons who have been harmed by governmental and societal actions in the past (a "suspect" class) or if the classification affects *fundamental rights*—particularly those rights the denial of which prevents the political process from working effectively, such as freedom of speech and the right to vote. This interpretation of the equal protection clause suggested the possibility that burdens might be put on the majority white population (a nonsuspect class) which could not be put on racial minorities (suspect classes). When it became apparent that the end of legal segregation did not mean the end of *de facto* segregation and did not assure that blacks and whites would be economically and socially equal, different governments and agencies developed "affirmative action" programs giving preferences to blacks and other minorities in such matters as hiring, promotion, and granting of contracts.

The record of the Court on the Constitutionality of affirmative action is mixed. When Allan Bakke, a white applicant, was twice denied admission to the medical school of the University of California at Davis, he brought suit arguing that the university had denied him his Constitutional rights by setting aside sixteen places in the entering class for minority students and admitting students whose qualifications were substantially below his own. A sharply divided Supreme Court held that while the explicit racial quota of the school violated either the equal protection clause of the Fourteenth Amendment or the Civil Rights Act of 1964 (the majority was divided in its opinion), race could be used as a criterion for admission provided it was only one of several factors taken into account. The decision condemned explicit quotas, but seemed to uphold more subtle preferences (*Regents of the University of California v. Bakke*, 1978).

Another case, decided a year after *Bakke*, lent additional support to preferences for minorities ("affirmative action" programs) when they are the result of private agreements and not governmental mandates. In *United Steelworkers of America v. Weber* (1979) the Court ruled that the Civil Rights Act of 1964 did not prohibit "all private, voluntary race-conscious affirmative action plans." As a result of an agreement between his union and the Kaiser Company, Weber, a white, had been passed over for a training program in preference for a black with less seniority. The Court argued that the literal reading of the Civil Rights Act that prohibited such preferences had to give way to the spirit of the act, which the Court thought was to advance the position of blacks in American society.

In the case of *Fullilove v. Klutznick* (1980) the Court seemed to uphold the Constitutionality of racial classifications in order to achieve broad social goals. The federal Public Works Employment Act of 1977 required that at least 10 percent of all the money granted for projects under the act be expended for minority business enterprises. This was the first time in American history that Congress had passed a law creating a broad legislative classification for entitlement to benefits based solely upon racial characteristics. By a 6–3 vote the Court held this classification Constitutional, arguing that the harm done the whites excluded from the benefits was minor and did not stigmatize them.

The Court decided many affirmative action cases during the 1980s, generally upholding the classification when it could be seen as a remedy for specific past discrimination and when its burden did not fall upon identifiable individuals (but only upon whites in general), and denying the classification when it could not be seen as such a remedy or where its burden fell upon a small class of specific people. Many of these decisions were decided by narrow margins. Sup-

port for affirmative action on the Court has, however, waned over the last decade. In 1989 the Court held unconstitutional a Richmond ordinance requiring city contractors to subcontract at least 30 percent of the dollar amount of each contract to "Minority Business Enterprises." The key to the decision was the holding that the "strict scrutiny" standard should apply to all racial classifications, including those that disadvantaged whites, made by state and local governments (*City of Richmond v. Croson Co.*, 1989). A similar decision was reached in 1995 in the case of *Adarand Constructors, Inc. v. Pena*, in which a federal set aside program for minority subcontractors in highway construction was declared unconstitutional, applying the *Croson* ruling to the federal government.

The sharp division within the Court over affirmative action reflects the division in the country as a whole. Proponents of affirmative action argue that past discrimination has created a situation which can be remedied only by using racial classifications. Temporary racial preference is justified as the only way to achieve racial equality. The alternative is to perpetuate a situation created by the unjust treatment of minorities. Opponents argue that affirmative action violates the basic principle of American law that individuals are responsible for their own actions and are not to be blamed or penalized because of the group to which they belong. They argue further that the acceptance of racial quotas will pit one racial group against another and will in the long run create vested interests in favor of the perpetuation of racial distinctions.

The struggle over this difference of principle is only partly being waged in the courts, which have generally played the role of allowing and disallowing what legislatures and administrative agencies have done rather than mandating certain policies. Opponents of affirmative action have taken their case to legislatures, seeking bans on such policies. In California in 1996, a public referendum added a provision to the California constitution ending affirmative action programs by any state agencies. All across the country, this issue is being discussed and reassessed. Although few pretend that the end of legal discrimination against blacks has resolved the issue of racial equality, how this situation

BOX 16.5

City of Richmond v. Croson Co. (1989)

The facts

In 1983 the Richmond City Council (blacks held 5 of the 9 seats on the Council) adopted the Minority Business Utilization Plan. This plan required prime contractors awarded construction contracts by the city to subcontract at least 30% of the dollar amount of the contract to businesses that were owned by American citizens who were "Blacks, Spanish-speaking, Orientals, Indians, Eskimos, or Aleuts." The Croson Company brought suit, arguing that the plan violated the equal protection clause of the Constitution.

The Court's opinion by Justice O'Connor

The Richmond Plan denies certain citizens the opportunity to compete for a fixed percentage of public contracts based solely upon their race. To whatever racial group these citizens belong, their "personal rights" to be treated with equal dignity and respect are implicated. . . .

Classifications based on race carry a danger of stigmatic harm. Unless they are strictly reserved for remedial settings, they may in fact promote notions of racial inferiority and lead to a politics of racial hostility. . . . [T]he standard of review under the Equal Protection Clause is not dependent on the race of those burdened or benefitted by a particular classification.

The dissenting opinion of Justice Marshall

It is a welcome symbol of racial progress when the former capital of the Confederacy acts forthrightly to confront the effects of racial discrimination in its midst. . . . Racial classifications "drawn on the presumption that one race is inferior to another or because they put the weight of government behind racial hated and separatism" warrant the strictest judicial scrutiny because of the very irrelevance of these rationales. By contrast, racial classifications drawn for the purpose of remedying the effects of discrimination . . . have a highly pertinent basis: the tragic and indelible fact that discrimination against blacks and other racial minorities in this Nation has pervaded our Nation's history and continues to scar our society.

The decision

The Court declared the Richmond Plan to be unconstitutional.

should be addressed remains one of the thorniest and most controversial questions in contemporary politics.

Rights of Immigrants

The protection of the rights of immigrants, who have become an increasingly large segment of the American population, raises many of the same problems that have faced racial and ethnic groups. It also raises some new problems. One major issue is illegal immigration, particularly from Mexico. It is difficult to calculate the number of illegal immigrants in the United States, as those who have entered illegally are not usually eager to make themselves known, but the number is in the millions. The Immigration and Naturalization Service does not have the resources to patrol the thousands of miles of our borders.

Once here, undocumented aliens may be open to manipulation and exploitation under the threat of exposing their status, may compete with Americans for jobs, and may place a burden on social services.

Congress passed the Immigration and Control Act of 1986 to try to deal with the multiple problems this situation presented. The act permitted those who could prove they had lived continuously in the United States since January 1, 1982, to apply for limited amnesty, and to gain permanent residency after showing minimum proficiency in English and knowledge of American government. It established fines and other penalties for employers who knowingly hire illegal aliens, or who, on the other hand, discriminate against legal residents who are foreign born. And it provided entrance to a certain number of aliens to serve as temporary farm workers.

This act, however, does not seem to have stemmed the tide of illegal immigration. The Court has also concerned itself with the problem. In 1982 it held unconstitutional a Texas law which denied state funds for education of illegal alien children. The majority ruled that no sufficiently important state purpose was served to justify distinguishing between citizens and illegal aliens in determining who was entitled to free public education, and hence that the statute violated the equal protection of the laws (*Pyler v. Doe*, 1982).

Equal Rights for Women

Women, like blacks, hispanics, and others, have found themselves the objects of discrimination in securing jobs, status, and equal treatment under the law. As in the other areas, the import of the nation's dedication to equality for the relationship between the sexes has been a matter of considerable debate. At the time of the founding and throughout the nineteenth century, women were generally denied full civil and political rights. Although there was nothing in the Constitution that restricted the right to vote to men, the state legislatures, which determined voting qualifications, universally denied the right to women. This denial generally rested on the argument that the political order was composed of families, not individuals, and that the differences between men and women made fathers and husbands the proper representatives of women.

Beginning in the 1840s women organized to achieve the right to vote. The movement for women's equality, like that of the blacks', could appeal to basic American principles to gain support. The Seneca Falls Convention of 1848, a crucial milestone in the national coordination of the women's movement, modeled its statement of principles on the Declaration of Independence. (It contained a statement that "all men *and women* are created equal.") The goal of women's suffrage was finally realized in the nation as a whole by the ratification of the Nineteenth Amendment prohibiting denial of the vote on account of sex in 1920. (Some states had previously granted women the vote.)

Even after gaining the right to vote, however, many inequalities continued to exist both in law and in practice. Some of these were based on the supposition that women required special protection, such as laws which limited the hours women could work but did not limit men. Others recognized what was thought to be women's special role in society, such as laws which preferred the mother when establishing custody in divorce cases. Many simply gave preferences to men, particularly in economic and business matters. Beginning in the 1950s, the women's movement gained new strength in its battle against inequality. At the same time, women were entering the work force in increasing numbers. This led to new laws requiring equal pay for equal work, prohibiting sex discrimination in employment and between students in schools receiving federal funds, and forbidding discrimination against pregnant women in the workplace.

A major effort was undertaken by feminist groups to secure passage of the Equal Rights Amendment to the Constitution. This amendment would have prohibited denying equality of rights under the law on account of sex. Although the proposed amendment initially received the overwhelming endorsement of Congress and swept through many state legislatures, the movement for its passage stalled and it was eventually defeated, despite an extension of the time limit for ratification by Congress.

While the defeat of the Equal Rights Amendment was a setback for the feminist movement, it did not necessarily show a widespread lack of support for equal rights for women in the United States. Not only did 35 states ratify the proposed amendment, but most people seemed to agree that women should have equal rights. There was much disagreement, however, about what those equal rights were, and many opponents of the amendment feared the answer that might be given by the courts. Particularly effective in the campaign against the amendment were the arguments that it might be read to require drafting women for combat duty or that it might undermine laws that protected women on the job. Opposition to the proposal was itself led and organized by women, and the Equal Rights Amendment became an issue that symbolized a struggle over a wide range of cultural issues.

Many of the goals desired by supporters of the Equal Rights Amendment are being achieved by legislative or court actions. The Supreme Court has not regarded sex classifications as inherently suspect, as they have racial classifications (discussed earlier), but they have moved in the direction of requiring a demonstration that the classification is substantially related to the achievement of some important governmental purpose. The Court has upheld the all-male draft with the argument that restriction of combat duties to men creates a reasonable distinction serving an important governmental interest that allows Congress to draft men but not women (*Rosteker v. Goldberg*, 1981). But it has barred many differences based on sex, such as state laws establishing different ages at which men and women become legal adults (*Stanton v. Stanton*, 1975). The Gulf War made clear that even the legal restriction of combat assignments to men becomes blurred as women move increasingly into support positions near or at the front.

Conclusion

Civil rights and liberties define limits on governmental action, specifying certain areas that lie beyond the reach of government and certain methods that government may or may not employ in acting on matters within its control. These limits help serve not only to define the character of liberty, but also to elaborate the meaning of equality. Other policies of government, as we have seen, also affect the nature of liberty and equality, but the concrete designation of rights and liberties is the most important foundation of these fundamental values of American society.

Although there is a wide area of consensus on rights and liberties, disagreements arise over certain claims to rights, over who possesses them, and over how they can be reconciled with other rights and duties. There have also been many conflicts over who should decide these questions. Rooted in important provisions of the Constitution, civil rights and liberties receive much of their definition and support from decisions of the courts. To this extent, the policymaking *process* for rights and liberties is decidedly

and peculiarly nonmajoritarian; one hesitates, however, to call it elitist in any traditional sense, for while the decisions are made by a small number of persons, they have for some time now usually been made not to aid a minority of the wealthy, but more often to aid individuals and groups that have suffered historical injustices. The protection of rights and liberties, however, is not exclusively the province of the judicial branch. Legislatures and executive officials and agencies have played important roles in determining civil rights policy, and organized citizens' groups have been instrumental in bringing about important changes. Thus one finds elements of majoritarian, pluralist, and bureaucratic decision making in the elaboration of rights and liberties. In a deeper sense, moreover, the security of rights and liberties rests ultimately on the majoritarian base of their support in public opinion as a fundamental constitutional element of the American system articulated in the Declaration of Independence.

Cases Cited

Abington School District v. Schempp, 374 U.S. 203 (1963)

Adarand Constructors, Inc. v. Pena, 115 S. Ct. 2097 (1995)

Alabama v. Shelton, (2002)

Arizona v. Fulminante, (1991)

Argersinger v. Hamlin, 407 U.S. 25 (1972)

Ashcroft v. Free Speech Coalition 535 U.S.—(2002)*

Brown v. Board of Education of Topeka, 347 U.S. 483 (1954)

Buckley v. Valeo, 424 U.S. 1 (1976)

Church of the Lukumi Babalu v. City of Hialeah, 508 U.S. 502 (1993)

City of Richmond v. Croson Co., 109 S. Ct. 706 (1989)

City of Boerne v. Flores (1997)

Civil Rights Cases, 109 U.S. 3 (1883)

Coker v. Georgia, 433 U.S. 584 (1977)

Cole v. Arkansas, 338 U.S. 345 (1948)

Communist Party of Indiana v. Whitcomb, 414 U.S. 441 (1974)

Dennis v. United States, 431 U.S. 494 (1951)

Duncan v. Louisiana, 391 U.S. 145 (1968)

Edwards v. Aguillard, 482 U.S. 578 (1987)

Escobedo v. Illinois, 378 U.S. 478 (1964)

Everson v. Board of Education, 330 U.S. 1 (1947)

Ex parte Milligen, 71 U.S. 2 (1866)

Florida v. Bostick, 501 U.S. 429 (1991)

Fullilove v. Klutznick, 100 S. Ct. 2758 (1980)

Furman v. Georgia, 408 U.S. 238 (1972)

Gideon V. Wainwright, 372 U.S. 335 (1963)

Gitlow v. New York, 268 U.S. 652 (1925)

Gregg v. Georgia, 428 U.S. 153 (1976)

Griswold v. Connecticut, 381 U.S. 479 (1965)

Hammer v. Dagenhart, 247 U.S. 251 (1910)

Harris v. New York, 401 U.S. 222 (1971)

In re Oliver, 333 U.S. 257 (1948)

Joseph Burstyn, Inc. v. Wilson, 343 U.S. 684 (1952)

Keyishian v. Board of Regents, 385 U.S. 589 (1967)

Klopfer v. North Carolina, 386 U.S. 213 (1967)

Kyllo v. U.S., 533 U.S. 27 (2001)

Lee v. Weisman, 505 U.S. 577 (1992)

Lemon v. Kurtzman, 403 U.S. 602 (1971)

Levitt v. Committee for Public Education, 413 U.S. 479 (1973)

Lochner v. New York, 198 U.S. 45 (1905)

Lyng v. Northwest Indian Cemetery Ass'n, 485 U.S. 439 (1988)

Mapp v. Ohio, 367 U.S. 643 (1961)

Miller v. California, 413 U.S. 15 (1973)

Milliken v. Bradley, 418 U.S. 717 (1974)

Miranda v. Arizona, 384 U.S. 436 (1966)

Molloy v. Hogan, 378 U.S. 1 (1964)

Mutual Film Corp v. Industrial Commission of Ohio, 236 U.S. 230 (1915)

Nebbia v. New York, 291 U.S. 502 (1934)

New York v. Ferber, 458 U.S. 747 (1982)

New York Times v. Sullivan, 376 U.S. 254 (1964)

New York Times Co. v. United States, 403 U.S. 713 (1971)

Nix v. Williams, 467 U.S. 431.

Oregon V. Elstad, 470 U.S. 298 (1985)

Plessy v. Ferguson, 163 U.S. 537 (1896)

Pointer v. Texas, 380 U.S. 400 (1965)

Pyler v. Doe, 102 S.Ct. 2382 (1982)

Regents of the University of California v. Bakke, 438 U.S. 269 (1978)

Reno v. American Civil Liberties Union (1997)

Reynolds v. United States, 98 U.S. 145 (1878)

Robinson v. California, 370 U.S. 660 (1962)

Roe v. Wade, 410 U.S. 113 (1973)

Rosteker v. Goldberg, 453 U.S. 57 (1981)

Santa Fe Independent School District v. Doe, 530 U.S. 290 (2000)

Schenck v. United States, 249 U.S. 47 (1919)

Sheppard v. Maxwell, 384 U.S. 333 (1966)

Sherbert V. Verner, 374 U.S. 398 (1963)

Slaughterhouse Cases, 16 Wall. 36 (1873)

Stanton v. Stanton, 421 U.S. 7 (1975)

Swann v. Charlotte Mecklenburg, 403 U.S. 1 (1971)

Terminiello v. Chicago, 337 U.S. 1 (1949)

Texas v. Johnson, 109 S. Ct. 2533 (1989)

Tinker v. Des Moines School District, 393 U.S. 503 (1969)

United States v. E. C. Knight, 156 U.S. 1 (1895)

United States v. Eichman, 110 S. Ct. 2404 (1990)

United States v. O'Brien, 391 U.S. 367 (1968)

United Steelworkers of America v. Weber, 443 U.S. 193 (1979)

Walz v. Tax Commission, 397 U.S. 664 (1970)

Wallace v. Jaffree, 472 U.S. 38 (1985)

Washington v. Texas, 338 U.S. 14 (1967)

Weeks v. United States, 232 U.S. 383 (1914)

West Coast Hotel v. Parrish, 300 U.S. 379 (1937)

Wickard v. Filburn, 317 U.S. 111 (1942)

Wisconsin v. Yoder, 406 U.S. 205 (1972)

Wolf v. Colorado, 338 U.S. 25 (1949)

Yates v. United States, 354 U.S. 298 (1957)

Zablocki v. Redhail, 434 U.S. 374 (1978)

*N.B. These cases have not yet been assigned a place in the U.S. Reports.

17

Foreign Policy

CHAPTER CONTENTS

Foreign affairs is the realm of politics that deals with a state's relations to the world outside its own borders—with other governments, worldwide agencies, or groups in other nations. Domestic affairs is the realm of politics that deals with the internal governance of a nation and the relations of citizens to each other and to their own government. In practice, of course, these two realms are not air-tight compartments. Foreign and domestic affairs continually interact with each other. This interaction can be as superficial as the boosts in popularity ratings presidents sometimes receive when they make highly-publicized trips to foreign capitals. Or it can be as serious as the intense domestic opposition to the Vietnam War, which made the military prosecution of the War more difficult and which forced an American withdrawal.

Despite the interconnections, it makes sense to treat foreign affairs separately from domestic affairs. The conduct of foreign affairs has a different character and logic to it that requires a different approach by both the constitution maker and statesman. Domestic policy focuses on what is best for ourselves and what we would choose on the grounds of justice or common interest; foreign policy often revolves around what we must do to assure our security and well-being in a world of sometimes hostile and threatening powers. Necessity here weighs far more heavily than it does in domestic affairs.

Basic Objectives of Foreign Policy

There are certain classic objectives that the United States, along with most other nations, pursues in foreign affairs. The first is the goal of providing for the common defense, since without security and independence no nation can control its own destiny. Security often depends heavily on a nation's military might, which in turn rests on both the quality of its armed forces and the capacity of its defense industry. A wide range of other factors, such as the skill of intelligence-gathering capabilities, the caliber of diplomacy, and of course overall economic health also affect the nation's security.

A second objective of foreign affairs is the promotion of a nation's interests in the world. Interests here include not only conventional economic objectives, such as protecting markets and sources of important raw materials, but also certain long-term global aims, such as safeguarding the world's environment and alleviating worldwide poverty. American foreign policy today extends to questions of world hunger, population, and the proper management of the earth's resources. Our involvement with each of these concerns affects our access in the long run to needed materials and to the global environment to which we are increasingly linked.

Finally, as a third objective, a nation may seek to promote certain ideas and values in the world, not only for security reasons but also because of its belief that they are good, or universally valid, or destined by the laws of history to prevail. Some nations are largely unconcerned with such matters and are content merely to be left alone. But certain nations have seen themselves as having a task that involves them in the world at large and in trying to shape the course of history. Feeling the obligation to spread the "light" of republican government, the United States has always been in this group. As George Washington declared in his first inaugural address, "the preservation of the sacred fire of liberty and the destiny of the republican model of government are . . . staked on the experiment entrusted to the hands of the American people." This same theme has been echoed in twentieth century inaugural addresses, from President Kennedy's avowal that America "shall pay any price, bear any burden, meet any hardship . . . to assure the survival and success of liberty," to President George H. Bush's assertion that "this country has meaning beyond what we see, and our strength is a force for good." How republicanism should be spread—and at what cost—are questions that have divided Americans, but a commitment to this goal has been evident in one form or another throughout our history.

The pursuit of these three objectives—security, global interests, and the promotion of republican ideas—occasionally conflict and do not result in perfectly consistent policies. Sometimes there are conflicts. For example, nations that are important to us for reasons of interest (or security) may have a less than enviable human rights records, forcing a choice between sacrificing economic gains and supporting republicanism. Such choices are often coupled with controversy, as when America supported authoritarian governments in South Korea, Spain, and the Philippines during the Cold War because of the importance of these nations to our security alliances, or today when America trades freely with China despite its human rights violations.

The character of foreign affairs makes it impossible to establish in the abstract hard and fast rules for pursuing these objectives. Much depends on the situation that prevails in the world and on the balance of forces. The options America had available to it in the nineteenth century, when it was a second-class power, differed from those it had during much of the twentieth century, when it was a major world power in life-and-death competition with the Soviet Union. And these in turn differ from the situation today, when America's power is greater and the focus is on regional conflicts rather than a world-wide ideological struggle. Clearly, relations of force greatly influence the way a nation goes about pursuing its objectives.

Because foreign affairs differ from domestic affairs, conducting foreign policy requires different capacities from the government. The founders accordingly established a (somewhat) different process for foreign policymaking. The Constitution gives the president more discretion in foreign than domestic affairs, and the Senate has certain specific powers, not shared with the House, in this domain. The laws have created special departments and agencies, such as the State Department, the Defense Department, the Central Intelligence Agency, and the National Security Council, to deal with the tasks of conducting foreign and security policy. Part of understanding foreign policy, therefore, involves a study of its special institutional arrangements and policymaking machinery.

The three elements of foreign affairs mentioned above—basic objectives, the world situation, and the machinery for decision making—form the core of any analysis of foreign policy. These elements are all interdependent, and we shall observe their interaction in the formation and conduct of American foreign policy.

Democracy and Foreign Policy: Some General Problems

How well is the United States equipped to handle its role as a major power in world affairs? As nations go, the involvement of the United States as a power in foreign affairs is fairly recent. For much of our history, we were physically isolated from the main arenas of diplomacy and were concerned chiefly with settling, civilizing, and industrializing a new continent. Foreign affairs were of significance only episodically. This situation changed with World War II, when the United States was thrust into a position of world leadership; and events since then have shown how deeply we are affected, politically and economically, by events beyond our borders.

How well any democratic nation can understand and cope with foreign affairs is another challenge. Consider how different international politics and American domestic politics have been. The United States has in its laws a set of rules designed to govern the relations of its citizens with one another and a government endowed with the right and the capacity to enforce these rules against those who violate them. Its citizens share a broad consensus on fundamental goals. But, in the international setting, these elements either are entirely absent or are present only in a very modest form.

The meeting of the different perspectives of foreign and domestic affairs can produce profound problems in American politics. Foreign policy operates in a world bound by few of the laws and norms of our political system. To pursue its objectives, the United States has had to use methods which, if applied domestically, would be regarded by most Americans as inappropriate. This tension is clear in the case of military power, which exists to deal with disputes that can be settled to its satisfaction only by the threat or use of armed force. The use of force contrasts sharply with the beliefs that govern domestic politics, where an entire system has been devised to avoid the resolution of conflict by force. Furthermore, in contrast to those instances in which the use of force in domestic politics is regarded as legitimate—when it is used by legal authority to enforce the law—international politics for the most part lacks a binding law and possesses no authority universally recognized as having the right to employ force against lawbreaking states. A basic tenet of our domestic political system is thus inapplicable to our relations with other peoples; we must depart from our principles in order to protect them. Here we find the difficult task posed by foreign policy. The nation must cope with a world in which the competition for power isn't cushioned by institutional safeguards and ethical norms as it is in domestic politics. Republican principles, if applied too strictly to the conduct of diplomacy, might place the United States at a serious disadvantage. But if the United States feels bound by no restrictions in its struggle with a threatening international environment, its foreign policy might repudiate the deepest principles for which the country stands. How frequently and how seriously can the United States compromise its principles in international politics before they begin to undermine in domestic politics as well?

Alexis de Tocqueville gave classic expression to the underlying difficulties that a liberal democratic system faces in the conduct of foreign policy. He wrote, "I have no hesitation in saying that in the control of society's foreign affairs democratic governments appear decidedly inferior to others."[1] Tocqueville cited three main problems: democracies are apt to project their own trusting nature on a world that is often governed by a harsh struggle for power and advantage; they tend to conduct an unstable foreign policy, changing their positions to accommodate the shifting sentiments of public opinion; and they find it difficult to keep secrets.

Democratic systems can, of course, counteract these tendencies by sound institutions and good diplomacy. But the weaknesses Tocqueville listed are always just beneath the surface, and learning from experience is a luxury that sometimes cannot be afforded. For example, pacifist tendencies in public opinion in Great Britain and France before World War II left those nations unprepared to face Nazi Germany in 1939.

The opposite side of the coin is that some nondemocratic regimes may be strong on the very points where democracies are weak. As closed societies, authoritarian or totalitarian systems are able to maintain secrets in a way that no democracy can; and they can sometimes ignore or control public opinion, extracting from society for military purposes a quantity of resources that seems almost impossible in a democratic system. Of course, democratic nations are not without important strengths, and authoritarian regimes certain vulnerabilities. Once a policy is adopted and agreed on, democracies can often produce striking results. The efforts by Great Britain and the United States during World War II are testimonies to the power and energy of a democratic people, once it is mobilized and committed to a task. Likewise, the hard bark of dictatorship often hides a rotting tree. Opposition and revolt are often lurking beneath the surface. Totalitarian systems can also destroy the creativity and economic strength needed for sustained struggle. Thus the greatest asset in foreign affairs of democratic nations compared to some totalitarian states derives from their domestic politics: democratic states have been able to earn the steadfast support of their citizens, while totalitarian states, despite tremendous efforts to engineer consent, have seen themselves threatened by the opposition of their own people. The mighty Soviet Empire, which was the military equal of the United States and its allies, fell for this reason.

The Founders and Foreign Policy

A primary reason for establishing a national government in 1787 was the inadequacy of the Articles of Confederation in conducting foreign policy. Even with the great oceans as protective shields, the founders feared that a weak and divided confederacy would invite intervention by European powers, perhaps with the support of state governments seeking to gain advantages against other states. The Constitution was created in large part to meet the requirements of conducting international affairs in the modern world.

The founders were firmly resolved that the conduct of foreign policy should be the province of the federal government and not the states. The Constitution bars the states from making treaties or agreements with foreign nations or from levying taxes on imports or exports. And it leaves little doubt about which level of government would possess the greater force. The federal government is given the power to raise armed forces and to assume control over the state militias when necessary to execute the law or protect the nation.

Having decided to make the conduct of foreign affairs the province of the federal government, the founders had then to determine how these powers would be exercised. Here they faced the challenge of finding the institutional arrangement that would preserve republican government at home while allowing for the conduct of an effective foreign policy. These two objectives were of course related, since, as Hamilton wrote, "no government could give us tranquility and happiness at home, which did not possess sufficient stability and strength to make us respectable abroad."[2] Still, this generality left open the question of just how much weight should be given to foreign policy concerns when these conflicted with certain republican ideals.

The Power to Conduct National Defense

Controlling the instruments of force in any society poses one of the great difficulties for any constitution maker. Force is needed to protect a nation, but what is to prevent those in command of this force from using it to take power over the governance of society? Indeed, many are the nations in which military commanders—or political figures who win control of the military—are the real governors of a nation.

Those of the founding generation had a genuine fear of an abuse of military power. As advocates of republican government, they worried that the few who controlled an extensive military force could overawe the rest of society. In the name of protecting republican principles, one group of delegates at the Constitutional Convention wanted to limit the size of the nations's professional armed forces in peacetime. (State militias, by contrast, were viewed as citizen armies that could protect society against military dictatorships.) Notwithstanding the popularity such a limitation would enjoy, the founders rejected it on the grounds that it would remove from government the power to perform one of its essential tasks: providing for the national defense. No one could know in advance what kind of forces

under what circumstances might be needed, and such decisions therefore had to be left to the discretion of those exercising power:

> It is vain to oppose constitutional barriers to the impulse of self-preservation . . . If one nation maintains constantly a disciplined army ready for the service of ambition or revenge, it obliges the most pacific nations who may be within reach of its enterprise to take corresponding precautions (*Federalist* 41)

Even this broad grant of power has not wholly resolved the potential for conflict between security claims and republican principles. At moments of crisis—the Civil War, World War I, and World War II—the federal government has assumed powers that would clearly be of dubious Constitutionality in peacetime, including the limitation and suppression of certain rights such as habeas corpus and freedom of speech. The courts have taken an ambivalent view of these actions, unwilling on the one hand to deny the government the means of self-defense, but reluctant on the other to admit that fundamental Constitutional rights can be abrogated in times of crisis.

The Institutional Machinery for Foreign Policymaking

In devising the institutional arrangement for the conduct of foreign policy, the founders were guided by two principles: to divide up and balance power among different institutions, and to concentrate certain key powers in a relatively strong and independent executive. The first of these principles was widely accepted by the populace at the time, but the second—given the fear of concentrated power in the monarch—took a good deal of persuasion.

The need for a strong executive became evident to some of the founders on the basis of their experience with the conduct of foreign affairs under the government of the Articles, which had no independent executive. There were several instances where, for want of an executive, America suffered minor humiliations or could not pursue its interests. Experience here was seconded by the ideas of the two great theorists of separation of powers—Locke and Montesquieu. They argued that the power to conduct foreign affairs was chiefly executive in nature, by which they meant that foreign affairs often involved a realm where discretion and quick action were needed and where decisions could not be closely guided by general rules or laws. An executive officer—in their times, the king—should therefore have great authority in directing foreign affairs.

Influenced by this thinking, the founders insisted on a unified executive with considerable discretion. Only an energetic presidency would be able to play the intricate game of statecraft on equal terms with other powers, and the founders praised the "decision, activity, secrecy, and despatch" that would allow this branch of government to take advantage of fleeting opportunities, adhere to bold plans, and maintain confidentiality. (*Federalist* 70) Still, taking into account the wishes of the American people and the character of a republican government, the founders did not grant the president anything like a plenary power to conduct foreign affairs. No single individual, freely chosen or not, should be endowed with such extensive powers. Moreover, in a popular system, no major enterprise in foreign affairs could be carried on for long without the active support of the people's representatives. The legislative branch had to be brought in to play a role.

Fearing tyranny if the executive were given full control of foreign policy, and ineffectiveness if this function were conferred upon the legislature, the founders therefore divided control over defense and foreign policymaking between the president and Congress. In this arena, more power was clearly given to the presidency than it possesses in domestic policymaking. With an eye to the respective strengths and weaknesses of each branch, the founders sought to take advantage of the strengths of both institutions by assigning to each the functions for which it was best suited. Some powers are granted to Congress under the lawmaking process, some are shared by the Senate alone with the president, and some are vested in the president.

Congress is given the power to declare war, which is not a law as such and therefore not subject to the president's veto (although it is difficult to imagine how a war could be prosecuted without the president's concurrence). Under the usual lawmaking power, Congress has the general power to lay taxes in order to "provide for the common defense." It is by law as well that the size of the armed forces, their character, and their budget are determined. A president on his own, therefore, has no power to add troops or increase military spending. Finally, Congress has the power to regulate commerce with foreign nations.

The special character of foreign affairs begins to be recognized in the case of solemn agreements reached among nations (treaties). The president makes treaties "by and with the consent of the Senate," by a two-thirds majority. With its smaller membership and longer terms, the Senate alone was thought better able to handle some of the special responsibilities connected with foreign affairs. The Senate also confirms the appointment of ambassadors, consuls, and high-ranking military officers.

The president clearly has a central role in the area of foreign and security affairs. The Constitution makes the president "commander in chief" of American armed forces. In this capacity, the founders understood that under certain circumstances a president might act—even if only defensively—to put the nation in conflict with another nation without, or prior to, a declaration of war. As noted, the president negotiates treaties, which begins to suggest the presidency's preeminent role in directing the nation's diplomacy. The president is also given the power to "receive Ambassadors and other public ministers," which has been interpreted as including the authority to decide whether a foreign government should be accorded diplomatic recognition, a decision that has sometimes had great importance. Finally, the president is vested by Article II with the "executive power," which presidents have regularly interpreted as providing a general power to conduct foreign affairs. This understanding derives from the view that the conduct of foreign affairs is included in the "executive power."

The founders did not try to settle everything about the conduct of foreign and security affairs in the Constitution. They established the institutions with their different and sometimes overlapping and conflicting claims to authority, leaving it to a process of ongoing development to determine the role of each institution. The Constitution has been described as an "invitation to struggle for the privilege of directing American foreign policy."[3] The division of powers in foreign policymaking between the president and the Congress—and even the courts in some instances—has many of the virtues of our political system: checks, balances, and possibilities for readjustment from multiple sources. It also has its inconveniences, and it is not always clear who speaks for the nation. The president takes the lead in negotiating American foreign policy, but sometimes to the great dismay of other nations the product of these negotiations can be modified or even nullified by Congress—as when President Wilson committed the United States to establishing a League of Nations after World War I, only to have this plan rejected by the Senate. In many areas, from foreign aid, to arms sales, to tariffs, foreign nations find that they must deal not only with the president but with the Congress as well. If the United States lacks the unity in foreign policymaking that some other nations possess, this is a price Americans pay for their conception of republican liberty.

The Founders' Conception of International Politics

The Constitution sets forth the federal government's powers and distributes authority in the foreign policymaking process, but it obviously does not define the nation's conception of international politics. The ends to be pursued have been a matter for definition and debate. During the founding era two very different views were articulated by Thomas Jefferson and Alexander Hamilton, and both have had an impact ever since on the way Americans think about foreign policy (see Box 17.1).

Jefferson favored the view that nations and individuals were—or, rather, could be—governed by the same ethical code. Traditional diplomatic practice, it was true, had fallen short of this rule: nations behaved much worse toward one another than did individuals. But this was the result of unrepresentative governments ruled by aggressive monarchs and selfish nobles who were used to practicing fraud and deceit. Honest, open, and responsible republican govern-

ment could, by its deeds and its example, introduce a higher standard of conduct into diplomacy than that of traditional conceptions of national interest. It was possible, Jefferson believed, to overcome the conflict in foreign policy between what republican principles demanded and expediency required.

Hamilton, by contrast, held that the rules governing behavior between nations and individuals must differ. Nations must of necessity be guided by harsher standards that considered their interest. As this was the standard that other nations would adopt, republican governments like America must regrettably learn to play by some of the same rules. Rather than seeking to overturn the diplomatic system which rested on these harsh realities (an unrealizable goal), Hamilton argued that the United States would have to make itself proficient in all the traditional diplomatic arts practiced by nonrepublican systems. Hamilton worried that his fellow countrymen, misled by the "dream of a golden age" of peace, might fail to make adequate provisions for protecting their own security.

Conflict between the Hamiltonian and Jeffersonian philosophies broke into the open in the 1790s in the debate over whether to honor the Franco-American Treaty of 1778 by supporting revolutionary France in its war against Great Britain. Was the United States, like an individual, bound by a debt of gratitude to a nation which had aided it in the past? Jefferson's Democratic-Republicans generally said yes. And they seemed to think that by following the noble sentiments of republicanism in the conduct of world affairs, they could remake the world of international politics in the image of American principles. Hamilton's Federalists generally said no to support for France, believing it was not in America's interest to ally itself with Britain's enemy when Britain ruled the seas. The conduct of international politics, they argued, could not be fundamentally changed by the new methods of republican diplomacy, so the country would have to accommodate itself to the realities of the outside world.

BOX 17.1

The Ongoing Debate Over Foreign Policy and Ethics

"I know but one code of morality for man whether acting singly or collectively. He who says I will be a rogue when I act in company with a hundred others but an honest man when I act alone, will be believed in the former assertion, but not in the latter. . . . Let us hope that our new government will take some . . . occasion to show that they mean to proscribe no virtue from the canons of their conduct with other nations." —Thomas Jefferson, 1789

"We have an inevitable role of leadership to play. . . . But our foreign policy ought not be based on military might nor political power nor economic pressures. It ought to be based on the fact that we are right and decent and honest and truthful and predictable and respectful; in other words, that our foreign policy itself accurately represents the character and ideals of the American people. But it doesn't. We have set a different standard of ethics and morality as a nation than we have in our own private lives as individuals who comprise the nation. And that ought to be changed." —Jimmy Carter, 1975

"It may be affirmed as a general principle, that the predominant motive of good offices from one nation to another is the interest or advantage of the Nations, which performs them. . . . The rule of morality is [in] this respect not exactly the same between Nations as between individuals. The duty of making [its] own welfare the guide of its action is much stronger upon the former than upon the latter. . . ." —Alexander Hamilton, 1793

"It is part of American folklore that, while other nations have interests, we have responsibilities; while other nations are concerned with equilibrium, we are concerned with the legal requirements of peace. We have a tendency to offer our altruism as a guarantee of our reliability. . . . Such an attitude makes it difficult to develop a conception of our role in the world. It inhibits other nations from gearing their policy to ours in a confident way—a `disinterested' policy is likely to be considered `unreliable.' . . . Principle, however lofty, must at some point be related to practice. . . . Interest is not necessarily amoral; moral consequences can spring from interested acts." —Henry Kissinger, 1968

Source: Julian Boyd, ed., *The Papers of Thomas Jefferson,* vol. 15 (Princeton, N.J.: Princeton University Press, 1958), p. 367; Jimmy Carter, *Public Papers of the President of the United States,* vol. 1 (Washington, D.C.: National Archives, 1977), pp. 71–72; Harold C. Syrett, ed., *Papers of Alexander Hamilton* (New York: Columbia University Press, 1969); Henry Kissinger, *American Foreign Policy* (New York: Norton, 1969), pp. 91–93.

Either one of these approaches to international affairs, if pursued dogmatically, could lead to failure or disaster, as events during the era of the Napoleonic Wars (1793–1815) demonstrated. The Federalist view that the needs of foreign policy had to override domestic scruples led to the enactment of the Alien and Sedition Acts of 1798, which attempted to halt domestic criticism of the Adams Administration's foreign policy. Here, the argument for the priority of foreign affairs was carried too far, resulting in a threat to fundamental liberties that in turn caused a huge domestic reaction against the oppressive measures of the national government that split the country. On the other hand, Republican attempts to conduct foreign affairs on the basis of Jeffersonian principles after 1800 led to Jefferson's disastrous "experiment" in international affairs—an embargo of trade with Britain and France in 1807. This policy, designed as a substitute for military action that would compel others to recognize American interests, failed to sway either of these warring nations. It severely disrupted the American economy and eventually helped to bring on what it had been designed to avoid—a war in 1812 with Great Britain, for which the United States was militarily unprepared.

Never were the alternatives more starkly posed. If the United States concluded that the "primacy of foreign policy" and the seriousness of outside threats demanded a yielding of its principles, it could lose liberties in areas of domestic life where foreign policy impinged upon them. If the United States assumed that the methods used in its domestic politics could be easily transferred to its foreign relations, it could be taken advantage of and blunder into situations where war or surrender were the only options. The choice here posed a problem that has continued throughout our history.

The Development of American Foreign Policy

The end of the Napoleonic Wars brought a much more favorable set of circumstances for the United States which left it relatively free to pursue its own moral and political consensus without fearing interference by powerful outside forces. Guided by what it called its "manifest destiny" to occupy North America from the Atlantic to the Pacific, the United States expanded across a vast continent. Because the continent was largely uninhabited, it could be subdued without many of the military and diplomatic methods that Americans criticized in other nations. For those who looked more closely, of course, the war against Mexico in 1848 and the constant fraud and force exercised against the Indian nations revealed the reality of a harsher imperial policy. Yet most Americans did not see these policies so much as a part of foreign affairs as part of a providentially inspired project to settle our own continent.

Sheltered by the British Navy, the United States could issue the Monroe Doctrine in 1823 to oppose further European colonization in the Americas, assert the rights of neutrals in wartime, and proclaim its principles concerning freedom of the seas with relative safety. It seemed plausible that American efforts to bring world politics under the rule of law were succeeding without resort to the practices of old-world diplomacy, such as spheres of influence or the balance of power. In pursuing its objective of promoting republican government in the world, America followed a policy of relying on its own example rather than involving itself in military adventures. Because it saw the liberalizing, democratizing trend of history moving in its direction, there was no reason to interfere with the building of the good society at home in order to hurry the process abroad. Thus in 1821, when presented with demands that the nation do something to aid Latin Americans

struggling to overthrow Spanish colonialism, Secretary of State John Quincy Adams replied:

> Wherever the standard of freedom and independence has been or shall be unfurled, there will be America's heart, her benedictions, and her prayers. But she goes not abroad in search of monsters to destroy. She is the well-wisher to the freedom and independence of all. She is the champion and vindicator only of her own.[4]

For most of the nineteenth century, the United States lived in a unique and protected set of circumstances. As James Bryce observed in 1889, "America lives in a world of her own. . . . Safe from attack, safe even from menace, she hears from afar the warring cries of European races and faiths."[5] This situation allowed Americans to speak in noble terms reminiscent of Jefferson, while living sheltered from the harsh realities of international politics. Americans could believe that by their isolation they were still promoting republican values throughout the world. And to some extent they were. But it was the happy set of circumstances more than anything else that allowed Americans to enjoy their successes. For nearly a century, the American people did not have to ponder the possible conflict in less favorable circumstances between an effective diplomacy and the preservation of their own liberties.

The Early Twentieth Century

The early twentieth century brought the United States into greater contact with the world. An American flirtation with imperialism outside the continental United States went on from about 1895 to 1905. Pursuit of this policy gained the country a handful of colonies—including the Philippines and Puerto Rico—as the result of a short and relatively painless war against Spain. It ended, however, before the ideas of leaders such as Theodore Roosevelt became accepted American beliefs.

Woodrow Wilson eventually proved as willing as Roosevelt to employ the power of the United States abroad, though at the service of different ends. Whereas Roosevelt had sought to join the traditional game of diplomacy in order to secure and protect hard and often materialistic national interests, Wilson went to war in order to promote American ideals and to punish those who flagrantly violated them in their domestic political institutions or their international conduct. Wilson adopted a view that had Jeffersonian overtones, although he allowed for the use of force in one great crusade designed to change the face of the world and make possible a new kind of diplomacy. In fighting World War I to "make the world safe for democracy," Wilson planned a peace afterwards in which the United States would play an ongoing role in a new world organization, the League of Nations. Jeffersonian ends were realizable, in Wilson's view, but only if the United States was prepared to commit its noble impulses to continuous involvement on the world scene.

Wilson's effort to create a new world order ended in failure. The Senate rejected the Versailles peace treaty, which Wilson personally had negotiated in Paris, because of opposition to the proposed form of the League of Nations. Leading senators like Henry Cabot Lodge were dubious of Wilson's great dreams and wary that the United States would have to sacrifice part of its independence to a new international body. The Senate's rejection of the League was in effect endorsed in the election of 1920, when Warren G. Harding was chosen president after opposing the League during the campaign. American foreign policy now changed directions. The actions of the United States were guided for the next twenty years by a policy of isolationism. The United States wished to have economic but not political or security ties to other countries. To the extent that these other countries imitated American domestic arrangements, they would be favorably regarded; if they chose not to do so, the United States might criticize them but would not attempt to persuade or force them to change their ways. In essence, American conduct was Jeffersonian in its determination not to let the demands of foreign policy interfere with its domestic concerns, but it lacked the concern with the outside world and the buoyant confidence in pressing America's example on the rest of the world that Jefferson's followers had displayed.

The Cold War

All this changed with the Second World War, a global upheaval that required a complete rethinking of American diplomacy. The United States, against its will and inclinations, was thrust onto the center stage of international affairs. From then on, the United States had to deal not with overmatched Indian tribes or a collapsing Spanish empire, but with powerful nations resolute in promoting their interests. The United States could no longer avoid the "corrupt" diplomacy of the old world. It was forced to deal with the new and unprecedented threats first of Nazism and Fascism and then of communism.

Three conditions defined the environment in which the United States found itself after World War II. First, there was a dramatic increase in the search for military security (and a difficulty of obtaining it). World War II marked the final collapse of a European balance of power that had protected American security since the days of Napoleon. If any nation was to counterbalance the Soviet Union in the postwar period, it was the United States. The term "Cold War" denoted a relationship of hostility between the United States and the Soviet Union deep enough to keep the world in a state of tension and fear, but in which the two antagonists never directly engaged in armed conflict. From the American perspective, the Cold War emerged out of a double (and largely overlapping) threat posed at the end of World War II: the ideology of communism and the increased power of the Soviet Union. Communism was deeply hostile to America's political, social, economic, and religious principles, while Soviet power threatened the freedom of other nations and ultimately that of the United States itself. The possession by both superpowers of nuclear weapons and the lack of any equal competitors made them both global powers, with a greater reach and more widespread interests than those held by dominant nations in previous eras. Yet the nature of the worldwide system of conflict and of modern weaponry made security, in the sense in which that term was used before World War II, all but impossible. The threat of immediate nuclear destruction deprived the United States of the margin of security that in the past had given it

---

BOX 17.2

Major Events in American Diplomacy in the Postwar Era

1945: Establishment of the United Nations.

1947: Announcement of the Truman Doctrine enunciating the policy of containment.

1948–51: The Marshall Plan, providing American financial assistance to Europe.

1949: Negotiation of the North Atlantic Treaty Organization (NATO).

1950–53: The Korean War between South Korea, supported by the United Nations (principally the United States) and North Korea, supported by China and the Soviet Union.

1953: Announcement of the doctrine of "massive retaliation," under which the United States threatened to respond to aggression supported by the Soviet Union by attacking the Soviet Union itself.

1962: The Cuban missile crisis, in which the United States and the Soviet Union went to the brink of nuclear war over the Soviet attempt to secretly place nuclear missiles in Cuba.

1964–73: United States involvement in the Vietnam War.

1972: Ratification of the SALT I agreement, limiting the strategic arsenals of the United States and the Soviet Union.

1972: Visit by President Nixon to communist China.

1979: Invasion of Afghanistan by Soviet forces.

1982–83: Extensive American involvement in Central America through open military assistance to the government of El Salvador and covert CIA support for rebels opposing the Nicaraguan regime.

1983: President Reagan announces Strategic Defense Initiative (Star Wars).

1989: Soviets withdraw from Afghanistan; hard-line communist governments fall in Poland, Hungary, East Germany, Czechoslovakia, Bulgaria, and Romania; Berlin Wall taken down.

1989: U.S. invades Panama and apprehends General Manuel Noriega on drug trafficking charges.

1991: U.S. leads an international coalition against Iraq in the Gulf War.

1995: The United States mediates the Dayton Accords in an attempt to bring peace to the former Yugoslavia. American troops are sent to Bosnia as peacekeepers.

1999: U. S. leads NATO attack against Serbian forces to protect Kosovars.

2001: Terrorists attack Pentagon and World Trade Center. War on terrorism begins in Afghanistan.

---

time to arm and prepare. Mobilization, far from being a wartime expedient, became continuous, and thus vastly more expensive.

Second, there was a breakdown in the minimal consensus on international norms that had existed during much of American history. The gulf in ideology that separated the United States from the Soviet Union made the international environment seem all the more threatening. Any setback for Washington and its allies could be interpreted as a defeat not only in terms of power but also for its most basic values. Disagreement between the world's two major powers on first principles also weakened the world's

institutional means for settling disputes; organizations like the United Nations depend for success on a certain level of consensus at least among the major powers. Thus, even as it complicated disputes over interests, ideological division also hindered their possible solution.

Finally, despite grave differences, the two superpowers also ironically came to share a common "interest" in avoiding the catastrophe of a nuclear war between themselves. The existence of nuclear weapons revolutionized international relations by placing new limits on how far major powers could go in expressing their hostility, which helps explain why, in a period of tremendous tension and suspicion, there was no hot war between Washington and Moscow. Repelled by their clashing interests and ideological enmity, the superpowers were simultaneously drawn together by their knowledge of the perils they both faced if their struggle should get out of hand.

Containment and the Cold War (1948–1968)
The postwar years tested American diplomacy and drew attention to geographical areas never before considered proper objects of American foreign policy. Faced with these new problems, the major political parties and most important leaders reached a consensus on the basic outlines of the conduct of foreign policy. This period of consensus can be dated from the presidential election of 1948, in which the two major candidates (Harry S. Truman for the Democrats and Thomas E. Dewey for the Republicans) adopted similar positions of strong opposition toward the Soviet Union, until President Lyndon Johnson's second term (1965–1968), when differences over the conduct of the war in Vietnam splintered the American populace and the Democratic party.

During the years of consensus, American public opinion was broadly united in support of containment as the proper course to follow in the Cold War. The policy of containment was adopted under a Democratic President (Harry S. Truman) and then embraced by a Republican President (Dwight Eisenhower). It was directed at "containing" communism and the Soviet Union—that is, at ensuring that communism and Soviet control did not expand to nations beyond those where communism was adopted or had been imposed at the end of World War II. Although essentially defensive in its strategy, containment nonetheless held out the hope that once the Soviet Union's prospects for expansion were blocked, it might begin to lose confidence in its ideology, prompting a modification of its system. Containment won broad public support and the backing of both political parties. It could be justified as a defense of both American principles and American interests, without being directly aggressive in character.

This consensus was also reflected in the emergence of a relatively small and informal group of like-minded people that came to be referred to as the "foreign policy establishment." Drawn from the world of finance, the great law firms, universities, private foundations, media, industry and labor unions, this informal group saw itself as helping to steer American foreign policy and to avoid partisan strife. This network was united by its interest in and knowledge of foreign affairs, and was influential in shaping public opinion and in providing experts for foreign policy and Defense Department posts in administrations of both parties. Although this group helped to lead public opinion, it could only operate inside of a broader public consensus. When the country divided over questions of foreign policy in the 1960s, consensus ended among members of the establishment as well.

In addition to the build-up of American military strength during this period, other instruments were employed to pursue America's interests. Alliance systems like the North Atlantic Treaty Organization (NATO), the Southeast Asia Treaty Organization (SEATO), and the Japanese-American Mutual Security Treaty were created to deter war. International organizations such as the International Monetary Fund (IMF), the International Bank for Reconstruction and Development (IBRD), and the General Agreement on Tariffs and Trade (GATT) were established to improve economic relations and facilitate trade. Through agencies like the Voice of America and Radio Free Europe, the United States directed information campaigns. Finally, America developed a much more substantial intelligence capacity in the CIA (Central Intelligence Agency) and began to use covert actions to promote security objectives. In Iran in 1953 and Guatemala in 1954, the CIA provided arms and logistical assistance to pro-U.S. forces which overthrew pro-communist or anti-western regimes.

There were instances when the United States either went to the brink of, or entered, warfare. In 1950, when the Soviet-sponsored regime in North Korea attacked its American-supported counterpart in South Korea, the United States organized an international response through the United Nations and threw its own forces into the battle. The U.S. suffered heavy casualties, especially when China entered the war to save North Korea. America fought through three more painful years until an armistice could be arranged that restored the situation to what it had been before the war. In Lebanon in 1958 and again in the Dominican Republic in 1965, Washington dispatched troops to small countries thought to be in danger of takeover by communist or communist-backed forces. In the Cuban missile crisis of 1962, the world came as close as it ever has to nuclear destruction. The prospect of a nuclear exchange between the superpowers appeared very real until the Soviet Union acceded to the United States' demand to remove the intermediate-range missiles it had installed in Cuba.

The longest and most difficult of these conflicts came in Vietnam. A gradually increasing series of commitments to South Vietnam under Presidents Truman, Eisenhower, and Kennedy culminated in full-fledged military involvement in that country's war with communist North Vietnam. It began under President Johnson and then continued under President Nixon. American participation ended with the negotiated withdrawal of American forces in early 1973. The war continued, however, and in the spring of 1975 the Saigon government fell to the North Vietnamese. The United States had lost more than 50,000 lives and spent billions of dollars in a losing cause.

The Postconsensus Years (1969–1980) The Vietnam War destroyed the foundation of support for the policy of containment. Bipartisanship dissolved into mutual recriminations over the conduct of the war and post-war America's role in the world. Many now denounced an activist posture for the United States, claiming that the United States not only was trying to act as the "world's policeman," but also was acting often on the wrong side. Looking back on history, some now argued that the Cold War had actually been more the responsibility of Washington than Moscow. A segment of American leadership and the public now rejected the policy of containment, calling for a less aggressive and less militarized foreign policy. They demanded that America focus not so much on the evils of communism as on the authoritarian or corrupt regimes that America had tolerated or supported in the name of containing communism.

As a result of the Vietnam War, the United States throughout much of the 1970s and 1980s was split apart by differences over foreign policy and the nation's place in the world. Every move in foreign policy brought dissension and recrimination. Foreign policy was argued in highly moralistic terms, with persons on each side vilifying the other. During the 1970s America's military superiority over the Soviet Union also disappeared as defense resources were diverted to the Vietnam War and as opposition to containment produced a reaction against military spending.

The incoming Nixon administration put forth the first attempted substitute for containment: detente. The objective, as President Nixon said, was to move "from an era of confrontation to an era of negotiation" through an emphasis on forces for cooperation between the superpowers.[6] While superpower relations would still be competitive, the Soviet Union could be dealt with pragmatically on the basis of its interests. There would be less ideological denunciation of communism and a tacit admission that America could live with communism if it seemed to renounce its revolutionary project. Trade and contact with the communist world would also build up connections and a web of interests, perhaps softening the character of communism. The assumption of the "deideologization" of Soviet policy meant that American policy could be less concerned with questions of ideology as well. The policy of detente was promoted by the practical step of establishing a relationship with communist China, which could serve as a useful counterweight to the greater power of the Soviet Union.

Nixon and his chief adviser Henry Kissinger intended our own de-emphasis on ideology as a way of preventing moralistic crusades in foreign policy that might drag the country into conflicts. Detente as practiced from 1969 to 1977 received widespread credit for being sober, judicious, and realistic. But the policy was also criticized as mistaken or amoral from both the Right and the Left. Conservative critics (mostly within the Republican party), argued that by refusing to be outspoken in condemning the tyranny of communism, the Nixon and Ford administrations were sapping the country's will to stand up to communism and to appreciate its threat. Liberal critics argued that by ignoring widespread human rights abuses throughout the world, but especially in authoritarian governments whom we supported because they were deemed strategically vital, the United States had lost its greatest strength—its moral position. Both conservatives and liberals felt that treating foreign policy simply as a matter of hard national interests was not enough.

The Carter administration became known for making the protection of "human rights" a key element of American foreign policy. Efforts at detente with the Soviets would be continued, but the United States would also conduct a campaign for human rights around the world. Opponents of the administration—including conservatives as well as many of the original architects of detente, such as Nixon and Kissinger—charged that Carter's emphasis on human rights was naive, because it failed to focus on the central problem: Soviet communism's threat to destroy the west and spread its totalitarianism system. This was the greatest danger to human rights. Foreign policy became a potent issue in the 1980 campaign and an important factor in President Carter's defeat.

The ongoing debate in this period had overtones of the early foreign policy struggle between Hamiltonians and Jeffersonians. The Nixon-Ford-Kissinger approach, like that of the Federalists of the 1790s, was to take national interest as the guide for American diplomacy and to look with suspicion on calls for morality in international politics. Members of the Carter administration, like the Democratic-Republicans of the 1800s, felt that the United States was bound by standards of personal morality much as any private person. In 1980 the voters questioned both courses by electing Ronald Reagan, who offered a foreign policy that wove together strands of both traditions.

Containment Renewed (1981–1989) President Reagan came to office pledging to "rearm America" and to draw a clear line again between liberal democracy and Communism. Reagan followed through with a substantial—and controversial—program of increased defense spending and an even more controversial campaign of drawing a clear moral line between liberal democracy and communism.

Containment of Soviet expansionism was restored to a central place in U.S. policy, and assistance was given to countries that seemed endangered by Soviet-sponsored subversion. President Carter's universalistic human rights policy was downplayed, at least initially, with the emphasis given instead to the threat posed by the Soviet Union and communism, not only to our own security but to human rights as well. The Reagan Administration, in fact, went somewhat beyond restoring containment and strengthening deterrence. Convinced that containment alone was defensive and passive, Reagan attempted on several levels to orchestrate a Western counteroffensive. He sought to rekindle an intense opposition to communism within the American public, at one point infuriating some of his critics by baldly referring to the Soviet Union as an "evil empire." Information campaigns aimed at the Soviet bloc were intensified, and greater controls on technology transfers were enforced. The Strategic Defense Initiative, a research program launched by Reagan in March 1983 to develop an effective defense against ballistic missiles, threatened to unbalance the power relationship and to engage the Soviets in a technological race where they were ill-equipped to compete.

The counteroffensive took its most dramatic form in the "Reagan Doctrine," a policy of supporting indigenous anti-communist guerrillas in an attempt to roll back Soviet influence in Afghanistan, Angola, Cambodia, and Nicaragua. The invasion of Grenada in 1983 by U.S. forces, which toppled a pro-Soviet regime, was a more direct manifestation of this roll-back policy. The Reagan Doctrine was highly controversial, largely because it was offensive in nature, and involved open military support for forces attempting to overthrow existing foreign governments.

The administration's generally Hamiltonian or power politics means, however, were in large measure put in the service of a Jeffersonian or "moral" ends. Reagan made a worldwide expansion of democracy a central theme of his foreign policy, built on a foundation that saw self-government and individual liberty not as American values but as universal values embraced and exemplified by America. The hoped-for victory against the Soviets in the Cold War was considered not merely an end in itself but a necessary precondition to a world of greater liberty. America also began to move—sometimes over the immediate objections of the Reagan administration—to support democratic alternatives to friendly but undemocratic governments when such alternatives were viable, such as in the Philippines in 1986.

The Reagan administration's foreign policy drew fire from several quarters. It was opposed by liberals who objected to its emphasis on military strength and foreign intervention, and its re-emphasis on the "evil" of Soviet Communism, which they thought would ignite a major conflict. Some "pragmatists" or realists also feared the ideological offensive as a dangerous "crusade." And there were congressional critics who feared that the frequent use of covert operations would reduce congressional influence over policy. Nevertheless, by the end of Reagan's presidency, much of the criticism had died down. The United States had gotten its way on many points. And far from growing worse, world tensions were subsiding. In fact, with reform-minded Mikhail Gorbachev in power in Moscow, the Cold War itself was entering a new and more benign phase.

The End of the Cold War and the Defining Characteristics of the Modern Era

President George H. Bush's Administration faced a dramatically changed situation in international politics. By the beginning of the 1990s, America's long-term objective—one which it had almost given up on as a practical goal—had come to pass. In July 1989, the Soviet Union repudiated the Brezhnev Doctrine, through which it had justified its 1968 invasion and occupation of Czechoslovakia. Within eighteen months all of the Communist states of Eastern Europe were moving toward free market capitalism and liberal democracy. Soon afterward, the United States witnessed the reunification of Germany and the collapse of the Soviet Union itself, with only Cuba and China remaining communist (but with the Chinese no longer trying to sell communist ideology to other nations). The downfall of the Soviet empire and communism was one of the most important historical transformations in the last two centuries.

The change took place in several stages. First Gorbachev himself initiated major changes inside the Soviet Union that were designed to reform and renew communism. Similar steps were taken inside some of the Eastern European satellite states. The process began to spin out of control, and instead of reforming communism people began to seek its demise. Some of the communist governments in Eastern Europe then fell, and the Soviet Union did not intervene to protect the communist regimes. Then the Soviet Union itself disintegrated, and communism was rejected. Today, no nation from the former Warsaw Pact claims to be communist. From an empire were carved out twenty-seven states (including the former Soviet republics and Eastern Europe). In addition, communism as an ideology has lost almost all of its attraction throughout the Third World.

There has been much speculation about the causes of this change. Some have argued that United States military preponderance throughout the 1980s drove the Soviet Union into submission, while others have maintained that Soviet economic mismanagement led to the empire's ultimate demise. Although it remains a matter of debate exactly how much American policies in the 1980s contributed to, or coincided with, the welcome turn of events, the overall steadfastness of American policy clearly had an impact on the collapse of the Soviet Union.

The early 1990s brought a change to the whole structure of international relations and of security policy as it had been known since World War II. As President George H. Bush declared in his 1991 State of the Union Address: "The end of the Cold War has been a victory for all humanity. . . . Europe has become whole and free—and America's leadership was instrumental in making it possible." The Soviet Union was no longer America's adversary and the United States offered its hand to the states that took its place.

In a 1993 address before the American Society of Newspaper Editors, President Clinton declared that "the opportunity lies before our nation . . . to answer the courageous call of Russian reform—as an expression of our own values, as an investment in our own security and prosperity . . . as a demonstration of our purpose in a new world."

As Americans celebrated success in the forty-year struggle against communism, they faced a new set of questions and a new challenge: what was America's role to be in the new world situation? The enormity of this long-term question was postponed by the organizing of a coalition of international military forces that ousted Iraq from Kuwait in 1991. In the aftermath of this war, President George H. Bush promised to work to create "a new world order" based on the universal recognition of the international rule of law, and backed up presumably by the United Nations and by American military might. The war demonstrated that even in a post-Cold War world there remained threats to American interests and security that would require the use of force. While superpower competition has ended, the world is neither peaceful nor stable.

The Gulf War also showed the importance of the United States to the creation and maintenance of the "new world order." America was the only power, on its own, that could project large amounts of force beyond its immediate geographical area. American military power dwarfed that of other nations and the United States remained the world's only "superpower." This has recently been reconfirmed with the so far successful prosecution of a war against the Al Qaeda terrorist network in the difficult and distant terrain of Afghanistan. And the form of government America espouses—liberal democracy—has been more widely acclaimed and has been embraced by more nations than ever before. Americans recognize the important role this nation plays in the world, and active public debate over foreign affairs by American leaders has recently increased dramatically.

The Post-Cold War World

America's preeminent objective during the Cold War was the protection of its national security and vital interests from the threats posed by the Soviet Union and its communist ideology. National security was defined predominantly in military-political terms, and there was a tendency to try to conduct foreign policy in a way that would insulate it from many domestic, economic interests. The end of the Cold War has transformed this situation.

One change of the post-Cold War world is a decline in the importance of ideology as a world-wide organizing principle. This change should help foster greater consensus on international norms, perhaps creating a more peaceful international arena. But it does not eliminate all threats to peace. Cultural, ethnic, and religious differences have in some cases taken the place of ideology, and states have begun to interact more exclusively on the basis of traditional and often antagonistic national interests.

A second change of the post-Cold War has been a strengthening of international and transnational organizations such as the United Nations, the European Community, and the Asia-Pacific Economic Cooperation. The expanded role for the United Nations has been the most striking part of this development. Paralyzed during the Cold War by the struggle between communism and liberal democracy, the United Nations has recently been used to play the role of peacekeeper in international crises and mediator of international issues.

Finally, economic concerns have assumed greater importance in world politics, as the world's nations have become increasingly interdependent. The end of the Cold War has made many states less willing to sacrifice economic interests in order to protect security concerns. American partners in Western Europe and Japan—recipients of American aid after World War II—have become keen economic competitors, and Europe itself continues to integrate economically. The definition of "national security" gradually has also been expanded to include some new, non-traditional issues such as protecting the environment and promoting international health.

With the greater emphasis today on these economic and non-traditional concerns, distinctions between foreign and domestic issues are no longer as clear they may once have seemed. During the nineteenth century diplomacy focused primarily on questions of "high politics"—the drawing of national boundaries, the extension of sovereignty over other countries or areas, issues of war and peace. Today, the United States government has committed itself to economic cooperation with its friends and allies, and this commitment sometimes conflicts with domestic economic concerns. The greater involvement of the federal government in regulating many more fields of activity than it did in the past forces it to weigh competing foreign and domestic demands. In addition, the other new issues that have been added to the policymaking agenda—the environment, energy, population, and food cannot be handled by diplomacy alone; all touch important domestic interests and require careful negotiations with other countries and continuous domestic political bargaining. In sum, domestic and foreign concerns have become ever more tightly linked with each other.

The 1990s Debate Over American Foreign Policy and the War on Terrorism

Faced with these new circumstances, American parties and leaders began trying to define a new general course for American foreign policy. With the Cold War over, people began asking, what now? The answer depends on a view of our own power, the nature of threats, and of what we wanted to try to accomplish in the world.

Some favored a policy of neo-isolationism. Proponents of this position argued that we had no major threat as we did during the Cold War and that therefore we can turn away from constant international involvement, focus on domestic issues, and protect our interests abroad only when it is necessary. American commitments abroad could be substantially reduced by withdrawing troops from Europe and Asia. America should end most of its ventures in peacemaking and nation-building, at least where any commitment of American troops or money were required. The world would continue to experience a great deal of disorder and strife, but little of this would affect America's vital interests. America should remain strong but detached, asserting itself only in the very few instances in which the national interest is clearly at stake.

Another group conceives of a new world order of human rights, peace, and morality in which America plays a substantial role in conjunction with various international organizations. In this view, American participation and leadership are essential parts of this new order, but the task of managing the new order does not require any extensive new military power or any new exercise of American will. Pursuing ethical issues and the interests of peace can be handled with the current level of commitment to foreign policy.

Finally, there are some who favored a policy of global leadership in which the exercise of American action and will are the decisive factors in achieving global peace and stability. Adherents of this view argued that the United States must be deeply involved in international affairs and must attempt to shape the world to promote liberal democratic values and American interests. America would have to assume a more active role, calling on other nations to follow its lead and being willing on occasion to act on its own. This policy would require a vigilant military and a willingness to take short-term risks in order to avoid what could develop into long-term problems. Accepting global leadership entails more responsibilities, but it offers new opportunities as well.

The crises in Bosnia and Kosovo in the 1990s brought some of these policy disputes to the surface by raising the question of when and under what conditions the United States should be willing to use military force in a post-Cold War world. Throughout much of the Cold War, this question had a fairly easy answer: the United States must be prepared to use force whenever and wherever the Soviet Union threatened its interests. But in the post-Cold War world, the answer is not so clear: should force be used to promote American values, like human rights and democracy, and to promote a world in which certain actions and forms of aggression are proven not to pay? Or should force only be used when America or its allies are directly attacked? How much military risk and national treasure is appropriate for each goal?

For the moment, events, or the force of necessity, have decided these questions and changed the character of foreign policy debate. After the terrorist attacks on the World Trade Center and the Pentagon on September 11, 2001, President George W. Bush has taken the position that

America must exercise global leadership, through a variety of military and economic means, to prevent terrorism. George W. Bush has argued for a proactive and aggressive foreign policy, rather than reactive or defensive one. The "Bush Doctrine" has three extremely ambitious tasks. America will (1) act preemptively against terrorist enemies and the regimes that support them; (2) reduce the threat of war among nations by maintaining its military supremacy, and build coalitions to solve regional conflicts; and (3) promote "tolerance and human rights" in Islamic and other countries where freedom is lacking. This doctrine marks a significant shift in American foreign policy from the largely defensive policy of containment to an aggressively internationalist one where America acts alone and calls on other countries to follow its lead.

The Foreign Policymaking Process in the Modern World

The Constitution divides the power to conduct foreign relations in a complex way between the president and the Congress and sets up a framework in which these two institutions exercise power—sometimes in harmony, sometimes in competition. On top of this, the challenges of the Cold War gave birth to new institutions for decision-making. This section analyzes the nation's foreign policymaking machinery within the executive branch, between the president and the Congress, and the general nature of policymaking in the foreign policy arena.

The Presidency and Growth of the Foreign Policymaking Machinery in the Executive Branch

Today, as before, the primary conduct of the nation's foreign policy falls to the president and the executive departments. Much of the goals are achieved under laws that have been passed. But there is much that law does not cover, and even where laws are involved they often remain ambiguous. However, the executive branch—and ultimately the president—has the greater authority in foreign policy.

The Problem of Unity The management of foreign policy since World War II has been greatly complicated by the growth in the size and complexity of the defense and national security apparatus. The executive branch in this period has been enlarged by the addition of new agencies, an expanded work force, and increased budgets. Much of this growth occurred in the nation's armed forces (which decreased in the 1990s), but it also has resulted from the performance of certain tasks on a wholly new scale, such as the collection and analysis of intelligence. In addition, the emphasis in foreign policy on economic, environmental, and health issues has brought into the process many agencies, such as the Commerce and Energy departments and the Environmental Protection Agency, that were previously concerned with only domestic matters.

This buildup in administrative structure threatens the unity and vigor needed for successful executive leadership in foreign affairs. The process of bargaining among contending agencies can be time-consuming and can result in decisions which, while unobjectionable to the agencies concerned, are ineffective. "A plurality in the Executive," Hamilton warned, "tends to conceal faults and destroy responsibility."[7] While the country has but one president at a time, the proliferation of agencies supposedly under presidential direction, but actually often pursuing goals of their own, has become in many cases the functional equivalent of a plural executive. Foreign policy must be negotiated within the United States government before it can be discussed with other nations.

Debates over the defense budget illustrate the problem. National security thinking holds that the defense budget should be based on a logical assessment of the threats facing the United States, from which defense planners determine about the size and type of military forces required and the equipment needed. In reality, the bureaucratic processes of the executive branch play an important role, as rivalry and logrolling occur among different bureaucratic agencies. Within the military, for example, the Navy may prefer an F-14 fighter and the Air Force the F-15. Money spent on equipment will mean less spent on training for peace-keeping missions abroad—keeping troops in Bosnia was one example—which may be favored by the State Department. In this way, bureaucratic rivalries complicate an already complex process. As another example, the increasing frequency of international discussions like the 1992 Earth Summit held in Rio de Janiero means the involvement of executive agencies like the Environmental Protection Agency and the Department of Energy.

The National Security Act of 1947 was an attempt to bring order to the foreign relations machinery. It created a National Security Council (NSC) to promote consultation among the agencies immediately concerned with foreign affairs (chiefly the State and Defense departments). The NSC would advise the president and help coordinate the implementation of presidential decisions. While the NSC constituted a determined effort to restore unity to policymaking, its success has been limited. Struggles among agencies and organizations over the direction of American foreign policy continue. And in a striking reversal of the original intentions of the National Security Act, during the Nixon and Carter Administrations the NSC Advisors—Henry Kissinger and Zbigniew Brzezinski—themselves became rivals of the State Department. The coordinating body, instead of providing for consultation, began to master the bodies it was designed to coordinate, acting as a "little State Department" in the White House. The policymaking role of the NSC was seen most dramatically in the Iran-Contra operation, when members of the NSC staff carried out an operation opposed by and unknown to the secretaries of State and Defense. As a result of the furor and investigations that followed this incident, the NSC has had its role scaled back to advice and coordination.

Another problem in certain areas of foreign policymaking is that bureaucratic agencies with a claim to be consulted have proliferated faster than the responses designed to restore some centralized control over them. For example, there are some thirty-five agencies and bureaus within the federal government that exercise some function within the so-called "intelligence" community, from the Central Intelligence Agency to the Department of Energy and, increasingly, to the Drug Enforcement Agency.

A degree of plurality within the executive in foreign policymaking has some positive effects. Struggles among agencies ensure that certain interests are represented and that differences can come to the president's attention. Many decisions today rest on such complex calculations that no central planner can easily take into account all the necessary considerations. Bureaucratic resistance sometimes provides a way for the benefits and costs of any policy to be more accurately weighed. But there obviously comes a point at which the struggles become more harmful than helpful and prevent the effective implementation of policies.

This picture of bureaucratic politics, while accurate in the main, should not be exaggerated. With sufficient attention and energy, presidents can usually impose a temporary unity of will on squabbling agencies, at least in certain areas. This may require working around certain agencies, excluding some from the loop, and exercising firm control at the top. A president, in short, often needs to be able to exercise a careful kind of diplomacy within the executive branch before he can exercise it effectively for the nation as a whole.

The Problem of Secrecy Secrecy is another quality of the executive that has been put in jeopardy by the size and complexity of modern foreign policymaking machinery. The larger the number of people privy to a secret, the more likely that it be exposed, inadvertently or by design. Leaks also become more frequent when there are differences on policy preferences among segments of the foreign policy bureaucracy. Agencies or individuals will leak secrets when public exposure will discredit and perhaps prevent implementation of policies they oppose. Recent presidents have expressed frustration over leaks of administration negotiating positions and have vowed to end them, but with only limited success. Secrecy has clearly not been the hallmark of the contemporary executive branch.

If protecting legitimate secrets is one problem, keeping too many things secret has been another. First, keeping secrets has become very expensive, and second, it is one thing for presidents and officials to use secrecy to protect policy options, but is another when agencies and officials use it to cover up mistakes or avoid scrutiny. The motto of policymakers often seems to be, "When in doubt, classify." Some executive orders and amendments to the Freedom of Information Act have reduced the number of officials who can classify documents and have tightened the regulations governing the type of classifications that can be applied. Still, there remain many instances in which secrecy is used as a veil to escape accountability.

The Intelligence Community   Secrecy is also used to protect the activities of intelligence services. These involve collecting information, which can include the use of such tactics as bribing, infiltration, and blackmail, as well as conducting covert operations that may be designed to de-stabilize certain governments or to infiltrate and destroy certain terrorist groups. The conduct employed in these instances sometimes goes well beyond the quieter diplomatic norms of earlier years, when Secretary of State Henry L. Stimson could sniff, "Gentlemen don't read other people's mail."

Many of these activities, of course, we never know about because the secrets have been kept. But many instances of controversial policies do become known, and there clearly have been cases of CIA abuses that were either imprudent or illegal or both. Some of these included botched assassination plots (now technically illegal), attempts to overthrow certain governments, the opening of mail from American citizens to selected foreign nations, and spying on American citizens by infiltrating certain protest groups.

The existence of intelligence services like the CIA raises perennial questions about the conflict between the democratic commitment to openness and the need for secrecy and the use of repugnant practices. Should all forms of covert action be outlawed, or should these methods be viewed as a necessary response to certain international threats? Some question whether any activities beyond the simple collection and analysis of information by normal means should be permitted at all. A disrespect for law and for the rights of others outside the United States, it is said, inevitably seeps back into this country, undermining the constitutional system that the intelligence community is sworn to protect. But

defenders of the intelligence community contend that intelligence is necessary for national defense and security, and that to be effective practices must be employed abroad that would be unacceptable if they were undertaken at home. If certain rules and norms of conduct are violated by other nations or by terrorist groups, can the United States afford not to employ some of the same methods? How else, for example, can terrorist groups be dealt with?

The debate on the American intelligence community has, as a practical matter, been narrowed to scrutinizing the terms and procedures under which the intelligence agencies operate. Congressional oversight has become far more important than before 1975, when scrutiny was left to a few members of the Armed Services committees of the two houses, who were told little, and frequently wanted to know less, about CIA operations. After revelations of extensive CIA misconduct in the mid-1970s, this attitude changed and Congress established new intelligence oversight committees in both houses. These committees require executive agencies to make full, and in some cases prior, reports of their activities. This system has achieved more political control over intelligence operations, but at the occasional expense of more leaks and a chilling effect on operations. We have yet to find a problem-free way of balancing the intelligence community's need for secrecy and democracy's need for open discussion.

The Role of Congress and the Separation of Powers in Today's Diplomacy

During the period of bipartisan consensus on containment that followed World War II, Congress ceded great discretion to the president in the conduct of foreign policy. But since the Vietnam War Congress has asserted a claim for much greater influence. Many of the major confrontations between the presidency and Congress in the 1970s and 1980s involved conflicts over the conduct of foreign policy.

The Constitution gives the Congress some important explicit powers in the conduct of foreign policy, in addition to its mighty power of the purse. The Senate has the power to approve treaties and presidential appointments, and

Congress is given the power to declare war. At the same time, Congress is not equipped as an institution to be as effective as the president in the foreign policy arena. The parochial views and interests of many of it members, the dispersion of power within and between both houses, and the impossibility of full access and control of intelligence makes the president comparatively more effective in foreign policy. The question remains nevertheless about what role Congress can and wishes to play under our Constitutional system.

Strengthened Congressional Tools The Vietnam War provided the motive for a new combativeness on the part of Congress in influencing the conduct of foreign affairs. Wishing to exercise more influence, Congress in the 1970s greatly expanded its staff support in the area of foreign affairs, both on its major committees and on the personal staffs of key members interested in foreign policy. This change freed representatives and senators from their previous dependence on information and analysis supplied by executive bureaucracies and enabled Congress to challenge the policies of executive agencies.

Increased congressional influence has been aided by an important general factor: an active foreign policy is costly. Control over the appropriations necessary to conduct foreign policy has given Congress a much greater voice in international affairs, and has increased the role of the House of Representatives, which has no part in the treaty ratification process. If, for example, the president wants to keep troops on a mission such as that in Afghanistan, Congress will have to approve the funding. This opens the door to congressional debate and to threats of a cut-off of funds, which could effectively terminate a presidential commitment.

Congress has made use of a number of mechanisms to assert more control. First, it has employed with new vigor its power of oversight and investigation, which it has sometimes employed to put administrations on the defensive and to influence popular opinion. Public hearings conducted in the late 1960s on the conduct of the Vietnam War, in the mid-1970s on abuses by the CIA, and in 1986–87 on the breakdown of presidential decision-making in the Iran-Contra episode are three striking examples in which the direction of the nation's foreign policy was influenced by congressional investigations. Quieter supervision, as in the ongoing oversight of the new intelligence committees, have been almost as important.

Second, Congress by legislation has determined that it will no longer permit secret executive agreements that bind the United States, in what amounts to security pacts with other nations. All executive agreements must now be transmitted to Congress within sixty days after they enter into force. In the same vein, Congress passed legislation that requires the administration to report to Congress the sale of arms to foreign nations and makes these transactions contingent on congressional approval.

Finally, Congress passed the War Powers Act of 1973, which goes to the heart of the president's power to use force and calls on the president to consult with Congress "in every possible instance" before introducing military forces into hostile situations. This legislation has never worked in quite the way that its originators intended, and presidents have ignored or challenged the Constitutionality of some of its provision. The law nevertheless remains on the books and has worked as a claim by members of Congress for the president to explain and justify more of his actions.

Congressional Responsibility in Foreign Policy
The main outlines of the debate on the responsibility that the Congress should assume today in making foreign policy are remarkably similar to the points debated at the Constitutional Convention in 1787. Opponents of the more assertive role of Congress have focused on two different critiques of congressional influence on the foreign policymaking process: its volatility and its rigidity. On the first count, they argue that the legislative branch is too likely to change its collective mind and that it responds too quickly to sudden shifts in the popular mood. Such vacillation, they argue, severely hampers American relationships with both allies and adversaries, neither of whom ever knows quite what to expect from Washington. Thus Presidents Nixon and Ford criticized Congress for its failure to uphold an American commitment by refusing to appropri-

ate the sums they requested for aid to South Vietnam and Cambodia. And President Reagan complained bitterly when Congress repeatedly cut off and then restored aid to the Nicaraguan contras.

To all this, Congress has responded with a vigorous defense of its role in the American constitutional system. Members of Congress insist that they are more like their constituents than are appointed executive officials, who need never face election at all. As representatives of the people, they must have the freedom to alter or terminate policies which they judge to be failing. This freedom must include the power to approve large-scale troop commitments and the power to decide annually, in the light of events abroad and economic conditions at home, how much the United States can afford to spend elsewhere.

Legislators have also been criticized for their rigidity in the requirements they place on executive officials. "Tying the president's hands" and "placing the president in a straitjacket" are two of the complaints most often heard against the attempts of Congress to regulate American foreign relations by law. Presidents have complained for years now of Congress's tendency to micromanage foreign policy, writing prohibitions, restrictions, and requirements into foreign aid bills and into appropriations measures that leave the president with no discretion to conduct an effective diplomacy. Members of Congress respond that while law may be a blunt instrument for dealing with the complexities of international relations, it would not have to be employed so often if executive officials were more responsive to congressional preferences. Congress must use what weapons it has.

With the Cold War over, the role of Congress in the foreign policy process will change once again. There will be new tensions and new issues forcing Congress to reassess its role in international affairs. The increased role of economics, the environment, and other global commons issues insures a larger congressional role in foreign policy but one that has not yet been clearly defined. Yet the recent emergence of terrorism as the primary security threat may strengthen the presidency.

Interest-Group Activity Another reason for the growing influence of Congress in foreign policymaking has been the decline in the distinction between foreign and domestic politics. Because of greater economic interdependency between the United States and other nations, economic interest groups that formerly dealt primarily with domestic concerns now are often equally concerned about foreign affairs. They may want to adjust tariff barriers, protect an area's security to ensure the safety of their investments, or promote friendly relations with a nation to enhance the possibilities of long-term trade. Such activities by economic interest groups, of course, are not new, but their scope has increased. The same can be said of ethnic groups, which, because of the more extensive role of the United States in the world, are constantly prodded to exercise a say in American foreign policy. Thus Jewish groups are concerned about American policy toward Israel, African-American groups take stands on American policy toward Africa, and groups of Hispanics have formed to deal with American policy toward Latin America.

The activity of interest groups is not limited, of course, to lobbying in Congress. But it has been stimulated by congressional resurgence in the foreign policymaking process, because Congress generally is the institution best suited to the representation of particular interests. The founders praised American pluralism and described the balancing of interests as a means of defending liberty. But they also sought to demonstrate the advantages of unity, especially when dealing with other nations. Representatives of interest groups bring valuable information, and members of Congress are generally willing to listen. Yet can one be certain that equilibrium is inevitably most desirable for the national interest? Is the national interest no more than the sum of the nation's special interests, especially in foreign affairs?

A Case Study: The Debate Over China

After Richard Nixon's opening to communist China in 1972, Beijing and Washington drew progressively closer, in large measure animated by the perception of a common enemy in the Soviet Union. By 1979, President Carter formally recognized the Peoples' Republic of China, and U.S. trade and military cooperation with China expanded further. Even President Reagan, who had long championed the rival non-communist Chinese government on Taiwan, visited Beijing in 1984. China's leaders, meanwhile, instituted free-market economic reforms, leading to hope in Washington that China was on the road to democracy.

But this hope was shattered in the spring of 1989. Inspired by the death of a pro-reform political figure, up to one million Chinese students—joined by workers and professionals—gathered in Tiananmen Square in Beijing in April and May, demanding political democratization to match the existing economic reforms. Hard-line elements within the Chinese Communist Party won an internal power struggle against those sympathetic to the students, declared martial law, and ordered the army to move against the demonstrators. On June 4, army troops attacked Tiananmen Square, dispersing the students and killing up to 5,000 persons on the spot. Up to 10,000 dissidents were arrested nationwide. Television cameras captured the demonstration and some of the massacres, sending these images into the homes of millions of Americans.

President George H. Bush was faced with the dilemma of how to respond. He had long supported a policy of cooperation with China, seeing it as a counterweight to the Soviets and a potentially important trading partner. Yet the demonstrators had been struggling for political freedom and had even raised a "Goddess of Liberty" statue patterned after our own Statue of Liberty. If the United States took a strong stand against the Chinese government, it risked destroying an important strategic and commercial relationship that had been carefully constructed following decades of hostility. If we remained silent, we would betray a commitment to liberal democratic government.

During the six-week long protest, Bush was only quietly supportive of the students, fearing that anything more might not only hurt ties with China but inflame the situation and lead to bloodshed. When the bloodshed came anyway, the administration condemned it but refused to make pronouncements that might upset relations with the Chinese government. After hesi-

tating, President Bush agreed to suspend military cooperation with China and to halt all arms sales. When the executions of those arrested began a few weeks later, the administration also proclaimed that "high-level contacts" with China would be suspended and that the U.S. would oppose new loans to China from international banks. No further economic sanctions were applied, despite demands from congressional Republicans and (especially) Democrats and a sizable Chinese-American community that the United States take more forceful action. Secretary of State James Baker defended this cautious policy by calling Sino-American ties "an important relationship which we should seek to preserve if we possibly can."[8]

The administration's determination to maintain that relationship, even in the face of strong congressional criticism, took several forms. U.S. opposition to international loans and the suspension of military assistance continued, but the self-imposed ban on high-level diplomatic contacts was broken when National Security Adviser Brent Scowcroft visited Beijing only months later. In the spring of 1990, President Bush agreed, over substantial congressional protest, to extend Most Favored Nation (MFN) trading status to China for another year, saying "The people of China who trade with us are the engine of reform. Our responsibility to them is best met not by isolating those forces . . . but by keeping open the channels of commerce."[9] Additionally, trade with China had doubled since 1987, and any reduction in that trade might hurt American prosperity more than it would hurt the Chinese regime. Congress continued its efforts to force what it saw as an overly conciliatory administration to keep up the pressure on China; the President continued gambling that his efforts to keep ties open to China would pay off in the long run, when China's elderly crop of leaders passes from the scene and is replaced by a new set of more liberal leaders influenced by their contacts with America.

The debate over China exemplifies many of the complexities of foreign policy which we have so far discussed: the conflicts of principle versus practical interest, and president versus Congress; the potential importance of domestic interests (like Chinese-Americans or businesses involved in foreign trade); the importance of security concerns (China as an indispensable counterweight to the Soviet Union) and ideology (the nature of the struggle within China between communism and liberalism, and the way it affected our perceptions and response); and the increasing impact of technologies that are making the world smaller and more interdependent, such as the communications technologies that put the massacre into Americans' living rooms, both reducing China's ability to deny the incident and increasing domestic pressure on the Bush administration to take some sort of action.

During the 1992 presidential campaign, Governor Clinton attacked President George H. Bush's policy and suggested that a Clinton administration would give higher priority to pressuring China through trade sanctions to improve its human rights record. But once in office President Clinton reversed his thinking and followed President George H. Bush's policy. Like George H. Bush, President Clinton continued to support economic openness toward China and has renewed most favored nation trading status in the face of continued human rights violations. This policy has been delicately continued by George W. Bush, despite a spy-plane flap early in his administration.

Conclusion

America's experience in foreign affairs has in general demonstrated that Hamilton was more correct than Jefferson: the relations among nations cannot be governed by the same maxims which Americans follow either in their private lives or in their domestic politics. Foreign policy differs dramatically from other areas of public policy in that it must deal with actors not subject to the Constitution, American laws, or American understandings of justice and right. Relations among nations are often based on force and fear rather than trust and goodwill. Yet Jefferson was in a way also right: foreign policy, because it affects our lives so deeply, cannot be considered wholly outside the American political system and its tenets of republicanism. This belief is all the more true today when diplomacy is no longer something confined to far-off embassies in exotic settings.

Conflicts between the need to conduct an effective foreign policy and the need to respect republican procedures have posed some of the most difficult problems of governance. Recognizing this conflict, the founders sought to provide an institutional framework that could help balance the competing objectives. The protective isolation that the United States enjoyed during much of the nineteenth century allowed Americans to avoid many of the difficulties of managing this system. But with the onset of World War II and America's engagement in the world as a major power, American political leaders had to relearn many of the founders' lessons and confront again the difficult problems of dealing with the balance between effective diplomacy and democratic values.

The striking changes in the international scene that have taken place since the end of the Cold War have altered the foreign policy setting in a way that holds out the prospect for lessening some of the tensions between democratic procedures and the effective conduct of foreign policy. Finding the right balance will nevertheless continue to be a challenge in the future, as America's role in dealing with new problems in the international arena is certain to be large and important. We may have won the Cold War against communist totalitarianism, but it is clear that we have much work ahead of us to win a stable and prosperous peace.

Chapter 17 Notes

1. Alexis de Tocqueville, *Democracy in America*, George Lawrence (trans.) (Garden City, N.Y.: Doubleday, 1969) p. 228.
2. Max Farrand (ed.), *The Records of the Federal Convention of 1787* vols. 1–4 (New Haven: Yale University Press, 1937).
3. Edward S. Corwin, *The President's Control of Foreign Relations* (Princeton: Princeton University Press, 1957), p. 171.
4. Walter LaFeber (ed.), *John Quincy Adams and the American Continental Empire* (Chicago: Quadrangle Books, 1965), p.45.
5. James Bryce, *The American Commonwealth* vols.1, 2 (New York: Macmillan, 1889).
6. Richard Nixon, *Public Papers of the Presidents of the United States* 1969 (Washington, D.C.: Office of the Federal Register, 1969), p. 9.
7. *Federalist* 70.
8. "Testing the Power of Dollar Diplomacy," *U.S. News and World Report*, July 3, 1989, p. 31.
9. "China: One Year later," *Time*, June 4, 1990, p. 59.

Appendixes

1

The Declaration of Independence

In Congress, July 4, 1776
The Unanimous Declaration of the
Thirteen United States of America

When, in the course of human events, it becomes necessary for one people to dissolve the political bands which have connected them with another, and to assume, among the powers of the earth, the separate and equal station to which the laws of nature and of nature's God entitle them, a decent respect to the opinions of mankind requires that they should declare the causes which impel them to the separation.

We hold these truths to be self-evident: That all men are created equal; that they are endowed by their Creator with certain unalienable rights; that among these are life, liberty, and the pursuit of happiness; that, to secure these rights, governments are instituted among men, deriving their just powers from the consent of the governed; that whenever any form of government becomes destructive of these ends, it is the right of the people to alter or to abolish it, and to institute new government, laying its foundation on such principles, and organizing its powers in such form, as to them shall seem most likely to effect their safety and happiness. Prudence, indeed, will dictate that governments long established should not be changed for light and transient causes; and accordingly all experience hath shown that mankind are more disposed to suffer, while evils are sufferable, than to right themselves by abolishing the forms to which they are accustomed. But when a long train of abuses and usurpations, pursuing invariably the same object, evinces a design to reduce them under absolute despotism, it is their right, it is their duty, to throw off such government, and to provide new guards for their future security. Such has been the patient sufferance of these colonies; and such is now the necessity which constrains them to alter their former systems of government. The history of the present King of Great Britain is a history of repeated injuries and usurpations, all having in direct object the establishment of an absolute tyranny over these states. To prove this, let facts be submitted to a candid world.

He has refused to assent to laws, the most wholesome and necessary for the public good.

He has forbidden his governors to pass laws of immediate and pressing importance, unless suspended in their operation till his assent should be obtained; and, when so suspended, he has utterly neglected to attend to them.

He has refused to pass other laws for the accommodation of large districts of people, unless those people would relinquish the right of representation in the legislature, a right inestimable to them, and formidable to tyrants only.

He has called together legislative bodies at places unusual, uncomfortable, and distant from the depository of their public records, for the sole purpose of fatiguing them into compliance with his measures.

He has dissolved representative houses repeatedly, for opposing, with manly firmness, his invasions on the rights of the people.

He has refused for a long time, after such dissolutions, to cause others to be elected; whereby the legislative powers, incapable of annihilation, have returned to the people at large for their exercise; the state remaining, in the mean time, exposed to all the dangers of invasions from without and convulsions within.

He has endeavoured to prevent the population of these states; for that purpose obstructing the laws for naturalization of foreigners; refusing to pass others to encourage their migrations hither, and raising the conditions of new appropriations of lands.

He has obstructed the administration of justice, by refusing his assent to laws for establishing judiciary powers.

He has made judges dependent on his will alone, for the tenure of their offices, and the amount and payment of their salaries.

He has erected a multitude of new offices, and sent hither swarms of officers to harass our people and eat out their substance.

He has kept among us, in times of peace, standing armies, without the consent of our legislatures.

He has affected to render the military independent of, and superior to, the civil power.

He has combined with others to subject us to a jurisdiction foreign to our constitution and unacknowledged by our laws, giving his assent to their acts of pretended legislation:

For quartering large bodies of armed troops among us;

For protecting them, by a mock trial, from punishment for any murders which they should commit on the inhabitants of these states;

For cutting off our trade with all parts of the world;

For imposing taxes on us without our consent;

For depriving us, in many cases, of the benefits of trial by jury;

For transporting us beyond seas, to be tried for pretended offenses;

For abolishing the free system of English laws in a neighboring province, establishing therein an arbitrary government, and enlarging its boundaries, so as to render it at once an example and fit instrument for introducing the same absolute rule into these colonies;

For taking away our charters, abolishing our most valuable laws, and altering fundamentally the forms of our governments;

For suspending our own legislatures, and declaring themselves invested with power to legislate for us in all cases whatsoever.

He has abdicated government here, by declaring us out of his protection and waging war against us.

He has plundered our seas, ravaged our coasts, burned our towns, and destroyed the lives of our people.

He is at this time transporting large armies of foreign mercenaries to complete the works of death, desolation, and tyranny already begun with circumstances of cruelty and perfidy scarcely paralleled in the most barbarous ages, and totally unworthy the head of a civilized nation.

He has constrained our fellow-citizens, taken captive on the high seas, to bear arms against their country, to become the executioners of their friends and brethren, or to fall themselves by their hands.

He has excited domestic insurrections amongst us, and has endeavored to bring on the inhabitants of our frontiers the merciless Indian savages, whose known rule of warfare is an undistinguished destruction of all ages, sexes, and conditions.

In every stage of these oppressions we have petitioned for redress in the most humble terms; our repeated petitions have been answered only by repeated injury. A prince, whose character is thus marked by every act which may define a tyrant, is unfit to be the ruler of a free people.

Nor have we been wanting in our attentions to our British brethren. We have warned them, from time to time, of attempts by their legislature to extend an unwarrantable jurisdiction over us. We have reminded them of the circumstances of our emigration and settlement here. We have appealed to their native justice and magnanimity; and we have conjured them, by the ties of our common kindred, to disavow these usurpations, which would inevitably interrupt our connections and correspondence. They, too, have been deaf to the voice of justice and of consanguinity. We must, therefore, acquiesce in the necessity which denounces our separation, and hold them, as we hold the rest of mankind, enemies in war, in peace friends.

We, therefore, the representatives of the United States of America, in General Congress assembled, appealing to the Supreme Judge of the world for the rectitude of our intentions, do, in the name and by authority of the good people of these colonies, solemnly publish and declare, that these United Colonies are, and of right ought to be, FREE AND INDEPENDENT STATES; that they are absolved from all allegiance to the British crown, and that all political connection between them and the state of Great Britain is, and ought to be, totally dissolved; and that, as free and independent states, they have full power to levy war, conclude peace, contract alliances, establish commerce, and do all other acts and things which independent states may of right do. And for the support of this declaration, with a firm reliance on the protection of Divine Providence, we mutually pledge to each other our lives, our fortunes and our sacred honor.

John Hancock [President]
John Adams
Samuel Adams
Josiah Bartlett
Carter Braxton
Charles Carroll
Samuel Chase
Abraham Clark
George Clymer
William Ellery
William Floyd
Benjamin Franklin
Elbridge Gerry
Button Gwinnett
Lyman Hall
Benjamin Harrison
John Hart
Joseph Hewes
Thomas Heyward Jr
William Hooper
Stephen Hopkins
Francis Hopkinson
Samuel Huntington
Thomas Jefferson
Francis Lightfoot Lee
Richard Henry Lee
Francis Lewis
Philip Livingston

Thomas Lynch Jr.
Thomas McKean
Arthur Middleton
Lewis Morris
Robert Morris
John Morton
Thomas Nelson Jr.
William Paca
Robert Treat Paine
John Penn
George Read
Caesar Rodney
George Ross
Benjamin Rush
Edward Rutledge
Roger Sherman
James Smith
Richard Stockton
Thomas Stone
George Taylor
Matthew Thornton
George Walton
William Whipple
William Williams
James Wilson
John Witherspoon
Oliver Wolcott
George Wythe

2

The Constitution of the United States of America

Preamble

We the People of the United States, in Order to form a more perfect Union, establish Justice, insure domestic Tranquility, provide for the common defence, promote the general Welfare, and secure the Blessings of Liberty to ourselves and our Posterity, do ordain and establish this Constitution for the United States of America.[1]

The legislature

ARTICLE I.

Division into Senate and House

Section 1 All legislative Powers herein granted shall be vested in a Congress of the United States, which shall consist of a Senate and House of Representatives.

House Membership

Section 2 The House of Representatives shall be composed of Members chosen every second Year by the People of the several States, and the Electors in each State shall have the Qualifications requisite for Electors of the most numerous Branch of the State Legislature.

No person shall be a Representative who shall not have attained to the Age of twenty five Years, and been seven Years a Citizen of the United States, and who shall not, when elected, be an Inhabitant of that State in which he shall be chosen.

Representatives and direct Taxes shall be apportioned among the several States which may be included within this Union, according to their respective Numbers, which shall be determined by adding to the

---

1. Note: The marginal notes provided are not part of the Constitution; they are included to help the reader locate different sections. Portions of the Constitution printed in *italic* have been superseded or changed by later amendments, as indicated in the footnotes.

whole Number of free Persons, including those bound to Service for a Term of Years, and excluding Indians not taxed, three-fifths of all other Persons.[2] The actual Enumeration shall be made within three Years after the first Meeting of the Congress of the United States, and within every subsequent Term of ten Years, in such Manner as they shall by Law direct. The Number of Representatives shall not exceed one for every thirty Thousand, but each State shall have at Least one Representative; and until such enumeration shall be made, the State of New Hampshire shall be entitled to chuse three, Massachusetts eight, Rhode-Island and Providence Plantations one, Connecticut five, New-York six, New Jersey four, Pennsylvania eight, Delaware one, Maryland six, Virginia ten, North Carolina five, South Carolina five, and Georgia three.

When vacancies happen in the Representation from any State, the Executive Authority thereof shall issue Writs of Election to fill such Vacancies.

House's power to impeach

The House of Representatives shall chuse their Speaker and other Officers; and shall have the sole Power of Impeachment.

Senate Membership

Section 3 The Senate of the United States shall be composed of two Senators from each State, *chosen by the Legislature thereof,*[3] for six Years; and each Senator shall have one Vote.

Immediately after they shall be assembled in Consequence of the first Election, they shall be divided as equally as may be into three Classes. The Seats of the Senators of the first Class shall be vacated at the Expiration of the second Year, of the second Class at the Expiration of the fourth Year, and of the third Class at the Expiration of the sixth Year, so that one third may be chosen every second Year; *and if Vacancies happen by Resignation, or otherwise, during the Recess of the Legislature of any State, the Executive thereof may make temporary Appointments until the next Meeting of the Legislature, which shall then fill such Vacancies.*[4]

No Person shall be a Senator who shall not have attained to the Age of thirty Years, and been nine Years a Citizen of the United States, and who shall not, when elected, be an Inhabitant of that State for which he shall be chosen.

Vice President's role in the Senate

The Vice President of the United States shall be President of the Senate, but shall have no Vote, unless they be equally divided.

The Senate shall chuse their other Officers, and also a President pro tempore, in the Absence of the Vice President, or when he shall exercise the Office of President of the United States.

Senate's power to try impeachment

The Senate shall have the sole Power to try all Impeachments. When sitting for the Purpose, they shall be on Oath or Affirmation. When the President of the United States is tried the Chief Justice

2. Modified by the Fourteenth Amendment, Section 2, and by the Sixteenth Amendment.
3. Superseded by the Seventeenth Amendment.
4. Modified by the Seventeenth Amendment.

shall preside: And no Person shall be convicted without the Concurrence of two thirds of the Members present.

Judgment in Cases of Impeachment shall not extend further than to removal from Office, and disqualification to hold and enjoy any Office of honor, Trust or Profit under the United States: but the Party convicted shall nevertheless be liable and subject to Indictment, Trial, Judgment and Punishment, according to Law.

Laws governing election of members of Congress

Section 4   The Times, Places and Manner of holding Elections for Senators and Representatives, shall be prescribed in each State by the Legislature thereof; but the Congress may at any time by Law make or alter such Regulations, except as to the Places of chusing Senators.

The Congress shall assemble at least once in every Year, and such Meeting shall be on the *first Monday in December, unless they shall by Law appoint a different day.*[5]

Internal rules of Congress

Section 5   Each House shall be the Judge of the Elections, Returns and Qualifications of its own Members, and a Majority of each shall constitute a Quorum to do Business; but a smaller Number may adjourn from day to day, and may be authorized to compel the Attendance of absent Members, in such Manner, and under such Penalties as each House may provide.

Each House may determine the Rules of its Proceedings, punish its Members for disorderly Behaviour, and, with the Concurrence of two thirds, expel a Member.

Each House shall keep a Journal of its Proceedings, and from time to time publish the same, excepting such Parts as may in their Judgment require Secrecy; and the Yeas and Nays of the Members of either House on any question shall, at the Desire of one fifth of those Present, be entered on the Journal.

Neither House, during the Session of Congress, shall, without the Consent of the other, adjourn for more than three days, nor to any other Place than that in which the two Houses shall be sitting.

Privileges and immunities of members

Section 6   The Senators and Representatives shall receive a Compensation for their Services, to be ascertained by Law, and paid out of the Treasury of the United States. They shall in all Cases, except Treason, Felony and Breach of Peace, be privileged from Arrest during their Attendance at the Session of their respective Houses, and in going to and returning from the same; and for any Speech or Debate in either House, they shall not be questioned in any other Place.

---

5.   Superseded by the Twentieth Amendment, Section 2.

Disabilities of members, ban on holding federal appointive offices

No Senator or Representative shall, during the Time for which he was elected, be appointed to any civil Office under the Authority of the United States, which shall have been created, or the Emoluments whereof shall have been encreased during such time; and no Person holding any Office under the United States, shall be a Member of either House during his Continuance in Office.

Procedure for enacting laws; president's veto power and method of overriding.

Section 7 All Bills for raising Revenue shall originate in the House of Representatives; but the Senate may propose or concur with Amendments as on other Bills.

Every Bill which shall have passed the House of Representatives and the Senate, shall, before it become a Law, be presented to the President of the United States; If he approve he shall sign it, but if not he shall return it, with his Objections to that House in which it shall have originated, who shall enter the Objections at large on their Journal, and proceed to reconsider it. If after such Reconsideration two thirds of that House shall agree to pass the Bill, it shall be sent, together with the Objections, to the other House, by which it shall likewise be reconsidered, and if approved by two thirds of that House, it shall become a Law. But in all such Cases the Votes of both Houses shall be determined by Yeas and Nays, and the Names of the Persons voting for and against the Bill shall be entered on the Journal of each House respectively. If any Bill shall not be returned by the President within ten Days (Sundays excepted) after it shall have been presented to him, the Same shall be a Law, in like Manner as if he had signed it, unless the Congress by their Adjournment prevent its Return, in which Case it shall not be a Law.

Every Order, Resolution, or Vote to which the Concurrence of the Senate and House of Representatives may be necessary (except on a question of Adjournment) shall be presented to the President of the United States; and before the Same shall take Effect, shall be approved by him, or being disapproved by him, shall be repassed by two thirds of the Senate and House of Representatives, according to the Rules and Limitations prescribed in the Case of a Bill.

Enumeration of the powers of Congress

Section 8 The Congress shall have Power To lay and collect Taxes, Duties, Imposts and Excises, to pay the Debts and provide for the common Defence and general Welfare of the United States; but all Duties, Imposts and Excises shall be uniform throughout the United States;

Borrowing

To borrow Money on the credit of the United States;

Commerce

To regulate Commerce with foreign Nations, and among the several States, and with the Indian Tribes;

Naturalization and bankruptcy

To establish a uniform Rule of Naturalization, and uniform Laws on the subject of Bankruptcies throughout the United States;

Money

To coin Money, regulate the Value thereof, and of foreign Coin, and fix the Standard of Weights and Measures;

To provide for the Punishment of counterfeiting the Securities and current Coin of the United States;

Post office

Patents and copyrights

Establish courts

Declare War

Raise army and navy

Call the militia

Authority over the District of Columbia

"Necessary and proper" clause

Enumeration of restraints of powers of Congress

Slave trade

Habeas corpus

No bill of attainder or ex post facto law

To establish Post Offices and post Roads;

To promote the Progress of Science and useful Arts, by securing for limited Times to Authors and Inventors the exclusive Right to their respective Writings and Discoveries;

To constitute Tribunals inferior to the supreme Court;

To define and punish Piracies and Felonies committed on the high Seas, and Offences against the Law of Nations;

To declare War, grant Letters of Marque and Reprisal, and make Rules concerning Captures on Land and Water;

To raise and support Armies, but no Appropriation of Money to that Use shall be for a longer Term than two Years;

To provide and maintain a Navy;

To make Rules for the Government and Regulation of the land and naval Forces;

To provide for calling forth the Militia to execute the Laws of the Union, suppress Insurrections and repel Invasions;

To provide for organizing, arming, and disciplining, the Militia, and for governing such Part of them as may be employed in the Service of the United States, reserving to the States respectively, the Appointment of the Officers, and the Authority of training the Militia according to the discipline prescribed by Congress;

To exercise exclusive Legislation in all Cases whatsoever, over such District (not exceeding ten Miles square) as may, by Cession of particular States, and the Acceptance of Congress, become the Seat of the Government of the United States, and to exercise like Authority over all Places purchased by the Consent of the Legislature of the State in which the Same shall be, for the Erection of Forts, Magazines, Arsenals, dock-Yards, and other needful Buildings;—And

To make all Laws which shall be necessary and proper for carrying into Execution the foregoing Powers, and all other Powers vested by this Constitution in the Government of the United States, or in any Department or Officer thereof.

Section 9 The Migration or Importation of such Persons as any of the States now existing shall think proper to admit, shall not be prohibited by the Congress prior to the Year one thousand eight hundred and eight, but a Tax or duty may be imposed on such Importation, not exceeding ten dollars for each Person.

The Privilege of the Writ of Habeas Corpus shall not be suspended, unless when in Cases of Rebellion or Invasion the public Safety may require it.

No Bill of Attainder or ex post facto Law shall be passed.

No Capitation, or other direct, Tax shall be laid, *unless in Proportion to the Census or Enumeration herein before directed to be taken.*[6]

No Tax or Duty shall be laid on Articles exported from any State.

---

6. Modified by the Sixteenth Amendment.

No Preference shall be given by any Regulation of Commerce or Revenue to the Ports of one State over those of another; nor shall Vessels bound to, or from, one State, be obliged to enter, clear, or pay Duties in another.

Appropriations and expenditures

No Money shall be drawn from the Treasury, but in Consequence of Appropriations made by Law; and a regular Statement and Account of the Receipts and Expenditures of all public Money shall be published from time to time.

No titles of nobility

No Title of Nobility shall be granted by the United States: And no Person holding any Office of Profit or Trust under them, shall, without the Consent of the Congress, accept any present, Emolument, Office, or Title, of any kind whatever, from any King, Prince, or foreign State.

Enumeration of restraints on the states

Section 10   No State shall enter into any Treaty, Alliance, or Confederation; grant Letters of Marque and Reprisal; coin Money; emit Bills of Credit; make any Thing but gold and silver Coin a Tender in Payment of Debts; pass any Bill of Attainder, ex post facto Law, or Law impairing the Obligation of Contracts, or grant any Title of Nobility.

No State shall, without the Consent of the Congress, lay any Imposts or Duties on Imports or Exports, except what may be absolutely necessary for executing its inspection Laws: and the net Produce of all Duties and Imposts, laid by any State on Imports or Exports, shall be for the Use of the Treasury of the United States; and all such Laws shall be subject to the Revision and Controul of the Congress.

No State shall, without the Consent of Congress, lay any Duty of Tonnage, keep Troops, or Ships of War in time of Peace, enter into any Agreement or Compact with another State, or with a foreign Power, or engage in War, unless actually invaded, or in such imminent Danger as will not admit of delay.

ARTICLE II

The executive

Section 1   The executive Power shall be vested in a President of the United States of America. He shall hold his Office during the Term of four Years, and, together with the Vice President, chosen for the same Term, be elected, as follows:

"Executive power" and term of office

Method of election

Each State shall appoint, in such Manner as the Legislature thereof may direct, a Number of Electors, equal to the whole Number of Senators and Representatives to which the State may be entitled in the Congress: but no Senator or Representative, or Person holding an Office of Trust or Profit under the United States, shall be appointed an Elector.

The Electors shall meet in their respective States, and vote by Ballot for two Persons, of whom one at least shall not be an Inhabitant of the same State with themselves. And they shall make a List of all the Persons voted for, and of the Number of Votes for each; which List they shall sign and certify, and transmit sealed to the Seat of the Government of the United States, directed to the President of the Senate. The President of the Senate shall, in the Presence of the Senate and House of Representatives, open all the Certificates, and the Votes shall then be counted. The Person having the greatest Number of Votes shall be the President, if such Number be a Majority of the whole Number of Electors appointed; and if there be more than one who have such Majority, and have an equal Number of Votes, then the House of Representatives shall immediately chuse by Ballot one of them for President; and if no Person have a Majority, then from the five highest on the List the said House shall in like Manner chuse the President. But in chusing the President, the Votes shall be taken by States, the Representation from each State having one Vote; a quorum for this Purpose shall consist of a Member or Members from two thirds of the States, and a Majority of all the States shall be necessary to a Choice. In every Case, after the Choice of the President, the person having the greatest Number of Votes of the Electors shall be the Vice President. But if there should remain two or more who have equal Votes, the Senate shall chuse from them by Ballot the Vice President.[7]

The Congress may determine the Time of chusing the Electors, and the Day on which they shall give their Votes; which Day shall be the same throughout the United States.

Qualifications for office

No Person except a natural born Citizen, or a Citizen of the United States, at the time of the Adoption of this Constitution, shall be eligible to the Office of President; neither shall any Person be eligible to that Office who shall not have attained to the Age of thirty five Years, and been fourteen Years a Resident within the United States.

In Case of the Removal of the President from Office, or of his Death, Resignation, or Inability to discharge the Powers and Duties of the said Office, the Same shall devolve on the Vice President, and the Congress may by Law provide for the Case of Removal, Death, Resignation or Inability, both of the President and Vice President, declaring what Officer shall then act as President, and such Officer shall act accordingly, until the Disability be removed, or a President shall be elected.[8]

Presidential salary

The President shall, at stated Times, receive for his Services, a Compensation, which shall neither be encreased nor diminished during the Period for which he shall have been elected, and he shall not receive within that Period any other Emolument from the United States, or any of them.

Oath of office

Before he enter on the Execution of his Office, he shall take the following Oath or Affirmation:—"I do solemnly swear (or affirm) that I will faithfully execute the Office of President of the United States, and will to the best of my Ability, preserve, protect and defend the Constitution of the United States."

7. Superseded by the Twelfth Amendment.
8. Modified by the Twenty-Fifth Amendment.

**Presidential powers
Commander in chief**

Section 2 The President shall be Commander in Chief of the Army and Navy of the United States, and of the Militia of the several States, when called into the actual Service of the United States; he may require the Opinion, in writing, of the principal Officer in each of the executive Departments, upon any Subject relating to the Duties of their respective Offices, and he shall have Power to grant Reprieves and Pardons for Offences against the United States, except in Cases of Impeachment.

Pardons

Treaties and appointment

He shall have Power, by and with the Advice and Consent of the Senate, to make Treaties, provided two thirds of the Senators present concur; and he shall nominate, and by and with the Advice and Consent of the Senate, shall appoint Ambassadors, other public Ministers and Consuls, Judges of the supreme Court, and all other Officers of the United States, whose Appointments are not herein otherwise provided for, and which shall be established by Law: but the Congress may by Law vest the Appointment of such inferior Officers, as they think proper, in the President alone, in the Courts of Law, or in the Heads of Departments.

The President shall have Power to fill up all Vacancies that may happen during the Recess of the Senate, by granting Commissions which shall expire at the End of their next Session.

State of the union

Section 3 He shall from time to time give to the Congress Information of the State of the Union, and recommend to their Consideration such Measures as he shall judge necessary and expedient; he may, on extraordinary Occasions, convene both Houses, or either of them, and in Case of Disagreement between them, with Respect to the Time of Adjournment, he may adjourn them to such Time as he shall think proper; he shall receive Ambassadors and other public Ministers; he shall take Care that the Laws be faithfully executed, and shall Commission all the Officers of the United States.

Convening Congress

**Receiving ambassadors
"Take care" clause**

Grounds for impeachment

Section 4 The President, Vice President and all civil Officers of the United States, shall be removed from Office on Impeachment for, and Conviction of, Treason, Bribery, or other high Crimes and Misdemeanors.

The judiciary

ARTICLE III

Federal courts; judicial tenure and salary

Section 1 The judicial Power of the United States, shall be vested in one supreme Court, and in such inferior Courts as the Congress may from time to time ordain and establish. The Judges, both of the supreme and inferior Courts, shall hold their Offices during good Behaviour, and shall, at stated Times, receive for their Services, a Compensation, which shall not be diminished during their Continuance in Office.

Jurisdiction of federal courts

Section 2 The judicial Power shall extend to all Cases, in Law and Equity, arising under this Constitution, the Laws of the United States, and Treaties made, or which shall be made, under their Authority;—to all Cases affecting Ambassadors, other public Ministers and Consuls;—to all Cases of admiralty and maritime Jurisdiction;—to Controversies to which the United States shall be a Party;—to Controversies between two or more States;—*between a State and Citizens of another State,*[9]—between Citizens of different States;—between Citizens of the same State claiming Lands under Grants of different States, and between a State, or the Citizens thereof, and foreign States, Citizens or Subjects.

In all Cases affecting Ambassadors, other public Ministers and Consuls, and those in which a State shall be Part, the supreme Court shall have original Jurisdiction. In all the other Cases before mentioned, the supreme Court shall have appellate Jurisdiction, both as to Law and Fact, with such Exceptions, and under such Regulations as the Congress shall make.

Trial by jury

The Trial of all Crimes, except in Cases of Impeachment, shall be by Jury; and such Trial shall be held in the State where the said Crimes shall have been committed; but when not committed within any State, the Trial shall be at such Place or Places as the Congress may by Law have directed.

Definition of treason and procedures for punishment

Section 3 Treason against the United States, shall consist only in levying War against them, or in adhering to their Enemies, giving them Aid and Comfort. No Person shall be convicted of Treason unless on the Testimony of two Witnesses to the same overt Act, or on Confession in open Court.

The Congress shall have Power to declare the Punishment of Treason, but no Attainder of Treason shall work Corruption of Blood, or Forfeiture except during the Life of the Person attainted.

Interstate relations

ARTICLE IV

Full faith and credit

Section 1 Full Faith and Credit shall be given in each State to the public Acts, Records, and judicial Proceedings of every other State. And the Congress may by general Laws prescribe the Manner in which such Acts, Records and Proceedings shall be proved, and the Effect thereof.

Privileges and immunities

Extradition

Section 2 The Citizens of each State shall be entitled to all Privileges and Immunities of Citizens in the several States.

A Person charged in any State with Treason, Felony, or other Crime, who shall flee from Justice, and be found in another State, shall on Demand of the executive Authority of the State from which he fled, be delivered up, to be removed to the State having Jurisdiction of the Crime.

9. Modified by the Eleventh Amendment

No Person held to Service or Labour in one State, under the Laws thereof, escaping into another, shall, in Consequence of any Law or Regulation therein, be discharged from such Service or Labour, but shall be delivered up on Claim of the Party to whom such Service or Labour may be due.[10]

Creation and admission of new states

Section 3 New States may be admitted by the Congress into this Union; but no new State shall be formed or erected within the Jurisdiction of any other State; nor any State be formed by the Junction of two or more States, or Parts of States, without the Consent of the Legislatures of the States concerned as well as of the Congress.

Control of national territories and property

The Congress shall have Power to dispose of and make all needful Rules and Regulations, respecting the Territory or other Property belonging to the United States; and nothing in this Constitution shall be so construed as to Prejudice any Claims of the United States, or of any particular State.

Guarantee to states

Section 4 The United States shall guarantee to every State in this Union a Republican Form of Government, and shall protect each of them against Invasion; and on Application of the Legislature, or of the Executive (when the Legislature cannot be convened) against domestic Violence.

Method of amending the Constitution

ARTICLE V

The Congress, whenever two thirds of both Houses shall deem it necessary, shall propose Amendments to this Constitution, or, on the Application of the Legislatures of two thirds of the several States, shall call a Convention for proposing Amendments, which, in either Case, shall be valid to all Intents and Purposes, as Part of this Constitution, when ratified by the Legislatures of three fourths of the several States, or by Conventions in three fourths thereof, as the one or the other Mode of Ratification may be proposed by the Congress; Provided that no Amendment which may be made prior to the Year One thousand eight hundred and eight shall in any Manner affect the first and fourth Clauses in the Ninth Section of the first Article; and that no State, without its Consent, shall be deprived of its equal Suffrage in the Senate.

Debts, supremacy, oaths

ARTICLE VI

Assumption of Confederation debts

All Debts contracted and Engagements entered into, before the Adoption of this Constitution, shall be as valid against the United States under this Constitution, as under the Confederation.

10. Superseded by the Thirteenth Amendment.

Supremacy of federal laws and treaties

This Constitution, and the Laws of the United States which shall be made in Pursuance thereof; and all Treaties made, or which shall be made, under the Authority of the United States, shall be the supreme Law of the Land; and the Judges in every State shall be bound thereby, any Thing in the Constitution or Laws of any State to the Contrary notwithstanding.

No religious test for office

The Senators and Representatives before mentioned, and the Members of the several State legislatures, and all executive and judicial Officers, both of the United States and of the several States, shall be bound by Oath or Affirmation, to support this constitution; but no religious Test shall ever be required as a Qualification to any Office or public Trust under the United States.

Method of ratification of the Constitution

ARTICLE VII

The Ratification of the Conventions of nine States, shall be sufficient for the Establishment of this Constitution between the States so ratifying the Same.

Done in Convention by the Unanimous Consent of the States present the Seventeenth Day of September in the Year of our Lord one thousand seven hundred and Eighty seven and of the Independence of the United States of America the Twelfth In witness whereof We have hereunto subscribed our Names,

Go. Washington—Presidt
and deputy from Virginia
New Hampshire
JOHN LANGDON
NICHOLAS GILMAN

Massachusetts
NATHANIEL GORHAM
RUFUS KING

Connecticut
WM. SAML. JOHNSON
ROGER SHERMAN

New York
ALEXANDER HAMILTON

New Jersey
WIL: LIVINGSTON
DAVID BREARLEY
WM PATERSON
JONA: DAYTON

Pennsylvania
B FRANKLIN
THOMAS MIFFLIN
ROB^T. MORRIS
GEO. CLYMER
THO^S FITZSIMONS
JARED INGERSOLL
JAMES WILSON
GOUV MORRIS

Delaware
GEO: READ
GUNNING BEDFORD JUN
JOHN DICKINSON
RICHARD BASSETT
JACO: BROOM

Maryland
JAMES M^CHENRY
DAN OF S^T THO^S JENIFER
DAN^L CARROLL

Virginia
JOHN BLAIR—
JAMES MADISON, JR.

North Carolina
W^M BLOUNT
RICH^D DOBBS SPAIGHT
HU WILLIAMSON

South Carolina
J. RUTLEDGE
CHARLES COTESWORTH PINCKNEY
PIERCE BUTLER

Georgia
WILLIAM FEW
ABR BALDWIN

Amendments I–X, known as the "Bill of Rights," ratified in 1791

Freedom of religion, speech, press, assembly

AMENDMENT I

Congress shall make no law respecting an establishment of religion, or prohibiting the free exercise thereof; or abridging the freedom of speech, or of the press; or the right of the people peaceably to assemble, and to petition the Government for a redress of grievances.

Right to bear arms

AMENDMENT II

A well regulated Militia, being necessary to the security of a free State, the right of the people to keep and bear Arms, shall not be infringed.

Restrictions on quartering of troops

AMENDMENT III

No Solider shall, in time of peace be quartered in any house, without the consent of the Owner, nor in time of war, but in a manner to be prescribed by law.

Prohibition on unreasonable searches and seizures

AMENDMENT IV

The right of the people to be secure in their persons, houses, papers, and effects, against unreasonable searches and seizures, shall not be violated, and no Warrants shall issue, but upon probable cause, supported by Oath or affirmation, and particularly describing the place to be searched, and the persons or things to be seized.

Rights of the accused; grand juries; double jeopardy; self-incrimination; due process; eminent domain

AMENDMENT V

No person shall be held to answer for a capital, or otherwise infamous crime, unless on a presentment of indictment of a Grand Jury, except in cases arising in the land or naval forces, or in the Militia, when in actual service in time of War or public anger; nor shall any person be subject for the same offence to be twice put in jeopardy of life or limb; nor shall be compelled in any criminal case to be a witness against himself, nor be deprived of life, liberty, or property, without due process of law; nor shall private property be taken for public use without just compensation.

Rights when on trial

AMENDMENT VI

In all criminal prosecutions the accused shall enjoy the right to a speedy and public trial, by an impartial jury of the State and district wherein the crime shall have been committed, which district shall have been previously ascertained by law, and to be informed of the nature and cause of the accusation; to be confronted with the witnesses against him; to have compulsory process for obtaining Witnesses in his favor, and to have Assistance of Counsel for his defense.

Trial by jury in common-law suits

AMENDMENT VII

In Suits at common law, where the value in controversy shall exceed twenty dollars, the right of trial by jury shall be preserved, and no fact tried by a jury, shall be otherwise reexamined in any Court of the United States, than according to the rules of the common law.

Bails, fines, and punishments

AMENDMENT VIII

Excessive bail shall not be required, nor excessive fines imposed, nor cruel and unusual punishments inflicted.

Rights retained by the people

AMENDMENT IX

The enumeration in the Constitution, of certain rights, shall not be construed to deny or disparage others retained by the people.

Powers reserved to the states

AMENDMENT X

The powers not delegated to the United States by the Constitution, nor prohibited by it to the States, are reserved to the States respectively, or to the people.

Ratified in 1795

AMENDMENT XI

Suits against the states

The Judicial power of the United States shall not be construed to extend to any suit in law or equity, commenced or prosecuted against one of the United States by Citizens of another State, or by Citizens or Subjects of any Foreign State.

Ratified in 1804

AMENDMENT XII

Election of the president and vice president

The Electors shall meet in their respective states and vote by ballot for President and Vice President, one of whom, at least, shall not be an inhabitant of the same state with themselves; they shall name in their ballots the person voted for as President, and in distinct ballots the person voted for as Vice President, and they shall make distinct lists of all persons voted for as President, and of all persons voted for as Vice President, and of the number of votes for each, which lists they shall sign and certify, and transmit sealed to the seat of the government of the United States, directed to the President of the Senate;—The President of the Senate shall, in the presence of the

Senate and House of Representatives, open all the certificates and the votes shall then be counted;—The person having the greatest number of votes for President, shall be the President, if such number be a majority of the whole number of Electors appointed; and if no person have such majority, then from the persons having the highest numbers not exceeding three on the list of those voted for as President, the House of Representatives shall choose immediately, by ballot, the President. But in choosing the President, the votes shall be taken by states, the representation from each state having one vote; a quorum for this purpose shall consist of a member or members from two-thirds of the states, and a majority of all the states shall be necessary to a choice. *And if the House of Representatives shall not choose a President whenever the right of choice shall devolve upon them, before the fourth day of March next following, then the Vice President shall act as President as in the case of the death or other constitutional disability of the President.*—[11] The person having the greatest number of votes as Vice President, shall be the Vice President, if such number be a majority of the whole number of Electors appointed, and if no person have a majority, then from the two highest numbers on the list, the Senate shall choose the Vice President; a quorum for the purpose shall consist of two-thirds of the whole number of Senators, and a majority of the whole number shall be necessary to a choice. But no person constitutionally ineligible to the office of President shall be eligible to that of Vice President of the United States.

AMENDMENT XIII

Ratified in 1865

Prohibition of slavery

Section 1 Neither slavery nor involuntary servitude, except as a punishment for crime whereof the party shall have been duly convicted, shall exist within the United States, or any place subject to their jurisdiction.

Section 2 Congress shall have power to enforce this article by appropriate legislation.

AMENDMENT XIV

Ratified in 1868

Citizenship; requirement of "due process" and "equal protection of the laws" by the states

Section 1 All persons born or naturalized in the United States and subject to the jurisdiction thereof, are citizens of the United States and of the State wherein they reside. No State shall make or enforce any law which shall abridge the privileges or immunities of citizens of the United States; nor shall any State deprive any person of life, liberty, or property, without due process of law; nor deny to any person within its jurisdiction the equal protection of the laws.

---

11. Superseded by the Twentieth Amendment, Section 3.

Section 2   Representatives shall be apportioned among the several States according to their respective numbers, counting the whole number of persons in each State, excluding Indians not taxed. But when the right to vote at any election for the choice of electors for President and Vice President of the United States, Representatives in Congress, the Executive and Judicial officers of a State, or the members of the Legislature thereof, is denied to any of the male inhabitants of such State, being *twenty-one*[12] years of age, and citizens of the United States, or in any way abridged except for participation in rebellion, or other crime, the basis of representation therein shall be reduced in the proportion which the number of such male citizens shall bear to the whole number of male citizens twenty-one years of age in such State.

Section 3   No person shall be a Senator or Representative in Congress, or elector of President and Vice President, or hold any office, civil or military, under the United States, or under any State, who, having previously taken an oath, as a member of Congress, or as an officer of the United States, or as a member of any State legislature, or as an executive or judicial officer of any State, to support the Constitution of the United States, shall have engaged in insurrection or rebellion against the same, or given aid or comfort to the enemies thereof. But Congress may by a vote of two-thirds of each House, remove such disability.

Section 4   The validity of the public debt of the United States, authorized by law, including debts incurred for payment of pensions and bounties for services in suppressing insurrection or rebellion, shall not be questioned. But neither the United States nor any State shall assume or pay any debt or obligation incurred in aid of insurrection or rebellion against the United States, or any claim for the loss of emancipation of any slave; but all such debts, obligations and claims shall be held illegal and void.

Section 5   The Congress shall have power to enforce, by appropriate legislation, the provisions of this article.

Ratified in 1870

AMENDMENT XV

Right to vote cannot be abridged on racial grounds

Section 1   The right of citizens of the United States to vote shall not be denied or abridged by the United States or by any State on account of race, color, or previous condition of servitude.

Section 2   The Congress shall have power to enforce this article by appropriate legislation.

12. Changed by the Twenty-Sixth Amendment.

Ratified in 1913

AMENDMENT XVI

Permits federal income tax

The Congress shall have power to lay and collect taxes on incomes, from whatever source derived, without apportionment among the several States, and without regard to any census or enumeration.

Ratified in 1913

AMENDMENT XVII

Popular election of senators

The Senate of the United States shall be composed of two Senators from each State, elected by the people thereof, for six years; and each Senator shall have one vote. The electors in each State shall have the qualifications requisite for electors of the most numerous branch of the State legislatures.

When vacancies happen in the representation of any State in the Senate, the executive authority of such State shall issue writs of election to fill such vacancies: *Provided*, That the legislature of any State may empower the executive thereof to make temporary appointments until the people fill the vacancies by election as the legislature may direct.

This amendment shall not be so construed as to affect the election or term of any Senator chosen before it becomes valid as part of the Constitution.

Ratified in 1919

AMENDMENT XVIII

Prohibition of manufacture and sale of liquor

Section 1 *After one year from the ratification of this article the manufacture, sale, or transportation of intoxicating liquors within, the importation thereof into, or the exportation thereof from the United States and all territory subject to the jurisdiction thereof for beverage purposes is hereby prohibited.*

Section 2 *The Congress and the several States shall have concurrent power to enforce this article by appropriate legislation.*

Section 3 This article shall be inoperative unless it shall have been ratified as an amendment to the Constitution by the legislatures of the several States, as provided in the Constitution, within seven years from the date of the submission hereof to the States by the Congress.[13]

Ratified in 1920

AMENDMENT XIX

Right to vote cannot be abridged on grounds of sex

The right of citizens of the United States to vote shall not be denied or abridged by the United States or by any State on account of sex.

13. Changed by the Twenty-Sixth Amendment.

Congress shall have power to enforce this article by appropriate legislation.

AMENDMENT XX

Terms of office

Section 1 The terms of the President and Vice President shall end at noon on the 20th day of January, and the terms of Senators and Representatives at noon on the 3rd day of January, of the years in which terms would have ended if this article had not been ratified; and the terms of their successors shall then begin.

Convening of Congress

Section 2 The Congress shall assemble at least once in every year, and such meeting shall begin at noon on the 3rd day of January, unless they shall by law appoint a different day.

Presidential Succession

Section 3 If, at the time fixed for the beginning of the term of the President, the President elect shall have died, the Vice President elect shall become President. If a President shall not have been chosen before the time fixed for the beginning of his term, or if the President elect shall have failed to qualify, then the Vice President elect shall act as President until a President shall have qualified; and the Congress may by law provide for the case wherein neither a President elect nor a Vice President elect shall have qualified, declaring who shall then act as President, or the manner in which who is to act shall be selected, and such person shall act accordingly until a President or Vice President shall have qualified.

Section 4 The Congress may by law provide for the case of the death of any of the persons from whom the House of Representatives may choose a President whenever the right of choice shall have devolved upon them, and for the case of the death of any of the persons from whom the Senate may choose a Vice President whenever the right of choice shall have devolved upon them.

Section 5 Sections 1 and 2 shall take effect on the 15th day of October following the ratification of this article.

Section 6 This article shall be inoperative unless it shall have been ratified as an amendment to the Constitution by the legislatures of three-fourths of the several States within seven years from the date of its submission.

AMENDMENT XXI

Prohibition repealed

Section 1 The eighteenth article of amendment to the Constitution of the United States is hereby repealed.

Section 2 The transportation or importation into any State, Territory, or possession of the United States for delivery or use therein of intoxicating liquors, in violation of the laws thereof, is hereby prohibited.

Section 3 This article shall be inoperative unless it shall have been ratified as an amendment to the Constitution by conventions in the several States, as provided in the Constitution, within seven years from the date of the submission hereof to the States by the Congress.

Ratified in 1951

Limitations on president's term of office

AMENDMENT XXII

Section 1 No person shall be elected to the office of the President more than twice, and no person who has held the office of President, or acted as President, for more than two years of a term to which some other person was elected President shall be elected to the office of the President more than once. But this Article shall not apply to any person holding the office of President when this Article was proposed by the Congress, and shall not prevent any person who may be holding the office of President, or acting as President, during the term within which this Article becomes operative from holding the office of President or acting as President during the remainder of such term.

Section 2 This article shall be inoperative unless it shall have been ratified as an amendment to the Constitution by the legislatures of three-fourths of the several States within seven years from the date of its submission to the States by the Congress.

Ratified in 1961

Presidential electors for the District of Columbia

AMENDMENT XXIII

Section 1 The District constituting the seat of Government of the United States shall appoint in such manner as the Congress may direct:

A number of electors of President and Vice President equal to the whole number of Senators and Representatives in Congress to which the District would be entitled if it were a State, but in no event more than the least populous State; they shall be in addition to those appointed by the States, but they shall be considered, for the purposes of the election of President and Vice President, to be electors appointed by a State; and they shall meet in the District and perform such duties as provided by the twelfth article of amendment.

Section 2 The Congress shall have power to enforce this article by appropriate legislation.

AMENDMENT XXIV

Section 1 The right of citizens of the United States to vote in any primary or other election for President or Vice President, for electors for President or Vice President, or for Senator or Representative in Congress, shall not be denied or abridged by the United States or any State by reason of failure to pay any poll tax or other tax.

Section 2 The Congress shall have power to enforce this article by appropriate legislation.

AMENDMENT XXV

Section 1 In case of the removal of the President from office or of his death or resignation, the Vice President shall become President.

Section 2 Whenever there is a vacancy in the office of the Vice President, the President shall nominate a Vice President who shall take office upon confirmation by a majority vote of both Houses of Congress.

Section 3 Whenever the President transmits to the President pro tempore of the Senate and the Speaker of the House of Representatives his written declaration that he is unable to discharge the powers and duties of his office, and until he transmits to them a written declaration to the contrary, such powers and duties shall be discharged by the Vice President as Acting President.

Section 4 Whenever the Vice President and a majority of either the principal officers of the executive departments or of such other body as Congress may by law provide, transmit to the President pro tempore of the Senate and the Speaker of the House of Representatives their written declaration that the President is unable to discharge the powers and duties of this office, the Vice President shall immediately assume the powers and duties of the office as Acting President.

Thereafter, when the President transmits to the President pro tempore of the Senate and the Speaker of the House of Representatives his written declaration that no inability exists, he shall resume the powers and duties of his office unless the Vice President and a majority of either the principal officers of the executive department or of such other body as Congress may by law provide, transmit within four days to the President pro tempore of the Senate and the Speaker of the House of Representatives their written declaration that the President is unable to discharge the powers and duties of his office. Thereupon Congress shall decide the issue, assembling within forty-eight hours for that purpose if not in session. If the Congress, within twenty-one days after receipt of the latter written declaration, or, if Congress is not in session, within twenty-one days after Congress is required to assemble, determines by two-thirds vote of both Houses that the President is unable to discharge the powers and duties of his office, the Vice President shall continue to discharge the same as Acting President; otherwise, the President shall resume the powers and duties of his office.

Ratified in 1971

Voting age set at 18 years old

AMENDMENT XXVI

Section 1   The right of citizens of the United States, who are eighteen years of age or older, to vote shall not be denied or abridged by the United States or by any State on account of age.

Section 2   The Congress shall have power to enforce this article by appropriate legislation.

Ratified 1992

Procedural limitations on pay raises for Congress

AMENDMENT XXVII

No law varying the compensation for the services of the Senators and Representatives shall take effect, until an election of Representatives shall have intervened.

3

The Federalist: Number 10 and Number 51

Note: *The Federalist* was a series of eighty-five essays published during the ratification debate (1787–1788) in support of the Constitution. The essays bore the pen name "Publius"; they were written by James Madison, Alexander Hamilton, and John Jay. *Federalist* 10 and *Federalist* 51, written by James Madison, are widely considered to be two of the most important papers in the series.

NUMBER 10

Among the numerous advantages promised by a well-constructed Union, none deserves to be more accurately developed than its tendency to break and control the violence of faction. The friend of popular governments never finds himself so much alarmed for their character and fate as when he contemplates their propensity to this dangerous vice. He will not fail, therefore, to set a due value on any plan which, without violating the principles to which he is attached, provides a proper cure for it. The instability, injustice, and confusion introduced into the public councils have, in truth, been the mortal diseases under which popular governments have everywhere perished, as they continue to be the favorite and fruitful topics from which the adversaries to liberty derive their most specious declamations. The valuable improvements made by the American constitutions on the popular models, both ancient and modern, cannot certainly be too much admired; but it would be an unwarrantable partiality to contend that they have as effectually

obviated the danger on this side, as was wished and expected. Complaints are everywhere heard from our most considerate and virtuous citizens, equally the friends of public and private faith and of public and personal liberty, that our governments are too unstable, that the public good is disregarded in the conflicts of rival parties, and that measures are too often decided, not according to the rules of justice and the rights of the minor party, but by the superior force of an interested and overbearing majority. However anxiously we may wish that these complaints had no foundation, the evidence of known facts will not permit us to deny that they are in some degree true. It will be found, indeed, on a candid review of our situation, that some of the distresses under which we labor have been erroneously charged on the operation of our governments; but it will be found, at the same time, that other causes will not alone account for many of our heaviest misfortunes; and, particularly, for that prevailing and increasing distrust of public engagements and alarm for private rights which are echoed from one end of the continent to the other. These must be chiefly, if not wholly, effects of the unsteadiness and injustice with which a factious spirit has tainted our public administration.

By a faction I understand a number of citizens, whether amounting to a majority or minority of the whole, who are united and actuated by some common impulse of passion, or of interest, adverse to the rights of other citizens, or to the permanent and aggregate interests of the community. There are two methods of curing the mischiefs of faction: the one, by removing its causes; the other, by controlling its effects.

There are again two methods of removing the causes of faction: the one, by destroying the liberty which is essential to its existence; the other, by giving to every citizen the same opinions, the same passions, and the same interests.

It could never be more truly said than of the first remedy that it was worse than the disease. Liberty is to faction what air is to fire, an ailment without which it instantly expires. But it could not be a less folly to abolish liberty, which is essential to political life, because it nourishes faction than it would be to wish the annihilation of air, which is essential to animal life, because it imparts to fire its destructive agency.

The second expedient is as impracticable as the first would be unwise. As long as the reason of man continues fallible, and he is at liberty to exercise it, different opinions will be formed. As long as the connection subsists between his reason and his self-love, his opinions and his passions will have a reciprocal influence on each other; and the former will be objects to which the latter will attach themselves. The diversity in the faculties of men, from which the rights of property originate, is not less an insuperable obstacle to a uniformity of interests. The protection of these faculties is the first object of government. From the protection of different and unequal faculties of acquiring property, the possession of different degrees and kinds of property immediately results; and from the influence of these on the sentiments and views of the respective proprietors ensues a division of the society into different interests and parties.

The latent causes of faction are thus sown in the nature of man; and we see them everywhere brought into different degrees of activity, according to the different circumstances of civil society. A zeal for different opinions concerning religion, concerning government, and many other points, as well of speculation as of practice; an attachment to different leaders ambitiously contending for pre-eminence and power; or to persons of other descriptions whose fortunes have been interesting to the human passions, have, in turn, divided mankind into parties,

inflamed them with mutual animosity, and rendered them much more disposed to vex and oppress each other than to co-operate for their common good. So strong is this propensity of mankind to fall into mutual animosities that where no substantial occasion presents itself the most frivolous and fanciful distinctions have been sufficient to kindle their unfriendly passions and excite their most violent conflicts. But the most common and durable source of factions has been the various and unequal distribution of property. Those who hold and those who are without property have ever formed distinct interests in society. Those who are creditors, and those who are debtors, fall under a like discrimination. A landed interest, a manufacturing interest, a mercantile interest, a moneyed interest, with many lesser interests, grow up of necessity in civilized nations, and divide them into different classes, actuated by different sentiments and views. The regulation of these various and interfering interests forms the principal task of modern legislation and involves the spirit of party and faction in the necessary and ordinary operations of government.

No man is allowed to be a judge in his own cause, because his interest would certainly bias his judgment, and, not improbably, corrupt his integrity. With equal, nay with greater reason, a body of men are unfit to be both judges and parties at the same time; yet what are many of the most important acts of legislation but so many judicial determinations, not indeed concerning the rights of single persons, but concerning the rights of large bodies of citizens? And what are the different classes of legislators but advocates and parties to the causes which they determine Is a law proposed concerning private debts? It is a question to which the creditors are parties on one side and the debtors on the other. Justice ought to hold the balance between them. Yet the parties are, and must be, themselves the judges; and the most numerous party, or in other words, the most powerful faction must be expected to prevail. Shall domestic manufacturers be encouraged, and in what degree, by restrictions on foreign manufacturers? are questions which would be differently decided by the landed and the manufacturing classes, and probably by neither with a sole regard to justice and the public good. The apportionment of taxes on the various descriptions of property is an act which seems to require the most exact impartiality; yet there is, perhaps, no legislative act in which greater opportunity and temptation are given to a predominant party to trample on the rules of justice. Every shilling with which they overburden the inferior number is a shilling saved to their own pockets.

It is in vain to say that enlightened statesmen will be able to adjust these clashing interests and render them all subservient to the public good. Enlightened statesmen will not always be at the helm. Nor, in many cases, can such an adjustment be made at all without taking into view indirect and remote considerations, which will rarely prevail over the immediate interest which one party may find in disregarding the rights of another or the good of the whole.

The inference to which we are brought is that the *causes* of faction cannot be removed and that relief is only to be sought in the means of controlling its *effects.*

If a faction consists of less than a majority, relief is supplied by the republican principle, which enables the majority to defeat its sinister views by regular vote. It may clog the administration, it may convulse the society; but it will be unable to execute and mask its violence under the forms of the Constitution. When a majority is included in a faction, the form of popular government, on the other hand, enables it to sacrifice to its ruling passion or interest both the public good and the rights of other citizens. To secure the public good and private rights against the danger of such a faction, and at the same time to preserve the spirit and the form of popular government, is then the great object to which our inquiries are directed. Let me add that it is the great desideratum by which alone this form of government can be rescued from the opprobrium under which it has so long labored and be recommended to the esteem and adoption of mankind.

By what means is this object attainable? Evidently by one of two only. Either the existence of the same passion or interest in a majority at the same time must be prevented, or the majority, having such coexistent passion or interest, must be rendered, by their number and local situation, unable to concert and carry into effect schemes of oppression. If the impulse and the opportunity be suffered to coincide, we well know that neither moral nor religious motives can be relied on as an adequate control. They are not found to be such on the injustice and violence of individuals, and lose their efficacy in proportion to the number combined together, that is, in proportion as their efficacy becomes needful.

From this view of the subject it may be concluded that a pure democracy, by which I mean a society consisting of a small number of citizens who assemble and administer the government in person, can admit of no cure for the mischiefs of faction. A common passion or interest will, in almost every case, be felt by a majority of the whole; a communication and concert results from the form of government itself; and there is nothing to check the inducements to sacrifice the weaker party or an obnoxious individual. Hence it is that such democracies have ever been spectacles of turbulence and contention; have ever been found incompatible with personal security or the rights of property; and have in general been as short in their lives as they have been violent in their deaths. Theoretic politicians, who have patronized this species of government, have erroneously supposed that by reducing mankind to a perfect equality in their political rights, they would at the same time be perfectly equalized and assimilated in their possessions, their opinions, and their passions.

A republic, by which I mean a·government in which the scheme of representation takes place, opens a different prospect and promises the cure for which we are seeking. Let us examine the points in which it varies from pure democracy, and we shall comprehend both the nature of the cure and the efficacy which it must derive from the Union.

The two great points of difference between a democracy and a republic are: first, the delegation of the government, in the latter, to a small number of citizens elected by the rest; secondly, the greater number of citizens and greater sphere of country over which the latter may be extended.

The effect of the first difference is, on the one hand, to refine and enlarge the public views by passing them through the medium of a chosen body of citizens, whose wisdom may best discern the true interest of their country and whose patriotism and love of justice will be least likely to sacrifice it to temporary or partial considerations. Under such a regulation it may well happen that the public voice, pronounced by the representatives of the people, will be more consonant to the public good than if pronounced by the people themselves, convened for the purpose. On the other hand, the effect may be inverted. Men of factious tempers, of local prejudices, or of sinister designs, may, by intrigue, by corruption, or by other means, first obtain the suffrages, and then betray the interests of the people. The question resulting is, whether small or extensive republics are most favorable to the election of proper guardians of the public weal; and it is clearly decided in favor of the latter by two obvious considerations.

In the first place it is to be remarked that however small the republic may be the representatives must be raise to a certain number in order to guard against the cabals of a few; and that however large it may be they must be limited to a certain number in order to guard against the confusion of a multitude. Hence, the number of representatives in the two cases not being in proportion to that of the constituents, and being proportionally greatest in the small republic, it follows that if the proportion of fit characters be not less in the large than in the small republic, the former will present a greater option, and consequently a greater probability of a fit choice.

In the next place, as each representative will be chosen by a greater number of citizens in the large than in the small republic, it will be more difficult for unworthy candidates to practice with success the vicious arts by which elections are too often carried; and the suffrages of the people being more free, will be more likely to center on men who possess the most attractive merit and the most diffusive and established characters.

It must be confessed that in this, as in most other cases, there is a mean, on both sides of which inconveniences will be found to lie. By enlarging too much the number of electors, you render the representative too little acquainted with all their local circumstances and lesser interests; as by reducing it too much, you render him unduly attached to these, and too little fit to

comprehend and pursue great wad national objects. The federal Constitution forms a happy combination in this respect; the great and aggregate interests being referred to the national, the local and particular to the State legislatures.

The other point of difference is the greater number of citizens and extent of territory which may be brought within the compass of republican than of democratic government; and it is this circumstance principally which renders factious combinations less to be dreaded in the former than in the latter. The smaller the society, the fewer probably will be the distinct parties and interests composing it; the fewer the distinct parties and interests, the more frequently will a majority be found of the same party; and the smaller the number of individuals composing a majority, and the smaller the compass within which they are placed, the more easily will they concert and execute their plans of oppression. Extend the sphere and you take in a greater variety of parties and interests; you make it less probable that a majority of the whole will have a common motive to invade the rights of other citizens; or if such a common motive exists, it will be more difficult for all who feel it to discover their own strength and to act in unison with each other. Besides other impediments, it may be remarked that, where there is a consciousness of unjust or dishonorable purposes, communication is always checked by distrust in proportion to the number whose concurrence is necessary.

Hence, it clearly appears that the same advantage which a republic has over a democracy in controlling the effects of faction is enjoyed by a large over a small republic—is enjoyed by the Union over the States composing it. Does this advantage consist in the substitution of representatives whose enlightened views and virtuous sentiments render them superior to local prejudices and to schemes of injustice? It will not be denied that the representation of the Union will be most likely to possess these requisite endowments. Does it consist in the greater security afforded by a greater variety of parties, against the event of any one party being able to outnumber and oppress the rest? In an equal degree does the increased variety of parties comprised within the Union increase this security. Does it, in fine, consist in the greater obstacles opposed to the concert and accomplishment of the secret wishes of an unjust and interested majority? Here again the extent of the Union gives it the most palpable advantage.

The influence of factious leaders may kindle a flame within their particular States but will be unable to spread a general conflagration through the other States. A religious sect may degenerate into a political faction in a part of the Confederacy; but the variety of sects dispersed over the entire face of it must secure the national councils against any danger from that source. A rage for paper money, for an abolition of debts, for an equal division of property, or for any other improper or wicked project, will be less apt to pervade the whole body of the Union than a particular member of it, in the same proportion as such a malady is more likely to taint a particular county or district than an entire State. In the extent and proper structure of the Union, therefore, we behold a republican remedy for the diseases most incident to republican government. And according to the degree of pleasure and pride we feel in being republicans ought to be our zeal in cherishing the spirit and supporting the character of federalists.

NUMBER 51

To what expedient, then, shall we finally resort, for maintaining in practice the necessary partition of power among the several departments as laid down in the Constitution? The only answer that can be given is that as all these exterior provisions are found to be inadequate the defect must be supplied, by so contriving the interior structure of the government as that its several constituent parts may, by their mutual relations, be the means of keeping each other in their proper places. Without presuming to undertake a full development of this important idea I will hazard a few general observations which may perhaps place it in a clearer light, and enable us to form a more correct judgment of the principles and structure of the government planned by the convention.

In order to lay a due foundation for that separate and distinct exercise of the different powers of government, which to a certain extent is admitted on all hands to be essential to the preservation of liberty, it is evident that each department should have a will of its own; and consequently should be so constituted that the members of each should have as little agency as possible in the appointment of the members of the others. Were this principle rigorously adhered to, it would require that all the appointments for the supreme executive, legislative, and judiciary magistracies should be drawn from the same fountain of authority, the people, through channels having no communication whatever with one another. Perhaps such a plan of constructing the several departments would be less difficult in practice than it may in contemplation appear. Some difficulties, however, and some additional expense would attend the execution of it. Some deviations, therefore, from the principle must be admitted. In the constitution of the judiciary department in particular, it might be inexpedient to insist rigorously on the principle: first, because peculiar qualifications being essential in the members, the primary consideration ought to be to select that mode of choice which best secures these qualifications; second, because the permanent tenure by which the appointments are held in that department must soon destroy all sense of dependence on the authority conferring them.

It is equally evident that the members of each department should be as little dependent as possible on those of the others for the emoluments annexed to their offices. Were the executive magistrate, or the judges, not independent of the legislature in this particular, their independence in every other would be merely nominal.

But the great security against a gradual concentration of the several powers in the same department consists in giving to those who administer each department the necessary constitutional means and personal motives to resist encroachments of the others. The provision for defense must in this, as in all other cases, be made commensurate to the danger of attack. Ambition must be made to counteract ambition. The interest of the man must be connected with the constitutional rights of the place. It may be a reflection on human nature that such devices should be necessary to control the abuses of government. But what is government itself but the greatest of all reflections on human nature? If men were angels, no government would be necessary. If angels were to govern men, neither external nor internal controls on government would be necessary. In framing a government which is to be administered by men over men, the great difficulty lies in this: you must first enable the government to control the governed; and in the next place oblige it to control itself. A dependence on the people is, no doubt, the primary control on the government; but experience has taught mankind the necessity of auxiliary precautions.

This policy of supplying, by opposite and rival interests, the defect of better motives, might be traced through the whole system of human affairs, private as well as public. We see it particularly displayed in all the subordinate distributions of power, where the constant aim is to divide and arrange the several offices in such a manner as that each may be a check on the other—that the private interest of every individual may be a sentinel over the public rights. These inventions of prudence cannot be less requisite in the distribution of the supreme powers of the State.

But it is not possible to give to each department an equal power of self-defense. In republican government, the legislative authority necessarily predominates. The remedy for this inconvenience is to divide the legislature into different branches; and to render them, by different modes of election and different principles of action, as little connected with each other as the nature of their common functions and their common dependence on the society will admit. It may even be necessary to guard against dangerous encroachments by still further precautions. As the weight of the legislative authority requires that it should be thus divided, the weakness of the executive may require, on the other hand, that it should be fortified. An absolute negative on the legislature appears, at first view, to be the natural defense with which the executive magistrate should be armed. But perhaps it would be neither altogether safe nor alone sufficient. On ordinary occasions it might not be exerted with the requisite firmness, and on extraordinary occasions it might be perfidiously abused. May not this defect of an absolute negative be supplied by some qualified connection between this weaker department and the weaker branch of the stronger department, by which the latter may be led to support the constitutional rights of the former, without being too much detached from the rights of its own department?

If the principles on which these observations are founded be just, as I persuade myself they are, and they be applied as a criterion to the several State constitutions, and to the federal Constitution, it will be found that if the latter does not perfectly correspond with them, the former are infinitely less able to bear such a test.

There are, moreover, two considerations particularly applicable to the federal system of America, which place that system in a very interesting point of view.

First. In a single republic, all the power surrendered by the people is submitted to the administration of a single government; and the usurpations are guarded against by a division of the government into distinct and separate departments. In the compound republic of America, the power surrendered by the people is first divided between two distinct governments, and then the portion allotted to each subdivided among distinct and separate departments. Hence a double security arises to the rights of the people. The different governments will control each other, at the same time that each will be controlled by itself.

Second. It is of great importance in a republic not only to guard the society against the oppression of its rulers, but to guard one part of the society against the injustice of the other part. Different interests necessarily exist in different classes of citizens. If a majority be united by a common interest, the rights of the minority will be insecure. There are but two methods of providing against this evil: the one by creating a will in the community independent of the majority—that is, of the society itself; the other, by comprehending in the society so many separate descriptions of citizens as will render an unjust combination of a majority of the whole very improbable, if not impracticable. The first method prevails in all governments possessing an hereditary or self-appointed authority. This, at best, is but a precarious security; because a power independent of the society may as well espouse the unjust views of the major as the rightful interests of the minor party, and may possibly be turned against both parties. The second method will be exemplified in the federal republic of the United States. Whilst all authority in it will be derived from and dependent on the society, the society itself will be broken into so many parts, interests and classes of citizens, that the rights of individuals, or of the minority, will be in little danger from interested combinations of the majority. In a free government the security for civil rights must be the same as that for religious rights. It consists in the one case in the multiplicity of interests, and in the other in the multiplicity of sects. The degree of security in both cases will depend on the number of interests and sects; and this may be presumed to depend on the extent of country and number of people comprehended under the same government. This view of the subject must particularly recommend a proper federal system to all the sincere and considerate friends of republican government, since it shows that in exact proportion as the territory of the Union may be formed into more circumscribed Confederacies, or States, oppressive combinations of a majority will be facilitated; the best security, under the republican forms, for the rights of every class of citizen, will be diminished; and consequently the stability and independence of some member of the government, the only other security, must be proportionally increased. Justice is the end of government. It is the end of civil society. It ever has been and ever will be pursued until it be obtained, or until liberty be lost in the pursuit. In a society under the forms of which the stronger faction can readily unite and oppress the weaker, anarchy may as truly be said to reign as in a state of nature, where the weaker individual is not secured against the violence of the stronger; and as, in the latter state, even the stronger individuals are prompted, by the uncertainty of their condition, to submit to a government which may protect the weak as well as themselves; so, in the former state, will the more powerful factions or parties be gradually induced, by a like motive, to wish for a government which will protect all parties, the weaker as well as the more powerful. It can be little doubted that if the State of Rhode Island was separated from the Confederacy and left to itself, the insecurity of rights under the popular form of government within such narrow limits would be displayed by such reiterated oppression of factious majorities that some power altogether independent of the people would soon be called for by the voice of the very factions whose misrule had proved the necessity of it. In the extended republic of the United States, and among the great variety of interests, parties, and sects which it embraces, a coalition of a majority of the whole society could seldom take place on any other principles than those of justice and the general good; whilst there being thus less danger to a minor from the will of a major party, there must be less pretext, also, to provide for the security of the former, by introducing into the government a will not dependent on the latter, or, in other words, a will independent of the society itself. It is no less certain than it is important, notwithstanding the contrary opinions which have been entertained, that the larger the society, provided it lie within a practicable sphere, the more duly capable it will be of self-government. And happily for the *republican cause,* the practicable sphere may be carried to a very great extent by a judicious modification and mixture of the *federal principle.*

4

Presidents and Congress

Year	President and Vice President	Party	Congress	House Majority Party	House Minority Party	Senate Majority Party	Senate Minority Party
1789–1797	George Washington John Adams	None	1st	38 Admin	26 Opp	17 Admin	9 Opp
			2nd	37 Fed	33 Dem-Rep	16 Fed,	13 Dem-Rep
			3rd	57 Dem-Rep	48 Fed	17 Fed	13 Dem-Rep
			4th	54 Fed	52 Dem-Rep	19 Fed	13 Dem-Rep
1797–1801	John Adams Thomas Jefferson	Fedederalist	5th	58 Fed	48 Dem-Rep	20 Fed	12 Dem-Rep
			6th	64 Fed	42 Dem-Rep	19 Fed	13 Dem-Rep
1801–1809	Thomas Jefferson Aaron Burr (to 1805) George Clinton (to 1809)	Democratic Republican	7th	69 Dem-Rep	36 Fed	18 Dem-Rep	13 Fed
			8th	102 Dem-Rep	39 Fed	25 Dem-Rep	9 Fed
			9th	116 Dem-Rep	25 Fed	27 Dem-Rep	7 Fed
			10th	118 Dem-Rep	24 Fed	28 Dem-Rep	6 Fed
1809–1817	James Madison George Clinton (to 1813) Elbridge Gerry (to 1817)	Democratic-Republican	11th	94 Dem-Rep	48 Fed	28 Dem-Rep	6 Fed
			12th	108 Dem-Rep	36 Fed	30 Dem-Rep	6 Fed
			13th	112 Dem-Rep	68 Fed	27 Dem-Rep	9 Fed
			14th	117 Dem-Rep	65 Fed	25 Dem-Rep	11 Fed
1817–1825	James Monroe Daniel D. Tompkins	Democratic-Republican	15th	141 Dem-Rep	42 Fed	34 Dem-Rep	10 Fed
			16th	156 Dem-Rep	27 Fed	35 Dem-Rep	7 Fed
			17th	158 Dem-Rep	25 Rep	44 Dem-Rep	4 Fed
			18th	187 Dem-Rep	26 Fed	44 Dem-Rep	4 Fed

*Died in Office +Resigned from Presidency #Resigned from Vice Presidency **Appointed VP under terms of the 25th Amendment.

Only members of two major parties in Congress are shown; omitted are independents, members of minor parties, and vacancies. Party Balance as of beginning of Congress.

Congresses in which one or both houses are controlled by a party other than that of the President are in bold print. During the administrations of George Washington and (in part) John Quincy Adams, Congress was not organized by formal parties.

Abbreviations: Admin=Administration supporters; AntiMas=Anti-Masonic; Dem=Democratic; Dem-Rep=Democratic-Republican; Fed=Federalist; Jack=Jacksonian Democrats; Nat Rep=National Republicans; Rep—Republican; Union=Unionist; Whig=Whig.

Year	President and Vice President	Party	Congress	House Majority Party	House Minority Party	Senate Majority Party	Senate Minority Party
1825–1829	John Quincy Adams John C. Calhoun	National-Republican	19th 20th	105 Admin **119 Jack**	97 Jack **94 Admin**	26 Admin **28 Jack**	20 Jack **20 Admin**
1829–1837	Andrew Jackson John C. Calhoun# (to 1832) (VP vacant 1832–1833)	Democrat	21st 22nd	139 Dem 141 Dem	74 Nat Rep 58 Nat Rep	26 Dem 25 Dem	22 Nat Rep 21 Nat Rep
	Martin Van Buren (1833–1837)		23rd 24th	147 Dem 145 Dem	53 AntiMas 98 Whig	20 Dem 27 Dem	20 Nat Rep 25 Whig
1837–1841	Martin Van Buren Richard M. Johnson	Democrat	25th 26th	108 Dem 124 Dem	107 Whig 118 Whig	30 Dem 28 Dem	18 Whig 22 Whig
1841	William H. Harrison* John Tyler	Whig					
1841–1845	John Tyler (VP Vacant)	Whig	27th 28th	133 Whig **142 Dem**	102 Dem **79 Whig**	28 Whig 28 Whig	22 Dem 25 Dem
1845–1849	James K. Polk George M. Dallas	Democrat	29th 30th	143 Dem **115 Whig**	77 Whig **108 Dem**	31 Dem 36 Dem	25 Whig 21 Whig
1849–1850	Zachary Taylor* Millard Fillmore	Whig	31st	**112 Dem**	**109 Whig**	**35 Dem**	**25 Whig**
1850–1853 (VP vacant)	Millard Fillmore	Whig	32nd	**140 Dem**	**88 Whig**	**35 Dem**	**24 Whig**

Year	President and Vice President	Party	Congress	House		Senate	
				Majority Party	Minority Party	Majority Party	Minority Party
1853–1857	Franklin Pierce William R. King* (VP vacant 1853–1857)	Democrat	33rd 34th	159 Dem **108 Rep**	71 Whig **83 Dem**	38 Dem 40 Dem	22 Whig 15 Rep
1857–1861	James Buchanan John C. Breckinridge	Democrat	35th 36th	118 Dem **114 Rep**	92 Rep **92 Dem**	36 Dem 36 Dem	20 Rep 26 Rep
1861–1865	Abraham Lincoln* Hannibal Hamlin (to 1865) Andrew Johnson (1865)	Republican	37th 38th	105 Rep 102 Rep	43 Dem 75 Dem	31 Rep 36 Rep	10 Dem 9 Dem
1865–1869	Andrew Johnson Richard M. Johnson	Republican	39th 40th	149 Union 143 Rep	42 Dem 49 Dem	42 Union 42 Rep	10 Dem 11 Dem
1869–1877	Ulysses S. Grant Schuyler Colfax (to 1873) Henry Wilson (to 1877)	Republican	41st 42nd 43rd 44th	149 Rep 134 Rep 194 Rep 169 Rep	63 Dem 104 Dem 92 Dem 109 Dem	56 rep 52 Rep 49 Rep 45 Rep	11 Dem 17 Dem 19 Dem 29 Dem
1877–1881	Rutherford B. Hayes William A. Wheeler	Republican	45th 46th	**153 Dem** **149 Dem**	**140 Rep** **130 Rep**	39 Rep **42 Dem**	36 Dem **33 Dem**
1881	James A. Garfield* Chester A. Arthur	Republican	47th	147 Rep	135 Dem	37 Rep	37 Dem
1881–1885	Chester A. Arthur (VP vacant)	Republican	48th	**197 Dem**	**118 Rep**	38 Rep	36 Dem

Year	President and Vice President	Party	Congress	House Majority Party	House Minority Party	Senate Majority Party	Senate Minority Party
1885–1889	Grover Cleveland Thomas A. Hendricks	Democrat	49th	183 Dem	140 Rep	**43 Rep**	**34 Dem**
			50th	169 Dem	152 Rep	**9 Rep**	**37 Dem**
1889–1893	Benjamin Harrison Levi P. Morton	Republican	51st	166 Rep	159 Dem	39 Rep	37 Dem
			52nd	**235 Dem**	**88 Rep**	47 Rep	39 Dem
1893–1897	Grover Cleveland Adlai E. Stevenson	Democrat	53rd	218 Dem	127 Rep	44 Dem	38 Rep
			54th	**244 Rep**	**105 Dem**	**43 Rep**	**39 Dem**
1897–1901	William H. McKinley* Garret A. Hoban (to 1901) Theodore Roosevelt (1901)	Republican	55th	204 Rep	113 Dem	47 Rep	34 Dem
			56th	185 Rep	163 Dem	53 Rep	26 Dem
1901–1909	Theodore Roosevelt (VP vacant (1901–1905) Charles W. Fairbanks (1905–1909)	Republican	57th	197 Rep	151 Dem	55 Rep	31 Dem
			58th	208 Rep	178 Dem	57 Rep	33 Dem
			59th	250 Rep	136 Dem	57 Rep	33 Dem
			60th	222 Rep	164 Dem	61 Rep	31 Dem
1909–1913	William H. Taft ames S. Sherman	Republican	61st	219 Rep	172 Dem	61 Rep	32 Dem
			62nd	**228 Dem**	**161 Rep**	51 Rep	41 Dem
1913–1921	Woodrow Wilson Thomas R. Marshall	Democrat	63rd	291 Dem	127 Rep	51 Dem	44 Rep
			64th	230 Dem	196 Rep	56 Dem	40 Rep
			65th	216 Dem	210 Rep	53 Dem	42 Rep
			6th	**240 Rep**	**190 Dem**	**49 Rep**	**47 Dem**

				House		Senate	
Year	President and Vice President	Party	Congress	Majority Party	Minority Party	Majority Party	Minority Party
1921–1923	Warren G. Harding* Calvin Coolidge	Republican	67th	301 Rep	131 Dem	59 Rep	37 Dem
923–1929	Calvin Coolidge (VP vacant 1923–1925) Charles G. Dawes (1925–1929)	Republican	68th	225 Rep	205 Dem	51 Rep	43 Dem
			69th	247 Rep	183 Dem	56 Rep	39 Dem
			70th	237 Rep	195 Dem	49 Rep	46 Dem
1929–1933	Herbert Hoover Charles Curtis	Republican	71st	267 Rep	167 Dem	56 Rep	39 Dem
			72nd	220 Dem	214 Rep	48 Rep	47 Dem
1933–1945	Franklin D. Roosevelt* John N. Garner (1933–1941) Henry A. Wallace (1941–1945) Harry S. Truman (1945)	Democrat	73rd	310 Dem	117 Rep	60 Dem	35 Rep
			74th	319 Dem	103 Rep	69 Dem	25 Rep
			75th	331 Dem	89 Rep	76 Dem	16 Rep
			76th	261 Dem	164 Rep	69 Dem	23 Rep
			77th	268 Dem	162 Rep	66 Dem	28 Rep
			78th	218 Dem	208 Rep	58 Dem	37 Rep
1945–1953	Harry S. Truman (VP vacant 1945–1949) Alben W. Barkley (1949–1953)	Democrat	79th	242 Dem	190 Rep	56 Dem	38 Rep
			80th	245 Rep	188 Dem	51 Rep	45 Dem
			81st	263 Dem	171 Rep	54 Dem	42 Rep
			2nd	234 Dem	199 Pop	49 Dem	47 Rep
1953–1961	Dwight D. Eisenhower Richard M. Nixon	Republican	83rd	221 Rep	211 Dem	48 Rep	47 Dem
			84th	232 Dem	203 Rep	48 Dem	47 Rep
			85th	233 Dem	200 Rep	49 Dem	47 Rep
			86th	283 Dem	153 Rep	64 Dem	34 Rep

				House		Senate	
Year	President and Vice President	Party	Congress	Majority Party	Minority Party	Majority Party	Minority Party
1961–1963	John F. Kennedy* Lyndon B. Johnson	Democrat	87th 88th	263 Dem 258 Dem	174 Rep 177 Rep	65 Dem 67 Dem	35 Rep 33 Rep
1963–1969	Lyndon B. Johnson (VP vacant 1963–1965)	Democrat	88th	258 Dem	177 Rep	67 Dem	33 Rep
	Hubert H. Humphrey (1965–1969)		89th 90th	295 Dem 247 Dem	140 Rep 187 Rep	68 Dem 64 Dem	32 Rep 36 Rep
1969–1974	Richard M. Nixon+ Spiro T. Agnew# (1969–1973)	Republican	91st 92nd	**243 Dem** **254 Dem**	**192 Rep** **180 Rep**	**57 Dem** **54 Dem**	**43 Rep** **44 Rep**
	Gerald R. Ford** (1973–1974)		93rd	**239 Dem**	**192 Rep**	**56 Dem**	**42 Rep**
1974–1977	Gerald R. Ford Nelson A. Rockefeller**		93rd 94th	**239 Dem** **291 Dem**	**192 Rep** **144 Rep**	**56 Dem** **60 Dem**	**42 Rep** **37 Rep**
1977–198l	James E. Carter Jr. Walter Mondale	Democrat	95th 96th	292 Dem 280 Dem	143 Rep 155 Rep	61 Dem 58 Dem	38 Rep 41 Rep
1981–1989	Ronald W. Reagan George H.W. Bush	Republican	97th 98th 99th 100th	**243 Dem** **269 Dem** **253 Dem** **257 Dem**	**192 Rep** **165 Rep** **182 Rep** **178 Rep**	53 Rep 54 Rep 53 Rep **54 Dem**	46 Dem 46 Dem 47 Dem **46 Rep**
1989–1993	George H.W. Bush J. Danforth Quayle	Republican	101st 102nd	**262 Dem** **268 Dem**	**173 Rep** **168 Rep**	**55 Dem** **56 Dem**	**45 Rep** **44 Rep**

Year	President and Vice President	Party	Congress	House		Senate	
				Majority Party	Minority Party	Majority Party	Minority Party
1993–2001	William J. Clinton Albert Gore	Democrat	103rd 104th 105th 106th	259 Dem **231 Rep** **227 Rep** **222 Rep**	175 Rep **203 Dem** **207 Dem** **211 Dem**	57 Dem **54 Rep** **55 Rep** **55 Rep**	43 Rep **46 Dem** **45 Dem** **45 Dem**
2001–	George W. Bush Richard Cheney	Republican	107th	221 Rep	212 Dem	50 Rep	50 Dem

5

Chief Justices of the Supreme Court

Chief Justice	Nominated by President	Date Sworn in as Chief Justice	End of Term as Chief Justice
John Jay	George Washington	October 19, 1789	June 19, 1795
John Rutledge	George Washington	August 12, 1795	December 14, 1795
Oliver Ellsworth	George Washington	March 8, 1796	December 15, 1800
John Marshall	John Adams	February 4, 1801	July 6, 1835
Roger B. Taney	Andrew Jackson	March 28, 1836	October 12, 1864
Salmon P. Chase	Abraham Lincoln	December 15, 1864	May 7, 1873
Morrison R. Waite	Ulysses S. Grant	March 4, 1874	March 23, 1888
Melville W. Fuller	Grover Cleveland	October 8, 1888	July 4, 1910
Edward D. White	William Howard Taft	December 19, 1910	May 19, 1921
William Howard Taft	Warren G. Harding	July 11, 1921	February 3, 1930
Charles Evans Hughes	Herbert Hoover	February 24, 1930	July 1, 1941
Harlan F. Stone	Franklin D. Roosevelt	July 3, 1941	April 22, 1946
Frederick M. Vinson	Harry S. Truman	June 24, 1946	September 8, 1953
Earl Warren	Dwight D. Eisenhower	October 5, 1953	June 23, 1969
Warren E. Burger	Richard Nixon	June 23, 1969	September 26, 1986
William H. Rehnquist	Ronald Reagan	September 26, 1986	

Subject Index

Index of Persons